THE INTERNATIONAL LEGAL FRAMEWORK AGAINST CORRUPTION

THE INTERNATIONAL LEGAL FRAMEWORK AGAINST CORRUPTION

States' obligations to prevent and repress corruption

Julio Bacio Terracino

intersentia
Cambridge – Antwerp – Portland

Intersentia Publishing Ltd.
Trinity House | Cambridge Business Park | Cowley Road
Cambridge | CB4 0WZ | United Kingdom
Tel.: +44 1223 393 753 | Email: mail@intersentia.co.uk

Distribution for the UK:
Hart Publishing Ltd.
16C Worcester Place
Oxford OX1 2JW
UK
Tel.: +44 1865 517 530
Email: mail@hartpub.co.uk

Distribution for the USA and Canada:
International Specialized Book Services
920 NE 58th Ave. Suite 300
Portland, OR 97213
USA
Tel.: +1 800 944 6190 (toll free)
Email: info@isbs.com

Distribution for Austria:
Neuer Wissenschaftlicher Verlag
Argentinierstraße 42/6
1040 Wien
Austria
Tel.: +43 1 535 61 03 24
Email: office@nwv.at

Distribution for other countries:
Intersentia Publishing nv
Groenstraat 31
2640 Mortsel
Belgium
Tel.: +32 3 680 15 50
Email: mail@intersentia.be

The International Legal Framework against Corruption. States' obligations to prevent and repress corruption
Julio Bacio Terracino

ISBN 978-1-78068-092-7
D/2012/7849/76
NUR 828

British Library Cataloguing in Publication Data. A catalogue record for this book is available from the British Library.

A Froukje, Luca y mi madre

ACKNOWLEDGEMENTS

This book is a revised version of my Ph.D. thesis, which I defended in 2010 at the Graduate Institute of International Studies in Geneva, Switzerland. Since then I work for the Organisation for Economic Co-operation and Development (OECD), yet the opinions expressed in this study are mine and do not engage the OECD or its member countries.

In writing this study, I have enjoyed the support of many people. I will not venture to thank them all individually here, yet I would like to express my gratitude to those to whom I owe special thanks.

First and foremost, I would like to express my deepest gratitude to my Ph.D. advisor Professor Andrew Clapham for his comments, encouragement and openness to exploring an uncharted topic in the field of international law. I also wish to thank the other members of my doctoral jury: Professor Nikos Passas of the School of Criminology and Criminal Justice at Northeastern University in Boston, Massachusetts, and Dr. Jean-Pierre Laviec of the Graduate Institute in Geneva. Furthermore, I am grateful to numerous people who contributed during the course of my research by discussing ideas and commenting on drafts, most notably Katharina Boele-Woelki, Ton Boele, El Cid Butuyan, Paco Cantu, Gillian Dell, Frank Fariello, Adrian Fozzard, Mark Johnson, Catherine Kessedjian, Facundo Perez Aznar, Deborah Ruiz Verduzo, Magdalena Sepúlveda Carmona, Jonathan Shapiro, Pietro Veglio, Deborah Wetzel and Dima Yared. I must also thank the Graduate Institute for awarding me a scholarship that facilitated my work.

Last, but certainly not least, I would like to thank my wife Froukje, who not only read and commented on every page of this study, but whose encouragement, support and inspiration throughout this undertaking made it all possible.

Julio Bacio Terracino
Paris, April 2012

CONTENTS

ABBREVIATIONS

ADB	Asian Development Bank
AU	African Union
AU Convention against Corruption	African Union Convention on Preventing and Combating Corruption
CoE	Council of Europe
CoE Civil Law Convention	Council of Europe Civil Law Convention on Corruption
CoE Criminal Law Convention	Council of Europe Criminal Law Convention on Corruption
COSP	Conference of the States Parties to the United Nations Convention against Corruption
ECHR	European Court of Human Rights
ECOWAS	Economic Community of West African States
ECOWAS Protocol against Corruption	Economic Community of West African States Protocol on the Fight against Corruption
EU	European Union
EU Convention against Corruption	Convention on the Fight against Corruption Involving Officials of the European Communities or Officials of Member States of the European Union
FATF	Financial Action Task Force
FCPA	United States Foreign Corrupt Practices Act
GRECO	Council of Europe Group of States against Corruption
GTZ	Deutsche Gesellschaft für Technische Zusammenarbeit
ICJ	International Court of Justice
MESICIC	OAS Mechanism for Follow-Up on the Implementation of the Inter-American Convention against Corruption
MLA	Mutual Legal Assistance
OAS	Organization of American States
OECD	Organization for Economic Cooperation and Development

OECD Convention	OECD Convention on Combating Bribery of Foreign Public Officials in International Business Transactions
OECD WGB	OECD Working Group on Bribery in International Business Transactions
OSCE	Organization for Security and Cooperation in Europe
SADC	Southern Africa Development Community
UN	United Nations
UNCAC	United Nations Convention against Corruption
UNDP	United Nations Development Programme
UNICRI	United Nations Interregional Crime and Justice Research Institute
UNODC	United Nations Office on Drugs and Crime
UNTOC	United Nations Convention against Transnational Organized Crime
US SEC	United States Securities and Exchange Commission
WTO	World Trade Organization

GENERAL INTRODUCTION

Corruption has become an enemy of humankind, which affects not only moral values, but also economic and social development in every sense. This has in turn served to make corruption an almost obligatory topic on the agenda of a number of international institutions, both governmental and non-governmental. Over the past fifteen years, corruption has been transformed from a predominantly national concern into a global political issue that is eliciting a global political response. International institutions have been the principal driving force in this respect and have succeeded in encouraging collaboration between States by mediating and defining international relationships and creating an international regime against corruption.

One of the most important consequences of the internationalization of corruption is the emergence of international regulation to combat corruption, particularly in the form of international treaties which have *de facto* added the subject of corruption to the international law agenda. It is clear that international law has the vocation of regulating corrupt acts that involve international aspects, such as so-called transnational corruption, or in other words the bribery of foreign public officials. International law, as the law governing relations between States, has traditionally addressed issues in which potential conflicts between States may arise. Indeed, that is almost certainly the reason why, in contrast with the present study, the great majority of scholarly works on corruption and the related international legal framework focus almost exclusively on the corrupt act of the bribery of foreign public officials.

Yet it is less clear why international law is also concerned with purely domestic corruption, or in other words corrupt practices carried out by a national of a State and taking place within its territory. Why has an issue that is normally considered to be entirely an internal affair of a State has become an issue of international law? Two main reasons may be advanced. The first, as is explained in detail in this study, is that corruption has received international attention in order to level the playing field in international commercial transactions and to improve economic and social development of developing countries. In addition, modern corrupt practices require a multilateral approach. While corruption may not in all cases necessarily be transnational, this may be the most effective approach to its repression. Even where domestic laws exist to combat corruption and the offence takes place wholly within the offender's own country, acts of corruption may have transnational consequences. The offender may flee the country to avoid prosecution, or may launder the proceeds of bribery in a foreign country where bank secrecy laws may help to hide traces. In this sense, corruption remains a national crime, but in its modern form requires international efforts for its suppression. However, while many modern corrupt practices have a transnational element, not all of them do. There is therefore another reason why purely domestic corrupt practices are regulated by international law.

A second reason for corruption becoming a topic in international law is related to developments within international law itself. International law was traditionally considered to be the law regulating relations between States, particularly with regard to territorial or jurisdictional issues. However, international law, as in the case of any other legal system, takes into account specialised problems of contemporary society. Its evolution into a so-called "international law of welfare" greatly expanded the scope of the topics that it covers.[1] As early as 1958, Wilfred Jenks, Director-General of the International Labour Organization (ILO), said that:

> "[The emphasis of international law is] increasingly shifting from the formal structure of the relationship between States and the delimitation of their jurisdiction to the development of substantive rules on matters of common concern vital to the growth of an international community and to the individual well-being of the citizens of its member States."[2]

The evolution of the tasks and dimensions of international law reflects the role that it plays in regulating conditions of well-being and promoting higher standards of living, full employment, economic and social progress and the development of all the members of the international community.[3] Even in 1947, issues such as human rights, labour, education, science and international financial matters were considered fields that were increasingly covered by international regulation.[4] International law has therefore changed from a "horizontal" international law of coexistence (concerned with the regulation and

---

1 Term used by Professor Röling: See Bernard Victor Aloysius Röling, *International Law in an Expanded World* (Amsterdam: Djambatan, 1960). See also, Wolfgang Gaston Friedmann, "Human Welfare and International Law: A Reordering of Priorities," in *Transnational Law in a Changing Society: Essays in Honor of Philip C. Jessup*, ed. Louis Henkin, Wolfgang Gaston Friedmann, and Oliver Lissitzyn (New York: Columbia University Press, 1972), 113–134.

2 C. Wilfred Jenks, *The Common Law of Mankind*, Library of World Affairs no. 41 (London: Stevens, 1958), 17.

3 Röling, *International Law in an Expanded World*.

4 Maurice Bourquin, "Pouvoir scientifique et Droit international," *Recueil des cours* 70, no. I (1947): 359.

formalization of inter-state diplomatic relations) to a "vertical" international law of cooperation (concerned with the elaboration of common objectives and rules in matters vitally affecting human welfare in our time).[5]

CORRUPTION: A NEW TRANSNATIONAL CRIME

The internationalization of corruption has resulted in the impressive total of fourteen international treaties. With the emergence of this body of international law, corruption has come to form part of the category of so-called transnational crimes, alongside other criminal activities, such as drug trafficking, human trafficking, the taking of hostages and the financing of terrorism.[6] Transnational crimes transcend international borders and the laws of several States, and have an impact on other countries.[7] International law, through treaties, defines transnational crimes and related offences and establishes obligations for the repression of such crimes in national jurisdictions. Usually, such treaties establish detailed rules relating to international cooperation in criminal matters, and specifically extradition and MLA, for the repression of those crimes. However, while international law provides common definitions and rules, it is up to national jurisdictions to repress the respective crimes on the basis of national law.

States have accordingly negotiated and adopted international anti-corruption treaties with a view to organizing inter-State cooperation to prevent and combat corruption. However, anti-corruption instruments, and particularly the UNCAC, also contain numerous provisions that are not related to inter-State cooperation, but are aimed at enhancing domestic institutional and legal frameworks to combat corruption. International law therefore not only assists inter-State cooperation in the enforcement of anti-corruption law, but also influences purely domestic action to combat corruption. The internationalization of corruption and the resulting international regulation have created an international legal framework against corruption, which is the focus of the present study.

---

5 Wolfgang Gaston Friedmann, *The Changing Structure of International Law* (London: Stevens & Sons, 1964), Chapter 6. For a similar view, see Anne-Marie Slaughter and William Burke-White, "The Future of International Law Is Domestic (or, The European Way of Law)," *Harvard International Law Journal* 47, no. 2 (2006): 327–352.

6 See, for example, Ilias Bantekas, "The Legal Nature of Transnational Financial Crime," in *International and European Financial Criminal Law*, ed. Ilias Bantekas and Giannis Keramidas (London: LexisNexis Butterworths, 2006), 1–19.

7 Gerhard Mueller, "Transnational Crime: Definitions and Concepts," *Transnational Organized Crime* 4, no. 3 & 4 (1998): 13. See also, Isabelle Fouchard, *Crime international: Entre internationalisation du droit et pénalisation du droit international*, PhD Thesis presented at the Graduate Institute of International and Development Studies (Geneva, 2008).

THE PURPOSE OF THIS STUDY

The international legal framework against corruption is composed of international rules designed specifically to combat corruption at the national and transnational levels, as well as other rules of international law that may be relevant to different aspects of prevention of corruption and the enforcement of anti-corruption law. For a full understanding of this international legal framework, it is necessary to examine, on the one hand, the interaction between existing general international legal rules and those specifically addressing corruption, which are mostly contained in international anti-corruption conventions, and, on the other hand, the legal adjustments that have been required at national level. It is accordingly useful to examine the international legal framework against corruption in terms of both international obligations and the main legal problems that may arise in the implementation of those obligations. What does international law require States to do in relation to corruption? And what happens if States do not meet their international obligations? The ultimate goal is to reinforce action to combat corruption, and it is also essential to examine what international law adds in that respect. Until now, there has been no comprehensive study on the international legal framework against corruption that has focused in particular on what international law can add in the fight against corruption.

The term "international legal framework against corruption" should be clarified. As stated earlier, this framework is composed of international obligations. However, the provisions of anti-corruption conventions do not all establish the same level of legal obligation. Many provisions are not obligations, but mere recommendations. In addition, an identical measure may not be accorded the same level of obligation in all treaties. A particular measure therefore may be mandatory in one treaty and optional in another. Consequently, the term international legal framework against corruption as used in this work encompasses all these provisions, and due note will be made whether the provision in question is an obligation or a recommendation. When a specific measure is accorded different levels of obligation in different treaties, the level applied by the UNCAC will prevail, yet due note of the level applied by other treaties will be made.

The present study therefore begins by tracing the emergence of the international legal framework against corruption and engages in a systematic analysis of its content. Evidently, this is not a neutral exercise. The underlying context of this study is the goal of advancing and enhancing action to combat corruption by preventing its occurrence and removing impunity. Against this background, the present study highlights the weaknesses and the innovative aspects of the international legal framework.

The study starts by examining the bases of the legal framework, with particular reference to certain definitional issues concerning the term corruption, which require clarification at the outset. Through a historical review, Chapter II shows the progress in the condemnation of corruption, including its ultimate transformation in recent years, namely the upgrading of anti-corruption to an issue of international concern. And it was the need to address the problem of corruption at the international level that paved the way for international regulation in the form of hard and soft law instruments. The international regulation of corruption, particularly in the form of treaties and resolutions of international organizations, is analysed in Chapter III and constitutes the main source of the international legal framework against corruption.

Once the bases of the international legal framework have been reviewed, the study turns to the more detailed analysis of its content. The scope of application of the international legal framework against corruption is outlined in Chapter IV, which examines the essential notion of public official and the definition of the corrupt acts of bribery, embezzlement, illicit enrichment, trading in influence and abuse of functions. Chapters V to VIII explore the international obligations of States relating to the prevention of corruption, criminal and civil jurisdiction, law enforcement and international cooperation in criminal matters and the recovery of assets.

Following the analysis of its content, it is necessary to examine the ways in which the international legal framework against corruption can be enforced. What happens if a State does not comply with its international obligations to combat corruption? As described in Chapter IX, there are two different mechanisms for the implementation and enforcement of international obligations relating to corruption: regular monitoring and, alternatively, international adjudication.

THE SCOPE OF THE PRESENT STUDY

The present study faces two main challenges. The first resides in the fact that an analysis of the international legal framework against corruption is by definition an international study, and its scope is therefore likely to be unmanageable. The study does not attempt to examine the interpretation, implementation and application of the international legal framework against corruption in every country of the world. For practical reasons, the number of legal systems studied is limited. Instead, the experience of the various countries is used to illustrate specific aspects of the international obligations arising out of the legal framework. In particular, the various approaches adopted by the different States to the interpretation, implementation and application of international obligations relating to corruption are helpful in obtaining a better understanding of the international legal framework.

The second challenge consists of the extremely broad scope of the notion of corruption. Corruption means different things to different people, and is often used as a catch-all term. For that reason, Chapter I devotes considerable attention to the issue of the definition of corruption and, for the purposes of the present study, focuses on the legal definition of the term. In this connection, the term "corruption" should be understood as grouping the offences of bribery, embezzlement, illicit enrichment, trading in influence and abuse of functions.

Moreover, the study does not cover corrupt practices occurring solely within the private sector, so-called "private-to-private corruption." As explained in Chapter I, international rules concerning this type of corruption are still in their infancy and tend to show that corruption in the private sector has not attained the same level of condemnation as corrupt practices involving the public sector. Finally, it should be noted that up to now there has not been developed any scientifically or academically sound ways of measuring corruption. No reference is therefore made in the present study to "levels" of corruption, including in monetary terms, or to the related indicators, such as Transparency International's Corruption Perception Index (CPI).

CHAPTER I
THE DEFINITION OF CORRUPTION REVISITED

INTRODUCTION

The excesses of the Wabenzi in certain African countries are well known.[8] In 2003–2004, the Government of Kenya spent at least 878 million Kenyan Shillings (ca. US$ 12 million) on the purchase of luxury cars for the personal use of government officials.[9] This and a variety of other acts are often reported as evidence of corrupt activity. However, is it proper to refer to these types of acts as corruption? Is it corruption if a government official drives a Mercedes Benz S600?

Most people would agree that the embezzlement of public assets or the acceptance of bribes by a public official entails corruption. But if an employee in a private company is bribed by a contractor of the company, is this also corruption? Most would still regard it as a corrupt act, but there exist a minority who hold that the term corruption is limited to acts that take place within the public sector. Others consider that corruption also encompasses such cases as when office supplies in a company go missing,[10] or when a public employee claims to be sick but goes on vacation.[11] There is evidently considerable disagreement on what constitutes corruption.

There is no single accepted definition of corruption. Indeed, there is a tendency to use the term loosely as a catch-all term. Thus, to avoid misguided generalizations, it is paramount to determine what exactly is meant by the term

---

8 A so-called wabenzi is a member of the African ruling class, usually an allegedly corrupt government official (or family member), so-called because they usually drive an imported vehicle (like a Mercedes Benz). In some Bantu languages "wa" means people of, and "benzi" makes reference to Mercedes Benz.

9 Kenya National Commission on Human Rights and Transparency International Kenya, *Living Large: Counting the Cost of Official Extravagance in Kenya*, Research Report on Wasteful Government Expenditure, 2006.

10 World Bank, *Helping Countries Combat Corruption: The Role of the World Bank*, 1997, 8–12.

11 Vito Tanzi, "Corruption around the World: Causes, Consequences, Scope, and Cures," in *Governance, Corruption, and Economic Performance*, ed. George T. Abed and Sanjeev Gupta (Washington, D.C.: International Monetary Fund, 2002), 25.

"corruption." The exercise of trying to define corruption is not a novelty. The great majority of studies on the topic in all fields usually begin with a section on "what is corruption." For some it is a vain endeavour and "the search for the true definition of corruption is, like the pursuit of the Holy Grail, endless, exhausting and ultimately futile..."[12] However, while it may appear that defining corruption is a mere semantic issue, and despite the numerous attempts to settle the issue, the present study still needs to dedicate a section to definitions. After approaching the concept of corruption, the paramount role of the law in its definition will become evident. In defining corruption at the international level, international law therefore becomes essential. A word on the private sector is also necessary since, according to some opinions, the term corruption cannot apply outside the public sector.

I. APPROACHING THE CONCEPT OF CORRUPTION

The term corruption comes from the Latin *corruptio,* which connotes destruction, moral decay, putridity or rottenness.[13] Historically the concept of corruption has always borne a moral connotation and has mostly referred to political and sexual behaviour.[14] In the political field, the traditional concept of corruption was strictly related to the morality of societies, rather than to actions of individuals. Western political thought has employed the notion of the corruption of the bad polity to characterize situations which are perceived as being marked by the decay of the moral and political order.[15] The moral health of societies was judged in terms of the distribution of wealth and power, relationships between leaders and followers, the sources of power and the moral right of rulers to rule.[16]

---

12 Graeme C. Moodie, "On Political Scandals and Corruption," *Government and Opposition* 15, no. 2 (April 1980): 209, citing Robert Williams, *The Problems of Corruption: A Conceptual and Comparative Analysis*, paper delivered to a Public Administration Committee Conference, York, 1976, 2.

13 The concept may have a physical significance, as in "[t]he destruction or spoiling of anything, *esp.* by disintegration or by decomposition with its attendant unwholesomeness and loathsomeness; putrefaction," or a moral significance, as in "moral deterioration or decay ... [the] [p]erversion or destruction of integrity in the discharge of public duties by bribery or favour..." *The Oxford English Dictionary*, Volume II: C, 1978, 1024–1025. A similar definition states: "état de ce qui est alteré, gâté; decomposition, putrefaction... [a]ction de pervertir moralement ... [a]ction de corrompre qqn en le soudoyant, en l'incitant à agir contre son devoir." *Grand Dictionnaire Encyclopédique Larousse*, tome 3: Christiania à Docte, 1982, 2652.

14 Robert Klitgaard, *Controlling Corruption* (Berkeley: University of California Press, 1988), 23.

15 Arnold J. Heidenheimer and Michael Johnston, eds., *Political Corruption: Concepts and Contexts*, 3rd ed. (New Brunswick, N.J: Transaction Publishers, 2002), 5.

16 Michael Johnston, "The Search for Definitions: The Vitality of Politics and the Issue of Corruption," *International Social Science Journal* 149 (1996): 322.

The traditional conception of corruption as a general disease of the body politic concerned political philosophers such as Thucydides, Plato, and Aristotle, and persisted into modern times in the political thought of Machiavelli, Montesquieu, and Rousseau.[17] Thucydides referred to the corruption of Athens when the Athenians invaded Melos, and stated that it was a decision that cast all of Athens, and not just its leaders, into a state of lost virtue and moral disrepute.[18] For Machiavelli, corruption undermined and ultimately destroyed the *virtú* of the citizen.[19] Nowadays, although at times shocking revelations about the misuse of political powers have revived associations between corruption and institutional decay, the modern concept of corruption is much narrower than the classical one, and is related to individual action or transactions. Corruption now refers to specific actions by individuals.

Etymologically, the concept of corruption makes reference to a situation or state of an object or a person. Yet all the modern notions of corruption, rather than such situation or state, describe the process that leads to that situation or state. This transformation is strictly linked to the development of the modern state. In the nineteenth century, with the modernization and bureaucratization in Western societies, the State came to be considered as a moral entity and the exercise of public authority as a duty.[20] Conceptions of public office as private property disappeared and public officials occupying a position of trust became bound by the duties of a fiduciary.[21] The Weberian bureaucracy and the development of the modern State resulted in corruption becoming a political

17 Carl J. Friedrich, "Corruption Concepts in Historical Perspective," in *Political Corruption: Concepts and Contexts*, ed. Arnold J. Heidenheimer and Michael Johnston, 3rd ed. (New Brunswick, N.J: Transaction Publishers, 2002), 17; Johnston, "The Search for Definitions: The Vitality of Politics and the Issue of Corruption," 322; Maryvonne Génaux, "Early Modern Corruption in English and French Fields of Vision," in *Political Corruption: Concepts and Contexts*, ed. Arnold J. Heidenheimer and Michael Johnston, 3rd ed. (New Brunswick, NJ: Transaction Publishers, 2002), 107–121.

18 Johnston, "The Search for Definitions: The Vitality of Politics and the Issue of Corruption," 323.

19 Friedrich, "Corruption Concepts in Historical Perspective," 18–19.

20 On the modernization and bureaucratization of the State and the effect on the notion of corruption, see also Chapter II below.

21 This was clearly a gradual transition and, in the early modern period, particularly in the seventeenth and eighteenth centuries, although some standards of public behaviour already existed, many practices that are corrupt only by modern standards were widely accepted. Most importantly and differently from today, public office was still considered to be an asset or private property subject to sale and rapacity. See, Jacob van Klaveren, "Corruption as a Historical Phenomenon," in *Political Corruption: Concepts and Contexts*, ed. Arnold J. Heidenheimer and Michael Johnston, 3rd ed. (New Brunswick, N.J: Transaction Publishers, 2002), 83–94; Koenraad W. Swart, "The Sale of Public Offices," in *Political Corruption: Concepts and Contexts*, ed. Arnold J. Heidenheimer and Michael Johnston, 3rd ed. (New Brunswick, N.J: Transaction Publishers, 2002), 95–106; Génaux, "Early Modern Corruption in English and French Fields of Vision." See also, Chapter II below.

pathology, rather than a global degeneration, and as such it could be defined in behavioural terms and the activities objected to could be outlawed.[22]

Hence, today the definition of corruption involves a process of spelling out classifications of behaviour,[23] and such behaviour is measured against a variety of standards. In this context, most definitions hold that corruption is the abuse of public office, power, or resources, for private benefit. However, what those types of behaviour or abuses are and the standards against which they should be measured are key to the dilemma.

Social scientists, and particularly political scientists, have approached this question from two different angles: they have defined corruption on the basis of either subjective or objective standards. On the subjective side, there are definitions that determine corrupt behaviour on the basis of public opinion or cultural standards.[24] Simply put, this implies that corruption is what the public considers to be corrupt. Subjective standards for the definition of corruption often appear to amount to a critique of overtly objective and legalistic definitions. Advocates of this approach hold that the advantage of subjective definitions is that they take into account local culture and what citizens define as corrupt, which in turn is helpful for effective law enforcement.[25] However, these definitions are blatantly unhelpful in arriving at a clear definition of corruption for several obvious reasons, and particularly because there is no single uniform public opinion on any issue, and even less on corruption, as there is no agreement as to who the public is, and because public opinion is very changeable, and probably manageable, over time.[26]

A great majority of social scientists have, however, defined corruption on the basis of objective standards. These definitions are often grouped into three categories: market centred, public interest centred, and public office centred.[27] Market centred definitions address corruption in terms of the theory of the market and were developed by authors dealing with earlier Western and contemporary non-Western societies, in which the norms governing public

---

22 Friedrich, "Corruption Concepts in Historical Perspective," 20.

23 Moodie, "On Political Scandals and Corruption," 209.

24 For studies on subjective standards to define corruption, see Michael Johnston, "Right and Wrong in British Politics: 'Fits of Morality' in Comparative Perspective," *Polity* 24, no. 1 (Autumn 1991): 1–25.

25 John Gardiner, "Defining Corruption," in *Political Corruption: Concepts and Contexts*, ed. Arnold J. Heidenheimer and Michael Johnston, 3rd ed. (New Brunswick, N.J: Transaction Publishers, 2002), 32–36.

26 Ibid.

27 Arnold J. Heidenheimer, "The Context of Analysis," in *Political Corruption: Readings in Comparative Analysis on Definition*, ed. Arnold J. Heidenheimer (New Brunswick: Transaction Books, 1970), 3–9.

officeholders were not clearly articulated or were non-existent.[28] These definitions broadly share the application of social or public choice methods to the analysis of corruption or, which amounts to the same, the use of economic methods and models for the analysis of politics.[29] However, it has been argued that market centred definitions are useful in understanding corruption and explaining the incidence of corruption, but not in defining it, as they still rely on prior conceptions of public office and the rules governing it.[30]

Another group of theorists define corruption in relation to the concept of public interest.[31] They focus on the effects of the act, and not its legal status. In other words, if an act is harmful to the public interest it is corrupt, even if it is legal; and if it is beneficial to the public, it is not corrupt even if it violates the law.[32] But even if the public interest could be shown to have a reasonably precise meaning, the definition of corruption and its consequences are intrinsically distinct issues.[33] Public interest definitions fail to define corruption and are inevitable broad and ambiguous.[34]

Most social scientists, however, have recourse to norms or rules of public office to define corruption. Public office centred definitions, also called legalistic definitions, can be illustrated by J.S. Nye's famous definition of corruption:

---

28 Van Klaveren's definition is usually considered to represent a market centred definition: "A corrupt civil servant regards his office as a business, the income of which he will...seek to maximize. The office then becomes a maximizing unit. The size of his income depends... upon the market situation and his talents for finding the point of maximal gain on the public's demand." Heidenheimer and Johnston, *Political Corruption*, 8. For other market oriented definitions, see Robert O. Tilman, "Emergence of Black-Market Bureaucracy: Administration, Development and Corruption in the New States," *Public Administration Review* 28, no. 5 (1968): 432–444; Nathaniel H. Leff, "Economic Development through Bureaucratic Corruption," *American Behavioral Scientist* 8, no. 3 (1964): 8–14.

29 Mark Philp, "Conceptualizing Political Corruption," in *Political Corruption: Concepts and Contexts*, ed. Arnold J. Heidenheimer and Michael Johnston, 3rd ed. (New Brunswick, N.J: Transaction Publishers, 2002), 49.

30 Ibid., 49–50.

31 Friedrich's definition of corruption illustrates public interest definitions: "The pattern of corruption can be said to exist whenever a powerholder who is charged with doing certain things, i.e. who is a responsible functionary or office-holder, is by monetary or other rewards not legally provided for, induced to take actions which favour whoever provides the rewards and thereby does damage to the public and its interest." Heidenheimer and Johnston, *Political Corruption*, 8–9.

32 Gardiner, "Defining Corruption," 31–32.

33 Johnston, "The Search for Definitions: The Vitality of Politics and the Issue of Corruption," 324.

34 Gardiner, "Defining Corruption," 30–32. It has also been stated that public interest definitions pre-judge the result of corruption and may preclude recognition of corruption until after the event only when the public interest can be clarified and judged. See, Gerald E. Caiden and Naomi J. Caiden, "Administrative Corruption," *Public Administration Review* 37, no. 3 (1977): 302.

> "Corruption is behavior which deviates from the formal duties of a public role because of private-regarding (personal, close family, private clique) pecuniary or status gains; or violates rules against the exercise of certain types of private-regarding influence. This includes such behavior as bribery (use of a reward to pervert the judgment of a person in a position of trust); nepotism (bestowal of patronage by reason of ascriptive relationship rather than merit); and misappropriation (illegal appropriation of public resources for private-regarding uses)."[35]

Hence, public office centred definitions are based on legal or formal rules of official conduct.[36] Reliance on the law to define corrupt behaviour, and as such corruption, has the main advantage of adding precision to the concept of corruption. Yet, as indicated in the next section, it has also been subject to disapproval.

There is clearly little agreement on the definition of corruption, or even on the approach that should be adopted for its definition. In addition to the traditional and behavioural definitions presented here, many more definitions and approaches exist. For example, Klitgaard has provided a famous equation as a definition: Corruption = Monopoly Power + Discretion – Accountability.[37] Another approach has been to define corruption by drawing upon a Principal-Agent-Client framework. Corruption is accordingly defined in the context of the relationship between a Principal (the public in general), an Agent (a public official), and a Client (a private individual with whom the agent interacts).[38] In the search for a definition of corruption, there has even been a resurgence of classical concerns about the moral health of societies, although now combined with modern notions of corrupt politics. This so-called neo-classical approach is concerned with corruption as a moral and political issue and defines it as the

---

35 Joseph S. Nye, "Corruption and Political Development: A Cost-Benefit Analysis," *American Political Science Review* 61, no. 2 (1967): 419.

36 See for example the work of David H. Bayley, "The Effects of Corruption in a Developing Nation," *Western Political Quarterly* 19, no. 4 (1966): 719–732; Hussein Alatas, *The Sociology of Corruption: The Nature, Function, Causes and Prevention of Corruption* (Singapore: D. Moore Press, 1968); Samuel P. Huntington, "Modernization and Corruption," in *Political Order in Changing Societies* (New Haven: Yale University Press, 1968), 59–71.

37 Yet his definition, rather than explaining what corruption is, highlights what causes corruption. Klitgaard, *Controlling Corruption*, 75. See also, UNDP, *Anti-Corruption*, Practice Note, February 2004 (in which UNDP also takes into account other factors, such as integrity and transparency, which work as a balance to monopoly and discretion. Thus, in this context, for UNDP the definition of corruption is: Corruption = (Monopoly Power + Discretion) – (Accountability + Integrity + Transparency)).

38 In this context, Klitgaard has stated: "this approach defines corruption in terms of the divergence between the principal's or the public's interests and those of the agent or civil servant: corruption occurs when an agent betrays the principal's interest in pursuit of her own." Klitgaard, *Controlling Corruption*, 24; Susan Rose-Ackerman, *Corruption: A Study in Political Economy*, 1978, 6–7. On principal-agent definitions, see also Arvind K. Jain, "Models of Corruption," in *Economics of Corruption*, ed. Arvind K. Jain (Boston: Kluwer Academic Publishers, 1998), 13–34.

abuse, according to the legal or social standards constituting a society's system of public order, of a public role or resource for private benefit.[39]

Another approach to studying corruption has been to concentrate on classifications, rather than definitions. Operational definitions of corruption are usually developed by beginning with a relatively broad definition, and then further specifying it by making classifications that render it into a workable concept. Probably the most well-known classification of corruption draws a distinction between grand and petty corruption. "Grand corruption" usually refers to corruption of heads of state, ministers, and high-level officials, which frequently involves large values.[40] On the other hand, "petty corruption" is everyday corruption at the lowest levels and refers to the corruption of junior officials, customs clerks, and traffic police, and generally involves relatively small values.[41] Certainly, the term corruption has been the subject of numerous classifications, and there are therefore many "types" of corruption, such as legislative,[42] business or corporate,[43] institutionalized,[44] endemic or systemic.[45]

---

39 For more on the neo-classical approach, see Johnston, "The Search for Definitions: The Vitality of Politics and the Issue of Corruption," 329–333.

40 The term 'grand corruption' is usually attributed to G. Moody Stuart and his book on grand corruption. However, Moody Stuart did not mean by grand corruption what it is understood by that term today. By 'grand corruption' he was referring to the bribery of foreign public officials by multinational corporations. See, George Moody-Stuart, *Grand Corruption: How Business Bribes Damage Developing Countries*, 3rd ed. (Oxford: WorldView Publishing, 1997).

41 Also called administrative or bureaucratic corruption, both Kaufmann and Bardhan have provided examples of variations of this type of corruption. See, Daniel Kaufmann, "Corruption: The Facts," *Foreign Policy*, no. Summer (1997): 117; Pranab Bardhan, "Corruption and Development: A Review of Issues," *Journal of Economic Literature* 35, no. 3 (September 1997): 1323.

42 Legislative corruption, or vote-buying, refers to the manner in which the voting behaviour of legislators and/or voters can be influenced. See, Susan Rose-Ackerman, *Corruption and Government: Causes, Consequences, and Reform* (Cambridge: Cambridge University Press, 1999), 127–142.

43 Business or corporate corruption occurs in relationships that exist between private businesses and suppliers or private service providers. It also involves illegal behaviour by corporate officials for private monetary gain. It may also be referred to as private-to-private corruption. See, Antonio Argandoña, "Private-to-private Corruption," *Journal of Business Ethics* 47, no. 3 (2003): 253–267. For more on this type of corruption, see section IV below.

44 Institutionalized corruption has been defined as the corruption of those who hold institutional positions and can influence institutional processes and actions, such as law enforcement personnel, and members of the judiciary. See, for example, M. Cherif Bassiouni and Eduardo Vetere, "Organized Crime and Its Transnational Manifestations," in *International Criminal Law: Crimes*, 2nd ed. (The Hague: Transnational Publishers, Inc., 1999), 883–903.

45 Endemic or systemic corruption occurs when corruption is an integrated aspect of the economic, social and political system. In reality, systemic corruption is not a special category of corrupt practice, but rather a situation in which the major institutions and processes of the state are routinely dominated and used by corrupt individuals, and in which most people have no alternative to dealing with corrupt officials. See, Michael Johnston, "Fighting Systemic Corruption: Social Foundations for Institutional Reform," *European Journal of*

II. THE PARAMOUNT ROLE OF THE LAW

It is therefore apparent that there are many different "types" of corruption, and also an endless list of definitions. However, it is possible to arrive at one definition that can be accepted by many scholars and in many fields of study, including the present study. The definition of corruption is composed of a descriptive core and a normative element.[46] There is relatively strong agreement on the descriptive core. Transparency International's definition of corruption is useful in reflecting the descriptive core: *corruption is the abuse of entrusted power for private gain*. However, this core needs to be measured against a normative element in order to determine the specific acts which constitute an abuse of entrusted power and what private gain is. As explained above, there is no agreement among scholars on which standard should be used. But, for the purposes of the present study, the normative element has to be the law.

Legal, or so-called public office centred definitions are indeed the most widely accepted by social scientists, although they are also heavily criticised, precisely because they rely on legal standards. Three main arguments have been raised against the legal element in defining corruption: (i) that many corrupt actions committed in politics fall outside the law;[47] and, conversely, (ii) some illegal and thus corrupt actions may be morally defensible;[48] and (iii) that powerful groups can influence law-making[49] and are likely to do so to legalize the practices on which their power depends.[50]

Development Research 10, no. 1 (June 1998): 85; Michael Johnston, *Syndromes of Corruption: Wealth, Power, and Democracy* (Cambridge: Cambridge University Press, 2005); Caiden and Caiden, "Administrative Corruption."

46 Daniel H Lowenstein, "Political Bribery and the Intermediate Theory of Politics," *UCLA Law Review* 32 (1984): 798–805.

47 See, for example, Philp, "Conceptualizing Political Corruption," 46.

48 See, for example, Gardiner, "Defining Corruption"; Rose-Ackerman, *Corruption: A Study in Political Economy*, 9.

49 See, for example, Larry L. Berg, Harlan Hahn, and John R. Schmidhauser, *Corruption in the American Political System* (Morristown, N.J.: General Learning Press, 1976), 5.

50 In practice, there are many other arguments against legally-based definitions, for example that they ignore broader issues of morality and justice and neglect important political values, such as leadership, citizenship, and accountability. However, in the present study, reference is only made to the strongest arguments. For further such views see, James C. Scott, *Comparative Political Corruption* (Englewood Cliffs, N.J: Prentice-Hall, 1972); John G. Peters and Susan Welch, "Political Corruption in America: A Search for Definitions and a Theory," *American Political Science Review* 72 (1978): 974–975; J. Patrick Dobel, "The Corruption of a State," *American Political Science Review* 72 (1978): 958–973; Moodie, "On Political Scandals and Corruption"; Mark Philp, "Defining Political Corruption," in *Political Corruption*, ed. Heywood Paul (Oxford: Blackwell, 1997), 20–46; Dennis Thompson, "Mediated Corruption: The Case of the Keating Five," *American Political Science Review* 87 (1993): 369–381.

For many critics, legal definitions are therefore too restrictive and leave out many practices that are corrupt but legal. This claim is made with reference, in particular, to certain practices to influence political or market decisions by political and economic elites. In this case, the critics appear to follow a romantic neo-classical definition of corruption.[51] For example, certain forms of political funding, which are legal in certain countries, are nevertheless said to be corrupt because they exert enormous influence in shaping institutions and policies which benefit private interests at the expense of broader public welfare.[52]

However, it is not very clear what these practices are, or the manner and criteria which should be used for their identification. In the field of political science, Michael Johnston, for instance has studied what he calls "influence market corruption," and in the field of economics Daniel Kaufmann has made reference to practices that he calls "legal corruption." Yet many of the examples provided are in fact illegal, and as such there is no doubt that they are corrupt, while other examples are legal and their corrupt nature is not convincing. For example, Johnston analyses in detail the inequalities in the electoral procedure in the United States and how the law has benefited the incumbent. But although such an outcome may be unjust and immoral, it is neither illegal nor corrupt.[53] The cases of so-called legal corruption are usually anecdotal and confined to a specific country, and to a historical and political context. It is not therefore possible to extract generalizations from these practices on their corrupt character.

---

51 In this sense, Scott indicates: "Our conception of corruption does not cover political systems that are, in Aristotelian terms, 'corrupt' in that they systematically serve the interests of special groups or sectors. A given regime may be biased or repressive; it may consistently favour the interests, say, of the aristocracy, big business, a single ethnic group, or a single region while it represses other demands, but it is not ipso facto corrupt unless these ends are accomplished by breaching the formal norms of office." Scott, *Comparative Political Corruption*, 5.

52 Daniel Kaufmann, "Corruption, Governance and Security: Challenges for the Rich Countries and the World," in *The Global Competitiveness Report 2004-2005* (Geneva: World Economic Forum, 2004), 90. In this sense, Johnston has stated: "Some systemic corruption problems might involve uses of wealth and power that are legal but still impair institutions and pre-empt the participation of others." Johnston, *Syndromes of Corruption: Wealth, Power, and Democracy*, 12.

53 See, Johnston, *Syndromes of Corruption: Wealth, Power, and Democracy*, chapter 4. Kaufmann provides an extremely broad definition of legal corruption and argues that such practices are legal but widespread on the basis of a survey of perceptions of corporations. See, Kaufmann, "Corruption, Governance and Security: Challenges for the Rich Countries and the World"; Daniel Kaufmann and Pedro C. Vicente, "Legal Corruption," 24 November 2005, available at http://papers.ssrn.com/sol3/papers.cfm?abstract_id=829844 (last visited 1 April 2012); Joel S. Hellman, Geraint Jones, and Daniel Kaufmann, *Seize the State, Seize the Day: State Capture, Corruption and Influence in Transition*, World Bank Policy Research Working Paper No. 2444, September 2000.

Most importantly, those who criticize legal definitions seem to be confusing two related, but intrinsically different concepts: law and morality. Indeed, many practices in politics, and particularly the way the private sector influences political decisions, can be considered immoral. There would appear to be a strong argument that it is immoral for the farming industry to lobby the U.S. Congress to keep its subsidies, at the expense of poor farmers in the developing world. But, is this really corrupt? Immoral practices may not be illegal. Most immoral ways of exerting influence are indeed criminalized, such as trading in influence and the abuse of functions. Other ways of exerting influence may remain in more of a grey area, immoral for some, but nevertheless legal.

However, institutionalized mechanisms exist to make assessments of such values. And this is precisely where the law comes in. The law is a formal mechanism of social control. Through criminalization, conduct that is deemed to harm societal values is proscribed.[54] Crimes consist of behaviour that the State has, for different reasons and at different times, decided is sufficiently serious to warrant being treated as crimes. It is this generalized societal consensus to criminalize certain forms of conduct that constitutes the legitimate voice in determining whether or not a specific act should be considered corrupt. Moreover, the problem may also be more of timing than of substance. Certain types of conduct that are immoral today and criticized by some as corrupt may be illegal tomorrow, if the necessary consensus is achieved for their criminalization.

The second claim against legal definitions of corruption argues that some illegal, and thus corrupt, actions may be morally defensible, and hence they should not be considered as corruption. In this sense, it has been claimed that "under certain circumstances, citizens may reasonably feel that an act which is legally defined as corruption is nevertheless a necessary tool to survive."[55] A famous example by Rose-Ackerman seems to reflect the dilemma behind this argument: "One does not condemn a Jew for bribing his way out of a concentration camp."[56] However, in this case, the fact that the victim paid a bribe to escape from the camp does not change, first, the inherent illegality of bribery, and second, the fact that it constitutes a corrupt act. Situations such as the one in the example are in fact taken into account by criminal law. The legal justification of duress would apply in this case, as the actor's circumstances are so difficult that his culpability

---

54 Crime is crime because it consists in wrongdoing which directly and in a serious degree threatens the security or well-being of society, and because it is not safe to leave it redressable only by compensation of the party injured. John Cyril Smith and Brian Hogan, *Criminal Law*, 7th ed. (London: Butterworths, 1992), 16.

55 Gardiner, "Defining Corruption," 39.

56 Rose-Ackerman, *Corruption: A Study in Political Economy*, 9.

for choosing criminal conduct is diminished in part or entirely.[57] The lesser evils defence could also be applied, which states that, if from an impartial standpoint the harm sought to be avoided by the criminal act is greater than the harm the act would cause, the actor is justified if he partakes in the criminal act (or what would otherwise be a criminal act).[58] Hence, the rule of law does provide a way out for cases of corruption that might be considered moral by some. Bribery is intrinsically corrupt, but in certain situations can be justified by society and as such, by the law. This does not, however, change the fact that the act remains corrupt.

A further argument against legally-based definitions holds that powerful groups can influence law-making. This is indeed true, but mainly in cases of another kind. While there are countless cases in which powerful groups have influenced law-making to their advantage, the cases referred to in this context are less numerous. These consist of cases in which powerful groups influence law-making in accordance with the substantive definition of corruption. Those who hold political power in any society are able to determine legality. For example, it has been said that Ferdinand Marcos rewrote sections of the Philippine Constitution to legalize his embezzlement of public assets.[59] Similarly, the former Italian Prime Minister Silvio Berlusconi is said to have changed the law so that his previously illegal practices of book-keeping were re-classified as legal,[60] and to be immune from criminal prosecution.

Such practices temporarily affect the definition of corruption in a particular situation or country. Although democratic systems and legislative processes can be and are abused by special groups or sectors, this is usually remedied in a later period. Abuse by powerful groups to influence law-making is one of the inherent flaws of democracy, but through the same democratic process another standard may be adopted, as a result of a counter-influence. In the case of the Philippines, for example, once Marcos had been ousted, the new Government of Corazon Aquino amended the Constitution and altered the provisions that had benefited Marcos' corruption. In Italy, the Constitutional Court repealed the immunity of Silvio Berlusconi in January 2004.

---

57 Larry Alexander, "The Philosophy of Criminal law," in *The Oxford Handbook of Jurisprudence and Philosophy of Law*, ed. Jules L. Coleman and Scott Shapiro (Oxford: Oxford University Press, 2002), 842–850.

58 Alexander, "The Philosophy of Criminal law."

59 See, Johnston, "The Search for Definitions: The Vitality of Politics and the Issue of Corruption," 323, citing Carbonell-Catilo, *The Dynamics of Manipulation and Violence in Philippine Elections: A Case of Political Corruption*, XIII World Congress, International Political Science Association, 1985.

60 Dieter Haller and Cris Shore, eds., *Corruption: Anthropological Perspectives* (London: Pluto, 2005), 4.

Democracy, and particularly legislative processes, must in the end balance the interests of different groups. This is inherent to democracy. The constant in changing societies and in changes in values is the law, understood as a system of rules that is designed to regulate social interaction.

III. THE INTERNATIONAL LAW DEFINITION OF CORRUPTION

The definition of corruption therefore consists of the combination of a descriptive core (abuse of entrusted power for private gain) and a normative element (the law which determines what actions constitute abuse of power for private gain). Evidently, as laws differ in every country, the definition of corruption varies from country to country.

However, current international conventions against corruption require States Parties to establish a number of offences as crimes of corruption in their domestic law, if these do not already exist. States with relevant legislation already in place have to ensure that the existing provisions define corruption and the related offences in conformity with the requirements of the relevant conventions, and if necessary they have to amend their laws. As a result, there is a process of the harmonization of domestic substantive law against corruption with the standards set out in international law. It is therefore important to examine international law for an indication of how corruption will eventually be defined in most legal systems and to arrive at the definition of corruption in the international sphere.

One of the sources of international law, treaty law, addresses the definition of corruption. In the same way as national legal systems, corruption itself is not criminalized, but is the term that groups together certain criminal acts which correspond to the descriptive core of corruption, the abuse of entrusted power for private gain. Yet international treaties have also accepted different approaches.

A first group of Conventions reflect the common error of interchangeably using the terms "corruption" and "bribery." For example, the UNTOC, in Article 8, under the heading "Criminalization of corruption," actually provides the definition of bribery. The CoE Civil Law Convention is similarly inaccurate.[61] The EU Convention against Corruption, in Article 2, entitled "Passive

[61] Article 2 of the CoE Civil Law Convention states: "For the purpose of this Convention, 'corruption' means requesting, offering, giving or accepting, directly or indirectly, *a bribe* or any other undue advantage or prospect thereof, which distorts the proper performance of any

corruption," provides the definition of passive bribery; and in Article 3, entitled "Active corruption," gives the definition of active bribery.[62] The EU Framework Decision on Combating Corruption in the Private Sector makes the same mistake.[63] In reality, these Conventions refer solely to the act of bribery, and should thus have been entitled conventions against bribery, and not corruption. In contrast, the OECD Convention truthfully reflects its title.

A second group of conventions fails to state explicitly that a given criminalized act amounts to corruption. This is the case of the UNCAC and the CoE Criminal Law Convention. For example, the UNCAC in Chapter III, "Criminalization and law enforcement," directly enumerates acts that are to be criminalized, without explicitly indicating that such acts constitute corruption. This can create confusion. Do all the acts under Chapter III amount to corruption? For example, should the "Laundering of proceeds of crime" under Article 23 and the "Obstruction of justice" under Article 25 be considered as constituting corruption? These instruments should establish a clearer differentiation between the actual acts that constitute corruption and the related offences that may not necessarily fit the same description.

A third group of instruments contain more explicit differentiations between corruption as a term grouping criminal acts and the actual acts that constitute corruption. Two such instruments are the ECOWAS Protocol against Corruption and the Inter-American Convention against Corruption. Both instruments provide in Article 6 entitled "Acts of corruption," a list of acts that constitute corruption. Two further instruments differentiate even more explicitly between corruption and the acts that constitute it. The African Union Convention against Corruption provides in Article 1 that "corruption" means the acts and practices including related offences proscribed in this Convention. Subsequently, Article 4 contains a list of acts of corruption, such as the bribery of a national public official, abuse of function, and embezzlement. An even clearer differentiation is provided by the SADC Protocol against Corruption, which distinguishes between corruption and the acts that constitute it, and also provides a general and residual definition of corruption. Article 1 provides that:

> 'Corruption' means any act referred to in Article 3 and includes bribery or any other behaviour in relation to persons entrusted with responsibilities in the public and private sectors which violates their duties as public officials, private employees,

---

duty or behaviour required of the recipient of the bribe, the undue advantage or the prospect thereof." (Emphasis added).

62 Precisely the same inaccuracy is present in the first and second Protocols to the Convention on the protection of the European Communities' financial interests.

63 Council Framework Decision 2003/568/JHA of 22 July 2003 on Combating Corruption in the Private Sector, Official Journal of the European Union L 192/54, 31 July 2003.

independent agents or other relationships of that kind and aimed at obtaining undue advantage of any kind for themselves or others.

It is clear from the above that corruption, defined as an individual and identifiable criminal act, does not exist either in national legal systems, or in the international legal system. Definitions of corruption always refer to a group of criminal offences. To discern the definition of corruption at the international level, it is therefore essential to identify these offences and how they are defined. Chapter IV below addresses this issue in detail.

IV. A WORD ON CORRUPTION IN THE PRIVATE SECTOR

A discussion of corruption in the private sector is inherent to any analysis of the definition of corruption. The term corruption usually entails the involvement of a private party (a citizen or corporation) and a public party (a public official). However, it is a matter of debate whether the term corruption should apply when a seemingly corrupt practice takes place solely within the private sector. A typical example is that of a company sales representative who gives money, gifts or other advantages (bribes) to the purchasing manager or buyer of a client company to win an order.[64] Also called private-to-private corruption or corporate corruption, such practices are viewed by some opinions as not being cases of true corruption, but as corporate or commercial criminality. This traditional approach to the definition of corruption rejects practices that do not involve the abuse of public power.[65] But this approach is increasingly losing ground and there is now almost general acceptance of private sector corruption as another of the "types" of corruption. This change is due in part to the increasingly widespread privatization of government services, the blurring of the separation between private and public functions, and the growth of international business transactions.[66] Some consider that corruption in the private sector

---

64 Argandoña, "Private-to-private Corruption," footnote 2. On corruption in the private sector, see for example François Vincke, "The Business Community's Attitude towards Corruption: Special Focus on Private-to-Private Corruption," in *Liber Amicorum: Commission Droit Et Vie Des Affaires* (Bruxelles: Bruylant, 1998), 177–194; Gunter Heine, Barbara Huber, and Tomas O. Rose, *Private Commercial Bribery: A Comparison of National and Supranational Legal Structures* (Freiburg: Edition iuscrim, 2003).

65 For example, Johnston states: "...we gain nothing by stretching our notions of corruption to include all forms of high-profile wrongdoing. We already have many concepts such as fraud, theft, and failure to perform fiduciary duties, that are readily applicable to the private sector." Johnston, *Syndromes of Corruption: Wealth, Power, and Democracy*, 13; Arvind K. Jain, "Corruption: A Review," *Journal of Economic Surveys* 15, no. 1 (February 1, 2001): 73.

66 Günter Heine, "Comparative Analysis," in *Private Commercial Bribery: A Comparison of National and Supranational Legal Structures*, ed. Günter Heine, Barbara Huber, and Thomas O Rose (Freiburg im Breisgau: Iuscrim, 2003), 608. See also, International Chamber of

undermines values such as trust, confidence and loyalty, which are necessary for the maintenance and development of social and economic relations, and that it ultimately damages society as a whole.[67]

Corruption in the private sector can take on a variety of forms, including bribery, dubious commissions, gifts and favours, the illegitimate use or trading of information, the use of undue influence to change a valuation or recommendation.[68] The core of the problem of corruption in the private sector is very similar to that of corruption involving the public sector. A manager or employee of a company acts disloyally in the performance of his or her duty towards the company, or against free competition and the market economy, taking advantage of his or her office or responsibility to obtain a benefit.

It is interesting that the evolution towards the definition as corporate corruption of what were once considered corporate crimes is illustrated by certain developments in national criminal law. Some countries have established criminal provisions against corruption in the private sector in their penal codes or in special laws, such as commercial codes.[69] Others, which follow a more traditional approach, have adopted specific criminal provisions against the corruption of public officials, but still adhere with regard to private sector corruption to civil remedies or self-regulation, labour law, or to traditional crimes, such as fraud management, misappropriation, fraudulent administration, or the forgery of documents.[70]

Commerce, *Memorandum to the OECD Working Group on Bribery in International Business Transaction*, Recommendations by the International Chamber of Commerce (ICC) on further provisions to be adopted to prevent and prohibit Private-to-Private Corruption, 13 September 2006.

67 CoE, Criminal Law Convention Explanatory Report, para. 52, available at http://conventions.coe.int/treaty/en/Reports/Html/173.htm (last visited 1 April 2012).

68 Argandoña, "Private-to-private Corruption," 255–256.

69 For example, Germany's Criminal Code has a chapter on "Crimes against Competition" criminalizing agreements restricting competition in relation to invitations to tender and the taking and offering of a bribe in business transactions, (StGB, Chapter XXVI, section 298, 299, and 300). Sweden (Criminal Code, Chapter 17, section 7) and the Netherlands (Criminal Code, section 328*ter*) provide for similar provisions. In the United States, corruption in the private sector, and particularly bribery, has mostly been criminalized at the state level. At the federal level, bribery in the sense of payments to private persons, has been criminalized only in relation to specific categories of persons, such as agents or employees of common carriers (Transportation Act of 1940, 49 U.S. Code section 1 (17)(b)), and contestants in television game shows (Communications Act, Amendments of 1960, 47 U.S. Code section 509(a)(2)).

70 For example, the Spanish Criminal Code does not make reference to corruption in the private sector, but includes a number of provisions on corporate crime (Title XIII, Chapter XIII). In France, bribery in the private sector is prohibited under the Labour Code, Art. L.152-6. See also, Heine, "Comparative Analysis," 611–612; Argandoña, "Private-to-private Corruption"; Rikki Stancich, "Deals in the Dark," *Ethical Corporation*, April 2008.

The criminalization of corruption in the private sector is aimed at protecting one or more of the following principles or interests: (i) the property and assets of the enterprise involved (the traditional approach); (ii) the employment relationship, in terms of loyalty, the integrity of the labour relationship between the employee and employer, the integrity of duties in business matters, or the integrity of fiduciary relationships; and (iii) free or fair competition and the proper functioning of the market.[71]

With these principles in mind, certain international legal instruments against corruption have addressed the issue of corruption in the private sector and are illustrative of the different views on this subject. The CoE Criminal Law Convention is intended to protect competition, private property interests, transparency in internal labour relationships, as well as "the trust, the confidence and the loyalty that are indispensable for private relationships to exist."[72] To this end, the Convention requires States Parties in their internal legislation to criminalize active and passive bribery in the private sector,[73] and money laundering of proceeds from bribery in the private sector,[74] as well as to take other measures in relation to accounting offences, participatory acts, sanctions, the cooperation of authorities, the protection of collaborators of justice and witnesses, the gathering of evidence, international cooperation, mutual assistance, and extradition.[75]

It should be noted that several States Parties have made declarations or reservations, particularly on the issue of the private sector. Belgium, for instance, regards bribery in the private sector as a criminal offence "only if such conduct was committed in view of the accomplishment or the omission of an act, without the knowledge and without authorization, as the case may be, of the board of

---

71 Heine, "Comparative Analysis," 612–617.

72 Barbara Huber, "Supranational Measures," in *Private Commercial Bribery: A Comparison of National and Supranational Legal Structures*, ed. Günter Heine, Barbara Huber, and Thomas O Rose (Freiburg im Breisgau: Iuscrim, 2003), 577, citing CoE Criminal Law Convention, Explanatory Report, para. 55.

73 CoE Criminal Law Convention, Arts. 7 and 8. Active bribery in the private sector is defined as follows: "...when committed intentionally in the course of business activity, the promising, offering or giving, directly or indirectly, of any undue advantage to any persons who direct or work for, in any capacity, private sector entities, for themselves or for anyone else, for them to act, or refrain from acting, in breach of their duties." Passive bribery in the private sector is defined as follows: "...when committed intentionally, in the course of business activity, the request or receipt, directly or indirectly, by any persons who direct or work for, in any capacity, private sector entities, of any undue advantage or the promise thereof for themselves or for anyone else, or the acceptance of an offer or a promise of such an advantage, to act or refrain from acting in breach of their duties."

74 CoE Criminal Law Convention, Art. 13.

75 CoE Criminal Law Convention, Arts. 14–27.

directors or of the general meeting, of the principal or of the employer."[76] This is a restrictive condition that is not present in the CoE Criminal Law Convention. Similarly, Portugal made a reservation declaring that it considers bribery in the private sector a criminal offence "only if the corruption in the private sector results in a distortion of competition or an economic loss for third persons."[77] Again, the negative effect of the corrupt act on third persons is not a requirement of the Convention. Poland also further restricts the definition of active and passive bribery in the private sector by reserving its right to apply the respective provisions "only in such case when the benefit or its promise is received by a person who has a leading position within an entity pursuing economic activity or by a person, who, due to his/her position or function, has an actual influence on taking decisions connected with activity of such an entity, in exchange for acting or abandonment, which can cause damage to its property, or for inadmissible preferential act, or action being unfair competition act."[78]

Although the CoE Civil Law Convention also applies to corruption in the private sector, it does not protect specific commercial interests or principles. The definition of bribery in this CoE Convention requires States Parties to provide in their domestic law "for effective remedies for persons who have suffered damage as a result of acts of corruption, to enable them to defend their rights and interests, including the possibility of obtaining compensation for damage."[79] States Parties have to provide in their internal law for the right to bring a civil action in corruption cases.[80] The Convention further regulates the statute of limitations for claims for compensation,[81] the protection of whistleblowers,[82] measures related to accounts and audits of companies,[83] effective procedures for the acquisition of evidence and interim measures in civil proceedings.[84] The Convention also provides that contracts providing for corruption should be declared null and void and that if consent to be bound by a contract is undermined by bribery the parties to such a contract should be able to request that it be declared void.[85]

76 See, Reservation of Belgium to the CoE Criminal Law Convention, available at http://conventions.coe.int/treaty/Commun/ListeDeclarations.asp?NT=173&CM=&DF=&CL=ENG&VL=1 (last visited 1 April 2012).
77 See, Reservation of Portugal to the CoE Criminal Law Convention, available at http://conventions.coe.int/treaty/Commun/ListeDeclarations.asp?NT=173&CM=&DF=&CL=ENG&VL=1 (last visited 1 April 2012).
78 See, Reservation of Poland to the CoE Criminal Law Convention, available at http://conventions.coe.int/treaty/Commun/ListeDeclarations.asp?NT=173&CM=&DF=&CL=ENG&VL=1 (last visited 1 April 2012).
79 CoE Civil Law Convention, Art. 1.
80 Ibid., Art. 3(1).
81 Ibid., Art. 7.
82 Ibid., Art. 9.
83 Ibid., Art. 10.
84 Ibid., Arts. 11 and 12.
85 Ibid., Art. 8.

In 2003, the European Union adopted a Framework Decision on Combating Corruption in the Private Sector (Framework Decision),[86] which recognizes that corruption in the private sector is a transnational problem. The aim of the Framework Decision is to protect competition in relation to the purchase of goods or commercial services with a view to economic development.[87] Similarly to the CoE Criminal Law Convention, the Framework Decision calls on States to criminalize active and passive bribery in the private sector,[88] and to take specific measures on penalties, sanctions, legal persons, and jurisdiction.[89] Member States are required to comply with the provisions of the Framework Decision before 22 July 2005 and to submit to the Council and the Commission the text of the implementing legislation.[90] However, only the Netherlands and Finland supplied their legislation to the Commission before the due date. A further 21 Member States have subsequently responded with, in some cases, incomplete information.[91]

At the regional level, outside Europe, only the AU has addressed the issue of corruption in the private sector. The AU Convention on Preventing and Combating Corruption provides a comprehensive framework and covers a range of criminal offences, including corrupt acts in the private sector.[92] It calls for measures on prevention, criminalization, regional cooperation, mutual legal assistance, and the recovery of assets.[93]

The UNCAC also deals with corruption in the private sector, but adopts a weaker approach. The Convention calls for preventive anti-corruption policies and practices, such as the development and maintaining by States of higher accounting and auditing standards in the private sector.[94] However, the Convention does not provide for the mandatory criminalization of such corrupt practices. States are only required to *consider* criminalizing bribery and

---

86 Council Framework Decision 2003/568/JHA of 22 July 2003 on Combating Corruption in the Private Sector, Official Journal of the European Union L 192/54, 31 July 2003. The Framework Decision repealed the Joint Action 98/742/JHA of 22 December 1998 adopted by the Council on the basis of Article K.3 of the Treaty on European Union, on corruption in the private sector, Official Journal of the European Union L 358, 31 December 1998.

87 Framework Decision, Preamble, para. 9.

88 Ibid., Art. 2.

89 Ibid., Arts. 3–7.

90 Ibid., Art. 9(1).

91 See, Commission of the European Communities, *Report from the Commission to the Council based on Article 9 of the Council Framework Decision 2003/568/JHA of 22 July 2003 on combating corruption in the private sector*, COM(2007) 328 final, 18 June 2007, available at http://eur-lex.europa.eu/LexUriServ/LexUriServ.do?uri=COM:2007:0328:FIN:EN:PDF (last visited 1 April 2012).

92 AU Convention against Corruption, Art. 11.

93 AU Convention against Corruption, Arts. 5, 16, 18, and 19.

94 UNCAC, Art. 12. This provision explicitly requires States Parties to disallow the tax deductibility of expenses that constitute bribes.

embezzlement in the private sector.[95] The timid approach adopted by the UNCAC, which is the latest international legal instrument on corruption, suggests that consideration of the abuse of power for private gain in the private sector is not yet generally accepted as a corrupt practice. Many States still follow the traditional approach of considering such practices as corporate criminality. As shown in this section, there is definitely a trend towards dealing with such practices as corruption. However, the rules adopted, and particularly international rules, are still at a rather infant stage in this respect.

This suggests that corruption in the private sector has not attained the same level of condemnation as corrupt practices involving the public sector. The principles and values that are protected by action to combat the two types of corruption also differ. As indicated above, private sector corruption restricts competition, betrays the bonds of duty and loyalty owed by an employee to an employer, violates corporate assets or shareholder interests, and ultimately damages society as a whole. In contrast, corruption involving the public sector directly harms society as a whole and seems to threaten more essential values, such as economic development, institutions and the values of democracy, justice and the rule of law, and the public trust vested in public officials. Although the approaches adopted to combat these different types of corruption may be related and interconnected, they still differ. For these reasons, and to maintain a narrow focus, the present study only concentrates on corruption involving the public sector.

CONCLUSION

It is by no means the aim of the present Chapter to exhaust the discussion on the definition of corruption. Countless approaches to this problem make it impossible to arrive at a universal definition. Political scientists, legal scholars, sociologists and economists see the issue of corruption through a different lens, and with a different purpose, and therefore define it differently. The notion of corruption undeniably needs to be adapted to each field of study. In the present study, corruption is therefore defined in legal terms.

In terms of the analysis of the international legal framework against corruption, only legal definitions can convey the real meaning of corruption. At times, the use of such definition may not always seem appropriate. Under these terms, a

---

95 UNCAC, Arts. 21 and 22. The UNTOC may also be mentioned as adopting a weak approach towards corruption in the private sector. Article 8 provides for the criminalization of corruption of public officials, however paragraph 2 of this Article provides that States Parties may wish to consider criminalizing other forms of corruption, which would allow for the criminalization of private sector corruption.

Wabenzi driving a Mercedes Benz S600 does not constitute corruption in legal terms, even though it may be immoral. However, corruption and immorality are two different things. In most parts of the world, it is society that decides through democratic processes which forms of behaviour are to be considered corrupt by declaring them illegal.

As a consequence, each legal system has a different definition of corruption. However, the internationalization of the problem of corruption is resulting in a process of the harmonization of domestic substantive law against corruption, with international law providing the standard. The definition of corruption in international law is a result of a combination of a descriptive core (abuse of entrusted power for private gain) and a normative element (the law determining the actions that constitute abuse of power for private gain). As a result, the different types of conduct or behaviour that are considered corrupt are central to any such definition. Chapter IV below examines these conducts in detail.

CHAPTER II

THE FIGHT AGAINST CORRUPTION UPGRADED TO THE INTERNATIONAL LEVEL

INTRODUCTION

Corruption has been condemned since time immemorial. However, over time the tone of its condemnation has evolved from being predominantly based on morality, to being founded today primarily on an empirical and objective basis. It would seem to be self-evident that corruption is universally condemned, and yet, as explained below, a minority of voices espouse an apologist approach towards corruption. This Chapter explores the different bases for the condemnation of corruption. The objective is to show how condemnation of corruption has evolved to its ultimate manifestation in recent years, namely the rise of anti-corruption to an issue of international concern.

In order to understand the historical development of the condemnation of corruption, it is necessary to make a distinction between bribery and other corrupt acts. Bribery was the first act to be rejected by society, although not all forms of bribery. As indicated below, bribery to obtain a public post was an accepted practice in Europe and other parts of the world until the nineteenth century. The situation was similar with other acts that today would be considered inherently corrupt. It is therefore important to bear in mind that modern definitions of corruption do not apply to what was considered corrupt in the past. Thus, the development of the condemnation of the various types of corrupt acts has been, and remains today, diverse.

I. FROM A MORALIST TO AN OBJECTIVE CONDEMNATION OF CORRUPTION

Corrupt practices can be traced back 5000 years, when bribery formed part of social behaviour.[96] Bribery constituted a form of mutually beneficial exchange,

---

96 John T. Noonan, *Bribes* (Berkeley: University of California Press, 1984), Part I.

or reciprocity, between two people. In ancient times, reciprocity used to be a cornerstone of human relationships in economic, social, political and personal matters. However, religious values, which led to changes in morality, gradually produced an anti-bribery ethic, and accordingly condemnation of corruption.

It is impossible to determine exactly when this anti-corruption ethic emerged.[97] But the evidence tends to suggest that condemnation of corruption in the form of bribery may have begun as early as 3000 B.C.[98] References to the condemnation of bribery can be found in several ancient sources, such as the Code of Hammurabi (Babylon, 2200 B.C.),[99] the Great Edict of Horemheb (Egypt, 1300 B.C.),[100] and Kautilya's Arthasastra (India, 400 B.C.).[101] Roman emperors in the fourth century legislated on several occasions between 316 A.D. and 398 A.D. against judicial corruption,[102] and held numerous trials on corruption, especially in provincial administrations.[103]

---

97 For historical accounts of corruption see, for example, Noonan, *Bribes*; Seppo Tiihonen, ed., *The History of Corruption in Central Government = L'histoire de la corruption au niveau du pouvoir central*, Cahier d'histoire de l'administration no. 7 (Amsterdam: IOS Press, 2003); Stephen Lovell, Alena V. Ledeneva, and A. B. Rogachevskiĭ, eds., *Bribery and Blat in Russia: Negotiating Reciprocity from the Middle Ages to the 1990s*, Studies in Russian and East European History and Society (Houndmills: Macmillan Press, 2000); Joel Hurstfield, *Freedom, Corruption, and Government in Elizabethan England* (Cambridge: Harvard University Press, 1973); Richard Harding, "Corruption and the Moral Boundaries of Patronage in the Renaissance," in *Patronage in the Renaissance*, ed. Guy Fitch Lytle and Stephen Orgel, Folger Institute Essays (Princeton, N.J: Princeton University Press, 1981), 47–64; Jeffrey K. Sawyer, "Judicial Corruption and Legal Reform in Early Seventeenth-Century France," *Law and History Review* 6 (1988): 95–117; Jean-Claude Waquet, *De la corruption: morale et pouvoir à Florence aux XVIIe et XVIIIe siècles* (Paris: Fayard, 1984); Upendra Thakur, *Corruption in Ancient India* (New Delhi: Abhinav Publications, 1979); Emmanuel Kreike and William C. Jordan, eds., *Corrupt Histories*, Studies in Comparative History (Rochester, NY: University of Rochester Press, 2004); Edward L. Glaeser and Claudia Dale Goldin, eds., *Corruption and Reform: Lessons from America's Economic History* (Chicago: University of Chicago Press, 2006).

98 Noonan, *Bribes*, xx.

99 See, The Code of Hammurabi 4 (Robert F. Harper trans. 1904) ("If a man (in a case) bear witness for grain or money (as a bribe), he shall himself bear the penalty imposed in that case."). John T. Noonan does not agree with interpreting the Code of Hammurabi as proscribing bribery. He claims that such interpretations are Western biased. Noonan, *Bribes*, 9–10. However, non-Western scholars have also interpreted the Code as covering bribery. See, Shaukat Ali, *Corruption: A Third World Perspective*, 2–3 (1985), cited in Philip M. Nichols, "Outlawing Transnational Bribery through the WTO," *Law and Policy in International Business* 28 (1997): 318, footnote 44.

100 The Edict proclaimed that any judge who took a reward from one litigant and failed to hear the adversary was guilty of a crime against justice and subject to capital punishment. See, Noonan, *Bribes*, 11.

101 The Arthasastra, an ancient Indian treatise on statecraft, economic policy and military strategy, has been interpreted as condemning bribe taking by civil servants in Mauryan India. See, Kautalya, *The Arthashastra*, trans. L. N Rangarajan, Penguin Classics (New Delhi: Penguin Books India, 1992), 294–303; Ajit Mishra, "Corruption: An Overview," in *The Economics of Corruption*, ed. Mishra Ajit (New Delhi: Oxford University Press, 2005), 4.

102 One of the most important decrees was Constantine's of 331 condemning the taking of an access payment. See, Noonan, *Bribes*, 90.

103 John Dickinson, *Death of a Republic; Politics and Political Thought at Rome 59–44 B.C* (New York: Macmillan, 1963).

This anecdotal ancient legislative evidence suggests a slow growth of the moral condemnation of corruption, cemented in religious values. In the Western world, this morality was strongly reinforced between the eleventh and sixteenth centuries.[104] This mostly occurred in the Church, where bribery was generally referred to by the term "simony." Nonetheless, corruption was not solely proscribed by Christianity.[105] It was condemned by the major religions, such as Buddhism,[106] Hinduism,[107] Islam,[108] Judaism,[109] Sikhism,[110] and Taoism.[111] Some time between 1000 A.D. and 1550 A.D., the anti-bribery ethic became a dominant idea in religious, legal, and literary expression.[112]

---

104 Noonan, *Bribes*, 139–310.

105 See the following two books of the Old Testament: *Deuteronomy* 16:19 ("Thou shalt not wrest justice…neither shalt thou take a bribe; for a bribe doth blind the eyes of the wise, and pervert the words of the righteous." American Standard Version); and *Exodus* 23:8 ("And thou shalt take no bribe: for a bribe blindeth them that have sight, and perverteth the words of the righteous." American Standard Version).

106 One of the Buddhist principles of ethical behaviour, or *sila* which makes reference to refraining from theft has been interpreted as covering bribery: "The second moral precept of refraining from taking what is not given … involves abstinence from all deceptive practices such as bribery that lead to social disintegration." See, U. Dhammaratana, "The Social Philosophy of Buddhism," in *The Social Philosophy of Buddhism*, Samdhong Rinpoche ed., 1972, p. 17–18, cited in Nichols, "Outlawing Transnational Bribery through the WTO," 321, footnote 53.

107 Thakur, *Corruption in Ancient India*, 14.

108 The Qur'an explicitly deals with corruption. *Sura* 2:188 states "And eat up not one another's property unjustly (in any illegal way e.g. stealing, robbing, deceiving, etc.), nor give bribery to the rulers (judges before presenting your cases) that you may knowingly eat up a part of the property of others sinfully." Taqi al-Din Hilali and Muhammad Muhsin Khan, trans., *Translation of the Meanings of the Noble Qur'an in the English Language* (Madinah, K.S.A: King Fahd Complex for the Printing of the Holy Qur'an, 1997). Islam as a religious doctrine has waged constant war against corruption… According to Islam, corruption is a sin for which there is no atonement. The Quran in unmistakable terms has pointed out that all those who indulge in corruption will be subject to eternal chastisement. Corruption is an immoral activity which deserves universal condemnation." Shaukat Ali, *Corruption: A Third World Perspective* (Lahore: Aziz Publishers, 1985), 49.

109 The Torah, the most holy of the sacred writings in Judaism, is accepted by Christianity as part of the Bible, comprising the first five books of the Old Testament. Hence, the two precepts against corruption in the Old Testament are common to Judaism, namely *Deuteronomy* 16:19 and *Exodus* 23:8.

110 "The main object of Sikh polity, it may again be emphasized, is 'righteous rule.' This can be achieved either by transforming the existing corrupt rulers on moral and ethical lines of religion through peaceful persuasions, or by replacing their corrupt rule by a 'just' regime if necessary, with the help of arms." Harbans Singh, *Degh, Tegh, Fateh: Socio-Economic & Religio-Political Fundamentals of Sikhism*, 1st ed. (Chandigarh: Alam Pub. House, 1986), 141.

111 One of the sacred texts of Taoism, "T'ai-Shang Kan-Ying P'ien", refers to bribe takers as evil doers. See, Daisetz Teitaro Suzuki and Paul Carus, trans., *T'ai-Shang Kan-Ying P'ien = [Taishang Gan Ying Pian] = Treatise of the Exalted One on Response and Retribution* (Chicago, Ill: Open Court Pub. Co, 1906), 56.

112 Noonan, *Bribes*, xx.

However, it was the arrival of the modern State administration in the nineteenth century and the notions of bureaucracy and "public interest" that gave a completely different meaning to the concept of corruption and provided great stimulus for its condemnation.[113] In pre-bureaucratic systems during the Middle Ages, office-holding was considered to be ownership of a source of income, to be exploited for rents or emoluments in exchange for the rendering of certain services. Similarly, in patrimonial systems, such as the Inca Empire, a ruler could legitimately engage in the self or family-centred distribution of the national income. Under such a system, by definition, corruption by ruling elites did not exist.[114] Similar situations of the sale of public office to the local aristocracy were common, although in different degrees and forms, in many countries in Europe, Asia, America, and Africa.[115]

In the nineteenth century, with the development of the modern state as a moral entity and the exercise of public authority as a duty, the conception of public office as private property disappeared, at least in theory.[116] This change occurred partly as a result of radical movements, such as the French Revolution. The idea that the office-holder must administer power for public ends and not for private benefit created a need for anti-corruption measures that would protect the public interest. This resulted in the first modern laws against corruption. For example, in Europe, the French Napoleonic Code of 1804 may be regarded as a landmark in this respect, with the introduction of strong penalties to combat corruption in public office. Evidently, the change in the moral perception of corruption did not mean that corrupt practices disappeared. On the contrary, during most periods of history certain corrupt practices have been regarded as permissible, or the penalties for them have been either fairly light, or generally not applied.

Therefore, until the twentieth century, corruption was viewed first as a moral failing and also, at times, as a violation of positive law, such as criminal legislation against bribery. But above all, the condemnation of corruption had an important moralistic connotation. Social scientists also approached the study of corruption from a moralistic perspective.[117] The cause of corruption was seen as incidental to the working of society and the result of evil and dishonest men

113 See also Chapter I above.

114 See, Jacob van Klaveren, "Corruption as a Historical Phenomenon," in *Political Corruption: Concepts and Contexts*, ed. Arnold J. Heidenheimer and Michael Johnston, 3rd ed. (New Brunswick, N.J: Transaction Publishers, 2002), 83–94.

115 Koenraad W. Swart, "The Sale of Public Offices," in *Political Corruption: Concepts and Contexts*, ed. Arnold J. Heidenheimer and Michael Johnston, 3rd ed. (New Brunswick, N.J: Transaction Publishers, 2002), 95–106.

116 Swart, "Political Corruption"; Lisa Hill, "Adam Smith and the Theme of Corruption," *The Review of Politics* 68, no. 4 (2006): 636–662.

117 Ronald E Wraith, *Corruption in Developing Countries* (London: Allen & Unwin, 1963); Gunnar Myrdal, "Corruption: Its Causes and Effects," in *Asian Drama: An Inquiry into the Poverty of Nations*, vol. 2, 3 vols. (New York: Twentieth Century Fund, 1968), 937–958;

gaining positions of power and trust.[118] The so-called moralists argued that to defeat corruption fundamental changes were needed in values and norms of honesty in public service.[119]

However, in the mid-twentieth century, research studies departed from the general moralistic and subjective approach that had been adopted towards corruption in the past. They paved the way to a more objective study of the phenomenon and explained its existence with reference to social mores and deficiencies in economic and political systems. Condemnation of corruption started to be based less on morality and more on empirical evidence of its negative consequences, and particularly its economic effects.

Many of the early economic studies on corruption focused on the principal-agent model of corruption, and on weaknesses in public institutions and policies that gave rise to rent seeking by public officials and the incubation of corrupt practices. The principal-agent model of corruption refers to the relationship between the principal (the public in general or citizens) and the agent (public official) who accepts a bribe from a private individual interested in a governmental good or service. Early research examined ways of motivating the agent to be honest, but did not analyse the economic consequences of corruption.[120] However, economic studies of corruption subsequently concentrated on the economic consequences of corrupt practices. This utilitarian condemnation of corruption concentrated on its negative effects on business development, public expenditure, domestic and foreign investment and economic growth.

Numerous studies have shown the detrimental effect of corruption on administrative performance and on economic and political development.[121]

Stanislav Andreski, *The African Predicament: A Study in the Pathology of Modernisation* (London: Joseph, 1968), 92–109.

118 Gerald E. Caiden and Naomi J. Caiden, "Administrative Corruption," *Public Administration Review* 37, no. 3 (1977): 301.

119 Pranab Bardhan, "Corruption and Development: A Review of Issues," *Journal of Economic Literature* 35, no. 3 (September 1997): 1335.

120 See, inter alia, Edward Banfield, "Corruption as a Feature of Government Organization," *Journal of Law and Economics* 18 (1975): 587–605; Susan Rose-Ackerman, "The Economics of Corruption," *Journal of Public Economics* 4 (1975): 187–203; Susan Rose-Ackerman, *Corruption: A Study in Political Economy*, 1978; Robert Klitgaard, *Controlling Corruption* (Berkeley: University of California Press, 1988); Robert Klitgaard, "Gifts and Bribes," in *Strategy and Choice*, ed. Richard Zeckhauser (Cambridge, Mass: MIT Press, 1991), 402; Jagdish N. Bhagwati, "Directly Unproductive, Profit-Seeking (DUP) Activities," *The Journal of Political Economy* 90, no. 5 (October 1982): 988–1002; Gary S. Becker, "Crime and Punishment: An Economic Approach," *Journal of Political Economy* 76, no. 2 (1968): 169–217; Anne Krueger, "The Political Economy of the Rent-Seeking Society," *The American Economic Review* 64, no. 3 (June 1974): 291–303.

121 David Gould and Jose A. Amaro-Reyes, *The Effects of Corruption on Administrative Performance: Illustrations from Developing Countries*, World Bank Staff Working Papers, no. 580, Management and Development Series (Washington D.C.: World Bank, 1983).

Cross-country studies have demonstrated the significant cost of corruption on investment and economic growth.[122] For example, it has been found that corruption distorts markets and the allocation of resources by acting as an arbitrary tax, by undermining the regulatory role of the government, and also by distorting the fundamental role of the government in such areas as the enforcement of contracts and the protection of property rights.[123] It has also been shown that corruption has a negative effect on resources allocation. It results in resource misallocation when the decision on how public funds are to be invested is taken by a corrupt government agency, which tends to choose activities that lend themselves more easily to corruption.[124] Thus, the misallocation of public funds has a pervasive effect on economic development. Corruption can also negatively affect private investment by undermining the incentive for entrepreneurs, who can expect to receive less for their efforts and who face greater uncertainty.[125]

Research has shown that corruption also affects the distribution of income and wealth. Higher corruption correlates to higher income inequality. Corruption evidently favours the wealthy. Biased tax systems, poor targeting of social programmes and their impact on asset ownership, human capital formation and education inequalities are just some of the consequences of corruption.[126] These in turn lead to inequality and greater poverty. Corruption also tends to exacerbate income inequalities, as it constitutes a tool by which those with power can hold on to it, to the exclusion of others.

Moreover, it should be emphasized that the objective condemnation of corruption is not only based on the negative economic consequences of corrupt practices. Numerous research studies have shown the detrimental effects of corruption on the legitimacy of political institutions and the values of democracy, justice and the rule of law and the public trust vested in public officials.[127] In addition, corruption has an adverse impact on service delivery.

---

122 Paolo Mauro, "Corruption and the Composition of Government Expenditure," *Journal of Public Economics* 69, no. 2 (1998): 263–279; Shang-Jin Wei, "How Taxing is Corruption on International Investors?," *Review of Economics and Statistics* 82, no. 1 (2000): 1–11; Martin Paldam, "The Cross-Country Pattern of Corruption: Economics, Culture and the Seesaw Dynamics," *European Journal of Political Economy* 18, no. 2 (2002): 215–240; Arvind K. Jain, "Corruption: A Review," *Journal of Economic Surveys* 15, no. 1 (February 1, 2001): 71–121.

123 Vito Tanzi, "Corruption Around the World: Causes, Consequences, Scope, and Cures," in *Governance, Corruption, and Economic Performance*, ed. George T. Abed and Sanjeev Gupta (Washington, D.C.: International Monetary Fund, 2002), 19–58.

124 In this sense, see Vito Tanzi and Hamid Davoodi, *Corruption, Public Investment, and Growth*, IMF Working Paper WP/97/139, 1997.

125 Kevin M. Murphy, Andrei Shleifer, and Robert W. Vishny, "The Allocation of Talent: Implications for Growth," *Quarterly Journal of Economics* 106, no. 2 (May 1991): 503.

126 Sanjeev Gupta, Hamid Davoodi, and Rosa Alonso-Terme, *Does Corruption Affect Inequality and Poverty?*, IMF Working Paper WP/98/76, 1998, 6.

127 Caiden and Caiden, "Administrative Corruption."

Corruption is associated with rising military spending as a share of Gross Domestic Product (GDP) and of total government expenditure, and with larger procurement outlays in relation to both GDP and government spending.[128] Conversely, corruption has been demonstrated to lower spending on health care and education services. Empirical studies show that a country's level of corruption is related to high rates of child and infant mortality, a higher percentage of low birth weight and higher drop-out rates in primary school.[129]

It has also been argued that corruption intensifies ethnic conflicts, as it does not seem to have contributed to class formation or to the development of social order. Instead, corruption intensifies existing interethnic conflicts and heightens competition among the various groups seeking to obtain a share of corrupt income.[130] It is also claimed that corruption erodes the legitimacy of honest elites and well-run institutions, and impedes development, thus being generally harmful to societies and government.[131] Corruption is said to have caused the crumbling of political regimes and paved the way for authoritarian administration, as has happened in Pakistan, Myanmar and China.[132]

Clearly, these are no more than a sample of the vast range of findings by studies of the consequences of corruption. They serve as an illustration of the radical change on which the condemnation of corruption is now cemented. Anti-corruption is no longer seen as principally an ethical issue. Increasingly, it has become an issue of economic development, competitiveness and political accountability.[133]

---

128 Sanjeev Gupta, Luiz de Mello, and Raju Sharan, *Corruption and Military Spending*, IMF Working Paper WP/00/23, 2000.

129 Sanjeev Gupta, Hamid Davoodi, and Erwin R. Tiongson, "Corruption and the Provision of Health Care and Education Services," in *Governance, Corruption and Economic Performance*, ed. George T. Abed and Sanjeev Gupta (Washington, D.C: International Monetary Fund, 2002), 245–279.

130 M. Shahid Alam, "Anatomy of Corruption: An Approach to the Political Economy of Underdevelopment," *American Journal of Economics and Sociology* 48, no. 4 (1989): 452–453.

131 Wraith, *Corruption in Developing Countries*; Myrdal, "Asian Dram"; George Charles Sumner Benson, *Political Corruption in America* (Lexington, Mass: Lexington Books, 1978).

132 Myrdal, "Asian Dram," 937–938. History is replete with examples of governments whose demise is attributable at least in part to corruption. These include the Roman Empire, the Ottoman Empire, and Imperial France. See, Charles Pinot Duclos, trans., *The History of Lewis XI: King of France* (London: Printed for C. Davis and P. Vaillant, 1746), 5; Ramsay MacMullen, *Corruption and the Decline of Rome* (New Haven: Yale University Press, 1988); Alan Warwick Palmer, *The Decline and Fall of the Ottoman Empire* (New York: M. Evans, 1992).

133 Michael Gadbaw, "International Anticorruption Initiatives: Today's Fad or Tomorrow's New World?," *American Society of International Law: Proceedings of the 91st Annual Meeting* (1997): 113.

II. CORRUPTION "APOLOGISTS": A RELATIVE CONDEMNATION OF CORRUPTION

A less moralistic and more objective approach to the study of corruption also opened the door to questioning the idea that all consequences of corruption are harmful. A minority of opinions broke away from the general condemnation of corruption and put forward theories on the potential benefits of corruption to political and economic development.[134] The most well-known and studied "corruption apologists" date from the 1960s and 1970s, most notably Leff, Huntington, and Nye.[135] However, similar claims had already been made by other authors in 1904.[136] These theories, known as revisionist or functionalist, did not claim that corrupt practices were generally beneficial to economic and political development. They accepted the detrimental consequences of corruption, but focused on the functionality or positive consequences of certain corrupt practices on the performance of least developed countries. This so-called "romantic view of corruption"[137] postulated two major positive effects of corruption, one on political development and the other on economic development.

In terms of political development, it has been claimed that corruption can have an integrationist effect, as certain corrupt practices, such as bribery, allow the integration of various groups into the political process who otherwise would not be able to participate. In many developing countries, interest groups are weak

---

134 See, David H. Bayley, "The Effects of Corruption in a Developing Nation," *Western Political Quarterly* 19, no. 4 (1966): 719–732; Gabriel Ben-Dor, "Corruption, Institutionalization, and Political Development: The Revisionist Theses Revisited," *Comparative Political Studies* 7, no. 1 (1974): 63–83; Samuel P. Huntington, "Modernization and Corruption," in *Political Order in Changing Societies* (New Haven: Yale University Press, 1968), 59–71; Nathaniel H. Leff, "Economic Development through Bureaucratic Corruption," *American Behavioral Scientist* 8, no. 3 (1964): 8–14; Joseph S. Nye, "Corruption and Political Development: A Cost-Benefit Analysis," *American Political Science Review* 61, no. 2 (1967): 417–427; James C. Scott, "The Analysis of Corruption in Developing Nations," *Comparative Studies in Society and History* 11, no. 3 (1969): 315–341; James C. Scott, "Corruption, Machine Politics and Political Change," *American Political Science Review* 63, no. 4 (1969): 1142–1159; Jose Veloso Abueva, "The Contribution of Nepotism, Spoils and Graft to Political Development," *East-West Center Review* 3 (1966): 45–54; O.P. Dwivedi, "Bureaucratic Corruption in Developing Countries," *Asian Survey* 7, no. 4 (1967): 245–253; Colin Leys, "What is the Problem about Corruption?," *Journal of Modern African Studies* 3, no. 2 (1965): 215–230.

135 Although the term "corruption apologists" has been used since at least 1910. See, Robert Clarkson Brooks, *Corruption in American Politics and Life* (New York: Dodd, Mead, 1910); Daniel Kaufmann, "Corruption: The Facts," *Foreign Policy*, no. Summer (1997): 114–131.

136 See, for example, Henry Jones Ford, "Municipal Corruption," *Political Science Quarterly* 19, no. 4 (December 1904): 673–686.

137 Vito Tanzi and Hamid Davoodi, "Corruption, Growth, and Public Finances," in *Governance, Corruption, and Economic Performance*, ed. George T. Abed and Sanjeev Gupta (Washington D.C.: International Monetary Fund, 2002), 197–198.

and political parties rarely allow the participation of elements outside the contending cliques. Consequently, graft may be the only institution that allows other interests to achieve inclusion and representation in the political process.[138] Unrepresented groups can gain political influence through corrupt means.[139] In this sense, it has been claimed that corruption can contribute to national integration and can be instrumental in the maintenance of a political system.[140] Moreover, thc proceeds of corruption are said to have been used to create viable political institutions, such as political parties, thereby strengthening political institutions and political development.[141]

In addition, several of the corruption apologists have also held that corruption can benefit economic development in several ways.[142] In many developing countries, economic expansion is hampered by imperfect government policies, government bureaucracy and inefficient and burdensome regulation.[143] Corruption may be a way of overcoming such barriers, with a positive effect on economic development. In the United States, during the 1870s and 1880s, corruption of state legislatures and city councils by railroad, utility and industrial corporations speeded up the growth of the American economy.[144] Another example is the differential response by the bureaucracies in Chile and Brazil to the price controls of food products introduced in the two countries during a period of high inflation in the early 1960s. While Chile enforced the freeze, resulting in the stagnation of food production, in Brazil a corrupt bureaucracy effectively sabotaged the freeze and production increased, to the benefit of consumers.[145] In the Soviet Union, certain types of corruption were considered functional and were tolerated in practice.[146] It has also been suggested that corruption increases investment, as it allows entrepreneurs to control risks and uncertainties and to introduce innovation, by making it

138 Leff, "Economic Development through Bureaucratic Corruption," 9.

139 Scott, "The Analysis of Corruption in Developing Nations," 325.

140 Nye, "Corruption and Political Development: A Cost-Benefit Analysis"; Robert Hislope, *When Being Bad is Good: Corrupt Exchange in Divided Societies*, Conference on Post Communist States and Societies: Transnational and National Politics (Maxwell School of Syracuse University, October 30, 2005). Hislope claims that in ethnically divided societies corrupt practices among ethnic party elites fosters durable multiethnic coalition government and thus reduces interethnic violence.

141 Huntington, "Modernization and Corruption."

142 Leff, "Economic Development through Bureaucratic Corruption"; David Osterfeld, *Prosperity Versus Planning: How Government Stifles Economic Growth* (New York: Oxford University Press, 1992).

143 Douglas A. Houston, "Can Corruption Ever Improve an Economy?," *Cato Journal* 27, no. 3 (2007): 325–342.

144 Huntington, "Modernization and Corruption."

145 Leff, "Economic Development through Bureaucratic Corruption," 11–12.

146 John M Kramer, "Political Corruption in the U. S. S. R.," *The Western Political Quarterly* 30, no. 2 (June 1977): 213–224; Konstantin M Simis, *USSR: The Corrupt Society: The Secret World of Soviet Capitalism* (New York: Simon and Schuster, 1982).

possible for economic innovators to introduce innovations before becoming politically established.[147] Corruption was also said to improve competition and efficiency, on the grounds that entrepreneurs who can afford the highest bribes to obtain licenses and favours from bureaucrats are the most efficient producers.[148]

In truth, the so-called corruption apologists were scholars who solely claimed that corruption in determined cases could have specific positive consequences on political or economic development. However, they triggered a tremendous amount of criticism and reaction.[149] A number of scholars have endeavoured to show that the alleged advantages brought by corruption are outnumbered by the resultant evils. It has been held that the revisionist theses failed to take into account the systemic character of corruption and did not adopt a dynamic perspective in relation to its effects.[150] The premise that corruption allows unrepresented groups to integrate into the political system does not hold, when in practice corruption in most cases creates a further barrier for the excluded and reinforces those in power. Unrepresented groups rarely possess the financial means and access to corrupt channels to promote their interests. Instead of producing national integration, corruption serves the interests of elites. Cases of corruption rarely involve those from underprivileged groups.[151] This results in a general distrust of political institutions, instead of them being strengthened, as maintained by the revisionists.

Similarly, the alleged economic benefits of corruption on development would also seem to be illusory. It is true that economic expansion is undermined by government bureaucracy and inefficient and burdensome regulation. However, at best corruption can only overcome these hurdles in the short-term. Bureaucrats and the governing elite usually expand bureaucracy and regulation as much as possible so that they can profit more fully from corruption. A famous study carried out by Kaufmann and Wei shows that bribes do not reduce red tape, but on the contrary serve to create greater bureaucratic burdens.[152] When

---

147 Leff, "Economic Development through Bureaucratic Corruption," 11.

148 Leff, "Economic Development through Bureaucratic Corruption," 11; Bayley, "The Effects of Corruption in a Developing Nation," 945.

149 See, for example, Alam, "Anatomy of Corruption: An Approach to the Political Economy of Underdevelopment"; Ben-Dor, "Corruption, Institutionalization, and Political Development: The Revisionist Theses Revisited"; Caiden and Caiden, "Administrative Corruption."

150 Alam, "Anatomy of Corruption: An Approach to the Political Economy of Underdevelopment."

151 Ben-Dor, "Corruption, Institutionalization, and Political Development: The Revisionist Theses Revisited," 72–74.

152 Daniel Kaufmann and Shang-Jin Wei, *Does "Grease Money" Speed Up the Wheels of Commerce?*, National Bureau of Economic Research Working Paper no. 7093, 1999; Alberto Ades and Rafael Di Tella, "The New Economics of Corruption: A Survey and Some New Results," *Political Studies* 45, no. 3 (1997): 496–515. Ades and Di Tella argue that corruption

bureaucrats realize that petty corruption can enhance their income, they are tempted to enact regulations that require increased interaction between managers and the bureaucracy, or they request "fees" for all the services they provide, even if they are supposed to be free. Hence, even if bribery speeds up individual transactions, the number of transactions required will tend to increase sufficiently to offset the efficiency with which each transaction is carried out. Moreover, small payments often lead to demands for larger payments.[153]

The problems that corruption can overcome may well exist precisely to provide increased opportunities for corruption and, as such, harm the economy instead of benefiting it. There does not appear to be a correlation between corruption and periods of rapid economic growth, indeed, just the opposite.[154] Furthermore, the granting of licenses and favours to entrepreneurs who can afford the highest bribes does not create competition and efficiency. The highest bidder is not necessarily the most efficient.[155] Higher bribes in the end may have to be financed by cheating on the terms of the contract, therefore transferring the costs to society.

Already in 1910, there were writers expressing opposition to the approach of the apologists.[156] Notwithstanding repeated attempts to bury such theories, there are still studies today claiming that corruption may produce positive outcomes.[157] For example, they criticize the current anti-corruption campaign because they question its negative consequences on development. Certain authors contest in particular the argument concerning the negative effects of corruption on economic development. For example, the Harvard Professor David Kennedy seems to accept that in developing countries the informal economy is more crucial than the formal economy. He adds that the anti-corruption campaign is aimed at rationalizing the informal economy and making it more transparent, and that this will hurt economic growth at least in the short or immediate term. Kennedy also argues that the connection between the elimination of corruption and development remains unclear and that no

acts like "sand-in-the-machine." Their research shows no benefits of corruption in countries mired in red tape.

153 Jain, "Corruption: A Review," 92.

154 Ben-Dor, "Corruption, Institutionalization, and Political Development: The Revisionist Theses Revisited," 70.

155 Susan Rose-Ackerman, "The Political Economy of Corruption," in *Corruption and the Global Economy*, ed. Kimberly Ann Elliott (Washington, DC: Institute for International Economics, 1997), 42.

156 Brooks, *Corruption in American Politics and Life*, chap. 1.

157 Some economists argue that in particularly confined circumstances corruption may promote faster growth. See, for example, Serguey Braguinsky, "Corruption and Schumpeterian Growth in Different Economic Environments," *Contemporary Economic Policy* 14, no. 3 (1996): 14–25; Houston, "Can Corruption Ever Improve an Economy?"; Hislope, *When Being Bad is Good: Corrupt Exchange in Divided Societies.*

economic theory predicts that a "not corrupt" regime leads to growth and development, rather than a stable low level equilibrium.[158] Reference is made to several cases of economic growth under corrupt regimes.[159]

The current anti-corruption campaign is also said to have had important political collateral damages. According to Moisés Naím, former Editor-in-chief of *Foreign Policy* magazine: "…the war on corruption is undermining democracy, helping the wrong leaders get elected and distracting societies from facing urgent problems."[160] It is argued that all the ills of nations are blamed on corruption and that, although it is true that corruption can be crippling, bringing an end to it does not necessarily resolve the deeper problems that afflict societies. Such a false belief can make it even harder to obtain public support for other indispensable public efforts. For example, tax reforms become impossible to pass when the general assumption is that any new public revenues will inevitably evaporate into corrupt hands. For Naím, the worst collateral damage caused by this fixation on corruption is the political instability that it can create and the false expectations that it produces. Many corrupt leaders have been ousted and replaced by other seemingly honest leaders with the expectation that development will follow. Yet, in many of these cases, the countries concerned remain corrupt and are still awaiting the promised progress.[161] Other authors are worried about anti-corruption campaigns producing excessive disaffection and disillusionment amongst citizens and the ensuing scepticism towards democracy.[162]

It is therefore not only the action taken to combat corruption that is challenged, but also the mere idea of combating corruption. However, neither of the main currents that challenge action against corruption favours allowing the spread of corruption throughout the world. Their criticism is aimed at re-shaping to varying degrees current anti-corruption policies, and particularly their international aspects. It is therefore safe to conclude that an empirical consensus has emerged on the detrimental effects of corruption on a wide range of societal variables.

---

158 David Kennedy, *The Dark Sides of Virtue: Reassessing International Humanitarianism* (Princeton, N.J: Princeton University Press, 2004), 163.

159 For example, Barry Hindess, "International Anti-Corruption as a Programme of Normalization," in *Governments, NGOs and Anti-Corruption: The New Integrity Warriors*, ed. Luís de Sousa, Peter Larmour, and Barry Hindes (New York, NY: Routledge, 2009), 27.

160 Moisés Naím, "Tunnel Vision on Corruption," *Washington Post*, February 20, 2005.

161 Ibid.5.

162 Staffan Anderson and Paul M. Heywood, "Anti-Corruption as a Risk to Democracy: On the Unintended Consequences of International Anti-Corruption Campaigns," in *Governments, NGOs and Anti-Corruption: The New Integrity Warriors*, ed. Luís de Sousa, Peter Larmour, and Barry Hindess (New York, NY: Routledge, 2009), 33–50.

III. THE 1990s: CORRUPTION IN THE AIR

As indicated earlier, the condemnation of, interest in, and studies on corruption date from ancient times.[163] However, in the 1990s this interest, particularly in the field of economics, reached another level. In the 1990s there was a true "corruption eruption"[164] as an issue. A combination of factors, such as the end of the Cold War and the accelerating trends towards globalization and world economic integration, the increasing economic liberalization and democratic reforms, as well as the emergence of the good governance agenda, are claimed to have caused the boom of corruption as a research and policy issue. During the 1990s, capital flows to emerging and developing countries began to originate predominantly in the private sector (multinational corporations and financial markets), replacing official transfers. Countries needed to be more transparent and accountable in the management of their economies to benefit from the growing international flows of capital, technology, and information.[165]

During the Cold War, official capital flows to developing countries were destined to maintain the political influence of the superpowers and their allies in strategic areas of the world. Hence, deficient economic performance, high tariffs and pervasive state intervention, combined with a lack of transparency or accountability by the countries receiving the capital mattered little for the distribution of bilateral official aid. In addition, developing countries were hardly affected by market retribution, as their influence was too small to matter.[166]

With the end of the Cold War, many developing countries lost their strategic privileges and began to be more exposed to the exacting requirements of market discipline. Countries began to compete to attract capital in an environment in which financial flows were driven by expected rates of return on investment. In order to attract foreign direct investment and to gain access to financial markets on reasonable terms, sound macroeconomic policies, a healthy regulatory environment and transparent and accountable institutions became essential conditions.[167] Such macroeconomic reforms were also related to the emergence

---

163 Even Plato dealt with corruption in *The Republic*. See, Judith Presler, "Plato's Solution to the Problem of Political Corruption," in *Philosophical Perspectives on Power and Domination*, ed. Laura Duhan Kaplan and Laurence F. Bove (Amsterdam; Atlanta, GA: Rodopi, 1997), 107–113.

164 Term borrowed from Moisés Naím, "The Corruption Eruption," *Brown Journal of World Affairs* 2, no. 2 (1995): 245–261.

165 George T. Abed and Sanjeev Gupta, "The Economics of Corruption: An Overview," in *Governance, Corruption, and Economic Performance*, ed. George T. Abed and Sanjeev Gupta (Washington, D.C.: International Monetary Fund, 2002), 1–4.

166 Ibid.

167 Ibid.

of the good governance agenda, which in turn also contributed greatly to the increased interest in corruption. This agenda, first endorsed by the World Bank, was aimed at increasing the productive capacity of the private sector as the engine of economic growth, or releasing market forces from regulatory controls. In the 1990s, good governance became a central part of development policy. During that period, action to combat corruption as a central aspect of the notion of good governance began to receive much more attention.

During the Cold War, many countries had concentrated on holding the line against communism and the development of real free markets and political competition was not a priority, if it was on the agenda at all. The fall of the Berlin Wall completely re-shaped priorities. The end of the Cold War and the demise of the communist threat also transformed internal political influences in developed countries. One example was Italy, where fear of communism had long led to public tolerance of notoriously high levels of corruption. However, with the end of the communist threat and the weakening of the once strong Italian Communist Party, the famous judicial investigation "*mani pulite*" (clean hands) began a nationwide examination in 1992 of corrupt practices in Italian politics.[168]

Interest and research into corruption also arose out of the growing availability of data measuring corruption which was developed in the late 1980s.[169] These data showed an increase in corrupt practices during the 1990s.[170] Tanzi argues that during the 1990s several countries experienced high taxes, a high level of public spending, and new governmental regulations and controls on economic activities. This gave bureaucrats the opportunity to engage in corruption.[171]

In addition, the 1990s were a period of numerous privatizations, which proved to be linked with corruption, particularly in Latin America and the transition economies with the so-called *nomenklatura* privatisations.[172] These corrupt

168 Patrick Glynn, Stephen J. Kobrin, and Moisés Naím, "The Globalization of Corruption," in *Corruption and the Global Economy*, ed. Kimberly Ann Elliott (Washington D.C.: Institute for International Economics, 1997), 9. On "mani pulite" see Donatella Della Porta and Alberto Vannucci, *Un Paese Anormale: Come La Classe Politica Ha Perso L'occasione Di Mani Pulite*, 1st ed., Saggi tascabili Laterza (Roma: GLF editori Laterza, 1999); Gabrio Forti, ed., *Il Prezzo Della Tangente: La Corruzione Come Sistema a Dieci Anni Da Mani Pulite* (Milano: Vita e Pensiero, 2003); Carlo Nordio, *Giustizia*, 1st ed. (Milano: Cantiere Italia, 1997).

169 Abed and Gupta, "The Economics of Corruption: An Overview," 4.

170 Tanzi, "Corruption Around the World: Causes, Consequences, Scope, and Cures," 22.

171 Ibid.

172 On "nomenklatura privatizations" and in general on corruption in privatizations, see Daniel Kaufmann and Paul Siegelbaum, "Privatization and Corruption in Transition Economies," *Journal of International Affairs* 50, no. 2 (1997): 419–458; Marshall Goldman, "The Pitfalls of Russian Privatization," *Challenge* 40, no. May-June (1997): 35–49; Luigi Manzetti and Charles Blake, "Market Reforms and Corruption in Latin America," *Review of International Political Economy* 3, no. Winter (1997): 662–697.

privatizations not only increased the level of corruption, but in addition, due to the scandals that they generated, also raised the level of perception among the general public.

Because corruption is by definition covert, there is no precise way of quantifying it; there is therefore no real way of knowing if it is increasing or decreasing. Yet, there is no doubt that in the 1990s the public's perception of corruption increased greatly because of the increase in publicity.[173] The growing role played by civil society and international organizations in publicizing the problem of corruption and trying to create anti-corruption movements also helped to attract more attention. Within international organizations, the international financial institutions became particularly interested in research into corruption and governance based on the concern that public spending and aid were not having the desired impact on poverty and social outcomes.[174]

It is a paradox that corruption is perceived to have increased in the 1990s when the global, political and economic circumstances created unprecedented conditions for its decline. The spread of democracy around the world in the late 1980s and throughout the 1990s is also said to have contributed to the rising importance of transparency in government operations. Between 1987 and 2000, the number of democratic states grew from 69 to 120, representing 63 per cent of the world population.[175] While democracies are not immune from corruption, they are usually considered more transparent than other systems in view of their more active national media and stronger legislatures with the power to hold leaders accountable.[176]

All of the above factors heightened interest in the phenomenon of corruption in general, and in particular in the economics of corruption. The expansion of research, particularly empirical research, carried out in the 1990s increasingly showed the devastating effects of corruption for both developed and developing countries.[177] As has been suggested, "the 1990s could be to corruption what the 1850s were to slavery: a decade of irreversible change."[178]

---

173 Naím, "The Corruption Eruption," 247.

174 Abed and Gupta, "The Economics of Corruption: An Overview," 5.

175 Ibid., 4, citing Freedom House, *Freedom in the World: The Annual Survey of Political Rights and Civil Liberties* (New York: Freedom House, various issues).

176 Glynn, Kobrin, and Naím, "The Globalization of Corruption," 11.

177 Kaufmann highlights the relevance of empirical research on corruption as being critical in stimulating, sustaining, and nourishing anti-corruption programmes. Policy action should be based on empirical research. Daniel Kaufmann, "Research on Corruption: Critical Empirical Issues," in *Economics of Corruption*, ed. Arvind K. Jain (Boston: Kluwer Academic Publishers, 1998), 129–137.

178 Glynn, Kobrin, and Naím, "The Globalization of Corruption," 26.

IV. CONCERN AT CORRUPTION GOES INTERNATIONAL

As indicated above, the condemnation of corruption has evolved over time from being predominantly based on morality to being founded on a more objective basis. However, most importantly, this evolution also led in the 1990s to an increase in the level of attention and condemnation of corruption. In turn, over the past fifteen years, the problem of corruption has been transformed from a predominantly national concern into a global political issue that is eliciting a global political response. But why is this happening now, if corruption has existed since time immemorial? And, why has action to combat corruption acquired such an international dimension?

The answer is complex and multifaceted. The first efforts to internationalize action against corruption were motivated by commercial interests with a view to levelling the playing field in international business transactions.[179] As trade and commercial barriers were lifted in developing countries, and state monopolies were privatized, multinational corporations competed for the new markets, sometimes bribing foreign public officials to secure business. Since 1977, when the Foreign Corrupt Practices Act (FCPA)[180] was enacted in the United States, criminalizing the bribery of foreign officials, American multinationals found themselves at a disadvantage, as equivalent legislation did not exist in other parts of the world.[181] Certain European multinationals could not only bribe foreign public officials to gain access to international markets, but such bribes were even tax deductible in their home countries. It was believed that US interests were substantially affected by this "commercial disadvantage,"[182] and in response the US Government began to work to level the playing field. As the competition in question was at the international level, the only way to ensure that all players (States) played by the same rules was by addressing the issue of corruption at the international level.

---

179 Some authors claim that this is the main, and probably the only motivation for the current fight against corruption in developed countries. See, for example, *Seminario internacional sobre la corrupción y la convención interamericana, Talleres de divulgación e implementación de la convención interamericana contra la corrupción* (Bogotá: Pontificia Universidad Javeriana, Facultad de Ciencias Jurídicas, 1999), 23.

180 FCPA, 15 U.S.C. §§78dd-(1)-(3), 78m, 78ff (2000).

181 Sweden also outlawed the bribery of foreign public officials at that time, although in a much more limited way than the United States. See, Nichols, "Outlawing Transnational Bribery through the WTO," 349–352.

182 The losses to US business were estimated by the US Commerce Department at US$ 100 billion between 1993 and 1996. See, Richard Lawrence, "US Anti-Corruption Drive Pays," *Journal of Commerce*, June 20, 1996; James Jr. Hines, *Forbidden Payment: Foreign Bribery and American Business after 1977*, NBER Working Paper 5266.

This is how the first discussions of action to combat corruption commenced in the United Nations and other international fora. The United States called on other countries to adopt legislation similar to the FCPA, and for some time, unsuccessfully negotiated such laws under the auspices of the United Nations. Although at first Europeans resisted, the United States ultimately won this bout of arm-wrestling by taking the issue to the OECD and forcing most European and other countries to criminalize the bribery of foreign public officials in international business transactions.

Moreover, it has also been argued that the international dimension of the fight against corruption emerged as a result of a "change of heart" by multinational corporations and the World Bank. Multinationals began seeing corruption as a hidden form of protectionism that excluded them from foreign markets, and the World Bank, which had avoided dealing with the "c" word (as corruption was known within the World Bank), started to come under pressure to ensure greater transparency and accountability in its programmes, and began including good governance among its conditionalities.[183]

As a result, the rise in concern about corruption has been criticized in a number of quarters as a creation of the First World international financial and development policy institutions. It is claimed that the international anti-corruption campaign proposes rule changes that will make local economies more accessible for foreign direct investment. The action taken to combat corruption is seen as an ideological project and an attempt to stigmatize some economic policies and legal regimes at the expense of others.[184]

Similarly, the current anti-corruption campaign is also criticized for considering corruption solely as a market distortion and as a means of discrimination against outside capital. It is argued that practices such as the distribution of licenses in developing countries, which privilege local actors, may be entirely predictable for local actors even if they are not in conformity with the published rules, and that this could well be the best policy for development. The anti-corruption campaign is aimed at dismantling such discretionary allocation practices

183 Ivan Krastev, "When 'Should' Does not Imply 'Can': The Making of the Washington Consensus on Corruption," in *Shifting Obsessions: Three Essays on the Politics of Anticorruption*, ed. Ivan Krastev (Central European University Press, 2004), 1–42.

184 David Kennedy, "The International Anti-Corruption Campaign," *Connecticut Journal of International Law* 14 (1999): 455–465; Ohnesorge, John K.M., "'Ratch'eting Up the Anti-Corruption Drive: Could a Look at Recent History Cure a Case of Theory-Determinism?," *Connecticut Journal of International Law* 14, no. 2 (1999): 467–473; Chantal Thomas, "Does the 'Good Governance Policy' of the International Financial Institutions Privilege Markets at the Expense of Democracy?," *Connecticut Journal of International Law* 14, no. 2 (1999): 551–562; James W. Williams and Margaret E. Beare, "The Business of Bribery: Globalization, Economic Liberalization, and the 'Problem' of Corruption," *Crime, Law and Social Change* 32 (1999): 115–146; Krastev, "Shifting Obsessions."

because they are not favourable or transparent to foreign investors. It is therefore implied that the anti-corruption campaign serves the purpose of the developed world to further spread and benefit from liberalization and deregulation, free trade and privatization in the developing world.[185]

This last argument is particularly unfaithful to the anti-corruption campaign. Certainly, many participants in the anti-corruption movement do have in mind the sole purpose of opening up developing markets for foreign investors, but are not the core actors in the campaign, nor do they represent its ideal.[186] But, most importantly, it is erroneous to believe that practices in a country which privilege local actors are necessarily predictable in that country and constitute the best policy for development. If the system is not transparent to foreign investors, it is most probably not transparent to the majority of local investors. Corruption ensures that opportunities stay in the hands of self-interested local elites. Although the anti-corruption campaign is seen in some quarters as benefiting foreign investors at the expense of local investors, if a broader perspective is adopted it is more likely that action to combat corruption will harm local corrupt elites and benefit everyone else.

Kennedy admits that, in the long run, it is politically and economically necessary for developing countries to gain the approval of foreign direct investors. And he also argues that this issue differs from the claim that development will be retarded without an anti-corruption campaign. Yet, how can the two be separated? Whatever the viewpoint adopted, foreign investors are needed for long-term development. As corrupt practices deter both foreign and local investment, it is therefore natural that an anti-corruption campaign stimulates transparency procedures which attract investors, thereby leading to economic development.

It is indeed the case that the international financial institutions played a primordial role in raising concern about corruption to the international level. This was simultaneously the cause and the result of the growing availability of empirical evidence of the harmful effects of corruption on economic and social development. This concern was then taken up by an increasing number of international organizations, which had the de facto effect of upgrading the issue of corruption to the international agenda.

---

185 Kennedy, "The International Anti-Corruption Campaign"; Williams and Beare, "The Business of Bribery: Globalization, Economic Liberalization, and the 'Problem' of Corruption."

186 Although there are those who claim that Transparency International, a major player in the current anti-corruption campaign, promotes a neo-liberal agenda and an institutional environment within developing countries that benefits international investors. See, Hindess, "Governments, NGOs and Anti-Corruption."

The internationalization of the concern at corruption was also motivated by globalization and the transnational aspects of modern corrupt practices. The emergence of an increasingly integrated international economy has enhanced the perception of corruption as a problem with inherently global ramifications. The broadening and deepening of global economic integration has strengthened the possibility that the effects of corruption will spread to the entire global economy. Globalization has both increased opportunities for corrupt practices and made detection more difficult due to the proliferation of electronic trade and off-shore financial centres.[187]

Moreover, the transnational aspect of corruption is not restricted to its economic dimension. Even where domestic laws exist to combat bribery and offences take place wholly within national confines, acts of corruption may have transnational consequences. Offenders may flee the country to avoid prosecution, or may launder the proceeds of bribery in a foreign country where bank secrecy laws may help to hide the traces. As indicated by the renowned international lawyer James Crawford: "[Corruption] cannot be resolved at a regional level, if, for no other reason than the "black" money which results from these activities will always end up elsewhere. It can only be addressed at general international level."[188] Already in 1976 the words of a US Senator expressed the emerging transnational aspect of corruption:

> "I would compare the problem of [international bribery] to the question of pollution. This is a pollution of the democratic processes and free enterprise processes of another kind. We found that we could not pass laws in just one state to prevent pollution because if we passed them in Illinois and did not in Indiana then steel companies in Indiana could still pollute Lake Michigan which washed the water upon the shores of ... Illinois. We had to pass national laws."[189]

---

187 Williams and Beare, "The Business of Bribery: Globalization, Economic Liberalization, and the 'Problem' of Corruption," 119; Kimberly Ann Elliott, "Corruption as an International Policy Problem: Overview and Recommendations," in *Corruption and the Global Economy*, ed. Kimberly Ann Elliott (Washington D.C.: Institute for International Economics, 1997), 175–235; Robert S. Leiken, "Controlling the Global Corruption Epidemic.," *Foreign Policy*, no. 105 (December 1996): 55.

188 James Crawford, "Prospects for the Codification and Development of International Law by the United Nations: The Work of the International Law Commission," *Finnish Yearbook of International Law*, no. IX (1998): 15.

189 Even though the Senator actually expressed this opinion in opposition to the unilateral criminalization of transnational bribery by the United States and only referred to the act of bribery of foreign public officials in international business transactions, his words would now also apply to purely domestic corrupt practices that have transnational consequences. Hearings on Multinational Corporations and U.S. Foreign Policy Before the Subcomm. on Multinational Corporations of the Senate Comm. on Foreign Relations, 94th Cong., 1st Sess. 157 (1976), cited in, David Slade, "Foreign Corrupt Payments: Enforcing a Multilateral Agreement," *Harvard International Law Journal* 22, no. 1 (1981): 127.

The last reason for the internationalization of the fight against corruption is therefore related to the practical means of combating it. In view of the transnational elements of many corrupt practices, a multilateral law enforcement approach is necessary to combat corruption effectively.

As indicated in this section, the international anti-corruption consensus resulted from the emergence of a coalition of global players who see their interest in focusing on corruption.[190] This was certainly both the cause and the result of the increased visibility of corruption. Yet this should not prevent recognition that international concern at corruption should be welcomed and, as demonstrated in this study can serve to revolutionize the means of combating corruption.

CONCLUSION

As outlined in the present Chapter, condemnation of corruption has been transformed over time. Morality and religious values have given way to an increasingly objective condemnation based on modern research methods and studies which have produced empirical evidence of the detrimental consequences of corruption. In turn, the ancient problem of corruption has become over the past fifteen years an issue of international concern that is eliciting a coordinated international response. The emergence of international regulation and the resulting international legal framework against corruption are part of the response.

The emergence of the international legal framework against corruption is therefore the result of a combination of values (moral and religious) and interests (economic and development). In other words, the highly political process of the negotiation of anti-corruption international instruments is a response to traditional normative values and the interests of global players. In turn, as will be shown throughout this study, the obligations arising from the international legal framework against corruption reflect a sometimes complicated interaction of interests and values. Certain anti-corruption obligations reflect the triumph of values over interests, while others are the result of a more pragmatic view of international politics and legalization. These and other issues relating to the international regulation are addressed in Chapter III below.

190 Krastev, "Shifting Obsessions," 13.

CHAPTER III
THE INTERNATIONAL REGULATION OF CORRUPTION

INTRODUCTION

At the same time, and as a consequence of becoming an issue of international concern, corruption began to be regulated by international law. As indicated in the previous Chapter, corruption became a global political issue and elicited a global political response. It received international attention in order to achieve a level playing field for commercial transactions, improve the economic, political, and social development of developing countries and also because in practice a multilateral approach against corruption offers enhanced effectiveness. The need to address the problem of corruption at the international level then paved the way for international regulation. Numerous so-called hard law and soft law anti-corruption instruments emerged from different international institutions. These constitute the main source of the international legal framework against corruption. To provide a context for the analysis contained in the rest of this study, it is necessary first to have a general idea of the existing regulation.

The most important of these instruments are undoubtedly the hard law international conventions which place a number of international obligations on States. This Chapter therefore begins by describing anti-corruption treaty law. However, the importance of soft law instruments should not be underestimated, as they also constitute an essential part of the international legal framework against corruption. As will be illustrated in later Chapters, soft law instruments emanating from international organizations supplement existing international obligations deriving from anti-corruption treaties by providing additional guidance and detail for the implementation of those obligations. The second section of this Chapter therefore explores the most important of these soft law instruments, the resolutions of international organizations dealing with corruption. Moreover, in the context of the internationalization of corruption and its international regulation, it is important to also address the development of the prohibition of corruption into a rule of transnational public policy.

I. ANTI-CORRUPTION TREATY LAW

There are fourteen international treaties or protocols covering the issue of corruption which have quasi-universal coverage. The UNCAC, now boasts 160 States Parties. Of 194 States in the world, this means that the UNCAC is applicable in 82 per cent of the globe, and several States that are not Parties to the UNCAC are nevertheless Parties to other anti-corruption conventions. For example, Germany is a Party to the OECD Convention, the EU Convention against Corruption and the EU Convention on the Protection of the European Communities' Financial Interests. If all of the anti-corruption treaties are taken into account together, their global coverage is therefore even broader. It is therefore necessary to analyse the common characteristics of these treaties and the types of obligations arising out of them.

1. TREATIES AGAINST CORRUPTION

1.1. *Chronology of anti-corruption treaties*

In March 1996, the Members of the OAS adopted the *Inter-American Convention against Corruption*, signalling the conclusion of the first anti-corruption treaty in the world.[191] In practice, the first treaty to address corruption, albeit indirectly, was adopted by the Member States of the European Union in the form of the *Convention on the Protection of the European Communities' Financial Interests* of 1995.[192] This Convention only deals with fraud affecting Community revenue and expenditure. However, it indirectly covers corruption since the definition of fraud covers the corrupt act of the embezzlement of the funds of the European Communities.[193] States are called upon to criminalize in their national law, *inter alia*, "the use or presentation of false, incorrect or incomplete

191 Inter-American Convention against Corruption (adopted at the third plenary session of the Organization of American States, 29 March 1996, entered into force 3 June 1997) 35 I.L.M. 724. The Convention was adopted in Caracas, Venezuela, on 29 March 1996. It entered into force on 6 March 1997. There are 33 States Parties to the Convention. All American States are Parties, with the exception of Barbados. The path to the Inter-American Convention began at the Miami Summit in 1994. The Declaration of Principles and the Plan of Action signed in Miami on 11 December 1994 clearly indicated that the issue of corruption extended further than bribery of foreign officials and that corruption was linked to the region's broader economic and political aspirations, namely development and democracy. Summit of the Americas, Declaration of Principles and Plan of Actions, 34 I.L.M. 808.

192 Convention drawn up on the basis of Article K.3 of the Treaty on European Union, on the Protection of the European Communities' Financial Interests, Official Journal C 316, 27 November 1995, 49, entered into force on 17 October 2002. See also, Explanatory Report on the Convention on the Protection of the European Communities' Financial Interests (Text approved by the Council on 26 May 1997), Official Journal C 191, 23 June 1997.

193 Convention on the Protection of the European Communities' Financial Interests, Art. 1.

statements or documents, which has as its effect the misappropriation or wrongful retention of funds from the general budget of the European Communities or budgets managed by, or on behalf of, the European Communities..."[194] In September 1996, this Convention was supplemented with the *Protocol to the Convention on the Protection of the European Communities' Financial Interests,* which deals specifically with corruption involving national and Community officials which damages, or is likely to damage, the European Communities' financial interests.[195] However, corruption in this Protocol is defined exclusively for the purpose of protecting the financial interests of the European Communities. Thus, for the purpose of this Protocol, for an act to be considered corruption it needs to damage or be likely to damage the European Communities' financial interests.[196] The relevance of the Protocol now is questionable, as the following year, in 1997, the Council of the European Union adopted the *Convention on the Fight against Corruption Involving Officials of the European Communities or Officials of Member States of the European Union.*[197] Although technically this was not the first legal instrument adopted by the European Union concerning corruption, it can be regarded as the most significant. In addition, in May 1997, the European Union adopted a *Second Protocol to the Convention on the Protection of the European Communities' Financial Interests,* intended to further supplement the Convention by requiring States to ensure that legal persons can be held liable and punished accordingly for fraud, active bribery and money laundering which damage or are likely to damage the European Communities' financial interests.[198]

---

194 States are called upon to criminalize in their national law, *inter alia*, "the use or presentation of false, incorrect or incomplete statements or documents, which has as its effect the misappropriation or wrongful retention of funds from the general budget of the European Communities or budgets managed by, or on behalf of, the European Communities..." Convention on the Protection of the European Communities' Financial Interests, Art. 1(1)(a).

195 Council Act of 27 September 1996 drawing up a Protocol to the Convention on the Protection of the European Communities' Financial Interests, Official Journal C 313, 23 October 1996, 2, entered into force 17 October 2002. See also, Explanatory Report on the Protocol to the Convention on the Protection of the European Communities' Financial Interests (Text approved by the Council on 19 December 1997), Official Journal C 11, 15 January 1998.

196 Protocol to the Convention on the Protection of the European Communities' Financial Interests, Arts. 2 and 3.

197 Council Act of 26 May 1997 drawing up, on the basis of Article K.3 (2) (c) of the Treaty on European Union, the Convention on the Fight against Corruption Involving Officials of the European Communities or Officials of Member States of the European Union, Official Journal C 195, 25 June 1997, 1. Entered into force on 28 September 2005. See also, Explanatory Report on the Convention on the Fight against Corruption Involving Officials of the European Communities or Officials of Member States of the European Union (Text approved by the Council on 3 December 1998), Official Journal C 391, 15 December 1998, 1.

198 Second Protocol, drawn up on the basis of Article K.3 of the treaty on European Union, to the Convention on the Protection of the European Communities' Financial Interests – Joint Declaration on Article 13 (2) – Commission Declaration on Article 7, adopted by Council Act of 19 June 1997, *Official Journal* C 221, 19 July 1997, 11, Arts. 3 and 4. The Protocol further covers issues of cooperation between the Member States of the European Union and the

Later in 1997, the OECD adopted the *Convention on Combating Bribery of Foreign Public Officials in International Business Transactions*, which only deals with the active bribery of foreign public officials.[199] This Convention is in principle open for accession by all States, whether or not they are Members of the OECD,[200] and in fact several Parties to the Convention are not Members of the OECD.[201] The following year in 1998, the CoE adopted the *Criminal Law Convention on Corruption*[202] and in 1999 the *Civil Law Convention on Corruption*.[203] The latter is the first attempt to define common international rules in the field of civil law and corruption. It requires States Parties to provide in their internal law for persons who have suffered damage as a result of corruption to have the right to initiate a civil action to obtain compensation.[204] In addition, the CoE Civil Law Convention also provides for State responsibility for bribery. In other words, States Parties have to provide in their internal law for appropriate procedures for persons who have suffered damage as a result of bribery by its public officials in the exercise of their functions so that they can claim compensation from the State.[205]

Commission of the European Communities, confiscation, and protection of personal data in investigations and prosecutions of fraud and corruption. Second Protocol to the Convention on the Protection of the European Communities' Financial Interests, respectively Arts. 6, 7, 5, 8, 9, 10, and 11.

199 Convention on Combating Bribery of Foreign Public Officials in International Business Transactions (adopted on 21 November 1997, entered into force 15 February 1999) 37 I.L.M. 1. As of 12 April 2012 its States Parties are: Argentina, Australia, Austria, Belgium, Brazil, Bulgaria, Canada, Chile, Czech Republic, Denmark, Estonia, Finland, France, Germany, Greece, Hungary, Iceland, Ireland, Israel, Italy, Japan, Republic of Korea, Luxembourg, Mexico, Netherlands, New Zealand, Norway, Poland, Portugal, Russian Federation, Slovak Republic, Slovenia, South Africa, Spain, Sweden, Switzerland, Turkey, United Kingdom and United States. For a historical development, see Mark Pieth, "Introduction," in *The OECD Convention on Bribery: A Commentary*, ed. Mark Pieth, Lucinda Low, and Peter J. Cullen (Cambridge University Press, 2007), 3–41; Alejandro Posadas, "Combating Corruption Under International Law," *Duke Journal of Comparative & International Law* 10, no. 2 (2000): 345–414; Padideh Ala'i, "The Legacy of Geographical Morality and Colonialism: A Historical Assessment of the Current Crusade against Corruption," *Vanderbilt Journal of Transnational Law* (2000): 877–932.

200 OECD, *Commentaries on the Convention on Combating Bribery of Foreign Public Officials in International Business Transactions*, DAFFE/IME/BR(97)20, 21 November 1997, para. 37.

201 These are: Argentina, Brazil, Bulgaria, Russian Federation and South Africa.

202 Criminal Law Convention on Corruption (adopted by the Committee of Ministers of the Council of Europe on 27 January 1999, entered into force 1 July 2002) 2216 U.N.T.S. 225. As of 12 April 2012, the Convention has 43 States Parties. For the complete list, see the CoE website: www.coe.int/ (last visited 12 April 2012). For the CoE's work leading to the adoption of the Convention, see, CoE, Criminal Law Convention Explanatory Report, Part II: Preparatory Work.

203 Civil Law Convention on Corruption (adopted by the Committee of Ministers of the Council of Europe on 4 November 1999, entered into force 1 November 2003) 2246 U.N.T.S. 3. As of 12 April 2012 the Civil Law Convention has 34 States Parties. For the complete list, see the CoE website: www.coe.int/ (last visited 12 April 2012).

204 CoE Civil Law Convention, Art. 3(1).

205 Ibid., Art. 5.

In 2000, the UN adopted the *Convention against Transnational Organized Crime* which, even though it is mainly targeted at organized crime, includes several provisions relating to the phenomenon of corruption.[206] In 2001, two anti-corruption treaties were adopted on the African continent, the *SADC Protocol against Corruption* and the *ECOWAS Protocol on the Fight against Corruption*,[207] and two years later the Heads of State at the African Union Summit held in Mozambique in 2003 adopted the *AU Convention on Preventing and Combating Corruption*.[208] Earlier in that year, the Member States of the CoE and other non-members had adopted an *Additional Protocol to the Criminal Law Convention* which extends the scope of the Criminal Law Convention to arbitrators in commercial, civil and other matters, as well as to jurors, thus supplementing the Convention's provisions protecting judicial authorities from corruption.[209] Finally, in 2003 the United Nations adopted the *UNCAC*, which is the most recent and significant international law instrument against corruption.[210] The UNCAC constitutes the most comprehensive anti-corruption treaty, as it covers a broad spectrum of corrupt practices and establishes numerous anti-corruption measures that are to be adopted by States Parties.

1.2. Common structure and content of anti-corruption treaties

While the above anti-corruption treaties vary in the detail of their provisions, with the exception of the CoE Civil Law Convention which, as indicated above, is inherently different, all the other conventions follow the line of the treaties on transnational crimes, such as the 1970 Convention for the Suppression of Unlawful Seizure of Aircraft[211] or the 1988 United Nations Convention against Illicit Traffic in Narcotic Drugs and Psychotropic Substances.[212] These

206 Convention against Transnational Organized Crime (adopted by the UN General Assembly by resolution 55/25 on 8 January 2001, entered into force 29 September 2003) 2225 U.N.T.S. 209.

207 Southern African Development Community Protocol against Corruption (adopted on 14 August 2001, entered into force on 6 July 2005), available at www.sadc.int/ (last visited 12 April 2012); Economic Community of West African States Protocol on the Fight against Corruption (adopted on 21 December 2001, not yet entered into force), available at www.ecowas.int/ (last visited 12 April 2012).

208 African Union Convention on Preventing and Combating Corruption (adopted by the 2nd Ordinary Session of the Assembly of the Union on 11 July 2003, entered into force 5 August 2006) 43. I.L.M. 1.

209 Additional Protocol to the Criminal Law Convention on Corruption (adopted by the Committee of Ministers of the Council of Europe on 15 May 2003, entered into force on 1 February 2005) E.T.S. 191. As of 12 April 2012, the Additional Protocol has 28 States Parties. For the complete list, see the CoE website: www.coe.int/ (last visited 12 April 2012).

210 Convention against Corruption (adopted by the UN General Assembly by resolution 58/4 on 31 October 2003, entered into force 14 December 2005) 2349 U.N.T.S. 41.

211 Convention for the Suppression of Unlawful Seizure of Aircraft, 860 U.N.T.S. 105, entered into force 14 October 1971.

212 Convention against the Illicit Traffic of Narcotic Drugs and Psychotropic Substances (UN Doc. E/CONF.82/15, 1988) 28 I.L.M. 493.

Conventions, as in the case of the anti-corruption Conventions, usually define one or more crimes that are to be criminalized in national law and establish certain rules aimed at enhancing international cooperation for national enforcement of the law against those crimes. Accordingly, the anti-corruption conventions have a more or less similar structure and content. Most of them provide for measures aimed at preventing corruption, such as calling on States to develop and maintain, inter alia, an anti-corruption body,[213] standards for the recruitment of personal for the public sector,[214] codes of conduct for public officials,[215] measures to prevent money laundering,[216] means to promote participation by civil society[217] and higher accounting and auditing standards in the private sector.[218]

In addition, the anti-corruption conventions require States Parties to criminalize corrupt practices in their domestic jurisdictions.[219] However, the corrupt acts subject to criminalization and the level of obligation vary in each convention. For example, on one side of the spectrum the OECD Convention only provides for the criminalization of the act of bribery of foreign public officials, while at the other end the UNCAC deals with several corrupt acts. Under the UNCAC, there are two groups of corrupt acts. The first consists of bribery of national public officials,[220] bribery of foreign public officials and officials of public international organizations[221] and the embezzlement of property by a public official.[222] States are required to criminalize these corrupt acts. The second covers corrupt practices that States are encouraged to consider as criminal offences, although they are not required to do so. These corrupt acts are: trading

213 For example, UNCAC, Art. 6; CoE Criminal Law Convention, Art. 20; ECOWAS Protocol against Corruption, Art. 5(h).

214 For example, UNCAC, Art. 7; Inter-American Convention against Corruption, Art. 3(5); SADC Protocol against Corruption, Art. 4(b).

215 For example, UNCAC, Art. 8; Inter-American Convention against Corruption, Art. 3(1); SADC Protocol against Corruption, Art. 4(a).

216 For example, UNCAC, Art. 14; CoE Criminal Law Convention, Art. 13; ECOWAS Protocol against Corruption, Art. 7; AU Convention against Corruption, Art. 6.

217 For example, UNCAC, Art., 13; Inter-American Convention against Corruption, Art. 3(11); SADC Protocol against Corruption, Art. 4(i); ECOWAS Protocol against Corruption, Art. 5(e); AU Convention against Corruption, Art. 12.

218 For example, UNCAC, Art. 12; OECD Convention, Art. 8; CoE Criminal Law Convention, Art. 14; SADC Protocol against Corruption, Art. 4(h).

219 For example, UNCAC, Arts. 15–25; Inter-American Convention against Corruption, Arts. 6–9; EU Convention against Corruption, Arts. 2 and 3; OECD Convention, Art. 1(1); CoE Criminal Law Convention, Arts. 2–12; SADC Protocol against Corruption, Art. 3; ECOWAS Protocol against Corruption, Art. 6; AU Convention against Corruption, Art. 4.

220 UNCAC, Art. 15.

221 Ibid., Art. 16.

222 Ibid., Art. 17.

in influence,[223] abuse of functions,[224] illicit enrichment,[225] bribery in the private sector[226] and embezzlement in the private sector.[227]

The Conventions also provide for a wide range of measures for the enforcement of anti-corruption law. For instance, States are called upon to exercise certain types of criminal and civil jurisdiction,[228] establish longer statute of limitations periods for corrupt acts,[229] institute the civil, criminal or administrative liability of legal persons,[230] protect witnesses, experts and victims,[231] and ensure that bank secrecy laws are not an obstacle to the enforcement of anti-corruption law.[232] The Conventions also contain detailed provisions on international cooperation in criminal matters. As is common in treaties concerning transnational crimes, they contain detailed provisions respecting extradition and mutual legal assistance.[233] In the context of international cooperation, the UNCAC has broken new ground with its provisions on the recovery of stolen assets, which is a fundamental principle of the Convention.[234] For this purpose, the Convention establishes various measures calling for international cooperation for the purpose of detecting the transfer of the proceeds of crime and determining the ownership of assets, as well as their confiscation, return and disposal.[235] The UNCAC is also the only anti-corruption treaty that urges States Parties to consider providing technical assistance to each other, in particular to developing countries. This means that States are called upon to

---

223 Ibid., Art. 18.

224 Ibid., Art. 19.

225 Ibid., Art. 20.

226 Ibid., Art. 21.

227 Ibid., Art. 22.

228 For example, UNCAC, Arts. 42 and 35; Inter-American Convention against Corruption, Art. 5; EU Convention against Corruption, Art. 7; OECD Convention, Art. 4; CoE Criminal Law Convention, Art. 17; SADC Protocol against Corruption, Art. 5; ECOWAS Protocol against Corruption, Art. 4; AU Convention against Corruption, Art. 13.

229 For example, UNCAC, Art. 29; OECD Convention, Art. 6.

230 For example, UNCAC, Art. 26; OECD Convention, Art. 2; CoE Criminal Law Convention, Art. 18; ECOWAS Protocol against Corruption, Art. 11.

231 For example, UNCAC, Art. 32; CoE Criminal Law Convention, Art. 22; ECOWAS Protocol against Corruption, Arts. 8 and 9.

232 For example, UNCAC, Art., 40, Inter-American Convention against Corruption, Art. 16; AU Convention against Corruption, Art. 17.

233 On extradition, see for example UNCAC, Art. 44; Inter-American Convention against Corruption, Art. 13; EU Convention against Corruption, Art. 8; OECD Convention, Art. 10; CoE Criminal Law Convention, Art. 27; SADC Protocol against Corruption, Art. 9; ECOWAS Protocol against Corruption, Art. 14; AU Convention against Corruption, Art. 15. On mutual legal assistance, see for example UNCAC, Art. 46; Inter-American Convention against Corruption, Art. 14; EU Convention against Corruption, Art. 8; OECD Convention, Art. 9; CoE Criminal Law Convention, Art. 26; SADC Protocol against Corruption, Art. 10; ECOWAS Protocol against Corruption, Art. 15; AU Convention against Corruption, Art. 18.

234 UNCAC, Chapter V.

235 Ibid., Art. 52–57.

provide both financial and material assistance to support anti-corruption programmes in developing countries.[236]

2. ANTI-CORRUPTION TREATY LAW OBLIGATIONS

An overview of the treaties against corruption shows that States Parties have assumed a wide range of international obligations. However, the provisions of the anti-corruption conventions do not all establish the same level of legal obligation. Indeed, many provisions are not obligations, but mere recommendations. Moreover, the same measure is not accorded the same level of obligation in all treaties. Some measures are mandatory in one treaty and optional in another. For example, the criminalization of an attempt and the preparation to commit an act of corruption is an optional recommendation under the UNCAC, but is mandatory under the Inter-American Convention against Corruption, the OECD Convention and the AU Convention against Corruption.[237] In this sense, anti-corruption treaties combine various types of obligations. The reasons for this approach are self-evident. When negotiating the treaties, agreement could not be reached among the negotiating parties on certain issues. Hence, as a compromise, in addition to traditional international legal obligations, which are mandatory, obligations of best endeavour and optional recommendations were included in the treaties.

2.1. Mandatory obligations to achieve a certain objective (obligations of result)

The mandatory provisions in anti-corruption conventions create obligations of different nature. Mandatory provisions may create obligations upon States to legislate or take action to attain a certain objective. For example, under the terms of certain anti-corruption treaties, States are required to adopt legislative and other measures to establish as a criminal offence the active bribery of foreign public officials.[238] States therefore have to achieve the objective of criminalizing this offence, regardless of the measures that the State may need to adopt or the obstacles that it may encounter.

---

236 Ibid., Art. 60–62.

237 UNCAC, Art. 27(2)-(3); Inter-American Convention against Corruption, Arts. 6(1)(e) and 7; AU Convention against Corruption, Arts. 4(1)(i) and 5(1). Under the OECD Convention, States Parties are required to criminalize an attempt and conspiracy to bribe a foreign public official to the same extent as an attempt and conspiracy to bribe a domestic official. OECD Convention, Art. 1(2).

238 For example, UNCAC, Art. 15; Inter-American Convention against Corruption, Art. 6(1)(a-b); and CoE Criminal Law Convention, Arts. 2 and 3.

2.2. *Mandatory obligations of best endeavour (obligations of conduct)*

Certain anti-corruption provisions under treaty law call upon States to *consider* applying certain measures or to *endeavour* to adopt certain measures. For example, States Parties to the UNCAC are required to consider adopting legislative and other measures to establish as a criminal offence the passive bribery of foreign public officials.[239] In this case, States are under the obligation to contemplate, or "think about" such measures, but are not required to achieve any specific result.

Clearly, this type of obligations complicates the assessment of compliance by States. How can it be established that a State has seriously considered a required action and in the end decided not to pursue it? It is not impossible in practice. There are, of course, ways of knowing whether a State has pondered a particular course of action required by an anti-corruption treaty. In the case of actions that require legislation, such as the creation of new criminal offences, States are therefore under the obligation to engage in the normal legislative debates and processes; and even if, upon completion of such legislative action, the required law is not approved, the State has still complied with its international obligation. In other words, the State has the obligation to submit the proposal to the legislative bodies.

There may, however, be mistrust about how genuine the effort is by the Government to meet its anti-corruption obligations of best endeavour, since in many cases such obligations are potentially aimed at the Government itself. It has therefore been argued that a "genuine effort" entails more than traditional parliamentary debates, and should, for example, include the hearing of experts by Parliament, public hearings with broad representation of civil society and expert reports circulated among the legal community, or even more ample forms of consultation, such as general referendums.[240]

Other obligations of best endeavour do not seem to require a formal legislative analysis to achieve the desired objective. For instance, in accordance with the UNCAC, States have to consider encouraging people to report to the national investigating and prosecuting authorities the commission of an offence.[241] States are not under the obligation to encourage people to report the commission of offences but to consider encouraging them to do so. Whether or not the State has made its best endeavour can be demonstrated for example, if discussions on the adoption of a programme for such purpose are held in the Ministry of Justice or other relevant Ministries.

239 UNCAC, Art. 16(2).
240 Guillermo Jorge, *The Romanian Legal Framework on Illicit Enrichment* (American Bar Association Central European and Eurasian Law Initiative (ABA/CEELI), July 2007), 53.
241 UNCAC, Art. 39(2).

Elsewhere, these provisions are referred to as optional requirements,[242] although they should not be confused with provisions that merely make recommendations to States Parties (see below, optional recommendations). States Parties are required to endeavour to adopt certain measures, and are therefore under a certain level of obligation, although it is of a different kind. In this case, States are usually required to consider applying or to endeavour to adopt a certain measure. While there is no obligation to achieve a specific result, States are under the obligation to at least consider or to endeavour to achieve a specific result (an obligation of conduct).

2.3. Optional recommendations

Anti-corruption treaties, particularly the UNCAC, also contain purely soft law norms, which amount to optional recommendations for States Parties. These provisions are usually drafted in the form of an authorization using the verb "may." For example, a State *may consider* a relevant anti-corruption treaty as the legal basis for extradition in respect of a corruption offence, if the State makes extradition conditional upon the existence of a treaty and receives a request from another State Party with which it has no extradition treaty.[243] Yet, these types of recommendations are not totally devoid of meaning. They are intended to indicate a desired means in relation to specific objectives of the fight against corruption. They constitute principles that are relevant to the interpretation and implementation of the Convention. While there is no total agreement among the States Parties on that particular issue to make it a mandatory obligation, there is still sufficient agreement for reference to be made to the issue in the treaty. In this connection, optional recommendations also serve the purpose of consolidating a convergence of approaches in relation to specific anti-corruption issues.

II. RESOLUTIONS ADOPTED BY INTERNATIONAL ORGANIZATIONS

In addition to anti-corruption treaties, an essential component of international regulation of corruption consists of soft law instruments, and particularly resolutions adopted by international organizations. As outlined below, there is a

[242] See, UNODC, *Legislative Guide for the Implementation of the United Nations Convention against Corruption* (Vienna, New York: United Nations, 2006).

[243] UNCAC, Art. 44(5); Inter-American Convention against Corruption, Art. 13(3); CoE Criminal Law Convention, Art. 27(2); OECD Convention, Art. 10(2); SADC Protocol against Corruption, Art. 9(4). While in all the above Conventions States have the option to consider the treaty as the legal basis for extradition, under the AU Convention against Corruption the obligation is mandatory, and States Parties have to consider the AU Convention against Corruption as the legal basis for extradition. AU Convention against Corruption, Art. 15(3).

plethora of resolutions adopted by various international organizations addressing different aspects of action to combat corruption. These resolutions are not only important in improving the understanding and implementation of treaty law obligations, but also offer insight into how concern for corruption developed within each organization.

1. THE UNITED NATIONS

It can be safely stated that the UNCAC is the most important anti-corruption instrument that has originated from the United Nations. Yet in the past the United Nations has adopted several resolutions that were predecessors to the UNCAC. This first set of resolutions adopted by the United Nations General Assembly attempted to place the issue of corruption within the United Nations and to begin framing United Nations policies against corruption. However, this proved difficult, as action to combat corruption within the United Nations was overshadowed by the antagonism between the northern and southern blocks.

In 1975, General Assembly Resolution 3514, entitled *Measures against Corrupt Practices of Transnational and Other Corporations, their Intermediaries and Others Involved* condemned all corrupt practices and directed the United Nations Commission on Transnational Corporations to make recommendations for eliminating corrupt practices.[244] As a result, the Commission on Transnational Corporations established the Ad Hoc Intergovernmental Working Group on Corrupt Practices (Working Group). In 1980, the Working Group completed a draft International Agreement on Illicit Payments. However, the international conference to finalize this agreement was never convened, as India, on behalf of the Group of 77, made the holding of the conference conditional upon the adoption of a Code of Conduct on Transnational Corporations. This code of conduct was, however, strongly opposed by the northern block, and consequently neither the International Agreement on Illicit Payments nor the Code of Conduct were adopted.[245]

Between 1975 and 1997, the United Nations adopted other instruments addressing corruption in an ancillary manner, such as a Code of Conduct for Law Enforcement Officials (General Assembly Resolution 34/169 of 17 December

244 UN General Assembly, Measures against Corrupt Practices of Transnational and Other Corporations, their Intermediaries and Others Involved, A/RES/3514(XXX), 15 December 1975.

245 For a detailed account on anti-corruption initiatives in the UN in the 1970s and 1980s, see Ala'i, "The Legacy of Geographical Morality and Colonialism: A Historical Assessment of the Current Crusade against Corruption"; Posadas, "Combating Corruption Under International Law."

1979), Recommendation on International Co-operation for Crime Prevention and Criminal Justice in the Context of Development (General Assembly Resolution 45/107 of 14 December 1990), and the International Code of Conduct of Public Officials (General Assembly Resolution of 12 December 1996).

It was not until 1997 that the General Assembly issued a resolution with substantial wording against corruption. Resolution 51/191 contained the *United Nations Declaration against Corruption and Bribery in International Commercial Transactions* which, as its name suggests, deals solely with one corrupt practice: the bribery of foreign public officials in international business transactions.[246] The adoption of such a resolution was hardly surprising, as the OECD Convention was adopted the same year. The General Assembly subsequently adopted resolutions urging Member States to ratify other existing conventions against corruption.[247] Finally, in 2001, the General Assembly adopted a resolution in which it decided to begin the elaboration of the United Nations Convention against Corruption.[248]

The General Assembly has supplemented the United Nations legal framework against corruption with several resolutions, all entitled *Preventing and combating corrupt practices and transfer of assets of illicit origin and returning such assets, in particular to the countries of origin, consistent with the United Nations Convention against Corruption.*[249] In these resolutions, the General Assembly usually condemns corruption, reiterates its commitment to preventing and combating corrupt practices at all levels, and urges all Governments to combat and penalize corruption, as well as the laundering of the proceeds of corruption. These resolutions also take note of the latest United Nations efforts to fight corruption and make reference to the issues of asset recovery, mutual legal assistance, technical assistance and international cooperation, actions by the private sector and the on-going process of designing the review of the implementation mechanisms of the UNCAC.

---

246 UN General Assembly, United Nations Declaration against Corruption and Bribery in International Commercial Transactions, A/RES/51/191, 21 February 1997.

247 For example, UN General Assembly, International Cooperation against Corruption and Bribery in International Commercial Transactions, A/RES/52/87, 2 February 1998; UN General Assembly, Action against Corruption and Bribery in International Commercial Transactions, A/RES/53/176, 25 January 1999.

248 UN General Assembly, An Effective International Legal Instrument against Corruption, A/RES/55/61, 22 January 2001.

249 See, UN General Assembly, Preventing and Combating Corrupt Practices and Transfer of Assets of Illicit Origin and Returning such Assets, in Particular to the Countries of Origin, Consistent with the United Nations Convention against Corruption, A/RES/63/226, 19 December 2008; A/RES/62/202, 19 December 2007; A/RES/61/209, 20 December 2006; A/RES/60/207, 22 December 2005; A/RES/59/242, 22 December 2004; A/RES/58/205, 23 December 2003; A/RES/57/244, 20 December 2002; A/RES/56/186, 21 December 2001; A/RES/55/188, 20 December 2000; and A/RES/54/205, 22 December 1999.

2. THE ORGANIZATION OF AMERICAN STATES

The Organization of American States has issued several resolutions and declarations concerning corruption. Most of them are resolutions of its General Assembly dealing with efforts relating to the adoption and implementation of the Inter-American Convention against Corruption. However, certain documents emanating from the OAS have set standards that supplement the Inter-American Convention against Corruption and form part of the Inter-American legal framework against corruption.

The first instrument to which reference should be made, the *Inter-American Democratic Charter,* sets out the underlying values for the work of the OAS.[250] The Inter-American Democratic Charter provides that the peoples of the Americas have a right to democracy and that their governments have an obligation to promote and defend it (Article 1). In addition, the Charter provides that transparency in government activities, probity and responsible public administration on the part of government are essential components of the exercise of democracy (Article 4). Another instrument developed by the OAS that has raised the Inter-American standards in combating corruption is the *Declaration of Nuevo Leon*, adopted in 2004 at the Special Summit of the Americas.[251] This Declaration, under its section on "Democratic governance" devotes several paragraphs to the issue of corruption, the Inter-American Convention against Corruption and the UNCAC. In this Declaration, the OAS States recognized the negative effects of corruption and pledged to intensify their efforts to combat it. They undertook to increase cooperation within the framework of the Inter-American Convention against Corruption and to promote transparency in political processes, in public financial management

[250] OAS General Assembly, Inter-American Democratic Charter, Resolution AG/RES. 1 (XXVIII-E/01), adopted at the 28th Special Session of the General Assembly, 11 September 2001.

[251] Special Summit of the Americas, Monterrey, Mexico, 12–13 January 2004. The Declaration aims to advance the "implementation of measures to combat poverty, to promote social development, to achieve economic growth with equity, and to strengthen governance in our democracies." Declaration of Nuevo Leon, Preamble, paragraph 1. Ever since the first Summit of the Americas was held in Miami in 1994, the Declarations and Plans of Action issued at the end of each Summit have addressed in part the issue of corruption. However, it was the Special Summit held in Mexico that dealt with corruption in a more detailed manner and where the most important commitments were made by Governments. See, First Summit of the Americas, Miami, United States, 9–11 December 1994, Declaration of Principles and Plan of Action; Second Summit of the Americas, Santiago, Chile, 18–19 April, 1998, Declaration of Principles and Plan of Action; Third Summit of the Americas, Quebec City, Canada, 20–22 April, 2001, Declaration of Principles and Plan of Action; Fourth Summit of the Americas, Mar del Plata, Argentina, 4–5 November 2005, Declaration of Mar del Plata; Fifth Summit of the Americas, Port of Spain, Trinidad and Tobago, 17–19 April 2009, Declaration of Commitment of Port of Spain. For more information on the Summits of the Americas, see www.summit-americas.org (last visited 12 April 2012).

and in government transactions. They also gave a commitment to deny safe haven to corrupt officials and those who corrupt them, cooperate in their extradition and asset recovery, and hold consultations in the event that adherence to the shared transparency and anti-corruption objectives is compromised to a serious degree in any American country.[252]

The *Declaration of Managua* reaffirms the values expressed in the Declaration of Nuevo Leon and contains similar commitments to strengthen efforts to combat corruption.[253] It is not strictly an instrument developed by the OAS, as it was adopted by the States Parties to the Inter-American Convention against Corruption. Together with the Declaration of Managua, the States concerned adopted the *Plan of Action of Managua on Additional Concrete Measures to Increase Transparency and Combat Corruption within the Framework of the Inter-American Convention against Corruption.*[254] This instrument contains a set of important and detailed commitments made by the States Parties to the Inter-American Convention against Corruption with a view to enhancing the effectiveness of the Convention. For this purpose, the States Parties reiterated commitments made under other Declarations, but added important elements which substantially improve the Inter-American anti-corruption legal framework. For example, they decided to begin consultations to consider whether it is necessary to adopt an instrument to facilitate the recovery of the proceeds of corruption and their return to their legitimate owners.[255] They also agreed to hold discussions to consider the possibility of encouraging the multilateral financial institutions to devote a percentage of annual public debt payments by States Parties to fund anticorruption programmes[256] and to take all appropriate steps to trace and identify the proceeds of illegal activities, where necessary lifting banking secrecy.[257]

Moreover, in 2003, at an OAS Special Conference on Security, the issue of corruption was addressed from a multidimensional perspective and was

252 The Plan of Action of this Declaration devotes a special chapter to combating corruption. Commitments were made therein in relation to the Inter-American Convention against Corruption, the Inter-American Program for Cooperation in the Fight against Corruption, as well as the strengthening of the Inter-American Network for Cooperation against Corruption, the strengthening of civil society participation in the respective states, and the adoption of policies, processes and mechanisms to protect public interests.

253 Organization of American States, Declaration of Managua, adopted at the fourth plenary session, OEA/Ser.K/XLI.1, EPICOR/doc.05/04 rev. 6, 9 July 2004.

254 Organization of American States, Plan of Action of Managua on Additional Concrete Measures to Increase Transparency and Combat Corruption within the Framework of the Inter-American Convention against Corruption, adopted at the Fourth Plenary Session, OEA/Ser.K/XLI.1, EPICOR/doc.04/04 rev. 5, 9 July 2004.

255 Ibid. para. 4.

256 Ibid. para. 16.

257 Ibid., para 1.

recognized as a threat to the security of States which undermines public and private institutions and trust in society, results in economic damage, compromises stability, erodes the rule of law and weakens the capacity of governments to respond to security threats. The Special Conference on Security adopted a *Declaration on Security in the Americas*, which addresses a wide range of issues, such as terrorism, extreme poverty, HIV/AIDS and trafficking in persons. With regard to corruption, States made a commitment to combat both passive and active corruption, the effects of which extend to different fields of State activity. Under the terms of the Declaration on Security in the Americas, "[...] cooperation, mutual legal assistance, extradition, and concerted action to combat corruption constitute a political and moral imperative. [The States concerned] pledged to strengthen the Follow-up Mechanism of the Inter-American Convention against Corruption and to support the United Nations Convention on this same question."[258]

Additional OAS instruments which supplement the legal framework to combat corruption include resolutions and declarations adopted by the OAS General Assembly. In the 1990s, the resolutions of the OAS General Assembly were mostly aimed at establishing a framework for addressing the issue of corruption and adopting the Inter-American Convention against Corruption.[259] Subsequently, once the Convention had been adopted, the resolutions of the General Assembly mostly dealt with setting up the monitoring mechanism for the Inter-American Convention against Corruption.[260] Nevertheless, once this

[258] Organization of American States, Special Conference on Security, Mexico City, Mexico, 27–28 October, 2003, Declaration on Security in the Americas, OEA/Ser.K/XXXVIII, CES/DEC.1/03 rev. 1, 28 October 2003, paragraph 31.

[259] For example, OAS General Assembly Resolution AG/RES 1159 (XXII-O/92) "Corrupt International Trade Practices" adopted at the Seventh Plenary Session 22 May 1992 (establishing that "corrupt practices can thwart the process of integral development by diverting resources needed to improve the peoples' economic and social conditions"); OAS General Assembly Resolution AG/RES 1294 (XXIV-O/94) "Probity and Public Ethics", adopted at the Tenth Plenary Session, 10 June 1994 (instructing the Permanent Council to establish a working group to study the matter of probity and public ethics. The Working Group was entrusted with the compilation and study of national legislation in effect with regard to matters of public ethics, the discussion of experiences in the control and oversight of existing administrative institutions, the development of a checklist of crimes related to public ethics as defined in national laws and the preparation of recommendations); and OAS General Assembly Resolution AG/RES 1346 (XXV-O/95) "Probity and Public Ethics", adopted at the Ninth Plenary Session, 9 June 1995 (Instructing the Chair of the Working Group on Probity and Public Ethics to prepare a draft Inter-American Convention against Corruption.).

[260] For example, OAS General Assembly Resolution AG/RES 1723 (XXX-O/00) "Enhancement of Probity in the Hemisphere and Follow-Up on the Inter-American Program for Cooperation in the Fight against Corruption", adopted at the First Plenary Session, 5 June 2000 (asking the OAS Permanent Council to analyse existing regional and international follow-up mechanisms with a view to recommending the most appropriate model to monitor the Inter-American Convention against Corruption.).

mechanism had been established, the General Assembly continued to adopt resolutions to promote this mechanism.[261] However, other resolutions and declarations of the OAS General Assembly set forth valuable standards that supplement the Inter-American Convention against Corruption in combating corruption. Two are particularly noteworthy.

OAS General Assembly Resolution 2222, *Cooperation among the Member States in the Fight Against Corruption and Impunity*, calls upon States to seek to surrender and extradite persons to the requesting State and to enforce the rules of international judicial cooperation so that extradition and mutual legal assistance are efficient, expeditious and effective.[262] The *Declaration of Quito on Social Development and Democracy, and the Impact of Corruption* reiterates previous commitments, although it is focused on the social impact of corruption.[263] The OAS States declare that development, democracy and the fight against corruption are closely inter-related.[264] Once again, the States undertook to deny safe haven to corrupt officials and those who corrupt them and to cooperate in their extradition and in the recovery and return of the proceeds.[265] The Declaration also emphasizes that corruption in the private sector may have a negative impact on economies,[266] and that the fight against

---

261 For example, OAS General Assembly Resolution AG/RES 1784 (XXXI-O/01) (recognised the importance of the MESICIC and the progress achieved by the Committee of Experts; requesting the General Secretariat of the OAS to fulfil the functions of the Secretariat of the MESICIC, as stipulated in the Document of Buenos Aires); OAS General Assembly Resolution AG/RES. 2022 (XXXIV-O/04) "Joint Efforts of the Americas in the Struggle against Corruption and Impunity", adopted at the Fourth Plenary Session, 8 June 2004 (linking the fight against corruption to the broader issue of democratic governance and asking the Inter-American Juridical Committee to prepare a report on the legal effects of giving safe haven to persons accused of corruption); OAS General Assembly Resolution AG/RES.2219 (XXXVI-O/06) "Follow-Up on the Inter-American Convention against Corruption and its Program for Cooperation", adopted by the Plenary at its Fourth Session, 6 June 2006 (asking States, *inter alia*, to participate in MESICIC, ratify or accede to the UNCAC and UNTOC, adapt their domestic law in order to comply with the commitments undertaken when ratifying or acceding to the Inter-American Convention against Corruption, and improve regional and bilateral mechanisms for mutual legal assistance in criminal matters); OAS General Assembly Resolution AG/RES. 2410 (XXXVIII-O/08) "Follow-Up on the Inter-American Convention against Corruption and the Inter-American Program for Cooperation in the Fight against Corruption", adopted by the Plenary at its Fourth Session, 3 June 2008 (asking States, *inter alia*, to participate in MESICIC, ratify or accede to the UNCAC and UNTOC, and adapt their domestic law in order to comply with the commitments undertaken when ratifying or acceding to the Inter-American Convention against Corruption).

262 OAS General Assembly Resolution AG/RES. 2222 (XXXVI-O/06) "Cooperation among the Member States in the Fight against Corruption and Impunity", adopted at the Fourth Session of the Plenary, 6 June 2006.

263 OAS Declaration of Quito on Social Development and Democracy, and the Impact of Corruption, AG/DEC. 36 (XXXIV-O/04), adopted at the Fourth Plenary Session, 8 June 2004.

264 Ibid., para. 1.

265 Ibid., para. 3.

266 Ibid., para. 4.

corruption should involve principles of the proper management of public affairs and public property, fairness, responsibility and equality before the law, and the fundamental principles of due process of law in criminal proceedings and in civil or administrative proceedings to adjudicate property rights.[267]

3. THE COUNCIL OF EUROPE

In addition to its international conventions, the CoE has developed other instruments setting standards to combat corruption. These instruments are non-binding for CoE Members, but function as recommendations from the CoE to its Members.

Through Resolution (97) 24, the Committee of Ministers of the CoE adopted in 1997 the *Twenty Guiding Principles for the Fight against Corruption.*[268] The principles were drafted by the Multidisciplinary Group on Corruption and are aimed at combining the forces of the Member countries of the CoE in the fight against corruption. The principles were the first step by the CoE in the fight against corruption and are a non-binding set of general guidelines which countries should apply in their domestic legislation and practice. They provide for a wide range of issues related to preventing and combating corruption. For example, States are called upon to take effective measures to prevent corruption; ensure coordinated criminalization; and ensure the independence and autonomy of those fighting corruption. Although the Guiding Principles are not binding, they carry the political weight of their masters, since their elaboration was ordered by the Heads of State and Government and the GRECO is currently entrusted with the task of monitoring their application.

Another instrument developed by the CoE is the *Model Code of Conduct for Public Officials.*[269] The Council recommended its Members to adopt national codes of conduct for public officials based on this model. The Model Code applies to persons employed by a public authority, but does not apply to publicly elected representatives, members of the government and holders of judicial office.[270] The purpose of the Model Code is "to specify the standards of integrity and conduct to

---

267 Ibid., para. 10.

268 CoE, Resolution (97) 24 on the 20 Guiding Principles for the Fight against Corruption, adopted by the Committee of Ministers on 6 November 1997 at its 101st Session.

269 CoE, Recommendation Rec (2000) 10 of the Committee of Ministers to Member States on codes of conduct for public officials, adopted by the Committee of Ministers at its 106th Session on 11 May 2000. See also, Recommendation Rec (81) 19 of the Committee of Ministers of the Council of Europe on the access to information held by public authorities; and Recommendation Rec (2000) 6 of the Committee of Ministers of the Council of Europe on the status of public officials in Europe.

270 Model Code of Conduct for Public Officials, Art. 1.

be observed by public officials, to help them meet those standards and to inform the public of the conduct it is entitled to expect of public officials."[271] The Model Code mostly contains general provisions. It establishes general principles, such as the principle that public officials should be honest, impartial, courteous and not act arbitrarily.[272] However, it also contains certain more detailed provisions regarding the reporting of unlawful, improper or unethical conduct, conflicts of interest, and the expected attitude to gifts and improper offers.[273] Although the Model Code was adopted in a non-binding recommendation of the Committee of Ministers, the GRECO monitors its implementation by Member States.

In 2003, the CoE adopted the *Common Rules against Corruption in the Funding of Political Parties and Electoral Campaigns*.[274] In this instrument, the CoE recommends Member States to adopt in their national legal systems rules in the field of the funding of political parties. The Common Rules deal with several issues, such as the need for State financial support to political parties to be objective, fair, and reasonable and should not impair their independence.[275] General principles concerning donations are outlined, such as the need to ensure that donations to political parties are made public and limited in value, as well as limited tax deductibility.[276] The Common Rules also establish rules regarding the funding of the electoral campaigns of candidates for election.[277] States should also provide for independent monitoring of the funding of political parties and electoral campaigns and the infringement of rules concerning such funding should be subject to sanctions.[278] As with all the other instruments, the GRECO is responsible for monitoring the implementation of the Common Rules.

4. THE ORGANISATION FOR ECONOMIC CO-OPERATION AND DEVELOPMENT

In addition to its Convention, the OECD has also produced other instruments dealing specifically with the question of corruption. Some of these instruments, all of which are non-binding for Member States, predate the Convention and

271 Ibid., Art. 3.
272 Ibid., Arts. 5 and 6.
273 Ibid., Arts. 12, 13, 18, and 19.
274 CoE, Recommendation Rec(2003)4 of the Committee of Ministers to member states on common rules against corruption in the funding of political parties and electoral campaigns, adopted by the Committee of Ministers on 8 April 2003 at the 835th Meeting of the Ministers' Deputies. See also, Recommendation 1516 (2001) on the financing of political parties, adopted on 22 May 2001 by the Council of Europe Parliamentary Assembly.
275 CoE, Common Rules against Corruption in the Funding of Political Parties and Electoral Campaigns, Art.1.
276 Ibid., Arts. 3 and 4.
277 Ibid., Arts. 8, 9 and 10.
278 Ibid., Arts. 14 and 16.

acted as precursors to it. The instruments existed as mere recommendations for States and are much wider in scope than the OECD Convention itself. The first of these instruments, which opened the way for the OECD Convention, is the *Recommendation of the Council on Bribery in International Business Transactions*, of 1994 (1994 Recommendation).[279] From the outset, the target has been quite narrow, namely concentrating on the bribery of foreign public officials. The 1994 Recommendation called on Member States to adopt a series of measures at the national and international levels in order to deter, prevent and combat bribery of foreign public officials in connection with international business.[280]

The *2009 Recommendation of the Council on Tax Measures for Further Combating Bribery of Foreign Public Officials in International Business Transactions* (Recommendation on Tax Measures)[281] succeeds the 1996 Recommendation of the Council on the Tax Deductibility of Bribes to Foreign Public Officials.[282] As indicated earlier, the issue of the tax deductibility of transnational bribes undermines fair competition in international markets. While American corporations, due to the existence of the Foreign Corrupt Practices Act, could not partake in bribery in their business dealings abroad, European corporations could not only do so legally (as it was not criminalized in their countries), but could also claim tax deductions in their countries for the expenses incurred when bribing foreign officials.[283] Both the 2009 and the 1996 Recommendations call on Member States to disallow the tax deduction of bribes to foreign public officials.

A further recommendation regarding corruption constituted an innovation for the Organization. The Recommendation dealt not only with bribery, but also with the issue of corruption in a broader sense and was concerned with its context beyond international business. The *Anti-Corruption Proposals for Bilateral Aid Procurement* is a Recommendation endorsed by the Development Assistance Committee (DAC Recommendation), and as its name indicates, refers

279 OECD, Recommendation of the Council on Bribery in International Business Transactions, adopted by the Council on 27 May 1994, C(94)75/FINAL.

280 In parallel with the later provisions of the OECD Convention and other recommendations, the 1994 Recommendation called for the examination and modification of criminal, civil and tax laws, as well as work on other issues, such as accounting, banking, and public subsidies, in order to deter and fight bribery. See, 1994 Recommendation, Provision III. Moreover, this early document already provided for a monitoring procedure to control its implementation by Member States.

281 OECD, Recommendation of the Council for Further Combating Bribery of Foreign Public Officials in International Business Transactions, Annex I, adopted by the Council on 25 May 2009, C(2009)64.

282 OECD, Recommendation of the Council on the Tax Deductibility of Bribes to Foreign Public Officials, adopted by the Council on 11 April 1996, C(96)27/FINAL.

283 See also, Chapter II.

to corrupt practices in bilateral aid-funded procurement.[284] Through this Recommendation, members of the Development Assistance Committee (DAC) are called upon to require anti-corruption provisions in their bilateral aid-funded procurements.[285] The DAC Recommendation also encourages States to promote the proper implementation of anti-corruption provisions in international development institutions, and to work closely with development partners to combat corruption in all development cooperation efforts.[286] Although the DAC Recommendation is non-binding, DAC Member States have responded by introducing, sometimes weak, anti-corruption clauses in their aid procurement contracts.[287] However, it would appear that the DAC Recommendation has not proved to be as effective as expected.[288]

Within the area of development cooperation, the OECD DAC has also issued the *Principles for Donor Action in Anti-Corruption.*[289] The Principles constitute basic guidelines and orientations to improve collective action by donors to combat corruption and supplement the *Policy Paper on Anti-Corruption: Setting an Agenda for Collective Action.*[290] The Principles cover the key areas and activities in which donors should work together to combat corruption. They emphasize the need to support and strengthen the capacity of civil society, as well as the need for OECD donors to undertake work in their own countries on areas such as the repatriation of assets, money laundering and the ratification and implementation of the UNCAC. Donor agencies are called upon to use the Principles to inform the design of anti-corruption policies and as a diagnostic tool for the assessment of governance on the ground.[291]

---

284 OECD, Anti-Corruption Proposals for Bilateral Aid Procurement, adopted by the Development Assistance Committee at its High Level Meeting, 6–7 May 1996, DCD/DAC(96)11/FINAL.

285 DAC Recommendation, para. 4.

286 DAC Recommendation, para. 4.

287 For instance, the United States introduced on 1 October 1996 the following anti-corruption provision in USAID-funded host country contracts for professional and technical services and equipment and materials: "No offer, payment, consideration, or benefit of any kind, which constitutes an illegal or corrupt practice, shall be made, either directly or indirectly, as an inducement or reward for the award of this contract. Any such practice will be grounds for cancelling the award of this contract and for such other additional actions, civil and/or criminal, as may be applicable", OECD Development Assistance Committee, *Follow-up report to the Recommendation on Anti-Corruption Proposals for Aid-Funded Procurement*, May 1997.

288 In 2003, a report of the Development Assistance Committee concluded that donors had made little progress in addressing corruption in development aid, notwithstanding the DAC Recommendation. "*Synthesis of Lessons Learned of Donor Practices in Fighting Corruption*", OECD Development Assistance Committee, DAC Network on Governance, 23 June 2003, DCD/DAC/GOVNET(2003)1.

289 Principles for Donor Action in Anti-Corruption, endorsed by the DAC at its meeting on 22 September 2006, DCD/DAC(2006)40/REV1.

290 Approved by the DAC at its meeting on 22 September 2006, available at www.oecd.org/dataoecd/2/42/39618679.pdf (last visited 12 April 2012).

291 The Paris Declaration on Aid Effectiveness also deals indirectly with corruption in development cooperation. Endorsed in 2005, the Paris Declaration goes beyond previous

The *2009 Recommendation of the Council for Further Combating Bribery of Foreign Public Officials in International Business Transactions* (2009 Recommendation),[292] succeeds the 1997 Revised Recommendation on Combating Bribery in International Business Transactions.[293] The 2009 Recommendation strengthens the OECD framework to combat bribery by supplementing the OECD Convention. The 1997 Revised Recommendation mostly reflected the contents of other existing anti-bribery and anti-corruption instruments.[294] The 2009 Recommendation reinforces earlier OECD instruments by emphasizing the implementation of the OECD Convention and provides guidance on good practices for that purpose. The Recommendation, for example, calls on States to: (i) adopt best practices to make companies liable for foreign bribery so that they cannot be misused as vehicles for bribing foreign public officials and they cannot avoid detection, investigation and prosecution for such bribery by using agents and intermediaries, including foreign subsidiaries, to bribe for them;[295] (ii) periodically review their policies and approach on small facilitation payments;[296] and (iii) to improve cooperation

agreements among donors and draws up a plan to help improve the quality and impact of development aid. In this context, donors undertake to provide even greater support to the anti-corruption efforts of developing countries, aligned with country-led initiatives and promoting local ownership of anti-corruption reforms. Specific areas of focus are developing countries programmes to strengthen procurement systems and financial management systems. See, Paris Declaration on Aid Effectiveness, High Level Forum, Paris, 28 February – 2 March, 2005.

292 Recommendation of the Council for Further Combating Bribery of Foreign Public Officials in International Business Transactions, adopted by the Council on 26 November 2009, available at www.oecd.org/document/13/0,3343,en_2649_34859_39884109_1_1_1_1,00.html (last visited 12 April 2012.

293 Revised Recommendation of the Council on Combating Bribery in International Business Transactions, adopted by the Council on 23 May 1997, C(97)123/FINAL.

294 In this sense, Member States are once again recommended to generally deter, prevent and combat bribery of foreign public officials, to deny tax deductibility of bribes, and to require anti-corruption provisions in bilateral aid-funded procurement. The Revised Recommendation does however contain certain provisions that are broader than the OECD Convention, for example with regard to public procurement and accounting requirements. With regard to procurement, paragraph VI makes several recommendations to Member countries, such as to support the work of the World Trade Organization to pursue an agreement on transparency in government procurement, to suspend from competition for public contracts enterprises determined to have incurred into transnational bribery, and to require anti-corruption provisions in bilateral aid-funded procurement. All of these provisions were not later transposed into the Convention, and States are not therefore required to give effect to them. Similarly, with regard to accounting requirements, the Revised Recommendation includes a long list of measures to be taken in relation to independent external auditing and internal controls. But the OECD Convention under Article 8 only refers to a few measures regarding the maintenance of books, records, accounts and financial statements of corporations.

295 2009 Recommendation, Annex I: Good Practice Guidance on Implementing Specific Articles of the Convention on Combating Bribery of Foreign Public Officials in International Business Transactions, para. B.

296 Ibid., paras. 6 and 7.

between countries for the sharing of information and evidence in foreign bribery investigations and prosecutions and the seizure, confiscation and recovery of the proceeds of transnational bribery.[297]

An additional instrument which forms part of the OECD's anti-corruption arsenal is the *Recommendation on Bribery and Officially Supported Export Credits.*[298] The objective of this instrument is to deter and combat bribery in international business transactions that benefit from official export credit support. The Recommendation calls for Member States to take certain measures, such as informing exporters and applicants, requesting support about the legal consequences of bribery in international business transactions and encouraging them to develop, apply and document appropriate management control systems that combat bribery, requiring exporters to provide a declaration that they have not been engaged or will engage in bribery in the transaction, and requiring exporters to disclose the identity of persons acting on their behalf in connection with the transaction and the amount and purpose of commissions and fees paid to such persons.[299]

Member States are also required to verify whether the exporter/applicant is listed on the publicly available debarment lists of the major international financial institutions.[300] Similarly, exporters/applicants are required to disclose whether they are under charge, or have been convicted within the last five years for violations of laws against bribery of foreign public officials.[301] Unfortunately, in cases where they have been debarred, charged or convicted, the Recommendation only requires Member States to apply enhanced due diligence.[302] In the event that bribery is discovered after support has been provided, States have to inform their enforcement authorities promptly and deny payment or seek the return of funds.[303]

The OECD has also addressed the issue of corruption more broadly and issued several instruments to strengthen integrity in the public sector. In this connection, through its *Recommendation on Enhancing Integrity in Public Procurement,*[304] the OECD provides policy-makers with principles for enhancing integrity throughout the entire public procurement cycle. The ten principles are

---

297 Ibid., para. 13.

298 Recommendation on Bribery and Officially Supported Export Credits, adopted by the OECD Council on 14 December 2006, TD/ECG(2006)24. This Recommendation is based on the 2006 Action Statement on Bribery and Officially Supported Export Credits adopted by the Working Party on Export Credit and Credit Guarantees on 9 May 2006, TD/ECG(2006)15.

299 Ibid., 1 (a), (b), and (e).

300 Ibid., 1 (c).

301 Ibid., 1 (d).

302 Ibid., 1 (f).

303 Ibid., 1 (i) and (k).

304 Recommendation of the Council on Enhancing Integrity in Public Procurement, C(2008)105, October 2008.

based on applying good governance to enhance integrity in public procurement. This includes the elements of transparency, good management, prevention of misconduct, accountability and control. The *Recommendation on Improving Ethical Conduct in the Public Service,*[305] *Recommendation for Managing Conflict of Interest in the Public Service,*[306] and *Recommendation on Principles for Transparency and Integrity in Lobbying,*[307] provide additional specific tools to prevent and combat corruption.

All the instruments described above are specifically designed as anti-corruption or integrity measures. Nevertheless, the OECD also targets corruption in more general terms through other less direct methods. While not always conceived with the sole purpose of combating corruption, other OECD instruments therefore also address corruption issues indirectly.[308]

5. THE ADB/OECD ANTI-CORRUPTION INITIATIVE FOR ASIA-PACIFIC

In the Asia-Pacific region, the OECD, together with the Asian Development Bank (ADB), has developed the ADB/OECD Anti-Corruption Initiative for Asia-Pacific. In the context of this Initiative, 28 Asian and Pacific economies, including China, are cooperating to build effective and sustainable anti-corruption mechanisms.[309] Together they have developed the Anti-Corruption Action Plan for Asia and the Pacific. The objective of the Initiative is to build sustainable legal and institutional frameworks to fight corruption. An integral part of the Action Plan is its implementation plan, through which participating countries have put into practice reforms to reverse corruption trends. The ADB and the OECD act as the Secretariat of the Initiative. Although not strictly a resolution adopted by an international organization, the Action Plan sets out goals and standards for sustainable safeguards against corruption in the economic, political and social spheres of the countries in the region and defines

---

305 Recommendation of the Council on Improving Ethical Conduct in the Public Service including Principles for Managing Ethics in the Public Service, C(98)70/Final, 23 April 1998.

306 Recommendation of the Council on OECD Guidelines for Managing Conflict of Interest in the Public Service, C(2003)107, 28 May 2003.

307 Recommendation of the Council on Principles for Transparency and Integrity in Lobbying, C(2010)16, 18 February 2010.

308 For example, the OECD Guidelines for Multinational Enterprises (DAFFE/IME/WPG(2000)15/FINAL) and the Principles of Corporate Governance (2004).

309 As of April 2012 the 28 participating economies are: Australia, Bangladesh, Bhutan, Cambodia, China, Cook Islands, Fiji Islands, Hong Kong, India, Indonesia, Japan, Republic of Kazakhstan, Republic of Korea, Kyrgyz Republic, Macao China, Malaysia, Mongolia, Nepal, Pakistan, Republic of Palau, Papua New Guinea, Philippines, Samoa, Singapore, Sri Lanka, Thailand, Vanuatu and Viet Nam.

the objectives of the participating countries in building sustainable legal and institutional frameworks to fight corruption.

6. THE EUROPEAN UNION

The European Union has also issued anti-corruption instruments in the form of resolutions of the European Parliament, which has adopted numerous resolutions and opinions on aspects of the fight against corruption.[310] The *Resolution on Combating Corruption in Europe* of 1995 was one of the first steps by the European Union to address the problem of corruption.[311] Through this ambitious Resolution, the European Parliament outlined many of the anti-corruption measures later adopted by the European Union. The Resolution called on the Commission, as well as the Council and Member States to take action against corruption in a wide variety of areas. It asked the Council to adopt measures to combat fraud and corruption that endangers the Community's financial interests,[312] called on Member States to criminalize bribery and abolish tax deductibility of bribes,[313] and recommended the adoption of several measures at different levels to improve the prevention and prosecution of corruption within the European Communities and in the jurisdictions of Members.[314] At that time the aim of the European Union was to develop its own policy of combating corruption which would enable it to establish the requisite preventive and repressive measures.

310 See, for example, European Parliament, Resolution of 15 November 1996 on the draft Council Act drawing up the Convention on the fight against corruption involving officials of the European Communities or officials of Member States of the European Union, Official Journal C 362, 2 December 1996, 321; Resolution of 20 November 1997 on the Action Plan to Combat Organized Crime, Official Journal C 371, 8 December 1997, 183; Opinion of 20 November 1997 on the draft joint action adopted by the Council on the basis of Article K.3 of the Treaty on European Union on making corruption in the private sector a criminal offence, Official Journal C 371, 8 December 1997, 193; Resolution of 17 February 1998 on the Commission's conduct in respect of alleged fraud and irregularities in the tourism sector, Official Journal C 80, 16 March 1998, 36; Resolution of 17 February 1998 on the Court of Auditor's Special Report No. 3/96 on tourist policy and the promotion of tourism, together with the Commission's replies, Official Journal C 80, 16 March 1998, 38; Resolution of 6 October 1998 on the Communication from the Commission to the Council and the European Parliament on a Union Policy against Corruption (COM(97)0192 C4-0273/97), Official Journal C 328, 26 October 1998, 46; and Resolution of 4 December 2003 on the Communication from the Commission to the Council, the European Parliament and the European Economic and Social Committee on a Comprehensive EU Policy Against Corruption (COM(2003) 317 - 2003/2154(INI)), Official Journal C 089 E, 14 April 2004, 110.

311 Resolution of 15 December 1995 on Combating Corruption in Europe, Official Journal C 017, 22 January 1996, p. 443.

312 Ibid., para. 2.

313 Ibid., paras. 5 and 6.

314 Ibid., paras. 8, 10, 12, 13, and 15.

The *Resolution on Aid Effectiveness and Corruption in Developing Countries* of 2005 is important as one of the early steps by the European Union to include the issue of corruption into development assistance.[315] It was realized that corruption obstructs the effectiveness of aid and therefore undermines the development goals of the European Union and slows down the pace of development in its partner countries.[316] In the Resolution, the European Parliament therefore calls on the Commission to focus more specifically in designing its development programmes on issues of accountability and transparency in order to avoid corruption.[317] The Resolution primarily expresses the intention of the European Union to regulate more thoroughly its provision of aid, particularly financial, to developing countries. For example, the European Parliament calls for more transparency in programmes for budget aid granted by the European Union, for example by publishing the relevant information about the aid spent in the recipient country and involving parliaments and civil society in this process.[318]

III. TRANSNATIONAL (OR TRULY INTERNATIONAL) PUBLIC POLICY

As indicated above, the internationalization of the phenomenon of corruption has resulted in international regulation, particularly in the form of anti-corruption treaties and soft-law instruments, such as resolutions adopted by international organizations. However, in the context of this internationalization and the ensuing international regulation, it is also important to address the development of the prohibition of corruption into a rule of transnational public policy.[319]

---

315 European Parliament, Resolution on Aid Effectiveness and Corruption in Developing Countries (2005/2141(INI)), Official Journal C 293 E, 2 December 2006, p. 316. See also, European Parliament, Report on Aid Effectiveness and Corruption in Developing Countries (2005/2141(INI)), Committee on Development: Rapporteur: Margrietus van den Berg, A6-0048/2006 Final, 27 February 2006.

316 Resolution on Aid Effectiveness and Corruption in Developing Countries, para. C.

317 Ibid., para. 1.

318 Ibid., paras. 12–15.

319 In international law, the notion of transnational public policy is also known as "international public order," "international *ordre public*," or "public order of the international community." See, Günther Jaenicke, "International Public Order," in *Encyclopedia of Public International Law*, ed. Rudolf Bernhardt, Consolidated library ed. (Amsterdam: North-Holland, 1992), 1348–1351.However, in the present study, preference is given to the term transnational public policy, as the most widely accepted term.

1. THE NOTION OF TRANSNATIONAL PUBLIC POLICY

Ordre public or public policy is known in many national legal systems, as well as in international law. National public policy or *ordre public interne* denotes the basic values of domestic law. Any rule of national law that may not be set aside by the will of the parties to a contract forms part of national public policy. A different concept is international public policy or *ordre public externe*, which is mainly used in private international law. Although called "international," it is no more than national public policy (although narrower in meaning) as applied to conflicts of laws and foreign awards, and its content and application remains subjective in each State. Rules of international public policy always prevail over conflicting rules of a foreign law.

In contrast, transnational public policy or "truly" international public policy embodies rules belonging to public policy pursuant to substantive rules of public international law.[320] While the issue of transnational public policy has mostly arisen in the context of commercial international arbitration, it is sometimes confused with a notion exclusive to the *societas mercatorum*, which is said to be governed by the *lex mercatoria*.[321] However, as explained below, transnational public policy applies to the international community as a whole, which is governed by international law.

Transnational, or truly international public policy is said to date at least from the last century, when two arbitral awards considered the role of transnational public policy, or to use the terminology of the period, the public policy of the "law of nations," in respect of slavery.[322] Moreover, as early as 1932, J.-P. Niboyet, in a

---

320 For more on the differences between national public policy, international public policy, and transnational or truly international public policy, see Jean-Baptiste Racine, *L'arbitrage commercial international et l'ordre public* (Paris: L.G.D.J., 1999), 233–436; Rudolf Bruns and Henry Motulsky, "Tendances et perspectives de l'arbitrage international (A propos de la réforme de la Convention de Genève de 1927)," *Revue Internationale de droit comparé* (1957): 717–727; Berthold Goldman, "Les conflits de lois dans l'arbitrage international de droit privé," *Recueil des cours* 109, no. 2 (1963): 347–485; Henri Rolin, "Vers un ordre public réellement international," in *Hommage d'une génération de juristes au Président Basdevant* (Paris: Pedone, 1960), 441–462; Catherine Kessedjian, "Transnational Public Policy," in *International Arbitration 2006: Back to Basics?*, ed. A. J. van den Berg, ICCA Congress Series (Alphen aan den Rijn, The Netherlands: Kluwer Law International, 2007), 857–870.

321 Abdulhay Sayed, *Corruption in International Trade and Commercial Arbitration* (The Hague, London, Boston: Kluwer Law International, 2004), 278 et seq.

322 These were two cases in which slaves who were being transported by the "owner" in ships (the Créole and Maria Luz) which failed to reach their original destination following (in the case of the "Créole") a revolt by the slaves and (in the case of the "Maria Luz") their liberation by the Japanese authorities. The awards had to analyse the rights of the "owners" and reached contrary conclusions, but both took into account a public policy of the law of nations. Pierre Lalive, "Transnational (or Truly International) Public Policy and International Arbitration," in *Comparative Arbitration Practive and Public Policy in Arbitration*, ed. Pieter Sanders,

course at the Hague Academy of International Law, referred to a public policy of international origin.[323]

Transnational public policy today represents an international consensus as to universal standards and accepted norms of conduct that must always apply. However, the rules and principles do not have to be strictly universal, as it is sufficient if they are shared by the large majority of national legal systems.[324] However, transnational public policy should not be confused with a juxtaposition of similar national public policies as meaning a "common public policy." Instead, it is a public policy of the international community.[325] The concept is said to comprise fundamental rules of natural law, *bonos mores*, principles of universal justice, *jus cogens* and the general principles of morality accepted by what are referred to as "civilized nations."[326] Transnational public policy serves the higher interests of the world community, the common interests of humankind, above and sometimes even contrary to the interests of individual nations.[327] It is important to differentiate the notion of transnational public policy from *jus cogens*.[328] The principles and rules that constitute a transnational public policy

International Council for Commercial Arbitration, Congress Series No. 3, VIIIth International Arbitration Congress, New York, 6–9 May 1986 (Deventer, The Netherlands: Kluwer Law and Taxation Publishers, 1987), 290.

323 Although he did not seem to support its application. J.-P. Niboyet, "Le rôle de la justice internationale en droit international privé: Conflit des lois," *Recueil des cours* 40, no. 2 (1932): 157–235.

324 Racine, *L'arbitrage commercial international et l'ordre public*, 360.

325 Berthold Goldman, La protection internationale des droits de l'homme et l'ordre public international dans le fonctionnement de la règle de conflit des lois, in International Institute of Human Rights, *René Cassin Amicorum Discipulorumque Liber* 463 (1969) cited in, Jacob Dolinger, "World Public Policy: Real International Public Policy in the Conflict of Laws," *Texas International Law Journal* 17, no. 2 (1982): 172. Hermann Mosler also emphasized that it is necessary to speak of a "public order of the international community", instead of "international public order." See, also, Hermann Mosler, *The International Society as a Legal Community* (Alphen aan den Rijn, The Netherlands: Sijthoff & Noordhoff, 1980), 17–18.

326 International Law Association, Committee on International Commercial Arbitration, Interim Report on Public Policy as a Bar to Enforcement of International Arbitral Awards, London Conference (2000). For more on transnational public policy or truly international public policy, see Lalive, "Transnational (or Truly International) Public Policy and International Arbitration"; Günther Jaenicke, "International Public Order," *Encyclopedia of Public International Law* II (1992): 1348–1351; Rolin, "Vers un ordre public réellement international"; C. Wilfred Jenks, "The Will of the World Community as the Basis of Obligation in International Law," in *Hommage d'une génération de juristes au Président Basdevant* (Paris: Pedone, 1960), 280–299; Kessedjian, "International Arbitration 2006."

327 Dolinger, "World Public Policy: Real International Public Policy in the Conflict of Laws," 172.

328 It is usually held that the definition of *jus cogens* (also called peremptory norms of general international law) is found in Article 53 of the Vienna Convention on the Law of Treaties: "...a norm accepted and recognized by the international community of States as a whole as a norm from which no derogation is permitted and which can be modified only by a subsequent norm of general international law having the same character." It is commonly held that the following are rules of *jus cogens*: the prohibition of aggression, slavery, genocide and torture, as well as basic rules of international humanitarian law. For an opinion that mixes the notion

are not confined to *jus cogens* norms, although principles and rules that are considered to be *jus cogens* certainly form the core of transnational public policy.[329]

More specifically, three categories of rules and principles have been put forward as constituting transnational public policy: (i) principles and rules relating to the formation and change of international law (e.g. the law of treaties); (ii) principles and rules relating to the organizational structure of the international community (e.g. principles of territorial integrity, equality of states; and (iii) principles and rules of substantive law which serve important interests of the international community and are considered essential for the protection of these interests by the international community.[330]

Turning specifically to the prohibition of corruption, a report of the International Law Association on public policy and international arbitration has explicitly stated that corruption, particularly in the form of bribery and trading in influence, form part of national, international and transnational public policy.[331] Moreover, other sources of evidence of transnational public policy, such as resolutions adopted by international organizations or codes of conduct in the private sector,[332] which reflect the widespread consensus around the world condemning corruption, further reaffirm that the prohibition of corruption is at the core of transnational public policy.[333] This has been stated repeatedly by numerous scholars.[334] Domestic courts, although generally refer to their own

of transnational public policy with *jus cogens*, see, Alexander Orakhelashvili, "International Public Order and the International Court's Advisory Opinion on Legal Consequences of the Construction of a Wall in the Occupied Palestinian Territory," *Archiv des Völkerrechts* 43, no. 2 (2005): 240–256.

329 Jaenicke, "International Public Order," 1348.

330 Ibid.; Kessedjian, "International Arbitration 2006."

331 International Law Association, Committee on International Commercial Arbitration, Interim Report on Public Policy as a Bar to Enforcement of International Arbitral Awards, London Conference (2000), 15, 22, 24, 25 and 32. See also, International Law Association, Committee on International Commercial Arbitration, Final Report on Public Policy, New Delhi Conference (2002), Recommendation 1(e).

332 According to C. Kessedjian, these are the main sources of evidence of transnational public policy. See, Kessedjian, "International Arbitration 2006," 861.

333 On the sources of transnational public policy, see Racine, *L'arbitrage commercial international et l'ordre public*, 367–376; Rolin, "Vers un ordre public réellement international," 448; Berthold Goldman, "Le droit applicable selon la Convention de la BIRD, du 18 mars 1965, pour le règlement des différends relatifs aux investissements entre Etats et ressortissants d'autres Etats," in *Investissements etrangers et arbitrage entre etats et personnes privees: La Convention B.I.R.D. du 18 Mars 1965*, CREDIMI (Paris: Pedone, 1969), 196. On the contrary, see Kessedjian, "International Arbitration 2006," 866.

334 Racine, *L'arbitrage commercial international et l'ordre public*, 393; Ahmed Sadek El-Kosheri and Philippe Le Boulanger, "L'Arbitrage face à la corruption et le trafic d'influence," *Revue de l'arbitrage* (1984): 3–18; Berthold Goldman, "L'action complémentaire des juges et des arbitres en vue d'assurer l'efficacité de l'arbitrage commercial international," in *Arbitrage*

international public policy, have also considered that corruption is contrary to transnational public policy. In the *European Gas Turbines v. Westman case*, the French Court of Appeal of Paris ruled that "a contract having influence-peddling or bribery as its motives or object is, therefore, contrary to French international public policy as well as to the ethics of international business as conceived by the largest part of the members of the international community."[335]

2. INTERNATIONAL ARBITRAL AWARDS

Numerous commercial arbitral awards have condemned corruption in the name of transnational public policy.[336] A first well-known and controversial award was rendered in 1963 by Judge Lagergren in ICC Case no. 1110.[337] Lagergren had to decide whether an agreement, entered into in 1959 between a company and an Argentinean businessman for the payment to that businessman of a 10 per cent commission for an energy project, also covered the sale of equipment by the same undertaking in Argentina in 1958 for a similar project. The arbitrator

---

international: 60 ans après, regard sur l'avenir (ICC publishing, 1984), 285–286; Eric Loquiun, "Les manifestations de l'ilicite," in *L'Illicité Dans Le Commerce International*, ed. Philippe Kahn and Catherine Kessedjian, Travaux du Centre de recherche sur le droit des marchés et des investissements internationaux (Paris: Litec, 1996), 256; Philippe Kahn, "Les principes généraux du droit devant les arbitres du commerce international," *Journal du droit international* 116, no. 2 (1989): 314 et seq.; Philippe Kahn, "A propos de l'ordre public transnational: Quelques observations," in *Mélanges Fritz Sturm offerts par ses collègues et ses amis à l'occacion de son soixante-dixième anniversaire*, ed. Jean-François Gerkens (Lausanne: Faculté de droit de Lausanne, 1999), 1539–1550; Lalive, "Transnational (or Truly International) Public Policy and International Arbitration," 291–294, especially para. 127; Kessedjian, "International Arbitration 2006," 869.

335 Sayed, *Corruption in International Trade and Commercial Arbitration*, 307, citing Measley's International Arbitration Report,Vol. 8, No. 11, November 1993, section B, 10.

336 For a detailed analysis of corruption as addressed in commercial arbitration, see Sayed, *Corruption in International Trade and Commercial Arbitration*; El-Kosheri and Le Boulanger, "L'Arbitrage face à la corruption et le trafic d'influence"; Pierre Mayer, "Le contrat illicite," *Revue de l'arbitrage* (1984): 205; Bruno Oppetit, "Le paradoxe de la corruption à l'épreuve du droit du commerce international," *Journal du droit international* (1987): 5–16; Pierre Mayer, "La règle morale dans l'arbitrage international," in *Études offertes à Pierre Bellet* (Paris: Litec, 1991), 414–426; Vincent Heuzé, "La morale, l'arbitre et le juge," *Revue de l'arbitrage* (1993): 179–198; Yves Derains, "La lutte contre la corruption – Le point de vue de l'arbitre international," in *Contribution au Congres AIJA, Montreux*, 1996; François Knoepfler, "Corruption et arbitrage international," in *Les contrats de distribution, Contributions offertes au Professeur Dessemontet*, ed. I. Cherpillod (Lausanne: Publication CEDIDAC 38, 1998), 357–380; José Rosell and Harvey Prager, "Illicit Commissions and International Arbitration: The Question of Proof," *Arbitration International* 15 (1999): 329–348; A. Timothy Martin, "International Arbitration and Corruption: An Evolving Standard," *Transnational Dispute Management* I, no. 2-May (2004).

337 ICC Case No. 1110, 1963, reproduced in Annex to J. Gillis Wetter, "Issues of Corruption before International Arbitral Tribunals: The Authentic Text and True Meaning of Judge Gunnar Lagergren's 1963 Award in ICC Case No. 1110," *Arbitration International* 10, no. 3 (1994): 282–294.

observed that the commissions to be paid involved enormous amounts of money. Lagergren stated:

> "[a]lthough these commissions were not to be used exclusively for bribes, a very substantial part of them must have been intended for such use. Whether one is taking the point of view of good government or that of commercial ethics it is impossible to close one's eyes to the probable destination of amounts of this magnitude, and to the destructive effect thereof on the business pattern with consequent impairment of industrial progress. Such corruption is an international evil; it is contrary to good morals and to an international public policy common to the community of nations."[338]

As a result of corruption and the gross violation of good morals and transnational public policy, Lagergren decided to decline his jurisdiction in the case.[339]

In ICC Case no. 3916 (*Loewe*), which was related to the payment of commissions, the arbitrator referred to Lagergren's award and concluded that the contract invoked was contrary to both French and Iranian international public policy and to what was considered to be morality in international affairs ("ce qui est considéré être la moralité dans les affaires internationales").[340] Another arbitral award that addressed the prohibition of corruption was ICC Case no. 7047 (*Westacre v. Jugoimport*), which related to the implementation of a "consultancy" contract. The Arbitral Tribunal recognized that legal provisions to combat corruption and bribery are part of the "ordre public international."[341] This was not denied in the subsequent proceedings of the Swiss Federal Tribunal, the Commercial Court in London and the English Court of Appeal, which left the "issue of illegality by reason of corruption to be determined by the ICC Arbitration."[342]

---

338 Ibid., Annex, para. 20.

339 This proved to be a highly controversial decision. Judge Lagergren was criticized for not declaring the nullity of the contract between the French company and the Argentinean businessman. The ruling was not followed in subsequent arbitral awards. See, Goldman, "Arbitrage international," 271; El-Kosheri and Le Boulanger, "L'Arbitrage face à la corruption et le trafic d'influence"; Lalive, "Transnational (or Truly International) Public Policy and International Arbitration". Yet, others agree with his decision because the parties had not claimed the illegality of the contract due to corruption. See, Mayer, "La règle morale dans l'arbitrage international," 379; Wetter, "Issues of Corruption before International Arbitral Tribunals: The Authentic Text and True Meaning of Judge Gunnar Lagergren's 1963 Award in ICC Case No. 1110."

340 Translation by the author. ICC Case No. 3916, Loewe, 1982, published in Sigvard Jarvin and Yves Derains, eds., *Collection of ICC Arbitral Awards 1974-1985*, 1st ed. (Kluwer Law International, 1994), 507–511.

341 *Westacre v. Jugoimport*, ICC Case No. 7047, Bulletin de l' Association suisse de l'arbitrage, 1995, p. 332.

342 *Westacre v. Jugoimport-SPDR Holding Co. Ltd. And Others*, [1998] 2 Lloyd's Law Reports, 111, 131.

Moreover, in ICC Case no. 7664 (*Frontier AG and Brunner Sociedade v. Thomson CSF)*, the Arbitral Tribunal decided that "a contract having trading in influence through bribery as its motive or object is contrary to French international public policy as well as to the ethics of international business as conceived by the largest part of states of the international community."[343] In another case, ICC case no. 8891, the Arbitral Tribunal found that "on the basis of the preceding considerations, the Arbitral Tribunal considers that a contract inciting or favouring the corruption of civil servants goes against transnational public policy and that, if such proves to be the object of the consultancy contract, it has no option other than to declare its nullity."[344] More recently, in ICSID Case *World Duty Free Company Ltd. v. Kenya,* the tribunal found:

> "In light of domestic laws and international conventions relating to corruption, and in light of the decisions taken in this matter by courts and arbitral tribunals, this Tribunal is convinced that bribery is contrary to the international public policy of most, if not all, States or, to use another formula, to transnational public policy. Thus, claims based on contracts of corruption or on contracts obtained by corruption cannot be upheld by this Arbitral Tribunal."[345]

The arbitral tribunals and the courts that have enforced or annulled the arbitral awards have consistently maintained that there is a transnational public policy, under which corrupt contracts are invalid and contrary to *bonos mores.*[346]

Although today it may seem self-explanatory, in the past the existence of a transnational public policy prohibiting corruption was doubted by some.[347] The

343 Translation by the author. Original in French: "un contrat ayant pour cause et pour objet l'exercice d'un trafic d'influence par le versement de pots-de-vin est [...] contraire à l'ordre public international français ainsi qu'à l'éthique des affaires internationales telle que conçue par la plus grande partie des Etats de la communautés internationale." ICC Case No. 7664 Frontier AG & Brunner Sociedades vs. Thomson CSF, 31 July 1996, para. 63, cited in Sayed, *Corruption in International Trade and Commercial Arbitration*, 306–307.

344 Translation by the author. Original in French: "[s]ur la base des considerations qui précèdent, le tribunal arbitral estime qu'un contrat incitant ou favorisant la corruption des fonctionnaires est contraire à l'ordre public transnational et que, si tel s'avère être l'objet du contrat de consultance, il n'a d'autre option que d'en constater la nullité." ICC Case No. 8891, 1998, *Journal du droit international*, Vol. 127(4), 2000 p. 1076–1084, 1080.

345 World Duty Free Company Ltd. v. Kenya, ICSID Case No. ARB/00/7, 4 October 2006, para. 157.

346 See also other cases, such as, ICC Case No. 2730, *Journal du Droit International* 1984, p. 914; ICC Case No. 5622 Hilmarton Ltd. v. Omnium de Traitement et de Valorisation S.A., 19 August 1988, 19 *Yearbook of Commercial Arbitration*, 1994, p. 105–123; and ICC Case No. 6248, 19 *Yearbook of Commercial Arbitration*, 1994, p. 124–140.

347 Oppetit, "Le paradoxe de la corruption à l'épreuve du droit du commerce international"; Bruno Oppetit, "Droit du commerce international et valeurs non marchandes," in *Etudes De Droit International En L'honneur De Pierre Lalive*, ed. Christian Dominicé, Robert Patry, and Claude Reymond (Bâle: Helbing & Lichtenhahn, 1993), 309–319; M. Béhar-Touchais, "Morale et contrats internationaux," in *La Morale Et Le Droit Des Affaires: Actes Du Colloque Organisé*

late Professor Bruno Oppetit stated that States have often facilitated the payment of commissions which constitute nothing more than corruption, and have not discouraged such "commissions" under the banner of commercial pragmatism.[348] As to the anti-corruption efforts of the United Nations and the OECD, Oppetit added that they give the false sense that there is universal consensus against corruption, but in truth their instruments lack operational value and do not create any legal obligation.[349] Finally, Oppetit considered that the arbitral awards condemning corruption in the name of transnational public policy were in reality mostly based on the will of the arbitrators and their own sentiment of justice.[350]

More than twenty years ago, when Oppetit expressed this opinion, this would have been (and was) controversial and a matter of scholarly debate. However, Oppetit's line of thought if followed today, it can be confirmed that the contrary is true. States have repeatedly expressed their opposition to corruption particularly in international commercial transactions, and there has been a multiplication of international treaties creating international legal obligations on States. Moreover, there has also been a proliferation of arbitral awards condemning corruption on the basis of transnational public policy.

Moreover, with regard to the claim that corruption is so widespread that it constitutes as such a real "trade usage" and hence demonstrates no real consensus that the prohibition of corruption forms part of transnational public policy, it should be recalled that, in some of the cases mentioned above, it was alleged that corruption was widespread either within the purchasing country or in the particular sector of activity. However, all the arbitral tribunals concluded that such facts did not alter in any way the legal consequences dictated by the prohibition of corruption.[351] They recognized that in some countries or sectors of activity, corruption is a common practice without which the award of a contract is difficult, or even impossible, but they always refused to condone such practices. It may therefore unquestionably be concluded that the prohibition of corruption is part of transnational public policy from which it is no longer possible to depart.

À l'Université Des Sciences Sociales De Toulouse Le 12 Mai 1995 (Paris: Montchrestien, 1996), 185.

348 Oppetit, "Le paradoxe de la corruption à l'épreuve du droit du commerce international."

349 Ibid., 16–17.

350 Ibid., 21.

351 See, ICC Case No. 1110, 1963, reproduced in Annex to Wetter, "Issues of Corruption before International Arbitral Tribunals: The Authentic Text and True Meaning of Judge Gunnar Lagergren's 1963 Award in ICC Case No. 1110.", paras. 19–20; ICC Case No. 3916, Loewe, 1982, published in Jarvin and Derains, *Collection of ICC Arbitral Awards 1974–1985*, 507–511.; ICC Case No. 8891, 1998, *Journal du droit international*, Vol. 127(4), 2000 p. 1083.

CONCLUSION

The international regulation of corruption, which started in the 1970s, but accelerated in the 1990s has created a sophisticated international legal framework. This Chapter has described how this international regulation developed through the adoption of anti-corruption conventions and the relevant resolutions of international organizations, and the emergence of the prohibition of corruption as a rule of transnational public policy. While the content of these instruments is examined in detail in the following Chapters of this study, the present Chapter provides a background to the international anti-corruption obligations.

As explained, the main component of the international legal framework against corruption is the anti-corruption conventions, which follow a fairly traditional approach to transnational criminal law by creating an international substantive and procedural network to deal with corruption more effectively. While this approach is not a novelty, as it has already been adopted for other transnational crimes, such as drug trafficking and unlawful acts against the safety of civil and maritime aviation, the anti-corruption conventions present certain particular features. There are fourteen legal instruments that deal with corruption, which at times overlap, yet do not contradict each other. Admittedly, some are more comprehensive than others. The UNCAC is by far the most important Convention as it establishes comprehensive obligations covering many aspects of action to combat corruption and has the potential of universal coverage. On the other hand, other anti-corruption conventions are more limited, such as the EU Convention against Corruption, which applies a narrow approach to the fight against corruption, and its impact in practice is not therefore significant.

In addition to international treaties, an essential part of the international regulation of corruption consists of the resolutions adopted by international organizations. These can be divided into two groups. The resolutions that are hortatory and only intended to reinforce the commitment to combat corruption, and those that are more practical and can assist in the implementation of treaty law obligations. The latter is the case, for example, of UN General Assembly Resolution 51/59, which adopted the International Code of Conduct for Public Officials, and the OECD Recommendation on Enhancing Integrity in Public Procurement.

Nevertheless, as indicated in the following Chapters, the international legal framework against corruption is not only composed of instruments as described in the present Chapter. Other hard law and soft law instruments which were not specifically or directly designed to combat corruption may also be relevant tools to assist in the interpretation and implementation of international anti-corruption obligations.

CHAPTER IV
THE SCOPE OF THE INTERNATIONAL LEGAL FRAMEWORK AGAINST CORRUPTION

INTRODUCTION

Corruption is commonly defined as the abuse of entrusted power for private gain. As indicated earlier, this solely constitutes the descriptive core and a normative element is essential to complete the definition. It is the law that constitutes the normative element and determines what actions constitute an abuse of power for private gain. As a result, the question of the actions covered and their definition is central to the scope of corruption as set out in the international legal framework. In addition to corrupt acts, the notion of public official is also essential in relation to the scope of corruption, as all corrupt acts inherently involve a public official.

This Chapter aims to answer those questions at the international level, and is therefore based on international law. Current international instruments against corruption require States Parties to establish a number of offences as crimes of corruption in their domestic law, if this has not already been done. States with relevant legislation already in place have to ensure that existing provisions define corruption and the related offences in conformity with the requirements of the respective instruments, and if necessary amend their laws accordingly. This constitutes the common ground for the analysis of international corrupt acts.

However, international instruments addressing corruption have taken different approaches to the criminalization of corrupt acts. Some international anti-corruption instruments solely call for the criminalization of the act of bribery.[352] Others are broader in scope and also call upon States Parties to criminalize acts of embezzlement, trading in influence, abuse of functions, illicit enrichment,

352 This is the case of the CoE Civil Law Convention, the OECD Convention, the EU Convention against Corruption, the EU Framework Decision on Combating Corruption in the Private Sector and the EU first and second Protocols to the Convention on the Protection of the European Communities' Financial Interests.

and other acts.[353] Both the UNCAC and the Inter-American Convention against Corruption establish different categories of acts. Under the UNCAC, it is mandatory for States Parties to criminalize bribery and embezzlement in their internal jurisdictions. The criminalization of a second group of acts is not mandatory, but preferred (trading in influence, abuse of functions, illicit enrichment, and corrupt acts in the private sector). The Inter-American Convention against Corruption follows a similar approach.[354]

As a result of the different levels of the requirement to criminalize the corrupt acts under the various instruments against corruption, there are grounds for claiming that the international definition of corruption only covers the acts that States Parties to the UNCAC are required to criminalize under all circumstances, namely bribery and embezzlement. Since other acts were not accepted by all the negotiating parties to UNCAC and their criminalization is not mandatory, their acceptance as corrupt acts at the international level is unclear. This study nevertheless addresses those acts, namely trading in influence, abuse of functions, and illicit enrichment, since their existence in the UNCAC is not entirely without significance. Although under the UNCAC it is not mandatory to criminalize them, it is nonetheless recommended. Moreover, several international instruments against corruption refer to such acts and, although their status in international law is unclear they are covered by anti-corruption legislation in many countries. It is possible to envisage that these acts will be criminalized in numerous States in the future. Moreover, the list of acts analysed here is not exhaustive. Progressive developments could extend the list to include other acts in the future.

I. THE NOTION OF PUBLIC OFFICIAL

The understanding of which individuals constitute a "public official" is central to the international legal framework against corruption, as corrupt acts almost by definition involve a public official. The UNCAC defines a public official as: "(i)

353 The CoE Criminal Law Convention criminalizes trading in influence. The UNCAC, the AU Convention against Corruption, the Inter-American Convention against Corruption, and the SADC Protocol against Corruption deal with the acts of embezzlement, trading in influence, abuse of functions, and illicit enrichment. The ECOWAS Protocol against Corruption includes all of these acts, except abuse of functions. The Inter-American Convention against Corruption also covers the improper use of classified or confidential information and the improper use of public property. The UNTOC refers to any other forms of corruption. UNTOC, Art. 8(2).

354 States Parties must criminalize: bribery of a national public official, and abuse of function. In contrast, States Parties have to consider criminalizing bribery of foreign public officials, illicit enrichment, embezzlement, improper use of classified or confidential information, improper use of public property, and trading in influence.

any person holding a legislative, executive, administrative or judicial office of a State Party, whether appointed or elected, whether permanent or temporary, whether paid or unpaid, irrespective of that person's seniority."[355] This definition includes heads of state, ministers and their staff, mayors, members of the military,[356] members of a public assembly exercising legislative or administrative powers, and judges, prosecutors, and holders of judicial office.[357] This applies to office at all levels and subdivisions of government from the national to the local level and to subnational governmental units of a self-governing nature, such as provincial or municipal, including where such bodies are not deemed to form part of the State.[358] The definition in the UNCAC also includes: "(ii) any other person who performs a public function, including for a public agency or public enterprise, or provides a public service, as defined in the domestic law of the State Party and as applied in the pertinent area of law of that State Party."[359] Teachers and doctors should therefore be considered as public officials. The UNCAC adds that public official should also mean "(iii) any other person defined as a 'public official' in the domestic law of a State Party.[360]

Hence, the determination of a person as a public official is related to whether the person works for any branch of the government (as in (i) above), the function of the person (as in (ii) above) or domestic law (as in (iii)). To identify a public official in the cases covered by (i) and (iii) is fairly straightforward, as it is sufficient to take into account objective criteria, such as whether the person is on the payroll of a branch of government, and merely examining the law would confirm whether the person in question is considered a public official under the law. However, it is more difficult to determine whether a person is a public official solely on the basis of her or his function.

355 UNCAC, Art. 2(a).

356 UN General Assembly, *Report of the Ad Hoc Committee for the Negotiation of a Convention against Corruption on the work of its first to seventh sessions: Addendum: Interpretative Notes for the Official Records (Travaux Préparatoires) of the Negotiation of the United Nations Convention against Corruption*, A/58/422/Add.1, 7 October 2003, para. 2.

357 See, CoE Criminal Law Convention Explanatory Report, paras. 27–29 and 44–45.

358 UN General Assembly, *Interpretative Notes for the Official Records (Travaux Préparatoires) of the Negotiation of the United Nations Convention against Corruption*, para. 3.

359 UNCAC, Art. 2(a).

360 Ibid. See also, CoE Criminal Law Convention Art. 1(a-b); AU Convention against Corruption, Art. 1; EU Convention against Corruption, Art. 1(c); ECOWAS Protocol against Corruption, Art. 1; SADC Protocol against Corruption, Art. 1; and the Inter-American Convention against Corruption, Art.1. In addition, for the purpose of some specific preventive obligations under the UNCAC, Chapter II, such as measures and systems requiring public officials to make declaration of assets or disciplinary measures, States are allowed to detract from the international definition and adopt a more restrictive definition of a public official. UNCAC, Art. 2(a). For the relevant preventive measures, see UNCAC, Chapter II, for example Art. 8(1) and (4–6).

At the outset, it should be noted that, even if a person is not defined as a public official in domestic law, if that person performs a public function she or he will be considered a public official.[361] Public functions include any activity in the public interest delegated by a government.[362] The delegation does not need to take a specific form. The person may be engaged under the authority of public or private law, or may have the status of an employee or act as a contractor only for the specific contract in question.[363] For example, private citizens involved in the provision of public services or who manage public funds are to be considered public officials.[364] Even members of royal families who in certain situations are not considered public officials and do not exercise any public function have to be regarded as public officials when they play a significant unofficial role in affairs of State.[365]

The term public service should not be understood as implying any judgment about the desirability of the activity in question from the point of view of social welfare or of other considerations. An activity is in the public interest where the overarching authority of the State stands behind it. For example, a historian entrusted by an administrative agency with the preparation of a report on an old building with a view to ascertaining its suitability for protection as part of the national heritage would qualify as a public official.[366]

In accordance with the definition of a public official, public agencies and enterprises should be considered as performing a public function, and as such employ public officials. A public agency is an entity constituted under public law to carry out specific tasks in the public interest.[367] A public agency is governed by public law and belongs to the national administration. In certain countries, trade unions, universities and religious communities are governed by public law and controlled by the government, and their officials are therefore public officials.[368]

---

361 UNODC, *Legislative Guide for the Implementation of the United Nations Convention against Corruption* (Vienna, New York: United Nations, 2006), para. 204.

362 OECD, *Commentaries on the Convention on Combating Bribery of Foreign Public Officials in International Business Transactions*, DAFFE/IME/BR(97)20, 21 November 1997, para. 12.

363 Ingeborg Zerbes, "Article 1: The Offence of Bribery of Foreign Public Officials," in *The OECD Convention on Bribery: A Commentary*, ed. Mark Pieth, Lucinda Low, and Peter J. Cullen (Cambridge University Press, 2007), 60.

364 However, some countries currently do not. See, El Salvador, Criminal Code, Art. 39; Panama, Constitution, Art. 299.

365 Courts in the United States in prosecutions under the FCPA have determined that, in certain cases, depending on the facts of the case, a member of a royal family may be considered a foreign public official. See, Stuart H. Deming, *The Foreign Corrupt Practices Act and the New International Norms*, International Practitioner's Deskbook Series (Chicago: Section of International Law and Practice, American Bar Association, 2005), 12.

366 Zerbes, "Article 1: The Offence of Bribery of Foreign Public Officials," 61.

367 OECD, *Commentaries on the Convention on Combating Bribery of Foreign Public Officials in International Business Transactions*, para. 13.

368 Zerbes, "Article 1: The Offence of Bribery of Foreign Public Officials," 61–62.

A public enterprise is a company controlled by the State. It should include any enterprise in which the government holds a majority stake, over which a government may exercise a dominant influence or which does not operate on a normal commercial basis without preferential subsidies or other privileges.[369] Executives, managers and employees of public enterprises are therefore considered to be public officials.[370]

It is also important to note that not all persons employed in the institutions carrying out public functions mentioned above are public officials. The key is the nature of their institutional function. To be considered a public official, a person must exercise state authority and have some substantive association with the policy or mandate of the institution.[371] This should be distinguished from ordinary tasks, such as cleaning or building maintenance. There may be borderline cases in which it is difficult to determine whether the person has a substantive association with the policy or mandate of the institution or not. In this sense, for example, it is difficult to know whether very low-level clerical or secretarial staff should be considered as public officials. This needs to be determined in each particular case. However, nothing prevents States from applying a more extensive approach. For example, in the Netherlands, even a tram driver and a security officer at a university have been considered public officials.[372]

The definition of a public official under the international legal framework against corruption is very broad indeed. States Parties to anti-corruption instruments are therefore required to incorporate this broad definition into their internal legislation, at least for the purposes of combating corruption. In certain States, this may be less simple than might initially be expected. Germany, for example, has not yet ratified the UNCAC because of this issue. Contrary to the provisions of the UNCAC, under German law, Members of Parliament are not regarded as public officials.[373] In addition, it should be noted that it is better for the definition of a public official to be included in the provisions respecting corruption offences so as to avoid having to have recourse to other statutes, such as legislation to

369 OECD, *Corruption: A Glossary of International Criminal Standards* (Paris: OECD Publishing, 2007), 31; Zerbes, "Article 1: The Offence of Bribery of Foreign Public Officials," 62–66.

370 OECD, *Commentaries on the Convention on Combating Bribery of Foreign Public Officials in International Business Transactions*, para. 14–15.

371 Zerbes, "Article 1: The Offence of Bribery of Foreign Public Officials," 69–70.

372 Supreme Court of the Netherlands, 1 December 1992, NJ 1993, 354; Supreme Court of the Netherlands, 18 May 2004, NJ 2004, 527, cited in OECD WGB, *The Netherlands: Review of Implementation of the Convention and 1997 Recommendation*, (Phase 1 Report), February 2001, 8; GRECO, *Third Evaluation Round: Evaluation Report on the Netherlands on "Incriminations (E.T.S. 173 and 191, GPC 2)"*, Greco Eval III Rep (2007) 8E, 13 June 2008, para. 86.

373 The bribing of a Member of Parliament is covered by a provision that only prohibits the buying or selling of votes for an election to the German or European Parliament. German Criminal Code, section 108.

combat corruption, the public service, or the public administration in different public authorities.

Although the international definition of public official is broad in scope, it does not cover officials of political parties or candidates for political office. This gap had already been identified when the OECD Convention was adopted, but up to now such persons have not been considered public officials.[374] Accordingly, under the international legal framework, unless they are considered a matter of private-to-private corruption, corrupt practices involving a person in anticipation of that person becoming a public official do not constitute criminal corrupt acts. At present, such acts are regulated purely by national law.

Lastly, when examining the notion of public official, two specific kinds of public officials should be analysed separately, namely foreign public officials and officials of public international organizations.

1. FOREIGN PUBLIC OFFICIAL

The international legal framework against corruption provides for a separate definition of foreign public officials. Such an official is defined as any person holding a legislative, executive, administrative or judicial office of a foreign country, whether appointed or elected, and any person exercising a public function for a foreign country, including for a public agency or public enterprise.[375] This definition is almost identical to the definition of a national public official; the comments made above therefore also apply in this instance. Evidently, one difference is that the term foreign public official refers to officials of a foreign State. This includes any organized foreign area or entity, even if it lacks certain elements of statehood, such as an autonomous territory or a separate customs territory. Palestine, Taiwan, or Northern Cyprus would for example fall under this definition.[376]

---

374 OECD, *Commentaries on the Convention on Combating Bribery of Foreign Public Officials in International Business Transactions*, para. 10.

375 UNCAC, Art. 2(b); CoE Criminal Law Convention, Arts. 5 and 6; OECD Convention, Art. 1(4)(a). None of the other international instruments against corruption contain a separate definition of foreign public official. The CoE Criminal Law Convention expands the notion of foreign public official to include members of foreign public assemblies, members of international parliamentary assemblies, and judges and officials of international courts. See Arts. 6, 9, 10, and 11.

376 Under the CoE Criminal Law Convention there is however an additional condition. In the case of proceedings involving a public official of another State, the prosecuting State may apply the definition of public official only insofar as that definition is compatible with its national law. This is to some extent a dual definition requirement. CoE Criminal Law Convention, Art. 1(c).

Moreover, although not a mandatory requirement of the international legal framework against corruption, it is preferred if States provide an autonomous definition of a foreign public official in their national legislation so as to avoid having to refer to the definition under the law in the country of the foreign public official.[377] The consideration of foreign law may present obstacles, as it is often difficult to ascertain and may contain loopholes.[378] The definition of foreign public official is mostly relevant to cases of transnational corruption. The intention behind having a separate definition of foreign public official is to provide guidance to States on how and when to regard foreign individuals as foreign public officials.

2. OFFICIAL OF A PUBLIC INTERNATIONAL ORGANIZATION

International organizations may also confer public office. A public international organization, usually referred to as an international organization, is an organization set up by agreement between two or more States.[379] It is different from a non-governmental organization (NGO), which is set up by individuals or a group of individuals (such as Greenpeace or Amnesty International).

An international civil servant or any person who is authorized by an international organization to act on its behalf is an official of a public international organization.[380] This includes members of parliamentary assemblies of international or supranational organizations (*e.g.* the European Parliament) and judges and officials of international courts (*e.g.* the International Court of Justice).[381] Whether a person is to be regarded as an official of an international organization depends on his or her function within the organization. As in the case of public officials, described above, not all persons employed by an international organization are to be regarded as officials of the organization. Solely persons who have a substantive association with the policy

377 For example, this is the case in Belgium. See, OECD WGB, *Belgium – Phase 2: Report on the Application of the Convention on Combating Bribery of Foreign Public Officials in International Business Transactions and the 1997 Recommendation on Combating Bribery in International Business Transactions*, 21 July 2005, para. 120–122.

378 Indeed, the OECD Convention, in Article 1, requires its States Parties to adopt an autonomous definition of a foreign public official.

379 According to the OECD, a public international organization includes any international organization formed by States, governments, or other public international organizations, whatever the form of organization and scope of competence. OECD, *Commentaries on the Convention on Combating Bribery of Foreign Public Officials in International Business Transactions*, para. 17.

380 UNCAC, Art. 2(c); CoE Criminal Law Convention, Art. 9; OECD Convention, Art. 1(4)(a). See also, CoE Criminal Law Convention, Explanatory Report, para. 57–61.

381 CoE Criminal Law Convention, Art. 10 and 11.

or mandate of the organization and who contribute substantively to its output are considered officials. Persons employed to perform routine tasks, such as cleaning and building maintenance, are not therefore regarded as officials of the international organization.

In view of the increasing importance and sweeping powers of international organizations in international politics, military relations and social and economic cooperation, it has been considered necessary for their officials to be subject to the international legal framework against corruption. However, international organizations and their officials usually enjoy immunities from jurisdiction so as to avoid interference in the exercise of their functions. Immunity is irrelevant in cases of prosecution for active corruption, or in other words the prosecution of a person who offers a bribe to an official of an international organization. However, whether or not the official can be prosecuted depends on the possibility of lifting his or her immunity.[382]

II. BRIBERY

The most representative act of corruption is bribery, defined as the intentional promise, offering or giving to a public official, or the intentional solicitation or acceptance by a public official, directly or indirectly, "of an undue advantage, for the official himself or herself or another person or entity, in order that the official act or refrain from acting in the exercise of his or her official duties."[383]

The types of bribery differ, depending on whether a national or foreign public official is involved, and whether it occurs with the public sector or solely in the private sector.[384] The above definition refers to bribery of national public officials, while the bribery of foreign public officials, also known as transnational bribery, adds an additional element, namely that the bribe is promised, offered, or given in order to obtain or retain business or other undue advantage in relation to the conduct of international business. Colloquial terms are often used to identify common bribery practices, such as "kickbacks," which occur when a

---

382 For more on immunity, see Chapter VI.

383 UNCAC, Art. 15. For almost identical definitions, see the AU Convention against Corruption, Art. 4(1)(a-b); Inter-American Convention against Corruption, Art. 6(1)(a-b); CoE Civil Law Convention, Art. 2; CoE Criminal Law Convention, Arts. 2 and 3; EU Convention against Corruption, Arts. 2 and 3; ECOWAS Protocol against Corruption, Art. 6(1)(a-b); and SADC Protocol against Corruption, Art. 3(a-b).

384 If the act of bribery is committed in the course of economic, financial or commercial activities and solely involves persons in the private sector, this is referred to as bribery in the private sector. See, UNCAC, Art. 21; AU Convention against Corruption, Art. 4(1)(e); CoE Criminal Law Convention, Arts. 7 and 8; SADC Protocol against Corruption, Art. 3(e). However, as already indicated, the present study does not address corrupt practices in the private sector.

public official gives a contract to a contractor who "kicks back" a percentage in exchange for being awarded the contract.

Bribery can also be defined in its active and passive forms. The act of offering a bribe is commonly referred to as active bribery, and the act of accepting the bribe as passive bribery, or extortion, although as explained below, extortion is a narrower concept and docs not cover all the situations encompassed by passive bribery. It is important to emphasize that active and passive bribery are separate offences for which prosecutions can be brought independently, and that there is no need for an agreement between the bribe-giver and the bribe-taker and/or consistency in the sentences for the two offences. For example, the acquittal of the bribe-giver should have no effect on the prosecution and possible conviction of the bribe-taker, and vice versa. Moreover, the two offenders, the bribe-giver and the bribe-taker, are not usually punished for complicity in the other's offence.

However, all types of bribery share the same elements, with the exception of transnational bribery which, as mentioned earlier, requires an additional element. The constituent elements of the corrupt act of bribery are examined in detail below.

1. INTENTIONALLY (*MENS REA*)

The mental or subjective element of bribery requires that the act must have been committed intentionally.[385] In other words, there must have been the intention to promise, offer, give, solicit, or accept a bribe for the purpose of altering the conduct of the public official in the course of his or her official duties. The intention is thus two-fold: resort to active or passive bribery, and to influence the conduct of the recipient, regardless of whether or not this actually occurred. The latter clause is especially relevant in the legislation of many countries, where the offering of money without a connection with a specific official act (*quid pro quo*) is not considered bribery and is sometimes not even illegal.[386] The element of intent therefore excludes several corrupt practices from being regarded as bribery. For example, if someone offers a gift to a public official without asking for any particular act in exchange, there is no intention to influence a specific act of the official, and hence no bribery.

---

385 However, certain international instruments do not refer to the element of intention. See, AU Convention against Corruption, CoE Civil Law Convention, and ECOWAS Protocol against Corruption.

386 See section 7 below.

To constitute the offence of bribery the element of intention is therefore needed, and there can accordingly be no bribery arising out of recklessness or negligence. Intentional bribery requires a certain degree of volition or conscious choice, and a certain degree of knowledge of the various elements of the offence. To act intentionally, the offender must have resolved to commit the crime, or to have reckoned with the occurrence of bribery. To act knowingly, the offender must have been aware that he or she was committing bribery him or herself, or through another person.

In bribery cases it is especially difficult to prove the element of intention as direct evidence (confession) is usually unavailable. The offender's mental state may therefore have to be inferred from objective factual circumstances,[387] such as when in public procurement a supplier tenders a bid for a contract and offers an expensive gift to the public official who is to choose the winning bid. It may then be inferred that the supplier had the intention to influence the decision of the public official. Concealment, or failure to report an event to the authorities, may also be taken as objective evidence of an intention to receive an advantage. It is therefore important for such inferences to be allowed by national criminal procedural laws.

2. PROMISE, OFFERING OR GIVING (*ACTUS REUS*)

As indicated above, one of the types of bribery is active bribery, which constitutes one of three actions; promising, offering, or giving a bribe. The "promise" makes reference to situations in which the bribe-giver undertakes to give a bribe later, usually once the public official has performed the act requested by the briber. "Offering" occurs when a bribe-giver indicates to the public official that she or he is ready to provide a bribe. "Giving" covers situations where the bribe-giver actually transfers the bribe to the bribe-taker.

An issue that is at times problematic concerning this element of the offence is whether the bribe has to be accepted by the bribe-taker. In certain countries acceptance is necessary, and without it the bribe-giver can only be prosecuted for attempted bribery.[388] It would also appear that in certain countries acceptance means that at least part of the bribe has reached the bribe-taker. The international

---

387 UNCAC, Art. 28.

388 For example, Latvia, Criminal Law, sections 323 and 15. See, GRECO, *Third Evaluation Round: Evaluation Report on Latvia on "Incriminations (E.T.S. 173 and 191, GPC 2)"*, Greco Eval III Rep (2008) 1E, 10 October 2008, para. 84. In Italy the acceptance of a bribe by an official is an essential element of the offence of bribery. If there is no acceptance or agreement, the practice is to prosecute for the offence of *istigazione alla corruzione* pursuant to Article 322 of the Criminal Code.

legal framework does not require such acceptance. However, the promise and offer of a bribe can be criminalized as an "attempt" to commit bribery.[389] In other countries, the offence of active bribery (promise, offering, or giving) is completed once an offer of a payment has been made.[390]

In certain countries, such as Mexico, it has been considered useful not to inhibit those who may potentially report acts of corruption with a view to encouraging within society in general the bringing of complaints against corrupt public officials. For that reason, Mexico only criminalizes the "spontaneous" giving of a bribe, and not cases where a bribe is given as a result of extortion or coercion by a public official.[391] Other countries also consider extortion and coercion as a defence for bribe-givers.[392] However, setting aside the fact that it can be extremely difficult to differentiate between extortion and solicitation, this defence is not in conformity with international standards, as neither the UNCAC nor any other international instrument envisages such a defence.[393]

There is still a general indulgent understanding that the bribe-taker (usually a public official) is "more guilty" than the bribe-giver. This is even reflected in certain legal provisions, such as in China, where significantly harsher penalties are envisaged for the solicitation and acceptance of bribes than for promising, offering or giving a bribe.[394] In this context, some countries have incorporated the defence of effective regret, under which the bribe-giver is not prosecuted if she or he voluntarily reports without delay to the authorities that she or he has

389 UNODC, *Legislative Guide for the Implementation of the United Nations Convention against Corruption*, para. 197.

390 For example, in France. GRECO, *Third Evaluation Round: Evaluation Report on France on "Incriminations (E.T.S. 173 and 191, GPC 2)"*, Greco Eval III Rep (2008) 5E, 19 February 2009, para. 14.

391 Mexico Federal Criminal Code, Art. 222, section II.

392 For example, Italy and its offence of *concussione*, whereby a public official abuses her or his function or power to oblige or induce an individual to unduly give or promise money or other assets to the official or a third party. The bribe-giver is considered a victim and is not prosecuted. Italian Criminal Code, Art. 317. For more on *concussione* and the related notion of *concussione ambientale*, see OECD WGB, *Italy – Phase 2: Report on the Application of the Convention on Combating Bribery of Foreign Public Officials in International Business Transactions and the 1997 Recommendation on Combating Bribery in International Business Transactions*, 29 November 2004, 33–36.

393 In this sense, see the recommendations made by the MESICIC Committee of Experts to Mexico to modify the definition of bribery. MESICIC Committee of Experts, *Final Report on Implementation in Mexico of the Convention Provisions Selected for Review in the Second Round, and on Follow-Up to the Recommendations Formulated to that Country in the First Round*, SG/MESICIC/doc.194/07 rev. 4, 29 June 2007, 31 and 36.

394 See, *Chinese Supplementary Regulations on Suppression of Corruption and Bribery 1998*, Promulgated by the Standing Committee of the National People's Congress on 21 January 21 1988, by Order Number 63 of President Li Xiannian of the People's Republic of China.

bribed a public official.[395] This defence also implies that the condemnation and prosecution of the bribe-taker is considered more serious or important than active bribery.[396] The effectiveness of this defence in combating corruption and encouraging the reporting of corruption has not been highly positive,[397] and it could be easily abused by bribe-givers, for instance by blackmailing the bribe-taker. For the purpose of strengthening action against corruption, it is important for the condemnation of active bribery to rise to the level of that of passive bribery.

3. SOLICITATION OR ACCEPTANCE (*ACTUS REUS*)

The "solicitation" or request of a bribe refers to the situation in which an official indicates to a person, implicitly or explicitly, that a bribe has to be given with the intention that the official act or refrain from taking action. To constitute an offence, it is irrelevant whether or not the solicitation was actually accepted or acted upon. The person solicited may not be aware of, or not have received the solicitation. Yet, by the mere fact of soliciting a bribe, the public official commits passive bribery.

The "acceptance" or receiving occurs when the official (directly or indirectly) essentially takes the bribe. The undue advantage is considered to have been accepted when there is a meeting of minds between the bribe-taker and the bribe-giver, or in other words, when consent has been given, even if the undue advantage is physically received or accepted later. But, what if the official accepts a gift without knowing that it is a bribe? And when she or he realizes, returns it? It would appear that acceptance means keeping the bribe for at least a certain time and that an official who, not having solicited it, immediately returns the gift to the sender would not have committed an offence.[398] However, the commentary

395 See for example, Spanish Penal Code, Art. 427, which exempts the bribe-giver from punishment in cases of active bribery if: (i) the bribe was solicited; (ii) the bribe-giver voluntarily reports the fact to the responsible investigative authority; and (iii) the report is made within ten days of the date of the facts. See also, Slovenian Criminal Code, Arts. 268(3 and 4), under which the court is even entitled to decide whether the confiscated bribe is to be returned to the bribe-giver. In Peru, even persons who are under investigation or already sentenced can obtain benefits if they provide information to the authorities about corrupt practices. Peru, Law 27.378, 20 December 2000.

396 However, not in all countries. For example, in Turkey the effective regret defence is applicable to both the bribe-giver and bribe-taker. See, Turkish Criminal Code, Art. 254(1).

397 In Spain, for example, the defence has only encouraged the reporting of one case of bribery. See, GRECO, *Third Evaluation Round: Evaluation Report on Spain on "Incriminations (E.T.S. 173 and 191, GPC 2)"*, Greco Eval III Rep (2008) 3E, 15 May 2009, para. 99.

398 CoE Criminal Law Convention, Explanatory Report, para. 43. In Turkey, a public official who receives a bribe, but then hands it over to the competent investigation authorities, is not prosecuted for the crime of bribery. Criminal Code, Art. 254(2).

to the EU Convention against Corruption states that the offence is committed even if the official returns the thing received.[399]

Several countries rely on the offences of extortion, coercion, or provocation to criminalize the elements of solicitation and acceptance. However, these concepts are not adequate as they involve a threat of injury,[400] whereas solicitation or acceptance of a bribe is also intended to cover situations in which there is no threat or violence by the public official.

4. DIRECTLY OR INDIRECTLY (INDIRECT BRIBERY)

Bribery can take place both directly and indirectly. While direct bribery is straightforward and does not imply any intermediary between the bribe-giver and bribe-taker, indirect bribery refers to bribery through an intermediary. An intermediary can be anyone, and does not need to be someone who is connected with the briber or the public official.

It is necessary to distinguish indirect bribery from other corrupt situations which may at first sight appear to constitute indirect bribery. These include cases in which a person promises, offers or gives a bribe to an intermediary in order to influence a public official who is not aware of the bribe. An example might be where a bribe is given to the wife of a public official to influence her husband to award a contract. Neither the wife nor the bribe-giver can be prosecuted for bribery, since not all the elements of the offence are constituted, particularly the fact that she is not a public official. Yet, such cases can be prosecuted for another corrupt act, namely trading in influence, which is discussed below in section V.

Indirect bribery may cover three different situations.

4.1. Bribery through intermediaries

One situation occurs when the *actus reus* is carried out through another person, for example where the bribe-giver utilizes another person to hand the bribe to the public official. In this case, the intermediary is more of an instrument or go-between, and there is no doubt about who is the real bribe-giver. It is important to distinguish between the liability of the intermediary and that of the bribe-giver or public official. An intermediary may be an innocent person who

399 Council of the European Union, *Explanatory Report on the Protocol to the Convention on the Protection of the European Communities' Financial Interests*, Official Journal C 011, 15 January 1998, 5–12, note 2.2.

400 OECD, *Corruption: A Glossary of International Criminal Standards*, 25.

unwittingly transmits the bribe to the official without knowledge of or intent to commit the offence.[401] However, when the intermediary consciously plays a role in the commission of the offence she or he becomes liable. Persons acting as intermediaries in relation to bribes can be prosecuted under the rules respecting aiding and abetting, although it is preferable to be prosecuted for a specific offence, such as "intermediation in bribery" in Estonia.[402] In addition, the liability of the bribe-giver and the public official is completely independent of that of the intermediary, and they remain liable irrespective of the culpability of the intermediary.[403]

4.2. Liability for a third party action

Indirect bribery also covers a second situation, namely liability for a third party action. In this case, the person does not expressly direct another person to engage in bribery, yet may still be liable and criminally responsible. Liability for this type of indirect bribery usually happens in two cases depending on the relationship with the intermediary: (i) when an independent intermediary (an agent) is appointed to act in the name of another person or company (the principal); and (ii) particularly in the context of international business, in relation to contracts concluded by a subsidiary for which the parent company is formally responsible.

In the first case, a principal hires a consultant, distributor or agent to represent her or his interests in a given situation, such as representation in a foreign country to win a contract. If the agent or consultant engages in bribery, this can entail the responsibility of the principal for indirect bribery. Although the intermediary is independent, the principal is still responsible, as anyone who creates a situation of risk is required to take the appropriate precautionary measures to prevent the occurrence of harm.[404] The theory of criminal law establishes the fundamental principle that a person can be liable for the acts of another only if she or he is able to control those acts and is also legally obliged to control them.[405] In addition, when an intermediary is involved, the bribe-giver or the public official must at least have knowledge thereof at some point. There must therefore be a certain level of awareness of the commission of the offence (i.e. intention or *mens rea*).[406] While section 1 above describes in general terms

---

401 Ibid., 39.

402 Latvia Criminal Law, section 322. Also, Estonia, Criminal Code, section 296 "arranging a receipt of gratuities."

403 For detailed information on bribery through intermediaries, see OECD, *Typologies on the Role of Intermediaries in International Business Transactions*, October 2009.

404 Zerbes, "Article 1: The Offence of Bribery of Foreign Public Officials," 125.

405 Ibid., 121.

406 Ibid.

the element of intention for the offence of bribery, there are certain specific features involved in identifying the intention to commit indirect bribery. Awareness of the commission of an offence can be inferred when someone knows or has serious grounds to believe that her or his agent is committing bribery, but does nothing to prevent it.[407] Intention for indirect bribery is also inferred when the principal or managers of a company deliberately close their eyes to the evidence that is before them of bribery by their agents or subsidiaries.[408]

4.3. *Bribery by foreign subsidiaries*

Experience has shown that it is important to prevent companies from using their foreign subsidiaries as intermediaries for paying bribes.[409] In cases of transnational bribery, the situation with regard to the liability of the principal for bribery carried out by or through a foreign subsidiary is far from clear, as international instruments do not specifically address this issue.[410] Nevertheless, such conduct should be considered prohibited in conformity with the spirit of the international instruments. As bribery through intermediaries is criminalized and complicity, incitement, aiding, and abetting in an act of bribery is also heavily criminalized, it is difficult to argue that foreign subsidiaries should be able to escape international regulation against corruption. Yet the key issue is how corporations and/or their employees can be held responsible for the corrupt conduct of their foreign subsidiaries?

At present, the liability of parent companies for the corrupt acts of their subsidiaries is regulated by national legislation, and although there are significant differences in the respective national laws, they nevertheless show some common trends. The United States has seen the greatest volume of litigation on this subject. In general, the condition for such liability rests on the claim that the subsidiary is so close to its parent that it is merely acting as a local intermediary. This situation has been found in cases where the subsidiary operates without independence, as an agency of the parent headquarters, and the management functions and all decisions are determined by headquarters.[411] When, behind the appearance of being an independent subsidiary, there is a real relationship of hierarchy with the headquarters and the parent company must

---

407 Ibid. For example, the FCPA defines knowledge as a state of mind in which a person is aware or has the firm belief. 15 USC, 78 dd-1(f)(2)(A).

408 Ibid., 122.

409 See, OECD, *Typologies on the Role of Intermediaries in International Business Transactions.*

410 The OECD has specifically stated that the role of subsidiaries in the bribery of a foreign public official is an important pending issue that needs to be addressed. OECD, *Decision of the Council Concerning Further Work on Combatting Bribery in International Business Transactions*, C(97)240/FINAL, 11 December 1997.

411 Zerbes, "Article 1: The Offence of Bribery of Foreign Public Officials," 130.

have known about the bribery or controlled the expenditure of the subsidiary, the parent company can be held liable for indirect bribery. In the United States, this is known as the notion of "wilful blindness" and "conscious disregard."[412]

Moreover, the liability of the parent company can also be inferred, even if the subsidiary is formally independent of the headquarters and is self-sufficient in its day-to-day functioning, if the headquarters has given an explicit instruction to engage in bribery. For example, the corporation Monsanto was sued by the US Securities and Exchange Commission (SEC) for violating the anti-bribery provisions of the FCPA because a senior Monsanto manager, based in the United States, had authorized and directed ("incentivized" in his own terms) an Indonesian consulting firm to make an illegal payment totalling US$50,000 to a senior official in the Indonesian Ministry of Environment.[413]

In addition, a duty of control can also entail the liability of the parent company.[414] In some States, a parent company is subject to certain statutory duties of supervision or due diligence, such as checking and approving accounts and company books, including the tracking of expenditure.[415]

5. UNDUE ADVANTAGE (DEFINITION OF A BRIBE)

It is not possible to provide an abstract definition of what constitutes an undue advantage or bribe. Ultimately, this depends on custom at a given time and has to be assessed taking into consideration the circumstances of the particular case. Yet, a general notion exists; a bribe places the public official or any other person, for example a relative, in a better position than she or he was before the commission of the offence and she or he or the other person is not entitled to that benefit.[416]

Under the offence of bribery, a bribe is defined as an undue advantage. Thus, not all advantages are prohibited, only those that are "undue". This should be interpreted as something that the recipient is not lawfully entitled to accept or receive. Since a public official is, as a general rule, remunerated by the State, its

412 Ugo Draetta, "The OECD Convention on Bribery of Foreign Public Officials and the Bribes Paid by Foreign Subsidiaries," *Revue de Droit des Affaires Internationales*, no. 1 (2004): 45.

413 Monsanto settled the action and agreed to pay a US$500,000 penalty. US SEC v. Monsanto Company, No. 05-0014 (D.D.C. complaint filed 6 January 2005), available at www.sec.gov/litigation/complaints/comp19023.pdf (last visited 10 April 2012).

414 For other bases for the liability of the parent company, see Draetta, "The OECD Convention on Bribery of Foreign Public Officials and the Bribes Paid by Foreign Subsidiaries," 47–50.

415 See, 15 US Code, section 78m(b)(2)(A).

416 CoE Criminal Law Convention Explanatory Report, para. 37.

organs, institutions or enterprises, any advantage granted by a private person or entity to a public official *ad personam* implies the presumption of its undue character.[417] However, if the advantage is permitted or required in the law or regulations of a country, including case law, it is not considered undue.[418] This does not mean that the advantage needs to be explicitly prohibited. However, it is due only if it is explicitly permitted.[419]

Whether the advantage has a value is determined by the application of a subjective, rather than an objective test. The requirement of undue advantage is satisfied if the thing has sufficient value in the mind of the person concerned that her or his action is influenced. Moreover, the element of undue advantage is constituted regardless of the value of the bribe, and whether it is of a pecuniary or non-pecuniary nature, tangible or intangible.[420] The definition of a bribe is therefore extremely broad and covers money, loans, shares in a company, food and drinks, sex, travel, obtaining a school place for a child, access to an exclusive club, or even information or advice that is valuable to the official.

A bribe constitutes a bribe even if the practice is widespread. There is agreement that the undue advantage or bribe is not dependent on perceptions of local custom or the tolerance of such payments by local authorities.[421] Kenya explicitly addresses this issue in its anti-corruption law: "In prosecution of an offence…it shall be no defence that the receiving, soliciting, giving or offering of any benefit is customary in any business, undertaking, office, profession or calling."[422]

Certain countries define bribes as "material and other advantages" or "bribes in any form," which does not necessarily include all non-pecuniary and intangible benefits.[423] For that reason, it is important for the definition contained in national legislation to cover all possible kinds of bribes.

When examining the notion of a bribe, two issues need to be highlighted and analysed separately: (i) how to distinguish between a bribe and a legitimate gift; and (ii) so-called facilitation payments.

---

417 Michael Kubiciel, "Core Criminal Law Provisions in the United Nations Convention against Corruption," *International Criminal Law Review* 9 (February 2009): 145.

418 OECD, *Commentaries on the Convention on Combating Bribery of Foreign Public Officials in International Business Transactions*, para. 8.

419 OECD WGB, *Australia: Review of Implementation of the Convention and 1997 Recommendation*, (Phase 1 Report), December 1999, 4 and 23.

420 UNODC, *Legislative Guide for the Implementation of the United Nations Convention against Corruption*, para. 196.

421 OECD, *Commentaries on the Convention on Combating Bribery of Foreign Public Officials in International Business Transactions*, para. 7.

422 Kenyan Anti-Corruption and Economic Crimes Acts, Act No. 3 of 2003, section 49.

423 OECD, *Corruption: A Glossary of International Criminal Standards*, 36.

5.1. *Gifts*

It should be emphasized that gifts and personal reciprocity form part of traditions throughout the world. Not only would it be impossible to eradicate them but, most importantly, there is a need to preserve them. Gifts as tokens of appreciation can actually benefit interaction between government officials and those subject to their authority. Although some may border on corruption, such as the Chinese tradition of *guanxi* which involves special connections and privileged relationships when doing business in China,[424] or the tradition in Korea of rice-cakes,[425] there seems little reason why the traditional ceremonial aspects of executive authority, which include tokens of appreciation, should not be maintained.

However, this does not mean that gifts should not be regulated. Indeed, gifts can produce a snowball effect and encourage corruption by giving the appearance that access to and the influence of officials is conditional upon the offering of favour and benefits. The obvious concern is how to criminalize all corrupt practices without including innocuous gifts? And, most importantly, how can a distinction be made between a legitimate gift and an undercover bribe?

States can always rely on the reasonable exercise of prosecutorial discretion. However, to avoid overcriminalisation, they should endeavour to draft their bribery provisions in such a way as to exclude trivial gifts, for example through provisions in administrative regulations that indicate the source and amount of permissible gifts, or the establishment of varying prohibitions based on the recipient's level of authority. It is argued that most public officials are unlikely to ever receive a gift as an undercover bribe, because they do not have the authority to set policy or establish regulations.[426] These are lower-level officials and should not be subject to a strict prohibition of gifts, as it can be assumed that most of the gifts that they receive will not be corrupt. However, officials at the highest levels of government should be subject to a stricter prohibition because of the significance of their authority, and any gift to such officials should therefore be

---

424 Vincent Johnson, "America's Preoccupation with Ethics in Government," *St. Mary's Law Journal* 30 (1999): 717. See also, Alan Smart and Carolyn L. Hsu, "Corruption or Social Capital? Tact and the Performance of Guanxi in Market Socialist China," in *Corruption and the Secret of Law*, ed. Monique Nuijten and Gerhard Anders (Aldershot, Hampshire, England: Ashgate, 2007), 167–189; Paul Steidlmeier, "Gift Giving, Bribery and Corruption: Ethical Management of Business Relationships in China," *Journal of Business Ethics* 20, no. 2: 121–132.

425 Joongi Kimand and Jong Bum Kim, "Cultural Differences in the Crusade against International Bribery," *Pacific Rim Law and Policy Journal* 6 (1997): 549.

426 Peter J. Henning, "Public Corruption: A Comparative Analysis of International Corruption Conventions and United States Law," *Arizona Journal of International and Comparative Law* 18, no. 3 (2001): 840–841.

subject to criminal prosecution.[427] In other words, for officials without authority, the definition of bribery should require the existence of a quid pro quo between the bribe and a specific act expected of the official, whereas for officials exercising higher levels of authority, the definition of bribery should not include such a requirement.

A number of countries have established clear rules on the acceptance of gifts by officials. Some countries have completely banned gifts or regulate the maximum allowable value of a gift or the maximum total value of gifts that an official may accept in any single year. For example, the Kyrgyz Law on the Civil Service does not allow any gift, apart from symbolic souvenirs at official events, and the Kazakh Law also bans all gifts, with the exception of gifts of up to US$ 15, which are permitted by criminal law (Article 311, Criminal Code).[428] In the United States,[429] Executive branch employees may not accept gifts given because of their official positions or from certain prohibited sources (such as persons who are seeking official action by, are doing business or seeking to do business with, or are regulated by the employee's agency, or have interests that may be substantially affected by the performance or non-performance of the employee's official duties).[430] However, public officials may accept a gift valued at US$20 or less, provided that the total value of gifts from the same person is not more than US$50 in a calendar year. They may also accept a gift motivated solely by family relationship or personal friendship, or modest refreshments, greeting cards, plaques and other items of little intrinsic value.[431]

With a view to circumventing these types of rules, corrupt parties have had recourse to more sophisticated and creative ways of hiding undue advantages so that they are not technically considered gifts. This is the case, for example, of expenditures for the promotion and advertisement of products. This practice, particularly widespread in the United States, consists of a manufacturer or promoter of a product organizing social events to show or test the new product. Bearing in mind that, to obtain authorization for the commercialization of a

---

427 Ibid.

428 Georgia allows gifts of up to US$ 50 if they are not related to an act of an official. In Azerbaijan, gifts of US$ 50 or more in value that are linked to the exercise of the duties have to surrender the gift or its equivalent value to the State. See, OECD, *Corruption: A Glossary of International Criminal Standards*, 36. For an interesting report on the regulation of gifts in South Africa, see Public Service Commission of South Africa, *Report on the Management of Gifts in the Public Service*, March 2008, available at www.info.gov.za/view/DownloadFileAction?id=94062 (last visited 10 April 2012).

429 References in this study to the United States only cover federal level or federal law, unless otherwise noted.

430 U.S. Code of Federal Regulations, Title 5, Part 2635 (Standards of Ethical Conduct for Employees of the Executive Branch) sections 201–205.

431 Ibid.

product, it is frequently necessary to obtain an official permit, the manufacturer often invites public officials to such events, covering all their costs, and sometimes also entertainment expenses and other gifts. This form of entertainment for public officials is designed to influence their decision in favour of the product in question.

In the United States, it has been decided to allow this type of practice, but limits have been imposed on what may be regarded as fair and tolerable expenditure. If the payments are reasonable and *bona fide* with a view to promoting or demonstrating the company's products, then it is not considered bribery. On the contrary, in the case *United States v Liebo,* the Justice Department brought a case against a US national who had paid for the honeymoon of a Nigerian official. The trip had no legitimate business connection and was part of a bribery scheme.[432]

Ultimately, it has to be decided on a case-by-case basis whether something constitutes a true gift, a marketing practice, or a bribe.[433] It should be emphasized that minimum gifts and socially accepted gifts are not regarded as undue.[434] For example, in Sweden, the Supreme Court ruled that small Christmas gifts, such as whisky bottles, a piece of salmon and chocolates from an entrepreneur to county officials of a value of approximately 100 SEK (US$13) annually were not improper.[435]

5.2. Facilitation payments

Facilitation payments, also known as "grease" payments, are a special kind of bribe in cases of transnational bribery that are subject to somewhat different rules. They are claimed to be small payments that are in conformity with socially accepted practices made to induce public officials to perform their functions, such as issuing licenses or permits. For example, giving US$20 to a customs official to perform an inspection procedure could be considered a facilitation payment. However, a payment is not considered to be a facilitation payment if it is unreasonably high or if it is related to decisions to award new business, continue a business relationship or perform an act that the official is not legally required to perform. For example, payments made to a customs official may

---

432 United States v. Liebo, 923 F.2d 1308, 1310–11 (8th Cir. 1991); Christopher F. Dugan and Vladimir Lechtman, "The FCPA in Russia and Other Fomer Communist Countries," *American Journal of International Law* 91 (1997): 381.

433 The US Department of Justice has issued guidance on this issue. For example, pilot or test versions of products may be distributed to foreign officials to test the products, but not for their personal use. US Department of Justice, release 02/11–12–1981.

434 CoE Criminal Law Convention Explanatory Report, para. 38.

435 Nytt Juridiskt Arkiv [NJA] [Swedish Supreme Court] 1981, p. 477; GRECO, *Third Evaluation Round: Evaluation Report on Sweden on "Incriminations (E.T.S. 173 and 191, GPC 2)"*, Greco Eval III Rep (2008) 4E, 19 February 2009, para. 14.

amount to a bribe if the goods are not allowed to be brought into the country or if the bribe is aimed at avoiding the payment of duties.

Although facilitation payments are indeed an undue advantage, and thus constitute the offence of bribery, in cases of transnational bribery the need for their payment in practice has been accepted as a defence against charges of bribery, at least by the OECD and the OAS.[436] States are not therefore required to prosecute bribery of a foreign public official when the bribe constitutes a facilitation payment.

Some Parties to the OECD Convention have established an explicit exception for facilitation payments, which are not considered bribes in their jurisdictions.[437] Others have not explicitly established such an exception, but apply it in practice.[438] However, the exception of facilitation payments has been problematic in terms of implementation, particularly with regard to its limits. Parties to the OECD Convention have interpreted it in the most varied of ways. In a number of

436 "Small 'facilitation' payments do not constitute payments made "to obtain or retain business or other improper advantage" within the meaning of paragraph 1 and, accordingly, are also not an offence. Such payments, which, in some countries, are made to induce public officials to perform their functions, such as issuing licenses or permits, are generally illegal in the foreign country concerned. Other countries can and should address this corrosive phenomenon by such means as support for programmes of good governance. However, criminalization by other countries does not seem a practical or effective complementary action." OECD, *Commentaries on the Convention on Combating Bribery of Foreign Public Officials in International Business Transactions*, para. 9. The Inter-American Convention against Corruption could also be interpreted as recognizing facilitation payments as an exception. Although the Convention does not explicitly establish an exception for facilitation payments, the report of the Inter-American Juridical Committee on model elements for inclusion in domestic implementing legislation implicitly recognizes that States Parties may be able to exclude facilitation payments from their implementing legislation. The Juridical Committee Report emphasizes that only bribery in relation to activities of an economic or commercial nature is intended to be covered by the Convention. This qualification could be viewed as excluding payments intended to expedite routine government activities. Lucinda A. Low, Andrea K. Bjorklund, and Kathryn Cameron Atkinson, "The Inter-American Convention against Corruption: A Comparison with the United States Foreign Corrupt Practices Act," *Virginia Journal of International Law* 38 (1997): 270.

437 For instance, Australia, Canada, Republic of Korea, and the United States. However, the precise method of implementation and the limit of what is permissible varies considerably from one State to the other. See, Australian Commonwealth Penal Code section 70.4; Canada, Corruption of Foreign Public Officials Act, 14 February 1999, section 3(4)-(5); Republic of Korea Foreign Bribery Prevention Act, 1997, Art. 3.2(b); United States, 15 US Code section 78dd-1(b), 78dd-2(b), 78dd-3(b).

438 For example, Japan where, although there is no explicit exception for facilitation payments, both the Ministry of Economy, Trade and Industry Guidelines (METI) to Prevent Bribery of Foreign Public Officials and the METI Guidebook on the Unfair Competition Prevention Law contain discussions on the acceptability of certain forms of facilitation payments. OECD WGB, *Japan – Phase 2: Report on the Application of the Convention on Combating Bribery of Foreign Public Officials in International Business Transactions and the 1997 Recommendation on Combating Bribery in International Business Transactions*, 7 March 2005, 39.

countries, the private sector has expressed dissatisfaction at the vagueness of the exception provided for in the OECD Commentaries and has accordingly developed different and sometimes confusing strategies to address the exception.[439] States have established differing requirements in relation to facilitation payments. Some indicate that they must be payments of minor value,[440] while others require that such payments are recorded.[441] Others have enlarged the scope of such payments to include "pecuniary and other advantages."[442]

In recent years, increasingly strong voices have begun to be raised in opposition to the tolerance of facilitation payments, and somewhat surprisingly, these are mostly from the private sector. It is claimed that facilitation payments are the slippery slope to more serious forms of corruption, that they impose additional costs on companies and citizens, and that they ultimately represent a double standard, as countries that permit such payments overseas do not allow them at home.[443]

In any case, the UNCAC makes no exception for facilitation payments, which means that current international law does not accept them and that States Parties cannot consider them as an exception and must treat them as bribes. However, for the moment, some States are maintaining the exception. It seems that they interpret facilitation payments as not being made for the purpose of obtaining or retaining business, and that they do not therefore fall under the definition of transnational bribery.[444] Nevertheless, to be in compliance with their international obligations and to criminalize transnational bribery in accordance with UNCAC, they need to eliminate the exception of facilitation payments. They are bribes that, even though they are of a minor amount, are inherently

---

439 OECD WGB, *Canada – Phase 2: Report on the Application of the Convention on Combating Bribery of Foreign Public Officials in International Business Transactions and the 1997 Recommendation on Combating Bribery in International Business Transactions*, 25 March 2004, para. 63.

440 Switzerland, Criminal Code, Article 322Octies.

441 Australia, Criminal Code, section 70.4(3).

442 Republic of Korea Foreign Bribery Prevention Act, 1997, Art. 3.2(b).

443 Antonio Argandoña, "Corruption and Companies: The Use of Facilitation Payments," *Journal of Business Ethics* 60, no. 3 (2005): 251–264; Robert Bailes, "Facilitation Payments: Culturally Acceptable or Unaccetably Corrupt?," *Business Ethics: A European Review* 15, no. 3 (2006): 293–298; Alexandra Wrage and Kerry Mandernach, "Facilitation Payments," in *Business against Corruption* (New York: United Nations Global Compact, 2006), 69–79; Alexandros Zervos, "Amending the Foreign Corrupt Practices Act: Repealing the Exemption for Routine Government Action Payments," *Penn State International Law Review* 25 (2006): 251. See also, *Resolution on Facilitation Payments*, adopted by the Transparency International Annual Membership Meeting Bali, Indonesia, 28 October 2007; International Chamber of Commerce, Commission on Anti-Corruption, *Combating Extortion and Bribery: ICC Rules of Conduct and Recommendations*, Art. 6 (although their view is quite flexible).

444 On this requirement, see section 8 below.

illegal in the country where they are made. The exception for these payments was negotiated at the OECD for practical reasons related to international business.

The argument behind the exception of facilitation payments was to avoid imposing unrealistic requirements on States.[445] This is understandable, as it is probably impossible for States to prosecute all cases of bribery of foreign public officials when the bribe consists of a small payment to induce a public official to perform her or his functions. However, this should be dealt with at the level of prosecutorial discretion and not through the establishment of such an artificial exception which amounts to a double standard.

6. FOR THE OFFICIAL OR ANOTHER PERSON OR ENTITY

This element of the offence of bribery refers to the recipient of the bribe. In a nutshell, it is irrelevant who the ultimate beneficiary of a bribe is. Bribes can be intended for the bribe-taker him or herself or for a third party (another person or entity), such as a relative of the bribe-taker or a political organization. The relationship of the public official to the beneficiary and the reasons why the official might want to benefit the third party are of no importance.[446] Unfortunately, some countries only seem to criminalize bribery when the bribe is for the official him or herself.[447]

A third party beneficiary of a bribe could also be the State itself, for example through a donation to a public fund. Yet, even bribes given to the State are prohibited. If the other elements of the offence of bribery are found, the fact that the State is a third party beneficiary does not alter the existence of a bribe. It has been argued that when the State is a beneficiary it is not injured (but enriched) and that hence there is no bribery. However, the error in this argument is to consider the damage to the State as an element of the offence, which it is not.[448]

---

445 Philip M. Nichols, "Corruption in the World Trade Organization: Discerning the Limits of the World Trade Organization's Authority," *N.Y.U. Journal of International Law and Politics* 28 (1995): 767.

446 However, Turkish law seems to require the existence of a relationship between the public official and the third party. See, OECD WGB, *Turkey – Phase 2: Report on the Application of the Convention on Combating Bribery of Foreign Public Officials in International Business Transactions and the 1997 Recommendation on Combating Bribery in International Business Transactions*, 7 December 2007, 49.

447 For instance, Latvia, although a Supreme Court decision seems to have overcome this lacuna. See, GRECO, *Third Evaluation Round: Report on Latvia*, para. 89. Also Estonia, Criminal Code sections 293, 294, 297, and 298. However, a draft amendment to the Criminal Code may solve this problem.

448 See, Zerbes, "Article 1: The Offence of Bribery of Foreign Public Officials," 98.

7. IN ORDER THAT THE OFFICIAL ACT OR REFRAIN FROM ACTING IN THE EXERCISE OF HIS OR HER OFFICIAL DUTIES (ACTS OF PUBLIC OFFICIALS)

This element of the offence of bribery refers to the overall purpose of the bribe, i.e. that in the exercise of his or her official duties the official acts or refrains from acting in accordance with the will of the bribe-giver.[449] This is the so-called element of *quid pro quo* (i.e. the action or omission by the official in response to the bribe). In addition, there are differences in national regulation as to whether or not the act or omission by the official constitutes a breach of his or her duties. The elements of quid pro quo and breach of duties are analysed below as constitutive parts of the offence of bribery.

7.1. Quid pro quo

The link between the bribe and the actions or omissions of an official is inherent to the definition of bribery. As indicated above, for the offence to occur there is no need for the official to actually act upon the bribe, but there must at least be a link between the bribe and the "intended" act or omission of the official. This also implies that the promise, offer, or solicitation of a bribe must take place before the official acts or refrains from acting in the exercise of his or her duties. The actual giving or acceptance of the bribe may take place subsequently.[450]

However, this element of the offence of bribery is controversial, as there is no agreement on what exactly is meant by quid pro quo. One approach links the bribe to *specific* acts or omissions by the public official, while another does not link the bribe to any specific act. Under the latter approach, it is sufficient if the bribe is linked to future and unspecified acts or omissions by a public official. The international legal framework against corruption is not specific as to which approach should be adapted and, as shown below, domestic jurisdictions are divided on the issue.

In the first case, the requirement of a causal link or *quid pro quo* between the bribe and a specific action or omission by the official could be extremely difficult to prove. Moreover, there are many cases of corruption in which this element is missing, for example when bribes are given regularly to a public official in exchange for "goodwill" and are not linked to any particular action or omission.[451] When there is no specific link or *quid pro quo*, the subjective

449 It is implied in this respect that the act or omission by the public official will benefit in some way the bribe-giver. However, this is not a requirement for the offence, and it does not therefore need to be proven.
450 CoE Criminal Law Convention Explanatory Report, para. 43.
451 OECD, *Corruption: A Glossary of International Criminal Standards*, 38.

element of intention (*mens rea*) is also missing (the intention to influence a particular conduct by the public official), and the offence of bribery is not therefore constituted.

In certain States, the *quid pro quo* is necessary to establish bribery, and when this element is missing the conduct usually falls under the definition of another type of criminal act. For example, in the United States, pursuant to 18 U.S. Code section 201(c), a bribe given to a public official which is not related to any specific act by the official does not constitute bribery, but may be subject to prosecution as an illegal gratuity.[452] The provision respecting illegal gratuities requires that the item of value given to the public official be "for or because of" the official's exercise of authority, but need not be related to a specific decision or act by the official.[453] However, the U.S. Supreme Court in the case *United States v Sun-Diamond*[454] eliminated the traditional distinction between bribery and a gratuity by requiring that in the case of a gratuity a clear link be established between a gift and a pending act by the official. In the case in question, the trade association Sun-Diamond was charged with violating, *inter alia,* 18 U.S. Code section 201(c)(1)(A), which prohibits the giving of "anything of value" to a present, past, or future public official "for or because of any official act performed or to be performed by such public official." The indictment asserted that Sun-Diamond gave illegal gratuities to the former Secretary of Agriculture while two matters in which it had an interest in receiving favourable treatment were pending before the Secretary. The indictment did not, however, allege a specific connection between either of those matters and the gratuities conferred, and this was contested by Sun-Diamond. The Court's ruling was based on the premise that it is impossible to distinguish between trivial and social gifts and corrupt gifts aimed at gaining the favour of an official. The Court chose to raise the standard to avoid over criminalizing socially accepted gifts by requiring in the case of a gratuity the establishment of a clear link between a gift and a pending act by the official. As a result, this ruling has been referred to as having effectively eliminated the crime of the giving of illegal gratuities.[455]

---

452 As a U.S. Court has stated: "[A] good will gift to an official to foster a favourable business climate, given simply with the 'generalized hope or expectation of ultimate benefit on the part of the donor,' does not constitute a bribe." United States v. Jennings, 160 F.3d 1006, 1013 (4th Cir. 1999), citing United States v. Johnson, 621 F.2d 1073, 1976 (10th Cir. 1980).

453 Hence, in a prosecution for the giving of an illegal gratuity, the government does not need to show that the gratuity was given in exchange for a specific official act. United States v. Secord (DC Dist Col) 726 F Supp 845; United States v. McDade (ED Pa) 827 F Supp 1153; United States v. Niederberger, 580 F.2d 63 (3d Cir.), cert. denied, 439 *U.S.* 980 (1978).

454 United States v. Sun-Diamond Growers of California, 526 U.S. 398.

455 See, Charles B. Klein, "What Exactly is an Unlawful Gratuity after United States v. Sun-Diamond Growers?," *George Washington Law Review* 68 (1999): 116–133; George D. Brown, "Putting Watergate Behind Us – Salinas, Sun-Diamond, and Two Views of the Anticorruption Model," *Tulane Law Review* 74 (2000): 747–813.

Clearly, in many States, to establish bribery *stricto sensu*, there has to be a link between the bribe and specific acts or omissions by the public official. This approach presents both advantages and disadvantages. One disadvantage is that, as indicated previously, many corrupt practices are left outside the definition of bribery and are not criminalized, such as when an official is repeatedly bribed without any link to an official act, but in order to earn his or her future good will. At the same time, the advantage of this approach is that it avoids overcriminalisation and leaves out of the definition of bribery cases of social or token gifts given to public officials. Both arguments were balanced by the U.S. Supreme Court in *Sun-Diamond* and it ultimately decided in favour of this advantage by requiring a quid pro quo even in cases of graft.

Nevertheless, bribery should be interpreted to cover situations in which undue advantage is given to a public official for the sole purpose of obtaining preferential treatment in the short or long term.[456] It seems that certain countries are actually moving in this direction. For example, in Switzerland "good will payments" or gifts with no direct relation to any favour yet given, but aimed at rendering the public official friendly and favourable are illegal. Although in Switzerland in the past there was a requirement of *quid pro quo*, Articles 322*quinquies* and 322*sexies* of the Swiss Criminal Code now provide that an undue advantage not directly for a specific commission or omission, which is contrary to the official's duties or exercise of discretionary powers, but merely with regard to the official's activities, constitute bribery.

Dutch criminal law adopts an alternative approach to criminalizing bribery without the requirement of *quid pro quo*. The clause "reasonably suspecting" was included into Articles 362, 363, and 364 of the Criminal Code in 2001, which now establish that a public official will also be held liable if it can be determined that he/she should have reasonably suspected that an advantage was received in return for an act or omission.[457]

It is inconceivable that bribes given regularly to a public official, but that are not connected to any specific act or omission by that official, should escape criminalization. In the end, it is only a matter of time. A bribe given today to a public official to buy "friendliness" will sooner or later be connected to an official act or omission. Nobody offers an advantage to a public official without

456 In this sense, see, Hoge Raad der Nederlanden [HR] [Supreme Court of the Netherlands], 20 June 2006, LJN AW3584, 01804/05.

457 For example, Article 362 provides that: "A prison sentence of not more than two years or a fine in the fifth category will be imposed on the public official: 1. Who accepts a gift, promise or service, knowing or reasonably suspecting that it is given, made or offered to him/her in order to induce him/her to do something or omit to do something in his/her service..." (unofficial translation).

expecting something in return. It can therefore be presumed that a bribe is connected to an act or omission by a public official, even if this cannot be demonstrated at a specific moment in time.

7.2. *Breach of duties*

An act or omission by an official does not have to be illegal *per se* or in breach of her or his duties. It does however need to be in the exercise of official duties, which means in the context of the official's duties in exercise of official powers. Even if the official acts in accordance with her or his official duties, it still constitutes an offence. For example if, in public procurement bidding, an official awards the contract to the best qualified supplier, bribery still occurs if the elements of the offence are constituted. For that reason, it is irrelevant to analyse what precisely constitutes the duty of an official. To enter into discussion of the duties of a public official in order to establish bribery would have created a considerable grey area which would have made prosecution very difficult in many cases.

The commentary to the OECD Convention and the *travaux préparatoires* of the UNCAC refer to this in relation to the bribery of foreign public officials and officials of public international organizations. They indicate that where the definition in national laws require that the bribe must be aimed at inducing a breach of the official's duty, it has to be understood that every public official has a duty to exercise judgment or discretion impartially and that this is an "autonomous" definition not requiring proof of the law or regulations of the particular official's country or international organization.[458] Although this passage does not completely resolve the issue, it does indicate the interpretation preferred by those negotiating the UNCAC.

Moreover, its inclusion in legal acts is important, because tolerance of this kind of corruption would undermine the confidence of citizens in the fairness of public administration.[459] Nevertheless, in certain countries a distinction is made as to whether the official acts in breach of duty or in accordance with her or his duty, or whether the official acts unlawfully or lawfully.[460] In the Russian Federation, there is a clear terminological distinction between *mzdoimstvo*, the

---

458 OECD, *Commentaries on the Convention on Combating Bribery of Foreign Public Officials in International Business Transactions*, para. 3; UN General Assembly, *Interpretative Notes for the Official Records (Travaux Préparatoires) of the Negotiation of the United Nations Convention against Corruption*, para. 24.

459 CoE Criminal Law Convention Explanatory Report, para. 39.

460 For example, Estonia, Criminal Code, sections 293, 294, 297, and 298. When the act is lawful it is called a gratuity, when unlawful it is called a bribe. Also in Bulgaria, Italy, the Netherlands, Poland, and Turkey.

receipt of remuneration to do what you are supposed to do anyway, and *likhoimstvo*, the receipt of remuneration for what you are not supposed to do.[461] However, this distinction is usually made for the purposes of applying different penalties.[462] The illegality or breach of duties in such cases constitutes an aggravating factor.

8. IN ORDER TO OBTAIN OR RETAIN BUSINESS OR OTHER UNDUE ADVANTAGE IN RELATION TO THE CONDUCT OF INTERNATIONAL BUSINESS (TRANSNATIONAL BRIBERY)

For a corrupt act to constitute the active bribery of a foreign public official or an official of an international organization, which is also called transnational bribery, a further element is required to constitute the offence: the goal of the bribe must be to obtain or retain business or other undue advantage in relation to the conduct of international business.[463] This eighth component constitutes an additional element to the offence of active bribery, hence transnational bribery possesses all the elements described above, but in addition the bribe must be promised, offered, or given: (i) in order to obtain or retain business or other undue advantage; and (ii) in relation to the conduct of international business.

---

461 Pranab Bardhan, "Corruption and Development: A Review of Issues," in *Journal of Economic Literature,* 35, No. 3 (September 1997): 1323.

462 For example, in the Netherlands, where the Criminal Code provides for a maximum of two years imprisonment when there is no breach of duty and a maximum of four years imprisonment when there is such a breach. Dutch Criminal Code, Arts. 177 and 363. In Turkey, under the old Criminal Code No. 765 the provision of a benefit to a public official to make her or him perform an act that she or he is normally required to make, or to omit an act which she or he is normally required not to make, was also considered bribery (Art. 211(1)). Under the new Criminal Code, however, such acts are not considered bribery but "abuse of duty" (Art. 257(3)). The penalty for the crime of abuse of duty is considerably less than for the crime of bribery. Abuse of duty carries a prison sentence of from one to two years, while the penalty for bribery is imprisonment from four to twelve years.

463 See, UNCAC, Art. 16(1); OECD Convention, Art. 1(1). Under the Inter-American Convention against Corruption, the criminalization of transnational bribery is a non-mandatory obligation. See, Art. 8. Conversely, under the CoE Criminal Law Convention, it is a mandatory obligation for States Parties and the definition of transnational bribery is broader as it does not require the element that the undue advantage be given to the official in the context of international business. CoE Criminal Law Convention, Art. 5. Similarly, it should be noted that within the EU this requirement is not necessary. Any bribe, and not only those given in order to obtain or retain business or other undue advantage in relation to the conduct of international business, that is promised or offered to any Community or national official, including any official of another Member State, is criminalized. EU Convention against Corruption, Art. 3.

The prohibition of transnational bribery in order to obtain or retain business is a fairly straightforward concept and it applies whether or not the company concerned is the best qualified bidder or is otherwise a company which could properly have been awarded the business.[464] As indicated earlier, it should be noted that payments made to expedite or to secure the performance of a routine governmental action by a foreign official (so-called facilitation payments) are not considered by certain States as payments made for the purpose of obtaining or retaining business.[465]

However, the prohibition of transnational bribery in order to obtain or retain *other undue advantage* requires some interpretation. According to the OECD Commentaries, it "refers to something to which the company concerned was not clearly entitled, for example, an operating permit for a factory which fails to meet the statutory requirements."[466] Other examples of undue advantages in the context of international business include the grant of subsidies or grants relating to business operations, the relaxing of environmental or other regulatory standards, tax breaks, etc.[467] In addition, the advantage must be undue, meaning that the person or company has no legitimate right to it. This also depends on the underlying official act from which it emanates. A legitimate business advantage must therefore have its roots in a legitimate official decision.[468]

This element of the offence also requires the conduct to be carried out *in relation to the conduct of international business.* Although Canada and Japan have interpreted business in vague terms and seem to exclude not-for-profit business, it is clear that the term "international business" includes both businesses for profit and not for profit.[469] In addition, the *travaux préparatoires* of the UNCAC indicate that this must be interpreted as including the provision of international aid.[470]

In view of the complex nature of most international business transactions, it is interesting to note a procedure that is available in the United States under which

---

464 OECD, *Commentaries on the Convention on Combating Bribery of Foreign Public Officials in International Business Transactions*, 4. The alleged necessity to engage in bribery in order to obtain or retain business or other undue advantage does not constitute a valid defence. Ibid., para. 7.

465 On facilitation payments, see section 5.2 above.

466 OECD, *Commentaries on the Convention on Combating Bribery of Foreign Public Officials in International Business Transactions*, para. 5.

467 Zerbes, "Article 1: The Offence of Bribery of Foreign Public Officials," 151.

468 Ibid., 152.

469 See the criticisms of the OECD WGB to Canada and Japan as a result of their interpretation of business as only covering for profit business. OECD WGB, *Canada – Phase 2 Report*, 28; OECD WGB, *Japan – Phase 2 Report*, 43.

470 UN General Assembly, *Interpretative Notes for the Official Records (Travaux Préparatoires) of the Negotiation of the United Nations Convention against Corruption*, para. 25.

an individual or company can request the opinion of the Department of Justice on proposed business conduct. The Foreign Corrupt Practices Act Opinion Procedure offers a rebuttable presumption that the conduct covered by the opinion does not violate the anti-bribery provisions.[471] These opinions are later made public, although the names of the parties and requestor are not identified. They therefore offer useful guidance on transactions and in determining how the Justice Department is likely to respond to certain factual circumstances.[472]

8.1. Passive transnational bribery

It is important to note that passive transnational bribery, or in other words the solicitation or acceptance of a bribe by a foreign public official or an official of a public international organization, does not require the bribe to be promised, offered, or given in order to obtain or retain business or other undue advantage, or in relation to the conduct of international business.[473] However, it should be further noted that under the UNCAC the criminalization of passive transnational bribery is only an obligation of best endeavour and that States Parties are only under the obligation to contemplate criminalizing the practice.[474] The *travaux préparatoires* indicate that the difference in the degree of obligation is not because delegations condoned or were prepared to tolerate the solicitation or acceptance of bribes by foreign public officials, but rather because the criminalization of such acts is already covered by the criminalization of passive bribery of domestic public officials.[475]

While in principle this is technically correct, the mandatory criminalization of the passive bribery of foreign public officials would have opened the door to the possibility of the prosecution of a foreign public official. This is of course a highly sensitive domain. The reticence in calling for mandatory criminalization of the practice is understandable, since it would subject all public officials to transnational prosecution for corruption. The implications for the sovereignty of States, particularly with regard to public officials, who represent the State itself, are insurmountable. Immunity problems would also be raised in this case, as in most States public officials enjoy sovereign immunity. Although, as explained below in Chapter VI, such immunity is not absolute in cases of corruption and may be lifted, it would undoubtedly create serious tensions between the States

---

471 15 US Code section 78dd-1.d, §§78–2.f.

472 For more on this procedure, see Deming, *The Foreign Corrupt Practices Act and the New International Norms*, 18–19.

473 UNCAC, Art. 16(2); CoE Criminal Law Convention, Art. 5.

474 UNCAC, Art. 16(2). However, under the CoE Criminal Law Convention and the EU Convention against Corruption, its criminalization is mandatory. CoE Criminal Law Convention, Art. 5; EU Convention against Corruption, Art. 2.

475 UN General Assembly, *Interpretative Notes for the Official Records (Travaux Préparatoires) of the Negotiation of the United Nations Convention against Corruption*, para. 28.

concerned. States are not yet ready to surrender their exclusive jurisdiction over the prosecution of their own public officials when they are accused of corruption. For these reasons, even if the criminalization of passive transnational bribery were mandatory, it is still highly unlikely that States would have massive recourse to the prosecution of foreign public officials.

8.2. Non-business related transnational bribery

As explained in this section, the offence of transnational bribery requires the goal of the bribe to be to obtain or retain business or other undue advantage in relation to the conduct of international business. Hence, a bribe offered or given to a foreign public official or an official of an international organization for non-business purposes does not constitute an offence under the international legal framework against corruption.

The origin of this requirement can be traced back to the United States FCPA, which also contains a similar condition. As indicated earlier, in response to growing scandals and evidence of American multinationals bribing foreign public officials to obtain business overseas, the United States Congress adopted the FCPA in 1977. The element that the bribe must be in order to obtain or retain business or other undue advantage in relation to the conduct of international business was inherent to what the United States was criminalizing and attempting to combat at that time. As the United States later raised the issue within the OECD, which resulted in the adoption of the OECD Convention, it is only natural that this element is also present in the OECD Convention. The OECD Convention is the model in criminalizing transnational bribery at the international level, and was in turn the model for the criminalization of that act in the UNCAC. The current international legal framework against corruption therefore ended up including the requirement that the bribe must be connected to international business.

However, the presence of this element is highly regrettable. As a result, acts of bribery of foreign public officials for non-business purposes are not covered by the definition of transnational bribery and are not therefore criminalized in international law. The bribery of foreign public officials should constitute an offence in all circumstances, and not solely in the context of international business. On the positive side, several countries already criminalize transnational bribery outside the context of international business.[476] However, they are the minority.

---

476 For instance, Belgium, Netherlands, Luxembourg, Hungary, Poland, Switzerland, Sweden, and the United Kingdom. Yet, many countries still only criminalize transnational bribery in the context of international business. See, for example, Argentina (Criminal Code,

Moreover, as indicated earlier, the requirement that the bribe must be given in order to obtain or retain business or other undue advantage in relation to the conduct of international business also applies to bribes offered or given to officials of public international organizations. This is even more unfortunate than in the case of foreign public officials. What is the relation between international business and officials of public international organizations? For example, the bribery of an official of the United Nations to influence the voting in an important political decision, or the bribery of an official so that an unqualified person is hired, would not constitute transnational bribery under the international legal framework against corruption. In view of the ever-growing fields of competence of public international organizations, it is important to combat such corrupt acts. Even though it is not a requirement under international law, it is of the utmost importance for States to criminalize the bribery of officials of public international organizations for non-business purposes.

III. EMBEZZLEMENT, MISAPPROPRIATION OR OTHER DIVERSION OF PROPERTY

In addition to bribery, probably the most common corrupt practice is the embezzlement of public property. Sometimes also called peculation, it is defined as the intentional embezzlement, misappropriation or other diversion by a public official, for her or his benefit or for the benefit of another person or entity, of any property, public or private funds or securities or any other thing of value entrusted to the public official by virtue of her or his position.[477]

The offence is constituted by different types of acts. To take or convert for one's own use another's money or property (embezzlement), or the unauthorized, improper, or unlawful use of money or property (misappropriation), of which the wrongdoer acquired possession lawfully by reason of her or his public office. By including the clause "other diversion of property", the offence is sufficiently broad in scope to include many practices that are not technically embezzlement or misappropriation.[478] This is the case, for example, of a public official who

Art. 258*bis*), Japan (Unfair Competition Prevention Law, Art. 10*bis*(1)), Mexico (Federal Criminal Code, Art. 222*bis*), Republic of Korea (Act on Preventing Bribery of Foreign Public Officials in International Business Transactions, Art. 3(1), and United States (15 US Code section 78dd- 1–3).

477 See, UNCAC, Art. 17; AU Convention against Corruption, Art. 4(1)(d); Inter-American Convention against Corruption, Art. XI(1)(d); ECOWAS Protocol against Corruption, Art. 6(1)(e); SADC Protocol against Corruption, Art. 3(d).

478 The term "diversion" was partly included to take into account the Spanish version of the UNCAC since, during the negotiations of the UNCAC, some Spanish-speaking delegations argued that "diversion" is distinct from "embezzlement" and "misappropriation." See, UN General Assembly, Ad Hoc Committee for the Negotiation of a Convention against

utilizes public funds or assets for private purposes, but returns them after use and does not appropriate the funds or assets. Similarly, the diversion of public property occurs when, for example, a public official at the municipal level uses the municipal tractor and an employee/driver of the municipality to turn over rocks and soil at her or his home.

Property is understood as assets of every kind, whether corporeal or incorporeal, movable or immovable, tangible or intangible, and legal documents or instruments attesting title to or interest in such assets.[479] The property must be entrusted to the public official by virtue of her or his position. This means that the public official must have material or juridical possession of the funds or assets in virtue of her or his position. If the public official acquires possession of public funds or assets by other means, for example fraudulently or unlawfully, and misappropriates those funds, it is not a case of embezzlement of public funds, as they were not entrusted to her or him by virtue of her or his position. The official instead acquired possession through other means and has probably committed another crime, such as larceny, but not embezzlement, misappropriation or other diversion of property.

The offence has been incorporated into the internal jurisdictions of States using different approaches. Some States, such as Germany, have not established a specific offence of embezzlement of public funds, but apply the general offence of misappropriation of any funds, whether public or private.[480] Switzerland has adopted a similar approach and, where the person embezzling is a public official and embezzles or misappropriates public funds or assets, this is considered to be an aggravating factor for which there is a stronger penalty.[481] In essence, these States consider the corrupt act of embezzlement to be a crime against property,

---

Corruption, Fourth Session, Vienna, 13–24 January 2003, *Revised Draft United Nations Convention against Corruption*, A/AC.261/3/Rev.2, 19 November 2002, p.25. For a contrary view, see Canada's declaration to the UNCAC in which it indicated that it was the understanding of the Canadian Government that the word "diversion" means embezzlement and misappropriation, which constitute the criminal offence of theft and fraud under current Canadian Law. Canada Declaration upon Ratification of the UNCAC, para. 2, available at http://treaties.un.org/pages/ViewDetails.aspx?src=TREATY&mtdsg_no=XVIII-14&chapter=18&lang=en (last visited 15 April 2012).

479 UNCAC, Art. 2(d); UN General Assembly, *Interpretative Notes for the Official Records (Travaux Préparatoires) of the Negotiation of the United Nations Convention against Corruption*, para. 6.

480 Germany did include the offence of embezzlement of public funds in its Criminal Code under section 350. However, the section was repealed in 1974 because it was considered that the offence of misappropriation under section 246 is applicable to whoever possesses funds or assets (of the State, of private individuals or legal persons) and has them under her or his administration by virtue of her or his position.

481 When the embezzler is a public official, the penalty is up to ten years of imprisonment, and five years when she or he is not a public official. Swiss Criminal Code, Title 2, Offences against Public Property, Art. 138.

regardless of whether the property belongs to a private person or the State. Other States, such as Argentina, have established a specific offence in their legislation for the embezzlement of public funds.[482] In this case, the crime is against public property. In other States, such as Costa Rica, the offence is against the integrity of the public official or public administration, instead of public property. It is interesting to note that the corrupt act of embezzlement may not be found in certain countries where public property is equivalent to the property of certain public figures. This is the case in certain absolute monarchies, such as Saudi Arabia or the Sultanate of Brunei, where the property of the State is the property of the royal family.

Where the crime of embezzlement is considered to be an offence against property (whether or not it is public), one element of the offence is damage to such property.[483] Where there is no damage, no offence is committed. In contrast, in States where there is a specific offence of embezzlement by a public official, because the crime is committed against the integrity of the public office and the public administration, there is no question of the element of damage.[484] Even where there is no damage, for example in cases where the public official returns the embezzled funds or assets, the offence has already been committed because integrity has been violated. The international legal framework against corruption does not provide for the element of damage in the offence of embezzlement. For States to comply with their international obligations, it is recommended that they establish a specific offence of embezzlement in the public sector in their internal legislation.

IV. ILLICIT ENRICHMENT

Illicit enrichment, also known as unexplained or excessive wealth, is defined as a significant increase in the assets of a public official that cannot reasonably be explained in relation to her or his lawful income.[485] However, this definition

---

482 Argentina Criminal Code, Art. 261; Costa Rica Criminal Code, Art. 354.

483 Several authors have argued that in order to constitute the crime of embezzlement the element of damage to property is needed. See for example, Sebastián Soler, *Derecho Penal Argentino* (Buenos Aires: Editorial La Ley, 1945), Vol. V, p. 205; Carlos Fontán Balestra, *Derecho Penal, Parte Especial*, 14th ed. (Buenos Aires: Abeledo-Perrot, 1995), 876.

484 Other authors have consistently argued that no damage is needed in the crime of embezzlement of public funds. See for example, Daniel P. Carrera, *Peculado (de bienes públicos y de trabajos o servicios, art. 261 del Cod. penal)* (Buenos Aires: Ediciones Depalma, 1968), 139; Carlos Creus, *Derecho Penal* (Buenos Aires: Editorial Astrea de A. y R. Depalma, 1983), Vol. II, p. 324.

485 UNCAC, Art. 20; Inter-American Convention against Corruption, Art. 9; ECOWAS Protocol against Corruption, Art. 6(3)(a). The AU Convention against Corruption lists illicit enrichment as a corrupt act under Article 4(1)(g) and Article 8, but does not provide a definition.

does not proscribe the conduct of the public official. Criminal acts by definition constitute an action or omission by an offender. A better definition of illicit enrichment holds that, when a public official during incumbency has acquired property that is manifestly disproportionate to her or his salary level and other lawfully earned income, such assets are presumed to have been unlawfully acquired, unless the official can justify their legitimacy.[486]

The definition of illicit enrichment lacks an important element, which is the temporal extension of the crime during the lifetime of the public official. It is relatively easy for corrupt public officials to conceal property or assets that they have embezzled during their tenure for after they are no longer public officials. For that reason, it is important for the crime of illicit enrichment to be applicable for a period of time following the departure of officials from their public functions. Some States provide for a two-year term,[487] yet a longer period would be preferable in view of the complex nature of this kind of crime and its high political significance. To prosecute corrupt officials it is sometimes necessary to wait for a change of political power and government, which may take longer than two years.

Illicit enrichment is an extraordinary criminal act that is only indirectly related to an illegal act by a public official. This illegal act may be any of a variety of criminal acts, such as accepting a bribe or embezzlement, but what is criminalized in the case of illicit enrichment is not the act as such, but the use of the proceeds from the illegal acts. In addition, the definition of illicit enrichment even specifies the evidentiary method to be used to determine whether the public official has used proceeds from a corrupt act to lead a lifestyle or acquire property that is disproportionate to her or his salary or other lawful income.

However, there is a reason for the existence of such a unique criminal act. Experience has shown that meeting the burden of proof in relation to corrupt acts is in most cases extremely difficult. Since most corrupt acts are consensual crimes (both parties agree to commit the crime), there are no direct victims. Although there are victims in practice, such as society in general, in most cases of corruption, the victims are not aware that they are victims. This absence of direct victims defies the traditional procedures of law enforcement of starting

486 The offence of illicit enrichment is usually defined as an action, but can also be defined as an omission, i.e. the lack of justification by the public official of unexplained wealth. For more on illicit enrichment as an omission, see Guillermo Jorge, *The Romanian Legal Framework on Illicit Enrichment* (American Bar Association Central European and Eurasian Law Initiative (ABA/CEELI), July 2007), 59–62. It is interesting to note that in Romania under the communist regime illicit enrichment was considered a crime that could apply to all individuals. Law 18/1968, in force until 1991.

487 For example, Colombia, Criminal Code, Art. 412; Argentina, Criminal Code, Art. 268(2).

investigations on the basis of a complaint by a victim. In many cases of corrupt acts, there are no witnesses, documents, or any other means of evidence. Successful prosecution mostly occurs when the parties are caught *in fraganti*, or when one unsatisfied party of the corrupt agreement is willing to cooperate with the prosecution. Successful prosecution is therefore dependent on disagreements between the participants in a corrupt deal.

The establishment of illicit enrichment as an offence addresses types of situation faced by the prosecutions when they have to prove that a public official solicited or accepted bribes in cases where the official's enrichment is so disproportionate to her or his lawful income that a *prima facie* case of corruption can be made.[488] As a result, some jurisdictions have established the offence of illicit enrichment.[489] However, illicit enrichment is a particularly controversial act of corruption because, according to some, the criminalization of such an act goes against the essential guarantees of a liberal criminal law system, national constitutions and international human rights law. This long-standing controversy is deserving of a separate and detailed analysis.

1. PRESUMPTION OF GUILT?

Many legal scholars have voiced opposition to the existence of the offence of illicit enrichment.[490] It has been called a crime of suspicion, because it allows the presumption of situations of guilt on the basis of unidentified facts.[491] It is

488 UNODC, *Legislative Guide for the Implementation of the United Nations Convention against Corruption*, para. 296.

489 Some countries go even further. It has been reported that in the Philippines, Indonesia and Thailand, civil governmental and civil society actors have engaged in the systematic monitoring of the lifestyles of public officials to detect cases of enrichment and subsequently trigger prosecution. See, ADB/OECD Anti-Corruption Initiative for Asia and the Pacific, *Anti-Corruption Policies in Asia and the Pacific: Progress in Legal and Institutional Reform in 25 Countries* (Manila: ADB/OECD Anti-Corruption Initiative for Asia and the Pacific, 2006), 40.

490 Dan Wilsher, "Inexplicable Wealth and Illicit Enrichment of Public Officials: A Model Draft That Respects Human Rights in Corruption Cases," *Crime, Law and Social Change* 45 (2006): 28; Jorge Federico Mikkelsen-Löth, *Enriquecimiento Ilícito: El Desafío Para La Ciencia Jurídico-penal En La Sociedad Actual De Enfrentar a La Corrupción En La Administración Pública* (Buenos Aires: La Ley, 2001); Francisco Pavón Vasconcelos, *Diccionario De Derecho Penal: Analítico-Sistemático* (México, D.F: Editorial Porrúa, 1997), 430–431; Marco Antonio Díaz de León, *Código Penal Federal Con Comentarios* (México, D.F: Editorial Porrúa, 1998), 383–384; Marcelo A. Sancinetti, *El Delito De Enriquecimiento Ilícito De Funcionario Público-- Art. 268 (2), C.P.: Un Tipo Penal Violatorio Del Estado De Derecho* (Buenos Aires: AD-HOC, 1994); Miguel Angel Inchausti, *Enriquecimiento Ilícito De Funcionarios: El Art. 268.2 Del Cód. Penal, Leyes 16.648 Y 25.188* (Buenos Aires: Ad Hoc, 2001).

491 Mikkelsen-Löth, *Enriquecimiento Ilícito*. An additional argument against the offence of illicit enrichment rests on the fact that this kind of crime could serve the purpose of political persecution and acts of revenge against public officials. For example, if a rival politician pays

argued that illicit enrichment runs counter to the principle of the presumption of innocence, reverses the burden of proof and infringes upon the guarantee against self-incrimination. For this reason, when international anti-corruption instruments require States to criminalize this act, a safeguard clause is always included, such as "subject to the State's constitution and the fundamental principles of its legal system."[492]

On the other hand, many support the offence of illicit enrichment. Many countries have established the offence and have used it successfully.[493] Despite the practical reasons for the existence of this crime, such as the difficulties in proving corrupt acts and the increasing need and demand to bring those who are corrupt to justice, as described below, a thorough legal examination of the concept of illicit enrichment proves that in reality this offence does not violate any of the basic legal guarantees of a liberal criminal law system. It does however alter the traditional understanding of the principle of presumption of innocence and the ensuing burden of proof on the prosecution.

The presumption of innocence is recognized in many national Constitutions and is at the core of international human rights law.[494] Any person who is charged with a criminal offence has the right to be presumed innocent until proven guilty

---

anonymously a debt of another public official and later accuses him of illicit enrichment (with the understanding that the decrease of debts is the same as increase of capital). It will be very difficult for the accused to demonstrate that he did not pay the debt, i.e. that he did not enrich himself outside his regular income. At the minimum, it will involve him in a trial that could hurt him politically, financially, and probably lead to his imprisonment.

492 For the different interpretations of this clause, see A. Posadas, "Combating Corruption Under International Law," *Duke Journal of Comparative & International Law,* Vol. 10, No. 2, Spring/Summer 2000, p. 384–386. On the basis of the clause "subject to its constitution and the fundamental principles of its legal system" Canada has made a reservation to the UNCAC whereby it states that the offence of illicit enrichment is incompatible with the Canadian Constitution, more specifically with the Canadian Charter of Rights and Freedoms, and therefore will not create such an offence. See, Canada Declaration upon Ratification of the UNCAC, para. 3.

493 For example, Argentina, Criminal Code, Art. 268(2); Bolivia, Criminal Code, forthcoming Art. 149 Bis (currently in the process of amending the Criminal Code); Costa Rica, Law against Corruption and Illicit Enrichment in the Public Function, Law No. 8422, 26 May 2004, Art. 45; Ecuador, Criminal Code, Chapter VIII, Provision Unnumbered following Art. 296 (incorporated by Art. 2 Law 6, 29 August 1985); Peru, Criminal Code, Art. 401; Mexico, Criminal Code, Art. 224; Paraguay, Law 2523/04; Pakistan, National Accountability Bureau Ordinance No. XVIII of 1999, 16 November 1999, as amended, para. 9(v); Colombia, Criminal Code, Art. 412; El Salvador, Criminal Code, Art. 447; Venezuela, Law against Corruption, Official Journal 5637, 7 April 2003, Arts. 46–51; Algeria, Law No. 06–01, 20 February 2006 on Prevention and Fight against Corruption, Art. 37. Also, in Bangladesh, Hong Kong, China, India, Malaysia, Nepal, Philippines, Singapore, and Thailand. See, ADB/OECD Anti-Corruption Initiative for Asia and the Pacific, *Anti-Corruption Policies in Asia and the Pacific*, 39.

494 For example, the Universal Declaration of Human Rights, Art. 11(1); International Covenant on Civil and Political Rights, Art. 14(2); Inter-American Convention on Human rights,

in accordance with the law. This comprises a number of rights and safeguards, including that the burden of proving the guilt of the accused rests with the State (the prosecution) and that any doubt should benefit the accused (*in dubio pro reo*).

However, this guarantee is far from being absolute. There are situations, such as in cases of strict liability offences, or when a confiscation order is issued, where the burden of proof is more flexible.[495] Crimes of strict liability normally arise where an activity is illegal, but is authorized under certain circumstances, for example, subject to the requirement to hold a license. In such cases, a legal burden can be imposed on the defendant, for example to prove that she or he has the licence.[496] Regulatory efficiency and common sense dictate that the prosecution should not be required to undertake the virtually impossible task of establishing that a defendant does not have a licence, when it is simpler for the defendant to establish that she or he has one.

With regard to illicit enrichment, the approach is different from that for crimes of strict liability. The offence of illicit enrichment rests on a presumption of facts and law. It has been interpreted that this presumption may be accepted under two conditions: when the presumption is not automatic, and when it is open to the defence to rebut the presumption.[497] The presumed fact is therefore that the property of the accused, which is manifestly disproportionate to her or his salary level and other lawfully earned income, originated in acts of corruption committed while in public office. Yet, such a presumption is not automatic, since it is incumbent on the prosecution to prove in the first place the elements of the presumption, normally that the property of the accused exceeds her or his salary level and other lawfully earned income. The accused then has the opportunity to rebut the presumption.

Illicit enrichment places an evidentiary burden on the accused, which means that the accused only needs to establish reasonable doubt as to her or his guilt. For this reason, the imposition of an evidentiary burden on the accused is hardly ever viewed as a violation of the presumption of innocence, but merely as an exception or alteration of the rule.[498]

Art. 8(2); European Convention on Human Rights, Art. 6(2); and the African Charter on Human and People's Rights, Art. 7(1).

495 In cases of strict liability offences or when a confiscation order is issued. See, Jorge, *The Romanian Legal Framework on Illicit Enrichment*, 40–42.

496 Wilsher, "Inexplicable Wealth and Illicit Enrichment of Public Officials: A Model Draft That Respects Human Rights in Corruption Cases," 31.

497 For an analysis of how this has developed in common and civil law countries, see Jorge, *The Romanian Legal Framework on Illicit Enrichment*, 44–48; Guy Stessens, *Money Laundering: A New International Law Enforcement Model* (Cambridge: Cambridge University Press, 2000), 71.

498 Ndiva Kofele-Kale, "Presumed Guilty: Balancing Competing Rights and Interests in Combating Economic Crimes," *The International Lawyer* 40, no. 4 (2006): 928.

Presumptions of fact or law have been accepted by every legal system. The European Court of Human Rights had the opportunity to address this issue in two cases and accepted presumptions of fact or law, as long as they are used within reasonable limits, which take into account the importance of what is at stake and maintain the rights of the defence.[499] However, additional arguments are needed to support presumptions of fact and law, as in both cases before the Court the presumptions of law were not the sole evidence relating to an element of the offence. The domestic courts had also relied upon corroborative evidence.

Other domestic court rulings are also instructive when they have specifically dealt with challenges to the offence of illicit enrichment as violating the principle of presumption of innocence and reversing the burden of proof. In *Attorney-General v Hui King-hong,*[500] the offence of illicit enrichment was contested by the defendant on the ground that it violated his right to be presumed innocent and that it placed the burden of proof on him. The Court of Appeal considered that the offence of illicit enrichment was dictated by necessity and went no further than necessary. Yet the Court of Appeal established certain restrictions to uphold the core of the presumption of innocence. It is for the prosecution to prove first beyond reasonable doubt the status of the accused as a public servant, her or his standard of living and total official emoluments during the charge period, and that her or his standard of living could not reasonably have been afforded out of her or his official emoluments during that period.[501] Only then is the defendant required to explain her or himself.[502]

In Argentina, in the case *Alsogaray, María Julia s/ recurso de casación e inconstitucionalidad*, the Supreme Court analysed the issue and determined that the offence of illicit enrichment does not violate the principle of presumption of innocence. The Court found that there is no presumption in the offence, since it is incumbent upon the prosecution to prove that the assets, property or life style of the public official cannot originate in her or his official emoluments or any other lawful income.[503]

---

499 *Salabiaku v. France*, Eur. Ct. H.R. (ser. A) 141-A (1988), para. 28; *Pham Hoang v France*, Eur. Ct. H.R. (ser. A) 243 (1992). Salabiaku concerned a national of Zaire (now the D.R.C) residing in France who was tried and convicted by French courts for violating Article 414 of the French Customs Code, which provides that "any person in possession of goods which he or she has brought into France without declaring them to customs is presumed to be legally liable unless he or she can prove a specific event of force majeure exculpating him." Salabiaku argued before the ECHR that by placing upon him an almost irrefutable presumption of guilt, the French courts had violated both his right to a fair trial and his right to be presumed innocent until proved guilty under the European Convention on Human Rights. The ECHR upheld the judgment of the French courts.

500 *Attorney General v. Hui King-hong* [1995] 1 H.K.C.L.R., 227.

501 Ibid. See also, *Attorney General v. Lee Kwong-Kut* [1993] A.C. 951.

502 See also, *Cheung Chee-kwong v. The Queen* [1971] 1 W.L.R. 1454.

503 A similar conclusion was reached by the Mexican Supreme Court in Case XXXIV/2002. Enriquecimiento Ilícito: La prueba circunstancial de ilicitud del incremento patrimonial que

Nevertheless, the world is divided on this issue and many countries strongly disapprove of the corrupt act of illicit enrichment. They include the United States, where presumptions of law and even evidentiary presumptions, such as in the offence of illicit enrichment, would be unconstitutional. This can be inferred from the case *County Court of Ulster County, New York v Allen*, which challenged the constitutionality of presumptions of law.[504] The Supreme Court accepted presumptions of law, but under strict limits requiring a close factual connection between the presumed and proven facts.[505] In other words, the presumed fact must follow from the proven fact beyond reasonable doubt and it therefore appears that the offence of illicit enrichment would not pass this test.[506] Similarly, certain countries, such as the United Kingdom, Canada and South Africa, have also accepted presumptions of law subject to restrictions, but still do not accept the act of illicit enrichment.[507]

Other jurisdictions have also rejected the offence of illicit enrichment. In Uruguay, during the parliamentary debate on Act No. 17.060 of 23 December 1998 on corruption, there were heated discussions as to whether to include the offence of illicit enrichment. The main argument against was that the offence

---

reconoce el artículo 224 del Código Penal Federal no es atentatoria del principio de presunción de inocencia, Pleno de la Suprema Corte de Justicia [S.C.J.N.] [Supreme Court], Semanario Judicial de la Federación y su Gaceta, Novena Época, Tomo XVI, Agosto 2002, Tesis P. XXXVII/2002. For a detailed criticism of this judgment, see Raúl F Cárdenas Rioseco, *El Delito De Enriquecimiento Ilícito Ante La Suprema Corte De Justicia De La Nación: Una Postura Inquietante* (México, D.F: Editorial Porrúa, 2003).

504 *County Court of Ulster County, New York v Allen*, 442 U.S. 140 (1979).

505 Ibid. 140, 172 (1979).

506 It is interesting to note that the US position against the offence of illicit enrichment is somewhat illogical, given that other provisions in United States law have recourse to similar presumptions and proscribe the failure to make proper financial disclosures and tax evasion. These are the so-called "net-worth", "bank deposits", and "cash expenditures" methods of proving tax evasion. The income of a defendant is calculated through an indirect method of proof. The amount of income a defendant allegedly received is shown circumstantially by adding the amounts of money deposited by the defendant over a period of time (the bank deposits method), calculating the increase in a defendant's visible wealth, such as new homes, automobiles, etc. (net-worth method), or documenting cash expenditures by a defendant (cash expenditure method). Pamela H. Bucy, "Criminal Tax Fraud: The Downfall of Murderers, Madams and Thieves," *Arizona State Law Journal* 29 (1997): 664–665; Henning, "Public Corruption: A Comparative Analysis of International Corruption Conventions and United States Law," 814–815. US law accepts the presumption that when these indirect methods of proof reveal an amount of income in excess of the defendant's income reported to the IRS, that he has not reported all of his income. The burden then rests with the defendant to rebut this presumption. Moreover, in indirect method cases, the government is not required to disprove every possible source of non-taxable income, or document the defendant's finances "to a mathematical certainty." Bucy, "Criminal Tax Fraud: The Downfall of Murderers, Madams and Thieves," 665; Henning, "Public Corruption: A Comparative Analysis of International Corruption Conventions and United States Law," 815.

507 See, Wilsher, "Inexplicable Wealth and Illicit Enrichment of Public Officials: A Model Draft That Respects Human Rights in Corruption Cases."

violated the principle of the presumption of innocence and shifted the burden of proof. The proposal to include illicit enrichment in the Act was rejected by one vote.

2. FLEXIBLE PRESUMPTION OF INNOCENCE AND EASING THE BURDEN OF PROOF

Presumptions or a flexible principle of presumption of innocence are not reserved solely for the crime of illicit enrichment. Similar legal techniques are used to demonstrate the criminal origin of the proceeds from drug trafficking and money laundering.[508] For example, in the case of money laundering, some civil law countries have resorted to indirect methods of proof by requiring the prosecution not to prove that the assets in question stem from a specific criminal offence or a specific type of crime, but rather that the money does not stem from legal income: salaries, inheritance, a loan, a gift, etc.[509] The criminalization of other types of conduct have followed a similar approach. For instance, the French Criminal Code also establishes certain offences which rest on a "flexible burden of proof", such as being unable to account for an income compatible with his lifestyle while living with a person habitually engaged in prostitution or while entertaining habitual relationships with one or more persons engaging in prostitution, which has been assimilated to the offence of procuring.[510] A similar approach has been applied in cases of the confiscation of proceeds of crime. A number of jurisdictions have accepted that, once the prosecution has established a *prima facie* case of the illicit origin of the proceeds, the burden shifts to the defence to prove the contrary.[511] A flexible interpretation of the principle of innocence and the burden of proof has therefore been applied in many cases, even in jurisdictions where the presumption of innocence of an accused person is held to be sacrosanct.[512]

The terms used in this discussion could also stir controversy. The expression "reversing the burden of proof" is inaccurate. At no moment is there truly a

---

508 For example, Article 5(7) of the United Nations Convention against the Illicit Traffic of Narcotic Drugs and Psychotropic Substances provides: "Each Party may consider ensuring that the onus of proof be reversed regarding the lawful origin of alleged proceeds or other property liable to confiscation, to the extent that such action is consistent with the principles of its domestic law and with the nature of the judicial and other proceedings."

509 Jorge, *The Romanian Legal Framework on Illicit Enrichment*, 16.

510 France Criminal Code, Art. 225-6, para. 3.

511 For example in Uganda. See, Prevention of Corruption Act, section 10. For a detailed account on confiscation and presumption of innocence see, Jorge, *The Romanian Legal Framework on Illicit Enrichment*, 17–21.

512 Kofele-Kale provides several cases under three different categories. See Kofele-Kale, "Presumed Guilty: Balancing Competing Rights and Interests in Combating Economic Crimes," 925–927.

shifting, but rather an easing of the burden of proof. It has been indicated in this respect that: "[t]o 'ease' the burden of proof should be viewed as drawing the right balance between the rights of the accused person and the interests of the community in situations where, without eroding the rights, common sense dictated that an explanation be sought from an official in possession of disproportionate wealth."[513]

Hence, when a person is accused of illicit enrichment, there is no presumption of guilt and the burden of proof rests with the prosecution, as it has to be demonstrated that the enrichment is beyond the official's lawful income. And this is far from being a simple task.[514] Only then is the defendant asked to provide a reasonable or credible explanation for the enrichment. Thus, this may be viewed as a rebuttal presumption, but never as a shifting of the burden of proof.[515]

3. THE GUARANTEE AGAINST SELF-INCRIMINATION

In addition to tensions with the principle of the presumption of innocence and the burden of proof, it is also argued that the offence of illicit enrichment infringes upon the guarantee against self-incrimination. This guarantee protects the accused from being compelled to testify against her or himself or to confess guilt.[516] This privilege is said to contain the right to remain silent, but illicit enrichment requires the defendant to give evidence, either oral or documentary, to exculpate her or himself.

---

513 Nihal Jayawickrama, Jeremy Pope, and Oliver Stolpe, "Legal Provisions to Facilitate the Gathering of Evidence in Corruption Cases: Easing the Burden of Proof," *Forum on Crime and Society (UNODC)* 2, no. 1 (2002): 30.

514 Kofele-Kale has listed what would be required of the prosecution at the very minimum:
- "Gather evidence, records or documents;
- Locate and identify witnesses and if the funds are scattered in various countries, prosecutorial staff will be required to move from one jurisdiction to the next to obtain the testimony of such key witnesses as bank officers and investigators will entail considerable expenses for the victim state;
- Take the testimonies or statements from persons with knowledge of the crime;
- Facilitate the personal appearance of witnesses;
- Effect searches and seizures;
- Examine objects and sites;
- Provide original or certified copies of relevant documents, records and items of evidence; Identify or trace property derived from the funds of illicit origin..." Kofele-Kale, "Presumed Guilty: Balancing Competing Rights and Interests in Combating Economic Crimes," 936.

515 UNODC, *Legislative Guide for the Implementation of the United Nations Convention against Corruption*, para. 297.

516 International Covenant on Civil and Political rights, Art. 14(3)(g); Inter-American Convention on Human Rights, Art. 8(2)(g) and (3).

However, this guarantee is not absolute, in the sense that inferences can be drawn from the silence of the defendant. The leading case of the ECHR on the matter is *Murray v UK*,[517] in which the Court found that the decision of an accused to remain silent throughout criminal proceedings may have implications when the trial court seeks to evaluate the evidence against him.[518] The ECHR then established the conditions under which drawing inferences from the silence of an accused is valid, namely that inferences should only be drawn after the prosecution has made out a prima facie case and that such inferences should follow common sense.[519]

Under these circumstances, adverse inferences may be drawn from a failure to declare income. If the evidence of the prosecution is sufficiently strong to call for an explanation which the defendant ought to be in a position to provide, then failure to do so "may as a matter of common sense allow the drawing of an inference that there is no explanation and the accused is guilty."[520] Moreover, the ECHR found that the drawing of reasonable inferences from the behaviour of the accused does not have the effect of shifting the burden of proof to the defence such as to infringe the principle of the presumption of innocence.

4. PUBLIC POLICY CONSIDERATIONS

This section has strived to show the legal bases of the offence of illicit enrichment, as it cannot be claimed that this crime violates the presumption of innocence and the ensuing guarantees of a fair trial. As indicated, illicit enrichment does however alter the traditional understanding of the presumption of innocence. The reasons for the alteration of this principle, the burden of proof and the guarantee against self-incrimination rest on several grounds. First, as indicated above, an evidentiary burden on the accused makes sense in relation to an element that would otherwise be difficult for the prosecution to prove given the defendant's superior access to information. Yet, although this is often argued in the present case, it is true for almost all crimes. In itself it does not therefore justify the alteration of such basic principles. The main reasoning lies elsewhere,[521] namely in public policy considerations. With the emergence or

517 *Murray v. U.K.*, 22 Eur. Ct. H.R. Rep. 29 (1996).

518 Ibid., para. 47.

519 Ibid., para. 51.

520 Ibid., para. 51.

521 A flexible approach to these principles and guarantees is also considered to be an effective way of balancing the equality-of-arms between the parties, since in cases of illicit enrichment the accused is likely to enjoy considerable advantages in terms of access to information, which creates an imbalance to the detriment of the prosecution in breach of the equality-of-arms principle. Kofele-Kale, "Presumed Guilty: Balancing Competing Rights and Interests in Combating Economic Crimes," 936–940.

escalation of organized crime, drug trafficking, terrorism and corruption, in many legal systems the operation of statutory presumptions of law or fact have been considered necessary for the effective administration of criminal justice. There is an increasing need for an effective and efficient legal framework for the investigation and prosecution of corruption and the offence of illicit enrichment has proven to be an effective and efficient component of such a legal framework.

V. TRADING IN INFLUENCE

The corrupt act of trading in influence may be defined as the intentional promise, offering or giving to a public official or any other person, or the intentional solicitation or acceptance by a public official or any other person, directly or indirectly, of an undue advantage in order for the public official or the person to abuse her or his real or supposed influence with a view to obtaining from an administration or public authority an undue advantage for the original instigator of the act or for any other person.[522] Trading in influence is also commonly divided into its active form (giving an advantage in exchange for influence) and its passive form (requesting or accepting an advantage in exchange for influence).

In other words, trading in influence refers to a corrupt trilateral relationship in which a person who has real or apparent influence on the decision-making of a public official exchanges this influence for a bribe. Even though the offences of trading in influence and bribery are very similar, in the case of trading in influence the recipient of the bribe is not the decision-maker or official, but an "influence peddler." The decision-maker or official may not even be aware of the existence of a bribe. The offence is therefore targeted, not at the decision-maker, but at "the close circle of the official or the political party to which he belongs and...the corrupt behaviour of those persons who are in the neighbourhood of power and try to obtain advantages from their situation..."[523] As a result, the offence of trading in influence is said to address so-called "background corruption."

---

522 See, UNCAC, Art. 18; CoE Criminal Law Convention, Art. 23. The Inter-American Convention against Corruption provides a rather different definition than the UNCAC. In Art. 11(1)(c) it refers to trading in influence solely to obtain a decision from a public authority, while the other Conventions refer to trading in influence to obtain a decision or action from a public authority. The OECD Convention does not cover the offence of trading in influence in such broad terms, but it does however cover the case in which a bribe is given to a government official for the official to use her or his office to influence the decision of another official. OECD, *Commentaries on the Convention on Combating Bribery of Foreign Public Officials in International Business Transactions*, para. 19.

523 CoE Criminal Law Convention Explanatory Report, para. 64–66.

Since the elements of the offence of trading in influence are very similar to those of bribery, the comments made above concerning bribery apply *mutatis mutandis* to trading in influence. The mental or subjective elements of this offence are therefore that the conduct must be intentional, and that it covers not only the giving or acceptance, but also the promise, offer, or solicitation of a bribe by an influence peddler directly or through an intermediary. The undue advantage or bribe may be tangible or intangible, and for the influence peddler her or himself or for another person or entity. In addition, the advantage has to be linked to her or his influence over an administration or public authority of the State, and it is irrelevant whether or not the influence is ultimately exerted and whether or not it leads to the intended result.[524]

As explained above, trading in influence is intended to encompass corrupt acts that are not covered by the offence of bribery. It is therefore important for States to criminalize this practice. However, for various reasons, the criminalization of trading in influence is still controversial in many countries. It should first be noted that its criminalization is not mandatory under the UNCAC and a number of States have opted not to criminalize it.[525] And even when it is criminalized, this has been done in a partial manner. Some countries have decided to apply the offence only to domestic public officials.[526] Hence, trading in influence is lawful when carried out to influence a decision by a foreign public entity. In the United Kingdom, trading in influence is not an offence, unless an agency relationship exists between the person who is offered the undue advantage and the person making the appointment, in which case it may constitute an offence under the Corruption Act 1906. These approaches do not seem to comply with the international legal framework.

In addition, it is important to differentiate between trading in influence and acknowledged forms of lobbying that are legal. Although there is no simple accepted definition of lobbying, the OECD has described it as "the existence of powerful interests – corporate, private or other jurisdictions such as sub-national governments – that make efforts to influence government decisions, in particular policy making, legislation or the award of contracts."[527] However, it is very

524 See, CoE Criminal Law Convention, Art. 12; AU Convention against Corruption, Art. 4(1)(f); ECOWAS Protocol against Corruption, Art. 6(1)(c&d); SADC Protocol against Corruption; Art. 3(f).

525 Under the CoE Criminal Law Convention, the criminalization of trading in influence is mandatory, but several States have made reservations to the Convention stating that they will not criminalize it: Armenia, Azerbaijan, Belgium, Denmark, Monaco, Netherlands and Sweden.

526 For example in France. See, GRECO, *Third Evaluation Round: Report on France*, para. 89.

527 OECD, *Lobbyists, Governments and Public Trust: Building a Legislative Framework for Enhancing Transparency and Accountability in Lobbying*, August 2008, 15.

difficult to generalize, as there are important differences in lobbying practices and regulations between countries.[528]

It is generally recognized that lobbying is an integral part of the political process, and it has certainly resulted in many grassroots issues being placed on the national agenda. Most States recognize that lobbying, as long as it is open and transparent, is a legitimate activity that lies at the very heart of the political process. However, in many countries, lobbying practices have become distorted into corrupt relationships between the lobbyists and those being lobbied. The growing economic power of lobbying groups has led governments to be held virtually hostage by entrenched lobbying organizations to the detriment of policy-making and the greater common good. An examination of lobbying practices is outside the scope of this study. Here it is sufficient to highlight the main differences between trading in influence and lobbying.

The principal difference lies in the fact that lobbying does not involve the promise, offering, giving, solicitation, or acceptance of an *undue advantage*. Thus, lawful lobbying consists of a person or group of persons who exercise their influence with a view to obtaining from an administration or public authority an advantage for the original instigator of the act or for any other person. The comments made above on undue advantage (bribes)[529] are therefore applicable and helpful in distinguishing between a legitimate lobbying practice and trading in influence. Another major difference between corrupt practices and lobbying lies in the fact that corrupt acts tend to benefit directly a small number of users, and usually a single user, while lobbying activities are usually carried out in order to benefit a group of users who share a specific interest.

Some countries have argued that the offence of trading in influence is unnecessary because, if lawful lobbying practices turn into corrupt acts through the provision of specific advantages to public officials in decision-making positions, the offence of bribery offers adequate protection. Yet, as explained above, the offence of bribery does not encompass the corrupt practices covered by the offence of trading in influence. It is therefore necessary to criminalize trading in influence.

---

528 For the different lobbying practices in developed and developing countries, see Raj Chari, Gary Murphy, and John Hogan, "Regulating Lobbyists: A Comparative Analysis of the United States, Canada, Germany and the European Union," *The Political Quarterly* 78 (September 2007): 422–438; Clive S. Thomas and Ronald J. Hrebenar, "Understanding interest groups, lobbying and lobbyists in developing democracies," *Journal of Public Affairs* 8, no. 1–2 (2008): 1–14; *Lobbying, Government Relations and Campaign Finance Worldwide: Navigating the Laws, Regulations and Practices of National Regimes* (Dobbs Ferry: Oceana Publications, 2005).

529 See section II.5 above.

VI. ABUSE OF FUNCTIONS

The corrupt act of abuse of functions or position may be defined as the intentional performance of or failure to perform an act, in violation of laws, by a public official in the discharge of her or his functions, for the purpose of obtaining an undue advantage for her or himself or for another person or entity.[530] This offence is similar to passive bribery (soliciting or accepting a bribe), but while bribery covers the mere fact of accepting or soliciting a bribe, the abuse of functions covers the action or omission of the public official.

Abuse of functions consists of three main elements: (i) the act or omission by the public official must form part of her or his official duties, and must therefore consist of an official act, meaning that private acts are not concerned; (ii) the objective of such act or omission must be to obtain an undue advantage for her or himself or for another person or entity; and (iii) such an act or omission must be intentional and unlawful. There accordingly need to be laws that proscribe the act or omission of the public official in question.

It should be recalled that the first two elements are also present in the offence of bribery. The comment made above in section II on bribery therefore apply here *mutatis mutandis*. The third element, namely that the act or omission by the public official must be unlawful, excludes criminalization of discretionary action of the public official. Corruption in the exercise of the discretion of a public official is addressed by other offences, most notably bribery. However, abuse of functions requires the official to act in a manner that is contrary to the law. In other words, the public official must act in breach of her or his duties. Cases that are prosecuted for abuse of functions can therefore also be prosecuted for bribery, since all the elements of abuse of functions are present in the offence of bribery. However, bribery cases in which the public official has not acted in breach of her or his duties cannot be prosecuted for abuse of functions.

It is important to emphasize that an offence of abuse of functions, as defined in the international legal framework, could never be established *verbatim* in domestic jurisdictions, as it would violate the principle of legality for lack of detail concerning the conduct that is prohibited.[531] The confusion over which types of conduct are prohibited by the offence of abuse of function is demonstrated by the responses of American States to the MESICIC.[532] The most

530 See, UNCAC, Art. 19; AU Convention against Corruption, Art. 4(1)(c); Inter-American Convention against Corruption, Arts. 6(1)(c) and 11(1)(a-b); SADC Protocol against Corruption, Art. 3(c).

531 Although Jamaican law does contain a similarly broad provision. See Corruption Prevention Act, Art. 14(1)(b), Act 18 of 2000.

532 See also, Henning, "Public Corruption: A Comparative Analysis of International Corruption Conventions and United States Law," 810–811, describing the confusion in the United States.

varied types of conduct are said to be covered by Article VI.1(c) of the Inter-American Convention against Corruption, which criminalizes abuse of function. States have referred in this context to embezzlement (actually covered by another provision of the Inter-American Convention, Article XI.d),[533] entering false data in information systems,[534] fraud or breach of trust,[535] or transactions incompatible with the performance of public functions.[536]

Abuse of functions may encompass various other types of conduct, such as improper disclosure by a public official of classified or privileged information and the improper use of public property.[537] The legislative guide for the implementation of the UNCAC provides as examples of the offence of abuse of functions, the improper demand or exemption in relation to taxes (French Criminal Code, Article 432–10), the taking of measures designed to obstruct the implementation of a law (French Criminal Code, Article 432–1), and corrupt use of official powers (Zambia Anti-Corruption Commission Act, §30).[538]

It may therefore be concluded that, in view of its broad scope, abuse of functions is understood as a quasi-residual corrupt act. Certain corrupt practices by public officials that do not fall under any of the other corrupt offences may be prosecuted on the ground of abuse of functions.

---

533 For example, MESICIC Committee of Experts, *Final Report on Implementation in the Republic of Colombia of the Convention Provisions Selected for Review in the Second Round, and on Follow-Up to the Recommendations Formulated to that Country in the First Round*, SG/MESICIC/doc.202/07 rev. 4, 7 December 2007, 35; MESICIC Committee of Experts, *Final Report on Implementation in the Federative Republic of Brazil of the Convention Provisions Selected for Review in the Second Round, and on Follow-Up to the Recommendations Formulated to that Country in the First Round*, SG/MESICIC/doc.225/08 rev. 4, 12 December 2008, 35; MESICIC Committee of Experts, *Final Report on Implementation in the Republic of Bolivia of the Convention Provisions Selected for Review in the Second Round, and on Follow-Up to the Recommendations Formulated to that Country in the First Round*, SG/MESICIC/doc.190/07 rev. 4, 28 June 2007, 18.

534 MESICIC Committee of Experts, *Brazil: Second Round Report*, 36.

535 MESICIC Committee of Experts, *Final Report on Implementation in Canada of the Convention Provisions Selected for Review in the Second Round, and on Follow-Up to the Recommendations Formulated to that Country in the First Round*, SG/MESICIC/doc.212/08 rev. 4, 27 June 2008, 46.

536 MESICIC Committee of Experts, *Final Report on Implementation in the Republic of Argentina of the Convention Provisions Selected for Review in the Second Round, and on Follow-Up to the Recommendations Formulated to that Country in the First Round*, SG/MESICIC/doc.181/06 rev.4, 15 December 2006, 32.

537 UN General Assembly, *Interpretative Notes for the Official Records (Travaux Préparatoires) of the Negotiation of the United Nations Convention against Corruption*, para. 31; Inter-American Convention against Corruption, Art. 11(1)(a-b). See also, 18 US Code section 205 proscribing the misuse of inside information by federal employees for personal gain.

538 UNODC, *Legislative Guide for the Implementation of the United Nations Convention against Corruption*, footnote 55.

CONCLUSION

This Chapter has completed the analysis of the international legal definition of corruption. The offences explored here constitute the normative element that determines what is considered an abuse of entrusted power for private gain at the international level. Ultimately, in international law, the term corruption means bribery, embezzlement, illicit enrichment, trading in influence, and abuse of functions. However, as indicated above, this list is not exhaustive and in practice only bribery and embezzlement are almost universally recognized as corrupt acts. The rest are widely accepted and their criminalization is requested by several international instruments, although they have not yet attained such universal acceptance.

States Parties to the various anti-corruption instruments are under an international obligation to criminalize those acts in their internal jurisdictions and have to follow the language of the instruments. The present Chapter has described the most common elements of each of the corrupt acts, with the objective of clarifying the exact content of the international obligations of States in relation to their criminalization.

Although Article 30(9) of the UNCAC provides that the description of offences is reserved for the domestic law of States Parties, in practice a State Party is requested to define the offences in its domestic law in an equivalent and not more restrictive way than described in the international instruments. This requirement arises from the provisions of the instruments themselves. For example, under the UNCAC, the provisions on criminalization begin by stating: "[e]ach State Party shall adopt [or shall consider adopting] such legislative and other measures as may be necessary to establish as a criminal offence, when committed intentionally." Immediately after this statement the UNCAC describes the offence. Hence, with the exception of illicit enrichment, in respect of which it is clearly indicated that the obligation of criminalization is subject to the Constitution of the State and the fundamental principles of its legal system, the other corrupt acts have to be defined in internal law in accordance with the anti-corruption instruments. This indirectly leads to the harmonization of the definitions of corrupt acts around the world.

CHAPTER V
ANTI-CORRUPTION PREVENTIVE MEASURES

INTRODUCTION

One of the principal components of the fight against corruption, at both the national and international levels, is the prevention of corruption. The international legal framework establishes several obligations for States relating to preventive measures. Most of these obligations concern institution-building, with the aim of strengthening public and private sector institutions and training those who work in them. Unfortunately, as will be seen in this Chapter, there is no part of the international legal framework against corruption that is more vague than that relating to the international obligations concerning the prevention of corruption. This does not, however, prevent certain measures making an undoubted contribution to reducing corruption.

I. PREVENTIVE ANTI-CORRUPTION POLICIES AND PRACTICES

The international legal framework against corruption requires States to introduce or maintain a series of coordinated and effective measures and policies against corruption aimed at the participation of civil society, the furtherance of the rule of law, the proper management of public interests, transparency and accountability. In this context, the international legal framework does not introduce specific legislative requirements, but rather calls on States to develop and maintain a series of measures and policies to prevent corruption. In this connection, there are a number of general obligations. States have to develop and implement or maintain effective anti-corruption policies that encourage the participation of society, reflect the rule of law and promote the sound and transparent administration of public affairs.[539] Such national anti-corruption policies can take different forms, such as explicit and comprehensive anti-corruption strategies, transparency or public integrity policies cutting across all

[539] UNCAC, Art. 5(1).

the public institutions of a specific country or sector, or a combination of public sector reforms.[540] In practice, these different forms are often combined. The main features of an effective anti-corruption policy are considered to be ownership, stakeholder participation, knowledge-based design, a holistic approach, priority setting, sequencing, coordination and monitoring.[541] Although the international legal framework does not require any specific type of anti-corruption policy, it is important for national policies to be fact-based, or in other words based on a risk assessment of the nature and extent of corruption and the available resources to fight it.[542] In addition, States have to collaborate with each other and international organizations for the promotion and development of measures for the prevention of corruption.[543]

States also have to endeavour to establish and promote effective practices aimed at the prevention of corruption.[544] This consists of a general encouragement to develop and introduce measures that can render preventive policies more effective in the specific context of each State. As part of the effort to establish effective anti-corruption policies, States are encouraged to evaluate the relevant legal instruments and administrative measures periodically with a view to determining their adequacy to prevent and combat corruption,[545] as technological, socio-economic and other circumstances may change over time and adjustments may be necessary. In addition, States are required to initiate, develop or improve specific training programmes for their staff who are responsible for preventing and combating corruption.[546]

---

540 Karen Hussmann, *Anti-Corruption Policy Making in Practice: What Can Be Learned for the Implementation of Article 5 of UNCAC?*, U4 Report 1:2007 (Bergen: Anti-Corruption Resource Centre, 2007), 20–25.

541 For an analysis of each of these elements, see Ibid., 29–36.

542 For details on the assessment of the nature and extent of corruption, see UNODC, *The Global Programme against Corruption: UN Anti-Corruption Toolkit*, 3rd ed. (Vienna: UNODC, 2004), 71–81.

543 UNCAC, Art. 5(4). Similarly, States have to inform the United Nations Secretary-General of the name and address of the authorities that can assist other States in the prevention of corruption. UNCAC, Art. 6(3).

544 UNCAC, Art. 5(2).

545 UNCAC, Art. 5(3).

546 UNCAC, Art. 60(1). Such training programmes could deal, *inter alia*, with the following areas: (a) effective measures to prevent, detect, investigate, punish and control corruption, including the use of evidence-gathering and investigative methods; (b) building capacity in the development and planning of strategic anti-corruption policy; (c) training competent authorities in the preparation of requests for mutual legal assistance; (d) evaluation and strengthening of institutions, public service management and the management of public finances, including public procurement, and the private sector; (e) preventing and combating the transfer of proceeds of corrupt acts and recovering such proceeds; (f) detecting and freezing of the transfer of proceeds of acts of corruption; (g) surveillance of the movement of proceeds of corrupt acts and of the methods used to transfer, conceal or disguise such proceeds; (h) appropriate and efficient legal and administrative mechanisms and methods for facilitating the return of proceeds of corrupt acts; (i) methods used in protecting victims and

1. ACCESS TO INFORMATION AND PARTICIPATION

As part of their preventive anti-corruption policies and practices, States are required to enhance transparency in their public administrations, including with regard to their organization, functioning and decision-making processes.[547] Examples of how States can enhance transparency in their public administration include:

(i) the adoption of procedures or regulations allowing members of the general public to obtain information on the organization, functioning and decision-making processes of the public administration and on decisions and legal acts that concern members of the public;
(ii) the simplification of administrative procedures to facilitate public access to the competent decision-making authorities; and
(iii) the publication of information on the risks of corruption in the public administration.[548]

Essential aspects of the obligation to enhance transparency in the public administration include allowing the public to have access to information concerning the public administration; raising public awareness regarding the existence, causes and gravity of and the threat posed by corruption; and promoting the active participation of individuals and groups outside the public sector (civil society, non-governmental organizations and community-based organizations) in the prevention of and action to combat corruption.[549] Examples of measures that can strengthen such participation include:

(i) enhancing the transparency of and promoting the contribution of the public to decision-making processes;
(ii) ensuring that the public has effective access to information;
(iii) undertaking public information activities that contribute to reducing tolerance of corruption, as well as public education programmes; and
(iv) respecting, promoting and protecting the freedom to seek, receive, publish and disseminate information concerning corruption, subject to certain

witnesses who cooperate with judicial authorities; and (j) training in national and international regulations and in languages. See, UNCAC, Art. 60(1)(a-j).

547 UNCAC, Art. 10.

548 UNCAC, Art. 10(a)-(c). Similarly, the AU Convention against Corruption establishes the right of access to information. See, AU Convention against Corruption, Art. 9.

549 UNCAC, Art. 13(1); UN General Assembly, *Report of the Ad Hoc Committee for the Negotiation of a Convention against Corruption on the work of its first to seventh sessions: Addendum: Interpretative Notes for the Official Records (Travaux Préparatoires) of the Negotiation of the United Nations Convention against Corruption*, A/58/422/Add.1, 7 October 2003, para. 16.

restrictions set out by law and necessity and in compliance with human rights obligations.[550]

There is almost universal agreement that access to information is a vital element in combating corruption as it attacks the core of corrupt practices, namely their secrecy, and enables citizens to ensure that their governments and public bodies are accountable. Access to information is recognized as a right.[551] Until recently, it was regarded as an obligation for States not to obstruct the flow of information, yet today the right is interpreted as a positive obligation of States to provide information.[552] This right is given effect in different ways by different countries, and no universal definition exists of access to information. However, on the basis of existing treaties, intergovernmental and civil society standards and declarations, the following are the main characteristics of the right to enjoy access to information.[553]

Access to information is the right of everyone and citizens should not be required to provide justification as to why the information is being sought. While access may be restricted by governments in certain situations, information is in principle public: access should be the rule, and restriction the exception. In addition, every public body should make readily available information about its functions and responsibilities, without the need for a request. Governments may only withhold information from public access if disclosure would cause demonstrable harm to legitimate interests, such as national security or privacy. These exceptions need to be clearly and specifically defined by law and there

550 UNCAC, Art. 13(1)(a-d); Ibid., para. 17. See, also, Inter-American Convention against Corruption Art. 3(11), where this consists of an obligation of best endeavour; and AU Convention against Corruption Arts. 5(8) and 12.

551 See, for example, UN General Assembly Resolution 59(I), adopted on 14 December 1946, U.N. Doc. A/RES/59/1/1946; Universal Declaration of Human Rights, Art. 19; International Covenant on Civil and Political Rights; Art. 19. Originally, the right to information or the right of access to information was regarded as a component of the right to freedom of expression.

552 This is how the most recent national laws define the right in Eastern Europe and Latin America. See also, *Claude Reyes et al. v. Chile*, Inter-Am. Ct. H.R. Serie C No. 151, Judgment of 19 September 2006, especially para. 77.

553 See, for example, CoE Convention on Access to Official Documents, 18 June 2009, which has not yet entered into force; United Nations Economic Commission for Europe Aarhus Convention on Access to Information, Public Participation and Access to Justice in Environmental Matters, which entered into force on 30 October 2001; Organization of American States, Inter-American Judicial Committee, Principles on the Right of Access to Information, CJI/RES. 147 (LXXIII-O/08), 7 August 2008; Council of Europe Recommendation 2002(2) on Access to Official Documents, adopted by the Committee of Ministers of the Council of Europe on 21 February 2002; the UNESCO Maputo Declaration on Fostering Freedom of Expression, Access to Information and Empowerment of People, 3 May 2008; Justice Initiative Ten Principles on the Right to Know; Article XIX, Public's Right to Know, Principles on Freedom of Information Legislation and *Model Freedom of Information Law*, 2001; Atlanta Declaration and Plan of Action for the Advancement of the Right of Access to Information; and Budapest Declaration on Right of Access to Information.

should be a right of appeal against any refusal of access. However, information should be released when the public interest outweighs any harm that might be occasioned by its release. As a general rule there is a strong presumption that information revealing corruption should be released in view of the high public interest in such information. Procedures for making requests should be simple, speedy and free, and it should be possible to request information concerning all public bodies. An independent authority, such as an ombudsperson or commissioner, should be established to review refusals, promote awareness and advance the right of access to information.

The obligations set out in the international legal framework against corruption concerning access to information should be interpreted in accordance with the above guidelines and in the light of the work carried out by the existing international movement that advocates the right of access to information.[554] Over 65 States already have laws on access to information, and some have even established the right at the constitutional level. To varying degrees, citizens have been able to use such laws to request information, hold public officials accountable and expose corruption.[555] There are strong examples from around the world from countries as diverse as Mexico, Japan, United Kingdom, Bosnia, India and the Philippines of the manner in which access to information has been used in exposing corruption. For example, the Mexican freedom of information law, which came into force in 2003, requires certain information including detailed budgets, to be published automatically by all bodies covered by the law.[556] One of those bodies is a publicly funded university, Instituto Politécnico Nacional, the recently-appointed director of which seized the opportunity of the new law to support his efforts to combat long-standing corruption in the university. In September 2003, the director opened to the public its payroll and budget, revealing that certain professors and employees of the university had received over-inflated salaries and increased suspiciously high expenditure on goods and services, such as US$400,000 for bags.[557]

In addition, participation of civil society plays undoubtedly a control role in combating corruption. Civil society organizations can operate as partners of the

---

554 See, for example, the work of Article XIX, the Freedominfo Portal: www.freedominfo.org (last visited 20 April 2012), which provides comprehensive information about freedom of information laws and movements around the world, and Access Info www.access-info.org (last visited 20 April 2012).

555 For more information, see Transparency International, *Using the Right to Information as an Anti-Corruption Tool*, 2006.

556 Helen Darbishire, "The Rights of Access to Information in Fighting Corruption: A Human Rights Perspective" (Paper presented at the review meeting of the International Council on Human Rights Policy on its project on Corruption and Human Rights, July 28, 2007), Annex A, available at www.ichrp.org/files/papers/127/131_-_Helen_Darbishire_-_2007.pdf (last visited 20 April 2012).

557 Ibid.

public sector to enhance the reach of anti-corruption programmes and point them towards priority areas. In addition, civil society organizations can hold the public sector accountable for not giving effect to or complying with its anti-corruption obligations. Several cases of best practice can be found for collaboration between civil society organizations and the public sector in the field of combating corruption. For example, in Pakistan, civil society organizations take part in the National Anti-Corruption Strategy Project, an advisory body to the Government consisting of representatives of the public sector, civil society, business, media and academic institutions.[558] In the Republic of Korea, the government assistance for civil society anti-corruption activities includes financial support.[559]

As indicated above, in addition to ensuring the right of the public to information and participation, States need to raise public awareness of corruption. This is extremely important, particularly to change public attitudes with a view to developing a firmer stance against corruption. Corruption is partly fuelled by the indifference and resignation of the population. Raising public awareness therefore provides support to those combating corruption and increases public pressure on the Government to commit itself more fully to addressing the problem of corruption. An innovative initiative in this respect was introduced in Hong Kong. The Independent Commission against Corruption (ICAC) produced a television drama series based on real corruption cases in which the detrimental consequences of corruption were vividly portrayed. The series was one of the most popular television programmes in Hong Kong.[560] In addition, demonstrating the negative effects of corruption is also key to effectively raising awareness of the issue. There is little purpose of reminding the general public of the existence of corruption if the ways in which corruption affects them, both as a society and individually, are not demonstrated clearly and precisely.

2. ANTI-CORRUPTION PREVENTIVE BODY

Anti-corruption bodies are at the core of preventive anti-corruption policies and practices. The creation of anti-corruption bodies required by the international legal framework against corruption is part of an institutional response to corruption. States have to enhance their institutional capacity to prevent corruption by setting up an anti-corruption body or bodies with responsibility

558 ADB/OECD Anti-Corruption Initiative for Asia and the Pacific, *Anti-Corruption Policies in Asia and the Pacific: Progress in Legal and Institutional Reform in 25 Countries* (Manila: ADB/OECD Anti-Corruption Initiative for Asia and the Pacific, 2006), 58.

559 Ibid., 60.

560 Alan Lai, "Building Public Confidence in Anti-Corruption Efforts: The Approach of the Hong Kong Special Administrative Region of China," *Forum on Crime and Society (UNODC)* 2, no. 1 (2002): 144.

for preventive measures and policies.[561] Such bodies can also assume law enforcement anti-corruption functions.[562] However, there is no need to create a new body if the functions and responsibilities required of States in relation to the prevention of corruption are already assigned to other existing agencies.[563] Indeed, most States already possess bodies in different sectors that perform anti-corruption prevention or law enforcement functions, although they are sometimes ineffective. Such bodies are most widespread in Asia and Africa, for example in Hong Kong,[564] Indonesia,[565] Bangladesh,[566] Kenya,[567] and Nigeria.[568] Where such bodies already exist, States may need to redefine existing

561 UNCAC, Art. 6(1). The Inter-American Convention against Corruption, contains a similar provision, although the requirement is limited to "best endeavour." See Inter-American Convention against Corruption Art. 3(9). See, also, CoE Criminal Law Convention Art. 20; AU Convention against Corruption, Art. 5(3).

562 UN General Assembly, *Interpretative Notes for the Official Records (Travaux Préparatoires) of the Negotiation of the United Nations Convention against Corruption*, para. 11. This is the case in many countries, for example, the Independent Commission against Corruption of the Hong Kong Special Administrative Region of China. Moreover, in many jurisdictions, the office of the ombudsman assumes the functions of an anti-corruption agency, including prosecution functions. For more information on anti-corruption law enforcement bodies, see Chapter VII.

563 UNODC, *Legislative Guide for the Implementation of the United Nations Convention against Corruption* (Vienna, New York: United Nations, 2006), para. 54. For the advantages and disadvantages of creating a new body, see UNODC and UNICRI, *Technical Guide to the United Nations Convention against Corruption* (Vienna, New York: United Nations, 2009), 8–9.

564 The Hong Kong Independent Commission against Corruption (ICAC) was established in 1974 and has gained a reputation for its success in dramatically reducing the level of corruption in Hong Kong's public service. It is also known for its intrusive methods of investigation. For more information, see Hong Kong ICAC's website: www.icac.org.hk/ (last visited 20 April 2012). See also, Jeremy Lo Kwok-chung, "Combating Corruption in Hong Kong," *Resource Material Series (UNAFEI)* 77 (March 2009): 3–10.

565 The Corruption Eradication Commission (KPK: *Komisi Pemberantasan Korupsi*) in Indonesia was created in 2002 by Law No. 30 of 2002 and has been highly successful as well as controversial in prosecution of high-level officials and businessmen and its wide use of intrusive investigative techniques, such as wire-taps without court orders. See, Sofie Arjon Schütte, "The Fight against Corruption in Indonesia," *Südostasien aktuell* 26, no. 4 (2007): 57–66; Norimitsu Onishi, "Corruption Fighters Rouse Resistance in Indonesia," *The New York Times*, July 25, 2009, www.nytimes.com/2009/07/26/world/asia/26indo.html?pagewanted=all (last visited 20 April 2012). For more information, see KPK's website: www.kpk.go.id (last visited 20 April 2012).

566 The Anti-Corruption Commission in Bangladesh (ACC) was created in 2004 by the Anti-Corruption Commission Act to replace the Anti-Corruption Bureau. For more information, see Institute of Governance Studies, BRAC University, "The Anti-Corruption Commission: Policy Note" (Institutions of Accountability Series, September 2007), available at www.igs-bracu.ac.bd/UserFiles/File/archive_file/ACC_Policy%20Note_Final.pdf (last visited 20 April 2012); Mohammad Ehsan, "When Implementation Fails: The Case of Anti-Corruption Commission (ACC) and Corruption Control in Bangladesh," *Asian Affairs* 28, no. 3 (2006): 40–63. See also, the ACC's website: http://acc.org.bd/ (last visited 20 April 2012).

567 The Kenya Anti-Corruption Commission (KACC) was created by the Anti-Corruption and Economic Crimes Act No. 3 of 2003.

568 The Economic and Financial Crimes Commission (EFCC) of Nigeria was created by the EFCC Establishment Act in 2004. For more information, see EFCC's website: http://efccnigeria.org/ (last visited 20 April 2012).

institutional arrangements in accordance with their international anti-corruption obligations.

The role that anti-corruption bodies can play in preventing corruption includes implementing, or overseeing and coordinating the implementation, of anti-corruption policies, or producing and disseminating knowledge about the prevention of corruption.[569] However, it should be emphasized that the implementation of anti-corruption policies is the responsibility of several institutions, and not of a single body. It has been aptly stated that, part of the reason for the failure of many anti-corruption policies is that overall responsibility for their implementation has been assigned to a national anti-corruption commission, without taking into account the fact that these institutions often lack the authority to demand action by other public sector or government agencies.[570] Responsibility for the implementation of the individual components of the anti-corruption policy rests with the respective sector or government agency, while the overall coordination and oversight function may be concentrated in a single agency.[571] This is a factor that States need to take into account when giving effect to their international obligations.

It is for this reason that the most important function of anti-corruption bodies is to coordinate anti-corruption policies. Experience shows that the oversight and monitoring dimension of national anti-corruption strategies or policies is often weak, formalistic, or non-existent.[572] States therefore need to ensure that the body or bodies entrusted with responsibility for the prevention of corruption carry out effective oversight and coordination at the intra-institutional, cross-institutional and national levels.[573] The additional function of these bodies, namely to prepare and disseminate knowledge about the prevention of corruption, can be interpreted in the broadest manner to include all types of knowledge for a variety of different audiences.[574]

In addition to establishing an anti-corruption body or bodies, States need to ensure their independence to guarantee that they can carry out their functions unimpeded by undue influences and provide them with adequate material

569 See, UNCAC, Art. 6(1)(a-b).

570 Hussmann, *Anti-Corruption Policy Making in Practice: What Can Be Learned for the Implementation of Article 5 of UNCAC?*, 42.

571 Ibid., 47–48.

572 Karen Hussmann, Hannes Hechler, and Miguel Peñailillo, *Institutional Arrangements for Corruption Prevention: Considerations for the Implementation of the United Nations Convention against Corruption Article 6* (U4 Anti-Corruption Resource Centre Report, 2009), 16.

573 See also ibid., 16–18.

574 Ibid., 19–21.

resources and training.[575] For this purpose, it is recommended that their independence and accountability should be established in law, rather than in executive decrees, which can easily be manipulated.[576] Moreover, the necessary independence of these bodies should be understood to refer to their functional and financial independence. Functional independence ensures that the body can carry out its functions without undue interference by any third party or the executive, while financial independence means that it is impossible for the government to impede or restrict the body's activities by reducing its budget.[577] States also need to ensure that the body is known to the public[578] and provide for public access to such body to report, including anonymously, any incident that may constitute an act of corruption.[579]

II. TRANSPARENCY MEASURES IN THE PUBLIC SECTOR

As part of their international obligations for the prevention of corruption, States are required to take measures and adopt systems for the achievement of the specific goal of transparency in the public sector. These measures can be grouped with action relating to public office, public finances and public procurement.

1. MEASURES RELATING TO PUBLIC OFFICE

The notion of public office is inherently connected to the definition of a public official. As indicated in Chapter IV, the understanding of which individuals constitute public officials, and hence holds a "public office," is central to the international legal framework against corruption. A person is regarded as a public official when he/she works for any branch of the government (any person holding a legislative, executive, administrative or judicial office, whether appointed or elected, whether permanent or temporary, whether paid or unpaid, irrespective of that person's seniority); or when he/she performs a public function, including for a public agency, or public enterprise or provides a public

---

575 UNCAC, Art. 6(2); CoE Criminal Law Convention, Art. 20.

576 UNODC and UNICRI, *Technical Guide to the United Nations Convention against Corruption*, 11.

577 See, Hussmann, Hechler, and Peñailillo, *Institutional Arrangements for Corruption Prevention: Considerations for the Implementation of the United Nations Convention against Corruption Article 6*, 21–22 citing the International Organisation of Supreme Audit Institutions (INTOSAI)'s classification of institutional independence.

578 UNCAC, Art. 13(2).

579 UNCAC, Art. 13(2). States should also consider encouraging their national and habitual residents to report corrupt offences to the national investigating and prosecuting authorities. UNCAC, Art. 39(2). See also Chapter VII.

service, such as teachers and doctors; or when he/she is defined as a public official in the domestic law of the State.[580]

Unfortunately, the international legal framework does not create particularly strong obligations for States with regard to public office. These concern the recruitment of public officials, codes of conduct, candidature for and election to public office and conflict of interests.

1.1. *Recruitment of public officials*

States are called upon to promote, *inter alia*, integrity, honesty and responsibility among their public officials.[581] To this end, States should try to adopt, maintain and strengthen systems for the recruitment, hiring, retention, promotion, and retirement of civil servants and non-elected public officials:

a) based on principles of efficiency, transparency, and objective criteria, such as merit, equity, and aptitude;[582]
b) that include adequate procedures for the selection and training of individuals for public positions, that are especially vulnerable to corruption;[583]
c) that include the rotation of individuals to other positions when their position is especially vulnerable to corruption;[584]
d) that promote adequate remuneration and equitable pay scales (in relation to the economic development of the State);[585] and
e) that promote education and training programmes to enable them to meet the requirements for the correct, honourable and proper performance of public functions and to enhance their awareness of the risks of corruption inherent in their functions.[586]

1.2. *Codes of conduct*

States are also required to endeavour to apply within their own institutional and legal systems codes or standards of conduct for the correct, honourable and proper performance of public functions.[587] With regard to codes of conduct,

580 For a detailed analysis of the definition of a public official, see Chapter IV.
581 UNCAC, Art. 8(1).
582 UNCAC, Art. 7(1)(a); Inter-American Convention against Corruption, Art. 3.5; AU Convention against Corruption, Arts. 7(4) and 5(4).
583 UNCAC, Art. 7(1)(b).
584 UNCAC, Art. 7(1)(b).
585 UNCAC, Art. 7(1)(c).
586 UNCAC, Art. 7(1)(d); Inter-American Convention against Corruption, Art. 3(3) and 3(12).
587 UNCAC, Art. 8(2); Inter-American Convention against Corruption, Art. 3(1)(h). This commitment is more stringent for States Parties of the AU Convention against Corruption. Pursuant to Article 7(2) of the AU Convention States Parties are required to create a body

although States are merely recommended to consider their implementation, experience shows that it is important for principles and ethical rules to be known and accepted by officials, and that codes of conduct serve that purpose. Some good practices include the development of codes of conduct through a process of consultation, the attachment of ethical rules to employment contracts and the regular implementation of awareness-raising initiatives.[588] Moreover, codes of conduct facilitate the resolution of dilemmas, offer responses to frequent questions that may arise in the course of work and clarify the standards and rules to be observed, thereby facilitating the identification and reporting of violations. Codes of conduct also serve to support the preparation and training of public officials.[589] When formulating all aspects of codes of conduct, States should take into account the existent initiatives,[590] such as the UN International Code of Conduct for Public Officials,[591] the Council of Europe Model Code of Conduct for Public Officials[592] and the OECD's Recommendation on Improving Ethical Conduct in the Public Service including the Principles for Managing Ethics in the Public Service.[593]

1.3. *Candidature for and election to public office*

In addition to the provisions on the recruitment of public officials and codes of conduct, the international legal framework also calls upon States to consider adopting legislative and administrative measures establishing criteria on candidature for and election to public office,[594] and to consider adopting legislative and administrative measures to enhance transparency in the funding of political parties and candidatures for elected public office.[595] The latter raises important concerns. The two principal risks in relation to political financing are that resources can distort electoral processes and that thus may improperly

---

mandated to establish a code of conduct, monitor its implementation and sensitize and train public officials on matters of ethics. For details of the implementation of codes of conduct, see UNODC and UNICRI, *Technical Guide to the United Nations Convention against Corruption*, 22–24.

588 UNODC, *Legislative Guide for the Implementation of the United Nations Convention against Corruption*, para. 91.

589 Ibid., para. 92.

590 UNCAC, Art. 8(3).

591 UN General Assembly resolution 51/59 of 12 December 1996, Annex.

592 CoE Recommendation No. R (2000) 10 on Codes of Conduct for Public Officials, Annex.

593 OECD Council Recommendation on Improving Ethical Conduct in the Public Service including the Principles for Managing Ethics in the Public Service, 1998-C(98)70/FINAL, 23 April 1998.

594 UNCAC, Art. 7(2).

595 UNCAC, Art. 7(3). Under the AU Convention against Corruption, this obligation is more stringent than a best endeavour. States Parties are obliged to adopt measures to prohibit the use of funds acquired through illegal and corrupt practices for the financing of political parties and to incorporate the principle of transparency into funding of political parties. AU Convention against Corruption, Art. 10.

influence the decisions taken by elected representatives.[596] It should be stated at the outset that there are no international standards respecting political financing. During the negotiation of the OECD Convention, the United States wanted to include in the Convention a provision requiring States to regulate political financing. However, agreement was not reached and the issue was left out of the Convention. A similar situation occurred during the negotiation of the UNCAC, and the compromise reached only requires States to *consider* taking measures to enhance transparency in political financing. No details are provided on what exactly these measures should include. On the basis of the research carried out by Transparency International and other organizations, standards for transparency in political finance can be organized on three levels: (i) accountability within parties: the requirement to use proper internal bookkeeping and accounting systems and keep party members properly informed; (ii) accountability to the State: the requirement for parties and candidates, donors and service providers to report on political finance transactions to State agencies (usually including limitations on the duration and cost of election campaigns, and on large private donations); and (iii) accountability to the public: the requirement to disclose all information on campaign finance (assets, income, and expenditure).[597] These indicators should therefore be taken into account by States if they attempt to enhance transparency in the funding of political parties and of candidates for elected public office.

1.4. Conflict of interests

As part of the obligations relating to public office, States are also encouraged to adopt, maintain and strengthen systems that promote transparency and prevent conflicts of interests in the public sector.[598] The OECD has defined conflict of interest as a conflict between the public duty and private interests of a public official, in which the public official has private-capacity interests which could improperly influence the performance of their official duties and responsibilities.[599] In this context, States are called upon to endeavour to establish measures and systems requiring public officials to declare to

596 Transparency International, *Accountability and Transparency in Political Finance: Why, How, and What For?*, TI Working Paper No. 01/2008, 2.

597 See, Transparency International, *Accountability and Transparency in Political Finance: Why, How, and What For?*; Transparency International, *Political Finance Regulations: Bridging the Enforcement Gap*, TI Policy Position No. 02/2009; Transparency International, *Standards on Political Funding and Favours*, TI Policy Position No. 01/2005; Transparency International and The Carter Center, *The Crinis Project: Money in Politics, Everyone's Concern*, 2007.

598 UNCAC, Art. 7(4); Inter-American Convention against Corruption Art. 3(1). On conflicts of interest, see Quentin Reed, *Sitting on the Fence: Conflicts of Interest and How to Regulate Them*, U4 Issue 2008:6 (Bergen: Anti-Corruption Resource Centre, 2008).

599 OECD, Recommendation of the Council on OECD Guidelines for Managing Conflict of Interest in the Public Service, C(2003)107, 28 May 2003.

appropriate authorities, *inter alia*, their outside activities, employment, investments, assets and substantial gifts or benefits from which a conflict of interest may result.[600] The obligation of disclosure can be established either by legislative means or as a contractual condition of employment. Ideally, not all public officials should be subject to disclosure procedures, but only officials at or above a specific level of seniority, or those in positions most likely to be exposed to corruption.[601] Such declarations should be made to specially established bodies, such as inspectors or auditors general, which are trusted with the authority to take any necessary action, and full public disclosure need only be made in cases where improper conduct is discovered.[602] In accordance with the UNCAC Technical Guide, if States establish a system for the disclosure and registration of assets and interests, they should ensure that:

- Disclosure covers all substantial types of income and assets of officials (all officials or those at a certain level of appointment or sector and/or their relatives);
- Disclosure forms allow for year-on-year comparisons of the financial situation of officials;
- Disclosure procedures should preclude the possibility of concealing officials' assets by other means or, to the extent possible, held by persons against whom a State Party may have no access (for example, overseas or held by a non-resident);
- A reliable system for income and asset control exists for all physical and legal persons - such as within the tax administration -in relation to persons or legal entities associated with public officials;

---

600 UNCAC, Art. 8(5). The Inter-American Convention against Corruption is broader in scope as it requires States to consider creating, maintaining, and strengthening systems for registering the income, assets and liabilities of persons who perform public functions in certain posts as specified by law and for making such registration public. See, Inter-American Convention against Corruption Art. 3(4). In Africa, this obligation is stronger, as States are under the obligation to require, and not just to consider requiring, all or designated public officials to declare their assets before, during and after their term in office. See, AU Convention against Corruption Art. 7(1).

601 UNODC, *The Global Programme against Corruption: UN Anti-Corruption Toolkit*, 251. However, certain countries, such as Bangladesh, India, Kazakhstan, Malaysia, and Pakistan, require all public officials to regularly disclose information about their assets. See, ADB/OECD Anti-Corruption Initiative for Asia and the Pacific, *Anti-Corruption Policies in Asia and the Pacific: Progress in Legal and Institutional Reform in 25 Countries*, 10; Richard Messick, *Income and Assets Declarations: Issues to Consider in Developing a Disclosure Regime*, U4 Issue 2009:6 (Bergen: Anti-Corruption Resource Centre, 2009), 10–12.

602 UNODC, *The Global Programme against Corruption: UN Anti-Corruption Toolkit*, 251. States should consider taking disciplinary or other measures against public officials who violate the codes or standards established in relation to conflicts of interest and the declaration of assets. UNCAC, Art. 8(6); Inter-American Convention against Corruption, Art. 3(2). The AU Convention against Corruption establishes the same obligation, but in stronger terms. See, AU Convention against Corruption, Art. 7(3).

- Officials have a strong duty to substantiate/prove the sources of their income;
- To the extent possible, officials are precluded from declaring non-existent assets, which can later be used as justification for otherwise unexplained wealth;
- Oversight agencies have sufficient human resources, expertise, technical capacity and legal authority for meaningful control; and
- Appropriate deterrent penalties exist for violations of these requirements.[603]

Systems of disclosure exist in different forms in a number of countries.[604] However, in practice, such systems have not played a significant role in preventing public officials from engaging in corrupt practices. Such failure is due to the fact that most countries have not established mechanisms to check the accuracy of the information provided by public officials. Moreover, a corrupt official can easily conceal assets by transferring them to relatives or friends, while actually retaining control of them, and disclosure systems usually only cover the public official and not her or his relatives.[605] Unfortunately, it is uncommon to learn that a senior public official has been taken to court for having falsified a declaration of assets. Nevertheless, disclosure remains an important obligation, as it acts as both a potential constraint on public officials engaging in corruption, creates considerable hurdles for them to enjoy illicitly acquired assets and may provide the starting point for holding a corrupt public official accountable.

2. MEASURES RELATING TO PUBLIC FINANCES

It is widely recognized that the nature and quality of the management of public finances to a large extent determines the ease with which corruption can

---

603 UNODC and UNICRI, *Technical Guide to the United Nations Convention against Corruption*, 25–26. For additional guidance on the development of a disclosure system, see Ruxandra Burdescu et al., *Stolen Asset Recovery: Income and Asset Declarations: Tools and Trade-Offs* (Washington, D.C.: World Bank, 2009); Messick, *Income and Assets Declarations: Issues to Consider in Developing a Disclosure Regime.* For guidance on managing conflict of interests, see OECD, *Toolkit for Managing Conflict of Interest in the Public Service*, available at www.oecd.org/dataoecd/5/48/49107986.pdf?contentId=49107987 (last visited 15 April 2012); OECD, *Managing Conflict of Interest in the Public Service: OECD Guidelines and Country Experiences*, available at http://oecd.org/dataoecd/54/31/48994419.pdf (last visited 15 April 2012).

604 For reviews of international experiences of asset disclosure, see Burdescu et al., *Stolen Asset Recovery: Income and Asset Declarations: Tools and Trade-Offs*; Aled Williams, "International Experience of Asset Declarations" (U4 Anti-Corruption Resource Centre Expert Answer, October 12, 2006); Marie Chene, "African Experience of Asset Declarations" (U4 Anti-Corruption Resource Centre Expert Answer, April 21, 2008).

605 However, some countries also require the declaration for the spouse and children. For example, Turkey (Law 3628 of 4 May 1990).

occur.[606] For that reason, under the international legal framework against corruption, States have mandatory obligations concerning the proper and transparent management of public finances. States are required to promote transparency and accountability in the management of public finances through measures that have to include procedures for the adoption of the national budget, timely reporting on revenue and expenditure, a system of accounting and auditing standards and related oversight, and an effective and efficient system of risk management and internal control.[607] States also have to adopt civil and administrative measures to preserve the integrity of accounting books, records, financial statements or other documents related to public expenditure and revenue and to prevent the falsification of such documents.[608]

In this respect, emphasis should be placed on the importance of the obligation to establish procedures for the adoption of the national budget which promote transparency and accountability in the management of public finances. The significance of this requirement is two-fold. On the one hand, there is mounting evidence that increased budget transparency is associated with better governance standards, less corruption and ultimately, improved economic and social outcomes.[609] On the other hand, this obligation merits special attention because the majority of States are currently not in compliance with it. A recent survey has shown that in most countries the public does not have access to the comprehensive and timely information needed to participate meaningfully in the budget process and to hold their government accountable.[610] States therefore need to radically improve the transparency of their budgetary process to meet their international anti-corruption obligations by making information available to the public in the four main phases of the budget process (formulation, approval, execution, and evaluation and audit).[611]

---

606 William Dorotinsky and Shilpa Pradhan, "Exploring Corruption in Public Financial Management," in *The Many Faces of Corruption: Tracking Vulnerabilities at the Sector Level*, ed. J. Edgardo Campos and Sanjay Pradhan (Washington, D.C: World Bank, 2007), 267.

607 UNCAC, Art. 9(2)(a-e); AU Convention against Corruption, Art. 5(4). Similarly, the Inter-American Convention against Corruption Art. 3(6) provides that States must consider adopting measures to create, maintain, and strengthen government revenue collection and control systems that deter corruption.

608 UNCAC, Art. 9(3); OECD Convention Art. 8(2).

609 See, for example, Daniel Kaufmann and Ana Bellver, *Transparenting Transparency: Initial Empirics and Policy Applications*, Policy Research Working Paper (Washington, D.C: World Bank, 2005); Farhan Hameed, *Fiscal Transparency and Economic Outcomes*, IMF Working Paper No. 05/225 (Washington, D.C: International Monetary Fund, 2005); Roumeen Islam, *Do More Transparent Governments Govern Better?*, Policy Research Working Paper No. 3077 (Washington, D.C: The World Bank, 2003).

610 See the Open Budget Index 2010, in which 79% of countries surveyed scored poorly in the assessment of the quantity and type of information available to the public in their budget documents. See, www.openbudgetindex.org (last visited 20 April 2012).

611 International Budget Partnership, *Open Budgets, Transform Lives: The Open Budget Survey 2010*, 2011. For additional ways of reducing corruption in the budget process, see Jan Isaksen,

In the formulation stage, governments should publish a pre-budget statement and establish a consultative process before the executive submits the budget proposal to the legislature.[612] The executive's budget proposal should also be made public, as well as the enacted budget.[613] Since the budget is usually a lengthy technical document, States should also publish a so-called "citizen's budget", a simplified summary of the budget in language that is accessible to the public.[614] During the execution phase, States should release implementation reports and an independent body should issue an annual audit report during the evaluation and audit stage.[615] The information made publicly available at each stage of the budget process determines the ability of civil society and other interested parties to influence and monitor the effectiveness of government policies as well as the transparency of the management of public finances.

A budget process in line with these standards would also comply with the other anti-corruption international financial obligations outlined above, namely the requirement to adopt measures for the timely reporting on revenue and expenditure and a system of accounting and auditing standards and related oversight. The latter role normally rests with the legislature and supreme audit institutions.[616] Although supreme audit institutions can play a key role in this respect, in most countries they face significant institutional, technical and political challenges.[617] Supreme audit institutions need to overcome these challenges and report their findings annually to the legislature and the general public, preferably in accordance with the guidelines issued by the International Organisation of Supreme Auditing Institutions (INTOSAI).[618]

The Budget Process and Corruption, U4 Issue 3:2005 (Bergen: Anti-Corruption Resource Centre, 2005).

612 International Budget Partnership, *Open Budgets, Transform Lives: The Open Budget Survey 2008*, 23–24.

613 Ibid., 24–25.

614 Ibid., 25.

615 Ibid., 26–28.

616 For measures relating to expenditure, see Geir Sundet, *Following the Money: Do Public Expenditure Tracking Surveys matter?*, U4 Issue 2008:8 (Bergen: Anti-Corruption Resource Centre, 2008).

617 Albert Van Zyl, Vivek Ramkumar, and Paolo de Renzio, *Responding to Challenges of Supreme Audit Instituions: Can Legislatures and Civil Society Help?*, U4 Issue 2009:1 (Bergen: Anti-Corruption Resource Centre, 2009).

618 INTOSAI is a non-governmental organization founded in 1953 which provides an institutionalized framework for supreme audit institutions to promote the development and transfer of knowledge, improve government auditing worldwide and enhance professional capacities. It has developed guidelines on auditing precepts (Lima Declaration) and on the independence of supreme audit institutions (Mexico Declaration). For more information, see its website: www.intosai.org (last visited 20 April 2012).

There are also a number of international, regional and national organizations and initiatives that are actively engaged on issues of public finance.[619] Although they do not normally focus on the role of public finance as an anti-corruption prevention measure, their work has produced research, standards, and tools that can be very beneficial in assessing the compliance of States with their public finance anti-corruption obligations.

3. MEASURES RELATING TO PUBLIC PROCUREMENT

In addition to public finance, other measures that States should take to enhance transparency in the public sector relate to public procurement. The awarding of contracts for goods or services, technically known as procurement, is acknowledged to be a process that is highly vulnerable to corruption. In many cases, procurement procedures may appear to be fair, although in reality they are manipulated to tilt the outcome in the direction of a favoured supplier. This is usually achieved by the purchaser (public official) through improper or unnecessary prequalification requirements, tailored specifications to fit a particular supplier, breach of confidentiality of the bid, or the invention of new criteria.[620] Since public procurement may account for 15–20% of public expenditure, and even as much as 70% (for example in Uganda),[621] the need to combat corruption in public procurement clearly constitutes a priority. Corruption in procurement results in unnecessary projects, substandard work or unnecessarily expensive work. For these reasons, numerous efforts are being made to reform procurement procedures by the World Bank, OECD and other related organizations.

3.1. *Appropriate systems of procurement*

The international legal framework against corruption therefore calls for the strong regulation of public procurement. States are required to establish appropriate systems of procurement, based on transparency, competition and objective criteria for decision-making that are effective, *inter alia,* in preventing

---

619 See, for example, the Public Finance sections of the World Bank and other IFI's; the OECD Budgeting and Public Expenditures and Public Finance sections; Public Expenditure and Financial Accountability (PEFA); Support for the Improvement of Governance and Management (SIGMA); International Public Sector Accounting Standards Board; Oxford Policy Management (OPM): Public Financial Management; the International Consortium on Governmental Financial Management (ICGFM); and the Collaborative Africa Budget Reform Initiative (CABRI).

620 For details of the ways in which public procurement can be manipulated, see OECD, Integrity in Public Procurement: Good Practice from A to Z, Paris, OECD Publishing, 2007; and UNODC, *The Global Programme against Corruption: UN Anti-Corruption Toolkit*, 262–263.

621 OECD, *Why is Procurement Important?*, Factsheet, December 2006.

corruption.[622] More specifically, systems of procurement need to meet five requirements. First, the public distribution of information relating to procurement procedures and contracts, including information on invitations to tender and relevant information on the award of contracts, must allow potential tenderers sufficient time to prepare and submit their tenders.[623] Second, the conditions for participation, including selection and award criteria and tendering rules, and their publication must be determined in advance.[624] This should cover all pertinent information that suppliers need to participate in the procedure, including any supplier qualification and pre-qualification requirements.[625] A third element of the procurement system is that decisions need to be taken in accordance with objective and predetermined criteria which allow the subsequent verification of the correct application of the rules or procedures.[626] Technical specifications are critical in this respect and should be objective, based on technical and quality characteristics (without reference to trademarks or other proprietary terms) and set out in the tender documents.[627]

In addition, as a fourth requirement, there have to exist effective systems of domestic review, including appeal, to ensure legal recourse and remedies in the event that the procurement rules or procedures are not followed.[628] In this context, it should be emphasized that, as indicated in Chapter VI, States need to ensure that entities or persons who have suffered damage as a result of an act of corruption have the right to initiate legal proceedings against those responsible for the damage in order to obtain compensation.[629] Accordingly, if procurement rules or procedures are not followed due to corruption, the affected tenderers are able to sue other parties, including the State, for the damaged suffered.[630] A fifth element of systems of procurement is that measures need to be established to regulate matters respecting the personnel responsible for procurement, such as the declaration of interests, screening procedures and training requirements.[631] In addition, legislation should require the declaration and registration of all interests, assets, hospitality and gifts. The elements indicated above in relation to

---

622 UNCAC, Art. 9(1); AU Convention against Corruption Art. 7(4) and 5(4). Under the Inter-American Convention against Corruption, this is an obligation of best endeavour. Inter-American Convention against Corruption, Art. 3(5).

623 UNCAC, Art. 9(1)(a).

624 UNCAC, Art. 9(1)(b).

625 COSP, *United Nations Convention against Corruption: Implementing Procurement-Related Aspects, Submitted by the United Nations Commission on International Trade Law*, CAC/COSP/2008/CRP.2, 15 January 2008, 12.

626 UNCAC, Art. 9(1)(c).

627 COSP, *United Nations Convention against Corruption: Implementing Procurement-Related Aspects*, 13.

628 UNCAC, Art. 9(1)(d).

629 UNCAC, Art. 35, CoE Civil Law Convention.

630 For more on civil litigation, see Chapter VI.

631 UNCAC, Art. 9(1)(e).

public office are also applicable in respect of public procurement. Moreover, the effective management of procurement staff should be based on the elements of appropriate terms and conditions of service, procedural controls (such as benchmarking performance, or the rotation of staff to avoid the perceived risk of inducements and lengthy incumbency), regular appraisals and confidential reporting.[632] Those are evidently only the minimum elements required and States are free to address additional issues. Moreover, these requirements should be taken into account at all administrative levels. However, there is an exception to the transparency of the procurement system; the provisions of the international legal framework against corruption cannot be construed as preventing a State from taking any action or not disclosing any information that it considers necessary for the protection of its essential interests related to national security.[633]

The international obligations of States in relation to public procurement may require amendments or new legislation or regulations, depending on the existing legal framework. Interestingly, South Africa has adopted provisions regulating public procurement at the highest level, namely in the Constitution.[634] When establishing appropriate systems of procurement, States should not only follow the international obligations described in this section, but also the myriad international legal instruments,[635] soft-law[636] and research studies on enhancing transparency in public procurement.[637] It would be impossible to analyse all

632 COSP, *United Nations Convention against Corruption: Implementing Procurement-related Aspects*, 14.

633 UN General Assembly, *Interpretative Notes for the Official Records (Travaux Préparatoires) of the Negotiation of the United Nations Convention against Corruption*, para. 13.

634 Section 187 of the 1994 South African Constitution provides that:

"(1) The procurement of goods and services for any level of government shall be regulated by an Act of Parliament and provincial laws, which shall make provision for the appointment of independent and impartial tender boards to deal with such procurements.

(2) The tendering system referred to in subsection (1) shall be fair, public and competitive, and tender boards shall on request give reasons for their decisions to interested parties.

(3) No organ of state and no member of any organ of state or any other person shall improperly interfere with the decisions and operations of the tender boards.

(4) All decisions of any tender board shall be recorded."

Pope, TI Source Book: Confronting Corruption: The Elements of a National Integrity System, 206.

635 Such as the WTO Amended Agreement on Government Procurement, or the EU procurement directives: Directive 2004/17/EC (contracts awarded in the utilities sectors) and Directive 2004/18/EC (contracts awarded by public authorities).

636 Such as the UNCITRAL Model Law on Procurement of Goods, Services, and Construction, or the OECD Recommendation of the Council on Enhancing Integrity in Public Procurement, [C(2008)105], 2008.

637 Such as the numerous reports and publications of the World Bank and the OECD. With regard to the World Bank see, for example, the several Country Procurement Assessment Reports which analyse the procurement policies, organization, and procedures of borrowing

these numerous initiatives here. Yet, the WTO merits a brief description as the issue of procurement has aroused controversial discussions in that forum. In addition, WTO rules are potentially global in scope and may be enforced through its notorious dispute settlement mechanism.

During the negotiation of the UNCAC, some delegations called for consistency between the UNCAC public procurement provisions and the relevant agreement in the WTO.[638] The WTO has recently amended its Agreement on Government Procurement, which did not concern with corruption at all.[639] The original Agreement was designed to make laws, regulations, procedures and practices for government procurement more transparent, mostly with the aim of ensuring that they did not protect domestic products or suppliers, or discriminated against foreign products or suppliers.[640]

In the past the WTO has endeavoured to deal specifically with the issue of transparency in government procurement in a more ambitious way.[641] However, the majority of Member States held that the rationale underlying a future agreement on transparency in government procurement should not be to combat corruption, nor should such a future agreement contain specific provisions on corruption.[642] Contrary to this approach, some commentators have argued that

---

countries, which are available at the World Bank's website. In relation to the OECD see, for example, *Bribery in Public Procurement: Methods, Actors and Counter-Measures*, 2007, *Integrity in Public Procurement: Good Practice from A to Z*, 2007, *Fighting Corruption and Promoting Integrity in Public Procurement*, 2005.

638 Ad Hoc Committee for the Negotiation of a Convention against Corruption, Second Session, Vienna, 17–28 June 2002, Revised Draft United Nations Convention against Corruption, A/AC.261/3/Rev.1, 1 March 2002, 13.

639 For details on the re-negotiation of the Agreement on Government Procurement, see www.wto.org/english/tratop_e/gproc_e/negotiations_e.htm (last visited 14 April 2012).

640 Agreement on Government Procurement, Annex 4(b) to the Marrakesh Agreement Establishing the World Trade Organization, done at Marrakesh on 15 April 1994, which took effect on 1 January 1996, Art. III. The Agreement has only been accepted by 41 Member States of the WTO, the majority of which are developed countries, although a number of Members are currently negotiating accession. The Agreement on Government Procurement is a Plurilateral Agreement, which means that its ratification or accession is negotiated separately and WTO Members can choose not to become Parties to it. For the list of States Parties, see, www.wto.org/english/tratop_e/gproc_e/memobs_e.htm (last visited 20 April 2012).

641 In 1996, mostly at the initiative of the United States, the WTO agreed to "establish a working group to conduct a study on transparency in government procurement practices, taking into account national policies, and, based on this study, to develop elements for inclusion in an appropriate agreement..." See, Singapore Ministerial Declaration, adopted on 13 December 1996 (WT/MIN(96)/DEC, 18 December 1996), para. 21. Since the preparatory work for the 1st Ministerial Meeting in Singapore, the US had tried to include the issue of bribery in international business transactions in the agenda of the WTO. Alejandro Posadas, "Combating Corruption Under International Law," *Duke Journal of Comparative & International Law* 10, no. 2 (2000): 403.

642 World Trade Organization, *Report of the Working Group on Transparency in Government Procurement to the General Council*, WT/WGTGP/7, 15 July 2003, para. 14; World Trade

in certain countries corruption is an even more serious barrier to trade than discrimination in procurement.[643] In 2004, the WTO General Council decided that "those issues [transparency in government procurement among others] will not form part of the Doha Work Programme and therefore no work towards negotiations (...) will take place within the WTO during the Doha Round."[644] Since then, the Working Group on Transparency in Government Procurement has been inactive.

Nevertheless, as stated earlier the WTO has recently amended the Agreement on Government Procurement which now establishes that procurement must be conducted in a transparent and impartial manner that avoids conflict of interest and prevents corrupt practices.[645] The amended Agreement is considerably stronger than the previous one. For example, it provides that a procuring entity must provide an unsuccessful supplier with an explanation of the reasons why the entity did not select its tender and the relative advantages of the successful supplier's tender, and that it must also publish award information.[646] These and other provisions could enhance efforts to reduce corruption in procurement procedures.

3.2. An appropriate balance of regulation

It should also be noted that the provisions of the international legal framework against corruption respecting public procurement do not apply to the award of all public contracts. Procurement systems may include appropriate threshold

---

Organization, *Report (1999) to the General Council*, WT/WGTGP/3, 12 October 1999, para. 111–115. See also, World Trade Organization, Work of the Working Group on the Matters Related to Items VI-XII of the List of the Issues Raised and Points Made, WT/WGTGP/W/33, 3 October 2002, paras. 79 and 84; World Trade Organization, Working Group on Transparency in Government Procurement, Report of the Meeting of 18 June 2003, WT/WGTGP/M/18, 7 July 2003.

643 Evenett has therefore suggested that WTO procurement disciplines and the work on transparency should focus on anti-corruption measures before tackling discrimination in procurement. Simon J. Evenett, "Multilateral Disciplines and Government Procurement," in *Development, Trade, and the WTO: A Handbook*, ed. Bernard M. Hoekman, Aaditya Mattoo, and Philip English (Washington, D.C: World Bank, 2002), 426; Simon J. Evenett and Bernard M. Hoekman, "Transparency in Government Procurement: What Can We Expect from International Trade Agreements?," in *Public Procurement: The Continuing Revolution*, ed. Sue Arrowsmith and Martin Trybus, International Economic Development Law, v. 15 (The Hague: Kluwer Law International, 2003), 269–280.

644 WTO General Council, July Decision of the General Council, paragraph 1(g), adopted on 1 August 2004 (WT/L/579, 2 August 2004).

645 World Trade Organization, Committee on Government Procurement, Adoption of the Results of the Negotiations under Article XXIV:7 of the Agreement on Government Procurement, following their Verification and Review, as Required by the Ministerial Decision of 15 December 2011 (Gpa/112), Paragraph 5, 2 April 2012, *Annex to the Protocol Amending the Agreement on Government Procurement*, Art. IV(4).

646 Ibid., Arts. XVI-XVII.

values in their application with a view to avoiding overly complex procedures for comparatively small amounts.[647] A highly structured bidding process does not allow the purchasing agency to engage in mutually beneficial negotiations with suppliers, through which the two parties can discuss and optimize technical and price solutions. A reform of procurement systems as part of a broader anti-corruption approach may have the effect of making them more rigid and sometimes over-regulated, and at the same time less efficient in terms of value for money, although promoting integrity and contributing to the general anti-corruption policy. Past experience suggests that excessive regulation can be counterproductive by increasing rather than diminishing vulnerability to corruption. Excessive regulation may also lead to errors and omissions, or frequent requests for exceptions, the approval or refusal of which can be non-transparent and difficult to monitor.[648] For this reason, many procurement guidelines and systems include thresholds below which simpler procedures may operate.[649] However, introducing flexibility into procurement systems also involves allowing a space for discretion, which is beneficial in avoiding an excessively rigid system and capturing optimal value, but at the same time raises the risk of subjectivity and corruption.[650]

Reconciling the two options can be difficult. In general, it is therefore considered that a more rigid system with a lower threshold is necessary for countries with a higher risk of corruption, while more flexible systems with a higher threshold can be envisaged in countries where corruption is less prevalent and where public officials show a higher degree of integrity.[651] A proper balancing of these elements and the circumstances that prevail in each particular State are the key to a transparent and competitive procurement system. Yet, at a minimum, such system should include the international obligations to combat corruption in relation to procurement that have been outlined in this section.

---

647 UNCAC, Art. 9(1); UNODC, *Legislative Guide for the Implementation of the United Nations Convention against Corruption*, para. 79.

648 COSP, *United Nations Convention against Corruption: Implementing Procurement-Related Aspects*, 10.

649 See, for example, Directives 2004/17/EC and 2004/18/EC, and the UNCITRAL Model Law.

650 COSP, *United Nations Convention against Corruption: Implementing Procurement-Related Aspects*, 10.

651 For example, in the United States, tendering is the exception rather than the rule. The US system relies heavily on a type of negotiated procurement that would give raise to extreme risks of corruption in other nations. The ability of the United States to use this type of flexible system, which allows for more efficient outcomes, is the result of a relatively strong system of integrity and enforcement. See, Christopher Yukins, "Integrating Integrity and Procurement: The United Nations Convention against Corruption and the UNCITRAL Model Procurement Law," *Public Contract Law Journal* 36, no. 3 (2007): 328.

III. TRANSPARENCY MEASURES IN THE JUDICIARY

It is generally recognized that, without the rule of law, efforts to combat corruption are largely futile. If the judiciary is not impartial, professional in its work and independent, the law cannot be relied upon as an important weapon to combat corruption. At the same time, the judiciary is widely regarded as one of the sectors most affected by corruption. Corrupt practices in the judiciary are highly complex and can range from acts involving judicial staff and judges with a view to influencing a particular case, to broader corrupt practices related to undue external interference, mostly involving the executive or the private sector. For this reason, the preventive measures set out in the international legal framework against corruption envisage anti-corruption measures in the judiciary.

The international obligation for the prevention of corruption in the judiciary is both simple and broad in scope. States are required to strengthen integrity and prevent opportunities for corruption among members of the judiciary, which may include the adoption of rules respecting to the conduct of members of the judiciary.[652] However, the international legal framework is silent about how integrity should be strengthened and corruption prevented in the judiciary. No details are provided concerning the exact measures to be taken by States. This is unfortunate, as it leaves the door open to a very broad range of measures. As a result, almost any type of measure taken by States in relation to the judiciary could be regarded as aimed at meeting the obligation of promoting integrity and preventing corruption. However, information abounds on how to interpret this obligation. To seek integrity in the judiciary, two elements are essential: independence from external influence and accountability to users and the general public.[653] Yet, these are also elements of the effective prevention of corruption. States therefore need to take measures relating to the procedures for judicial appointment, tenure and other career-related issues, as well as non-career related issues, such as the issuing of summonses, securing evidence, the obtaining of bail, the expedition of cases and the delaying of cases.[654] This is because the two main aspects to preventing corruption in the judiciary consist of the appointment and promotion of judges and other personnel, and the work for

652 UNCAC, Art. 11(1). In States where prosecution services do not form part of the judiciary, but enjoy independence similar to that of the judicial service, States may also strengthen integrity and prevent opportunities for corruption among members of the prosecution service. UNCAC, Art. 11(2). However, if prosecution services are placed under the executive branch of government or the judiciary, they are already covered by other obligations.

653 Jessica Schultz, *The UNCAC and Judicial Corruption: Requirements and Avenues for Reform*, U4 Brief No. 18 (Bergen: Anti-Corruption Resource Centre, 2009), 2.

654 UNODC and UNICRI, *Technical Guide to the United Nations Convention against Corruption*, 47; UNODC, *The Global Programme against Corruption: UN Anti-Corruption Toolkit*, 110–119.

which they are responsible. Judicial appointments and promotions therefore need to be carried out in a transparent manner, namely on merit and subject to established criteria.[655] The judicial process needs to be open and accessible, and has to include the elements of an effective administration of court proceedings, such as reasoned judgments, the prominent display of notices describing procedures and proceedings, an efficient system of maintaining court records, etc.[656]

Moreover, the prevention of corruption in the judiciary depends on a broad range of actors: if the security services do not function, or if the police, lawyers or prison officials are corrupt, the integrity of the courts will be compromised.[657] With a view to enhancing integrity and preventing corruption in the judiciary, States should also take into account the relevant international instruments, such as the Bangalore Principles of Judicial Conduct (2002), the UN Handbook on Practical Anti-Corruption Measures for Prosecutors and Investigators (2005), the UN Guidelines on the Role of Prosecutors (1990), and the 1999 International Association of Prosecutors' Standards of Professional Responsibility and Statement of the Essential Duties and Rights of Prosecutors. These instruments provide high-quality guidelines for an efficient and transparent judicial system.[658]

IV. TRANSPARENCY MEASURES IN THE PRIVATE SECTOR

The relationship between corruption and the private sector is far reaching and complex. In a nutshell, private enterprises can both fuel corruption and suffer its consequences. It is widely recognized that private enterprises are at the origin of many corrupt practices, such as bribery or trading in influence in public procurement. High monetary penalties have also been imposed on private companies for taking part in corrupt practices, as illustrated by the US$ 1.6 billion penalty to be paid by the German corporation Siemens for its notorious corrupt practices around the world.[659]

655 UNODC and UNICRI, *Technical Guide to the United Nations Convention against Corruption*, 49–50.

656 UNODC and UNICRI, *Technical Guide to the United Nations Convention against Corruption*, 49–50; Transparency International, *Global Corruption Report 2007: Corruption in Judicial Systems* (Cambridge: Cambridge University Press, 2007), xxv-xxvii.

657 Schultz, *The UNCAC and Judicial Corruption: Requirements and Avenues for Reform*, 2.

658 For a comprehensive analysis of corruption in judicial systems, see Transparency International, *Global Corruption Report 2007: Corruption in Judicial Systems.*

659 U.S. Department of Justice, *Siemens AG and Three Subsidiaries Plead Guilty to Foreign Corrupt Practices Act Violations and Agree to Pay $450 Million in Combined Criminal Fines*, Press Release, 15 December 2008. Siemens has stated that the internal inquiry and related

Simultaneously, the private sector is subject to the destructive force of corruption, which undermines fair competition, reduces economic growth and political development, and ultimately strangles the very existence of private enterprise. For that reason, the strengthening of corporate integrity is acknowledged to be beneficial to both the private sector itself (the so-called business case) and public policy against corruption.[660] The international legal framework against corruption therefore addresses the enhancement of the potential of the private sector to combat corruption.

States are called upon to prevent corruption involving the private sector, enhance accounting and auditing standards in the private sector and provide effective, proportionate and dissuasive civil, administrative or criminal penalties for failure to comply with such measures.[661] To achieve these ends, States can choose from a variety of measures, such as: promoting cooperation between law enforcement and private entities;[662] promoting the development of standards and procedures, such as codes of conduct and good practice guides; promoting transparency among private entities; preventing the misuse of procedures regulating private entities, such as procedures relating to subsidies or licences; preventing conflicts of interest, particularly with regard to the employment of public officials in the private sector (the so-called revolving door problem); and ensuring that private enterprises have adequate internal auditing controls.[663]

A further measure to prevent corruption that should be taken by States is to disallow the tax deductibility of expenses corresponding to bribes and, where appropriate, other expenses incurred in furtherance of corrupt conduct.[664] The issue of tax deductibility is mostly relevant to transnational bribes, as it is clearly prohibited to deduct from taxes any bribes given to local public officials. In the

---

legal fees have cost it more than US$ 1 billion. Siri Schubert and Christian Miller, *At Siemens, Bribery Was Just a Line Item*, New York Times, 20 December 2008.

660 For a comprehensive and interdisciplinary study on corruption and the private sector, see Transparency International, *Global Corruption Report 2009: Corruption and the Private Sector* (Cambridge: Cambridge University Press, 2009).

661 UNCAC, Art. 12(1). The AU Convention against Corruption is more specific than the UNCAC concerning this obligation. Under the AU Convention against Corruption, States have to establish mechanisms to encourage participation by the private sector in action to combat unfair competition, compliance with tender procedures and property rights and generally the prevention of companies from paying bribes to win tenders. See, AU Convention against Corruption, Art. 11. See, also, CoE Civil Law Convention, Art. 10(1) and 10(2).

662 States are also called upon to encourage cooperation between national law enforcement authorities and entities of the private sector, in particular financial institutions, relating to matters involving the commission of acts of corruption (UNCAC, Art. 39(1)). See also Chapter VII.

663 UNCAC, Art. 12(2)(a-f).

664 UNCAC, Art. 12(4); OECD, Recommendation of the Council on the Tax Deductibility of Bribes to Foreign Public Officials, Adopted by the Council on 11 April 1996, C(96)27/FINAL; Inter-American Convention against Corruption, Art. 3(7).

past, in certain countries, many corporations used to deduct from taxes the bribes given to foreign public officials, since such bribery was not criminalized. At least until July 1988, the following countries allowed the deduction from taxable revenue of bribes paid to foreign public officials: Australia, Austria, Belgium, France, Germany, Luxembourg, New Zealand, Sweden and Switzerland.[665] Today, the prohibition of the tax deductibility of bribes is (in theory) an established anti-corruption rule.

In addition, States are also required to review their laws and regulations respecting the maintenance of books and records, the disclosure of financial statements and accounting and auditing standards, and have to prohibit certain accounting practices known to be susceptible to abuse. States therefore need to take measures to prohibit the following acts carried out for the purposes of committing corruption: (i) the establishment of off-the-books accounts;[666] (ii) the making of off-the-books or inadequately identified transactions;[667] (iii) the recording of non-existent expenditure;[668] (iv) the entry of liabilities with incorrect identification of their objects;[669] (v) the use of false documents;[670] and (vi) the intentional destruction of bookkeeping documents earlier than foreseen by the law.[671]

A number of the measures mentioned in this section are already promoted in anti-corruption initiatives driven by the private sector, such as the World Economic Forum Partnership against Corruption Initiative, the International Chamber of Commerce Rules of Conduct and Recommendations on Combating Extortion and Bribery, and the Transparency International Business Principles for Countering Bribery. Although these types of initiatives are designed by and directed at the private sector, they do enhance the prevention of corruption and accounting and auditing standards in the private sector, as advocated by the

665 See *Hearings on Convention on Combating Bribery of Foreign Public Officials in International Business Transactions*, S. Exec. Rep. 105–19 at 12 (1998), cited in Posadas, "Combating Corruption Under International Law," 143. Further evidence of the acceptance of the tax deductibility of bribes is contained in the Inter-American Convention against Corruption, where the prohibition of such tax deductibility is a matter of best endeavour. See, Inter-American Convention against Corruption, Art. 3(7).

666 UNCAC, Art. 12(3)(a); OECD Convention Art. 8(1). The expression "off-the-books accounts" refers to transactions which do not appear in any of the financial records kept by a company.

667 UNCAC, Art. 12(3)(b); OECD Convention Art. 8(1).

668 UNCAC, Art. 12(3)(c); OECD Convention Art. 8(1).

669 UNCAC, Art. 12(3)(d); OECD Convention Art. 8(1).

670 UNCAC, Art. 12(3)(e); OECD Convention Art. 8(1).

671 UNCAC, Art. 12(3)(f). For more information on anti-corruption accounting measures, see, for example, Gregory S. Bruch and Akita N. Adkins, "Article 8: Accounting," in *The OECD Convention on Bribery: A Commentary*, ed. Mark Pieth, Lucinda A Low, and Peter J. Cullen (Cambridge University Press, 2007), 377–405; Stuart H Deming, "Potent and Broad-Ranging Implications of the Accounting and Record-Keeping Provisions of the Foreign Corrupt Practices Act," *Journal of Criminal Law and Criminology* 96 (2005): 465.

international legal framework, which indirectly benefits the fight against corruption as a whole. When implementing the international obligations described in this section, States should therefore also take these initiatives into account.

V. PREVENTION OF MONEY LAUNDERING

The connection between corruption and money laundering is self-evident.[672] For those who engage in corruption to enjoy the benefits of their illicit activities, they have to hide the origin of the funds. However, the link between corruption and money laundering is not only related to laundering the proceeds of corruption. Money laundering methods also encourage corruption by providing a platform to hide the origin of bribes. It also has a corrupting effect on national and international financial systems.[673] A comprehensive anti-corruption strategy therefore also needs to include action to prevent and combat the laundering of the proceeds of corruption.[674]

In a nutshell, money laundering consists of disguising the illegal origin of the proceeds of crime. This is done essentially in three stages: introducing the proceeds of crime into the financial system ("placement"); engaging in various transactions intended to disguise the origin of and the path taken by the money ("layering"); and thereby integrating the money into the legitimate economy through apparently legitimate transactions ("integration").[675] Of the three stages, it is most critical to impede the first, as once the assets are introduced into the financial system it becomes much harder or even impossible to trace them.[676] Accordingly, the international legal framework against corruption contains measures aimed at preventing such activities, enlisting the assistance of financial institutions and others in detecting transactions that may be of

---

672 The UN General Assembly has repeatedly expressed concern about the links between corruption and other serious forms of crime, including money laundering. See, *inter alia*, Action against Corruption, A/RES/51/59, 12 December 1996; Action against Corruption, A/RES/54/128, 28 January 2000; An Effective International Legal Instrument against Corruption, A/RES/55/61, 22 January 2001; Preventing and Combating Corrupt Practices and Illegal Transfer of Funds and Repatriation of such Funds to the Countries of Origin, A/RES/55/188, 25 January 2001; Terms of Reference for the Negotiation of an International Legal Instrument against Corruption, A/RES/56/260, 9 April 2002; and Preventing and Combating Corrupt Practices and Illegal Transfer of Funds and Repatriation of such Funds to the Countries of Origin, A/RES/57/244, 7 February 2003.

673 UNODC, *The Global Programme against Corruption: UN Anti-Corruption Toolkit*, 440.

674 See David A Chaikin and J. C Sharman, *Corruption and Money Laundering: A Symbiotic Relationship* (New York: Palgrave-Macmillan, 2009).

675 UNODC, *Legislative Guide for the Implementation of the United Nations Convention against Corruption*, para. 127.

676 Ibid., para. 128.

criminal origin and facilitating the tracing of the funds involved in such transactions.[677]

States need to institute a comprehensive domestic regulatory and supervisory regime in order to deter and detect all forms of money laundering.[678] They should consider using as a guide in the establishment of this regulatory and supervisory regime the relevant initiatives undertaken by multilateral organizations against money laundering.[679] As a minimum, this regime must require banks and non-bank financial institutions to ensure: (i) effective customer identification; (ii) accurate record-keeping; and (iii) a mechanism for the reporting of suspicious transactions.[680]

These requirements cover banks and other financial institutions (such as insurance companies and securities firms), including persons, both natural or legal, which provide services for the transmission of money or values, and also to other bodies particularly susceptible to money laundering.[681] Such other bodies may include intermediaries, which in some jurisdictions may include stock brokerage firms, other securities dealers, currency exchange bureaux and currency brokers.[682] The regime should apply not only to banking institutions, but also to areas of commerce where the high turnover and large volumes make money laundering likely. For example, experience shows that money laundering activities have taken place in the real estate sector and in trade in commodities, such as gold, precious stones and tobacco. As a result, the list of institutions established in many fora is being expanded beyond financial institutions to

677 Ibid., para. 129.

678 UNCAC, Art. 14(1)(a).

679 UNCAC, Art. 14(4). The *travaux préparatoires* of UNCAC indicate that this provision referes in particular to the Forty Recommendations and the Eight Special Recommendations of the Financial Action Task Force on Money Laundering, as revised in 2003 and 2001, respectively, and in addition to other existing initiatives by regional, inter-regional, and multilateral organizations against money laundering, such as the Caribbean Financial Action Task Force, the Commonwealth, the Council of Europe, the Eastern and Southern African Anti-Money Laundering Group, the European Union, the Financial Action Task Force of South America against Money Laundering, and the Organization of American States. UN General Assembly, *Interpretative Notes for the Official Records (Travaux Préparatoires) of the Negotiation of the United Nations Convention against Corruption*, para. 21. On the combat against money laundering, see also the following initiatives: United Nations Convention against Illicit Traffic in Narcotic Drugs and Psychotropic Substances, 1988; UNTOC; United Nations Convention for the Suppression of the Financing of Terrorism of 1999; Security Council resolutions 1267 (1999) of 15 October 1999, 1373 (2001) of 28 September 2001 and 1377 (2001) of 12 November 2001 on the financing of terrorist acts; Council of Europe Convention on Laundering, Search, Seizure and Confiscation of the Proceeds from Crime, 1990.

680 UNCAC, Art. 14(1)(a).

681 UNCAC, Art. 14(1)(a).

682 UN General Assembly, *Interpretative Notes for the Official Records (Travaux Préparatoires) of the Negotiation of the United Nations Convention against Corruption*, para. 18.

include businesses and professions related to real estate and commodities.[683] In this connection, the regulatory and supervisory regime for natural and legal persons that provide services for the transmission of money or values is aimed at addressing concerns about both formal remitters and informal value-transfer systems, such as the *hawala*.[684] These kinds of systems are especially vulnerable to abuse by criminals, including persons engaged in corruption, and are being increasingly closely regulated for the purpose of detecting money laundering, terrorist financing and other offences.[685]

1. KNOW-YOUR-CUSTOMER OBLIGATIONS AND ENHANCED DUE DILIGENCE FOR PEPs

Customer identification entails the requirement to identify and document holders of accounts in financial institutions and all parties to financial transactions. Records should contain sufficient information for the identification of the parties and the nature of the transaction, and of the specific assets and amounts or values involved, and to permit the tracing of the source and destination of all funds or other assets.[686] These are the so-called "know-your-customer" rules. In addition, banks and financial institutions should enhance the due diligence procedures for politically exposed persons (PEPs), their family members and close associates.[687] It is left to each State to decide who should be

683 See, for example, Recommendation 18 of the FATF Forty Recommendations and Interpretative Note to Recommendation 18 which extends, under certain conditions, the requirements of customer due diligence and record-keeping to casinos, real estate agents, dealers in precious metals and stones, lawyers, notaries, other independent legal professionals and accountants and trust and company service providers. Similar requirements are set forth in Article 1 of Directive 2005/60/EC adopted by the European Parliament and the Council of the European Union, 26 October 2005.

684 UNODC, *Legislative Guide for the Implementation of the United Nations Convention against Corruption*, para. 141. *Hawala* means transfer in Arabic, and is also known as *hundi*. It consists of an informal value transfer system based on the performance and honour of an important network of money brokers, which are primarily located in the Middle East, North Africa, the Horn of Africa, and South Asia. For more information, see Nikos Passas, "Formalizing the Informal? Problems in the National and International Regulation of Hawala," in *Regulatory Frameworks for Hawala and Other Remittance Systems* (Washington, D.C: International Monetary Fund, 2005), 8–9.

685 For a critical view of the over-regulation of informal value transfers see, for example, Nikos Passas, "Fighting Terror with Error: The Counter-Productive Regulation of Informal Value Transfers," *Crime, Law and Social Change* 45 (2007): 315–366.

686 UNODC, *Legislative Guide for the Implementation of the United Nations Convention against Corruption*, para. 145. For a detailed analysis of customer identification, see Guy Stessens, *Money Laundering: A New International Law Enforcement Model* (Cambridge: Cambridge University Press, 2000), 146–157.

687 UNCAC, Art. 52(1). See also, FATF Recommendation No. 12 and Interpretative Note to Recommendation 12, available at www.fatf-gafi.org (last visited 22 April 2012). The term "close associates" is deemed to encompass persons or companies clearly related to individuals

regarded as a PEP. However, there are certain guidelines. A PEP is a natural person in a senior political position who has a degree of control or influence over public assets, such as Heads of State or Government, ministers, members of Parliament, senior civil servants, senior government, judicial on military officials, senior executives of State-owned enterprises, among others.[688] More specifically, regulatory authorities and banks should require a declaration of beneficial ownership, request asset and income disclosure forms, undertake a periodic review of PEP customers and avoid setting limits on the time a PEP remains a PEP.[689] Such measures constitute an additional hurdle and make it difficult for senior public officials to launder the proceeds of corrupt practices. Unfortunately, as indicated by the FATF evaluations, the majority of States do not comply with the politically exposed persons recommendation. Customer identification is central to the effective prevention of money laundering and, as indicated in a recent report by the NGO Global Witness, there are numerous cases in which banks have failed to apply due diligence and have, almost deliberately, done business with corrupt regimes.[690] With a view to facilitating the implementation of such measures, States should:

a) issue advisories regarding the types of persons for whose accounts enhanced scrutiny is expected, the types of accounts and transactions to which particular attention should be paid and account opening, maintenance and record-keeping measures for such accounts;[691] and
b) notify financial institutions of the identity of particular persons for whose accounts enhanced scrutiny is expected.[692] Since it may be difficult for financial institutions to know when a client is also a PEP, States should identify them and disseminate the information to financial institutions.

---

who are entrusted with prominent public functions. UN General Assembly, *Interpretative Notes for the Official Records (Travaux Préparatoires) of the Negotiation of the United Nations Convention against Corruption*, para. 50.

688 See definition of PEP in the Wolfsberg Principles, available at www.wolfsberg-principles.com/ (last visited 22 April 2012); Basel Committee on Banking Supervision, Customer Due Diligence for Banks, 2001, available at www.bis.org/publ/bcbs77.pdf (last visited 22 April 2012); and the FATF's 40 Recommendations (as amended on 16 February 2012), available at www.fatf-gafi.org (last visited 22 April 2012). For a more detailed analysis of the PEP concept, see Hans-Peter Bauer, "How to Deal with Politically Exposed Persons," in *Recovering Stolen Assets*, ed. Mark Pieth (Bern: Peter Lang, 2008), 195–217.

689 See, Theodore S. Greenberg et al., *Stolen Asset Recovery: Politically Exposed Persons: A Policy Paper on Strengthening Preventive Measures* (Washington D.C.: World Bank, 2009).

690 Global Witness, *Undue Diligence: How Banks Do Business with Corrupt Regimes*, March 2009.

691 UNCAC, Art. 52(2)(a). The obligation to issue advisories may be fulfilled by the State or by its financial oversight bodies. UN General Assembly, *Interpretative Notes for the Official Records (Travaux Préparatoires) of the Negotiation of the United Nations Convention against Corruption*, para. 52.

692 UNCAC, Art. 52(2)(b).

This sort of guidance from national authorities is particularly helpful to financial institutions in their efforts to comply with regulatory requirements. In this context, States should also ensure that financial institutions maintain adequate records over an appropriate period of time of accounts and transactions involving persons to whom enhanced scrutiny is applied, which should as a minimum contain information relating to the identity of the customer, as well as, in so far as possible, of the beneficial owner.[693] This measure is important, as it obliges States to maintain an evidentiary record. States may also provide guidance to financial institutions on the appropriate procedures to apply and on whether specific risks require the application and implementation of such provisions: (i) to accounts of a particular value or nature; (ii) to its own citizens, as well as to citizens of other States; and (iii) to officials with a particular function or seniority.[694] It should be emphasized that these measures apply both to domestic and to foreign public officials.[695] Such measures are essential to facilitate investigations and the identification of assets, and their possible return in the future.

2. ACCURATE RECORD KEEPING AND REPORTING SUSPICIOUS TRANSACTIONS

The requirement of accurate record-keeping refers to the keeping for a specified minimum period of time records of clients and transactions. FATF recommends at least five years.[696] Suspicious transactions should be reported to the Financial Intelligence Unit (FIU) or any other designated agency. Suspicious transactions should be understood to include unusual transactions which, by reason of their amount, characteristics and frequency, are inconsistent with the business activity of the customer, exceed the normally accepted parameters of the market or have no clear legal basis, and which could constitute or be connected with unlawful activities in general.[697] Such anti-money laundering (AML) preventive provisions are based on a due diligence regulatory approach. This is key, since effective AML has to be based on self-regulation. Moreover, it is important to bear in mind that, for as long as the financial system continues to reward its employees for attracting new business, but does not reward them for being

693 UNCAC, Art. 52(3).

694 UN General Assembly, *Interpretative Notes for the Official Records (Travaux Préparatoires) of the Negotiation of the United Nations Convention against Corruption*, para. 49.

695 UNODC, *Legislative Guide for the Implementation of the United Nations Convention against Corruption*, para. 692.

696 See, Stessens, *Money Laundering: A New International Law Enforcement Model*, 157–159.

697 UN General Assembly, *Interpretative Notes for the Official Records (Travaux Préparatoires) of the Negotiation of the United Nations Convention against Corruption*, para 19; Stessens, *Money Laundering: A New International Law Enforcement Model*, 159–178.

cautious when dealing with clients, the flow of illegal proceeds will continue to corrupt individuals and institutions alike.[698]

3. SHELL BANKS, FIUS AND OTHER MISCELLANEOUS AML PREVENTIVE MEASURES

One of the most widely used financial vehicles to hide assets in the international financial system is the so-called "shell bank." States therefore also need to prevent the establishment of banks that have no physical presence and are not affiliated to a regulated financial group ("shell banks").[699] The *travaux préparatoires* of UNCAC indicate that physical presence, means meaningful mind and management located within the jurisdiction. The simple existence of a local agent or low-level staff would not constitute physical presence. Management is understood to include administration (books and records).[700]

States are also under the international obligation to consider the establishment of a financial intelligence unit (FIU) to serve as a national centre for the collection, analysis and dissemination of information regarding potential money laundering.[701] Since the 1990s, many States have established such units as part of their regulatory, police or other authorities, with a wide range of structures, responsibilities, functions and departmental affiliation or independence. The Egmont Group (the informal association of FIUs) has defined such units as central, national agencies responsible for receiving (and, where so permitted, requesting), analysing and disseminating to the competent authorities disclosures of financial information: (a) concerning suspected proceeds of crime; or (b) as required by national legislation or regulation, in order to combat money laundering and the financing of

---

698 UNODC, *The Global Programme against Corruption: UN Anti-Corruption Toolkit*, 440 citing Oliver Stolpe, *Geldwäsche and Mafia*, Kriminalistik, No. 2, 2000, p. 99 and 101. However, in a minority of cases banks, and most importantly bank employees, have been sanctioned for money laundering, including certain employees of Swiss banks who faced serious civil penalties for allowing the Abacha funds to be deposited in their banks. ADB/OECD Anti-Corruption Initiative for Asia and the Pacific, *Controlling Corruption in Asia and the Pacific*, 179.

699 Moreover, States may wish to consider imposing a requirement on financial institutions: (i) to refuse to enter into or continue a correspondent banking relationship with "shell banks"; and (ii) to guard against establishing relations with foreign financial institutions that permit their accounts to be used by "shell banks." UNCAC, Art. 52(4).

700 UN General Assembly, *Interpretative Notes for the Official Records (Travaux Préparatoires) of the Negotiation of the United Nations Convention against Corruption*, para. 54.

701 UNCAC, Art. 14(1)(b) and 58. For details on the elements that States should include in legislation establishing the FIU, see UNODC, *Legislative Guide for the Implementation of the United Nations Convention against Corruption*, para. 159.

terrorism.[702] Although the establishment of FIUs is not required by law, it is strongly recommended.[703]

States also have to ensure that all agencies involved in combating money laundering have the capacity to cooperate and exchange information at the national and international levels.[704] As part of the effort to develop the capacity to provide effective international cooperation, States are required to consider the introduction of feasible measures to monitor the cross-border movement of cash and other monetary instruments.[705] They should also consider the implementation of measures requiring financial institutions, including money remitters to: include on forms for the electronic transfer of funds and related messages accurate and meaningful information on the originator; maintain such information throughout the payment chain; and apply enhanced scrutiny to transfers of funds that do not contain complete information on the originator.[706]

This section has described the international anti-corruption obligations concerning the prevention of money laundering. As indicated, these measures should be understood as building upon existing, and more detailed, anti-money laundering obligations, such as those arising out of the Financial Action Task Force. In addition to prevention, as indicated in Chapter VII below, the international legal framework also requires States to criminalize money laundering, particularly where the original offence is a corrupt act.

VI. INTERNATIONAL COOPERATION

International cooperation, or technical assistance, is not strictly a preventive measure. However, in the majority of cases, international cooperation in the form of technical and financial support focuses on the design and implementation of anti-corruption policies, the strengthening of institutions and the development of capacity. Accordingly, although international cooperation is partly provided to actually combat corruption, such as in issues of asset recovery, in most cases it serves a preventive purpose through the creation of an environment that will impede corruption in the future. Moreover, as

---

702 Egmont Group, *Interpretative Note Concerning the Egmont Definition of a Financial Intelligence Unit*, available at www.egmontgroup.org/ (last visited 22 April 2012).

703 UNODC, *Legislative Guide for the Implementation of the United Nations Convention against Corruption*, para. 764.

704 UNCAC, Art. 14(1)(b). In addition, States are encouraged to develop and promote global cooperation between judicial, law enforcement and financial regulatory authorities in order to combat money laundering. UNCAC, Art. 14(5).

705 UNCAC, Art. 14(2).

706 UNCAC, Art. 14(3).

shown below, most of the international anti-corruption obligations relating to international cooperation are connected to preventive measures. In the present study international cooperation is mainly understood as a preventive tool to combat corruption.

The international legal framework places numerous obligations upon States in terms of international cooperation, but few such obligations require States to attain a specific result. Moreover, most of these obligations are exceedingly broad in scope, and several appear to address the same issues. It is therefore useful to group the international cooperation obligations in the field of combating corruption under the various means of cooperation. A first group of obligations is aimed at the provision of assistance for the implementation of other anti-corruption obligations, particularly in relation to the prevention of corruption.[707] States therefore need to make concrete efforts to the extent possible and in coordination with each other, as well as with international and regional organizations:

(a) to enhance their cooperation at various levels with developing countries, with a view to strengthening the capacity of the latter to prevent and combat corruption;[708]
(b) to enhance financial and material assistance to support the efforts of developing countries to prevent and fight corruption effectively and to help them implement the UNCAC successfully;[709]
(c) to provide technical assistance to developing countries and countries with economies in transition to assist them in meeting their needs for the implementation of UNCAC;[710]
(d) to encourage and persuade other States and financial institutions as appropriate to join them in international cooperation efforts, in particular

707 States are called upon to take measures conducive to the optimal implementation of the UNCAC, to the extent possible, through international cooperation. UNCAC, Art. 62(1).

708 UNCAC, Art. 62(2)(a).

709 UNCAC, Art. 62(2)(b). States may also conclude bilateral or multilateral agreements or arrangements on material and logistical assistance, taking into consideration the financial arrangements necessary for the means of international cooperation provided for by the UNCAC to be effective and for the prevention, detection and control of corruption. UNCAC, Art. 62(4).

710 In order to assist developing countries and countries with economies in transition to meet their needs for the implementation of the UNCAC, States Parties should also try to make adequate and regular voluntary contributions to an account specifically designated for that purpose in a United Nations funding mechanism. As of April 2012, such a special account has not been created. States Parties may also give special consideration, in accordance with their domestic law and the provisions of the UNCAC, to contributing to that account a percentage of the money or of the corresponding value of proceeds of crime or property confiscated in accordance with the UNCAC. UNCAC, Art. 62(2)(c).

by providing more training programmes and modern equipment to developing countries;[711]

(e) to consider establishing voluntary mechanisms with a view to contributing financially to the efforts of developing countries and countries with economies in transition for the application of the UNCAC through technical assistance programmes and projects.[712]

A second group of international obligations relate to international cooperation in training and the exchange of information with a view to combating corruption. These obligations are numerous and mostly require States to consider taking measures relating to international cooperation, although they are not legally obliged to achieve any specific result. In this context, States are called upon to consider affording one another, especially for the benefit of developing countries, the widest measure of technical assistance, material support and training, in all areas of preventing and combating of corruption.[713] States also have to consider affording one another training and assistance and the mutual exchange of relevant experience and specialized knowledge, which will facilitate international cooperation between States in the areas of extradition and mutual legal assistance.[714] In addition, States are under the international obligation to strengthen efforts to maximize operational and training activities in international and regional organizations and in the framework of relevant bilateral and multilateral agreements or arrangements.[715] In the context of information exchange, States are called upon to consider developing and sharing with each other and through international and regional organizations statistics,

711 UNCAC, Art. 62(2)(d).

712 UNCAC, Art. 60(7). States are also called upon to consider making voluntary contributions to the United Nations Office on Drugs and Crime for the purpose of fostering, through the Office, programmes and projects in developing countries with a view to implementing the Convention. UNCAC, Art. 60(8). Indeed, several countries have made such contributions. For example, during the period 2008–2009, over US$7 million was donated to UNODC for anti-corruption action. See, COSP Third Session, *Preliminary Proposals for Possible Technical Assistance Activities to Respond to Needs Identified by States Parties through the Self-Assessment Reports: Discussion paper prepared by the Secretariat*, CAC/COSP/2009/5, 8 October 2009, 8–9.

713 UNCAC, Art. 60(2); Inter-American Convention against Corruption, Art. 14(2); AU Convention against Corruption, Art. 18(4). In addition, States have to consider assisting one another, upon request, in conducting evaluations, studies and research relating to the types, causes, effects and costs of corruption in their respective countries, with a view to developing, with the participation of competent authorities and society, strategies and action plans to combat corruption. UNCAC, Art. 60(4); AU Convention against Corruption, Art. 18(3).

714 UNCAC, Art. 60(2). States may also cooperate in providing each other with the names of experts who could assist in the recovery of proceeds of corruption. UNCAC, Art. 60(5).

715 UNCAC, Art. 60(3). States are also required to consider using subregional, regional and international conferences and seminars to promote cooperation and technical assistance and to stimulate discussion on problems of mutual concern, including the special problems and needs of developing countries and countries with economies in transition. UNCAC, Art. 60(6).

analytical expertise concerning corruption and information with a view to developing, insofar as possible, common definitions, standards and methodologies, as well as information on best practices to prevent and combat corruption.[716]

Another way for States to cooperate combating corruption is through the UNCAC Conference of the States Parties (COSP).[717] Obviously, this only applies to States Parties to the UNCAC. The objectives of the COSP constitute a third group of obligations in relation to international cooperation to combat corruption and include:

(a) facilitating technical assistance and information exchange activities, including by encouraging the mobilization of voluntary contributions;[718]
(b) taking note of the technical assistance requirements of States Parties with regard to the implementation of the UNCAC and recommending any action it may deem necessary in that respect;[719]
(c) facilitating the exchange of information among States Parties on patterns and trends in corruption and on successful practices for preventing and combating it and for the return of proceeds of crime;[720]
(d) cooperating with relevant international and regional organizations and mechanisms and non-governmental organizations, making use of relevant information produced by other international and regional mechanisms in order to avoid unnecessary duplication of work;[721] and
(e) reviewing periodically the implementation of the UNCAC by its States Parties and making relevant recommendations.[722]

As shown in this section, the international obligations respecting international cooperation are numerous and are intended to regulate a wide variety of matters.

---

716 UNCAC, Art. 61.

717 The objectives of the Conference of the States Parties are to improve the capacity of and cooperation between States Parties to achieve the objectives set forth in the UNCAC and to promote and review its implementation. UNCAC, Art. 63. Most of the international conventions against corruption set up an organ with similar objectives as the UNCAC's Conference of the States Parties, particularly to monitor implementation. CoE Civil Law Convention, Art. 14; CoE Criminal Law Convention, Art. 24; OECD Convention, Art. 12; AU Convention against Corruption, Art. 22, SADC Protocol against Corruption, Art. 11. Moreover, States must provide the Conference of the States Parties with information on its programmes, plans and practices, as well as on legislative and administrative measures to implement this Convention, as required by the Conference of the States Parties. UNCAC, Art. 63(6).

718 UNCAC, Art. 63(4)(a).

719 UNCAC, Art. 63(4)(g).

720 UNCAC, Art. 63(4)(b).

721 UNCAC, Art. 63(4)(c-d). The COSP may also consider information received from relevant non-governmental organizations. UNCAC, Art. 63(6).

722 UNCAC, Art. 63(4)(e).

The international legal framework reinforces existing initiatives and creates quasi-legal obligations. However, although they consist of obligations, as observed earlier, most of them call upon States to consider adopting certain measures, and there is therefore no obligation to achieve a specific objective. Moreover, the few obligations that require States to adopt certain measures do so in such broad terms and usually with the qualification "to the extent possible" with the effect that it is virtually impossible to hold States accountable for non-compliance. International cooperation to combat corruption is not new.[723] A number of countries have consistently provided technical assistance in this field, as have international organizations, such as the World Bank, OECD, UNDP and UNODC. The main challenge today is how to coordinate the existing and growing international technical cooperation programmes to combat corruption.[724]

CONCLUSION

Preventive measures have the potential to make corruption riskier and more difficult, while at the same time laying the basis for enforcement of anti-corruption laws. The international obligations examined in this Chapter for the prevention of corruption are far from constituting a strong and complete package of measures that can realistically prevent corruption. Unfortunately, most of the obligations only call on States to try to adopt measures, but do not impose a requirement to achieve the necessary result with a view to the meaningful prevention of corruption. Nevertheless, these types of obligations are not completely devoid of any relevance. As already indicated in Chapter III, States are required to endeavour to adopt the preventive measures and can be held accountable if no attempt is made on their part to try to adopt such measures.

Anti-corruption international obligations relating to preventive measures do address some of the usual systemic weaknesses which facilitate corrupt practices and if, well implemented, could significantly reinforce the institutions necessary to prevent corruption. In this connection, the provision on access to information

723 All the major donors have been funding anti-corruption projects in developing countries for years. See, for example, an analysis of anti-corruption projects funded by GIZ. GTZ, *Supporting the Implementation of the United Nations Convention against Corruption: What Technical Assistance Can Do: South Africa, Ghana, Indonesia and Latin American Countries*, 2007.

724 See also Karen Hussmann and Miguel Peñailillo, *How can Technical Assistance Support the Implementation of UNCAC?*, U4 Background Paper for the International Cooperation Workshop on Technical Assistance for the Implementation of UNCAC, Montevideo, May 2007 (Bergen: Anti-Corruption Resource Centre, 2007).

can have a particularly positive influence in the fight against corruption. Yet the timid approach of the international legal framework towards furthering transparency in the private sector and especially in the judiciary makes it hard to envisage long term prevention of corrupt practices. Without an independent, impartial and well functioning judiciary the prevention and repression of corruption becomes more difficult.

CHAPTER VI

CRIMINAL AND CIVIL JURISDICTION OVER CORRUPTION

INTRODUCTION

As noted in the previous Chapter, the prevention of corruption is of great importance, but it is likely to fail without effective prosecution and punishment for corrupt acts. A central pillar of the international legal framework against corruption is therefore the criminalization and enforcement of laws against corruption. The anti-corruption conventions offer a combination of substantive and procedural anti-corruption law. They aim to reinforce domestic substantive criminal law and to strengthen the necessary procedures for effective anti-corruption law enforcement. This Chapter is concerned with jurisdictional issues considered as the first stage in the enforcement of anti-corruption law.

The subject of criminal and civil jurisdiction merits detailed examination, not only because it is at the heart of law enforcement, but also because past anti-corruption legal proceedings, and the lack thereof, have shown the complexity of jurisdictional issues in the enforcement of anti-corruption law. Modern corrupt practices have an inherent transnational element which not only makes it difficult to investigate them, but which also creates challenges to the traditional jurisdictional grounds for combating crime. When a person in one country bribes a high level public official in another country, which State has criminal jurisdiction over the offence? If a third person suffers damage as a result of such bribery, can that person sue one or both parties, and in the courts of which State? Can the public official invoke immunity to avoid both the criminal and civil jurisdiction? In the enforcement of anti-corruption law, a number of issues relating to jurisdiction require clarification. As explained in this Chapter, the international obligations arising out of the international legal framework against corruption provide guidance in this respect.

I. CRIMINAL JURISDICTION

As noted throughout this study, the international legal framework against corruption requires States to adopt numerous anti-corruption laws, including criminal laws, which they are also required to enforce. As explained in this section, there are several obligations for States in relation to their anti-corruption criminal jurisdiction. At the outset, it should be noted that there is no obligation upon States to change the ways in which they exercise their criminal jurisdiction. For States which normally allow prosecutorial discretion, this is respected by the international legal framework. However, although States may allow prosecutorial discretion, the international legal framework reminds them that such discretionary legal power needs to be exercised to maximize the effectiveness of law enforcement measures in respect of corrupt offences and with due regard to the need to deter the commission of such offences.[725] Moreover, such discretion needs to be exercised on the basis of professional motives and should not be subject to improper influence by political interests.[726]

Moreover, the international legal framework has not altered anything for States that do not allow prosecutorial discretion. In most civil law countries, prosecutors are obliged to investigate reported crimes over which the courts have jurisdiction. This also applies to corruption. Certain countries also allow private parties to initiate criminal actions, either in their own capacity or by prompting prosecutorial or judicial investigation. This is called "*constitution de partie civile*" in French and "*querella*" in Spanish and consists of the victim petitioning the State to redress harm resulting from criminal conduct. Actions of this kind can therefore lead to criminal sanctions, although they may also have the advantage of allowing the award of civil damages to victims.[727] Victims in civil law countries therefore become parties to the case, and cases may be maintained even in the presence of objections by the prosecution authorities. This also applies to corruption proceedings.[728]

---

725 UNCAC, Art. 30(3).

726 OECD, *Commentaries on the Convention on Combating Bribery of Foreign Public Officials in International Business Transactions*, DAFFE/IME/BR(97)20, 21 November 1997, para. 27.

727 See, Open Society Justice Initiative, *Legal Remedies for the Resource Curse: A Digest of Experience in Using Law to Combat Natural Resource Corruption* (New York: Open Society Institute, 2005), 24. For a contrary view in the context of corruption, see Daniel Dommel, "Les défis de la corruption" (Transparency International Working Paper, 1999).

728 Similarly, the international legal framework against corruption requires States to enable the views and concerns of victims to be presented and considered at an appropriate stage of criminal proceedings in a manner not prejudicial to the rights of the defence (UNCAC, Art. 32(5)). In practice, many States allow for victims to appear (other than as witnesses) and express themselves. In general, this is allowed following the conviction of the accused in order to avoid any finding prejudicial to the eventual outcome in the case. UNODC, *Legislative Guide for the Implementation of the United Nations Convention against Corruption* (Vienna, New York: United Nations, 2006), para. 450.

However, in practice, private parties initiating criminal proceedings for corruption would appear to face considerable obstacles, particularly in establishing legal standing. For example, in France non-governmental organizations in cooperation with individuals have attempted to initiate a series of criminal proceedings against the Presidents of Gabon, Republic of Congo, and Equatorial Guinea for their purchase of luxurious real estate and cars in France with funds that allegedly had been embezzled from their States.[729] Yet the French courts have systematically rejected these cases due to lack of legal standing. Although certain countries allow private parties to initiate criminal actions, this may prove especially difficult in cases of corruption in which proof of damage or of an affected legal right may not be possible. This is examined in more detail in section II below.

1. GROUNDS FOR CRIMINAL JURISDICTION

The international obligations relating to the criminal jurisdiction of States in respect of corrupt acts do not revolutionize similar obligations arising out of other international law regimes. As examined below, States may exercise their criminal jurisdiction on the basis of various grounds, namely territorial, nationality, protective and universal.

1.1. Territorial jurisdiction

The basic principle of criminal jurisdiction is that a crime that is committed in a State's territory is justiciable in that State. This applies the essential territoriality of sovereignty, the sum of the legal competences of a State. It is the most commonly exercised and least controversial basis for criminal jurisdiction. Accordingly, States are under the international obligation to establish their jurisdiction over corrupt acts when the offence is committed in whole or in part in their territory,[730] or on board a vessel flying the flag of the State or on an aircraft registered under the law of the State,[731] which are generally understood as extensions of the territory.

---

729 See, Sherpa, *Biens mal acquis*, available at www.asso-sherpa.org/index.php?page=corruption &ssmenu=actions&id=26 (last visited 29 April 2012).

730 Territory is defined by geographical areas separated by borderlines from other areas and united under a common legal system and it includes the airspace above the land, the earth beneath it, and up to twelve miles of the territorial sea adjacent to the coast. Vaughn Lowe, "Jurisdiction," in *International Law*, ed. Malcolm D. Evans, 2nd ed. (Oxford: Oxford University Press, 2006), 342.

731 UNCAC, Art. 42(1)(a) and (b); Inter-American Convention against Corruption, Art. 5(1); CoE Criminal Law Convention, Art. 17(1)(a); OECD Convention, Art. 4(1); AU Convention against Corruption, Art. 13(1)(a); UNODC, *Legislative Guide for the Implementation of the United Nations Convention against Corruption*, para. 41. The United States does not exercise

In corruption cases, the issue in relation to territorial jurisdiction is how to determine "the place" where the corrupt act was committed. At the outset, it should be recalled that it is not necessary for an offence as a whole to be committed exclusively on the territory of a State for it to be able to establish jurisdiction. If only parts of the offence, for example the acceptance or the offer of a bribe, are committed on its territory, a State may still exercise jurisdiction.[732] For example, the jurisdictional provisions of the FCPA were originally strictly territorial, requiring the use of the mail or another instrumentality of interstate or foreign commerce in furtherance of the improper payment. This was indeed a broad basis of territoriality, prosecution could take place simply on the basis of telephone calls or e-mail transmissions with a US nexus, or the use of the banking system. It was not necessary for the entirety of the corrupt act to take place in the United States, as a single act in furtherance of the offence would suffice. While the UNCAC only provides that the act must be "committed in the territory", without stipulating whether this means the whole or part of the act, it should be understood that the commission of a corrupt act inherently covers the possibility that solely a part of the act is actually committed in the territory of the State. A restrictive interpretation of the phrase "committed in the territory" to mean the commission of the entire corrupt act in the territory of a State would render territorial jurisdiction almost impossible, in view of the increase in globalized relations over the past two decades.

In cases where several parts of a corrupt practice are carried out in different States, all such States therefore have territorial jurisdiction. It is generally agreed by scholars that territorial jurisdiction has spawned two variants (subjective and objective) to take into account criminal practices committed in two or more countries.[733] Under the principle of subjective territoriality, a State exercises jurisdiction over a crime in which one element is committed in that State, or if the crime is considered to have originated in that State, but to have been completed abroad. A second principle is the "effects doctrine", or objective territoriality, which refers to the ability of a State to assert jurisdiction over

plenary jurisdiction over offences that are committed on board ships flying its flag or aircraft registered under its laws. Accordingly, the US has made a reservation to this provision in the UNCAC, whereby it reserves the right not to exercise jurisdiction with respect to offences that are committed on board ships flying its flag or aircraft registered under its laws. See, United States Reservation to the UNCAC, para. 2, available at http://treaties.un.org/Pages/ViewDetails.aspx?src=IND&mtdsg_no=XVIII-14&chapter=18&lang=en (last visited 29 April 2012).

732 CoE Criminal Law Convention Explanatory Report, para. 79.

733 Edwin D. Dickinson, ed., "Harvard Research in International Law: II: Jurisdiction with Respect to Crime," *American Journal of International Law Supplement* 29 (1935): 484–487; Michael Akehurst, "Jurisdiction in International Law," *British Yearbook of International Law* 46 (1972): 152–156; Lowe, "Jurisdiction," 343–345; Ilias Bantekas and Susan Nash, *International Criminal Law*, 2nd ed. (London [etc.]: Cavendish Publ, 2003), 144–149.

certain acts committed by foreign nationals outside its jurisdiction in cases where the conduct has an effect within the State, and therefore focuses on the location of the effects of the act, not the location of the act itself.[734]

The place where a corrupt act is committed may be any of the following:

- The location of the corruptor when the *pactum* is agreed upon;
- The location of the corrupted when the *pactum* is agreed upon;
- The location where the payment starts from (for example, a bank in another State);
- The location where the payment ends up (for example, a bank in a third State);
- The location where the account holder is located (for example, an offshore company);
- The location where the act by the corrupted is performed; and
- The location where the effect of the act of corruption is produced.[735]

The complex nature of many corrupt practices clearly requires a broad interpretation of criminal territorial jurisdiction under which an extensive physical connection to the corrupt act is not required.[736] States should therefore extend territorial jurisdiction to cover corrupt acts that occur overseas but have an impact within their State, or where only a small part of the conduct constituting the offence occurs in their territory.

1.2. Nationality jurisdiction

As described above, territorial jurisdiction in respect of corruption is quite broad. Nevertheless, the international legal framework against corruption also refers to other bases of jurisdiction. States are encouraged to exercise their jurisdiction even when neither a part of the corrupt act, nor its effects are produced in their territory.

States are encouraged to exercise jurisdiction over corrupt acts when they are committed by their nationals abroad.[737] This is the active nationality (or

---

734 However, the effects doctrine and objective territoriality are not exactly the same concepts. While objective territoriality requires some element of intraterritorial conduct, the effects doctrine, as applied by the United States, does not require any intraterritorial conduct to take place in the State. See, Lowe, "Jurisdiction," 344–345.

735 Marc Henzelin, *Looking for a Forum*, Paper presented at the IBA Anticorruption Conference: The Awakening Giant of Anti-Corruption Enforcement (Paris, May 4, 2005), 6.

736 In the context of the bribery of foreign public officials, see OECD, *Commentaries on the Convention on Combating Bribery of Foreign Public Officials in International Business Transactions*, para. 25.

737 UNCAC, Art. 42(2)(b); Inter-American Convention against Corruption, Art. 5(2); CoE Criminal Law Convention, Art. 17(1)(b); EU Convention against Corruption, Art. 7(1)(b-d)

personality) approach to jurisdiction, which is mostly prevalent in civil law countries, as well as some common law jurisdictions. Some States even assume jurisdiction over persons who are not nationals, but who are residents of or domiciled in the State and have committed certain crimes abroad.[738] The special case of transnational bribery needs to be highlighted in relation to this approach to jurisdiction. This specific corrupt act is inherently extraterritorial, and it is therefore surprising that, with the exception of the African Union Convention and the SADC Protocol, all the other anti-corruption instruments do not envisage a compulsory jurisdiction for this crime when committed by the nationals of a State abroad.[739] Although in some cases bribes are offered, promised or given to a foreign public official or an official of an international organization without the briber ever leaving her or his country of nationality, in many situations this occurs in a foreign country, usually the country of nationality or residence of the official. For this reason, and taking into account the fact that States are under the international obligation to criminalize active transnational bribery,[740] States need to establish their criminal jurisdiction over their nationals, as a minimum, when they engage in transnational bribery.

In addition to jurisdiction on the basis of active personality or nationality, States can establish passive nationality (or personality) jurisdiction, whereby States exercise jurisdiction over corrupt acts committed against their own nationals.[741] This has traditionally been contested as a ground for jurisdiction by certain international law scholars and States.[742] However, particularly in view of the current upsurge in transnational crime and terrorist activity, it is now meeting

and 7(2). Under the AU Convention against Corruption and the SADC Protocol against Corruption, this is a mandatory obligation. See, AU Convention against Corruption, Art. 13(1)(b), and SADC Protocol against Corruption, Art. 5(1)(b). States are in principle free to regulate who their nationals are. Nationality is normally granted to anyone born in the territory (also known as *jus soli*) or to children of whom one or both of the parents are themselves nationals of the State (known as *jus sanguinis*). The nationality of corporations is also a matter to be regulated by each State. In general, common law States accord nationality to companies on the basis of their incorporation in the territory of the State, regardless of where the actual business or management of the company is carried out. Civil law States tend to confer nationality on the basis of the place where the company has the seat of its management. See, Lowe, "Jurisdiction," 345–346.

738 For example, Denmark, Finland, Malaysia, Netherlands, Norway, Russian Federation, Sweden and UAE. See also, Inter-American Convention against Corruption, Art. 5(2); AU Convention against Corruption, Art. 13(1)(b).

739 Under the OECD Convention, States Parties are obliged to establish jurisdiction to prosecute their nationals for bribery of a foreign public official where such States have jurisdiction to prosecute their nationals for offences committed abroad. See, OECD Convention, Art. 4(2).

740 See, UNCAC, Art. 16(1); UNODC, *Legislative Guide for the Implementation of the United Nations Convention against Corruption*, para. 213.

741 UNCAC, Art. 42(2)(a).

742 See, Robert Cryer, *An Introduction to International Criminal Law and Procedure* (Cambridge: Cambridge University Press, 2007), 42; Ian Brownlie, *Principles of Public International Law*, 6th ed. (Oxford: Oxford University Press, 2003), 302; Frederick A. Mann, "The Doctrine of

with relatively little opposition.[743] The passive nationality ground for jurisdiction should not be confused with "diplomatic protection", which refers to the right of a State to intervene diplomatically or to raise an international claim on behalf of its nationals against another State. It is important to clarify what should be understood by a corrupt act committed "against" a national. Reference is clearly made in this respect to cases in which a corrupt act produces a victim, i.e. someone that is harmed by the corrupt act in any way. For example, when company A is excluded from a procurement procedure in a foreign State because another foreign company (company B) has bribed the public official making the selection, the State of nationality of company A may want to assert jurisdiction on the case on the basis of passive nationality. However, in many cases of corruption it is very difficult to identify a specific harm or victim. As a result, criminal jurisdiction on the basis of passive nationality may not be so valuable for anti-corruption purposes.

1.3. Protective jurisdiction

Furthermore, in accordance with the international legal framework against corruption, States may also exercise criminal jurisdiction when a corrupt act is committed against the State itself.[744] This refers to the so-called protective principle, which recognizes the power of a State to assert jurisdiction over a limited range of crimes committed by foreign nationals outside its territory in cases where the crime prejudices the State's vital interests, including its economic interests, national security, counterfeiting the State's currency and espionage.[745] This ground for jurisdiction is relevant to combating corruption as a corrupt act organized and perpetrated in a foreign State may have detrimental effects on the vital interests of another State, and particularly on its security and economic interests. For example, corruption in the granting of visas or immigration papers in one country for entry into another may affect the security interests of the latter country. Jurisdiction on the basis of the protective principle is important in cases of corruption because in many cases it is difficult to establish jurisdiction on any other basis. For example, in a famous case in Lesotho,[746] in which the

---

Jurisdiction in International Law," *Recueil des cours* 111, no. I (1964): 39. The United States is one of the countries that has contested this approach.

743 See Arrest warrant of 11 April 2000 (Democratic Republic of the Congo v. Belgium), Judgment, I.C.J. Reports 2002, 3 (Joint Separate Opinion of Judges Higgins, Kooijmans and Buergenthal, para. 47, and Separate opinion of President Guillaume, para 16).

744 UNCAC, Art. 42(2)(d); AU Convention against Corruption, Art. 13(1)(d).

745 Lowe, "Jurisdiction," 347–348.

746 This case concerned corruption in the World Bank funded Lesotho Highlands Water Project, in which contractors and consultants had bribed the authorities of the Project, most notably its chief executive Masupha Sole, in exchange for profitable contracts. The Lesotho authorities prosecuted both M. Sole and the bribers. Here, reference is made to the case against Masupha Sole.

prosecution only had evidence that money had been paid secretly into Swiss accounts belonging to the accused, the inability of the prosecution to prove where the alleged corrupt agreements had been concluded led to a particularly important ruling on jurisdiction. The judge held that it had been a State official from Lesotho who had been involved in the bribes and that the harm that resulted from them related to Lesotho. This gave Lesotho jurisdiction.[747] The Court of Appeals upheld the decision and found:

> "The Crown argued that [jurisdiction] was sufficiently established by the harmful consequences immediately inflicted upon the integrity of public administration in Lesotho by the conclusion of the corrupt agreements. We agree. The development scheme administered by the LHDA is ... of great importance to Lesotho, and indeed, to the Southern African Development Community. It involves Lesotho's international relations and is central to its economic future. Its success and integrity matter vitally to this country. Corrupt agreements by its chief executive with its international contractors, if established, would be a cancer at its heart."[748]

In addition, with regard to the offence of money laundering, the international legal framework against corruption provides that States may also wish to establish jurisdiction when the offence constitutes participation, association or conspiracy to commit, attempt to commit, aiding, abetting, facilitating and counselling or laundering of proceeds of corruption committed outside its territory in connection with the laundering of proceeds of corruption in its territory.[749]

1.4. Universal or quasi-universal jurisdiction

The international legal framework further provides that States may exercise their criminal jurisdiction on any other basis established in accordance with their domestic law.[750] This clause begs the question of the acceptance for corruption of one additional recognized basis of jurisdiction, namely universal jurisdiction. Under universal jurisdiction, a State would assert jurisdiction over a corrupt act committed by non-nationals against non-nationals outside its territory and having no connection to or impact on the State. Universal jurisdiction is based solely on the nature of the crime and is generally recognized for a very limited list of crimes, such as piracy, war crimes and genocide.[751]

---

747 Rex v. Ephraim Masupha Sole [High Court of Lesotho] 20 May 2002, available at www.ipocafrica.org/index.php?option=com_content&view=article&id=71&Itemid=66 (last visited 29 April 2012).

748 Ephraim Masupha Sole v. The Crown [Court of Appeal of Lesotho], 14 April 2003, para. 21, available at www.ipocafrica.org/index.php?option=com_content&view=article&id=71&Itemid=66 (last visited 29 April 2012).

749 UNCAC, Art. 42(2)(c).

750 UNCAC, Art. 42(6).

751 See, for example, Rosalyn Higgins, *Problems and Process: International Law and How We Use It* (Oxford: Clarendon Press, 1994), 58; Princeton University Program in Law and Public

However it is uncertain whether corruption offences fall within this category of serious crimes meriting universal jurisdiction, as corruption cannot be considered to be crime offensive to the international community as a whole or at least not in the same way as war crimes or genocide. There are nevertheless those who argue that major cases of corruption, such as a President embezzling millions of dollars from State assets, should be subject to universal jurisdiction.[752] However, up to now they have failed to make a convincing argument for extending universal jurisdiction to corruption crimes. Their claims are based on the extremely serious detrimental effects of corruption, which they compare to the effects of genocide and similar crimes. Yet, while the consequences of corruption can be and have proved to be disastrous,[753] they cannot in any way be compared to the consequences of crimes such as genocide or crimes against humanity. Despite the fact that the negative effects of corruption may be quantitatively massive in economic and social terms, genocide and similar crimes constitute atrocities that shock the conscience of humanity as whole and cannot be measured in quantitative terms.

The nature of the crime of corruption does not therefore meet the threshold usually required for crimes subject to be universal jurisdiction. However, nor does the crime of piracy, which has far less detrimental effects on society than corruption. And yet piracy is normally considered to be a crime for which universal jurisdiction is possible, not because of its nature, but because it is committed on the high seas where no State has jurisdiction. Accordingly, in order to combat piracy, all States are given jurisdiction. This is a practical basis for universal jurisdiction which is lacking in cases of corruption, since corrupt acts are always committed in one or more jurisdictions. A characteristic of corruption cases is the lack of political willingness or ability, which results in impunity. Unfortunately, this is not a sufficient ground to elevate corruption to the group of crimes that are subject to universal jurisdiction, and international law does not appear to recognize universal jurisdiction for corruption.

Nevertheless, in view of the emergence of the international legal framework against corruption, including the several multilateral treaties against corruption,

---

Affairs, *The Princeton Principles on Universal Jurisdiction*, 2001; Institut de Droit International, dix-septième commission, *La compétence universelle en matière pénale à l'égard du crime de génocide, des crimes contre l'humanité et des crimes de guerre*, Resolution of 26 August 2005.

752 See, inter alia, Ndiva Kofele-Kale, *International Law of Responsibility for Economic Crimes: Holding Heads of State and Other High Ranking State Officials Individually Liable for Acts of Fraudulent Enrichment* (The Hague: Kluwer Law International, 1995), 344–350; Chile Eboe-Osuji, "Kleptocracy: A Desired Subject of International Criminal Law that is in Dire Need of Prosecution by Universal Jurisdiction," in *African Perspectives on International Criminal Justice*, ed. Edward K Kwakwa and Evelyn A. Ankumah (Accra: Africa Legal Aid, 2005), 121–132.

753 On the consequences of corruption, see Chapter II.

a form of quasi-universal jurisdiction has emerged between the parties.[754] As described in this section, States may prosecute offenders on the basis of a number of stated jurisdictional grounds, ranging from territoriality to nationality, and protective principles. This, together with the obligation to extradite or prosecute (discussed below), creates a treaty based quasi-universal jurisdiction over corruption. The intention of the international legal framework is to expand the jurisdiction of States with a view to ensuring that serious transnational crimes do not go unprosecuted as a result of jurisdictional gaps.[755]

2. THE PROBLEM OF CONCURRENT JURISDICTIONS

It should be noted that the various bases for jurisdiction are often interweaved in practice. This could lead to the problem of concurrent jurisdiction, not only for criminal, but also civil jurisdiction. For example, in 2004, the Norwegian oil company Statoil was prosecuted in its home country and fined US$3 million for trading in influence in the Islamic Republic of Iran in connection with its earlier pursuit of oil concessions in that country.[756] Subsequently, as Statoil was also listed in the United States, the US SEC and the US Department of Justice both prosecuted the company for the same conduct. The case in the United States was ultimately resolved through a settlement in late 2006, in which the company agreed to pay a fine of US$ 21 million to the US authorities, against which it received credit for the fine paid to the Norwegian authorities.[757] Concurring jurisdiction is problematic since, as shown by this example, it may lead to a person being tried twice for the same offence. This contravenes the national constitutional, criminal and international human rights principle of *ne bis in idem* (also called double jeopardy). The international legal framework against corruption does not resolve the issue of concurring jurisdictions and its possible effect on the principle of *ne bis in idem*. While the OECD, EU and AU anti-corruption conventions seem to oppose trying a person twice for the same offence,[758] the UNCAC provides no clarification. In fact, the UNCAC can be

754 On quasi-universal jurisdiction, see Malcolm Nathan Shaw, *International Law*, 6th ed. (Cambridge [etc]: Cambridge University Press, 2008), 673–680; Lowe, "Jurisdiction," 349–351.

755 UNODC, *Legislative Guide for the Implementation of the United Nations Convention against Corruption*, para. 519.

756 International Bar Association, *Report of the Task Force on Extraterritorial Jurisdiction*, 2009, 211–212, available at www.ibanet.org (last visited 29 April 2012).

757 For this and other cases of concurrent jurisdiction, such as Siemens, TSKJ, Lesotho Highlands Water Project, see Ibid., 211–217.

758 The OECD Convention, in Article Art. 4(3), provides that consultation should be carried out among concurring States with "a view to determining the most appropriate jurisdiction for prosecution." The EU Convention, Article 9(2), refers to centralizing the prosecution in a single Member State where possible; and the AU Convention against Corruption, in Article 13.3 provides that a person shall not be tried twice for the same offence.

interpreted as accepting multiple concurrent jurisdictions. Article 42(5) provides that the competent authorities of concurring jurisdictions "shall, as appropriate, consult one another with a view to coordinating their actions." In general international law, the *ne bis in idem* principle traditionally does not apply between sovereign States.[759] Yet this seems to be changing, and certain international treaties and a number of scholars have advocated transnational *ne bis in idem* protection.[760] Accordingly, when enforcing anti-corruption law, States have to take the *ne bis in idem* principle into account. Where they assert jurisdiction over a corruption case that has been or is simultaneously being investigated or prosecuted in another State, as a minimum they need to take into account the foreign proceedings, particularly with regard to the punishment or penalty.

3. THE OBLIGATION TO EXTRADITE OR PROSECUTE

In line with what is almost standard practice in regard to international and transnational crimes, the international legal framework against corruption requires States to extradite or prosecute alleged offenders of corrupt acts, also known as the *aut dedere aut judicare* obligation. Specifically, States are required to establish their jurisdiction over corrupt acts when the alleged offender is present in their territory and they do not extradite such a person on the ground that the person is one of their nationals.[761] Indeed, many States are prohibited by their constitutions from extraditing their own nationals. States are also encouraged to exercise jurisdiction when the alleged offender is in their territory and they do not extradite her or him for any other reason.[762]

While the "extradite" part of the *aut dedere aut judicare* obligation is fairly straightforward, and is discussed in detail in Chapter VIII, the "prosecute" part of the obligations needs clarification. The obligation to prosecute should be

---

759 Immi Tallgren and Astrid Reisinger Coracini, "Article 20: Ne Bis In Idem," in *Commentary on the Rome Statute of the International Criminal Court -Observers' Notes, Article by Article-*, ed. Otto Triffterer, 2nd ed. (Munich: Verlag C.H.Beck, 2008), 673–674. The United Nations Human Rights Committee has stated that the rule of *ne bis in idem* does not exclude prosecutions for the same offence in different States. See, UN HRC Communication 204/1986 *A. P. v. Italy* [2 November 1987] para. 7.3.

760 See, for example, Convention of 19 June 1990 applying the Schengen Agreement of 14 June 1985 between the Governments of the States of the Benelux Economic Union, the Federal Republic of Germany and the French Republic on the Gradual Abolition of Checks at their Common Borders, 30 I.L.M. 84 (1991); Alexander Poels, "A Need for Transnational Non Bis In Idem Protection in International Human Rights Law," *Netherlands Quarterly of Human Rights* 23, no. 3 (2005): 329–347; Dax R. Lopez, "Not Twice for the Same: How the Dual Sovereignty Doctrine is Used to Circumvent Non Bis In Idem," *Vanderbilt Journal of Transnational Law* 33 (2000): 1263–1312.

761 UNCAC, Arts. 42(3) and 44(11); Inter-American Convention against Corruption, Art. 5(3); CoE Criminal Law Convention, Art. 17(3); AU Convention against Corruption, Art. 13(1)(c).

762 UNCAC, Art. 42(4).

understood in reality as an obligation to submit the case to the competent authorities of a State for the purposes of prosecution.[763] The duty is not to prosecute, let alone to punish, and States retain their prosecutorial discretion.[764] To this end, the relevant authorities have to take decisions and conduct proceedings in the same manner as in the case of any other offence of a grave nature under the domestic law of that State, and the States concerned are required to cooperate with each other, particularly on procedural and evidentiary aspects to ensure the efficiency of the prosecution.[765] Moreover, in order to meet the obligation to prosecute when extradition is refused, they are also required to allocate adequate human and budgetary resources to enable effective domestic prosecution.[766]

Regrettably, the *aut dedere aut judicare* obligation, as set out in the international legal framework against corruption, is considerably more limited than the equivalent obligation under other regimes (such as in the Hague Convention for the Suppression of Unlawful Seizure of Aircraft).[767] The obligation to prosecute is only subsidiary to that of extradition. This means that prosecution only occurs if: (1) the alleged offender is not extradited on the basis that she or he is a national of the requested State; *and* (2) if such prosecution is demanded by the requesting State. This subsidiarity is a result of the preference in practice for extradition instead of the exercise of jurisdiction by a State foreign to the place where the crime was committed. It is often very difficult in practice to try a person for an offence committed outside the territorial jurisdiction of a court. Yet realistically prosecution is the best option in cases where States, mostly of the civil law tradition, cannot extradite their nationals. Conversely, if the State refuses to extradite the alleged offender on other grounds, such as human rights concerns, or refuses extradition simply without giving a reason, or if the requesting State does not call on the requested State to prosecute the accused, there is no subsidiary obligation to prosecute the alleged offender.

Moreover, the obligation to extradite or prosecute in the anti-corruption regime is not in line with obligations relating to criminal jurisdiction. As indicated above, States are only obliged to establish territorial jurisdiction. It is therefore possible that some States will not be able to comply with the *aut dedere aut judicare* obligation when the corrupt act can only be prosecuted under

763 UNCAC, Art. 44(11).
764 This is the traditional understanding of the clause "to prosecute" in *aut dedere aut judicare* obligations.
765 UNCAC, Art. 44(11).
766 UNODC, *Legislative Guide for the Implementation of the United Nations Convention against Corruption*, para. 568.
767 See, Hague Convention for the Suppression of Unlawful Seizure of Aircraft, 1970, 860 U.N.T.S. 105, Art. 4(2).

extraterritorial jurisdiction. For States to be able to meet the obligation to extradite or prosecute, they therefore need to make provision in their domestic legislation for extraterritorial jurisdiction for corruption cases, especially when jurisdiction is based on the active nationality ground. Clearly, the notion of *aut dedere aut judicare* contained in the anti-corruption regime is defined so restrictively that it does not constitute a significant and effective tool in combating corruption and avoiding impunity and safe haven States.

II. CIVIL JURISDICTION

Although much less well-known than criminal prosecution, civil litigation for corruption, through which a victim of a corrupt act sues a corrupt person to obtain compensation for the damage suffered, is also known to exist. This has arisen in the majority of cases around the principal-agency relationship and the concept of fiduciary duty.[768] These legal proceedings are normally referred to as civil proceedings and apply civil law.[769] Albeit with substantive and procedural differences, civil proceedings are recognized in every legal system throughout the world. In contrast with criminal law, civil law is a branch of law that is the general part of private law and deals with disputes between individuals and/or organizations, in which compensation may be awarded to the victim.[770] In civil law proceedings, the law usually applied is the law of tort in common law systems and the law of non-contractual obligations in civil law jurisdictions, as well as labour law, environmental law, agency law and commercial/corporate law.

Yet it was only with the Council of Europe Civil Law Convention, and subsequently the UNCAC, that this practice became part of the international legal framework against corruption. States are therefore under the international obligation to ensure that entities or persons who have suffered damage as a result of an act of corruption have the right to initiate legal proceedings against those

---

768 See, Colin Nicholls, Tim Daniel and John Hatchard, *Corruption and Misuse of Public Office* (Oxford: Oxford University Press, 2006), 228.

769 However, the criminal-civil distinction is not always obvious. See, for example, Mary M. Cheh, "Constitutional Limits on Using Civil Remedies To Achieve Criminal Law Objectives: Understanding and Transcending the Criminal-Civil Law Distinction," *Hastings Law Journal* 42 (1991): 1325–1413.

770 As indicated earlier, although most States make a distinction between their criminal and civil law jurisdictions, a number of States of the civil law tradition allow civil claims to be made in the course of criminal proceedings in order for the victim to recover damages. This is usually called *action civile* in French or *querella* in Spanish and is accepted for example, in Argentina, Bolivia, Bulgaria, China, Colombia, Denmark, France, Germany, Italy, Poland, Romania, Russian Federation, Senegal and Sweden.

responsible for the damage in order to obtain compensation.[771] This clearly does not guarantee victims compensation or restitution, but requires legislative or other measures to provide for procedures whereby compensation or restitution can be sought or claimed. In other words, States must provide in their internal laws for the right to bring a civil action in corruption cases and the court or jury, in each individual case, decides whether or not the conditions for compensation are fulfilled.[772]

In addition, the international legal framework against corruption encourages States to assist each other in investigations of and proceedings in civil and administrative matters relating to corruption.[773] States have to allow another State to initiate civil action in their courts to establish title to or ownership of property acquired through the commission of a corrupt act.[774] This is important because, as recalled earlier, many cases of corruption have a certain international element, and the allegedly person corrupt and/or the assets may have disappeared abroad. International regulation of civil litigation is therefore necessary. When dealing with cases of corruption involving international elements, several problems may arise, such as obtaining evidence, recognizing and enforcing foreign judgments, and even uncertainties as to the applicable law. States can assist each other in investigations for civil proceedings relating to corruption through the application of existing international legal instruments in this field, such as the Brussels I Regulation and the New Lugano Convention on Jurisdiction and Enforcement of Judgments in Civil and Commercial Matters of 2000 and 2007 respectively,[775] the 1965 Hague Convention on the Service Abroad of Judicial and Extra-Judicial Documents in Civil or Commercial Matters[776] and the 1970 Hague Convention on the Taking of Evidence Abroad in Civil or Commercial Matters.[777]

771 UNCAC, Art. 35, CoE Civil Law Convention. The CoE Civil Law Convention was specifically drafted to address civil jurisdiction in the enforcement of anti-corruption law, but only for the act of bribery. CoE Civil Law Convention, Art. 3(1).

772 CoE Civil Law Convention Explanatory Report, para. 35.

773 UNCAC, Art. 43(1). Under the CoE Civil Law Convention this is not an obligation of best endeavour, but is mandatory. States are required to cooperate in civil proceedings in cases of corruption, especially for the service of documents, obtaining evidence abroad, jurisdiction, recognition, and enforcement of foreign judgments and litigation costs. CoE Civil Law Convention, Art. 13.

774 UNCAC, Art. 53(a). See also Chapter VIII.

775 EU Council Regulation (EC) No. 44/2001 of 22 December 2000 on Jurisdiction and the Recognition and Enforcement of Judgments in Civil and Commercial Matters, Official Journal of the European Communities L 12/1, 16 January 2001; Convention on Jurisdiction and Enforcement of Judgments in Civil and Commercial Matters, Official Journal of the EU L 339/3, 21 December 2007.

776 Hague Convention on the Service Abroad of Judicial and Extra-Judicial Documents in Civil or Commercial Matters (adopted 15 November 1965) 658 U.N.T.S. 163.

777 Hague Convention on the Taking of Evidence Abroad in Civil or Commercial Matters (adopted on 18 March 1970) 847 U.N.T.S. 231.

Civil litigation presents several advantages in corruption cases. One of the main problems with the enforcement of anti-corruption criminal law is that the institutions and officials responsible for the enforcement of criminal law may themselves be corrupt, resulting in the State being unwilling to combat corruption. Alternatively, such institutions or officials may not be corrupt themselves, but may be under-resourced, and the State may therefore be unable to fight corruption. Civil litigation can help to circumvent these situations and, while it cannot replace the enforcement of traditional criminal law against corruption, it might enhance it. For instance, evidence developed in civil litigation may be useful in subsequent criminal prosecutions, or may alert prosecutors to situations which should be investigated.[778] Those affected by corruption can sue the perpetrators under civil law, which therefore effectively empowers victims to take action at their own initiative. This offers the advantage of making the control of corruption partly self-enforcing. So-called "privatized law enforcement" effectively unleashes the power of private civil litigation and collateral legal and administrative sanctions on persons who engage in corrupt practices.[779] Other advantages of civil proceedings include the possibility of establishing liability on the basis of civil standards, without the requirement of a criminal conviction of the offender. Civil law proceedings may therefore be preferred because the civil law burden of proof is lower than that under criminal law.[780] Under the civil law burden of proof, it must be shown that, on a balance of probabilities the defendant engaged in corruption (as opposed to proving this "beyond reasonable doubt").[781]

However, civil litigation may also present disadvantages. Some potential litigants may effectively be excluded due to a lack of resources, lack of access to legal counsel, and for other reasons. Corporations as civil litigants can decide whether to sue, settle or discontinue proceedings on the basis of business or economic criteria which may not be in line with the government's overall anti-corruption strategy. A civil action may also conflict with parallel criminal proceedings or with government policy. Rules are therefore required to resolve such problems. Moreover, civil litigation can be abused and it is therefore necessary for the respective rules to ensure that civil litigation in corruption cases is not used for other purposes. The impact of allegations of corruption in harming reputations

---

778 Lucinda A. Low, *The United Nations Convention against Corruption: The Globalization of Anticorruption Standards*, Paper presented at the Conference of the IBA The Awakening Giant of Anticorruption Enforcement (London, May 4, 2006), 17.

779 Ibid.

780 On the difference between civil and criminal standards generally, see Cheh, "Constitutional Limits on Using Civil Remedies To Achieve Criminal Law Objectives: Understanding and Transcending the Criminal-Civil Law Distinction."

781 For other benefits of civil and administrative, as opposed to criminal remedies, see Bryane Michael, "Suing against Corruption: The Role of Civil Law" (Policy Innovations, July 23, 2007), available at www.policyinnovations.org. (last visited 29 April 2012).

mean that civil litigation can be a potent weapon. Higher initial standards of proof, such as those used in some types of defamation cases, may therefore become necessary.[782]

In any case, civil litigation forms part of the network of avenues for achieving accountability and justice, and consequently combating corruption. Victims are empowered and therefore bring pressure to bear on authorities in the fight against corruption. Moreover, civil litigation may create greater openness for the reporting of corruption, as the compensation that can be awarded to the victims may also act as an incentive for the denunciation of corruption. However, for civil litigation to have the desired positive effect on the enforcement of anti-corruption law, it is important to raise awareness among the population of this possibility for combating against corruption. It is also important that, in addition to the victim being compensated, the judgment is made public so that civil law enforcement performs a preventive role. The most important elements of civil litigation are analysed below.

1. CIVIL LIABILITY

Despite differences in terminology and approach, three main conditions would generally be required in every legal system to engage the liability of a person under civil jurisdiction:

(i) the defendant intentionally or negligently committed an act of corruption, or failed to take reasonable steps to prevent the act of corruption;
(ii) the plaintiff suffered a damage; and
(iii) there is a causal link between the act of corruption and the damage.[783]

The actor must therefore have acted intentionally or negligently for liability to be recognized. This is usually referred to as fault liability. An actor is considered to have acted intentionally if she or he voluntarily took a course of action knowing that it was more than likely to result in harm. A negligent actor should have foreseen the risk, and it is not necessary to establish a motive, malicious intention or desire to inflict harm.[784] In addition to fault liability, most legal systems also contain exceptional rules respecting strict (no fault) liability in relation to specific types of activity or damage, under which an actor can be held liable even

782 Low, *The United Nations Convention against Corruption: The Globalization of Anticorruption Standards*, 17.
783 See also, CoE Civil Law Convention, Art. 4.
784 International Commission of Jurists Expert Panel on Corporate Complicity in International Crimes, *Corporate Complicity and Legal Accountability: Volume 3 Civil Remedies* (Geneva, 2008), 12–17.

if the conduct was not negligent or intentional.[785] This is the case, for example, of the vicarious liability of the employer for the damage that an employee causes to a third party. The employer is responsible if, for example, she or he neglected to organize his company adequately or failed to exert appropriate control over employees.[786]

The second condition for the establishment of civil liability is that there must be damage to the victim. It is generally considered that damage has to be specific to a person or group of persons, as opposed to generalized harm suffered by the entire population. The damage or harm must also have been caused to an interest of the victim that is protected by law, such as life, physical or mental integrity or property rights.[787]

Furthermore, in civil litigation for a conduct to constitute a cause of harm, there must be a third condition, namely a causal connection between the conduct in question and the harm. To determine the existence of a causal connection, it is necessary to establish whether or not the conduct was a *sine qua non* condition, or in other words conduct without which the harm would not have occurred.[788] Once this has been established, the court determines whether the connection warrants liability. As the consequences of an act can theoretically stretch into infinity, most legal systems place a limit upon legal responsibility.[789] This needs to be borne in mind in corruption cases, because corrupt acts may ultimately affect a wide range of human needs. The damage should be an ordinary, and not an extraordinary consequence of corruption. This means that the connection between a corrupt act and the harm produced to a victim must be at a certain degree of approximation. If the link is too indirect or remote, the court will most probably not find civil liability for the damage caused. For example, loss of profit by an unsuccessful competitor, who would have obtained the contract if an act of corruption had not been committed, is an ordinary consequence of corruption and normally gives rise to compensation.[790] In contrast, an example of a remote connection which would not generally be compensated might consist of the unsuccessful competitor falling down the stairs and breaking a leg in disappointment at the loss of the contract.[791]

785 Ibid., 10., citing for example, French Civil Code, Art. 1384; German Civil Code, Chapter 3, section 1; Brazilian Civil Code, Arts. 932 and 933.

786 Ibid.

787 Ibid., 10–11.

788 Ibid., 22.

789 Ibid., 21–22.

790 CoE Civil Law Convention Explanatory Report, para. 45.

791 CoE Civil Law Convention Explanatory Report, para. 45.

2. PERSONAL CIVIL JURISDICTION

In general, a person who can establish the above elements of civil liability can bring a civil claim. As is the case in most domestic jurisdictions, the international legal framework against corruption recognizes the right of "entities and persons" who have suffered damage to bring a civil claim. These are deemed to include States, as well as legal and natural persons.[792] The State may also sue in civil courts as a wronged individual, for example in respect of a contractual dispute with a multinational company. Reference should be made to an innovative provision in Costa Rica which enables the State to sue corrupt persons for "social damage" on behalf of the Costa Rican population.[793] Indeed recently, the company Alcatel-Lucent, a French-American communications company, agreed to pay the Costa Rican State US$ 10 million in compensation for the social damage caused by its corrupt practices.[794]

The principal-agent model is helpful in analysing who may be a claimant in a corruption proceeding.[795] The principal may suffer in a variety of ways as a result of a bribe taken by an agent, as the principal may have to pay more or may be deprived of some type of benefit.[796] While many civil claims for corruption arise within the traditional agency relationship, such as between trustee and beneficiary, partner and co-partner, director and company, employee and employer, legal practitioner and client, there are also claimants that are not directly involved in the relationship between principal-agent, most notably rival bidders, or in other words the company that fails to obtain a valuable contract through the corrupt activity of a competitor.[797]

Plaintiffs should also bear in mind that suits are only accepted by courts if they are brought within a limitation period. Most legal systems provide for two types of periods of limitation for plaintiffs to initiate civil proceedings. Plaintiffs are usually required to commence proceedings: (i) within a fixed period of becoming aware of the act giving rise to the claim or damage (known as the relative

---

792 UN General Assembly, *Report of the Ad Hoc Committee for the Negotiation of a Convention against Corruption on the work of its first to seventh sessions: Addendum: Interpretative Notes for the Official Records (Travaux Préparatoires) of the Negotiation of the United Nations Convention against Corruption*, A/58/422/Add.1, 7 October 2003, para. 37; CoE Civil Law Convention Explanatory Report, para. 27.

793 Costa Rica Criminal Procedural Code, Art. 38.

794 Reuters, UPDATE 1-Alcatel-Lucent to pay $10 mln in Costa Rica case, 21 January 2010, available at www.reuters.com/article/idUSN2121041320100121?type=marketsNews (last visited 29 April 2012).

795 For such an approach, see Nicholls, Daniel, and Hatchard, *Corruption and Misuse of Public Office*, 229–233.

796 Ibid., 229–230.

797 Ibid., 231–233.

period), and (ii) within a longer fixed period from the time the act giving rise to the claim or damage took place, regardless of the date of knowledge by the plaintiff (known as the absolute period). Beyond these periods proceedings may not be commenced. States are free to establish these periods for corruption as they see fit. For Parties to the CoE Civil Law Convention, these periods should be at least three and ten years, respectively.[798]

The defendants in civil litigation can also be any natural or legal person or entity, including the State itself. Within the principal-agent relationship, the defendants in claims arising out of corruption are principally the dishonest agent and the person paying the bribe. However, those who have assisted in the corrupt act and those who have handled property obtained as a result of that act may also be defendants.[799] The civil liability of legal persons is analysed below in Chapter VII. In the present context, reference should be made to the civil liability of the State. The CoE Civil Law Convention provides for State responsibility for bribery. In this sense, States Parties have to establish in their internal law appropriate procedures so that persons who have suffered damage as a result of an act of bribery by public officials in the exercise of their functions can claim compensation from the State.[800] Suing the State to seek compensation for acts that have caused damage is recognized in many legal systems. Although most governments cannot be sued in private civil courts, most countries have administrative tribunals which can award damages similar to those of a civil court. Each State is free to establish the conditions and procedures for filing claims against the State for damage caused by corruption committed by public officials in the exercise of their functions. And, States may, and many do, establish the possibility in their internal laws for the State to sue public officials for the reimbursement of any loss for which they are found responsible.

3. CLASS ACTIONS FOR CORRUPTION

In the context of civil jurisdiction, it is interesting to explore the possibility of bringing class actions for corruption "à la Erin Brockovich."[801] This is an important issue in civil litigation related to corruption. Do or should domestic legal systems permit class actions? The possibility of this type of action is

---

798 CoE Civil Law Convention, Art. 7.

799 See also Nicholls, Daniel, and Hatchard, *Corruption and Misuse of Public Office*, 233–234.

800 CoE Civil Law Convention, Art. 5.

801 Erin Brockovich is a famous paralegal in the United States, known to a global audience as a result of the Hollywood movie by the same name and charmingly played on screen by the actress Julia Roberts. She was instrumental in bringing a class action for harm resulting from environmental exposure to toxic chemicals, which was settled in 1996 awarding to the victims of over US$300 million, one of the largest settlements paid in a class action lawsuit in US history.

essential in corruption cases, because many corrupt practices result in widespread damage across the population. A class action claim begins in the same way as any other action, with the plaintiff bringing a claim against the defendant, but the plaintiff sues on her or his behalf and on behalf of a number of other persons seeking relief in claims showing common issues of law or fact.[802] All members of the class action are bound by the result of the litigation and share any remedy or compensation. Class actions have mostly been used in the United States to remedy group harms, such as mass injuries caused by defective products, or environmental exposure to toxic chemicals or mass financial losses resulting from violations of anti-trust, securities and other consumer protection statutes. Even though the legal system in the United States is most famous in providing for class actions, several other countries also envisage some form of class action system, such as Australia, Canada, Indonesia, Israel and Sweden.[803] An increasing number of countries are now accepting some form of collective or class action.

Although not envisaged in the international legal framework, nothing prevents class actions or other forms of representative or group litigation from being brought before a court in a corruption case. Many cases of corruption result in widespread damage for groups of persons, and sometimes even the whole population. In such cases, and when the effect of corruption on victims is too modest to merit an individual claim, or when an individual claim is impossible due to the inequality between the plaintiff and defendant, victims may consider suing under existing forms of class actions, including at the transnational level.[804] Most importantly in corruption cases, class actions offer the possibility for groups of people to challenge powerful and usually corporate defendants. Those who engage in corrupt practices are usually powerful and well connected, and may have recourse to further corrupt acts to preserve their privileged situation. In many cases, it is in practice unrealistic to bring an individual claim against such "persons." Class actions empower individuals with relatively modest claims that would be impractical against powerful defendants. Class actions and other forms of collective litigation can therefore contribute to the deterring corporate and institutional corruption.

---

802 International Law Association, Committee on International Civil Litigation and the Interests of the Public, *Report on Transnational Group Actions*, Submitted to the ILA 73rd Conference, Rio de Janeiro, 17–21 August, 2008, 5.

803 For a detailed analysis of class actions and other forms of representative and group litigation in numerous countries, see The Globalization of Class Actions: An international conference co-sponsored by Stanford Law School and The Centre for Socio-Legal Studies, Oxford University 12, 13 & 14 December 2007, papers available at www.law.stanford.edu/calendar/details/1066/ (last visited 29 April 2012).

804 For more on class actions particularly at a transnational level, see International Law Association, *Report on Transnational Group Actions*.

4. COMPENSATION

The international legal framework against corruption does not specify how entities or persons who have suffered damage as a result of an act of corruption should be compensated. States therefore follow the practice of their courts in compensating damages in civil proceedings.[805] In general, civil litigation is not aimed at punishing, but is designed to offer two types of remedy. First, it provides a remedy requiring a return to the way things were before the act, the *status quo ante*, so as to restore the position of an injured party. Second, it provides a remedy to compensate an injured party for the harm suffered. Compensation is determined according to the loss sustained by the victim(s) in each particular case, and should not be limited to a standard payment. Such compensation varies according to the nature of the damage and may cover material damage or *damnum emergens* (the actual reduction in the economic situation of the person who has suffered damage), loss of profit or *lucrum cessans* (the profit that could reasonably have been expected without the corrupt act) and non-pecuniary loss (non-material economic loss, such as loss of reputation).[806] In the case of bribery, for example, the claimant could seek the restitution of the amount of the bribe, as well as any profits accruing from the bribe. For example, if a public official "invests" the bribes received in real estate which increases in value, the State could claim restitution of the bribes, as well as the profit accruing from them.[807] However, it is doubtful whether a claimant could seek the profits made from a contract obtained through a bribe.[808] While material damage and loss of profit are compensated financially, non-pecuniary loss may also be compensated through other means, such as the publication of the judgment at the cost of the defendant,[809] the justifiable dismissal of a corrupt employee, or rescission, voidability or termination of contract. Moreover, certain domestic laws, particularly in the United States, may apply punitive damages in addition to compensation in cases where compensation is deemed an inadequate remedy and in order to reform or deter the defendant and others from engaging in similar conduct.

With a view to securing and avoiding concealment or dissipation of assets, most States also allow plaintiffs in civil proceedings to apply to the court for interim orders to preserve their rights and interests (for example, for the preservation or

---

805 For example, for a detailed analysis of practice in the United Kingdom, see Nicholls, Daniel and Hatchard, *Corruption and Misuse of Public Office*, 235–250.

806 CoE Civil Law Convention Explanatory Report, para. 38.

807 See, *Attorney-General for Hong Kong v. Reid* [1994] 1 AC 324, PC, cited in Nicholls, Daniel and Hatchard, *Corruption and Misuse of Public Office*, 237.

808 See, Ibid., 241–242.

809 CoE Civil Law Convention Explanatory Report, para. 37.

custody of the property during the course of civil proceedings).[810] Moreover, if the plaintiff has by her or his own fault contributed to the damage or to its aggravation, the compensation may be reduced or disallowed.[811]

5. EXTRATERRITORIAL CIVIL JURISDICTION

Civil claims have arisen in which some States, and particularly the United States, have sought to apply their laws outside their territory. This is commonly regarded as the exercise of extraterritorial jurisdiction and it usually requires some kind of link between the forum and the litigation. The *travaux préparatoires* for the UNCAC referred to a legitimate relationship between the corrupt act and the State in which the proceedings are brought.[812] However, no explanation was given as to what constitutes a legitimate relationship in this context.

Most States exercise civil jurisdiction: (i) over acts (tort or non-contractual obligation) committed in their respective jurisdictions (although this is territorial rather than extraterritorial jurisdiction); (ii) when the residence or domicile of the defendant is in their respective jurisdictions; or (iii) when the parties consent to their jurisdiction. While the third ground is fairly straightforward and most frequently occurs because the parties have agreed on the forum prior to a dispute, the first and second grounds merit more detailed analysis.

The first ground refers to the place where the act (tort) was committed. However, States have different understandings of how to determine the place of commission of an act. The main difference is whether they take into account solely the place where the act was committed,[813] or also where the effects (damage) are produced. In some States, mostly of a common law tradition, as well as those covered by the Brussels regime,[814] committing a tort within the jurisdiction of a State can include situations in which the cause of the action arose within the jurisdiction, because the damage caused by the tort was suffered there, even if the place where the defendant's initial conduct occurred was outside the forum State.[815] Claimants therefore have the choice of suing in either

810 See also, CoE Civil Law Convention, Art. 12.

811 CoE Civil Law Convention, Art. 6.

812 UN General Assembly, *Interpretative Notes for the Official Records (Travaux Préparatoires) of the Negotiation of the United Nations Convention against Corruption*, para. 38.

813 For example in Argentina, Brazil, Russian Federation and Spain.

814 The Brussels regime is composed of the 1968 Brussels Convention on Jurisdiction and the Enforcement of Judgments in Civil and Commercial matters (27 September 1968) and the 2000 Brussels Regulation on Jurisdiction and the Recognition and Enforcement of Judgments in Civil and Commercial Matters (Council Regulation (EC) No. 44/2001, 22 December 2000).

815 According to the European Court of Justice, the place where the tort is committed "must be understood as being intended to cover both the place where the damage occurred and the

forum. In reality, this is not extraterritorial jurisdiction, but the exercise of territorial jurisdiction through the application of the "effects doctrine."

With regard to the second ground relating to the domicile or residency of the defendant, when the defendant is a company, most national legal systems require the company to be domiciled or incorporated into its jurisdiction, although sometimes the link may be less formal and take the form of a business activity or financial holdings in the jurisdiction. Certain States, particularly common law States, but also some civil law systems, such as Venezuela, broaden the domicile ground and also exercise jurisdiction when the defendant is present in their territory, even for a brief visit (so-called "tag jurisdiction" in the United States).[816] When a defendant is present in the forum, courts in common law countries automatically have jurisdiction and there does not need to be a connection between the forum and either the defendant or the substance of the action. The presence of corporations is established when the entity carries on business (which does not necessarily have to be related to the principal object of the business) at a fixed and definite place, including when a local agent is used.[817] Moreover, some States define domicile broadly to encompass the presence of the defendant in the territory.

Only a very few States, such as France, Belgium and Finland, recognize jurisdiction on the basis of the plaintiff's and/or defendant's nationality.[818] Certain states, such as Germany, the Russian Federation and Sweden, authorize jurisdiction based on the presence of property within the forum. Some countries require to be a connection between the claim and the defendant's property, while others establish that the value of the property within the forum must at least exceed the costs of enforcing a potential judgment.[819]

The exercise of extraterritorial jurisdiction remains controversial.[820] Some States are considered plaintiff-friendly jurisdictions, and have therefore become

place of the event giving rise to it." Case 21/76, Handelskwekerij Gj Bier NV v. SA Mines de Potasse d'Alsace [1976] E.C.R. 1735, para. 24–25.

816 See, for example, *Maharanee of Baroda v. Wildenstein* [1972] 2 QB 283 (UK CA), cited in International Bar Association, *Report of the Task Force on Extraterritorial Jurisdiction*, 97.

817 See, for example, The Theodohos [1977] 2 Lloyd's Rep 428 (QBD (Adm Ct)); Commonwealth Bank v. White [1999] VSC 262 (Australia), cited in Ibid., 98.

818 See, Germany, Zivilprozessordnung (Civil Procedure Code), section 23; Denmark, Danish Administration of Justice Act, section 246(3); Finland, Finish Code of Judicial Procedure, Chapter 10 section 1; Norway, Civil Procedure Act, sections 4–3(2); Sweden, Code of Judicial Procedure, Chapter 10 section 3; Russian Federation, RSFSR (Civil Procedure Code), Art. 402(2).

819 Ibid.

820 Efforts at the international level to agree on principles governing extraterritorial civil jurisdiction have so far been unsuccessful, as shown by the failure of States to agree on the Draft Hague Convention on Jurisdiction and Foreign Judgments in Civil and Commercial

magnets for litigation, even in cases where there is little connection between the legal issues and the jurisdiction in which they are to be tried. For example, courts in the United States demonstrate broad acceptance of personal jurisdiction and attract foreign litigants wishing to take advantage of the more generous awards of damages, extensive discovery rules and the contingent fee system. In many cases, victims choose the forum that offers the best chance of adequate remedy and reparation. This is the practice known as "forum-shopping", which is not necessarily pernicious. It is actually in the interest of justice to provide parties with a reasonable degree of choice as to where to bring cases with transnational elements. This is especially true in the case of corruption when civil suits cannot realistically be brought in the State where the corrupt act actually took place. If the corrupt party is, for example, a high-level public official or figure with influence in the judiciary, the victim is likely to be denied access to justice or a fair proceeding. Moreover, where the defendant is a company domiciled in another jurisdiction, the victim may choose the jurisdiction that offers greater assurance of compliance with the judgment. A similar situation arises where the defendant's assets are in a jurisdiction other than where the corrupt act took place. Effective compensation for the damage suffered may only be realistic if the defendant is sued in the jurisdiction where the assets are located. Nevertheless, establishing extraterritorial civil jurisdiction can be particularly complex.

5.1. United States Alien Tort Claims Act

In any analysis of extraterritorial civil litigation, reference has to be made to the renowned United States Alien Tort Claims Act (ATCA).[821] The ATCA allows non-US citizens to file suits against both natural and legal persons in the United States who are alleged to have violated the law of nations or a treaty to which the United States is a party. A number of recent ATCA cases involve corruption in the exploitation of natural resources (oil and mining companies). However, these lawsuits have generally focused primarily on the human rights consequences of corrupt activities in the extractive industry, rather than on the corruption itself.[822] The question therefore remains as to whether corrupt acts could themselves be redressed in US courts under the ATCA?

Matters in 2001. The various approaches to civil jurisdiction adopted by States were at that time irreconcilable, especially between the United States and European countries. In Europe, greater consensus with respect to the scope of extraterritorial tort jurisdiction has emerged through the Brussels regime. Nevertheless, the adoption of the Hague Convention on Choice of Court Agreements in 2005 may foreshadow increasing agreement on extraterritorial civil jurisdiction. See, Convention on Choice of Court Agreements (adopted 30 June 2005) 44 I.L.M. 1294.

821 Alien Tort Statute, 28 US Code section 1350.

822 See, for example, Presbyterian Church of Sudan v. Talisman Energy, 244 F.Supp. 2d 289, 296 (S.D.N.Y. 2003); Doe I. v. Unocal Corp. 963 F. Supp. 880 (C.D.Cal. 1997); dismissed by Doe v. Unocal Corp., 110 F. Supp. 2d 1294 (C.D. Cal. 2000) remanded by John Doe I v. Unocal Corp.,

The United States is party to most of the anti-corruption treaties, including the UNCAC. It might therefore be assumed that certain cases of corruption could be brought before a United States court as a violation of the ATCA. However, since the 2004 US Supreme Court Judgment *Sosa v. Alvarez-Machain*,[823] the possibility of civil litigation in corruption cases under the ATCA is almost zero. The Supreme Court found in this case that a private party would not have a remedy under the ATCA for a violation of a non-self-executing treaty.[824] In this context, it should be emphasized that the United States made a Declaration to the UNCAC specifying that the provisions of the UNCAC are non-self executing (with the exception of the extradition and MLA provisions) and that none of the provisions of the UNCAC create a private right of action.[825] Indeed, most of the provisions of the UNCAC may be regarded as a non-self-executing, probably with the exception of Articles 44 and 46, as most Articles in the treaty require States Parties to adopt legislative measures in national law. The UNCAC itself therefore specifies that it is non-self-executing. It is therefore difficult to envisage a cause being brought under the ATCA for a violation of the UNCAC.[826]

5.2. *Forum non conveniens*

When analysing extraterritorial civil litigation, it is necessary to refer to one of the major legal techniques for declining jurisdiction, namely *forum non conveniens*. Under this doctrine of judicial discretion, a court may refuse an action by a plaintiff within its jurisdiction when it determines that a case would be better brought in another forum, due for example to reasons of language or

---

395 F.3d 932 (9th Cir. Cal. 2002) vacated, rehearing, en banc, granted by Doe v. Unocal Corp., 395 F.3d 978, 2003 (9th Cir. 2003) affirmed by Doe v. Unocal Corp., 248 F.3d 915 (9th Cir. Cal. 2001) in the related case, National Coalition Government of Burma v. Unocal, Inc., 176 F.R.D. 329 (C.D. Cal. 1997).

823 Sosa v. Alvarez-Machain, 124 S.Ct. 2739 (2004).

824 Ibid., 2763. There are usually considered to be two kinds of treaties in terms of their application: self-executing, which do not require additional legislative action to have effect in domestic law; and non-self-executing, which require additional implementing legislation to have legal effect and to be enforceable in domestic courts.

825 United States Declaration to the UNCAC, para. 2, available at http://treaties.un.org/Pages/ViewDetails.aspx?src=IND&mtdsg_no=XVIII-14&chapter=18&lang=en (last visited 29 April 2012).

826 Civil litigation arising out of the famous FCPA has also been rejected (Lamb v. Phillip Morris, Inc., 915 F.2d 1024 (6th Cir. 1990), cert. denied, 111 S. Ct. 961 (1991)). However, another United States law that opens the door for civil litigation for corruption in US courts is the Racketeer Influenced and Corrupt Organizations (RICO) Act. RICO permits civil suits by private plaintiffs who have been harmed by the acquisition or investment activities of a racketeering enterprise, where the defendants have engaged in a pattern or racketeering activity, i.e. the commission on at least two occasions of an offence traditionally associated with organized crime, such as murder, kidnapping, bribery, or money laundering. Most importantly, a RICO action requires proof that the activities of the enterprise were the likely cause of harm to the plaintiff.

the location of defendants or evidence.[827] This doctrine is mostly known in common law jurisdictions. However, several civil law countries, such as Norway and Sweden, do recognize a limited power to decline jurisdiction where the case has insufficient connection with the forum or where its pursuit would constitute an abuse.[828]

Experience has shown that courts enjoy a fairly wide degree of discretion to refuse jurisdiction when invoking this doctrine, and this defence has been used successfully to foreclose litigation in a foreign jurisdiction to recover allegedly corrupt funds. In the *Islamic Republic of Iran v. Pahlavi,*[829] it was alleged that the defendant had accepted bribes and misappropriated, embezzled or converted US$ 35 billion in Iranian funds. The Court of Appeals of NYC upheld the dismissal of the suit based on *forum non conveniens*, despite the fact that the Islamic Republic of Iran did not have a suitable alternate forum.[830] Four suits were brought before US courts, and they were all dismissed on the basis of *forum non conveniens*.

In cases of corruption, this doctrine may provide courts with an easy way out of dealing with difficult, high-profile and politically sensitive cases. The doctrine may also prevent victims from having access to the sole jurisdiction where they might obtain a remedy. The local forum could be the nation in which the corruption occurred, where plaintiffs would most probably face judges favourable to the corrupt government officials. Yet courts cannot apply the doctrine unrestrictedly. In considering whether there is a more appropriate forum abroad, the courts have to seek the forum with which the action has the most real and substantial connection. However, they also have to consider the convenience or expense of litigating in a local forum rather than a foreign one, the availability of witnesses, the place of residency of the parties and, most importantly, whether the plaintiff would obtain justice in the foreign jurisdiction.[831] In the European Union, the courts of Member States have to allow proceedings to commence if the defendant is domiciled in their jurisdiction or if the harm occurred within their jurisdiction, even if the plaintiff is domiciled in a foreign State.[832] It should

---

827 Ronald A Brand and Scott R Jablonski, *Forum Non Conveniens: History, Global Practice, and Future under the Hague Convention on Choice of Court Agreements* (New York: Oxford University Press, 2007), 1.

828 International Law Association, Committee on International Civil and Commercial Litigation, Third Interim Report: *Declining and Referring Jurisdiction in International Litigation*, London Conference, 2000, 8. For more information on *forum non conveniens* in both common law and civil law systems, see Brand and Jablonski, *Forum Non Conveniens*.

829 Republic of Iran v. Pahlavi, 62 N.Y.2d 474, 477 (1984), cert. denied, 469 U.S. 1108 (1985).

830 Kofele-Kale, *International Law of Responsibility for Economic Crimes*, 282.

831 International Bar Association, *Report of the Task Force on Extraterritorial Jurisdiction*, 103.

832 Case C-412/98, Group Josi Reinsurance Company S.A. v. Universal General Insurance Company (UGIC), ECJ, 13 July 2000, E.C.R. 2000 I-05925. The Brussels Convention on Jurisdiction and the Enforcement of Judgments in Civil and Commercial Matters, 27 September 1968.

be emphasized that, if there is no meaningful and reasonably accessible alternate forum in which access to justice for the victim is a real possibility, then the doctrine may not be legitimately applied.[833] Indeed, *forum non conveniens* is not accepted under the Brussels Regime.[834] Courts therefore have to consider whether the alternate foreign forum is adequate and available, and the public interests of the local and foreign fora.[835]

III. BARRIERS TO JURISDICTION

As indicated in this Chapter, there are a number of international obligations concerning jurisdiction that are aimed at strengthening capacities in national jurisdictions for the enforcement of anti-corruption law. Notwithstanding these obligations, there are certain barriers to the exercise of adjudicatory jurisdiction over corruption offences that have an important effect on legal enforcement. Some of these barriers and their interpretation in the context of the international legal framework against corruption are examined in other Chapters, such as statutes of limitations. Here, particular attention is paid to barriers to jurisdiction that have proved to be the most effective in impeding adjudicatory jurisdiction, namely immunities, the act of State doctrine and amnesties.

1. IMMUNITIES FROM JURISDICTION

Since corruption inherently involves public officials, their immunities and jurisdictional privileges can be an important barrier in combating corruption. Indeed, experience has shown that immunities have often been abused by corrupt public officials.[836] In many cases, immunity has turned into impunity. For that reason, it is important to eliminate or prevent corrupt public officials from shielding from judicial accountability for corrupt acts.[837] Unfortunately, the international legal framework against corruption does not address the issue of immunities adequately. It simply requires States to maintain an appropriate balance between any immunities or jurisdictional privileges accorded to their public officials for the performance of their functions and the possibility of effectively investigating, prosecuting and adjudicating corrupt offences.[838] It

833 Brand and Jablonski, *Forum Non Conveniens*, 102.

834 Case C-281/02, Andrew Owusu v. N.B. Jackson, trading as 'Villa Holidays Bal-Inn Villas' and Others, 1 March 2005, E.C.R. 2005 I-01383.

835 Piper Aircraft Co. v. Reyno, 454 US 235 (1981) 241.

836 For a Latin American account, see Latin Leaders' Legal Escape Hatch, *The Washington Post*, 24 May 2004.

837 UNODC, *Legislative Guide for the Implementation of the United Nations Convention against Corruption*, para. 387.

838 UNCAC, Art. 30(2); AU Convention against Corruption, Art. 7(5).

would appear that States enjoy almost unfettered discretion regarding immunities.[839] They are solely subject to the requirement of an "appropriate balance between immunities and adjudication." This balance could be interpreted as an obligation "to limit immunity from investigation, prosecution or adjudication of corruption offences to the degree necessary in a democratic society."[840] However, what does this obligation entail in practice?

In order to understand in detail what is required of States, an examination is necessary of immunities at the national level, applied internally and regulated by national law, and immunities applied at the international level, as regulated by international law.

1.1. Immunities at the national level

There are no rules of international law concerning immunities within a State. This issue is normally regulated in national laws, and usually in the constitution. In most national legal systems, there are two sorts of immunity: non-liability for votes and opinions expressed in the exercise of duties (freedom of expression) and inviolability (especially immunity from investigation, prosecution and adjudication).[841] Under much national legislation, heads of state and other officials (such as the President, Members of Parliament, government ministers and judges) enjoy immunity from investigation, prosecution, and adjudication, either during their term of office or permanently. Other office holders do not enjoy immunities, but benefit from some form of jurisdictional privilege (for example, they may only be investigated or prosecuted by, or with the consent of, a high-ranking official or committee). Public officials are granted immunities at the national level so as to ensure their independence, protect them from malicious prosecution and safeguard the proper functioning of State institutions.[842]

The problem arises when these immunities are abused, either in law or in practice, when they may act as a barrier to jurisdiction. A way of avoiding the abuse of immunities is to review whether the immunities granted are sufficient and do not go beyond their objectives. Immunities should be limited to what is strictly necessary for the office held. They therefore need to be analysed with respect to the three main aspects of immunities: who enjoys them, their scope and the procedure to lift them. With regard to the first aspect, States should

---

839 In this sense, see also UNCAC Art. 30(9).

840 Council of Europe, Committee of Ministers, Resolution (97) 24: On the Twenty Guiding Principles for the Fight against Corruption, 6 November 1997, Guiding Principle 6.

841 UNODC and UNICRI, *Technical Guide to the United Nations Convention against Corruption* (Vienna, New York: United Nations, 2009), 85.

842 Ibid., 85–87.

restrict the list of privileged public officials, and preferably grant limited immunity which does not cover corrupt or otherwise criminal behaviour whether conducted in a private or an official capacity. In many countries, there are an exceedingly large number of beneficiaries of immunities at the national and even the local levels, comprising not only a wide range of public officials, but also, *inter alia,* candidates for the Presidency,[843] parliamentary candidates,[844] and civil servants in general.[845] It is also important for States to ensure that immunities that apply to one person do not frustrate the prosecution and adjudication of cases involving other persons implicated in corruption.[846]

The scope of the immunities granted also needs to be taken into account. It has been argued that the obligation to apply an appropriate balance between immunities and adjudication requires States to adopt a "functional" concept of immunities, or in other words that immunity is attached to the office and not to the office holder.[847] Accordingly, balanced, and therefore legitimate immunities should only be those that are necessary to safeguard the functioning of the institutions of State.[848] States may wish to apply immunities only with regard to acts committed in the performance of the duties of a public official only where the official has performed the roles and responsibilities of the office as established by law, and during her or his time in office, and not when the official has left office.[849] Immunities should also be of limited duration. They should apply only while an official is in office and not indefinitely. In many countries, immunities are not functional in their nature, and even officials involved in a car accident because of speeding have escaped prosecution, although driving was not part of their official duties.[850] Countries should also consider suspending any applicable statutes of limitation while an official is immune from prosecution. This would ensure that prosecution is not barred by the time an official leaves office. Moreover, persons who enjoy immunity should only be protected against prosecution, but not against investigation. Proper investigation and evidence gathering is necessary for the potential lifting of immunities.

---

843 For example, in the Russian Federation. See, GRECO, *Joint First and Second Evaluation Rounds: Evaluation Report on the Russian Federation*, Greco Eval I-II Rep (2008) 2E, 5 December 2008, para. 175.

844 For example, in Armenia. See, GRECO, *Joint First and Second Evaluation Rounds: Evaluation Report on Armenia*, Greco Eval I-II Rep (2005) 2E, 10 March 2006, para. 56.

845 For example, in Turkey. See, GRECO, *Joint First and Second Evaluation Rounds: Evaluation Report on Turkey*, Greco Eval I-II Rep (2005) 3E, 10 March 2006, para. 98.

846 UNODC and UNICRI, *Technical Guide to the United Nations Convention against Corruption*, 87.

847 Ibid., 85.

848 Ibid.

849 Ibid., 85–86.

850 OECD, *Corruption: A Glossary of International Criminal Standards* (Paris: OECD Publishing, 2007), 51.

Most national laws envisage the possibility of lifting immunities in the case of criminal conduct by the office-holder. This may take different forms, such as the lifting of immunity by the institution concerned (a Parliamentary decision in respect of one of its Members, or a decision by the Parliament in respect of a Head of State or by a constitutional court). In many States, these procedures are highly complex and involve predominantly individual decision-makers.[851] Procedures to lift immunities vary highly among States, only general comments can therefore be made in this respect. Countries should ensure that the processes are transparent and publicly accountable. For example, effective procedures are needed for the lifting of immunities, which should not allow for politically motivated discretion, should be expeditious, based on objective criteria and should avoid conflicts of interests in the decision to waive immunity.[852]

1.2. Immunities at the international level

In addition to immunity under national laws, the State itself and certain categories of State officials also enjoy immunities at the international level. In other words, they cannot be prosecuted in foreign courts due to the immunity granted under international law.[853] At the international level, immunities are founded on the inviolability of the State and its agents as a means of promoting peaceful inter-State relations.[854] It is usually agreed that there are three types of immunity under international law: functional (also called *ratione materiae*), personal (also called *ratione personae*) and State (or sovereign) immunity.

a. Immunity from prosecution

Functional immunity protects *de jure* or *de facto* State agents from prosecution in other countries for acts committed within the context of their official duties.[855] Hence, a person who commits a criminal offence in performing an act of State is immune from prosecution, even after the person ceases to perform acts of State. This immunity is justified under customary international law by the fact that the actions of such persons are imputed to the State and not the individual.[856] Functional immunity is linked to a position, rather than a specific

---

851 For example, in Estonia. See, GRECO, *First Evaluation Round: Evaluation Report on Estonia*, Greco Eval I Rep (2001) 7E Final, 14 September 2001, para. 143.

852 UNODC and UNICRI, *Technical Guide to the United Nations Convention against Corruption*, 86.

853 The comments made in this section apply *mutatis mutandi* to public international organizations and their officials.

854 Ian Brownlie, *Principles of Public International Law*, 7th ed. (Oxford: Oxford University Press, 2008), 326–327.

855 Antonio Cassese, *International Criminal Law*, 2nd ed. (Oxford: Oxford University Press, 2008), 303–304.

856 Ibid., 303.

person. Therefore, the moment the accused leaves office, she or he is liable to be prosecuted for crimes committed before or after the term in office. The person could therefore be prosecuted for corrupt acts carried out before or after being in office. However, if the person is suspected of committing corrupt acts during the term of office, is she or he subject to functional immunity? The answer to this question depends on whether exceptions to the rule of functional immunity are accepted. If the immunity is linked to the official position rather than the individual, and since corruption does not involve an act carried out while a person is engaged in official capacity, but rather in a personal capacity, the accused could not benefit from functional immunity. Corruption is never part of official State policy, even if it is committed massively by certain members of the government. Corruption is always committed in a personal capacity for personal benefit. However, whether functional immunities can be overridden for non-official acts, such as corruption, is still uncertain.

In contrast, personal immunity, including diplomatic immunity, protects some categories of State officials (heads of State, heads of Government, diplomatic agents and ministers of foreign affairs)[857] from the civil or criminal jurisdiction of foreign national courts for all acts, both public and private, while they are in office.[858] Personal immunity is justified on the grounds that such officials and diplomats require a certain amount of independence to be able to exercise their functions effectively.[859] This type of immunity ends when the person leaves office, as it is not a right of the individual, and it may be waived by the State.[860] Consequently, acts of corruption by these categories of officials cannot be prosecuted in foreign courts while they are in office, unless the State waives their personal immunity.

State (or sovereign) immunity protects the State itself (as opposed to State officials) and acts as a bar to the civil and administrative jurisdiction of States in respect of claims by courts of foreign States. State immunity is not generally considered to be absolute and national courts have challenged it in cases relating to the commercial activity of States. Accordingly, only the acts of States

---

857 These are the categories of State officials who benefit from personal immunity according to the International Court of Justice. See, Arrest Warrant of 11 April 2000 (Democratic Republic of the Congo v. Belgium), Judgment, I.C.J. Reports 2002, 3, para. 51: "in international law it is firmly established that … certain holders of high-ranking office in a State, such as the Head of State, the Head of Government and Ministers of Foreign Affairs, enjoy immunities from jurisdiction in other States, both civil and criminal."

858 Cassese, *International Criminal Law*, 304.

859 Ibid., 303.

860 Similarly, States should encourage public international organizations to waive the immunities of their officials in appropriate cases. See UN General Assembly, *Interpretative Notes for the Official Records (Travaux Préparatoires) of the Negotiation of the United Nations Convention against Corruption*, para. 23.

undertaken in a sovereign capacity (so called *jure imperii*) are considered immune from the jurisdiction of foreign States, while acts undertaken in a private or commercial capacity (so-called *jure gestionis*) are not protected by State immunity.[861] Moreover, State immunity does not protect a foreign State from prosecution in the courts of another State by persons who have suffered damage or injury arising out of an act by the foreign State's in its own territory.[862] This would apply if a person sought compensation from a State in a foreign court for damage suffered as a result of corruption (State responsibility). Similarly to functional immunity, such corruption could not be considered an official act carried out during the course of official duties, and a corrupt act cannot be an act of *jure imperii* in the context of State immunity.[863]

As a result, immunities from jurisdiction as regulated in international law should not constitute a significant barrier to jurisdiction in relation to corruption. State immunities do not apply in cases of corruption, since corruption can never be considered an act carried out in an official or sovereign capacity, but rather an act committed in a personal or private capacity in view of a private interest. If functional immunity is interpreted as allowing an exception for private acts, the enforcement of anti-corruption law would also not be restricted by functional immunities. On the other hand, in the case of heads of State, heads of Government, diplomatic agents and ministers of foreign affairs, jurisdiction for their alleged participation in corrupt acts is barred by personal immunities while they are in office, unless their State waives their immunity. Once such officials leave office, however, it should be able to exercise jurisdiction over them since, as explained above, their alleged corrupt acts are not protected by functional immunities.

b. Immunity from confiscation

In addition to prosecution and punishment of corrupt officials in foreign courts, immunities are also relevant to confiscation procedures in foreign countries. The confiscation of funds that belong to a person enjoying immunity creates a different problem from physical restraint. The confiscation of funds is exercised "*in rem*" and not "*in personam*", even if the owner or beneficiary of the funds enjoys immunity under customary international law. In confiscation procedures,

---

861 United Nations Convention on Jurisdictional Immunities of States and Their Property, adopted by UN General Assembly Resolution 59/38, 16 December 2004 (not yet entered into force), Art. 10; Brownlie, *Principles of Public International Law*, 332–336.

862 UN Convention on Jurisdictional Immunities of States and Their Property, Art. 12; Ibid., 336.

863 See below, Tribunal fédéral [Federal Court] affaire République du Kazakhstan, 8 December 2000, réf. 1P.582/2000, consid. 2 c), p. 9, partially reproduced in Lucius Caflisch, "La Pratique Suisse en Matière de Droit International Public 2000," *Revue suisse de droit international et de droit européen* 11, no. 4 (2001): 573–678.

the rules of international law regarding immunities have been interpreted in different ways. The experience of Switzerland is instructive, due to its significant case law on these matters, arising out of the large number of Heads of State that have held, or hold some of their assets in Swiss bank accounts. In Switzerland, the assets of former Heads of State have been successfully confiscated in a number of cases, although in such cases it has been the State itself that has requested the confiscation and waived the immunity of the former Head of State.[864] However in the *Marcos* case,[865] Switzerland held that former Heads of State should only enjoy functional immunity, that is immunity for acts carried out in the exercise of their official duties.[866] However, the Swiss Tribunal did not elaborate on what should be understood by acts carried out in the exercise of official duties. The Government of the Philippines had argued that acts of illicit enrichment do not constitute acts carried out in the exercise of official duties.[867]

The Swiss courts further elaborated on this in the *Kazakhstan* case.[868] A judge in Belgium requested the Swiss authorities to seize several bank accounts in the context of a criminal investigation in Belgium into money laundering. The bank accounts were under the name of offshore companies, yet the banks had been informed that the economic beneficiary was the then President of Kazakhstan and the former Prime Minister, as well as their respective families. The judge of first instance (*juge d'instruction*) in Geneva, after analysing the numerous bank transfers, concluded that *a priori* the funds seemed to constitute laundering of the proceeds of corruption and decided to seize the funds and bank documents. The Republic of Kazakhstan invoked its State immunity. However, in subsequent

---

864 For example in the cases of Haile Selasié (1974), Pahlevi (1979), Ceausescu (1987), Marcos (1988), Traoré (1991), Layne (1996), Mobutu (1997), Bhutto (1997), Karadzic (1997), Suharto (1998) and Abacha (1999). On the immunity of former Heads of State and the confiscation of their assets, see Joe Verhoeven and Claude Reymond, "Sur la récuperation à l'étranger des sommes détournées par d'anciens chefs d'Etat," in *Etudes De Droit International En L'honneur De Pierre Lalive*, ed. Christian Dominicé and Robert Patry (Bâle: Helbing & Lichtenhahn, 1993), 357–373.

865 Tribunal federal [Federal Court] Ferdinand and Imelda Marcos v. Office fédéral de la police, 2 November 1989, ATF 115 Ib 496, 498–503, partially reproduced in Lucius Caflisch, "La Pratique Suisse en Matière de Droit International Public 1990," *Revue suisse de droit international et de droit européen* 1, no. 4 (1991): 533–537; Lucius Caflisch, "La Pratique Suisse en Matière de Droit International Public 1998," *Revue suisse de droit international et de droit européen* 9, no. 4/5 (1999): 691–700.

866 Marc Henzelin, "L'immunité pénale des chefs d'Etat en matière financière. Vers une exception pour les actes de pillage de ressources et de corruption?," *Revue suisse de droit international et de droit européen* 12, no. 2 (2002): 195–196.

867 Tribunal fédéral [Federal Court] Ferdinand and Imelda Marcos v. Office fédéral de la police, 2 November 1989, ATF 115 Ib 496, 5(d).

868 Tribunal fédéral [Federal Court] affaire République du Kazakhstan, 8 December 2000, réf. 1P.582/2000, 9, partially reproduced in Caflisch, "La Pratique Suisse en Matière de Droit International Public 2000," 589–591. See also, Tribunal fédéral [Federal Court] affaire République du Kazakhstan, 25 June 2001, réf. 1A.94/2001.

instances, Swiss courts found that the bank account holders (the offshore companies) considered by Kazakhstan as performing State tasks could not benefit from immunity unless their tasks were *jure imperii* and not if they were *jure gestionis*.[869] The Swiss Federal Supreme Court (Tribunal fédéral) found that:

> "under the restrictive approach that prevails in Switzerland, the principle of immunity of foreign States is not an absolute rule. The foreign State may invoke the principle of immunity if it acted under its sovereignty (*iure imperii*). If, however, it acted as the holder of a private right, as a private individual, it may be subject to Swiss jurisdiction."[870] (Author's translation)

In order to identify whether an act is *jure imperii* or *jure gestionis*, the Supreme Court used the criterion of the "inherent nature of the act." The key, according to the court, is to know whether the act is exercised by the public authority or whether it is an act that could be performed by two private individuals. The Supreme Court considered that Kazakhstan had had recourse to offshore companies and had therefore acted as a private party.[871]

With regard to sitting Heads of State, in the past Switzerland strictly deferred to their immunity as Heads of State even if the assets clearly had their origins in corruption.[872] However, Swiss justice has managed to overcome the hurdle of immunity in cases where a Head of State is only the beneficiary of a Swiss bank account and the funds are under the name of a third party. In the *Bongo* case,[873] the President of Gabon, Omar Bongo, had deposited US$ 1.5 million in Switzerland in a bank account under a Panamanian company. The Swiss courts granted the seizure of the funds under a mutual legal assistance request from France and indicated that only the Panamanian company could contest the seizure of the funds. Since Omar Bongo was not the account holder, but a beneficiary, he could not intervene in the proceedings and could not accordingly

---

869 For a criticism of this approach, see Henzelin, "L'immunité pénale des chefs d'Etat en matière financière. Vers une exception pour les actes de pillage de ressources et de corruption?," 203–209.

870 Tribunal fédéral [Federal Court] affaire République du Kazakhstan, 8 December 2000, réf. 1P.582/2000, 9, partially reproduced in Caflisch, "La Pratique Suisse en Matière de Droit International Public 2000," 589–591, originally "selon la conception restrictive qui prévaut en Suisse, le principe de l'immunité des Etats étrangers n'est pas un règle absolue. L'Etat étranger peut invoquer le principe de l'immunité de juridiction s'il a agi en vertu de sa souveraineté (iure imperii); si, en revanche, il a agi comme titulaire d'un droit privé, au même titre qu'un particulier, il peut être soumis à la juridiction suisse."

871 Tribunal fédéral [Federal Court] affaire République du Kazakhstan, 25 June 2001, réf. 1A.94/2001, consid. 4(d), 12–13.

872 See, Henzelin, "L'immunité pénale des chefs d'Etat en matière financière. Vers une exception pour les actes de pillage de ressources et de corruption?," 191–196.

873 Tribunal fédéral [Federal Court] A. et B. c. Chambre d'accusation de Genève, 8 March 1999, réf. 1P.631/1998 and 1P.633/1998, partially reproduced in La Semmaine Judiciaire, 1999 I, p. 427.

invoke his immunity as a sitting Head of State. Consequently, Heads of State wishing to use the Swiss banking system need to do so in their own name to be able to claim immunity. If they hide their identity, they cannot claim immunity.[874] Nevertheless, if the bank in Switzerland is duly informed that a Head of State is the beneficiary, the immunity may be upheld.[875]

In the case of sitting heads of State, there are arguments in favour of not protecting their bank accounts with immunity when the funds appear to have their origin in a criminal activity, and particularly corruption.[876] Along the same lines, the *Institut de Droit International* adopted a resolution in 2001 on "Immunities from Jurisdiction and Execution of heads of State and of Government in International Law," calling for an exception to the principle of the immunity of heads of State in cases where there are doubts concerning the legal nature of the means by which the funds or assets held by, or on behalf of, the head of State were appropriated.[877] In the case of former heads of State, the situation is simpler, since the State itself either waives the immunity of the former head of State, or her or his corrupt act and the proceeds are considered an act committed outside the official duties, and cannot therefore be attributed to the State and protected by immunity. In any case, a paradox arises if the immunity granted to heads of State by the State itself on behalf and in the

---

874 However, this finding goes against a well known immunity rule whereby a Head of State travelling incognito in the territory of another country will be automatically protected by immunity as soon as his identity is known by the authorities of the foreign State. See, Alvaro Borghi, "Corruption et immunité des dirigeants politiques," in *Les traités internationaux contre la corruption: L'ONU, l'OCDE, le Conseil de l'Europe et la Suisse*, ed. Tiziano Balmelli and Bernard Jaggy (Lausanne, Bern, Lugano: Editions interuniversitaires suisses – Edis, 2004), 104.

875 See Tribunal fédéral [Federal Court] affaire République du Kazakhstan, 8 December 2000, réf. 1P.582/2000, 9.

876 Christian Dominicé, "Quelques Observations sur l'immunité de Juridiction Pénale de l'ancien Chef d'Etat," *Revue Générale de Droit International Public* 103, no. 2 (1999): 307; P. Gully-Hart, "The Function of State and Diplomatic Privileges and Immunities in International Cooperation in Criminal Matters: The Position of Switzerland," *Fordham International Law Journal* 23 (2000): 1342; Borghi, "Corruption et immunité des dirigeants politiques."

877 The relevant provisions are as follows:

> "2. When serious doubt arises as to the legality of the appropriation of a fund or any other asset held by, or on behalf of, the Head of State, nothing in these provisions prevents the State authorities of the territory on which those funds or other assets are located, from taking provisional measures with respect to those funds or assets, as are necessary for the maintenance of control over them while the legality of the appropriation remains insufficiently established.
>
> 3. In conformity with their obligations of cooperation, States should take all appropriate measures to combat illegal practices, in particular to clarify the origin of deposits and dealings in assets and to supply all relevant information in this respect."

Institut de Droit International, Immunities from Jurisdiction and Execution of Heads of State and of Government in International Law, Art. 4, 26 August 2001.

interests of the population results in a *de facto* shield for a corrupt head of State, thereby rendering the State and its population defenceless victims.[878]

2. ACT OF STATE DOCTRINE

Although not *stricto sensu* a jurisdictional immunity, the act of State doctrine has proved to be an additional barrier to jurisdiction over corrupt acts. Under this doctrine, the civil courts in a country refrain from judging the acts of a foreign State that are carried out within its own territory.[879] This doctrine has mainly developed in common law jurisdictions, particularly in the United States, but equivalent approaches are adopted in some civil law countries. The act of State doctrine is not a rule of international law, but a judicial self-restraint doctrine.[880] It is based on the argument that the courts of a State may not interfere in its political and foreign policy,[881] that the determination of the validity of a foreign official act is a political rather than a legal act for which courts are ill-suited[882] and the respect that one sovereign State owes to the independence of another.[883]

Whether corrupt acts can constitute an act of State and are therefore immune from review in the courts of another State is still a matter of controversy. An act of State is a sovereign act performed within the territory of a State. The act of State doctrine normally does not preclude judicial review of the extraterritorial effects of such acts.[884] Many corruption cases are not fully executed within the territory of one State. When the proceeds of corruption are hidden in bank accounts in a foreign State, the latter has the right to determine the legality or illegality of those assets, which is intrinsically linked to the way in which they were acquired. Moreover, in such cases, in view of the emergence of the international legal frameworks against money laundering and against

878 Borghi, "Corruption et immunité des dirigeants politiques," 102.

879 The United States Supreme Court first announced the act of State doctrine in 1897 in Underhill v. Hernandez, 168 U.S. 250 (1897). The following is the relevant passage: "Every sovereign state is bound to respect the independence of every sovereign state, and the courts of one country will not sit in judgment on the acts of the government of another done in his own territory." For a case in the United Kingdom, see Buttes Gas v. Hammer, (1981) 3 AER 616 and (1982) AC 888.

880 The doctrine can be set aside or put forward by the Executive, asking either that it not be used or that it be used in cases where it does not apply. See, Brigitte Stern, "Immunities for Heads of State: Where Do We Stand?," in *Justice for Crimes against Humanity* (London: Hart Publishing, 2003), 77.

881 See for example, Susana Siderman De Blake et al v. The Republic of Argentina, 965 F 2d 699 (1992) (US Court of Appeals, 9th Cir.).

882 See for example, Banco Nacional de Cuba v. Sabbatino, 376 US 398 (1964).

883 This is the comity rationale. See, Underhill v. Hernandez, 168 U.S. 250 (1897).

884 See, for example, Liu v. Republic of China, 892 F.2d 1419, 1432 (9th Cir. 1989), p. 1433; Maltina Corp. v. Cawy Bottling Co., 462 F.2d 1021, (5th Cir. 1972), p. 1025.

corruption, States are also under international obligations to prevent the introduction of criminal funds into their financial system. As indicated earlier, States have to establish a regulatory and supervisory regime that requires banks and non-bank financial institutions to ensure effective customer identification, accurate record-keeping and a mechanism for the reporting of suspicious transactions.[885] Most importantly, States are required to criminalize money laundering offences, such as the concealment or disguise of the nature, source, location, disposition, movement or ownership of the proceeds of crime.[886] As noted earlier, States are required to apply money laundering offences to proceeds generated by corrupt acts committed outside the jurisdiction of the State.[887] Hence, corrupt acts carried out in one State could be considered a predicate offence for AML prosecution in another State. The outcome of all these obligations is that when funds or assets belonging to a former or sitting head of State are located in a foreign State, that latter State has the right and duty to examine whether those funds are derived from corrupt or other criminal acts. Ultimately the courts of a State, where called upon to do so, can judge such acts by the former or sitting head of State.

In addition, as already indicated in the section on immunities, corrupt acts cannot be considered as sovereign acts, and cannot therefore be regarded as acts of State.[888] However, that has not been the uniform interpretation in the case law of the United States. For example, in 1983, in *Clayco Petroleum Corp. v. Occidental Petroleum Corp.*[889] and in 1988 in *Republic of Philippines v. Marcos (so-called Marcos II)*,[890] US courts held that adjudication by US courts over these cases which allegedly involved corruption in foreign countries was barred by the act of State doctrine because the claims by the plaintiffs required analysis of acts by a foreign sovereign. Specifically, in *Clayco*, the US Court of Appeal for the Ninth Circuit held that the act of State doctrine barred an antitrust suit against

---

885 UNCAC, Art. 14(1)(a).

886 UNCAC, Art. 23(1)(a)(ii); Inter-American Convention against Corruption Arts. 7 and 6(1)(d); AU Convention against Corruption, Art. 6(b).

887 UNCAC, Art. 23(2)(a-c); OECD Convention, Art. 7; CoE Criminal Law Convention Art. 13.

888 Sovereign acts have been interpreted as not covering: commercial acts (see for example, Alfred Dunhill v. Republic of Cuba, 425 US 682 (1976), 15 IL; 735, ILR 66, 212); flagrant violations of important rules of international law, most notably human rights violations (see for example, Filartiga v. Pena Irala, 630 F.2d 876, 889–890 (2d Cir. 1980); confiscation of property (see for example in the United Kingdom, Kuwait Airways Corp. (KAC) v. Iraqi Airways Co. (IAC) and others, House of Lords, 16 May 2002, UKHL 19.) or violation of public policy (see, for example, Government of India, Ministry of Defence (Revenue) Division v. Taylor (1955) 1 All ER 292, cited in Hazel Fox, "International Law and Restraints on the Exercise of Jurisdiction by National Courts of States," in *International Law*, ed. Malcolm D. Evans, Second Edition. (Oxford: Oxford University Press, 2006), 384.).

889 Clayco Petroleum Corp. v. Occidental Petroleum Corp, 712 F.2d 404 (9th Cir. 1983), cert. denied, 104 S. Ct. 703 (1984).

890 Republic of Philippines v. Marcos, 818 F 2d 1473 (9th Cir 1988).

Occidental Petroleum, which had allegedly bribed a foreign government official to obtain an off-shore oil concession.[891] The court argued that proof of Clayco's claim would require it to review the propriety of the granting of the oil concession by the foreign government, which is precisely an act of a foreign sovereign and is thus barred by the act of State doctrine.[892] Similarly, in *Marcos II,* the Government of the Philippines was seeking the seizure and confiscation of all of the assets of Marcos around the world.[893] The US court in the Ninth Circuit ruled that adjudication was barred by the act of State doctrine because the activities of Marcos consisted of public and governmental action that fell under the doctrine, even if they were illegal.[894] Not surprisingly, this ruling raised a fair amount of criticism.[895] The court erroneously concluded that the corrupt dealings of Marcos were public, whereas US courts had long recognized the distinction between the public and private acts of a foreign official and had ruled that the act of state doctrine only protects official public actions.[896]

In contrast, US courts have in the majority of cases ruled in favour of regarding corruption as an exception or limitation to the act of State doctrine. In the context of the Marcos saga, in *Republic of Philippines v. Marcos (so-called Marcos I),*[897] the US Court of Appeals in the Second Circuit ruled that the defendants had failed to show that their acts were public acts protected under the doctrine.[898] Already in the 1960s, in *Jimenez v. Aristeguieta,*[899] a US court had

---

891 Clayco Petroleum Corp. v. Occidental Petroleum Corp, 712 F.2d 404 (9th Cir. 1983), cert. denied, 104 S. Ct. 703 (1984).

892 Ibid., 406. For a similar case and ruling, see Hunt v. Mobil Oil Corp., 550 F2d 68 (2d Cir. 1977), cert. denied, 434 U.S. 984 (1978). However, for a similar case in which the US Supreme Court reached the contrary conclusion, see below Kirkpatrick and Co., Inc., v. Environmental Tectonics Corp. Int.

893 The Philippine Government brought an action in the United States alleging that while Marcos was in power he converted approximately US$1.5 billion in assets belonging to the Philippine Government through corrupt acts. Assets allegedly belonging to Marcos were discovered in the United States and around the world.

894 Republic of Philippines v. Marcos, 818 F 2d 1473 (9th Cir 1988), 1490.

895 Kofele-Kale, *International Law of Responsibility for Economic Crimes*, 288–291, citing Tacie A Sundack, Note, Republic of Philippines v. Marcos: the Ninth Circuit Allows a Former Ruler to Invoke the Act of State Doctrine Against a Resisting Sovereign, 38 *American University Law Review* 225, 247 (1988); William J. Ritter, Case Comment, International Relations-Act of State Doctrine-Marcos' Assets as Act of Philippine State, 11 *Suffolk Transnational Law Journal* 501 (1988); Douglas J. Chu, Note, Marcos Mania: The Crusade to Return Marcos' Billions to the Philippines Through the Federal Courts, 18 *Rutgers Law Journal* 217 (1986); A.C. Robitaille, Note, The Marcos Cases: A Consideration of the Act of State Doctrine and the Pursuit of the Assets of Deposed Dictators, 9 *Boston College Third World Law Journal,* 81, 85 (1989). See, also Joel Simon, "Clayco Petroleum Corp. v. Occidental Petroleum Corp.: Should there be a Bribery Exception to the Act of State Doctrine?," *Cornell International Law Journal* 17 (1984): 407–427.

896 Kofele-Kale, *International Law of Responsibility for Economic Crimes*, 290.

897 Republic of Philippines v. Marcos, 806 F.2d 344 (2d Cir. 1987).

898 Ibid., 359.

899 Jimenez v. Aristeguieta, 311 F.2d 547 (5th Cir. 1962), cert. denied sub nom. Jimenez v. Hixon, 373 U.S. 914 (1963).

held that it is "only when officials having sovereign authority act in an official capacity that the Act of State Doctrine applies."[900] In this case, the Venezuelan Government lodged a request with the United States for the extradition of Marcos Perez Jimenez, former President of Venezuela, who at that time was exiled in Miami and had allegedly enriched himself through corrupt acts while in office. The court held that a dictator's illegal acts and the receipt of money and securities with knowledge of their unlawful origin were for private financial gain and exceeded his official authority.[901] Consequently, the doctrine did not bar his extradition.

In *Sage International, Ltd v. Cadillac Gage Co.*,[902] a US corporation, Sage, sued another U.S. corporation, Cadillac, in the US District Court for the Eastern District of Michigan to recover damages for loss of income caused by its exclusion from entering the armoured car market in fifteen foreign countries due to Cadillac's participation in an illegal kickback scheme in those countries.[903] Cadillac requested the court to dismiss Sage's claim on the grounds that the act of State doctrine barred inquiry into the reasons why foreign governments bought Cadillac cars rather than Sage's cars.[904] The court balanced the need for justice among the litigants against the risk to US foreign relation, and ruled against the application of the act of State doctrine.[905] The court also argued that the doctrine does not apply when the case involves charges of corruption relating to the acts of a foreign government.[906]

In *W.S. Kirkpatrick and Co., Inc., v. Environmental Tectonics Corp. Int.*,[907] the US Supreme Court had to decide whether the act of State doctrine bars a court from entertaining a cause for action that requires imputing to foreign officials a corrupt motivation in the performance of an official act. In this case, Kirkpatrick had by bribing Nigerian public officials obtained a contract for the construction and equipment of an aero-medical centre in an air force base in Nigeria. Environmental Tectonics, as the unsuccessful bidder, sued Kirkpatrick for damages. Kirkpatrick sought the dismissal of the complaint on the ground that the action was barred by the act of State doctrine. The case eventually reached the Supreme Court, which found that in the case the court was not being asked to determine the legality of the acts of the Nigerian officials, but merely whether those acts occurred, and that the act of State doctrine did not therefore apply.[908]

900 Ibid.
901 Ibid.
902 Sage International, Ltd v. Cadillac Gage Co., 534 F.Supp. 896 (E.D. Mich. 1981).
903 Ibid., 898.
904 Ibid.
905 Ibid., 909.
906 Ibid., 910.
907 W.S. Kirkpatrick and Co., Inc., v. Environmental Tectonics Corp. Int., 493 U.S. 400.
908 Ibid., 406.

Moreover, the Supreme Court added that the underlying grounds for the doctrine, namely international comity and non-interference in the political and foreign policy of the State, are not a doctrine in themselves and cannot be interpreted to expand the doctrine.[909]

Domestic courts are barred from considering cases involving foreign cases where the claims turn on the legality or otherwise of the actions of foreign sovereigns on their own territory. Yet corrupt practices by heads of State and heads of government, as illustrated by the United States case law, are not considered sovereign acts. Corrupt acts are not public acts (Marcos I), but private financial gain exceeding official authority (Jimenez). Corruption has been accepted as an exception to the act of State doctrine (as in Sage). This is even affirmed by States themselves. For instance, in the Marcos case the Philippine Ministry of Foreign Affairs sent a note verbal to the United States stating that the act of State doctrine did not cover any acquisition of personal wealth by the Marcos spouses given that such acquisition did not constitute a public governmental or official act of the Philippine Government, even if such enrichment was achieved through the use or claimed use of government authority.[910] Here, an analogy could be made with jurisdictional immunities. The rationale behind the immunity from jurisdiction and act of State doctrines are similar, namely to respect the sovereignty of foreign States, which necessarily includes the acts of State bodies. However, as indicated in the previous section, corrupt acts are normally excluded from functional and State immunity since they do not constitute acts undertaken in an official or sovereign capacity. Similarly, corrupt practices cannot be covered by the act of State doctrine because they are not acts carried out by the sovereign. Additionally, as observed in the previous section, state immunity does not protect a foreign State from actions in the courts of another State by persons who have suffered damage or injury arising out of the act in question.[911] This clearly covers situations in which persons can sue former heads of State to recover damages arising out of corrupt practices.

When the legal argument is not sufficient to forestall the application of the act of state doctrine in corruption cases, policy considerations should be given prominence. If the truth be told, the act of State doctrine functions more as an escape hatch. The diversity of outcomes in case law shows that the doctrine is open to broad interpretation which tends to obscure the underlying policy considerations. Account should therefore be taken of anti-corruption policy considerations as an additional ground in endeavouring to ensure that the act of state doctrine is not applied in corruption cases.

---

909 Ibid., 409.

910 Tribunal fédéral [Federal Court] Ferdinand and Imelda Marcos v. Office fédéral de la police, 2 November 1989, ATF 115 Ib 496, 5(d).

911 Brownlie, *Principles of Public International Law*, 336.

3. AMNESTIES

Amnesties constitute a further barrier to criminal jurisdiction over corruption, they are intended to produce a clean slate and artificially create a new starting point, especially when States are going through periods of transition.[912] There have been several instances of amnesty for corruption. Probably the most renowned case is the amnesty granted in Hong Kong in 1977. The Hong Kong Independent Commission against Corruption (ICAC) had been set up in 1974, mainly in response to police corruption. ICAC's strong stand against corruption, particularly in the police force, resulted in frequent clashes with the police. Events escalated in 1977, when 2000 police officers demonstrated and the ICAC's headquarters was attacked, resulting in injury to several officers. The police threatened to go on strike and the Governor of Hong Kong decided to grant a partial amnesty for all minor crimes committed prior to 1977.[913] This amnesty has been considered successful because it was partly instrumental in the subsequent effective work of the ICAC in reducing drastically the level of corruption in Hong Kong. Clearly, the exact role played by the amnesty in the success of the ICAC is difficult to establish. It is believed that the amnesty enabled the ICAC to focus on the future, rather than being overwhelmed with a backlog of cases, and allowed it to conduct its work on a fresh footing and build public support without being tainted by the accusation of a witch-hunt of past wrongdoers.[914]

Most amnesties relating to corruption offences were not, however, confined to corruption. They were granted as part of a broader amnesty for other crimes, such as human rights violations, in the context of conflict resolution. This was the case, for example, in South Africa and Uganda, where perpetrators of crimes could apply for amnesty once they had fully disclosed their role and the crimes committed during the conflict.[915] Corruption was not therefore specifically

---

912 Black's Law Dictionary defines amnesty as "[a] sovereign act of forgiveness for past acts, granted by a government to all persons (or to certain classes of persons) who have been guilty of crime or delict, generally political offenses, -treason, sedition, rebellion, draft evasion,- and often conditioned upon their return to obedience and duty within a prescribed time." Henry Campbell Black, Joseph R Nolan, and Jacqueline Nolan-Haley, *Black's Law Dictionary: Definitions of the Terms and Phrases of American and English Jurisprudence, Ancient and Modern*, 6th ed. (St. Paul: West Pub. Co, 1990), 82–83.

913 More specifically, the amnesty stated: "In future the ICAC would not normally act on complaints or evidence relating to offenses committed before 1st January 1977, except in relation to persons who had already been interviewed (and allegations of an offense put to them), persons against whom warrants had been issued, and persons outside of Hong Kong on 5th November." See, ICAC, *Annual Report of the Independent Commission Against Corruption*. (Hong Kong: Government Printer, 1977), 9.

914 Jeremy Pope, *TI Source Book: Confronting Corruption: The Elements of a National Integrity System* (Berlin: Transparency International, 2000), 100.

915 In South Africa, this was through the Truth and Reconciliation Commission and its Amnesty Committee set up under the Promotion of National Unity and Reconciliation Act, No. 34 of 1995. In Uganda, there was the Amnesty Act 2000 and Amnesty Commission. Similar non-

targeted by the amnesty law. In Uganda, for example, the Amnesty Act provided that amnesty would be granted for "any other crime in furtherance of the war or armed rebellion ... or assisting or aiding the conduct or prosecution of the war or armed rebellion."[916] This clause could be understood as including corrupt acts. Nevertheless, the success of these amnesties in terms of the enforcement of anti-corruption law is virtually impossible to measure. Their achievement is measured in relation to resolving conflicts and bringing peace, rather than in terms of how well the corruption problem was addressed in the aftermath of the conflict.

Amnesties for corruption will continue to give rise to debate. A number of amnesties for corruption have been proposed and vehemently rejected by public opinion. In Pakistan, for example, a controversial amnesty for corruption was granted by Presidential Decree in 2007 to public officials who had been accused of corruption between 1986 and 1999.[917] However, in July 2009, the Supreme Court of Pakistan ruled that the Decree needed to be approved by Parliament and, in view of the increasing pressure and opposition, it was finally abandoned. The use of amnesties in corruption cases, as for any other crime for that matter, clearly gives rise to a fair amount of controversy.

Although most States have the power to grant amnesties in accordance with their constitutional framework for crimes committed within their jurisdiction, the question arises as to whether this is consistent with the international legal framework against corruption. While there is no specific international rule against amnesties for corruption offences, they may conflict with certain international obligations. As already noted in this study, a State is under the international obligation to: establish territorial criminal jurisdiction over corrupt acts;[918] prosecute alleged offenders when they are present in the territory of the State and it does not extradite such persons on the grounds that they are nationals of that State;[919] apply prescribed sanctions, taking into account the gravity of the offence;[920]and ensure that entities or persons who have suffered

corruption specific processes were set in motion by the Truth and Reconciliation Commissions in Sierra Leone, Democratic Republic of Congo and Liberia.

916 Uganda Amnesty Act 2000, s. 3(1)(c) and (d).

917 National Reconciliation Ordinance of 5 October 2007.

918 UNCAC, Art. 42(1)(a-b); Inter-American Convention against Corruption, Art. 5(1); CoE Criminal Law Convention, Art. 17(1)(a); OECD Convention, Art. 4(1); AU Convention against Corruption, Art. 13(1)(a); UNODC, *Legislative Guide for the Implementation of the United Nations Convention against Corruption*, para. 41.

919 UNCAC, Art. 42(3); Inter-American Convention against Corruption, Art. 5(3); CoE Criminal Law Convention, Art. 17(3); AU Convention against Corruption, Art. 13(1)(c).

920 UNCAC, Art. 30(1). The CoE Criminal Law Convention, the EU Convention, and the OECD Convention call for effective, proportionate and dissuasive sanctions which in the case of natural persons, should include deprivation of liberty. CoE Criminal Law Convention; Art. 19(1); EU Convention, Art. 5(1); OECD Convention, Art. 3(1).

damage as a result of an act of corruption have the right to initiate legal proceedings against those responsible for the damage in order to obtain compensation.[921]

Any amnesty granted for corruption offences might well conflict with these anti-corruption obligations. However, it is necessary in this respect to make a distinction between the criminal law obligations referred to above and the obligation to ensure that civil remedies are available for the victims of corruption. The latter obligation is clearly violated in cases of amnesties. When a State grants an amnesty for corruption offences against civil proceedings, the victims of corruption are denied the right to initiate legal proceedings to obtain compensation from those responsible for the damage. However, criminal law obligations may not be violated by amnesties, as States are not subject to an unconditional requirement to prosecute and sanction. As indicated above, the obligation to prosecute should be understood in reality as a requirement to submit the case to the competent authorities for the purpose of prosecution.[922] The duty is not to prosecute, let alone to punish, and States retain their prosecutorial discretion.[923] Nor is prosecutorial discretion an unfettered obligation. It should be exercised to maximize the effectiveness of law enforcement measures in respect of corrupt offences and with due regard to the need to deter the commission of such offences.[924] Moreover, such discretion needs to be exercised on the basis of professional motives, and should not be subject to improper influence by concerns of a political nature.[925] Although amnesties are distinct from prosecutorial discretion, the underlying rationale behind both is similar. States have clearly retained prosecutorial discretion as a back door in case prosecution is undesirable. That same back door can be used by States to escape criminal prosecution and the application of sanctions for corruption if an amnesty is merited.

In analysing amnesties, contextual and policy considerations are important so as not to adopt a purely legalistic approach in an area that is partly legal and partly political. Amnesties may indeed be justified when corruption is systemic and widespread among low-level officials. Where large numbers of low-level officials are involved, a general amnesty followed by re-training may well be seen as preferable to the costs associated with large numbers of prosecutions and the

921 UNCAC, Art. 35; CoE Civil Law Convention, Art. 3(1).
922 UNCAC, Art. 44(11).
923 This is the traditional understanding of the clause "to prosecute" in *aut dedere aut judicare* obligations.
924 UNCAC, Art. 30(3).
925 OECD, *Commentaries on the Convention on Combating Bribery of Foreign Public Officials in International Business Transactions*, para. 27.

replacement of large numbers of public officials.[926] They may help towards the danger of public expectations of retributive justice overwhelming the capacity of the authorities and corruption reform being jeopardized if those in positions of power implicated in the investigation and prosecution of allegations of past corruption. It may well be preferable for a government to seek a fresh start through a limited or general amnesty with a view to making a clean break with the past and focusing scarce resources on the implementation of anti-corruption reforms. There may also be cases in which an amnesty can serve as a negotiation tool, in the same way as they are used and relatively well accepted negotiations to end violent conflicts. It may also be argued that amnesties could also serve the purpose, in specific cases, of encouraging senior officials to return the proceeds of their crimes. The return of highly needed assets to developing countries may be preferable to simply keeping offenders in prison for a number of years.

On the other hand, amnesties also present the risk of a general erosion of deterrence and the rule of law, which may in turn encourage future acts of corruption in the expectation that they too will be excused or ignored.[927] Most importantly, amnesties are usually strongly opposed by public opinion and may have the effect of polarizing society, thereby fuelling conflict instead of solving it. For that reason, it is difficult and imprudent to generalize about the acceptability of amnesties in the context of the international legal framework against corruption. The viability and legality of amnesties in relation to corruption therefore need to be evaluated on a case-by-case basis.

CONCLUSION

This Chapter has examined the jurisdictional issues related to the enforcement of anti-corruption law. Although the complexity of many corrupt practices and their transnational elements present challenges for criminal and civil jurisdiction, the international legal framework against corruption has only taken up those challenges to a certain extent. International obligations relating to jurisdiction constitute a traditional set of measures with a minimum degree of novelty. Criminal jurisdiction for corruption remains largely territorial, although States may choose to apply extraterritorial grounds, such as active or passive nationality and the essential interests of the State. With regard to immunities, States are only required to apply an appropriate balance between immunities and adjudication, which may in the end result in little change in practice.

---

926 UNODC, *The Global Programme against Corruption: UN Anti-Corruption Toolkit*, 3rd ed. (Vienna: UNODC, 2004), 435.

927 Ibid., 437.

Nevertheless, as indicated in this Chapter, these provisions need to be interpreted in a way that reinforces the enforcement of anti-corruption law. Criminal territorial jurisdiction has to be interpreted broadly so that an extensive physical connection to the corrupt act is not required. States are also encouraged to exercise their criminal jurisdiction, even in cases where neither a part of the corrupt act, nor its effects, occurs in their territory. Moreover, the interpretation of the law of immunities shows that, in the majority of cases, jurisdictional immunities do not constitute a barrier to prosecution or litigation in relation to corruption.

The international legal framework has to some extent enhanced the use of certain tools which are serving to reinforce action to combat corruption. The most important jurisdictional aspect of international law against corruption is undoubtedly the reinforcement of civil litigation against corruption, including at the international level. Moreover, the international legal framework has indirectly created a form of quasi-universal jurisdiction. States may prosecute offenders on the basis of a number of specific jurisdictional grounds, ranging from territoriality to nationality, and protective principles. This, together with the obligation to extradite or prosecute, has created a treaty based quasi-universal jurisdiction over corruption.

CHAPTER VII
ENFORCEMENT OF ANTI-CORRUPTION LAW

INTRODUCTION

Corruption is mainly regarded as a crime, and as such action to combat corruption partly rests on a rational theory of crime control. It is therefore believed that the probability of engaging in corruption depends primarily on the penalty imposed and on the likelihood of being caught.[928] For that reason, both at the national and, more recently at the international level, law enforcement has played a prominent role in combating corruption. However, there are many critics of such a law enforcement-centred approach. It has been argued that, because corruption is not merely a crime, but also affects economic and moral issues, the law and its enforcement are an ill-equipped approach to tackling corruption.[929] It has also been claimed that anti-corruption law enforcement creates an unhappy population or a nation of outlaws.[930] It is also argued that corruption is a symptom of a disease at the core of individual and institutional values, and that law enforcement approaches simply touch upon the symptoms, without ever addressing the disease.[931] These claims have their merits. Corruption is much more than a simple crime, and law enforcement is not a universally effective tool in combating it. Centuries of corrupt practices around the world, despite the criminalization of corruption, prove that law enforcement is not the ultimate solution. However, it is still the most important method that societies have put in place to contain undesirable conduct such as corruption

928 On this rational theory of crime control, see, Gary S. Becker, "Crime and Punishment: An Economic Approach," *Journal of Political Economy* 76, no. 2 (1968): 169–217.

929 Catherine Kessedjian, "La norme juridique est-elle apte à lutter contre la corruption?," in *Souveraineté étatique et marchés internationaux à la fin du 20ème siècle: A propos de 30 ans de recherche du CREDIMI: Mélanges en l'honneur de Philippe Kahn*, vol. 20, Travaux du Centre de recherche sur le droit des marchés et des investissements internationaux (Dijon: Litec, 2000), 602–603 and 607.

930 Gabriel Ben-Dor, "Corruption, Institutionalization, and Political Development: The Revisionist Theses Revisited," *Comparative Political Studies* 7, no. 1 (1974): 69.

931 Seminario internacional sobre la corrupción y la convención interamericana, *Talleres de divulgación e implementación de la convención interamericana contra la corrupción* (Bogotá: Pontificia Universidad Javeriana, Facultad de Ciencias Jurídicas, 1999), 235. For a similar view, see John T. Noonan, *Bribes* (Berkeley: University of California Press, 1984), 546–547.

insofar as possible. In this discussion, it is necessary to make a distinction between the underlying causes of corruption and corrupt acts themselves. It is true that, if corruption is considered as encompassing its underlying causes, then it is a complex issue that goes beyond a criminal activity. However, if the underlying causes are set aside, then what is left is solely a criminal act and as such, law enforcement is the way to deal with it. The underlying causes of corruption, as with any other crime, will never be dealt with through law enforcement. Nor is that the objective of law enforcement. The causes need to be addressed though other methods unrelated to law enforcement. Yet, on the one hand, while the underlying causes of corruption, and other criminal activity for that matter, continue to be studied and tackled, on the other hand law enforcement remains the principal means of identifying, punishing, and indirectly deterring criminal activity such as corruption.

This Chapter addresses the host of provisions and measures that contribute to the effective identification, apprehension, prosecution, adjudication and sanctioning of those engaged in corruption.

I. MISCELLANEOUS OBLIGATIONS

The international legal framework against corruption imposes numerous obligations on States relating to a number of different aspects of the national law enforcement system against corruption. While some of these obligations are more complex and controversial in nature, and are a novelty for certain legal systems, those analysed in this section tend to be more straightforward and easier to implement for the majority of States, and are therefore examined in less detail.

1. CRIMINALIZATION OF CORRUPT ACTS

The first and most basic international obligation of anti-corruption law enforcement is to criminalize corrupt acts. All other law enforcement obligations are contingent on the criminalization of corruption. States have to establish a number of offences as crimes in their domestic law, if they do not already exist. In this connection, States need to criminalize the bribery of national public officials and the solicitation or acceptance of a bribe by national public officials;[932] the bribery of foreign public officials or officials of public

---

932 UNCAC, Art. 15; Inter-American Convention against Corruption Arts. 6(1)(a-b) and 7; AU Convention against Corruption, Art. 4(1)(a-b) and 5(1); CoE Criminal Law Convention, Art. 2 and 3. The CoE Criminal Law Convention also provides separately for the obligation to criminalize the active and passive bribery of a member of any domestic public assembly exercising legislative or administrative powers. See, CoE Criminal Law Convention, Art. 4.

international organizations;[933] and the embezzlement, misappropriation or other diversion of property by a public official.[934] States are also encouraged, although not legally required, to criminalize the solicitation or acceptance of a bribe by foreign public officials and officials of international organizations,[935] bribery and embezzlement within the private sector,[936] trading in influence,[937] abuse of functions[938] and the illicit enrichment of a public official.[939]

933 UNCAC, Art. 16(1); OECD Convention, Art. 1(1); CoE Criminal Law Convention, Art. 5 and 9. The CoE Criminal Law Convention criminalizes separately the active and passive bribery of members of parliamentary assemblies of international or supranational organizations of which the party is a member, of any holders of judicial office or officials of any international court whose jurisdiction is accepted by the Party, and a member of any public assembly exercising legislative or administrative powers in any other State. See, CoE Criminal Law Convention, Arts. 6, 10 and 11. The Inter-American Convention against Corruption provides for the criminalization of foreign public officials, but not officials of public international organizations. See, Inter-American Convention against Corruption Art. 8. The AU Convention against Corruption does not explicitly provide for the criminalization of bribery of foreign public officials. However, in Article 19(1), it requires States Parties to collaborate with the countries of origin of multinationals to criminalize and punish the practice of secret commissions and other forms of corrupt practices during international trade transactions.

934 UNCAC Art. 17; AU Convention against Corruption, Art. 4(1)(d) and 5(1). A similar provision is found in the Inter-American Convention against Corruption, although as a best endeavour obligation. See, Inter-American Convention against Corruption Art. 11(1)(d). The Inter-American Convention against Corruption also provides for a specific type of diversion of property, namely the improper use of state property, which States Parties undertake to consider criminalizing. See, Inter-American Convention against Corruption Art. 11(1)(b).

935 UNCAC, Art. 16(2). The criminalization of the passive bribery of foreign public officials is mandatory under the CoE Criminal Law Convention. See, Art. 5.

936 UNCAC, Art. 21. Under the CoE Criminal Law Convention and AU Convention against Corruption States Parties are obliged to criminalize this offence. See, CoE Criminal Law Convention, Arts. 7 and 8; and AU Convention against Corruption, Arts. 4(1)(e), and 5(1). States should also consider criminalizing the embezzlement of property in the private sector. UNCAC, Art. 22.

937 UNCAC, Art. 18, Inter-American Convention against Corruption Art. 11(1)(c). Under the CoE Criminal Law Convention, States Parties are required to criminalize active and passive trading in influence by domestic public officials, members of domestic public assemblies, foreign public officials, members of foreign public assemblies, officials of international organizations, members of international parliamentary assemblies, and judges and officials of international courts. See, Art. 12. Similarly, under the AU Convention against Corruption, States Parties are required to criminalize active and passive trading in influence. See, AU Convention against Corruption, Arts. 4(1)(f) and 5(1).

938 UNCAC, Art. 19. Under the Inter-American Convention against Corruption and AU Convention against Corruption, States Parties are required to criminalize the abuse of functions. See, Inter-American Convention against Corruption, Art. 7 and 6(1)(c); and AU Convention against Corruption, Arts. 4(1)(c). and 5(1). The Inter-American Convention against Corruption also establishes a specific type of abuse of functions, namely the improper use of classified or confidential information, which States Parties undertake to consider criminalizing. See, Inter-American Convention against Corruption Art. 11(1)(a).

939 UNCAC, Art. 20. The Inter-American Convention against Corruption and AU Convention against Corruption also require the criminalization of illicit enrichment, although in stronger terms, as States Parties have to criminalize it, and not simply consider doing so. See, Inter-American Convention against Corruption, Art. 9; and AU Convention against Corruption, Arts. 4(1)(g), 5(1), and 8.

As indicated Chapter IV, the international legal framework against corruption provides detailed definitions of these offences, with which States have to comply in their domestic law.[940] Even if States already have the relevant legislation, they need to ensure that the existing provisions comply with the international legal framework and to amend their laws, where necessary.[941] In addition to criminalizing the commission of a corrupt act, States also need to criminalize participation in such an act as an accomplice, assistant or instigator,[942] and may go further by criminalizing an attempt and/or the preparation of an act of corruption.[943] States also have to criminalize the obstruction of justice in proceedings or in the exercise of official duties by a justice or law enforcement official in relation to the commission of corrupt acts or related offences.[944]

The criminalization of offences is important for States to be able to prosecute and sanction offenders.[945] Moreover, as indicated in Chapter VIII, since a number of States make extradition and mutual legal assistance conditional upon the existence of dual criminality, a fairly harmonized worldwide definition of the corrupt acts is also necessary for effective international cooperation in criminal matters.

---

940 International anti-corruption law has adopted the so-called "functional equivalence" principle, by which the legal framework establishes a standard to be met by States, but does not require them to use identical terms in domestic law. See also Chapter IX.I below.

941 For more on the implementation by States of the obligation to criminalize corrupt acts, see Chapter IV.

942 UNCAC, Art. 27(1); Inter-American Convention against Corruption, Art. 6(1)(e) and 7; CoE Criminal Law Convention, Art. 15; OECD Convention, Art. 1(2); AU Convention against Corruption, Art. 4(1)(i) and 5(1).

943 UNCAC, Art. 27(2–3). Under the Inter-American Convention against Corruption and AU Convention against Corruption, States Parties are obliged to criminalize any participation, collaboration or attempt to commit a corrupt act. See, Inter-American Convention against Corruption, Art. 6(1)(e) and 7; AU Convention against Corruption, Art. 4(1)(i) and 5(1). Similarly, under the OECD Convention, States Parties are obliged to criminalize any attempt or conspiracy to bribe a foreign public official to the same extent as any attempt or conspiracy to bribe a domestic official. See, OECD Convention, Art. 1(2).

944 UNCAC, Art. 25. The CoE Criminal Law Convention further calls upon States to establish liability (criminal or other) for accounting offences, such as the creation or using of an invoice or any other accounting document or record containing false or incomplete information, and unlawfully omitting to make a record of a payment, when committed intentionally in order to commit, conceal or disguise an act of corruption. See Art. 14. On money-laundering as a corruption related offence, see below the section on Money Laundering.

945 It has also been argued that these offences should not be criminalized. It has been claimed that the criminalization of corruption offences could actually worsen corruption in the developing world, as when a large segment of a country's population engages in corruption, its criminalization is tantamount to creating a nation of outlaws. See, Bryane Michael, *Suing against Corruption: The Role of Civil Law,* Policy Innovations, 23 July 2007, available at www.policyinnovations.org (last visited 29 April 2012).

2. CRIMINALIZATION OF MONEY LAUNDERING

There is an intrinsic link between corruption and money laundering. For those who commit corruption to enjoy the benefits of their illicit activities, they need to hide the origin of their funds and eventually convert them into legal funds. Money laundering is therefore an important tool for corrupt offenders, as already indicated in Chapter V. Effective anti-money laundering (AML) policies and measures create an important barrier that offenders find it difficult to overcome. These measures are therefore one of the best means of supporting action to combat corruption, as offenders who manage to evade anti-corruption law enforcement may be subject to anti-money-laundering law enforcement.

In addition to measures to prevent money laundering discussed in Chapter V, the international legal framework against corruption places an additional requirement on States: to criminalize money laundering that has its origins in a corrupt act. Under the terms of the UNCAC, which follows the definition of the offence of money laundering in the 1988 UN Convention against Illicit Traffic in Narcotic Drugs and Psychotropic Substances and other international instruments, States are required to criminalize the following acts:

a) the conversion or transfer of the proceeds of crime;[946]
b) the concealment or disguise of the true nature, source, location, disposition, movement or ownership of the proceeds of crime;[947]
c) the acquisition, possession or use of the proceeds of crime (subject to the basic concepts of the national legal system);[948] and
d) participation in, association with or conspiracy to commit, attempts to commit and aiding, abetting, facilitating and counselling the commission of any money laundering offences (subject to the basic concepts of the national legal system).[949]

It is important to recall that the proceeds of crime consist of any property derived from or obtained, directly or indirectly, through the commission of an offence.[950] States have to apply these money laundering offences to the proceeds

---

946 UNCAC, Art. 23(1)(a)(i); AU Convention against Corruption, Art. 6(a).

947 UNCAC, Art. 23(1)(a)(ii); Inter-American Convention against Corruption, Arts. 7 and 6(1)(d); AU Convention against Corruption, Art. 6(b).

948 UNCAC, Art. 23.1(b)(i); Inter-American Convention against Corruption, Arts. 7 and 6(1)(d); AU Convention against Corruption, Art. 6(c).

949 UNCAC, Art. 23(1)(b)(ii). States are also encouraged to criminalize the concealment or continued retention of property that is the result of a corrupt act. UNCAC, Art. 24; AU Convention against Corruption, Art. 4(1)(h) and 5(1). Under the AU Convention against Corruption, States Parties are obliged to criminalize this act.

950 UNCAC, Art. 2(e).

of corrupt acts and a wide range of predicate offences.[951] There are therefore two distinct crimes, the corrupt act (the predicate offence), which produces proceeds for the persons involved in the act, and the laundering of such proceeds. Nevertheless, money-laundering offences are understood to be independent and autonomous offences and a prior conviction for the predicate offence is not necessary to establish the illicit nature or origin of the assets laundered.[952] The illicit nature or origin of the assets and any knowledge, intent or purpose may be established during the course of the prosecution for money laundering and may be inferred from objective factual circumstances.[953]

It should also be noted that States are required to apply these money laundering offences to proceeds generated by corrupt acts committed outside the jurisdiction of the State.[954] Accordingly, corrupt acts carried out in one State may be considered predicate offences for the purpose of an AML prosecution in another State. However, dual criminality may be necessary. In other words, offences committed outside the jurisdiction of a State only constitute predicate offences when the relevant conduct is a criminal offence under the domestic law of the State where it was committed and would also be a criminal offence under the domestic law of the State bringing charges for money laundering.[955] While dual criminality in this context is common practice in several States, such as Argentina,[956] New Zealand[957] and Switzerland,[958] in other States, for example Spain and Italy,[959] dual criminality is not required. It is extremely important for States to establish the extraterritoriality of predicate offences, as most money laundering cases involve an international element, since the proceeds of corruption are often laundered in another jurisdiction.

In addition to criminalizing the intentional commission of money laundering originating from a corrupt act, States are also required to criminalize, subject to the basic concepts of their legal system, participation in, association with or conspiracy to commit attempts to commit, and aiding, abetting, facilitating and

---

951 A predicate offence is any offence as a result of which proceeds have been generated that may become the subject of a money-laundering offence. UNCAC, Art. 2(h).

952 UN General Assembly, *Report of the Ad Hoc Committee for the Negotiation of a Convention against Corruption on the work of its first to seventh sessions: Addendum: Interpretative Notes for the Official Records (Travaux Préparatoires) of the Negotiation of the United Nations Convention against Corruption*, A/58/422/Add.1, 7 October 2003, para. 32.

953 Ibid.

954 UNCAC, Art. 23(2)(a-c); OECD Convention, Art. 7; CoE Criminal Law Convention Art. 13.

955 UNCAC, Art. 23(2)(c). However, dual criminality is not required under the CoE Convention on Laundering, Search, Seizure and Confiscation of the Proceeds from Crime. See, Art. 6(2)(a).

956 See, Argentine Criminal Code, Art. 279.4.

957 See, New Zealand Crimes Act 1961, section 257A (6A).

958 See, Swiss Criminal Code, Art. 305*bis* (3).

959 See, Spanish Criminal Code, Art. 301.4, and Italian Criminal Code, Arts. 9 and 10.

counselling the commission of money-laundering.[960] Clearly, the widest forms of participation need to be criminalized. This is necessary because third parties are often involved in money laundering. Offenders who have obtained the proceeds of crime usually need to resort to intermediate financial institutions to be able to launder them. As the role of third parties is so prominent in certain money laundering cases, the criminalization of their participation in the commission of the crime would appear to be essential.[961]

The international legal framework against corruption builds on earlier and parallel anti-money laundering initiatives.[962] And, partly as a result of these initiatives, many States have already criminalized money laundering. However, the key element is for such legislation to establish corrupt acts as predicate offences. The Financial Action Task Force (FATF) has already recommended States to consider corruption and bribery as predicate offences to money laundering and, through a system of peer evaluation, States have amended their AML legislation *inter alia*, to include bribery and corruption as predicate offences.[963] Many States already have laws on money laundering, but there are many variations in the definitions of predicate offences. Some States limit predicate offences to drug trafficking and a few other offences (for example, Qatar which does not include corrupt acts),[964] other States have a long list of offences or define predicate offences generically as including all crimes (such as the Russian Federation and Mexico),[965] or all crimes are subject to a defined penalty threshold (for example, in Turkey where predicate offences are those for which the minimum punishment is one year or more of imprisonment, thereby including corrupt acts).[966]

Consequently, although there is already a trend to globalize AML legislation and expand predicate offences to include a wide range of acts, including corruption, the international legal framework against corruption is contributing to this trend. States with criminal legislation against money laundering which do not regard corruption as a predicate offence need to amend their legislation

960 UNCAC, Art. 23(1)(b)(ii).

961 For examples of the prominent roles of certain intermediaries in money laundering, most notably banks, see Global Witness, *Undue Diligence: How Banks Do Business with Corrupt Regimes*, March 2009.

962 In particular, the Forty Recommendations and the Nine Special Recommendations of the Financial Action Task Force on Money Laundering (FATF). For more on this and other anti-money laundering initiatives, see Chapter V above.

963 FATF, Recommendation 3, Interpretative Note to Recommendation 3and General Glossary (Designated categories of offences). For the many FATF mutual evaluation reports, see FATF's website: www.fatf-gafi.org (last visited 29 April 2012).

964 See, Article 2 of the Law (28) of 2002, as amended in 2003.

965 See, Russian Federation Criminal Code, Art 174, 174.1, 175; Mexico Federal Criminal Code, Art. 400*bis*.

966 See, Turkish Criminal Law No. 5237 of 2005, Art. 282.

accordingly. States without criminal legislation against money laundering need to reform their criminal law to include money laundering as a crime and corrupt acts as a corresponding predicate offence.

3. ANTI-CORRUPTION LAW ENFORCEMENT BODY

The international legal framework against corruption requires the existence of specialized bodies at the national level to prevent corruption and enforce anti-corruption law.[967] With regard exclusively to law enforcement, States have to ensure the existence of a body or persons specialized in combating corruption through law enforcement, and grant such body or persons: (i) the necessary independence to carry out their functions effectively without any undue influence; and (ii) appropriate training and resources to carry out their tasks.[968]

With varying degrees of success, a number of States have already established such specialized bodies. As indicated in Chapter V, this practice has been most widespread in Asia and Africa; for example in Indonesia, Bangladesh, Kenya and Nigeria.[969] The Hong Kong Independent Commission against Corruption (ICAC) is probably the most famous and successful experience in this respect.[970] There even exist local anti-corruption law enforcement bodies, such as the New South Wales Independent Commission against Corruption, whose jurisdiction is limited to the state of New South Wales, the largest state in Australia.[971]

---

967 On anti-corruption bodies responsible for preventive measures and policies, see Chapter V above.

968 UNCAC, Art. 36. In addition to the existence of an anti-corruption law enforcement body, States are also required to encourage the cooperation between such body or bodies and other public authorities and public officials (UNCAC, Art. 38). In this connection, States are also asked to encourage cooperation between national law enforcement authorities and entities of the private sector, in particular financial institutions, relating to matters involving the commission of acts of corruption (UNCAC, Art. 39(1)). The role of the private sector in the enforcement of anti-corruption law should not be underestimated. It is often competitors who observe irregularities and suspicious transactions in the course of their routine commercial activities. Persons specializing in specific contexts or operations are well placed to identify uncommon patterns that may serve as indicators of corrupt practices (UNODC, *Legislative Guide for the Implementation of the United Nations Convention against Corruption* (Vienna, New York: United Nations, 2006), para. 481). Anti-corruption authorities would benefit from such insights and could more easily draw attention to priority sectors.

969 For information about the anti-corruption bodies in these countries, see Chapter V above.

970 The Hong Kong Independent Commission against Corruption (ICAC) was established in 1974 and is reputed for its success in dramatically reducing the level of corruption in Hong Kong's public service. It is also known for its intrusive methods of investigation. For more information, see the Hong Kong ICAC's website: www.icac.org.hk/ (last visited 29 April 2012). See also, Jeremy Lo Kwok-chung, "Combating Corruption in Hong Kong," *Resource Material Series (UNAFEI)* 77 (March 2009): 3–10.

971 The New South Wales ICAC was established in 1988 by the Independent Commission Against Corruption Act. For more information, see New South Wales ICAC's website: www.icac.nsw.

In practice, the international legal framework does not require States to create such institutions. States may choose to provide specialized expertise within existing structures of the police, prosecution offices and courts.[972] Most States have adopted this approach. For example, Japan has created specialized investigation departments within prosecutors' offices in the major cities.[973]

As indicated in Chapter V, the creation of anti-corruption bodies is part of an institutional response to corruption. States are also required to create anti-corruption bodies that are entrusted with preventive measures and policies. However, experience so far has not convincingly shown that these bodies are effective in combating corruption. In fact, in only very limited cases have they proved to be effective, most notably the Hong Kong ICAC.[974]

4. SPECIAL INVESTIGATIVE TECHNIQUES

It is widely agreed that in cases of corruption, normal and less intrusive investigative techniques are simply not effective or are excessively risky to those involved. The international legal framework against corruption therefore specifically endorses the special investigative techniques of controlled delivery, undercover operations and electronic surveillance to combat corruption.

gov.au (last visited 29 April 2012). See also, John Pritchard, "Introduction to the New South Wales Independent Commission against Corruption," *Resource Material Series (UNAFEI)* 69 (July 2006): 202–226.

972 For more information on alternatives to implement this obligation, see UNODC and UNICRI, *Technical Guide to the United Nations Convention against Corruption* (Vienna, New York: United Nations, 2009), para. 113–117.

973 ADB/OECD Anti-Corruption Initiative for Asia and the Pacific, *Anti-Corruption Policies in Asia and the Pacific: Progress in Legal and Institutional Reform in 25 Countries* (Manila: ADB/OECD Anti-Corruption Initiative for Asia and the Pacific, 2006), 44.

974 For more on anti-corruption bodies, agencies and commissions, see Luís de Sousa, *Anti-Corruption Agencies: Between Empowerment and Irrelevance* (European University Institute Working Papers, RSCAS 2009/08, 2009); John Heilbrunn, *Anti-Corruption Commissions: Panacea or Real Medicine to Fight Corruption?* (World Bank Institute, 2004); Alan Doig, David Watt, and Robert Williams, *Measuring "Success" in Five African Anti-Corruption Commissions: The Cases of Ghana, Malawi, Tanzania, Uganda and Zambia*, U4 Anti-Corruption Resource Centre Research Report (Bergen: Chr. Michelsen Institute, May 2005); UNDP, *Institutional Arrangements to Combat Corruption: A Comparative Study* (Thailand, 2005); Jon Quah, *Defying Institutional Failure: Learning from the Experiences of Anti-Corruption Agencies in Four Asian Countries* (Centre for Research and Studies on Sociology (CIES), Conference: Empowering Anti-Corruption Agencies: Defying Institutional Failure and Strengthening Preventive and Repressive Capacities, May 14, 2008), SpringerLink; Michael Johnston, "A Brief History of Anticorruption Agencies," in *The Self-Restraining State: Power and Accountability in New Democracies*, ed. Andreas Schedler, Larry Diamond, and Marc F. Plattner (Boulder, Colorado: Lynne Rienner Publishers, Inc., 1999), 217–226; Patrick Meagher, *Anti-Corruption Agencies: A Review of Experience* (Center for Institutional Reform and the Informal Sector, March 2004); OECD, *Specialised Anti-Corruption Institutions: Review of Models* (Paris: OECD, 2007).

Controlled delivery is an investigative tool that is already in use in several countries, particularly to combat drug trafficking.[975] It is defined by the UNCAC in the following terms:

> "...the technique of allowing illicit or suspect consignments to pass out of, through or into the territory of one or more States, with the knowledge and under the supervision of their competent authorities, with a view to the investigation of an offence and the identification of persons involved in the commission of the offence."[976]

Undercover operations may be defined as an investigation involving a series of related undercover activities (investigative activities involving the use of an assumed name or cover identity) by an undercover employee (agent) over a period of time by infiltrating a criminal organization to gather evidence.[977] Electronic surveillance refers to listening devices or the interception of the communications of the persons being investigated. It performs a similar function to undercover operations and is often preferable where such operations are excessively risky to the investigation or the safety of investigators. Additional special investigative techniques include preventive arrest and integrity tests. In Peru, for example, for crimes related to organized crime, such as corruption, arrest may occur at the pre-judicial stage, before the beginning of the judicial proceedings. In cases of strict necessity and urgency the judge may, at the request of the office of the Prosecutor, order preventive arrest for up to 15 days.[978] Integrity tests are also being increasingly widely used as an investigative tool in anti-corruption investigations[979] and consist of random or "intelligence-led" tests on persons or institutions.[980]

States are required to envisage these and other investigative techniques, which are particularly useful for the investigation and prosecution of corruption cases.

---

975 For example at the European level, article 22 of the Convention on Mutual Assistance And Cooperation Between Customs Administrations and article 12 of the Convention on Mutual Assistance in Criminal Matters between the Member States of the European Union, state that Member States will undertake to ensure that controlled deliveries may be permitted in their territories in relation to criminal investigations into extraditable offences.

976 UNCAC, Art. 2(i), which takes the definition from Art. 1(g) of the 1988 UN Convention against Illicit Traffic in Narcotic Drugs and Psychotropic Substances.

977 International Training Course on "Effective Methods to Combat Transnational Organized Crime in Criminal Justice Processes" Group 1 Phase 2 Report, "Special Investigative Tools to Combat Transnational Organized Crime (TOC)," *Resource Material Series (UNAFEI)* 58 (December 2001): 232.

978 Peru, Law 27.379, 20 December 2000.

979 For more on integrity testing, see UNODC, *The Global Programme against Corruption: UN Anti-Corruption Toolkit*, 3rd ed. (Vienna: UNODC, 2004), 396–406.

980 For more on this practice in the United Kingdom, see Colin Nicholls, Tim Daniel, and John Hatchard, *Corruption and Misuse of Public Office* (Oxford: Oxford University Press, 2006), 153–154.

Several countries which still do not use these special techniques therefore have to incorporate them into their jurisdictions and carry out training for law enforcement officers on how best to utilize such techniques. However, when incorporating these investigative techniques and regulating their use, States must be mindful of certain possible constraints. Special investigative techniques have to be consistent with the law, and particularly the right to a fair trial, from which the requirement of the proper administration of justice is inferred.[981] This right is so prominent in democratic societies that it cannot be sacrificed for the sake of expediency. This usually means that investigative techniques have to be subject to clear restrictions and safeguards so as not to breach constitutional rights, which has different implications for different investigative techniques. For example, electronic surveillance, such as wire tapping, interception of telecommunications and access to computer systems, which can be a threat to the human right to privacy, have to be approved by a court following a request from the police or prosecutor's office. This is normally standard procedure in most countries. In the case of undercover operations, law enforcement officials need to be careful not to engage in incitement, also called entrapment, whereby the undercover agents exert an influence on a person which may incite an offence that would otherwise not have been committed. In many jurisdictions, entrapment is a valid defence against criminal guilt. The ECHR overturned a bribery judgment by the courts of Lithuania because the defendant was found to have been incited by *agents provocateurs* (undercover agents) to accept the bribe.[982] A test to avoid entrapment would be if:

> "(i) The investigators have reasonable grounds to suspect the target or targets of involvement in a certain kind of offence, or at least the investigators have reasonable grounds to suspect people frequenting a particular location to be thus involved; and
> (ii) The investigators are duly authorized to carry out the operation in compliance with appropriate Codes of Practice, etc; and
> (iii) The undercover agent (agents) do no more than provide the target or targets with an unexceptional opportunity to commit the offence."[983]

Special investigative techniques are particularly useful in dealing with sophisticated organized criminal groups in view of the dangers and difficulties inherent in gaining access to their operations and gathering information and evidence for use in prosecutions.[984] States are therefore required to allow for the

---

981 On the right to a fair trial, see, for example, Universal Declaration on Human Rights, Art. 10; International Covenant on Civil and Political rights, Art. 14; European Convention on Human Rights, Art. 6; and generally Amnesty International, *Fair Trials Manual*, 1998.

982 Ramanauskas v. Lithuania, Eur. Ct. H.R., Judgment of 5 February 2008 (not yet published).

983 Nicholls, Daniel, and Hatchard, *Corruption and Misuse of Public Office*, 152.

984 For more on anti-corruption special investigative techniques, see Leslie Gielow Jacobs and Benjamin B. Wagner, "Retooling Law Enforcement to Investigate and Prosecute Entrenched

appropriate use by competent authorities of special investigative techniques within their territories, and also have to allow for the admissibility in court of the resulting evidence.[985]

5. PIERCING BANK SECRECY

Investigations into corruption often necessitate access to bank accounts to trace bribes and obtain incriminating evidence. Investigation into corruption may therefore be seriously impaired in countries with traditional rules of bank secrecy. The principle of bank secrecy rests on the right to privacy. Bank secrecy originated in Switzerland and is intended to protect the financial privacy of citizens from unauthorized access by other private persons or by the State. Hence, bank secrecy means that banks are under the obligation to refuse to disclose customer information to private third parties and only to allow specified access by the public authorities upon proper legal authority.[986] States differ with regard to the protection afforded by bank secrecy laws. In most States, a breach of bank secrecy is regarded as a private law issue and a breach of contract, while in others the protection of banking information is a public interest matter and a breach of bank secrecy constitutes a criminal offence.[987]

Corruption: Key Criminal Procedure Reforms for Indonesia and Other Nations," *University of Pennsylvania Journal of International Law* 30, no. 1 (2008): 183; International Training Course on "Effective Methods to Combat Transnational Organized Crime in Criminal Justice Processes" Group 1 Phase 2 Report, *Special Investigative Tools to Combat Transnational Organized Crime (TOC)*; Nicholls, Daniel, and Hatchard, *Corruption and Misuse of Public Office*, 131–154.

985 UNCAC, Art. 50(1). Decisions to use controlled delivery at the international level may, with the consent of the States Parties concerned, include methods such as intercepting and allowing the goods or funds to continue intact or be removed or replaced in whole or in part. UNCAC, Art. 50(4).

986 For example, Article 47 of the Swiss Federal Banking Act of 8 November 1934 provides that:
"1. Any person who, in his or her capacity as a member of a body, employee, proxy, liquidator or commissioner of a bank, observer for the Banking Commission, or a member of a body or an employee of an authorized auditing firm, has revealed a secret that was entrusted to him or her or of which he or she had knowledge by means of his or her practice or employment, any person who has incited another to violate professional secrecy, shall be punished by imprisonment for a maximum of six months or by a fine not exceeding 50,000 francs.
2. If the offender acted in negligence, the punishment shall consist of a fine not exceeding 30,000 francs.
3. Violation of secrecy remains punishable even when the practice or employment has terminated or the holder of the secret no longer works in the banking industry.
4. Reserved are the provisions of the federal and cantonal legislation ruling on the obligation to inform authorities and testify in court."

987 For a different vision on bank secrecy, see Guy Stessens, *Money Laundering: A New International Law Enforcement Model* (Cambridge: Cambridge University Press, 2000), 314–318.

As the regulation of bank secrecy can hamper the investigation and prosecution of corruption, the international legal framework against corruption attempts to restrict it for both transnational and national investigations. At the transnational level, in accordance with the international legal framework, in international investigations, prosecutions and judicial proceedings in relation to corruption offences, States cannot deny mutual legal assistance to another State on the ground of bank secrecy.[988] At the national level, States have to ensure that, in the case of domestic criminal investigations of acts of corruption, their legal system contains appropriate mechanisms to overcome obstacles arising out of bank secrecy laws.[989] This requires States to regulate in detail who has authority to have access to bank information, under what circumstances and the procedure required.[990] However, under no circumstances may bank secrecy be an obstacle to an investigation on corruption. States need to specify the standard of proof for lifting bank secrecy, the deadlines for the courts to decide whether to lift secrecy and the procedure to appeal against judicial decisions.

It is important to be able to pierce bank secrecy during the investigatory stage in a criminal procedure *before* the account holder is formally charged with an offence. In the past, traditional laws on bank secrecy did not allow banks to reveal to the law enforcement authorities any account holder information, unless a court order had been issued, and only when the holder had been formally charged with an offence. Such a restrictive bank secrecy law would today go against what is required of States, as the international legal framework against corruption refers to criminal *investigations* of acts of corruption, and not only prosecutions. The reasoning for this is self-evident. It is extremely difficult to charge a suspect of a corrupt offence without obtaining prior detailed information on his or her accounts and transactions.

An additional important element in overcoming obstacles arising out of bank secrecy laws is for the bank not to notify its customers of any judicial request for information concerning their accounts. Once the customer is informed, it is easy to destroy evidence and/or remove or transfer assets. In certain countries, banks used to be obliged to notify their clients in such cases. However, as a result of the international legal framework against corruption, banks are now prohibited from disclosing to their customers the fact that law enforcement authorities have requested information on their financial activities.[991]

---

988 See also Chapter VIII.

989 UNCAC, Art. 40; CoE Criminal Law Convention, Art. 23(3).

990 See also UNODC and UNICRI, *Technical Guide to the United Nations Convention against Corruption*, 124–129.

991 See, for example, the case of Armenia. For the old regime, see Law on Banking Secrecy of 1996, Arts. 10, 13, and 16. For the new regime, see Law on Banking Secrecy of 2007, Arts. 10 and 11.

II. REPORTING CORRUPTION

Corruption is usually regarded as a victimless crime, in the sense that, even though it always produces victims, either the population generally, or a group, or individual natural or legal persons, in most cases these victims are not aware of the corrupt practice and/or that they are victims. The traditional means of bringing criminal cases to the attention of the authorities through reporting by the victim is therefore of little use in combating corruption. A second problem inherent to corruption is that it flourishes in a culture of inertia, secrecy and silence. Yet, most cases of corruption are not truly secret. Although there may well be witnesses or someone knows something, for different reasons, frequently related to fear of retaliation, the person(s) with information choose to remain silent. In order to combat corruption effectively, it is therefore necessary to break that culture and find alternative creative ways of encouraging the denunciation of corruption. For this purpose, the international legal framework against corruption follows the growing trend of recognizing that the encouragement of the reporting of corrupt practices to the authorities, and the protection of the reporting persons who report such practices, and of any witnesses to the case, are key factors in breaking the secrecy surrounding corrupt practices.

1. ENCOURAGING REPORTING

The international legal framework against corruption establishes relatively weak obligations in respect of the reporting of corrupt acts. States are under no obligation to establish any system that will meaningfully increase the reporting of corruption cases. They are simply required to consider encouraging their nationals and residents to report the commission of acts of corruption to the law enforcement authorities,[992] and to consider establishing measures and systems to facilitate the reporting by public officials of acts of corruption to the appropriate authorities when such acts come to their notice in the performance of their functions.[993] It is a growing practice in many States to place a duty on certain public officials and/or individuals to report suspicious transactions to the appropriate authorities.[994] For example, in India it is mandatory for any person, regardless of occupation or professional status, to report any act of corruption committed by a public servant. Failure to do so constitutes a criminal offence.[995] The Council of Europe Model Code of Conduct for Public Officials provides that public officials should report to the competent authorities if they are aware of

---

992 UNCAC, Art. 39(2).

993 UNCAC, Art. 8(4).

994 UNODC, *Legislative Guide for the Implementation of the United Nations Convention against Corruption*, para. 486.

995 Indian Criminal Procedure Code, 1973, section 39.

breaches of the code by other officials.[996] In other jurisdictions, such as Hong Kong, China, Japan, Malaysia, Singapore, Thailand and Vietnam, only public officials are under the obligation to report corruption.[997]

Other countries do not require individuals and/or public officials to report corruption, but offer rewards for relevant information. In this connection, some scholars propose that States should allow *qui tam* actions when enforcing the law against corruption.[998] This consists of a type of action in the United States under the False Claims Act,[999] which allows a private individual with knowledge of fraud committed against the US Federal Government to bring a suit on its behalf and receive a portion (usually about 15–25%) of any recovered damages or fine imposed. For example, in September 2009, a former sales representative of the pharmaceutical company Pfizer earned US$51.5 million for his role as a whistleblower in a lawsuit against the company.[1000] Clearly, such rewards encourage people to step forward and they also recognize the contribution of whistleblowers and the difficulties that sometimes they have to endure physically, mentally and socially when they decide to come forward. The use of financial rewards is a valid way of encouraging people to report corrupt practices. However, this has to be covered by strict rules to avoid abuse and time-consuming false reporting.

Under the international legal framework, States are also required to encourage persons who participate or who have participated in the commission of an offence to supply information for investigative and evidentiary purposes and to provide specific assistance to deprive offenders of the proceeds of crime and to recover such proceeds.[1001] One way of achieving this is to mitigate the punishment of an accused person, or to grant immunity from prosecution to a person who provides substantial cooperation in the investigation or prosecution of an offence.[1002] The UNCAC even suggests adopting such measures at the

---

996 Council of Europe, Codes of Conduct for Public Officials, Recommendation Rec(2000)10, adopted by the Committee of Ministers of the Council of Europe on 11 May 2000 and explanatory memorandum, Art. 12.

997 ADB/OECD Anti-Corruption Initiative for Asia and the Pacific, *Anti-Corruption Policies in Asia and the Pacific*, 49.

998 See Indira Carr, "Fighting Corruption through Regional and International Conventions: A Satisfactory Solution?," *European Journal of Crime, Criminal Law and Criminal Justice* 15, no. 2 (2007): 145–148; Bryane Michael, *Drafting Implementing Regulations for International Anti-Corruption Conventions*, QEH Working Paper Series, Working Paper 150: 20–24.

999 False Claims Act, 31 US Code section 3729 et seq.

1000 Reuters, *Pfizer whistleblower's ordeal reaps big rewards*, 2 September 2009, available at www.reuters.com/article/newsOne/idUSN021592920090902 (last visited 29 April 2012).

1001 UNCAC, Art. 37(1).

1002 UNCAC, Art. 37(2); UNCAC, Art. 37(3). For details on the procedure of how to mitigate punishment, see UNODC and UNICRI, *Technical Guide to the United Nations Convention against Corruption*, 119–120.

international level. States are therefore encouraged to consider entering into agreements or arrangements with other States regarding the potential granting by the other State Party of the mitigation of punishment or of immunity to a person who participates or has participated in the commission of an offence and can provide substantial cooperation to the competent authorities of the State concerned.[1003]

The mitigation of punishment or the provision of immunity to persons involved in corruption is accepted in several countries[1004] and organizations.[1005] It is a practice that is widely used in the United States through cooperation agreements.[1006] One example was in Nigeria, when the Government of Olusegun Obasanjo, which took power after Abacha's death, issued Decree No. 53 which offered amnesty to public officials coming forward and disclosing information about looted assets and surrendering those assets. However, the mechanism of mitigating the punishment of an accused or providing immunity is foreign to most civil law countries. Nevertheless, certain countries with a civil law tradition have already introduced reforms to their criminal procedures, which borrow these mechanisms from the common law tradition.[1007] For example, Peru has embraced the approach of granting immunity or sentence reductions to accused persons.[1008]

1003 UNCAC, Art. 37(5).

1004 For example in Mongolia, Nepal, Republic of Korea, and the Philippines. See, ADB/OECD Anti-Corruption Initiative for Asia and the Pacific, *Anti-Corruption Policies in Asia and the Pacific: Progress in Legal and Institutional Reform in 25 Countries*, 50.

1005 There is a growing trend to provide for so-called "voluntary disclosure programmes" in certain organizations. For example, the World Bank Integrity Vice-Presidency created such programme to encourage corporations and individuals that have been involved in corruption in World Bank financed projects to report their past corrupt acts. Participants of the World Bank Voluntary Disclosure Programme undertake to: (1) not engage in misconduct in the future; (2) disclose to the Bank the results of an internal investigation into past fraudulent, corrupt, collusive, or coercive acts in Bank-financed or supported projects or contracts; and (3) implement a robust internal compliance program which is monitored by a Bank-approved compliance monitor.

1006 Cooperation agreements are usually negotiated as part of a plea bargain, in which the defendant is required to admit guilt for one or more criminal offences, and to incur some type of criminal liability. As part of the agreement, the defendant agrees to fully and truthfully cooperate with the prosecution, including disclosing information and providing testimony in court. See, Jacobs and Wagner, *Retooling Law Enforcement to Investigate and Prosecute Entrenched Corruption*, 32.

1007 On the introduction of different forms of plea bargaining in Argentina, France, Germany and Italy, see Maximo Langer, "From Legal Transplants to Legal Translations: The Globalization of Plea Bargaining and the Americanization Thesis in Criminal Procedure," *Harvard International Law Journal* 45, no. 1 (2004): 1–64.

1008 Peruvian Act No. 27378 of 20 December 2000. For details on this Act, see Nelly Calderon Navarro, "Fighting Corruption: The Peruvian Experience," *Journal of International Criminal Justice* 4 (2006): 488–509.

2. WHISTLEBLOWER PROTECTION

An additional means of encouraging the reporting of corruption cases is to establish protection for persons who report from repression or retaliation. The international legal framework against corruption requires States to consider incorporating into their domestic legal systems appropriate measures to provide protection for persons who report in good faith and on reasonable grounds to the competent authorities any facts concerning acts of corruption.[1009] However, the level of protection under the international legal framework offered to persons reporting cases of corruption is not clear. While the UNCAC does not create a mandatory obligation on States to establish such protection, all the other regional conventions against corruption require States to establish appropriate protection. For States that are Parties to the regional conventions, the situation is straightforward, as they have to adopt legislation or measures that protect reporting persons. However, States that are parties only to the UNCAC may choose not to establish such protection once they have considered incorporating it into their legal system. The non-mandatory approach adopted by the UNCAC towards the protection of reporting persons is regrettable. "Whistleblowing protection" although still in its infancy, is increasingly recognized as an essential anti-corruption mechanism and a key factor in promoting a culture of public accountability and integrity.

Technically, whistleblower protection only refers to the protection of disclosure by employees in the public and/or private sector, as opposed to reports by any member of the public. Another important characteristic of whistleblowing is that it frequently covers a public interest dimension, as the wrongdoing often represents a direct threat to the security, health or safety of others.[1010] Special protection for employees is justified for several reasons. First, although members of the public may also experience reprisals or retaliation, employees require stronger legal protection, as their institutional connection to their employer makes them especially vulnerable to retaliation.[1011] Indeed, experience has shown that employees who report wrongdoing may be subject to intimidation, harassment, dismissal and even violence by the employer or other fellow employees. Second, employees are also more likely to detect misconduct, fraud and corruption in the course of their duties than outsiders,

---

[1009] UNCAC, Art. 33; Inter-American Convention against Corruption, Art. 3(8).Under the CoE Civil Law Convention and AU Convention against Corruption States Parties are required to establish appropriate protection for persons reporting corruption. See, CoE Civil Law Convention, Art. 9; and AU Convention against Corruption, Art. 5(6). For a similar provision, see CoE Criminal Law Convention, Art. 22(a).

[1010] See, Marie Chene, *Good Practice in Whistleblowing Protection Legislation (WPL)*, (U4 Anti-Corruption Resource Centre Expert Answer, July 2009), 3.

[1011] Ibid., 2.

as they have access to critical information for which it is worth blowing the whistle.[1012]

An increasing number of countries are adopting whistleblowing protection legislation, although only a few have adopted comprehensive laws.[1013] The majority of countries that have adopted some form of whistleblower protection have done so as part of sectoral laws, such as the Law on Civil Servants (Croatia), anti-corruption laws (Kenya), labour law (Slovakia), or laws on access to information (Montenegro). There are large variations across countries with regard to the disclosures that are protected. Some countries limit protection to public officials (Canada), others to private sector employees (Japan) and others protect both the public and private sectors (United Kingdom, New Zealand and South Africa). Some countries restrict protection to employees (South Africa), while others extend protection to external consultants and contractors (United Kingdom). Evidently, the wider the scope of the disclosures protected, the more protection is granted to potential whistleblowers, and the more efficient the anti-corruption mechanism is likely to be. With regard to the issue of which disclosures are to be protected, opinions are mixed concerning anonymous whistleblowing.[1014] However, it is important for anonymous reporting to be accepted, particularly in developing countries, where the institutional environment and protection is weak and the mere existence of a law will not provide sufficient protection.[1015] Indeed, the UNCAC provides that anonymous reporting is to be accepted by its States Parties.[1016]

With regard to the type of wrongdoing in respect of which whistleblowers should be protected, at a minimum all corrupt acts should be covered. However, it is important for whistleblowing protection laws to cover a broader scope of types of wrongdoings, and not exclusively corruption. This range would include abuse of authority, violation of laws and ethical standards, danger to public health or safety, gross waste and maladministration. Ideally, States should also establish protection measures for whistleblowers when they report acts of corruption that might not be recognized as crimes, but could be subject to administrative

1012 Ibid.

1013 Those with comprehensive legislation are, for example: Canada, Public Servants Disclosure Protection Act; Japan, Whistleblower Protection Act; New Zealand, Protected Disclosures Act; Romania, Act on the Protection of Whistleblowers; South Africa, Protected Disclosures Act; United Kingdom, Public Interest Disclosure Act; and United States, Whistleblower Protection Act.

1014 For details on these opinions, see David Banisar, "Whistleblowing: International Standards and Developments" (Instituto de Investigaciones Sociales UNAM, March 2006), 60–65.

1015 On the specifics of whistleblowing in Africa, see William De Maria, "Whistleblower protection: Is Africa ready?," *Public Administration And Development* 25, no. 3 (2005): 217–226.

1016 UNCAC, Art. 13(2).

investigation.[1017] The law should also provide for at least two levels of institutions to which whistleblowers can report their suspicions, preferably one within the organization for which the whistleblower works, and a second external level if their disclosures to the first do not produce appropriate results.[1018]

The nature and extent of protection should be commensurate with possible retaliation. Whistleblowers should be protected from dismissal, suspension, disciplinary and other forms of workplace sanctions and discrimination, including petty harassment and stigmatization. They should also enjoy career protection, institutional recognition of reporting, transfer within the same organization or relocation to a different organisation.[1019] In certain cases, the identity of whistleblowers needs to be kept confidential. Measures to protect whistleblowers from workplace retaliation need to be compatible with national labour law, particularly where employers are able to dismiss employees without reason.

It is also central, with a view to attaining the objective of the protection of whistleblowing, to raise awareness of the existence of the law and to change public attitudes towards whistleblowing. Whistleblowing should be regarded as an act of loyalty to the organization and to the public interest, rather than an act of personal disloyalty.[1020] Most importantly, the introduction of whistleblowing legislation can only be effective when it is tailored to the specific circumstances of the country (its institutional, economic and cultural environment), including the factors that influence the propensity to report. However, experience shows that laws alone will not encourage people to report corrupt acts. Legal measures have to go hand-in-hand with action. It is essential for laws to be enforced and administered actively, and that this is readily apparent.

1017 MESICIC has stressed on this point when reviewing the anti-corruption legislation of several countries. See, for example, MESICIC Committee of Experts, *Final Report on Implementation in Mexico of the Convention Provisions Selected for Review in the Second Round, and on Follow-Up to the Recommendations Formulated to that Country in the First Round*, SG/MESICIC/doc.194/07 rev. 4, 29 June 2007, 26; MESICIC Committee of Experts, *Final Report on Implementation in the Republic of Guatemala of the Convention Provisions Selected for Review in the Second Round, and on Follow-Up to the Recommendations Formulated to that Country in the First Round*, SG/MESICIC/doc.217/08 rev. 4, 27 June 2008, 29; MESICIC Committee of Experts, *Final Report on Implementation in the Republic of Argentina of the Convention Provisions Selected for Review in the Second Round, and on Follow-Up to the Recommendations Formulated to that Country in the First Round*, SG/MESICIC/doc.181/06 rev.4, 15 December 2006, 28.

1018 UNODC, *The Global Programme against Corruption: UN Anti-Corruption Toolkit*, 450; Paul Latimer and A.J. Brown, "Whistleblower Laws: International Best Practice," 2009, 10–18.

1019 UNODC, *Legislative Guide for the Implementation of the United Nations Convention against Corruption*, para. 453.

1020 Howard Whitton, *Making Whistleblower Protection Work: Elements of an Effective Approach* (U4 Anti-Corruption Resource Centre Brief, December 2008), 2.

3. LEGAL OBSTACLES TO REPORTING CORRUPTION: DEFAMATION LAWS

Whistleblowing protection laws need to take into account the potential legal obstacles to the disclosure of information. Contracts of employment may include confidentiality or loyalty clauses which, if violated, even by disclosing corrupt practices, may lead to termination of employment or liability for damages.[1021] In this connection, special reference should be made to the obstacle of defamation or "insult" laws. In general terms, defamation is the issuance of a false statement about another person, which causes that person to suffer harm. It is usually prohibited under domestic legislation and a number of criminal codes contain provisions penalizing those who knowingly come forward with false allegations. Due to the special stigma that an allegation of corruption can bring upon a person, certain anti-corruption legal instruments, particularly in the African continent, make special reference to defamation. In Uganda, the Prevention of Corruption Act makes it an offence to give false information (section 21). Algeria, Lesotho, Malawi and Zambia, have all adopted provisions prohibiting the making of false and malicious reports against innocent persons.[1022] Even the AU Convention against Corruption, in Article 5(7), and the SADC Protocol against Corruption, in Article 4(1)(f), require States Parties to punish false reporting of corruption.

In addition to the strong stigmatization that comes with an accusation of corruption, it should be noted that false and malicious reports are sometimes made by those seeking to conceal their own wrongdoing. It is therefore important for States to establish some type of defamation offence in order to protect innocent persons from false allegations of corruption. However, defamation offences can also act as a double-edged sword, as they have also proved to deter whistleblowing of corrupt practices in particular, and freedom of expression in general. This happens especially in countries where the judiciary is not independent.[1023]

1021 For a comprehensive account of legal obstacles, see Banisar, "Whistleblowing: International Standards and Developments."

1022 Algeria, Law no. 06–01 of 20 February 2006 on Prevention and the Fight against Corruption, Art. 46; Lesotho, section 48 of the Prevention of Corruption and Economic Offences Act; Malawi, sections 14 and 49 of the Corrupt Practices Act; Zambia, section 24 of the Anti-Corruption Act.

1023 For example, in Indonesia, two anti-corruption activists were accused of criminal defamation by the Attorney-General after questioning gaps in his annual budget. See, Asian Human Rights Commission, Urgent Appeal Case: AHRC-UAC-148–2009, 6 November 2009, available at www.ahrchk.net/ua/mainfile.php/2009/3305/ (last visited 29 April 2012). A similar situation occurred in Bahrain, see International Freedom of Expression Exchange Alert, 16 July 2009, available at www.ifex.org/bahrain/2009/07/16/sabt_defamation_charge/ (last visited 29 April 2012).

As a result of the controversial nature of defamation laws, as explained above, anti-corruption practitioners are divided as to whether to advocate or oppose such laws. Yet the existence of different types of defamation laws is undeniable, and it would be unrealistic to demand their repeal, particularly because such laws are relevant in many spheres outside action against corruption. However, those in the anti-corruption movement who oppose defamation laws are in practice only calling for the strict regulation of the laws.[1024] It is important for whistleblower laws to provide for some test of legitimacy, and for them to be administered so as to distinguish between genuine and false reporting. In this respect, most laws and international treaties refer to the protection of persons reporting wrongdoing who act *in good faith* and on reasonable grounds. For example, Malaysia, Singapore and Thailand offer immunity against criminal proceedings for false accusations and defamation if the information was disclosed in good faith.[1025] The outcome, evidence and motives of the whistleblower should be of no significance, provided that the can satisfy the good faith test: an honest belief held on reasonable grounds that their disclosure was true at the time it was made.[1026]

An effective whistleblowing protection law needs to take into account these obstacles and other legal hurdles to disclosure, and to protect "good faith" whistleblowers from civil and criminal liability. This should include regulation of ways of relieving whistleblowers from civil liability for defamation or breach of confidentiality and statutory secrecy provisions.

4. PROTECTION OF WITNESSES

Witnesses also play a key role in the enforcement of anti-corruption law. Although, at first sight, whistleblowers may be confused with witnesses, in reality they come at different stages of the investigation. As explained earlier, whistleblowers usually trigger the investigation and proceedings, whereas witnesses are persons who are in possession of information that is important for the judicial or criminal proceedings and can help to certify important considerations of the crime or event. Even though in most corruption cases the whistleblower may also be regarded as a witness, that is not always the case and a person who draws attention to the wrongdoing may not have sufficient information for the criminal proceedings. The law should therefore take the difference between whistleblowers and witnesses into account. However, a law

---

1024 See, for example, UNDP, *Anti-Corruption Practice Note*, February 2004, 11.

1025 ADB/OECD Anti-Corruption Initiative for Asia and the Pacific, *Anti-Corruption Policies in Asia and the Pacific: Progress in Legal and Institutional Reform in 25 Countries*, 51.

1026 Whitton, *Making Whistleblower Protection Work: Elements of an Effective Approach*, 3.

that protects witnesses may not be efficient in protecting whistleblowers, and they both therefore require specific protection provisions.

The protection afforded to witnesses in corruption cases by the international legal framework is considerably stronger than that for whistleblowers. States are under the obligation to provide effective protection against potential retaliation or intimidation of witnesses, experts and victims, insofar as they are witnesses, and as appropriate for their relatives and other persons close to them, who give testimony concerning acts of corruption, and for accused persons who provide substantial cooperation in the investigation or prosecution of an offence.[1027] Many States already have legislation protecting witnesses establishing numerous different means of protection, such as police protection, relocation or the provision of a new identity. For example, in Hong Kong, China, Korea, Philippines and Thailand, provision is made for different types of witness protection.[1028] However, there are no witness protection mechanisms in other States. To meet their anti-corruption international obligations, they firstly need to adopt witness protection measures and, secondly ensure that these measures are "effective." The meaning of effective witness protection may be analysed on the basis of the UNODC publication "Good Practices for the Protection of Witnesses."[1029]

The effective protection of witnesses may involve procedures for their physical protection, such as their relocation and permitting limitations on the disclosure of information concerning their identity and whereabouts.[1030] Experience shows that effective protection schemes are varied and are applied in proportion to the seriousness and importance of the security situation of the individual. For the most serious life-threatening situations, in which protection cannot be ensured by other means, the witness will be covered by a witness protection programme. Such programmes only exist in a few countries and normally consist of the creation of a new identity for the witness, her or his resettlement in a new area

1027 UNCAC, Arts. 32(1), 32(4), 37(4). See, also, CoE Criminal Law Convention, Art. 22(a-b); AU Convention against Corruption, Art. 5(5). See also, Resolution of the Council of the European Union of 23 November 1995 on the Protection of Witnesses in the Fight against Organized Crime, Official Journal C 327, 7 December 1995, 5–5; Council of Europe, Recommendation Rec(2005)9 of the Committee of Ministers to Member States on the Protection of Witnesses and Collaborators of Justice, 20 April 2005. The criminalization of obstruction of justice, as required under the UNCAC, Art. 25, also indirectly further protects witnesses in anti-corruption criminal proceedings.

1028 ADB/OECD Anti-Corruption Initiative for Asia and the Pacific, *Anti-Corruption Policies in Asia and the Pacific: Progress in Legal and Institutional Reform in 25 Countries*, 52. For provisions in the European region, see Gert Vermeulen, ed., *EU standards in witness protection and collaboration with justice* (Maklu, 2005).

1029 UNODC, *Good Practices for the Protection of Witnesses in Criminal Proceedings Involving Organized Crime* (Vienna, New York: United Nations, 2008).

1030 UNCAC, Art. 32(2)(a).

and the creation of a substitute life story.[1031] As witness protection programmes are expensive and labour-intensive, many countries cannot and do not adopt them. States are therefore called upon to consider entering into agreements with other States for the relocation of witnesses, experts and victims witnesses who give testimony concerning acts of corruption and, as appropriate, their relatives and other persons close to them.[1032] Such international cooperation for the protection of witnesses is already envisaged by certain countries, such as Canada and Colombia, and is actively promoted by the Organization of American States.[1033]

However, in the majority of cases witnesses, do not face life-threatening risks and suffer a lesser degree of intimidation and violence, such as verbal threats, harassment and property damage. For situations of this kind, a witness protection programme may not be appropriate and other measures proportional to the threat, and of limited duration, should be applied, such as temporary change of residency, police escort, a change of telephone number and the monitoring of mail and telephone calls.[1034]

Other witness protection measures involve procedural protection. In other words, protection measures are aimed at the development of evidentiary rules allowing witness testimony to be given in a manner that ensures the safety of the witness.[1035] Procedural protection measures ensure that witnesses testify free of intimidation and fear for their lives and include the use of a pre-trial statement instead of in court testimony, testimony via closed-circuit television or videoconferencing, voice and face distortion, or anonymous testimony.[1036] In giving effect to such procedural measures, due consideration needs to be given to balancing the protection of witnesses against the basic right of defendants to a fair trial. In some States, the giving of evidence without the physical presence of witnesses, or while shielding their identity, may have to be reconciled with constitutional or other rules allowing defendants the right to confront the accuser.[1037] Protective procedural measures may affect the right of defendants to

[1031] On witness protection programmes, see UNODC, *Good Practices for the Protection of Witnesses in Criminal Proceedings Involving Organized Crime*, 43–87.

[1032] UNCAC, Art. 32(3).

[1033] See, OAS General Secretariat, Department of Legal Cooperation of the Secretariat for Legal Affairs, *Study on Cooperation on the Protection of Victims and Witnesses*, OEA/Ser.K/XXXIV, PENAL/INF.1/09, 23 March 2009.

[1034] UNODC, *Good Practices for the Protection of Witnesses in Criminal Proceedings Involving Organized Crime*, 29–31.

[1035] UNCAC, Art. 32(2)(b).

[1036] For a more detailed analysis of these procedural measures, see UNODC, *Good Practices for the Protection of Witnesses in Criminal Proceedings Involving Organized Crime*, 31–41.

[1037] UNODC, *Legislative Guide for the Implementation of the United Nations Convention against Corruption*, para. 445.

a fair trial and prevent them from challenging the testimony of witnesses directly. States therefore need to balance between the two competing obligations, namely to protect witnesses and to uphold the rights of the defendant. Courts may be called upon to develop solutions specific to each case.

It would appear that anonymous witnesses, under certain restrictions, may be in compliance with international human rights law. The ECHR has found that "the use of statements made by anonymous witnesses is not under all circumstances incompatible with the Convention … [when] the handicaps under which the defence laboured were sufficiently counterbalanced by the procedures followed by the judicial authorities."[1038] In this case, the questioning of an anonymous witness in the presence of counsel by an investigating judge who was aware of the identity of the witness, even if the defence was not, was regarded as a procedure that sufficiently balanced the anonymity of the witness. The Court also recalled that a conviction should not be based solely or to a decisive extent on anonymous statements.[1039] The International Tribunal for the Former Yugoslavia (ICTY) has also accepted that, in certain situations, the identity of the witnesses may be withheld from the accused and his counsel.[1040]

Moreover, the international legal framework provides for a broad range of persons who may be covered by protection, namely witnesses, experts, victims witnesses, their relatives and persons close to them, as well as accused persons who cooperate in the investigation or prosecution. However, these persons are also defined in restrictive terms since, with the exception of accused persons, they are to be protected only when they provided testimony in trial or court hearings concerning corrupt acts or related offences. This restrictive approach is unfortunate, as it fails to take into account the complexities of the investigation and prosecution of corruption cases in relation to which persons who may not necessarily provide testimony may still collaborate in the investigation or prosecution and accordingly be at risk of intimidation or retaliation. This is the

---

1038 Doorson v. The Netherlands (1996) 22 Eur. Ct. H.R. 330, para. 69–72.

1039 Ibid., para. 76. In other cases, the European Court of Human Rights has also ruled against anonymous witnesses by stating that they constituted a violation of the right to a fair trial. See, Kostovski v. The Netherlands (1989) 12 Eur. Ct. H.R. 434, Windisch v. Austria (1990) 13 Eur. Ct. H.R. 281, Lüdi v. Switzerland (1992) 15 Eur. Ct. H.R. 173.

1040 See, for example, Prosecutor v. Dusko Tadic, Case No. IT-94-I-T, Decision on the Prosecutor's Motion for Protective Measures for Victims and Witnesses, 10 August 1995; Prosecutor v. Tihomir Blaskic, Case No. IT-95-14, ICTY T.Ch. I, Decision on the Application of the Prosecutor dated 17 October 1996 requesting Protective Measures for Victims and Witnesses, 5 November 1996. This ICTY approach has been subject to criticism. See, Monroe Leigh, "The Yugoslav Tribunal: Use of Unnamed Witnesses against Accused," *The American Journal of International Law* 90, no. 2 (April 1996): 235–238. For a defence of the ICTY's decision and in favour of accepting anonymous witnesses under certain circumstances, see Christine M. Chinkin, "Due Process and Witness Anonymity," *The American Journal of International Law* 91, no. 1 (January 1997): 75–79.

situation, for example, of persons who provide key evidence, such as incriminating documentation or an expert opinion, but who are not ultimately called upon to testify. As a result, even if not legally required by the international legal framework, when States are giving effect to the obligation to protect witnesses they need to take this into account and provide for the protection of witnesses, experts, victims witnesses, their relatives and persons close to them in cases in which they *cooperate*, which covers a broader range of situations than solely providing testimony.

III. STATUTES OF LIMITATIONS

Statutes of limitations are statutory rules establishing the period within which a criminal or civil action can be brought against a defendant. Given the fact that, once the period of limitation, also known as the prescription period, has expired, it is no longer possible to proceed against the respective offence, regardless of the weight of evidence or the seriousness of the offence, the period of limitation constitutes an overarching issue for the effective enforcement of anti-corruption law.

1. STATUTES OF LIMITATIONS AS OBSTACLES TO THE ENFORCEMENT OF ANTI-CORRUPTION LAW

The periods of limitation for corruption offences have traditionally been relatively short in comparison with other offences. There are indications that these restrictive periods have amounted to a considerable obstacle in combating corruption and may have the effect of strengthening impunity for corruption. Although, until now cases in which investigations or prosecutions have been barred by statutes of limitations have not been properly documented, there have been sporadic reports of corruption cases closed due to the expiry of the limitation period. For example, in Italy, a British lawyer accused of accepting a bribe of US$600,000 from the Prime Minister, Silvio Berlusconi, in return for giving false evidence in two corruption trials in the late 1990s was barred from prosecution due to the expiry of the limitation period.[1041] As the bribe took place in November 1999 (although the exact timing of the bribe is disputed), the Italian Court of Cassation found that the charges had expired under a ten-year statute of limitations. It is interesting to note that the limitation period had been shortened by Mr. Berlusconi's previous government.

1041 BBC News, *Mills Bribery Conviction Quashed*, 25 February 2010, available at http://news.bbc.co.uk/go/pr/fr/-/2/hi/uk_news/8535837.stm (last visited 29 April 2012).

More specifically, two main areas of conflict can be identified between statutes of limitations and the enforcement of anti-corruption law. First, short periods of limitation overlook the fact that many corruption offences do not come to light for many years, for example when there is a change of regime or when an official leaves his or her post. As noted earlier, corruption is usually regarded as a victimless crime, in the sense that, even though it always produces victims, the victims are in most cases not aware of the corrupt practice and/or that they are victims. The traditional means of bringing criminal cases to the attention of authorities through reporting by the victim does not therefore function in cases of corruption. Moreover, corruption cases are often extremely complex and require the gathering of extensive evidence and complicated accounting and financial analysis, all of which usually require a long time.

A second area of conflict between statutes of limitations and the enforcement of anti-corruption law consists of international cooperation in criminal matters (mutual legal assistance and extradition) due to the requirement of dual criminality, or simply because some countries may not provide cooperation if the prosecution of the offence is barred by a statute of limitation. The requirement of dual criminality is traditionally a basic principle of international cooperation, especially in the field of extradition, under which the conduct that is the subject of a cooperation request has to be recognized as criminal offence in both the requesting and the requested State.[1042] Although, dual criminality does not mean that the offence needs to be defined in both countries in exactly the same terms, it may be considered that when the limitation period for an act has expired in another country, the act is no longer criminalized and the lack of dual criminality may therefore impede cooperation. This interpretation considers the principle of dual criminality as a principle of dual punishability. For example, the UN Model Treaty on Extradition provides that extradition should not be granted if the person whose extradition is requested has, under the law of either Party, become immune from prosecution for lapse of time.[1043] Similarly, under the EU Arrest Warrant, countries may refuse extradition where the criminal prosecution or punishment of the requested person is statute-barred according to the law of the executing Member State and the acts fall within the jurisdiction of that Member State under its own criminal law.[1044]

Nevertheless, it is important to note that national law and practice varies in this respect and not all countries consider punishability as part of dual criminality. The Dutch authorities, for example, have interpreted this in the opposite sense.

1042 For more on double criminality, see Chapter VIII.

1043 Model Treaty on Extradition, A/RES/45/116, Annex, 14 December 1990, amended by A/RES/52/88, 12 December 1997, Art. 3(e).

1044 Council Framework Decision of 13 June 2002 on the European Arrest Warrant and the Surrender Procedures between Member States, Art. 4(4).

For the Netherlands, the requirement of dual criminality means that the offence is also an offence under the law of the foreign jurisdiction, but not that it would have been possible in practice to prosecute the crime in the foreign jurisdiction in question.[1045] The Supreme Court ruled that it is irrelevant that the statute of limitation in the foreign jurisdiction has run out for the offences in question.[1046]

In contrast, other States refuse international cooperation on the basis of statutes of limitations. On the same day that a devastating earthquake hit Haiti in January 2010, the Swiss Supreme Court ruled that the US$ 4.6 million kept by the family of the former ruler of Haiti, Jean-Claude Duvalier, in Swiss bank accounts, which had been frozen since 1986, could not be returned to Haiti since the limitation period for the criminal offence had elapsed.[1047] Haiti never convicted any of the Duvalier family in its domestic courts, which makes it difficult for the Swiss authorities to provide legal assistance. Swiss legislation allows procedures for the recovery of assets without a conviction in the victim country only where the assets have been held by a criminal organization. Although Swiss Courts did not deny that the Duvalier family had acted as a criminal organization, it ruled that the statute of limitation for the charges of organized crime had run out in 2001, 15 years after the overthrow of Jean-Claude Duvalier as ruler of Haiti in 1986.[1048] Although this case does not technically concern a corrupt offence (the offence in this case was the establishment of a criminal organization) and the limitation period was in effect quite long (15 years), it does illustrate the relevance of statutes of limitations as potential obstacles in international anti-corruption investigations and prosecutions, as well as the recovery of corrupt assets. This is particularly relevant in contemporary action to combat corruption since, given the increasingly transnational aspect of corruption, it is widely recognized that mutual legal assistance and extradition are essential tools in the enforcement of anti-corruption laws.

2. ADEQUATE AND LONG STATUTES OF LIMITATIONS

In view of the above, the international legal framework against corruption does not require States to establish a period of limitation. However, if they do, certain standards have to be met. The OECD Convention provides that statutes of limitations applicable to the offence of bribery of foreign public officials have to

1045 Hoge Raad der Nederlanden [HR] [Supreme Court of the Netherlands], 18 December 2001, NJ 2002, 300.

1046 Ibid.

1047 Tribunal fédéral [Federal Court], Fondation Brouilly v. Office federal de la justice, 12 January 2010, 1C_374/2009.

1048 Ibid.

allow for an "adequate period of time for the investigation and prosecution of the offence."[1049] The UNCAC requires States to establish a long statute of limitations period in which to commence proceedings for corruption offences and to establish a longer statute of limitations period or provide for the suspension of the statute of limitations where the alleged offender has evaded the administration of justice.[1050]

The terms "adequate" and "long" are clearly open to interpretation. In OECD Members, the statute of limitations period for the offence of bribery of foreign public officials ranges from two to fifteen years, yet the OECD WGB did not specify what an "adequate" period is. The analysis made by the OECD WGB does not reveal a specific benchmark for the period of limitation. In examining the assessment of the OECD WGB, it should be borne in mind that it concerns an offence of particular difficulty. Foreign bribery investigations normally rely on MLA, which may take many months (and sometimes years). It may therefore be expected that the OECD WGB will be inclined to demand longer periods that may not be applicable to domestic corruption offences. Evidently, the adequacy of the limitation period has been interpreted in the context of the general conditions in each country for the enforcement of national criminal law. The adequacy of the limitation period is also related to the existence of relevant procedural rules. For example, statutes of limitations are considered more adequate when there are provisions allowing the suspension or interruption of the period for certain procedural acts (such as arrests and requests for mutual legal assistance)

As is the case in most common law systems, the non-existence of statutes of limitations allows ample time for the investigation and prosecution of complex cases.[1051] However, if the legal system does establish a statute of limitations, as in most civil law jurisdictions, a period of over five years may be considered acceptable for the effective enforcement of anti-corruption law.[1052] However, a

---

1049 OECD Convention, Art. 6.

1050 UNCAC, Art. 29. However, Belgium has made a reservation to the UNCAC declaring that it will not extend or suspend the statute of limitations period when the alleged perpetrator has evaded the administration of justice. See, Belgian reservation to the UNCAC, available at http://treaties.un.org/Pages/ShowMTDSGDetails.aspx?src=UNTSONLINE&tabid=2&mtdsg_no=XVIII-14&chapter=18&lang=en#EndDec (last visited 29 April 2012).

1051 For example, Canada and the United Kingdom have not established statutes of limitations.

1052 For example, fifteen years in Switzerland were considered adequate, while the OECD WGB expressed doubts about the five years in the Republic of Korea and the United States. See OECD WGB, *Switzerland – Phase 2: Report on the Application of the Convention on Combating Bribery of Foreign Public Officials in International Business Transactions and the 1997 Recommendation on Combating Bribery in International Business Transactions*, 24 December 2004, 27; OECD WGB, *Korea – Phase 2: Report on the Application of the Convention on Combating Bribery of Foreign Public Officials in International Business Transactions and the 1997 Recommendation on Combating Bribery in International Business*

period of three years should be regarded as inadequate. For example, the OECD WGB has found in the cases of Japan, France and Hungary that their limitation period of three years is too short.[1053] Similarly, GRECO also considered that the three year period for bribery in France was inadequate.[1054] In Albania, a three year period for bribery in the private sector was also considered too short, and in Latvia, a period of two years for the offence of trading in influence was also regarded as inadequate by GRECO.[1055]

GRECO found the time limits for prosecution in Lithuania to be reasonably long.[1056] However, it is the way that they are calculated which poses certain problems: in particular, the limitation period runs until the day of the delivery of a possible conviction (and not of the accusation or initiation of criminal proceedings, as in other countries); accordingly, there would appear to be a great reluctance by the prosecutorial authorities to file a case in court even six months before the statute elapses.[1057] Moreover, as it is not possible to suspend the calculation of the time limit, except in cases where the offender has taken steps to evade the consequences of his or her actions (for example, by hiding), it is claimed that defendants and lawyers use this to delay unnecessarily the proceedings (for example through repeated sickness on the days of court hearings).[1058]

Statutes of limitations should also be flexible in terms of the grounds for their suspension, extension and interruption. For example, in Finland, periods of

---

Transactions, 5 November 2004, 34; OECD WGB, *United States – Phase 2: Follow-Up Report on the Implementation of the Phase 2 Recommendations on the Application of the Convention and the 1997 Recommendation on Combating Bribery in International Business Transactions*, 1 June 2005, 4, 13.

1053 OECD WGB, *Japan – Phase 2: Report on the Application of the Convention on Combating Bribery of Foreign Public Officials in International Business Transactions and the 1997 Recommendation on Combating Bribery in International Business Transactions*, 7 March 2005, 55; OECD WGB, *France – Phase 2: Report on the Application of the Convention on Combating Bribery of Foreign Public Officials in International Business Transactions and the 1997 Recommendation on Combating Bribery in International Business Transactions*, 22 January 2004, 39; OECD WGB, *Hungary – Phase 2: Report on the Application of the Convention on Combating Bribery of Foreign Public Officials in International Business Transactions and the 1997 Recommendation on Combating Bribery in International Business Transactions*, 6 May 2005, 35.

1054 GRECO, *Third Evaluation Round: Evaluation Report on France on "Incriminations (E.T.S. 173 and 191, GPC 2)"*, Greco Eval III Rep (2008) 5E, 19 February 2009, 19, 28.

1055 GRECO, *Third Evaluation Round: Evaluation Report on Albania on "Incriminations (E.T.S. 173 and 191, GPC 2)"*, Greco Eval III Rep (2008) 7E, 15 May 2009, 16; GRECO, *Third Evaluation Round: Evaluation Report on Latvia on "Incriminations (E.T.S. 173 and 191, GPC 2)"*, Greco Eval III Rep (2008) 1E, 10 October 2008, 29.

1056 GRECO, *Third Evaluation Round: Evaluation Report on Lithuania on "Incriminations (E.T.S. 173 and 191, GPC 2)"*, Greco Eval III Rep (2008) 10E, 2 July 2009, 25.

1057 Ibid.

1058 Ibid.

limitation may be extended for a maximum of one year if: (i) the pre-trial investigation of the offence requires special time-consuming investigative measures due to which the investigation would clearly be incomplete at the time the statute of limitation expires; (ii) the offence has come under pre-trial investigation at an exceptionally late date; and (iii) the person to be summoned as a defendant is a fugitive from justice.[1059] In all cases, the extension of the period of limitation has to be in the public interest. However, an extension of one year was considered too short in one case by GRECO.[1060]

Limitation periods of three years or less do not therefore seem to meet the standards of the international legal framework for the investigation and prosecution of corruption. A period of over three years, and preferably five or more years, have been considered more in line with such international standards. Nevertheless, limitation periods have to be assessed in their context, taking into account the general conditions of enforcement of national criminal law and the overall coherence of national systems. Thus, in certain circumstances the OECD WGB has even criticized a five-year (or higher) threshold. This is the case, for example, in Belgium, Greece and Italy where there are known to be lengthy delays in the criminal justice process, which may in turn result in otherwise adequate limitations periods leading to the expiry of investigations and prosecutions of foreign bribery cases.[1061]

IV. SANCTIONS

The application of sanctions is the benchmark of a well-functioning law enforcement mechanism. An essential element of the enforcement of anti-corruption law is therefore the sanctioning of offenders.[1062] The international legal framework against corruption not only provides for traditional criminal

1059 Finish Criminal Code, Chapter 8, section 4.

1060 GRECO, *Third Evaluation Round: Evaluation Report on Finland on "Incriminations (E.T.S. 173 and 191, GPC 2)"*, Greco Eval III Rep (2007) 2E, 7 December 2007, 21.

1061 OECD WGB, *Belgium – Phase 2: Report on the Application of the Convention on Combating Bribery of Foreign Public Officials in International Business Transactions and the 1997 Recommendation on Combating Bribery in International Business Transactions*, 21 July 2005, 26; OECD WGB, *Greece: Review of Implementation of the Convention and 1997 Recommendation*, (Phase 1 Report), July 1999, 33; OECD WGB, *Italy – Phase 2: Report on the Application of the Convention on Combating Bribery of Foreign Public Officials in International Business Transactions and the 1997 Recommendation on Combating Bribery in International Business Transactions*, 29 November 2004, 37.

1062 When applying sanctions, it is important that States take measures to address the consequences of corruption, although with due regard to the rights of third parties acquired in good faith. In this connection, States may consider corruption a relevant factor in legal proceedings to annul or rescind a contract, withdraw a concession or other similar instrument or take any other remedial action. See, UNCAC, Art. 34.

sanctions (imprisonment and fines), but also for civil, administrative, and disciplinary sanctions. Proceedings of a civil, administrative or disciplinary nature are alternative, but essential ways of enforcing anti-corruption law. While the international legal framework leaves the penalties to be imposed for corrupt acts under domestic law to the discretion of States,[1063] it does provide certain guidelines as to what penalties are acceptable.

1. CRIMINAL SANCTIONS

The international legal framework against corruption is founded on the traditional understanding that criminal law should serve the purpose of reintegrating the criminal into society, as well as providing retribution for the victims and society in general. This is clearly demonstrated by the international obligations relating to criminal sanctions. First, States are required to endeavour to promote the reintegration into society of persons convicted of a corrupt act.[1064] Second, States are also under an international obligation to apply prescribed sanctions that take into account the gravity of the offence.[1065] Sanctions should be sufficiently severe to deter or dissuade the offender and others from committing the offence, but not so heavy as to be disproportionate to the gravity of the offence.[1066] The gravity of the offence may not be determined only by the value of the bribe, but by taking into account such other factors, as the seniority of those involved, the sphere in which the offences occur and the level of trust attached to the public official.[1067] When applying a penalty, States may also take into consideration the criminal record of an alleged offender in another State.[1068] For this purpose, States need to allow foreign States to have access to their criminal registers.

1063 UNCAC, Art. 30(9).

1064 UNCAC, Art. 30(10).

1065 UNCAC, Art. 30(1). The CoE Criminal Law Convention, the EU Convention and the OECD Convention provide for effective, proportionate and dissuasive sanctions and, in the case of natural persons, should include deprivation of liberty. CoE Criminal Law Convention; Art. 19(1); EU Convention, Art. 5(1); OECD Convention, Art. 3(1). States also have to ensure that they will be able to apply the criminal sanction once the proceedings are over. In this connection, States must seek to ensure that pre-trial and pre-appeal release conditions take into consideration the need for the presence of defendants at criminal proceedings (UNCAC, Art. 30(4)).

1066 UNODC, *Legislative Guide for the Implementation of the United Nations Convention against Corruption*, para. 383. The gravity of the offence must be taken into account when considering early release or parole of convicted persons. UNCAC, Art. 30(5).

1067 UNODC and UNICRI, *Technical Guide to the United Nations Convention against Corruption*, 83.

1068 UNCAC, Art. 41.

A guideline to determine the acceptable level of a sanction is to compare it with the penalty applied for other economic crimes, such as theft and fraud. With regard to the act of bribery of foreign public officials, it is mandatory for Parties to the OECD Convention to apply a penalty that is comparable to that applicable for the bribery of their own public officials.[1069] Furthermore, if the corrupt act is to be considered a serious offence, States need to provide for a maximum penalty of at least four years deprivation of liberty.[1070] Another important factor to consider is whether the sanctions are sufficient to enable effective mutual legal assistance and extradition.[1071] Most countries can only seek and provide extradition and mutual legal assistance for crimes that are punishable by sufficiently severe sanctions. States therefore have to ensure that the sanctions for corrupt acts meet this threshold.

When prescribing the sanctions for corrupt acts, it has been argued that it is important to bear in mind the asymmetry between active and passive participants in a corrupt act. It may be useful in this respect to recall the concepts of active and passive corruption. For example, with regard to bribery, the act of offering a bribe is commonly referred to as active bribery and the act of accepting the bribe as passive bribery. Susan Rose-Ackerman, a Professor at Yale and an expert on anti-corruption, has made reference to this asymmetry with regard to bribery. She argues that, for sanctions to have a truly deterrent effect, they have to be linked to the benefits obtained by the parties to the corrupt practice and that their role (active or passive) must therefore be taken into account.[1072] The sanctions imposed on public officials (as bribe-takers) should be linked to the size of the pay-offs they receive (the bribe) and the probability of detection. In contrast, bribers must be sanctioned on the basis of their gains (their additional profits, for example), and not the size of the bribe.

Nevertheless, it is important to bear in mind in this connection that the asymmetry between the active and passive sides of a corrupt act is not translated into a different level of condemnation. While the sanctions may differ depending on the particular case, the condemnation should be the same. As stated above, there is still a general understanding that the bribe-taker (usually a public official) is "more guilty" than the bribe-giver. This is even reflected in certain legal provisions, for example in China, where significantly harsher penalties are envisaged for the solicitation and acceptance of bribes than for promising,

1069 OECD Convention, Art. 3(1).

1070 UNODC, *Legislative Guide for the Implementation of the United Nations Convention against Corruption*, para. 272.

1071 OECD Convention, Art. 3(1).

1072 Susan Rose-Ackerman, *Corruption and Government: Causes, Consequences, and Reform* (Cambridge: Cambridge University Press, 1999), 54–55.

offering or giving a bribe.[1073] However, there is currently a trend in the anti-corruption movement towards equalizing the level of condemnation (and sanctions, where applicable) between the active and passive participants in a corrupt act. For the purpose of strengthening action to combat corruption, it is important for the condemnation of active bribery to rise to the level of that of passive bribery. In any case, nothing in the international legal framework requires a distinction to be made in relation to sanctions for both sides in a corrupt act, although nor is there any provision prohibiting such a distinction.

2. CIVIL AND ADMINISTRATIVE SANCTIONS

Sanctions for corrupt acts need not be limited to criminal penalties, such as fines and imprisonment. Civil, administrative and disciplinary sanctions may also be applied.[1074] However, in cases in which States are required to establish a certain form of conduct as a criminal offence, they may also establish civil, administrative or disciplinary sanctions although they cannot replace criminal sanctions. In this respect, as the international legal framework provides for the mandatory criminalization of the corrupt acts of bribery and embezzlement, it would not be possible for States to establish solely civil and administrative sanctions for those crimes. For example, a person convicted (criminally) for a corrupt act may also be disqualified from public office, or from any office in an enterprise owned in whole or in part by the State.[1075]

Most States establish administrative and disciplinary sanctions for persons involved in corrupt acts, and particularly for public officials in the regulations covering public administration. States have well-developed disciplinary proceedings for civil servants who do not comply with their duties. Disciplinary proceedings are sometimes conducted in parallel with criminal proceedings, and sometimes a criminal proceeding will preclude disciplinary action. In general, public officials accused of committing a corrupt act can be sanctioned by disciplinary penalties, and may be removed, suspended or reassigned.[1076] Civil and administrative sanctions for non-public officials may include exclusion from entitlement to public benefits or aid, disqualification from participation in public procurement or privatization, from the practice of other commercial activities, or they may be placed under judicial supervision.[1077] Specifically in

1073 See, Chinese Supplementary Regulations on Suppression of Corruption and Bribery 1998, Promulgated by theStanding Committee of the National People's Congress on 21 January 1988, by Order Number 63 of President Li Xiannian of the People's Republic of China.

1074 OECD Convention, Art. 3(4).

1075 UNCAC, Art. 30(7).

1076 UNCAC, Art. 30(6).

1077 OECD, *Commentaries on the Convention on Combating Bribery of Foreign Public Officials in International Business Transactions*, DAFFE/IME/BR(97)20, 21 November 1997, para. 24.

the case of legal persons, fines (criminal and non-criminal) are undoubtedly the sanction most frequently used. Other sanctions include exclusion from contracting with the Government, also called debarment or blacklisting (for example in the areas of public procurement, aid procurement and export credit financing forfeiture), confiscation, restitution, debarment or closing down of legal entities; as well as the withdrawal of certain advantages, suspension of certain rights, prohibition of certain activities, publication of the judgment, the appointment of a trustee, or the requirement to establish an effective internal compliance programme.[1078] As is the case with sanctions for natural persons, the sanctions applied to legal persons should be comparable to those applicable for other serious economic crimes, such as theft and fraud.[1079]

Civil and administrative proceedings and sanctions offer certain advantages. In such proceedings, there is a lower burden of proof, and it may be possible to sanction a corrupt act under a civil or administrative proceeding that could not be criminally sanctioned because of lack of evidence. The criminal prosecution of corruption requires the prosecution to prove *beyond a reasonable doubt* that the accused participated in a corrupt act, while in civil or administrative proceedings there is normally a less stringent burden of proof. The guilt of the accused must be proved *on a balance of probabilities*. It has been argued that, for this reason, law enforcement agencies would have more success implementing the international conventions against corruption if they chose to pursue certain corruption offences as disciplinary or administrative infractions.[1080]

Criminal sanctions may undoubtedly not be sufficient. In order to ensure the consistency of the overall legal system, the condemnation of corruption has to be translated into all relevant fields of law: private law, tax law, competition law, administrative law, law of contracts, law of torts, and law of dispute resolution. The law in all these areas has to contribute to a consistent reaction to corrupt practices.[1081] The whole legal system needs to ensure that corruption does not pay.

1078 UNODC, *Legislative Guide for the Implementation of the United Nations Convention against Corruption*, para. 338; OECD, *Commentaries on the Convention on Combating Bribery of Foreign Public Officials in International Business Transactions*, para. 24; Second Protocol to the Convention on the Protection of the European Communities' Financial Interests, Art. 4(1)(a-d).

1079 For an analysis of sanctions in the OECD context, see Mark Pieth, "Article 2 The Responsibility of Legal Persons," in *The OECD Convention on Bribery: A Commentary*, ed. Mark Pieth, Lucinda A. Low, and Peter J. Cullen (Cambridge University Press, 2007), 194–203.

1080 Bryane Michael and Habit Hajredini, "The Effective Implementation of International Anti-Corruption Conventions," *eucrim*, no. 3–4 (2007): 129–130.

1081 UNODC and UNICRI, *Technical Guide to the United Nations Convention against Corruption*, 109.

V. FREEZING, SEIZURE, AND CONFISCATION

The practice of confiscation, in the sense of the legal seizure of property without compensation by a government or other public authority, can be traced back to the Roman Empire. However, it was only in the late 1980s that there was a resurgence of interest in confiscation as a means of crime prevention and repression. This went hand-in-hand with the rising interest in the criminalization of drug trafficking and money laundering. In turn, a number of international instruments, starting with the 1988 Drug Trafficking Convention,[1082] the Council of Europe Money Laundering Convention,[1083] the FATF Recommendations,[1084] the UNTOC,[1085] and more recent anti-corruption instruments, have required States to enact legal provisions providing for the confiscation of instrumentalities and the proceeds of crime.[1086]

As a result, the freezing, seizure and confiscation of the proceeds of crime are measures that are already recognized in several criminal fields, and particularly money laundering, drug trafficking and organized crime. What do these criminal activities have in common? They all constitute crimes that generate a profit, so-called acquisitive crimes, in the case of which criminalization does not adequately punish or deter offenders. Despite being imprisoned, offenders are still able to enjoy their ill-obtained assets for personal use or to fund further illegal activities. Therefore, many States provide for confiscation procedures, which are the most important legal tool to deprive offenders of their criminal gains and constitute an essential element for an effective punishment and deterrence.

1. CONFISCATION

The term confiscation, which includes forfeiture, where applicable, is defined as the permanent deprivation of property by order of a court or other competent authority.[1087] Property covers a wide range of assets and is understood as composing assets of every kind, whether corporeal or incorporeal, movable or

---

1082 Convention against the Illicit Traffic of Narcotic Drugs and Psychotropic Substances (U.N. Doc. E/CONF.82/15, 1988) 28 I.L.M. 493, Art. 5.

1083 CoE Convention on Laundering, Search, Seizure and Confiscation of the Proceeds from Crime and on the financing of terrorism (adopted 16 May 2005) C.E.T.S. 198.

1084 FATF Recommendation No. 4, available at www.fatf-gafi.org (last visited 29 April 2012).

1085 UNTOC (Arts. 12–14).

1086 See also the Convention for the Suppression of the Financing of Terrorism (GA Res. 109, UN GAOR, 54th Sess., Supp. No. 49, UN Doc A/54/49 (Vol. I) (1999), S. Treaty Doc. No. 106–49 (2000), adopted 9 Dec. 1999, entered into force 10 Apr. 2002) 39 I.L.M. 270, and Security Council Resolution 1373 (2001).

1087 UNCAC and UNTOC, Art. 2(g).

immovable, tangible or intangible, and legal documents or instruments evidencing title to or interest in such assets.[1088] There are three types of confiscation: the traditional type of confiscation of the instrumentalities of crime (instruments used to perpetrate the crime) and the confiscation of the objects of crime (goods subjected to the criminal behaviour). Another type of confiscation is that of the proceeds of crime or in other words, the confiscation of the financial gains obtained through criminal activities.[1089] It is this last form of confiscation, of an inherently punitive character, which constitutes a novelty, and which has mainly emerged in the money laundering and drug trafficking regimes.

The international legal framework against corruption, following in the footsteps of the framework for money laundering and drug trafficking, calls for strong confiscation regimes envisaging the identification, freezing, seizure and confiscation of funds and property acquired by means of corruption. States are required to take a number of measures for this purpose. First, they have to take measures to enable the confiscation of the proceeds of crime deriving from acts of corruption, or of property the value of which corresponds to that of such proceeds.[1090] This provision accepts both object-based and value-based confiscation systems. In a nutshell, object-based confiscation is the confiscation of the exact assets obtained through the offence, while under value-based confiscation, the assets confiscated consist of any asset belonging to the offender or over which the offender exercises control, determined by the value that the offender may have gained by engaging in the offence.[1091]

A value-based or mixed confiscation model is preferable as it presents several advantages to purely object-based systems. Value-based confiscation avoids the need to prove the relationship between the offender's property and the offence as it may be enforced against assets that are not directly related in any way with criminal activity. Value-based confiscation also avoids concerns with direct or indirect proceeds, or with intermingled legal and illegal assets, and it does not affect the rights acquired by bona fide third parties.[1092] States should therefore give priority to value-based confiscation systems.

1088 UNCAC and UNTOC, Art. 2(d).

1089 UNCAC defines the proceeds of crime as "any property derived from or obtained, directly or indirectly, through the commission of an offence." UNCAC and UNTOC, Art. 2(e).

1090 UNCAC, Art. 31(1)(a); CoE Criminal Law Convention, Art. 19(3); OECD Convention, Art. 3(3), AU Convention against Corruption, Art. 16(1)(b); SADC Protocol against Corruption, Art. 8(1)(a).

1091 UNODC and UNICRI, *Technical Guide to the United Nations Convention against Corruption*, 93–94.

1092 For a detailed analysis of object-based and value-based confiscation, see Stessens, *Money Laundering: A New International Law Enforcement Model*, 31–38.

Mark Pieth, chairman of the OECD WGB, has pointed to a difficulty related to the identification of proceeds in cases of transnational bribery which can also be extended to other corrupt acts.[1093] Pieth rightly points out that, in situations facilitated by corrupt acts, it may be difficult to identify the proceeds of corruption. This is because the concept of the proceeds of crime is taken from the fight against illicit drug-trafficking, where it is relatively easy to identify the profit made by the offender. However, as Pieth indicates, in the case of a contract obtained by giving a bribe, but which is otherwise legal, it may be difficult to determine the proportion of the benefit that constitutes the proceeds of the crime. In this and other cases of corruption, it may be very difficult to assess the financial benefit deriving from corruption. Even though, under civil law jurisdictions, the view is gaining ground that a contract obtained through corruption is null and void,[1094] and thus it could be argued that all the profit made through the contract is to be considered the proceeds of crime, the situation is far from clear in practice. For cases in which the influence of the bribe on the contract has been established on the basis of evidence, Pieth proposes to allow the courts to exercise discretion in determining the amount to be confiscated in cases where the exact value of the gain cannot be established.[1095] However, there is no comprehensive solution to this issue.

In addition to envisaging the confiscation of the proceeds of crime, States have the obligation to ensure the confiscation (also called forfeiture in this case) of property, equipment or other instrumentalities used in or destined for use in acts of corruption.[1096] Instrumentalities are any property used or intended to be used in any manner wholly or in part to commit a criminal offence.[1097] This is the most traditional type of confiscation, with which most States are already familiar, and it is therefore only necessary to emphasize the need for States to extend this type of confiscation to the instrumentalities of corrupt acts.

1093 Mark Pieth, "Article 3(3) Seizure and Confiscation," in *The OECD Convention on Bribery: A Commentary*, ed. Mark Pieth, Lucinda A. Low, and Peter J. Cullen (Cambridge University Press, 2007), 259–260.

1094 In accordance with the UNCAC, States may consider corruption a relevant factor in legal proceedings to annul or rescind a contract, withdraw a concession or other similar instrument or take any other remedial action. See, UNCAC, Art. 34. For a contrary view, see Mathias Nell, *Contracts Induced by Means of Bribery: Should they Be Void or Valid?* (University of Passau, 2008), available at http://ideas.repec.org/p/bav/wpaper/042_nell.html (last visited 29 April 2012).

1095 Pieth, "Article 3(3) Seizure and Confiscation," 259–260.

1096 UNCAC, Art. 31(1)(b); CoE Criminal Law Convention, Art. 19(3); OECD Convention, Art. 3(3).

1097 Council of Europe Convention on Laundering, Search, Seizure and Confiscation of the Proceeds from Crime and on the Financing of Terrorism, Art. 1(c).

2. PROCEDURAL AND OTHER CONSIDERATIONS

States are also required to take measures to enable the identification, tracing, freezing or seizure of the proceeds and instrumentalities of corruption for the purpose of their eventual confiscation.[1098] A pre-requisite for effective confiscation is the existence of a system of preliminary measures to identify and immobilize property for the purposes of confiscation. Freezing or seizure is defined as the act of temporarily prohibiting the transfer, conversion, disposition or movement of property or temporarily assuming custody or control of property on the basis of an order issued by a court or other competent authority,[1099] for example by blocking bank accounts or objects being physically seized by the police. This is normally carried out through court freezing orders, also called *Mareva* injunctions, which in certain countries operate *in rem* with regard to specific assets and in others *in personam* in respect of all of a person's assets.[1100] For this purpose, it is extremely important for law enforcement authorities to have the necessary investigative powers and tools to monitor property and have access to documentation.[1101]

States are required to regulate the administration of frozen, seized, or confiscated property,[1102] for example by ensuring that professionals with skills in relation to the type of property can be appointed for management and administrative purposes. Experience has shown that this provision, which was not contained in earlier conventions dealing with confiscation, is essential for effective international cooperation for the confiscation and recovery of assets.[1103] States also have to ensure the application of confiscation powers to transformed or converted property and proceeds that have been intermingled with legitimately obtained property (to the value of the proceeds in question) and to income or other benefits derived from the proceeds.[1104] This provision covers situations in which the proceeds or instrumentalities have been mingled with legitimate proceeds or converted into different forms. It also covers situations in which there are "secondary proceeds," or those deriving from the original proceeds,

---

1098 UNCAC, Art. 31(2); CoE Criminal Law Convention, Art. 23; AU Convention against Corruption, Art. 16(1)(a); SADC Protocol against Corruption, Art. 8(1)(b).

1099 UNCAC and UNTOC, Art. 2(f).

1100 For more on seizure and freezing, see Trevor Clayton Hartley, *International Commercial Litigation: Text, Cases and Materials on Private International Law* (Cambridge: Cambridge University Press, 2009), 403–448.

1101 For a detailed analysis of the required investigative powers, see UNODC and UNICRI, *Technical Guide to the United Nations Convention against Corruption*, 96–97; Pieth, "Article 3(3) Seizure and Confiscation," 256.

1102 UNCAC, Art. 31(3).

1103 UNODC, *Legislative Guide for the Implementation of the United Nations Convention against Corruption*, para. 412–413.

1104 UNCAC, Art. 31(4–6). See, also CoE Criminal Law Convention, Arts. 19(3) and 23; OECD Convention, Art. 3(3); AU Convention against Corruption, Arts. 16(1)(a-b), and 17(1).

which may encompass material benefits, as well as legal rights and interests of an enforceable nature,[1105] such as bank interest. States therefore have to envisage situations in which proceeds are mingled or converted, or where there are secondary proceeds, and need to establish procedures for their confiscation. As noted above, a value-based confiscation system would avoid any problem with these situations.

The international legal framework against corruption establishes additional obligations on States related to confiscation.[1106] States are required to empower their courts or other competent authorities to order that bank, financial or commercial records be made available or seized, even when bank secrecy laws are applicable.[1107] These procedural law requirements are intended to facilitate the implementation of other obligations relating to confiscation. Bank records, financial records, such as those of other financial services companies, and commercial records, such as records of real estate transactions, shipping lines, freight forwarders and insurers, must be subject to compulsory production, for example through production orders and search and seizure or similar means.[1108] Moreover, in accordance with the principle set out in the international legal framework against corruption that bank secrecy should not be an impediment to the effective enforcement of anti-corruption law or international cooperation, bank secrecy may not be used as a justification for not producing financial and commercial records.

In confiscation procedures, it is also important to bear in mind the situation of third parties. Freezing, seizure and confiscation should not prejudice the rights of *bona fide* third parties,[1109] meaning individuals who had no knowledge of the offence and no connection with the offender. This means that the property of third parties that has been acquired in good faith cannot be confiscated. Conversely, confiscation should be permitted where the third party had knowledge of the provenance of the funds or was negligent in acquiring them. It is interesting to note that certain countries do not consider as *bona fide*, third

---

1105 UN General Assembly, *Report of the Ad Hoc Committee on the Elaboration of a Convention against Transnational Organized Crime on the work of its first to eleventh sessions: Addendum: Interpretative notes for the official records (travaux préparatoires) of the negotiation of the United Nations Convention against Transnational Organized Crime and the Protocols thereto*, A/55/383/Add.1, 3 November 2000, para. 23.

1106 In the case of transnational confiscation procedures, specific international cooperation mechanisms are necessary to enable States to give effect to foreign freezing and confiscation orders. UNCAC, Arts. 55 and 57. See also Chapter VIII.

1107 UNCAC, Art. 31(7); CoE Criminal Law Convention, Art. 23; AU Convention against Corruption, Art. 17(1); SADC Protocol against Corruption, Art. 8(2).

1108 UNODC, *Legislative Guide for the Implementation of the United Nations Convention against Corruption*, para. 421.

1109 UNCAC, Art. 31(9).

parties persons who have received property as a gift, inheritance or without adequate remuneration.[1110]

The international legal framework also explicitly allows States to adopt a measure that is controversial, although considered common in certain countries, namely requiring an offender to demonstrate the lawful origin of alleged proceeds of crime or of other property liable to confiscation.[1111] In other words, States may wish to consider shifting the burden to the defendant of proving that the alleged proceeds of crime were actually derived from legitimate sources. This is a concept that is already applied in several jurisdictions, particularly for drug trafficking, money laundering, and organized crime. The principle of the presumption of innocence and the adoption of a flexible approach to the burden of proof is discussed in Chapter IV. In the present context, it is sufficient to add this reversal of the burden of proof relates only to the criminal (corrupt) origin of the proceeds for the purposes of their confiscation and does not pertain to the guilt of the accused. The reversal of the burden of proof in this respect has been procedurally embedded in special confiscation procedures applied only when the accused has been found guilty.[1112]

There are significant variations in the methods and approaches adopted by different legal systems in relation to confiscation. The purpose of confiscation varies between States. For some countries, confiscation serves a punitive purpose offering additional deterrence (Bulgaria), while in others the purpose is restitution (Netherlands, Sweden), and in yet others the goal is to cut off the financing of further illegal activities (Switzerland).[1113] However, in most cases it constitutes a punitive measure.[1114] Other variations relate to the range of offences with respect to which confiscation can take place, whether the system is object or value-based, the requirement of a prior conviction of the offender, the required standard of proof (criminal or lower civil level), whether and the conditions under which third party property is subject to confiscation and the power to confiscate the products or instrumentalities of crime.[1115]

1110 Pieth, "Article 3(3) Seizure and Confiscation," 262.

1111 UNCAC, Art. 31(8).

1112 For an analysis of how this provision collides with the human right to a fair trial, see Stessens, *Money Laundering: A New International Law Enforcement Model*, 68–74.

1113 Pieth, "Article 3(3) Seizure and Confiscation," 255. For the confiscation procedures in Lesotho, Malawi, Mauritius, Namibia, South Africa, Tanzania, Zambia, and Zimbawe, see Philliat Matsheza, Heather Mupita, and Kenyatta Nyirenda, eds., *SADC Anti-Corruption Laws: A Case for Harmonisation* (Harare: Human Rights Trust of Southern Africa, 2004), 67–78.

1114 See, Stessens, *Money Laundering: A New International Law Enforcement Model*, 50–56.

1115 UNODC, *Legislative Guide for the Implementation of the United Nations Convention against Corruption*, para. 401.

Most systems require a conviction as a prerequisite for confiscation and the proceedings following conviction are generally of a civil nature (employing the civil standard of proof). However, an increasing number of countries are adopting separate regimes that are independent of criminal conviction-based confiscation (so-called *in rem* confiscations) under which assets can be confiscated through civil proceedings relating to the property itself, in which no one needs to be convicted of an offence (for example Colombia, Germany, South Africa and the United States).[1116] In other words, the government sues the item of property, not the person, and the owner is effectively a third party claimant. Once the government establishes probable cause that the property should be subject to forfeiture, it is for the owner to prove that this is not the case. At no time does the owner have to be judged guilty of any crime.

The international legal framework against corruption is not aimed at resolving variations between States and leaves it for them to regulate the details of their confiscation procedures in accordance with their domestic legal system. As described above, it does however set out some minimum standards that States must follow, although these are quite general. States therefore have a wide range of policy options available for the implementation of their international obligations related to confiscation procedures.

VI. LIABILITY OF LEGAL PERSONS

It is widely recognized that the imposition of liability in respect of legal persons is particularly important in corruption cases because such crimes are frequently committed by, through or under the cover of legal entities.[1117] In addition, as corporate structures become increasingly large and complex, it is often difficult to hold one or more individuals in a company responsible for a particular decision. Legal persons also often have elaborate financial structures and accounting practices which make it easier to conceal corrupt acts and the identity of decision-makers. This concern is not theoretical or related only to potential risks. Numerous cases have been reported in which legal entities have been involved in corrupt acts. The establishment of the liability of legal entities will also have a deterrent effect on corruption because damage to reputation and monetary sanctions can be very costly for legal persons. For these and other

[1116] Ibid., paras. 400–401.

[1117] This applies to many types of criminal activity. For this reason, several international conventions outside the field of corruption provide for the liability of legal persons. See, UNTOC, Art. 10; CoE Convention on the Protection of the Environment through Criminal Law (adopted 4 November 1998) C.E.T.S. 172, Art. 9; Financial Action Task Force (FATF) Recommendation No. 3 and Interpretative Note to Recommendation 3.

reasons, the view has gained ground that standards establishing the liability of legal persons for corruption are indispensable.

Accordingly, under the international legal framework against corruption, States are required to establish the liability of legal persons for participation in corrupt offences. Legal persons can take a variety of forms and an effective scheme for imposing liability therefore has to cover a wide range of entities. The definition of a legal person in the international legal framework against corruption refers back to domestic law. For example, Article 1(d) of the CoE Criminal Law Convention provides that: "legal person" shall mean any entity having such status under the applicable national law..." It would appear, however, that legal persons include corporations, partnerships, societies, associations, foundations and not-for-profit bodies.[1118] Public entities, such as ministries, local bodies and public international organizations are excluded from the definition of legal persons, as their responsibility is usually covered by specific regulations and administrative law.[1119] However, where the State has endowed public entities (state-owned or state-controlled) with powers to conclude contracts on its behalf, they should be considered legal persons.[1120]

The liability of legal persons may be criminal, civil or administrative.[1121] In addition, legal persons held liable for corrupt acts must be subject to effective, proportionate and dissuasive sanctions, which may be criminal, civil or administrative.[1122] The international legal framework leaves States a wide range of sanctions to apply. However, the liability of legal persons in general, and their criminal liability in particular, is a controversial legal issue around the world. The principle that corporations cannot commit crimes (*societas delinquere non potest*) is still upheld in a number of countries. Only common law systems and certain other countries accept the criminal responsibility of legal persons. The international legal framework does not therefore require States to establish the *criminal* liability of legal persons for participation in a corrupt act. As indicated above, States may choose between criminal, civil or administrative liability, thereby accommodating the various legal systems and approaches.

The debate is not currently centred so much on whether to establish liability for legal entities in cases of corruption, but on the modalities of how such liability

1118 OECD, *Corruption: A Glossary of International Criminal Standards*, 2007, 59.
1119 CoE Criminal Law Convention Explanatory Report, para. 31.
1120 Pieth, "Article 2 The Responsibility of Legal Persons," 186.
1121 UNCAC, Art. 26(1) and (2).
1122 UNCAC, Art. 26(4); OECD Convention; Art. 3(2), CoE Criminal Law Convention, Art. 19(2); Second Protocol to the Convention on the Protection of the European Communities' Financial Interests, Art. 4. For more on sanction respecting legal persons, see section IV above.

should be applied in practice. The key is to understand how the liability of legal persons is engaged. It is necessary in this respect to examine the rules governing the attribution of responsibility and the manner in which a corrupt act is connected to a legal person, as well as the role of due diligence in establishing liability.

1. ATTRIBUTION OF RESPONSIBILITY

The difficulty in establishing the liability of a legal person rests on the collective decision-making process in legal entities. The liability of a legal person for a corrupt act also depends on the position held by the natural person who commits or carries out the act. The question that arises is when an act by a natural person can be attributed to a legal person. There are essentially three major approaches to this question. However, it should be noted that the majority of States apply not one approach, but a combination of two.

One rule of attribution consists of the so-called identification theory, according to which only acts by persons holding a leading position engage the liability of the legal person.[1123] These may be persons who have the power to represent the legal person, take decisions on its behalf or exercise control within the legal person.[1124] This also includes persons to whom particular functions of the legal person have been delegated so that these functions can be performed without supervision. Liability also arises when a person in a leading position has delegated authority to a subordinate, or directs or supervises a subordinate. In addition, there is an obligation to extend liability to cases in which a lack of supervision within a legal person makes it possible to commit the corrupt act.[1125] Legal persons are therefore also liable for omissions by persons in leading positions to exercise supervision over the acts committed by subordinates acting on behalf of the legal entity. The identification theory has been criticized for being too narrowly focused on the senior officials of a company and accordingly favouring larger companies in which decisions are taken by lower level staff.[1126] To varying degrees, Austria, Canada, France, Germany, Italy and the United Kingdom apply some version of the identification theory.[1127]

1123 Celia Wells, "Corporate Criminal Responsibility," in *Research Handbook on Corporate Legal Responsibility*, ed. Stephen Tully (Edward Elgar Publishing, 2007), 151–152.

1124 CoE Criminal Law Convention, Art. 18. For a discussion of this in the OECD context, see Pieth, "Article 2 The Responsibility of Legal Persons," 188–189.

1125 CoE Criminal Law Convention, Art. 18(2); Second Protocol to the Convention on the Protection of the European Communities' Financial Interests, Art. 3(2).

1126 Pieth, "Article 2 The Responsibility of Legal Persons," 179–180.

1127 For example, in Germany, the person who commits the offence must be the authorized organ of the legal person, a member of such an organ or a fully authorized representative, or someone who holds a leading position. Italy may impose liability for acts performed by

A second rule of attribution is based on an agency principle (or *respondeat superior* in the United States), which applies vicarious liability. Any employee can engage the liability of a legal person when acting within the scope of his or her duties and for the benefit of the corporation.[1128] Vicarious liability does not require proof that the accused knew or could reasonably have known that the act was wrong, and does not recognize any excuse of honest and reasonable mistake. The legal person is not exonerated if it prohibited the illegal behaviour in company by-laws or if it had set up compliance programmes. The approach of vicarious liability has been criticized as being both too broad, and thus entailing the liability of legal persons whenever an individual employee is at fault, even where the company itself was faultless, and too narrow, since liability still needs to be triggered by the fault of an individual related to the legal person.[1129]

A third rule of attribution relates to "corporate culture" or due diligence. However, in practice, it does not constitute a rule of attribution as it does not refer to the attribution of liability to a legal person through the acts of employees or persons in leading positions. It is more an objective theory. Australia imposes liability on a legal person where a "corporate culture" exists in the legal person that directs, encourages, tolerates or leads to the offence or the legal person fails to create and maintain a corporate culture that requires compliance with the relevant law.[1130] Switzerland makes reference to a "lack of reasonable organizational measures" as one element leading to the liability of a legal person.[1131] This rule of attribution has shifted from a subjective focus (the

---

persons in senior positions who carry out "activities of representation, administration or management of the body or one of its organizational units having financial and operational autonomy." For an analysis of legislation on the liability of legal persons in these countries, see OECD WGB, *Germany: Review of Implementation of the Convention and 1997 Recommendation*, (Phase 1 Report), April 1999, 5; OECD WGB, *Italy: Review of Implementation of the Convention and 1997 Recommendation*, (Phase 1 Report), April 2001, 11; OECD WGB, *Austria - Phase 2: Report on the Application of the Convention on Combating Bribery of Foreign Public Officials in International Business Transactions and the 1997 Recommendation on Combating Bribery in International Business Transactions*, 16 February 2006, 39; OECD WGB, *Canada - Phase 2: Report on the Application of the Convention on Combating Bribery of Foreign Public Officials in International Business Transactions and the 1997 Recommendation on Combating Bribery in International Business Transactions*, 25 March 2004, 30–31; OECD WGB, *France: Review of Implementation of the Convention and 1997 Recommendation*, (Phase 1 Report), December 2000, 12–13; OECD WGB, *United Kingdom: Review of Implementation of the Convention and 1997 Recommendation*, (Phase 1 Report), April 1999, 5.

1128 Wells, "Corporate Criminal Responsibility," 150–151.

1129 Pieth, "Article 2 The Responsibility of Legal Persons," 179, citing, Wells C. *Criminal Responsibility of Legal Persons in Common Law Jurisdictions*, OECD Room Document DAFFE/IME/BR(2000)22, Paris, 4, and Heine G., *Corporate Liability Rules in Civil Law Jurisdictions*, OECD Room Document DAFFE/IME/BR(2000)23, Paris, 4.

1130 OECD WGB, *Germany - Phase 1 Report*, 5; OECD WGB, *Australia: Review of Implementation of the Convention and 1997 Recommendation*, (Phase 1 Report), December 1999, 9–10.

1131 Swiss Criminal Code, Art. 100*quater*.

behaviour of leading persons or employees) to an objective focus (a deficiency of the legal person independent of the behaviour of leading persons or employees).[1132] Under this system, the legal person avoids liability if it establishes adequate organizational concepts, an appropriate corporate culture and engages in credible compliance efforts.

The international legal framework against corruption does not require States to use any particular rule of attribution. Most instruments against corruption are silent on this subject with the exception of the CoE Criminal Law Convention and the EU Second Protocol to the Convention on the Protection of the European Communities' Financial Interests, which both refer to the identification theory although with a slightly broader scope. This is because, in addition to envisaging the attribution of liability to persons in leading positions, the two instruments add that where the lack of supervision or control by a person in a leading position has made the commission of a corrupt act possible, the legal person should also be held liable.[1133] States Parties to these two instruments therefore need to envisage for this type of rule of attribution, as a minimum. However, nothing prevents them from applying rules of attribution that result in the broader liability of legal persons. States that are not parties to these instruments are free to apply the rule of attribution of their choice. From the perspective of effectiveness, many scholars advocate the third rule of attribution based on corporate culture or due diligence,[1134] which offers the advantage of attributing a more active role to legal persons in the prevention of corruption since, in order to avoid risks, they have to establish effective due diligence and compliance programmes.

When describing the rules for the attribution of liability it is important to emphasize that, irrespective of the rule applied by the State, the liability of legal persons has to be independent of the conviction of the natural person who has committed the act.[1135] It may not be possible to prosecute the natural person who perpetrated the corrupt act or to identify specific individuals within the

---

1132 The criminal liability of legal persons in the Republic of Korea and Japan follow this rule of attribution. OECD WGB, *Germany – Phase 1 Report*, 5; OECD WGB, *Korea: Review of Implementation of the Convention and 1997 Recommendation*, (Phase 1 Report), July 1999, 7; OECD WGB, *Japan: Review of Implementation of the Convention and 1997 Recommendation*, (Phase 1 Report), May 2002, 7.

1133 CoE Criminal Law Convention, Art. 18(2); Second Protocol to the Convention on the Protection of the European Communities' Financial Interests, Art. 3(2).

1134 James Gobert, "Controlling Corporate Criminality: Penal Sanctions and Beyond," *Webjournal of Current Legal Issues*, no. 2 (1998): 12; Pieth, "Article 2 The Responsibility of Legal Persons," 193; Celia Wells, *Corporations and Criminal Responsibility*, 2nd ed. (Oxford: Oxford University Press, 2001).

1135 UNCAC, Art. 26(3). See, also, CoE Criminal Law Convention, Art. 18; OECD Convention, Art. 2.

legal person. The regime for imposing liability upon legal persons should not require the prior or simultaneous identification, prosecution or conviction of a natural person. The inverse situation is also explicitly envisaged by the international legal framework against corruption. The imposition of liability upon legal persons has to be without prejudice to the criminal liability of any natural person.[1136]

2. CONNECTION BETWEEN THE CORRUPT ACT AND THE LEGAL PERSON

The question of when an act of a natural person can be attributed to the legal person as discussed in the previous section is intrinsically linked to the subject covered by this section. Does any corrupt act by a natural person engage the liability of the legal person? The answer is straightforward. A legal person is held liable for corrupt acts committed by its employees when there is a connection between the act and the legal person, but not when the corrupt act is for a personal benefit, for example in the case of an employee bribing a public official in order to obtain subsidized housing. In this case, there is no connection with the legal person. In other words, the requirement is usually that the corrupt act must have been committed for the *benefit* of the legal person, and not in the interest of the employee.[1137] However, this is sometimes difficult to determine and has been interpreted in several ways. In some countries, the corrupt act has to be linked to the business of the legal person ("in relation to," "in connection with," or "in the course of its operations").[1138] Another approach is to require a general interest test ("on behalf of," "in the name of," "in furtherance of the interest of," or "for the gain of").[1139] Although there is no uniform implementation of this requirement among States, it is clear that the closer the link, the easier it is to demonstrate the liability of the legal person.

3. DUE DILIGENCE

When assessing liability, many jurisdictions take into consideration whether a legal person has exercised due diligence in supervising and controlling its employees. As indicated earlier, in some States compliance with due diligence by a legal person may completely exclude its liability (corporate culture), while in

1136 UNCAC, Art. 26(3).
1137 CoE Criminal Law Convention, Art. 18.
1138 Pieth, "Article 2 The Responsibility of Legal Persons," 187, citing as examples Iceland, Japan, Republic of Korea and United Kingdom.
1139 Ibid., citing as examples Belgium, Canada, Finland, France, Germany, Italy, Mexico, Norway, Portugal, Switzerland, and United States.

others it can be used as a legal defence. Due diligence is necessary to promote preventive measures by legal persons and because in practice it is difficult for many legal persons to control every act by each employee. The respective procedures vary among countries. In general, due diligence requires a legal person to take certain measures, such as the application of a code of conduct, an efficient internal auditing control, compliance programmes, effective training and enforcement. However, most States that have introduced a due diligence concept define it in general terms. Legal persons are required to "pay due attention or exercise proper supervision to prevent corruption" (Korea), "take all reasonable and necessary organizational measures to prevent corruption" (Switzerland), or create a "compliance culture" (United States).[1140] Due diligence is also applied in different ways as a legal defence. For example, in Italy and Korea, the legal person is completely exonerated where due diligence is demonstrated.[1141] In the United States, due diligence is not a defence, but only a mitigating factor in sentencing.[1142] There is therefore a trend among legal entities to adopt some form of preventive measures, such as more effective management and supervisory structures to avoid committing corrupt acts.

CONCLUSION

One of the main problems in controlling corruption is inadequacy of enforcement of anti-corruption law. Impunity for corrupt acts is widespread around the world. For that reason, hope and reliance on the capacity of traditional law enforcement approaches for corruption has been lost. Nevertheless, law enforcement still constitutes an essential element in combating corruption. As a result, the international legal framework against corruption gives a great deal of importance to law enforcement and has placed on States a wide variety of international obligations in relation to the enforcement of anti-corruption law. As seen in this Chapter, several of these obligations consist of traditional elements of law enforcement mechanisms, with which most States are already familiar. This is the case, for example, of the criminalization of corrupt acts and the application of criminal sanctions. However, the strength of the international legal framework in regard to law enforcement rests on the more innovative elements with which most States are not familiar, but which are particularly useful in combating corruption, such as using special investigative

1140 OECD WGB, *Korea - Phase 2 Report*, 35; OECD WGB, *Switzerland - Phase 2 Report*, 37–39; OECD WGB, *United States - Phase 2: Report on the Application of the Convention on Combating Bribery of Foreign Public Officials in International Business Transactions and the 1997 Recommendation on Combating Bribery in International Business Transactions*, October 2002, 17–18.

1141 OECD WGB, *Italy - Phase 2 Report*, 43; OECD WGB, *Korea - Phase 2 Report*, 36.

1142 OECD WGB, *United States - Phase 2 Report*, 17.

techniques, enhancing the reporting of corrupt practices, providing for adequate and long statutes of limitations, stepping up confiscation regimes and providing for the liability of legal persons. Indeed, as shown in this chapter, the international legal framework against corruption has already influenced many national jurisdictions, sometimes to the core of their law enforcement mechanisms. Countries which have historically refused to criminalize legal persons, have now introduced the concept into their legal systems, or at least some form of non-criminal responsibility. The effect of the international legal framework on national legal systems is clearly significant.

However, as also shown throughout this Chapter, many of the international provisions on the enforcement of anti-corruption law are non-mandatory, and constitute mere recommendations. One particular Article in the UNCAC is telling about the non-mandatory nature of certain provisions. Article 30(9) provides that "[n]othing contained in this Convention shall affect the principle that the description of the offences … or other legal principles controlling the lawfulness of conduct is reserved to the domestic law of a State Party and that such offences shall be prosecuted and punished in accordance with that law." Nevertheless, at the end of the day this provision does not seem to add any new element to the host of provisions for the enforcement of anti-corruption law. This provision, if interpreted in the context of the object and purpose of the UNCAC and other anti-corruption conventions, does not alter any of the obligations resting on States, as described in this Chapter. Notwithstanding this provision, States are still required, for example, to apply sanctions for corrupt acts taking into account the gravity of the offence. By the same token, where States have merely been encouraged to adopt certain measures, but are not legally required to do so, as in the case of criminalizing the act of illicit enrichment, the Article 30(9) does not take away any element of obligation that was not present in the first place. It may therefore be concluded that Article 30(9) has no impact on the international obligations relating to the enforcement of anti-corruption law.

CHAPTER VIII

INTERNATIONAL COOPERATION IN CRIMINAL MATTERS AND ASSET RECOVERY

INTRODUCTION

On 14 September 2000, anyone watching television in Peru would have been surprised to see Mrs. Susana Higuchi, the ex-wife of the then President Alberto Fujimori, presenting a video showing Vladimiro Montesinos, the head of the Peruvian secret service and Fujimori's right hand man, bribing an opposition legislator with US$15,000 in cash. The broadcast of this video triggered a political and legal scandal with international ramifications.[1143] Both Fujimori and Montesinos fled Peru and found refuge, Fujimori in Japan and Montesinos in Venezuela. Bank accounts with millions in corrupt funds were discovered in Switzerland, Luxembourg, the Cayman Islands, United States, Uruguay and many other countries. The Peruvian authorities were then faced with an international legal quandary. Both of the accused needed to be extradited, evidence of their corrupt acts had to be secured from many different jurisdictions and the stolen assets needed to be traced and repatriated from other countries. The legal struggle of the Peruvian authorities to prosecute both Fujimori and Montesinos and recover the stolen assets is evidence of the paramount role of international cooperation in criminal matters for effective anti-corruption investigation, prosecution and asset recovery.

The modern world provides persons engaging in corruption with several ways of escaping prosecution and justice. Globalization allows offenders to cross borders more easily, break up transactions and obscure investigative trails, and to seek a safe haven for themselves and for the proceeds of crime. The prevention of corruption and the enforcement of the respective laws cannot therefore be

---

[1143] For more information on the case against Fujimori and Montesinos, see José Ugaz, "Caso Fujimori - Montesinos," in *Transparencia y Probidad Pública: Estudios de Caso en América Latina*, ed. José Zalaquett and Alex Muñoz (Santiago: Andros Impresores, 2008), 99–112; Ronald Gamarra, "A Leader Takes Flight: The Indictment of Alberto Fujimori," in *Prosecuting Heads of State*, ed. Ellen L. Lutz and Caitlin Reiger (Cambridge: Cambridge University Press, 2009), 95–110.

achieved without cooperation between States in criminal matters. Accordingly, the international legal framework against corruption establishes numerous international obligations with a view to enhancing domestic legal and institutional frameworks for fostering international cooperation in criminal matters.

There is no general rule in international law requiring States to cooperate in criminal matters. Although cooperation is possible in some cases on the basis of national legislation, reciprocity or comity, international cooperation generally occurs on the basis of a treaty between the States concerned. As a result, many States already have a relatively strong legal basis for requesting or providing international cooperation in criminal matters, since they are parties to applicable regional or bilateral treaties.[1144] A number of the rules on international cooperation arising from the international legal framework against corruption are subsidiary to existing international instruments on international cooperation,[1145] and the international obligations that have been established supplement such treaties or apply in the absence of such a treaty.

This Chapter describes and analyses the international obligations of States relating to international cooperation. The most important aspect of any discussion of international cooperation are undoubtedly extradition and mutual legal assistance (MLA). However, as explained below, in the context of action to combat corruption, asset recovery is probably an even more pressing concern in international cooperation. Finally, certain miscellaneous obligations relating to international cooperation in criminal matters are also examined.

I. EXTRADITION

As perpetrators of corruption may flee a jurisdiction to avoid prosecution, extradition proceedings are necessary to bring them to justice in the prosecuting State. Extradition, as one of the principal forms of international cooperation in criminal matters, is a formal and, most frequently, treaty-based procedure, leading to the return or delivery of fugitives to the jurisdiction in which they are

---

1144 Multilateral treaties such as the European Convention on Extradition (adopted on 13 December 1957) 359 U.N.T.S. 273, and its two Additional Protocols of 1975, 1161 U.N.T.S. 450, and 1978, 1496 U.N.T.S. 328; the European Convention on Mutual Assistance in Criminal Matters (adopted on 20 April 1959) 472 U.N.T.S. 185 and its two Additional Protocols of 1978, 1495 U.N.T.S. 350 and 2001, 2297 U.N.T.S. 24; the Convention on the Transfer of Proceedings in Criminal Matters (adopted on 15 May 1972) 1137 U.N.T.S. 30; the Inter-American Convention on Mutual Assistance in Criminal Matters (adopted 23 May 1992) A-55; the Inter-American Convention on Extradition (adopted 5 February 1981) B-47; the ECOWAS Convention on Mutual Assistance in Criminal Matters (adopted 29 July 1992) 2329 U.N.T.S. 301.

1145 UNCAC, Art. 46(7); CoE Criminal Law Convention, Art. 25(1)-(2).

wanted. Although in some instances in the absence of a treaty, extradition may be granted voluntarily or on the basis of reciprocity, this does not happen frequently. For that reason, States have negotiated multilateral and bilateral treaties on extradition, and most States are today parties to one or more such treaties.[1146]

1. COMPLEMENTARY AND SUBSIDIARY EXTRADITION INTERNATIONAL OBLIGATIONS

The international legal framework against corruption addresses the issue of extradition in order to support and supplement pre-existing extradition arrangements. The intention is to expand the extradition treaty network and reinforce national legislation with a view to ensuring the existence of appropriate legal frameworks to facilitate extradition. States are called upon to conclude agreements or arrangements to carry out or to enhance the effectiveness of extradition.[1147] Nevertheless, the international legal framework does not add much innovation to existing extradition arrangements and obligations.

States that do not make extradition conditional on the existence of a treaty need to ensure that corruption offences are deemed extraditable, provided that the condition of dual criminality is fulfilled.[1148] States also have to recognize all corruption offences as being extraditable between States Parties to the UNCAC.[1149] If its domestic law so allows, a State may grant the extradition of a person for a corruption offence even if the offence is not punishable under its own domestic law, or in other words without the condition of dual criminality.[1150]

On the other hand, States which make extradition conditional on the existence of a treaty need to ensure that all corruption offences are extraditable in any

1146 Examples include the Inter-American Convention on Extradition, the European Convention on Extradition, the ECOWAS Convention on Extradition, and the Extradition Agreement of the League of Arab States.

1147 UNCAC, Art. 44(18).

1148 UNCAC, Art. 44(1).

1149 UNCAC, Art. 44(7); Inter-American Convention against Corruption, Art. 13(4); CoE Criminal Law Convention, Art. 27(3); AU Convention against Corruption, Art. 15(4); SADC Protocol against Corruption, Art. 9(5). In the absence of an applicable treaty, domestic legislation in many countries allows extradition to countries with which they have no treaty obligations. While this approach is welcome, it does not create binding obligations under international law. A State which enacts such legislation has no international obligation to extradite a person to another State.

1150 UNCAC, Art. 44(2). Furthermore, States may apply these extradition rules if the request for extradition includes several separate offences, at least one of which is extraditable under the UNCAC and some of which are not by reason of their period of imprisonment, but are related to offences established in accordance with the UNCAC. UNCAC, Art. 44(3).

extradition treaty existing between States Parties to the anti-corruption instruments.[1151] States also have to include corruption offences as extraditable offences in every extradition treaty to be concluded.[1152] If a State makes extradition conditional on the existence of a treaty and receives a request from another State Party with which it has no extradition treaty, the State may consider the UNCAC, or another anti-corruption treaty to which they are Parties, as the legal basis for extradition in respect of a corruption offence.[1153]

Moreover, if States use the UNCAC or the Inter-American Convention against Corruption as the legal basis for extradition, they cannot consider any of the corrupt offences as political offences and refuse extradition on that basis.[1154] This provision is important in the context of corruption because prosecutions for corruption are often intermingled with politics. The international legal framework against corruption accordingly shows a trend towards the restriction of political offences as a ground for refusing extradition. In this connection, it should be noted that the initial text of the UN Model Treaty on Extradition, as adopted in 1990, clearly included this as a mandatory ground for refusal of extradition (Article 3(a)). However, the revised version included a further restriction to ensure that the political offence exception was not applied in cases of serious crimes for which States had assumed the obligation, pursuant to any multilateral convention, to prosecute where they refused extradition.[1155] Corruption offences fall into this category of crimes that are subject to the

1151 By virtue of this provision, offences are automatically deemed to be included in existing extradition treaties. Hence, there is no need to amend such treaties. However, if treaties are considered subordinate to domestic extradition legislation under the legal system of a particular State and its current legislation is not sufficiently broad to cover all offences established in accordance with the UNCAC, amending legislation may be required. UNODC, *Legislative Guide for the Implementation of the United Nations Convention against Corruption* (Vienna, New York: United Nations, 2006), para. 558.

1152 UNCAC, Art. 44(4); Inter-American Convention against Corruption, Art. 13(2); CoE Criminal Law Convention, Art. 27(1); OECD Convention, Art. 10(1); AU Convention against Corruption, Art. 15(2); SADC Protocol against Corruption, Arts. 9(2) and 9(3).

1153 UNCAC, Art. 44(5); Inter-American Convention against Corruption, Art. 13(3); CoE Criminal Law Convention, Art. 27(2); OECD Convention, Art. 10(2); SADC Protocol against Corruption, Art. 9(4). While under all of the above Conventions, States have the option to consider the treaty as the legal basis for extradition, under the AU Convention against Corruption, the obligation is mandatory for States Parties. States therefore have to consider the AU Convention against Corruption as the legal basis for extradition. AU Convention against Corruption, Art. 15(3). Moreover, States Parties to the UNCAC which make extradition conditional upon the existence of a treaty have to inform the Secretary-General of the UN at the time of the deposit of their instrument of ratification, acceptance or approval of or accession whether they will take the UNCAC as the legal basis for cooperation on extradition with other States Parties. Otherwise, they have to seek to conclude treaties on extradition with other States. UNCAC, Art. 44(6).

1154 UNCAC, Art. 44(4); Inter-American Convention against Corruption, Art. 17.

1155 UNODC and UNICRI, *Technical Guide to the United Nations Convention against Corruption* (Vienna, New York: United Nations, 2009), 150.

requirement of extradition or prosecution. Although not yet a legal requirement, the development of international law indicates that when States use treaties other than the UNCAC or the Inter-American Convention against Corruption as a legal basis for extradition, they should not refuse extradition on the grounds that the offence may be politically motivated.

In the extradition process for a corruption offence, States have to guarantee fair treatment at all stages of the proceedings, including enjoyment of all the rights and guarantees provided by the law of the State in the territory of which the person is present.[1156] Moreover, States have to make an effort to expedite extradition procedures and to simplify the respective evidentiary requirements in respect of any corruption offence.[1157] At the request of another State, a State may also, upon being satisfied that the circumstances so warrant and are urgent, take a person whose extradition is sought and who is present in its territory into custody or take other appropriate measures to ensure his or her presence at extradition proceedings.[1158]

States may clearly still refuse extradition for corruption offences, but the reasons considered to be valid are restricted. For example, States have no obligation to extradite an alleged offender where there are substantial grounds for believing a fugitive will be subject to discrimination.[1159] However, a State cannot refuse a request for extradition on the sole ground that the offence is also considered to involve fiscal matters.[1160] Historically, most extradition treaties excluded tax and fiscal offences from the scope of extraditable offences. This had its origin in the view that revenue or fiscal offences, in contrast with criminal offences, were matters relating to internal regulation.[1161] However, this view has lost ground in recent years, and there is a growing tendency to make fiscal offences extraditable. Moreover, before refusing extradition, the State has to consult with the requesting State to provide it with ample opportunity to present its opinions and to provide information relevant to its allegation.[1162]

1156 UNCAC, Art. 44(14). The AU Convention against Corruption contains a similar provision which specifically refers to the minimum guarantees of a fair trial under international human rights law. AU Convention against Corruption, Art. 14.

1157 UNCAC, Art. 44(9).

1158 UNCAC, Art. 44(10); Inter-American Convention against Corruption, Art. 13(7); AU Convention against Corruption, Art. 15(7); SADC Protocol against Corruption, Art. 9(8).

1159 UNCAC, Art. 44(15).

1160 UNCAC, Art. 44(16).

1161 Gavan Griffith and Claire Harris, "Recent Developments in the Law of Extradition," *Melbourne Journal of International Law* 6 (2005): 36.

1162 UNCAC, Art. 44(17).

2. THE OBLIGATION TO EXTRADITE OR PROSECUTE

As already indicated in Chapter V, in line with the almost standard practice in regard to transnational crimes, the international legal framework against corruption also establishes the State obligation to extradite or prosecute alleged offenders of corrupt acts, also known as the *aut dedere aut judicare* obligation. At the request of the Party seeking extradition, a State must submit a case without undue delay to its competent authorities for the purpose of prosecution if an alleged offender is found in its territory and the State does not extradite the person solely on the ground that the alleged offender is one of its nationals.[1163] A State is required to grant extradition in accordance with the obligations described in this section or, if the State refuses extradition on the ground that the accused is one of its national, it has to prosecute the accused in accordance to the comments made in Chapter VI.

The *aut dedere aut judicare* obligation as set out in the international legal framework against corruption is considerably more limited than the equivalent obligation under other regimes (such as the Hague Convention for the Suppression of Unlawful Seizure of Aircraft).[1164] The obligation to prosecute is only subsidiary to extradition. As already noted, the reason for this subsidiarity is that in practice extradition is preferred to the exercise of jurisdiction by a State which is not the country where the crime was committed. It is often very difficult in practice to try a person for an offence committed outside the territorial jurisdiction of a domestic court. Yet prosecution is in practice the best option in the case of States, mostly with civil law systems, which cannot extradite their nationals.

A State is not bound by the obligation to extradite or prosecute if it refuses extradition on any other grounds, for example that the request has been made for the purpose of prosecuting or punishing a person on account of that person's

1163 UNCAC, Art. 42(3) and 44(11); Inter-American Convention against Corruption, Art. 13(6); CoE Criminal Law Convention, Art. 27(5); OECD Convention, Art. 10(3); AU Convention against Corruption, Art. 15(6); SADC Protocol against Corruption, Art. 9(7); EU Convention against Corruption, Art. 8(2). The State Party may extradite or surrender one of its nationals upon the condition that the person will be returned to serve the sentence imposed as a result of the trial or proceedings for which the extradition or surrender was sought and the requesting State accepts this condition and other appropriate terms. Such conditional extradition is sufficient to discharge the obligation of extradition or prosecution. UNCAC, Art. 44(12). Similarly, if extradition sought for purposes of enforcing a sentence is refused because the person sought is a national of the requested State, the latter State, upon application of the requesting State, has to consider the enforcement of the sentence imposed under the domestic law of the requesting State or the remainder thereof. UNCAC, Art. 44(13).

1164 See, Hague Convention for the Suppression of Unlawful Seizure of Aircraft, 1970, 860 U.N.T.S. 105, Art. 4(2).

sex, race, religion, nationality, ethnic origin, or political opinions.[1165] Extradition may be refused in these circumstances on condition that such a ground for refusal is specified in the extradition treaty in force with the requesting State or, in the absence of a treaty, in the domestic law governing extradition.[1166]

II. MUTUAL LEGAL ASSISTANCE

Modern corrupt practices often involve mobile actors, participants in more than one country or transactions that cross national borders. National authorities are therefore increasingly in need of the assistance of other States for the successful investigation, prosecution, and punishment of corruption offenders. States accordingly have to provide each other with legal assistance in gathering evidence for use in the investigation and prosecution of corruption. This is commonly known as mutual legal assistance (MLA) and normally includes the power to summon witnesses, compel production of evidence and other documents, issue search warrants and serve process. A State may seek and provide MLA through various types of arrangements, including bilateral treaties, multilateral treaties and domestic legislation.[1167] It is important to note that a State has no obligation to provide MLA to another State under customary international law. For that reason, a number of States have enacted laws which enable them to provide such assistance and increasingly have recourse to bilateral and multilateral treaties to facilitate the provision of MLA against transnational criminal activity.[1168]

Such treaties commonly list the type of assistance to be provided, the rights of the requesting and requested States, the rights of alleged offenders and the

---

1165 UNCAC, Art. 44(15).

1166 UNODC, *Legislative Guide for the Implementation of the United Nations Convention against Corruption*, para. 583.

1167 For details on the rich U.S. experience and MLA treaties, see Bruce Zagaris, *International White Collar Crime: Cases and Materials* (Cambridge: Cambridge University Press, 2010), 256–300.

1168 For example, the CoE Convention on Mutual Assistance in Criminal Matters and its two Additional Protocols of 1978 and 2001, Inter-American Convention on the Taking of Evidence Abroad of 1975 and its Additional Protocol of 1984, Inter-American Convention on Mutual Assistance in Criminal Matters of 1992 and its Optional Protocol of 1993; ECOWAS Convention on Mutual Assistance in Criminal Matters of 1992; the EU Convention on Mutual Assistance in Criminal Matters of 2000 and its Protocol of 2001; and the 1983 Arab League Convention on Mutual Assistance in Criminal Matters. There are also multilateral instruments on mutual legal assistance with regard to particular offences, such as the UNTOC (Art. 18), the UN Convention against Illicit Traffic in Narcotic Drugs and Psychotropic Substances (Art. 7), the CoE Convention on Laundering, Search, Seizure and Confiscation of the Proceeds from Crime (Arts. 8–10), and the CoE Convention on Cybercrime (Art. 3).

procedures to be followed in making and executing requests. These instruments enhance law enforcement by enabling the authorities to obtain evidence abroad in a way that is admissible domestically, supplementing other arrangements for the exchange of information and resolving certain complications between States with different legal traditions.[1169] Although there is no need for a treaty and effective internal legislation may be sufficient for the provision of legal assistance, there are several advantages to MLA treaties.[1170] Most importantly, treaties oblige a requested State to cooperate under international law. They also contain detailed provisions on the procedure to be followed for cooperation and therefore offer greater certainty and clarity than a non-treaty based procedure. Most States are now parties to MLA treaties and many States have adopted legislation for the provision of MLA to countries with which they have no treaty relations. Such legislation often contains provisions on sending, receiving, considering and executing requests that are similar to those in treaty-based schemes.

In this respect, international Conventions against corruption build on existing MLA treaties and legislation. There are two groups of obligations, depending on whether or not a State in question is covered by a MLA treaty.

1. COMPLEMENTARY INTERNATIONAL OBLIGATIONS RELATING TO MLA

Where an MLA treaty is in force between States Parties to the UNCAC, the rules of the treaty apply and are supplemented by certain obligations arising out of the UNCAC. These include the requirement for States to afford each other the widest measure of MLA in investigations, prosecutions and judicial proceedings in relation to corruption offences.[1171] Moreover, States cannot decline MLA on the grounds of bank secrecy.[1172] The international legal framework also broadly

---

1169 UNODC, *Legislative Guide for the Implementation of the United Nations Convention against Corruption*, para. 587.

1170 In some cases, a mutual legal assistance procedure has been effective even in the absence of a treaty between the States in question. Examples include the Abacha case between Switzerland and Nigeria and the case between Peru and the Cayman Islands for the recovery of the assets stolen by Montesinos.

1171 UNCAC, Art. 46(1); Inter-American Convention against Corruption, Art. 14(1); CoE Criminal Law Convention, Art. 26(1); OECD Convention, Art. 9(1); AU Convention against Corruption, Art. 18(1); SADC Protocol against Corruption, Art. 10(1). States are encouraged to conclude bilateral or multilateral agreements or arrangements that serve the purposes of, give practical effect to or enhance mutual legal assistance. UNCAC, Art. 46(30).

1172 UNCAC, Art. 46(8); Inter-American Convention against Corruption, Art. 16(1); CoE Criminal Law Convention, Art. 26(3); OECD Convention, Art. 9(3); AU Convention against Corruption, Art. 17(3). The Inter-American and AU Conventions add that the requesting State cannot use any information received that is protected by bank secrecy for any purpose other than the proceeding for which that information was requested unless so authorized by

establishes the type of MLA that may be requested, namely for: obtaining or taking statements; serving judicial documents; executing searches and seizures, and freezing; examining objects and sites; providing information, evidence and expert evaluations; providing documents and records for the identification, tracing or seizure of the proceeds of crime or property; facilitating the appearance of witnesses; the recovery of assets; and any other type of assistance not contrary to domestic law.[1173] In addition, with regard to MLA, international law encourages States to transmit information relating to criminal matters spontaneously to a competent authority in another State where they believe that such information could assist in inquiries or criminal proceedings.[1174]

States are under the same obligations to the fullest extent possible in proceedings in which a legal person may be held liable.[1175] For a State that does not recognize the criminal liability of legal persons, dual criminality may raise obstacles if it is requested to provide MLA to another State where a legal person is subject to criminal prosecution. The State may refuse to cooperate in such cases. States are only required to provide MLA "to the fullest extent possible," and many States do not therefore provide MLA when the investigation or prosecution involves a legal person. Certain States that do require dual criminality have addressed the problem by relying on illegal conduct committed by a natural person in the case or if the requesting State indicates that the conduct giving rise to the request can be attributed to a natural person, thereby satisfying the dual criminality requirement. For example, if Japan receives a request for MLA in a case in which a legal person is the object of an investigation, it will ask the requesting State to change the object of the investigation to a natural person, even if the identity of the natural person is not known.[1176] Although as indicated in this study, the international legal framework against corruption places several obligations on States to enhance the liability of legal persons, it has not supplemented those provisions with a matching solid system for MLA.

---

the requested State. Inter-American Convention against Corruption, Art. 16(2); AU Convention against Corruption, Art. 17(2).

1173 UNCAC, Art. 46(3).

1174 UNCAC, Art. 46(4). The competent authorities receiving the information have to comply with a request that the information remain confidential or with restrictions on its use. However, this does not prevent the receiving State Party from disclosing in its proceedings information that is exculpatory to an accused person. In such a case, the receiving State Party has to notify the transmitting State Party prior to the disclosure, or without delay after the disclosure. UNCAC, Art. 46(5).

1175 UNCAC, Art. 46(2); OECD Convention, Art. 9(1).

1176 ADB/OECD Anti-Corruption Initiative for Asia and the Pacific, *Mutual Legal Assistance, Extradition and Recovery of Proceeds of Corruption in Asia and the Pacific*, 172.

2. SUBSIDIARY INTERNATIONAL OBLIGATIONS RELATING TO MLA

The above obligations apply in all cases. However, where there is no MLA treaty in force between the countries concerned, States Parties to the anti-corruption instruments have to follow the whole set of obligations arising out of the anti-corruption treaties (especially UNCAC) respecting requests, execution and refusal.[1177]

2.1. Requests for MLA

Requests for MLA, and any communication related thereto, have to be transmitted to the central authorities designated by States Parties.[1178] Such requests must be made in writing or, where possible, by any means capable of producing a written record, in a language acceptable to the requested State Party and under conditions allowing that State Party to establish authenticity.[1179] In urgent circumstances, and where agreed by the States Parties, requests may be made orally, but have to be confirmed in writing forthwith. Moreover, a request for MLA has to be executed in accordance with the domestic law of the requested State Party,[1180] and contain:

(a) the identity of the authority making the request;
(b) the subject matter and nature of the investigation, prosecution or judicial proceeding to which the request relates and the name and functions of the authority conducting the investigation, prosecution or judicial proceeding;
(c) a summary of the relevant facts, except in relation to requests for the purpose of service of judicial documents;

1177 UNCAC, Art. 46(6)–(7).

1178 States are required to designate a central authority that has the responsibility and power to receive requests for mutual legal assistance and either to execute them or to transmit them to the competent authorities for execution. However, a State may require that such requests and communications be addressed to it through diplomatic channels and, in urgent circumstances, where the States Parties agree, through the International Criminal Police Organization, if possible. UNCAC, Art. 46(13); Inter-American Convention against Corruption, Art. 18 (although the designation of a central authority is not mandatory); CoE Criminal Law Convention, Art. 29; OECD Convention, Art. 11; AU Convention against Corruption, Art. 20. Where a State Party has a special region or territory with a separate system of mutual legal assistance, it may designate a distinct central authority that has the same function for that region or territory. Moreover, States have to notify the Secretary-General of the relevant international organization of the central authority designated and the acceptable languages at the time it deposits its instrument of ratification, acceptance or approval of or accession to the Convention.

1179 UNCAC, Art. 46(14).

1180 UNCAC, Art. 46(17).

(d) a description of the assistance sought and details of any particular procedure that the requesting State Party wishes to be followed;
(e) where possible, the identity, location and nationality of any person concerned; and
(f) the purpose for which the evidence, information or action is sought.[1181]

As is usual in MLA treaties, the international legal framework against corruption also provides for the principle of speciality. In other words, States may not transmit or use information or evidence furnished by the requested State Party for investigations, prosecutions or judicial proceedings other than those stated in the request without the prior consent of the requested State Party.[1182] Moreover, the requesting State is under an obligation not to use any information received that is protected by bank secrecy for any purpose other than the proceedings for which that information was requested, unless authorized to do so by the requested State.[1183] However, the requesting State Party can disclose in its proceedings information or evidence that is exculpatory to an accused person.[1184]

2.2. *Execution of MLA*

A State may transfer a person who is being detained or is serving a sentence in its territory and whose presence in another State is requested for purposes of identification, testimony or otherwise providing assistance in obtaining evidence for investigations, prosecutions or judicial proceedings in relation to offences covered by the UNCAC.[1185] However, the transfer can only be carried out if the person freely gives his or her informed consent and the competent authorities of both States agree.[1186] A State may also, at the request of another State Party,

---

1181 UNCAC, Art. 46(15). The requested State Party may request additional information when it appears necessary for the execution of the request. UNCAC, Art. 46(16).

1182 UNCAC, Art. 46(19). A State may require that the requested State Party keep confidential the fact and substance of the request, except to the extent necessary to execute the request. If the requested State Party cannot comply with the requirement of confidentiality, it has to promptly inform the requesting State. UNCAC, Art. 46(20).

1183 UN General Assembly, *Report of the Ad Hoc Committee for the Negotiation of a Convention against Corruption on the work of its first to seventh sessions: Addendum: Interpretative Notes for the Official Records (Travaux Préparatoires) of the Negotiation of the United Nations Convention against Corruption*, A/58/422/Add.1, 7 October 2003, para. 43.

1184 UNCAC, Art. 46(19). In this case, the requesting State Party has to notify and consult with the requested State Party prior to disclosure and if, in an exceptional case, advance notice is not possible, the requesting State Party must inform the requested State Party of the disclosure without delay.

1185 UNCAC, Art. 46(10).

1186 UNCAC, Art. 46(10)(a) and (b). In addition, the State Party to which the person is transferred has to comply with several obligations, namely: (a) to keep the person transferred in custody, unless otherwise requested or authorized by the State Party from which the person was transferred; (b) without delay implement its obligation to return the person to the custody of

when an individual is in its territory and has to be heard as a witness or expert by the judicial authorities of another State Party, organize a hearing to take place by video conference if it is not possible or desirable for the individual in question to appear in person in the territory of the requesting State Party.[1187] However, these provisions may require legislative changes, such as the adoption of legislative powers allowing the authorities to compel the attendance of a witness, amendments to evidentiary rules and the expansion of perjury offences.[1188]

States have to respond to the request for MLA promptly and take as full account as possible of any deadlines suggested by the requesting State Party for which reasons are given.[1189] The requested State Party has to respond to reasonable requests by the requesting State Party on the status, and progress in its handling, of the request.[1190] However, the requested State may postpone MLA on the ground that it interferes with an on-going investigation, prosecution, or judicial proceeding.[1191]

---

the State Party from which the person was transferred as agreed beforehand, or as otherwise agreed, by the competent authorities of both States Parties; and (c) not require the State Party from which the person was transferred to initiate extradition proceedings for the return of the person. The person transferred shall receive credit for service of the sentence being served in the State from which he or she was transferred for time spent in the custody of the State Party to which he or she was transferred. See, UNCAC, Art. 46.11. Moreover, unless the State Party from which a person is to be transferred so agrees, that person, may not be prosecuted, detained, punished or subjected to any other restriction of his or her personal liberty in the territory of the State to which that person is transferred in respect of acts, omissions or convictions prior to his or her departure from the territory of the State from which he or she was transferred. UNCAC, Art. 46(12). A similar impediment applies to persons who are not being detained or imprisoned and agree to give evidence in a proceeding or to assist in an investigation, prosecution or judicial proceeding in the territory of the requesting State Party. See, UNCAC, Art. 46(27).

1187 UNCAC, Art. 46(18). States Parties may agree that the hearing shall be conducted by a judicial authority of the requesting State Party and attended by a judicial authority of the requested State Party.

1188 For more on the changes that may be required, see, UNODC, *Legislative Guide for the Implementation of the United Nations Convention against Corruption*, para. 629.

1189 States have to provide to the requesting State Party copies of government records, documents or information in their possession that under their domestic law are available to the general public. UNCAC, Art. 46.29(a). At its discretion, the requested State Party may provide to the requesting State Party in whole, in part or subject to such conditions as it deems appropriate, copies of any government records, documents or information in its possession that under its domestic law are not available to the general public. UNCAC, Art. 46(29)(b).

1190 UNCAC, Art. 46(24). The ordinary costs of executing a request shall be borne by the requested State Party, unless otherwise agreed by the States Parties concerned. UNCAC, Art. 46(28). However, developing countries may encounter difficulties in meeting even some of the ordinary costs and should be provided with appropriate assistance to enable them to meet this requirement. UN General Assembly, *Interpretative Notes for the Official Records (Travaux Préparatoires) of the Negotiation of the United Nations Convention against Corruption*, para. 44.

1191 UNCAC, Art. 46(25).

Although dual criminality is usually a condition for providing legal assistance, States are required to take into account the overall purposes of the UNCAC in responding to requests for legal assistance in the absence of dual criminality.[1192] Moreover, although States may decline to render assistance on the ground of absence of dual criminality, where consistent with the basic concepts of their legal system, they have to render assistance that does not involve coercive action.[1193] It is clear that the intention of the UNCAC is to promote the provision by States of legal assistance even in the absence of dual criminality.[1194] This departs from earlier Conventions, such as UNTOC, under which the provision of MLA without dual criminality was left to the discretion of the State concerned.[1195]

2.3. Refusal of MLA

A State can clearly refuse MLA, and the international legal framework sets out broad reasons for so doing. MLA may be refused: (i) if the request is not made in conformity with the provisions of the UNCAC; (ii) if the requested State Party considers that execution of the request is likely to prejudice its sovereignty, security, *ordre public* or other essential interests; (iii) if the authorities of the requested State Party would be prohibited by its domestic law from carrying out the action requested with regard to any similar offence, had it been subject to investigation, prosecution or judicial proceedings under their own jurisdiction; and (iv) if it would be contrary to the legal system of the requested State Party relating to MLA for the request to be granted.[1196] In practice, these provisions leave the door open for the refusal of MLA on countless grounds. However, before refusing MLA or postponing it, the requested State Party is required to consult with the requesting State Party to consider whether assistance may be granted subject to such terms and conditions as it deems necessary. If the requesting State Party accepts assistance subject to those conditions, it has to comply with the conditions.[1197] On the other hand, as indicated earlier, States

---

1192 UNCAC, Art. 46(9)(a).

1193 UNCAC, Art. 46(9)(b). Such assistance may be refused in cases of a trivial nature (*de minimis*) or where the assistance is available under the other provisions of the Convention.

1194 See, Article 46(9)(c). Conversely, the OECD Convention clearly provides that dual criminality shall be deemed to exist if the offence for which the assistance is sought is within the scope of the Convention, even where States make mutual legal assistance conditional upon the existence of dual criminality. OECD Convention, Art. 9(2).

1195 UNTOC, Art. 18(9).

1196 UNCAC, Art. 46(21). The reasons for the refusal of mutual legal assistance have to be given to the requesting State. UNCAC, Art. 46(23). The CoE Criminal Law Convention is more restrictive in respect of the grounds on which mutual legal assistance may be refused. It provides solely that a State may refuse mutual legal assistance if it believes that compliance with the request would undermine its fundamental interests, national sovereignty, national security or ordre public. CoE Criminal Law Convention, Art. 26(2).

1197 UNCAC, Art. 46(26).

may not decline MLA on the grounds of bank secrecy,[1198] or on the sole ground that the offence is also considered to involve fiscal matters.[1199]

3. INSUFFICIENT LEGAL FRAMEWORK FOR MLA

Anti-corruption conventions are primarily intended to promote the creation by States of a solid legal framework that allows the provision of broad legal assistance. Such a legal framework is useful in avoiding some of the known obstacles to the provision of effective legal assistance, such as legal barriers and political unwillingness. In the absence of uniform procedures for the provision of MLA, different legal systems, and the incompatibility of systems for police cooperation, investigation and prosecution, may result in lengthy and cumbersome or unsuccessful procedures. Indeed, the unavailability of mutual assistance from a foreign jurisdiction in which a foreign bribe transaction occurs has been regarded as the "single most important reason for terminating an investigation" into foreign bribery.[1200] Evidently, the MLA legal framework promoted by the anti-corruption conventions does not break new ground in this field, and largely follows the usual MLA provisions found in existing treaties. No major changes can be expected in respect of anti-corruption MLA, even if States duly comply with their international obligations.

However, a strong MLA framework does not avoid the fact that certain States have no practical means of providing and requesting assistance. Many developing countries do not have a domestic framework in place and lack basic human and financial resources, expertise and the legal infrastructure to request or provide assistance effectively in a corruption case. Under these circumstances, the existence of a legal framework alone is not sufficient. In these cases international cooperation in criminal matters needs to be combined with the international obligations relating to technical assistance with a view to strengthening the capacity to provide and request MLA.

1198 UNCAC, Art. 46(8); Inter-American Convention against Corruption, Art. 16(1); CoE Criminal Law Convention, Art. 26(3); OECD Convention, Art. 9(3); AU Convention against Corruption, Art. 17(3). The Inter-American and AU conventions add that the requesting State cannot use any information received that is protected by bank secrecy for any purpose other than the proceeding for which that information was requested unless so authorized by the requested State. Inter-American Convention against Corruption, Art. 16(2); AU Convention against Corruption, Art. 17(2).

1199 UNCAC, Art. 46(22).

1200 OECD WGB, *Mid-Term Study of Phase 2 Reports: Application of the Convention on Combating Bribery of Foreign Public Officials in International Business Transactions and the 1997 Recommendation on Combating Bribery in International Business Transactions*, 2006, 108.

III. ASSET RECOVERY

Following the death of her husband, Maryam Abacha, wife of the military dictator Sani Abacha, who ruled Nigeria from 1993 until 1998, was arrested trying to leave the country with 38 suitcases filled with US dollars and pounds sterling. It is not generally known how millions of dollars in assets can be transferred abroad. However, in many instances of corruption this happens in the least sophisticated way possible, simply by putting millions of banknotes in a suitcase and travelling abroad. The billions embezzled by the Abacha family were mostly removed in cash from the Central Bank of Nigeria. Abacha would ask his National Security Adviser to write to him urgently requesting funds for vague and unspecified purposes. Abacha would then countersign the letter, which his National Security Adviser presented to the Central Bank for payment.[1201] The money would then be transported abroad, mostly by the Abacha family themselves.

The Abacha example illustrates a recurrent feature of many corrupt practices: the proceeds of corruption are often hidden in a foreign State, usually in so-called "financial centres." Part of the efforts required to combat corruption therefore consist of tracing and repatriating the proceeds of corruption back to the State of origin, which is frequently in dire need of those assets. There have been some successful asset recovery procedures, such as the US$ 1.3 billion returned to Nigeria which were part of the assets stolen by Sani Abacha, and the US$ 658 million retuned to the Philippines which were part of the assets stolen by ex-President Ferdinand Marcos. However, while much attention has been paid to these cases, in overall terms, the recovery of corrupt assets remains an extremely complex and difficult procedure that is mainly unsuccessful.

Better international regulation of asset recovery procedures was therefore needed and there are now several international obligations on States relating to the transfer of assets of illicit origin and facilitating the return of such assets to

---

1201 The following is an example of such a letter:
"SPECIAL ALLOCATION OF FUNDS
1. Due to some security problems requiring immediate solution and implementation, I am constrained to ask from your Excellency to kindly give consideration in approving funds to deal with the situation. The situation as I informed you is desperate and imminent. It has to be dealt with properly and urgently. These nagging problems which are in bad taste and not in our national interest, involve some countries within and outside Africa.
2. Kindly approve Ten million Pound Sterling [£10m], Fifty million Dollars [$50m] and Two Hundred and fifty million Naira [N250m]. The funds are urgently required to solve this enormous task.
3. Please approve."

Tim Daniel and James Maton, "Recovering the Proceeds of Corruption: General Sani Abacha – A Nation's Thief," in Recovering Stolen Assets, ed. Mark Pieth (Bern: Peter Lang, 2008), 66.

the States of origin.[1202] The UNCAC states that the return of assets constitutes one of its fundamental principles.[1203] It is probably in this respect that the international legal framework against corruption is most "revolutionary." And it is the provisions on asset recovery which have attracted most developing countries' ratifications.

The basic obligation requires States to afford one another the widest measure of cooperation and assistance for the return of assets.[1204] However, there is no standard procedure for the return of assets deriving from corruption. Asset recovery is driven by pragmatic considerations. The international legal framework therefore sets out a range of options from which States can choose. As indicated below, most obligations relating to the recovery of assets focus primarily on the measures to be taken by the requested State rather than the requesting State. They are most relevant to States that have traditionally "received" funds from overseas, namely financial centres. For easier analysis, the obligations relating to the recovery of assets may be subdivided into action to prevent the transfer of assets, enhance the direct recovery of property or facilitate mechanisms for the recovery of property through international cooperation.

1. PREVENTION OF THE TRANSFER OF ASSETS

By preventing the transfer of assets, the international legal framework against corruption attempts to address two obstacles to asset recovery: the difficulty of identifying the proceeds of corruption and the need for evidence. The measures to prevent the transfer of assets build on general preventive measures relating to corruption, especially those concerning the prevention of money laundering. Therefore, this section largely restates what was indicated in Chapter V. A series of measures are specified which States have to introduce to prevent more effectively and detect transfers of the proceeds of crime. States therefore have to cooperate with one another for the purpose of preventing and combating the transfer of proceeds of corruption offences and of promoting ways and means of recovering such proceeds.[1205]

1.1. Know-your-customer obligations

The following provisions should be seen in the context of the more general regulatory and supervisory regime that States have to establish against money

1202 See, Stolen Asset Recovery (StAR) Initiative, *Stolen Asset Recovery: Towards a Global Architecture for Asset Recovery* (Washington D.C.: World Bank, 2009).
1203 UNCAC, Art. 51.
1204 UNCAC, Art. 51.
1205 UNCAC, Art. 58.

laundering, in which customer identification, record-keeping and reporting requirements feature prominently.[1206] Specifically, States need to require financial institutions to:

(a) verify the identity of customers;
(b) to take reasonable steps to determine the identity of beneficial owners of funds deposited into high-value accounts; and
(c) to scrutinise accounts sought or maintained by or on behalf of individuals who are, or have been, entrusted with prominent public functions (PEPs), their family members and close associates.[1207]

These obligations are identical to those described earlier concerning the prevention of money laundering and effective customer identification. The duty of financial institutions to know their customers is not new, and forms part of long-standing internationally accepted standards of due diligence and the prudential management of financial institutions.[1208] Offenders often hide their transactions and criminal proceeds behind false names or those of third parties. The requirement is to make reasonable efforts to determine the beneficial owner of funds. As indicated in Chapter V, customer identification entails the requirement of the identification and documentation of holders of accounts in financial institutions and all parties to financial transactions. Records need to contain sufficient information to identify the parties and the nature of the transaction, the specific assets and the amounts or values involved, and to allow the tracing of the source and destination of all funds or other assets.[1209] These are the so-called "know-your-customer" rules. Moreover, customer identification includes the identification of beneficial owners. In order to prevent the use of third persons to hold the proceeds of crime on behalf of corrupt individuals, States also have to take reasonable steps to determine the beneficial owner of funds deposited in highly valued accounts.[1210] It is common a practice for

[1206] See also Chapter V.

[1207] UNCAC, Art. 52(1). The term "close associates" is deemed to encompass persons or companies clearly related to individuals entrusted with prominent public functions. UN General Assembly, *Interpretative Notes for the Official Records (Travaux Préparatoires) of the Negotiation of the United Nations Convention against Corruption*, para. 50.

[1208] See, for example, the FATF Forty Recommendations available at www.fatf-gafi.org/ (last visited 29 April 2012) and the Basle Committee on Banking Supervision "Prevention of criminal use of banking system for the purpose of money laundering" and "Customer due diligence for banks" available at www.bis.org/ (last visited 31 January 2012).

[1209] UNODC, *Legislative Guide for the Implementation of the United Nations Convention against Corruption*, 145. For a detailed analysis of customer identification, see Guy Stessens, *Money Laundering: A New International Law Enforcement Model* (Cambridge: Cambridge University Press, 2000), 146–148.

[1210] A beneficial owner is a person "who does not have title to property but has rights in the property which are the normal incident of owning the property. The persons for whom a trustee holds title to property are the beneficial owners of the property, and the trustee has a

criminals not to open bank accounts under their own name, but under that of someone else (usually a legal person), while constituting themselves as the beneficial owners. In cases of highly valued accounts, States therefore need to require financial institutions to identify the beneficial owner who ultimately controls the funds.[1211]

1.2. Enhanced due diligence for PEPs

In addition, banks and financial institutions need to carry out enhanced due diligence in the case of politically exposed persons (PEPs), their family members and close associates.[1212] Although the enhanced due diligence for PEPs has already been described in Chapter V, it is however useful to restate in this section the international obligations relating to PEPs as they are pertinent to the recovery of assets.

The decision as to who is to be regarded as a PEP is left to each State. However, there are certain guidelines. A PEP is a natural person in a senior political position who has a degree of control or influence over public assets, such as Heads of State or Government, Ministers, Members of Parliament, senior civil servants, senior government, judicial, and military officials, senior executives of state-owned enterprises, among others.[1213] More specifically, regulatory authorities and banks need to require a declaration of beneficial ownership, request asset and income disclosure forms, undertake o periodic review of PEP customers and avoid setting limits on the time an individual remains a PEP.[1214] These measures constitute an additional hurdle and make it difficult for senior public officials to launder the proceeds of corrupt practices. Unfortunately, as indicated by FATF evaluations, the majority of States do not comply with the recommendations relating to politically exposed persons. Customer identification is central to the effective prevention of money laundering and, as indicated in a recent report by the NGO Global Witness, there are numerous

---

fiduciary responsibility to them." Henry Campbell Black, Joseph R Nolan, and Jacqueline Nolan-Haley, *Black's Law Dictionary: Definitions of the Terms and Phrases of American and English Jurisprudence, Ancient and Modern*, 6th ed. (St. Paul: West Pub. Co, 1990), 156.

1211 For a more detailed analysis of the identification of beneficial owners, see Stessens, *Money Laundering: A New International Law Enforcement Model*, 148–157.

1212 UNCAC, Art. 52(1); FATF Recommendation No. 12 and Interpretative Note to Recommendation 12.

1213 See the definition of PEP in the Wolfsberg Principles, available at www.wolfsberg-principles.com/ (last visited 31 January 2012); Basel Committee on Banking Supervision, Customer Due Diligence for Banks, 2001, available at www.bis.org/publ/bcbs77.pdf (last visisted 31 January 2012); and the FATF's 40 Recommendations (as amended on 16 February 2012), available at www.fatf-gafi.org (last visited 29 April 2012). For a more detailed analysis of the PEP concept, see Hans-Peter Bauer, "How to Deal with Politically Exposed Persons," in *Recovering Stolen Assets*, ed. Mark Pieth (Bern: Peter Lang, 2008), 195–217.

1214 See, Theodore S. Greenberg et al., *Stolen Asset Recovery: Politically Exposed Persons: A Policy Paper on Strengthening Preventive Measures* (Washington D.C.: World Bank, 2009).

cases in which banks have failed to apply due diligence and have, almost deliberately, done business with corrupt regimes.[1215] As indicated in Chapter V, in order to facilitate implementation of such measures, States have to:

(a) issue advisories regarding the types of persons for whose accounts enhanced scrutiny is expected, the types of accounts and transactions to which particular attention should be paid and account-opening, maintenance and record-keeping measures for such accounts;[1216] and
(b) notify financial institutions of the identity of particular persons for whose accounts enhanced scrutiny is expected.[1217] Since it may be difficult for financial institutions to know when a client is a PEP, States need to identify them and disseminate information to financial institutions.

This sort of guidance from national authorities is particularly helpful to financial institutions in their efforts to comply with the regulatory requirements. In this context, States also need to ensure that financial institutions maintain adequate records, over an appropriate period of time, of accounts and transactions involving the persons to whom enhanced scrutiny is applied, which should, as a minimum, contain information relating to the identity of the customer as well as, as far as possible, of the beneficial owner.[1218] This measure is important as it obliges States to maintain an evidentiary record. States may also need to provide guidance to financial institutions on the appropriate procedures to be applied and on whether certain risks require the application and implementation of these provisions: (i) to accounts of a particular value or nature; (ii) to its own citizens, as well as to citizens of other States; and (iii) to officials with a particular function or seniority.[1219] It should be emphasized that these measures apply to both domestic and foreign public officials.[1220] They are essential to facilitate investigations and the identification and possible future return of assets.

1.3. Shell banks, financial disclosure, and FIUs

One of the most widely used financial vehicles to hide assets in the international financial system is the so-called "shell bank." States therefore also need to

---

1215 Global Witness, *Undue Diligence: How Banks Do Business with Corrupt Regimes*, March 2009.

1216 UNCAC, Art. 52(2)(a). The obligation to issue advisories may be fulfilled by the State or by its financial oversight bodies. UN General Assembly, *Interpretative Notes for the Official Records (Travaux Préparatoires) of the Negotiation of the United Nations Convention against Corruption*, para. 52.

1217 UNCAC, Art. 52(2)(b).

1218 UNCAC, Art. 52(3).

1219 UN General Assembly, *Interpretative Notes for the Official Records (Travaux Préparatoires) of the Negotiation of the United Nations Convention against Corruption*, para. 49.

1220 UNODC, *Legislative Guide for the Implementation of the United Nations Convention against Corruption*, para. 692.

prevent the establishment of banks that have no physical presence and are not affiliated to a regulated financial group ("shell banks").[1221] The *travaux préparatoires* of UNCAC indicate that physical presence means meaningful mind and management located within the jurisdiction. The simple existence of a local agent or low-level staff would not constitute physical presence. Management is understood to include administration (books and records).[1222]

As already indicated in relation to preventive measures, in the context of asset recovery States are also required to consider establishing financial disclosure systems for appropriate public officials and appropriate sanctions for non-compliance. As noted in Chapter V, States have to endeavour to establish measures and systems requiring public officials to make declarations to appropriate authorities regarding, *inter alia*, their outside activities, employment, investments, assets and substantial gifts or benefits from which a conflict of interest may arise.[1223] With a view to preventing the transfer of the proceeds of corruption, States are also required to consider permitting their competent authorities to share the information resulting from disclosure procedures with authorities in other States when necessary to investigate, claim and recover the proceeds of corruption offences.[1224] In addition, States may require public officials to disclose ownership of foreign accounts. More specifically, States have to consider requiring appropriate public officials with an interest in or control over a financial account in a foreign country to: (i) report that relationship to the appropriate authorities; (ii) maintain appropriate records related to such accounts; and (iii) provide for sanctions for non-compliance.[1225]

States are also required to consider establishing a financial intelligence unit (FIU) to be responsible for receiving, analysing and disseminating to the competent authorities reports of suspicious financial transactions.[1226] As indicated in Chapter V, since the 1990s, many States have established such units as part of their regulatory, police or other authorities, with a wide range of structures, responsibilities, functions and departmental affiliation or independence. The Egmont Group (the informal association of FIUs) has defined such units as central, national agencies responsible for receiving (and, where so permitted, requesting), analysing and disseminating to the competent

1221 Moreover, States may consider requiring their financial institutions: (i) to refuse to enter into or continue a correspondent banking relationship with "shell banks"; and (ii) to guard against establishing relations with foreign financial institutions that permit their accounts to be used by "shell banks". UNCAC, Art. 52(4).

1222 UN General Assembly, *Interpretative Notes for the Official Records (Travaux Préparatoires) of the Negotiation of the United Nations Convention against Corruption*, para. 54.

1223 For detailed information on disclosure systems, see Chapter V.

1224 UNCAC, Art. 52(5).

1225 UNCAC, Art. 52(6).

1226 UNCAC, Art. 14(1)(b) and 58.

authorities disclosures of financial information: (a) concerning suspected proceeds of crime; or (b) as required by national legislation or regulation, in order to combat money laundering and the financing of terrorism.[1227] Although, the establishment of FIUs is not required by law, it is strongly recommended.[1228]

2. DIRECT RECOVERY OF PROPERTY

International obligations relating to the direct recovery of assets refer to the recovery of property through civil proceedings. For certain States and in certain situations a criminal conviction may be unattainable, and civil litigation is therefore the only method of recovering stolen assets. As indicated earlier, the international legal framework against corruption provides for, and actively promotes, civil litigation and civil confiscation procedures.[1229] In the context of asset recovery, such proceedings have to be made available to foreign States. States must therefore allow another State to initiate civil action in their courts to establish title to, or ownership of, property acquired through a corruption offence.[1230] In other words, foreign States need to be granted legal standing in the courts of another State. The civil case before the courts of the United Kingdom against Frederick Chiluba, who governed Zambia from 1991 to 2002, constitutes a good example of such proceedings.[1231] The civil recovery procedure was brought by the Attorney General of Zambia for and on behalf of the Republic of Zambia against Chiluba and his associates in the Chancery Division of the High Court in London because much of the stolen money was held in bank accounts in London. On 4 May 2007, Chiluba and his co-defendants were found guilty of stealing US$ 46 million.[1232]

Moreover, States are required to permit their courts to order those who have committed corruption offences to pay compensation or damages to another State that has been harmed by such offences.[1233] This innovative provision departs from the notion that the proceeds from corruption should be recovered only for the purposes of confiscation and requires States to ensure that their courts can recognize the right of victim States to seek recovery of compensation or

1227 Egmont Group, *Interpretative Note Concerning the Egmont Definition of a Financial Intelligence Unit*, available at www.egmontgroup.org (last visited 31 January 2012).

1228 UNODC, *Legislative Guide for the Implementation of the United Nations Convention against Corruption*, para. 764.

1229 See Chapter on Law Enforcement (confiscation) and Jurisdiction (civil jurisdiction).

1230 UNCAC, Art. 53(a).

1231 Attorney General of Zambia for and on behalf of the Republic of Zambia v. Meer Care and Desai and Ors [2007] EWHC 952.

1232 Ibid.

1233 UNCAC, Art. 53(b).

damages.[1234] The international legal framework against corruption does not, however, regulate how foreign States which have suffered damage as a result of an act of corruption should be compensated.[1235] The intention of civil proceedings is to recover assets acquired through corruption or damages from corrupt activities through a ruling that may be enforced against legitimately acquired assets or those of doubtful provenance.

As already indicated, the international legal framework against corruption encourages victims of corruption to sue those responsible to recover what they have lost. In respect of the recovery of property, this is extended to foreign States and the comments made in Chapter VI regarding civil litigation apply *mutatis mutandis*. However, attention needs to be drawn to one matter. As with any civil litigation, a connection to the desired jurisdiction is generally required for the commencement of civil proceedings. In the context of asset recovery, this is demonstrated by the fact that the corruptly acquired assets are in the jurisdiction or have passed through the jurisdiction in which the case is brought.[1236] In other words, the presence of assets acquired corruptly provides the necessary jurisdiction to sue those responsible.

The international legal framework also requires States to provide legal standing to other States so that they can claim, as a third party in a confiscation procedure, ownership of assets acquired through a corrupt act.[1237] As one State may not always be aware of the existence of proceedings in a foreign State, such as the prosecution of a company charged with the bribery of a public official of that State, it is necessary to notify the State concerned of its right to stand and prove its claim.[1238]

3. MECHANISMS FOR THE RECOVERY OF PROPERTY THROUGH INTERNATIONAL COOPERATION

While recovery of assets may be achieved indirectly through civil proceedings, the traditional way of repatriating stolen assets has been through international

1234 UNODC and UNICRI, *Technical Guide to the United Nations Convention against Corruption*, 203–204.

1235 For more on compensation, see Chapter VI.

1236 See, for example, the cases in the United Kingdom of the Islamic Republic of Pakistan v. Asif Ali Zardari and others [2006] EWHC 2411 (Comm); the Federal Republic of Nigeria v. Joshua Chibi Dariye and another [2007] EWHC 708 (Ch); and Attorney-General for and on behalf of the Republic of Zambia v. Meer Care and Desai and Ors [2005] EWHC 2102, cited in Tim Daniel and James Maton, "Civil Proceedings to Recover Corruptly Acquired Assets of Public Officials," in *Recovering Stolen Assets*, ed. Mark Pieth (Bern: Peter Lang, 2008), 246.

1237 UNCAC, Art. 53(c).

1238 UNODC and UNICRI, *Technical Guide to the United Nations Convention against Corruption*, 205.

cooperation in criminal matters between the respective States. The key for effective asset recovery is therefore a robust system of international cooperation. States therefore have to consider concluding bilateral or multilateral agreements or arrangements to enhance the effectiveness of international cooperation for asset recovery.[1239] Such agreements could contain commitments and go further than the requirement of international anti-corruption obligations.

3.1. *Confiscation*

As already noted in Chapter VII, the international legal framework against corruption requires the establishment of a basic regime for the domestic freezing, seizure and confiscation of assets. This is a prerequisite for international cooperation and the return of assets. Domestic infrastructure paves the way for cooperation in matters of confiscation and the international obligations described below build on that structure and cover issues arising out of requests for confiscation from another State.

Experience has shown that there are two possible approaches to the execution of international requests for seizure and confiscation. Either evidence can be submitted by the requesting State in support of an application for a domestic order, or the requesting State's order can be executed directly as a domestic order. While the former is standard practice in this type of procedure, the latter may be more controversial, as it implies that a State has to recognize an order issued by the courts of another State. Fortunately, the international legal framework requires States to accept the latter, which serves to expedite requests for seizure and confiscation. Direct enforcement is much less resource intensive, avoids duplication and is significantly more effective in providing the assistance sought on a timely basis.[1240] States have to permit their competent authorities to give effect to an order of confiscation issued by a court of another State.[1241] Under this obligation, States have to entrust domestic authorities with the capacity to recognize and act on an order of confiscation issued by another State. Such an order of confiscation should be interpreted broadly as including monetary confiscation judgments, but should not be read as requiring the enforcement of an order issued by a court that does not have criminal jurisdiction.[1242] Moreover, States are required to permit their authorities to order

1239 UNCAC, Art. 59.

1240 UN Office for Drug Control and Crime Prevention, Report of the Informal Expert Working Group on Mutual Legal Assistance Casework Best Practice (Vienna, 2001), section 7.8, available at https://www.unodc.org/tldb/pdf/Practical%20_Guide_MLA_2001.pdf (last visited 31 January 2012).

1241 UNCAC, Art. 54(1)(a).

1242 UN General Assembly, *Interpretative Notes for the Official Records (Travaux Préparatoires) of the Negotiation of the United Nations Convention against Corruption*, para. 57.

the confiscation of such property of foreign origin by adjudication of money laundering or other offences within their jurisdiction or by other procedures authorized under domestic law.[1243] This involves confiscation on the grounds of money laundering, as opposed to convictions for predicate offences. This obligation would be fulfilled by a criminal proceeding that could lead to confiscation orders.[1244] In addition, States are required to allow their competent authorities to adopt provisional measures to be taken at the request of another State with a view to the enforcement of freezing or confiscation orders. More specifically, States have to allow their competent authorities to freeze or seize property upon a freezing or seizure order issued by a competent authority of a requesting State in relation to property that may eventually be subject to confiscation.[1245] In this case, the State also has to act on or recognize an order issued in another State. States also have to allow their competent authorities to freeze or seize property upon request when there are sufficient grounds for taking such actions and the property would eventually be subject to confiscation.[1246]

States that receive a request from another State for confiscation in relation to corruption offences are required, to the greatest extent possible, to submit to their competent authorities either: (i) the request to obtain an order of confiscation and give effect to it;[1247] or (ii) an order of confiscation issued by a court of the requesting State party insofar as it relates to proceeds of crime situated in the territory of the requested Party, with a view to giving effect to it to the extent requested.[1248] Following a request made by another State with jurisdiction over a corruption offence, States have to take measures to identify,

---

1243 UNCAC, Art. 54.1(b).

1244 UN General Assembly, *Interpretative Notes for the Official Records (Travaux Préparatoires) of the Negotiation of the United Nations Convention against Corruption*, para. 58.

1245 UNCAC, Art. 54(2)(a).

1246 UNCAC, Art. 54(2)(b). States should also consider taking additional measures to permit their authorities to preserve property for confiscation, such as on the basis of a foreign arrest or criminal charge related to the acquisition of such property. UNCAC, Art. 54(2)(c). Under the AU Convention against Corruption, this obligation is mandatory. See, AU Convention against Corruption, Art. 16(1)(a).

1247 UNCAC, Arts. 55(1)(a), 31(1), 31(5)-(7). In addition to the standard content of a request for mutual legal assistance, including the irrelevance of bank secrecy, the request of the requesting State should contain a description of the property to be confiscated, including, to the extent possible, the location and, where relevant, the estimated value of the property and a statement of the facts relied upon by the requesting State Party sufficient to enable the requested State Party to seek the order under its domestic law. UNCAC, Arts. 55(3)(a) and 46(15).

1248 UNCAC, Art. 55(1)(b). In addition to the standard content of a request for mutual legal assistance, including the irrelevance of bank secrecy, a request from the requesting State should contain a legally admissible copy of an order of confiscation upon which the request is based issued by the requesting State Party, a statement of the facts and information as to the extent to which execution of the order is requested, a statement specifying the measures taken by the requesting State Party to provide adequate notification to bona fide third parties and to trace and freeze or seize proceeds of crime, property, equipment or other instrumentalities for the purpose of confiscation by the requesting or the requested State.[1249] However, a State may refuse cooperation or lift provisional measures relating to confiscation if the requesting State does not provide sufficient and timely evidence or if the property is of minimal value.[1250]

States also have to consider allowing the confiscation of property of foreign origin by adjudication of money-laundering or other offences within their jurisdiction or by other procedures under domestic law without a criminal conviction in cases in which the offender cannot be prosecuted by reason of death, flight or absence or in other appropriate cases.[1251] This refers to non-conviction-based confiscation and it is highly regrettable that it is not a mandatory provision in the international legal framework against corruption. Although more and more States are incorporating non-conviction-based confiscation into their legal systems, the majority still require a criminal conviction prior to confiscation. However, for many reasons, criminal conviction may be unattainable. Corrupt leaders may have protected themselves by means of legal abuses, such as lifelong immunity (Pinochet), or the corrupt official might have died (Abacha) or fled the country (Fujimori). Moreover, there might be no political will or insufficient evidence to satisfy a criminal standard of proof.[1252] In such cases, States in which a prior criminal conviction is required to execute a confiscation order are *de facto* denying the repatriation of assets to the States of origin.

The international legal framework against corruption also promotes spontaneous cooperation. States are encouraged to inform other concerned States proactively when they believe that information may be useful in initiating or conducting investigations, prosecutions or judicial proceedings or might lead to a request by that State for the recovery of assets.[1253] This kind of spontaneous cooperation took place between Switzerland and Peru, with Switzerland providing the names

---

ensure due process and a statement that the confiscation order is final. UNCAC, Arts. 55(3)(b) and 46(15).

1249 UNCAC, Art. 55(2). In addition to the standard content of a request for mutual legal assistance, including the irrelevance of bank secrecy, a request from the requesting State should contain a statement of the facts relied upon by the requesting State Party and a description of the actions requested and, where available, a legally admissible copy of an order on which the request is based. UNCAC, Arts. 55(3)(c) and 46(15).

1250 UNCAC, Art. 55(7). However, before lifting any provisional measure, the requested State Party shall, wherever possible, give the requesting State Party an opportunity to present its reasons in favour of continuing the measure. UNCAC, Art. 55(8).

1251 UNCAC, Art. 54(1)(c). Under the AU Convention against Corruption this obligation is mandatory. See, AU Convention against Corruption, Art. 16(3).

1252 For detailed information on non-criminal-based confiscation, see Theodore S. Greenberg et al., *Stolen Asset Recovery: A Good Practice Guide for Non-Conviction Based Asset Forfeiture* (World Bank Publications, 2009).

1253 UNCAC, Art. 56; CoE Criminal Law Convention, Art. 28.

of the account holders and the dates of transactions in the context of the investigation against Montesinos and unilaterally froze bank accounts allegedly belonging to him.[1254]

Finally, if a State makes the taking of the above measures concerning international cooperation for purposes of confiscation conditional on the existence of a treaty, it has to consider the UNCAC the necessary and sufficient treaty basis.[1255]

3.2. *Return of assets*

The return of assets does not mean the "automatic" return of assets. The provisions in this section are only applicable when an order of confiscation has been issued and a judgment enforced, subject to the procedures respecting MLA. No reference is made in this respect to a separate mechanism for recovery. The return of assets refers to the last step in the long process of asset recovery.

The international legal framework against corruption provides for the repatriation of confiscated assets to the requesting State.[1256] The international obligations recognize a set rules for the disposal of proceeds based on the type of corruption offence involved, the strength of the evidence and the claims presented, and the rights of prior legitimate owners of the property and victims other than the State. In cases of the embezzlement of public funds or the laundering of embezzled funds, States are required, in accordance with the rules respecting MLA and international cooperation for asset recovery, to return confiscated property to the requesting State.[1257] The obligation to return assets is valid on condition that the confiscation was executed properly and on the basis of a final judgment in the requesting State. However, the judgment may be waived by the requested State.[1258] Obviously, in cases of embezzlement the claim of pre-existing property ownership is very strong. However, this provision is an innovation and departs from the traditional practice in transnational criminal law under which confiscated assets were within the control of the State executing the confiscation order, or alternatively the practice of asset sharing as a an incentive to cooperation.[1259]

1254 Asset Recovery Knowledge Centre, *Efforts to Recover Assets Looted by Vladimiro Montesinos of Peru*, August 2007, available at www.assetrecovery.org/kc/resources/org.apache.wicket. Application/repo?nid=1aafec73-a345-11dc-bf1b-335d0754ba85 (last visited 31 January 2012).

1255 UNCAC, Art. 55(6).

1256 With regard to the return of assets, States have to enable their authorities to return confiscated property at the request of another State, in accordance with their fundamental legal principles and taking into account bona fide third party rights. UNCAC, Art. 57(2).

1257 UNCAC, Art. 57(3)(a).

1258 UNCAC, Art. 57(3)(a).

1259 See for example, UNTOC (Art. 14) and the UN Convention against Illicit Traffic in Narcotic Drugs and Psychotropic Substances (Art. 5(5)). See also, for example the Federal Asset

On the other hand, when confiscation arises out of a corrupt act other than embezzlement, for example bribery, the return of assets is more difficult. In such cases, a State has to return the confiscated property to the requesting State when the latter reasonably establishes its prior ownership or when the requested State recognizes damage to the requesting Party.[1260] Moreover, confiscation has to have been properly executed and on the basis of a final judgement in the requesting State Party. The requested State Party could waive such a judgment. For example, in the return of assets from Switzerland to Peru in the Montesinos case, Switzerland did waive the judgment in Peru.

In other words, in order to transfer or return the confiscated assets to the requesting State, the requesting State must demonstrate its prior ownership or to have suffered damage as a result of the corrupt act. Proceeds from bribery may, for example, involve criminal harm caused to the State, but the proceeds are not funds to which the State was ever entitled. Claims to these proceeds would be of a compensatory nature rather than based on pre-existing property ownership. Claims by prior legitimate owners and other victims of the corruption offences therefore need to be considered alongside those of the State.[1261] In all other cases, the State executing the confiscation is not obliged to return the confiscated assets to another State, although it has to give priority consideration to returning confiscated property to the requesting State, returning such property to its prior legitimate owners or compensating the victims of the crime.[1262]

Moreover, where appropriate, unless States decide otherwise, the requested State may deduct reasonable expenses incurred in investigations, prosecutions or judicial proceedings leading to the return or disposition of confiscated property.[1263] It should be emphasized that the obligation to return assets minus reasonable expenses is distinct from arrangements for asset sharing. For that reason, States cannot rely on domestic provisions in respect of asset sharing in order to deduct expenses incurred in proceedings. They need to review existing legislation and amend it as appropriate to allow the return of assets minus reasonable expenses.

During the negotiations of the UNCAC, discussion arose on whether the country returning the assets should be allowed to set conditions to the requesting State on the use of the funds. Originally the draft UNCAC stipulated that where

Sharing Act of 19 March 2004 in Switzerland (Loi fédérale sur le partage des valeurs patrimoniales confisquées, RS 312.4).

1260 UNCAC, Art. 57(3)(b).

1261 UNODC, *Legislative Guide for the Implementation of the United Nations Convention against Corruption*, 264.

1262 UNCAC, Art. 57(3)(c).

1263 UNCAC, Art. 57(4).

appropriate, recovered assets were to be returned to the requesting State with the requirement, for example, that the assets be used to support anti-corruption initiatives or programmes. This provision was not accepted by the delegations and was ultimately deleted.[1264] The obvious intention was to prevent returned assets being subject to further corruption. However, the establishment of such conditions would constitute an infringement of several fundamental principles of international law, and particularly the sovereignty of the requesting State.

The international legal framework against corruption therefore only adopts an optional approach to determining the use of returned funds. States may conclude mutually acceptable arrangements, on a case-by-case basis, for the final disposal of confiscated property.[1265] For example, under an agreement between Kazakhstan, Switzerland and the United States with World Bank support, approximately US$84 million of funds recovered in a complex corruption case between Kazakhstan and American and European oil companies were returned to Kazakhstan on condition that they were used exclusively for development projects involving poor children.[1266] These types of agreements have been concluded on several occasions, for example, when the assets stolen from Peru by Montesinos were returned by the United States, and when the assets embezzled by Abacha were returned by Switzerland to Nigeria.[1267]

IV. MISCELLANEOUS OBLIGATIONS

The international legal framework against corruption establishes several obligations that can be grouped under the heading miscellaneous. At the outset, it should be recalled that States are under the general obligation to cooperate in criminal matters in accordance with the relevant provisions of the international anti-corruption conventions.[1268] States are also required to consider entering into bilateral or multilateral agreements or arrangements on a variety of issues,

---

1264 See, UN General Assembly, Ad Hoc Committee for the Negotiation of a Convention against Corruption, Third Session, Vienna, 30 September-11 October 2002, *Revised Draft United Nations Convention against Corruption,* A/AC.261/3/Rev.1/Add.1, 5 July 2002, Article 71.

1265 UNCAC, Art. 57(5).

1266 See, World Bank Press Release *Frozen funds to Help Kazakh Youth under New International Agreement,* No:2007/360/ECA; The World Bank Europe and Central Asia Region. News Release No:2008/07/KZ.

1267 For more information on monitoring the return of assets, see Pietro Veglio and Peter Siegenthaler, "Monitoring the Restitution of Looted State Assets: The Role of Multilateral Development Banks (MDBs)," in *Recovering Stolen Assets*, ed. Mark Pieth (Bern: Peter Lang, 2008), 315–329; Stolen Asset Recovery (StAR) Initiative, *Stolen Asset Recovery: Management of Returned Assets: Policy Considerations* (Washington D.C.: World Bank, 2009).

1268 UNCAC, Art. 43(1); CoE Criminal Law Convention, Art. 25; AU Convention against Corruption, Art. 19(5); EU Convention against Corruption, Art. 9(1).

such as direct cooperation between their law enforcement agencies,[1269] the establishment of joint investigative bodies,[1270] the use of special investigative techniques in the context of cooperation at the international level[1271] and the transfer to their territory of persons sentenced to imprisonment or other forms of deprivation of liberty for corruption offences so that they can complete their sentence there.[1272] Moreover, for the purposes of judicial efficiency, States are required to consider the possibility of transferring proceedings to another State for the prosecution of a corruption offence in cases where such transfer is considered to be in the interests of the proper administration of justice, and particularly in cases where several jurisdictions are involved, with a view to concentrating the prosecution.[1273] Other miscellaneous obligations can be grouped under the following issues related to international cooperation: dual criminality, cooperation in civil and administrative proceedings and law enforcement cooperation.

1269 In the absence of such agreements or arrangements, States Parties to the UNCAC may consider the treaty to be the basis for mutual law enforcement cooperation in respect of corruption offences. In addition, whenever appropriate, States Parties have to make full use of agreements or arrangements, including international or regional organizations, to enhance the cooperation between their law enforcement agencies. UNCAC, Art. 48(2).

1270 In relation to matters that are the subject of investigations, prosecutions or judicial proceedings in one or more States, the competent authorities concerned may establish joint investigative bodies. In the absence of such agreements or arrangements, joint investigations may be undertaken by agreement on a case-by-case basis. The States involved have to ensure that the sovereignty of the State Party in whose territory such investigation is to take place is fully respected. UNCAC, Art. 49.

1271 Special investigative techniques include controlled delivery, electronic surveillance or other forms of surveillance, and undercover operations. For more information on these techniques, see Chapter VII. Moreover, the respective agreements or arrangements have to be concluded and implemented in full compliance with the principle of sovereign equality of States and carried out strictly in accordance with the terms of those agreements or arrangements. UNCAC, Art. 50(2). In the absence of such an agreement or arrangement, decisions to use such special investigative techniques at the international level must be made on a case-by-case basis. When necessary, the decision to use special investigative techniques may take into consideration financial arrangements and understandings with respect to the exercise of jurisdiction by the States Parties concerned. UNCAC, Art. 50(3).

1272 The transfer of sentenced persons is generally aimed at the social rehabilitation of the person, who can be transferred to serve his or her sentence in a more familiar environment. See, UNCAC, Art. 45. See also, Council of Europe Convention on the Transfer of Sentenced Persons 1985; and the Model Agreement on the Transfer of Foreign Prisoners, adopted by the Seventh United Nations Congress on the Prevention of Crime and the Treatment of Offenders in 1985.

1273 UNCAC, Art. 47; EU Convention against Corruption, Art. 9(2). See also, UN Convention against Illicit Traffic in Narcotic Drugs and Psychotropic Substances, Art. 8; UNTOC, Art. 21; European Convention on the Transfer of Proceedings in Criminal Matters; UN Model Treaty on the Transfer of Proceedings in Criminal Matters.

1. DUAL CRIMINALITY

The concept of dual criminality is very important in the context of international cooperation in criminal matters. The double criminality requirement is traditionally a basic principle of international cooperation, especially in the field of extradition. The principle of dual criminality requires the conduct that is the subject of a cooperation request to be recognized as a criminal offence in both the requesting and requested State. However, dual criminality should not be interpreted in a strict or overly restrictive way. The acts need not be defined in exactly the same terms. States have to cooperate whenever dual criminality is considered a requirement, irrespective of whether the laws of the requested State place the offence within the same category of offences or denominate the offence using the same terminology as in the requesting State, if the conduct giving rise to the offence for which assistance is sought is a criminal offence under the laws of both States.[1274] Nevertheless, the dual criminality requirement can amount to an obstacle to international cooperation, particularly in cases involving offences that may not exist in all countries, such as illicit enrichment. For example, the extradition of an alleged corrupt financier from the Bahamas to the United States on charges of bribing public officials in Azerbaijan in the late 1990s was rejected by courts in the Bahamas because bribing a foreign public official is not a crime under Bahamian criminal law.[1275] However, in this case, the Bahamas incurred in international responsibility as it was not in compliance with its international obligations, as it is Party to the UNCAC, and should therefore have criminalized the offence of bribing foreign public officials.

In the case of illicit enrichment, the dual criminality impediment can be circumvented where the cooperation is considered to pertain to the illegal conduct that leads to enrichment (if known), such as bribery, rather than illicit enrichment itself. This should satisfy the requirement of dual criminality requirements. In addition, to render dual criminality more flexible, the international legal framework against corruption requires States to provide MLA of a non-coercive nature, even in the absence of dual criminality.[1276] The UNCAC does not provide guidance on what constitute coercive measures, although the *travaux préparatoires* indicate that the requested State must define

1274 UNCAC, Art. 43(2). See also, UN Model Treaty on Extradition, UN General Assembly Resolution 45/116, amended by Resolution 52/88, Art. 2(2).

1275 David McFadden, *Bahamas Rejects US Extradition Bid for Financier*, ABC News, 9 February 2010.

1276 UNCAC, Art. 46(9)(b). It is clear that the UNCAC is intended to promote the provisions of legal assistance even in the absence of dual criminality. See, Article 46(9)(c). Conversely, the OECD Convention clearly provides that dual criminality shall be deemed to exist if the offence for which the assistance is sought is within the scope of the Convention, even where States make mutual legal assistance conditional upon the existence of dual criminality. OECD Convention, Art. 9(2).

that concept taking into account the purpose of the UNCAC, namely to promote and strengthen efficient and effective action to combat corruption, and the related international cooperation.[1277] Non-coercive measures could be for example taking evidence from voluntary witnesses or providing publicly available documents. In the case of coercive measures, the requested State may waive dual criminality. With regard to extradition, States Parties also have discretion to extradite in the absence of dual criminality.[1278] Clearly, the intention is to ease difficulties associated with the application of the double criminality requirement.

2. INTERNATIONAL COOPERATION IN CIVIL AND ADMINISTRATIVE PROCEEDINGS

Although international cooperation in criminal matters refers obviously to cooperation in criminal proceedings,[1279] the international legal framework also establishes relatively weak cooperation obligations in relation to non-criminal proceedings, namely civil and administrative proceedings. States are encouraged to assist each other in investigations of and proceedings in civil and administrative matters relating to corruption.[1280] In this connection, States are required to cooperate in accordance with existing international legal instruments on international cooperation in civil and commercial matters.[1281] These conventions should also be applicable in corruption cases that involve an international element. This is important since, as indicated earlier, the international legal framework actively promotes civil litigation in relation to

---

1277 UN General Assembly, *Interpretative Notes for the Official Records (Travaux Préparatoires) of the Negotiation of the United Nations Convention against Corruption*, para. 42. See UNCAC, Art. 1.

1278 UNCAC, Art. 44(2).

1279 It should be noted that the Second Additional Protocol to the European Convention on Mutual Assistance in Criminal Matters (2001) extends its scope to cover administrative proceedings that may give rise to proceedings before a court having jurisdiction in particular in criminal matters (Art. 1(3)). A similar provision is contained in the 2000 European Union Convention on Mutual Assistance in Criminal Matters (Art. 3(1)).

1280 UNCAC, Art. 43(1). Under the CoE Civil Law Convention this is mandatory and not an obligation of best endeavour. States have to cooperate in civil proceedings in cases of corruption, especially for the service of documents, obtaining evidence abroad, jurisdiction, recognition, and enforcement of foreign judgments and litigation costs in accordance with relevant international instruments on civil and commercial matters to which they are Parties. CoE Civil Law Convention, Art. 13.

1281 Such as the Brussels Convention of 1958, and the Brussels Regulation of 2000 and the Lugano Conventions of 1988 and 2007 on Jurisdiction and Enforcement of Judgements in Civil and Commercial Matters, the 1965 Hague Convention on the Service Abroad of Judicial and Extra-Judicial Documents in Civil or Commercial Matters, the 1970 Hague Convention on the Taking of Evidence Abroad in Civil or Commercial Matters, and the Hague Conventions on Civil Procedures of 1954 and 1980.

corruption. In such proceedings, it may be necessary to have recourse to the legal assistance of another State. Moreover, since in many countries legal persons cannot be subject to criminal proceedings, but only to civil or administrative proceedings, it is important that in such proceedings against legal persons States are able to provide each other with cooperation in civil and administrative matters.

3. LAW ENFORCEMENT COOPERATION

Other miscellaneous obligations relating to international cooperation refer to cooperation for law enforcement. States have traditionally been reluctant to cooperate with foreign law enforcement agencies. Moreover, the diversity of approaches and priorities in law enforcement in the various States constitutes a major challenge to harmonization and the promotion of cooperation among law enforcement agencies. The international legal framework promotes close cooperation between law enforcement authorities as an important tool for the successful investigation of transnational corruption. States are required to cooperate closely with one another to enhance the effectiveness of law enforcement action to combat corrupt acts.[1282] In particular, States have to:

(a) enhance and, where necessary, establish channels of communication between their respective law enforcement agencies in order to facilitate the exchange of information;[1283]
(b) cooperate with other States in their inquiries concerning: (i) the identity, whereabouts and activities of specific persons; (ii) the movement of the proceeds of crime or property derived from the commission of corruption offences, and of property, equipment or other instrumentalities used or intended for use in the commission of offences;[1284]
(c) provide, where appropriate, necessary items or quantities of substances for analytical or investigative purposes;[1285]
(d) facilitate effective coordination between their competent agencies and promote the exchange of personnel and other experts, including the posting of liaison officers;[1286]

1282 UNCAC, Art. 48(1).

1283 UNCAC, Art. 48(1)(a). For example, States are called upon to exchange, where appropriate, information with other States concerning specific means and methods used to commit corruption offences, including the use of false identities, forged, altered or false documents and other means of concealing activities. UNCAC, Art. 48(1)(d).

1284 UNCAC, Art. 48(1)(b).

1285 UNCAC, Art. 48(1)(c).

1286 UNCAC, Art. 48(1)(e).

(e) coordinate administrative and other measures taken as appropriate for the purpose of early identification of corrupt offences.[1287]

The trial in Zambia against former President Chiluba constitutes a good example of the importance of international cooperation in law enforcement. Technical advice from US experienced prosecutors, as well as (controversial) financial support to the Zambian Task Force prosecuting Chiluba, helped the inexperienced and under-resourced Zambian authorities and were vital to carry out the trial.[1288]

CONCLUSION

The obligations concerning international cooperation in criminal matters established in the international legal framework not only cover traditional forms of cooperation, such as extradition, MLA and law enforcement cooperation, but also other relatively new options in transnational criminal justice, including the transfer of proceedings in criminal matters, assistance in establishing joint investigative bodies and cooperation for the appropriate use of special investigative techniques. Nevertheless, it cannot be claimed that there has been a revolution in the new international obligations concerning international cooperation. International anti-corruption obligations relating to extradition supplement pre-existing extradition treaties. The obligations differ according to whether or not States make extradition conditional on the existence of a treaty. When they do not, or in other words when they rely on their own laws, States have to ensure that corrupt acts are extraditable offences under their national law, preferably, even in the absence of dual criminality. The States concerned should therefore be equipped with a solid legal framework for extradition. On the other hand, States which make extradition conditional on the existence of a treaty are required to regard corrupt acts as being included in all extradition treaties existing between the States Parties to the anti-corruption conventions. Clearly, a State may still refuse extradition, except on the grounds of the nationality of the offender. As explained above, the obligation on States to extradite or prosecute corrupt individuals is relatively weak.

In contrast, although the international obligations relating to MLA in themselves constitute traditional provisions, they have the positive effect of extending their application among all the States Parties to the UNCAC. The international

1287 UNCAC, Art. 48(1)(f).

1288 For more on this trial and the role of international technical assistance, see Paul Lewis, "Shifting Legitimacy: The Trials of Frederick Chiluba," in *Prosecuting Heads of State*, ed. Ellen L. Lutz and Caitlin Reiger (Cambridge: Cambridge University Press, 2009), 130–150.

obligations respecting MLA also supplement pre-existing MLA treaties. States covered by an MLA treaty have to apply the rules of the treaty, with only minor obligations arising from the international legal framework against corruption, for example that they cannot decline MLA on the ground of bank secrecy. However, States that are not parties to any MLA treaty are required to apply all the UNCAC obligations in respect of MLA which cover all relevant MLA issues, such as the making and execution of requests and grounds for refusal. Unfortunately, international law cannot resolve the problem that many developing States simply do not have the means to provide effective MLA. This is an issue that needs to be considered in future, particularly under the umbrella of the international obligations respecting technical assistance.

As indicated in this chapter, most obligations relating to extradition and MLA remain at a traditional level and have not created extraordinary legal tools for States to cooperate better in the investigation and prosecution of corruption. But the same is not true of the obligations concerning asset recovery. The return of assets in the past essentially depended on the good will of the State in which the assets were found. Certain instruments, such as the Second Additional Protocol to the European Convention on Mutual Assistance in Criminal Matters (Art. 12) and bilateral treaties (Switzerland-US of 25 May 1973), and certain provisions of national law provide for the possibility of return, but there is no obligation. The international legal framework creates this obligation, although only for assets stolen through the embezzlement of public funds. In the case of all other corrupt acts, the requesting State needs to demonstrate its ownership of the assets or its right to compensation. In addition, the international legal framework against corruption creates a framework to enhance the practical aspects of recovery. It specifies how cooperation and assistance should be provided, how the proceeds of corruption are to be returned to a requesting State and how the interests of other victims or legitimate owners are to be considered. Notwithstanding its flaws, the international legal framework against corruption constitutes a step forward towards a more solid web of legal tools to enhance international cooperation in criminal matters relating to corruption. Time will tell whether this will be reflected in actual practice.

CHAPTER IX

IMPLEMENTATION AND ENFORCEMENT OF INTERNATIONAL ANTI-CORRUPTION OBLIGATIONS

INTRODUCTION

Based on the preceding analysis of the international legal framework against corruption, it is now necessary to examine the ways in which it can be enforced. As indicated throughout this study, States are under numerous international obligations relating to corruption. The implementation of the international anti-corruption obligations of States usually consists of adapting their national laws, legal systems and practice to the international standard set by the international legal framework.

However, what happens if a State does not comply with international anti-corruption commitments? As described below, there are two different mechanisms for the implementation and enforcement of international anti-corruption obligations. With a view to both monitoring and assisting in the implementation of the international legal framework against corruption, the respective international instruments establish follow-up mechanisms. However, alternatively, the international legal framework against corruption can be enforced through international adjudication.

I. IMPLEMENTATION ISSUES

The implementation process, also known as domestication, lies at the heart of the fulfilment of international obligations. Implementation and accountability are now regarded as essential elements of normative declarations, whether soft or hard law. States Parties are called upon to take the necessary measures, including legislative and administrative measures, to ensure the implementation of their obligations.[1289] In other words, States are required to give effect to their

---

[1289] UNCAC, Art. 65.

international anti-corruption obligations. Moreover, the provision of international cooperation and technical assistance aimed at the implementation of anti-corruption conventions is also an international obligation.[1290] States therefore have to cooperate and participate in technical assistance programmes, to the extent possible, with a view to enhancing implementation at the national level.

In the context of implementation, it should be emphasized that anti-corruption treaties have adopted the so-called "functional equivalence" principle, in accordance with which they establish a standard to be met by States Parties, but do not require them to utilize their precise terms in domestic laws.[1291] States Parties may use various approaches to fulfil their obligations. In other words, States Parties are required to achieve equivalence to the requirements of the treaties in terms of the overall legal effects produced by their legal systems.[1292] To monitor compliance, the simple corroboration of legal texts is not therefore sufficient. A holistic appraisal is necessary of the law in operation, including informal rules and practices, as well as the functions assumed by other legal institutions.

With regard to implementation, apart from external elements and conditions, such as political will and the technical capacity of States Parties, the implementation of anti-corruption treaties may face two different challenges that are inherent to the treaties themselves. A first challenge to the implementation of anti-corruption treaty law is the existence of treaty provisions that contain broad and vague language. Evidently, the objective of reaching consensus has resulted in a number of vacuous or highly ambiguous provisions in the conventions. This may make it difficult to monitor effectively compliance by States with their international anti-corruption obligations and may constitute an easy escape route for States from their international obligations through the adoption of meaningless measures which appear on the surface to meet the respective requirements. Clearly, the more the obligation is specifically detailed, the easier it is to monitor State compliance. Yet, as shown in this work, in most cases it is fairly straightforward to interpret what is required from States to

---

1290 UNCAC, Art. 62.

1291 Although this principle is only explicitly mentioned in the Preamble to the OECD Convention and its official commentary (paragraph 2), other anti-corruption conventions may also be interpreted as implying that their domestic implementation has to be carried out in conformity with a functional equivalence. See, for example, UNCAC Art. 30(9). On functional equivalence, see Mark Pieth, "Preventing Corruption: A Case Study," in *Les chemins de l'harmonisation pénale = Harmonising Criminal Law*, ed. Mireille Delmas-Marty et al., vol. 15, UMR de droit comparé de Paris (Paris: Société de législation comparée, 2008), 231–234.

1292 Mark Pieth, "Introduction," in *The OECD Convention on Bribery: A Commentary*, ed. Mark Pieth, Lucinda Low, and Peter J. Cullen (Cambridge University Press, 2007), 27–30.

implement vague international obligations where such obligations are interpreted in conjunction with the object and purpose of anti-corruption treaties and, most importantly, in the context of other relevant international instruments.

Second, several articles in treaties contain safeguard clauses that operate as filters in relation to the obligations of States Parties in the case of conflicting constitutional or fundamental rules. Certain provisions accordingly only constitute obligations upon States Parties, where they are not in conflict with their Constitution and the fundamental principles of their legal system,[1293] not contrary to the domestic law of the requested State Party,[1294] where such a requirement is consistent with the fundamental principles of their domestic law and with the nature of judicial and other proceedings,[1295] or to the extent permitted by the basic principles of its domestic legal system.[1296] While these clauses are also a result of compromises in the negotiating process, they go against a basic principle of international treaty law: "[a] party may not invoke the provisions of its internal law as justification for its failure to perform a treaty."[1297] A State cannot even rely on its own Constitution to evade obligations incumbent upon it under international law or treaties that are in force.[1298] However, this widely accepted principle of international law has unfortunately been overruled by treaty law against corruption. In such cases, national law takes on relevance as a condition limiting international obligations.[1299] In practice, clauses of this type transform mandatory obligations into optional recommendations and

1293 For example, UNCAC, Art. 20.

1294 For example, UNCAC, Art. 46(17).

1295 For example, UNCAC, Art. 31(8).

1296 For example, UNCAC, Art. 50(1).

1297 Vienna Convention on the Law of Treaties, 1155 U.N.T.S. 331, Art. 27. The principle had already been affirmed before the adoption of the Vienna Convention. See for example, The Greco-Bulgarian "Communities", Advisory Opinion, 1930, P.C.I.J. (Ser. B), No. 17, 31 July, 32; Free Zones of Upper Savoy and the District of Gex, P.C.I.J. (Ser. A) No. 24 (Order of 6 December 1930), 12; and ibid., Judgment, 1932, P.C.I.J. (Ser. A/B) No. 46, 7 June, 167. See also, Draft Articles on Responsibility of States for Internationally Wrongful Acts, adopted by the International Law Commission at its Fifty-third Session, in 2001, *Yearbook of the International Law Commission*, 2001, vol. II, Part Two, Art. 32.

1298 Treatment of Polish Nationals and Other Persons of Polish Origin or Speech in the Danzig Territory, Advisory Opinion, 1932, P.C.I.J. (Ser. A/B) No. 44, 24.

1299 See also the United States reservation to the UNCAC in which it declares that due to its fundamental principle of federalism, state and local prevention and law enforcement may not be entirely in compliance with the obligations arising the UNCAC. United States Reservation to the UNCAC, para. 1, available at http://treaties.un.org/Pages/ShowMTDSGDetails.aspx?src=UNTSONLINE&tabid=2&mtdsg_no=XVIII-14&chapter=18&lang=en#EndDec (last visited 29 April 2012). The Netherlands has objected to this reservation as it creates uncertainty as to what extent the United States accepts being bound by the obligations under the UNCAC. See, Dutch Objection to the Reservation made by the United States, available at http://treaties.un.org/Pages/ShowMTDSGDetails.aspx?src=UNTSONLINE&tabid=2&mtdsg_no=XVIII-14&chapter=18&lang=en#EndDec (last visited 29 April 2012).

create inequality of obligations between States Parties. Most importantly, they also have the effect of reducing the scope of the anti-corruption conventions.

II. MONITORING AND FOLLOW-UP

The biggest challenge faced in relation to the international legal framework against corruption is how to ensure its implementation. Anti-corruption conventions address this issue through the establishment of mechanisms to monitor implementation. Evidently, they are far from enforcement mechanisms. Monitoring is based on collaboration and repeated peer-review controls which are aimed at identifying non-compliance, including treaty violations, and finding soft means of achieving compliance (mostly through recommendations and peer pressure). Although monitoring implementation is extremely important in a practical sense, in a strict legal sense, if a State does not comply with its obligations it automatically incurs international responsibility.

As indicated above, mechanisms that monitor implementation do not simple corroborate legal texts, but also monitor the law in operation, including informal rules and practices. However, in practice monitoring mechanisms have proved more efficient in providing information about the adoption of legal texts than about their actual application and their overall effect on anti-corruption efforts at national level. This can be partly explained by the fact that the majority of States Parties to anti-corruption conventions experience difficulties in providing qualitative and quantitative data that would allow for a more objective evaluation of the implementation of the conventions.[1300] Hence, the development and use of performance indicators seems especially valuable to monitor the implementation of anti-corruption conventions.[1301] Uncooperative States Parties or the provision of unreliable information are further obstacles to an effective monitoring mechanism. This has been addressed by the different monitoring bodies using "subtle" diplomatic approaches as they do not possess coercive powers.

There are currently six mechanisms to review the implementation of anti-corruption treaties. One concern with so many mechanisms is the unavoidable duplication of efforts and the reporting fatigue that it creates among States. For example, the United States is reviewed by the procedures of the OECD, the Council of Europe, the OAS and the United Nations. Unfortunately, up to now there has been no harmonization of procedures and, despite repeated calls for

---

1300 Miguel Peñailillo, *How Prepared Are We to Assess Real Implementation of Anti-Corruption Conventions? Lessons from the Americas*, U4 Issue 3:2009 (Bergen: Anti-Corruption Resource Centre, 2009).

1301 Ibid., 22–29.

collaboration, there is little meaningful collaboration in practice between these bodies. The following is a brief analysis of existing monitoring and follow-up mechanisms under the anti-corruption conventions.[1302]

1. OECD CONVENTION

The OECD Convention set up a programme to monitor its implementation which was the first such anti-corruption follow-up mechanism.[1303] This monitoring process consists of on site visits and evaluations of the legislation and structures of each country with a view to ensuring the effective implementation and enforcement of the Convention. Country monitoring is carried out by the OECD WGB.[1304] The mandate of the OECD WGB is to carry out systematic country monitoring of the implementation of the OECD Anti-Bribery Convention and the 2009 Recommendation.[1305] As a result, the Working Group has issued numerous reports and recommendations on the situation in each country.

For each country reviewed, a draft report is prepared which is submitted to a Working Group consultation. This report is based on information provided by the country under examination as well as information collected by the OECD Secretariat and two other countries who act as "lead examiners" either through independent research or through expert consultation during on site visits. The outcome of the Working Group consultation is the adoption of the final country report, which contains an evaluation of the country's laws and practices to combat foreign bribery. Prior to issuing the final report, the country reviewed has the opportunity to read the report and to comment on it. The country can express its dissent, which will be reflected in the final report, but cannot prevent the adoption of the evaluation by the Working Group.[1306]

The restricted membership of the OECD, together with the few non-Members that have been admitted as parties to the OECD Convention, have made it possible to develop probably the most efficient anti-corruption monitoring mechanism. Changes in the national law of States Parties have materialized in

1302 The ECOWAS Convention is not mentioned in this section as it has no monitoring or follow-up mechanism.

1303 OECD Convention, Art. 12.

1304 The OECD Investment Committee established the Working Group on Bribery in May 1994. It is composed of government experts from the participating countries. It meets five times a year at the Paris Headquarters of the OECD.

1305 OECD, Recommendation of the Council for Further Combating Bribery of Foreign Public Officials in International Business Transactions, adopted by the Council on 26 November 2009.

1306 The reports on each country can be found on the OECD's website, at www.oecd.org.

practice as a result of the OECD peer review.[1307] Although this is already a first step towards the effective implementation of the OECD Convention, enforcement in the form of prosecution is still rare in the majority of parties.[1308] This illustrates the ultimate challenge of implementing anti-corruption conventions, namely to attain the necessary level of political commitment so as to really combat corruption, not only by reforming laws in accordance with the conventions, but also by giving effect to them in practice.[1309]

2. THE COUNCIL OF EUROPE CONVENTIONS

The CoE anti-corruption conventions are monitored by the Group of States against Corruption (GRECO) established in 1999 for that purpose.[1310] The Statute of GRECO provides that its objective is to improve the capacity of its members to fight corruption through a dynamic process of mutual evaluation and peer pressure.[1311] Any State that becomes a Party to the Criminal or Civil Law Conventions on Corruption automatically accedes to GRECO.[1312] The

---

1307 For a summary record of the most important legislative changes arising from the OECD monitoring mechanism, see OECD WGB, *Mid-Term Study of Phase 2 Reports: Application of the Convention on Combating Bribery of Foreign Public Officials in International Business Transactions and the 1997 Recommendation on Combating Bribery in International Business Transactions*, 2006.

1308 Fritz Heimann and Gillian Dell, *Transparency International Progress Report 2009: Enforcement of the OECD Convention on Combating Bribery of Foreign Public Officials in International Business Transactions* (Berlin: Transparency International, June 23, 2009).

1309 For details on the OECD monitoring mechanism, see Pieth, "Preventing Corruption: A Case Study," 236–244.

1310 The Committee of Ministers at its 102nd Session on 4 May 1998 adopted Resolution (98) 7 authorizing the partial and enlarged agreement establishing the GRECO. Partial Agreements allow members to abstain from participating in a course of action advocated by other members. On 1 May 1999, the representatives in the Committee of Ministers of Belgium, Bulgaria, Cyprus, Estonia, Finland, France, Germany, Greece, Iceland, Ireland, Lithuania, Luxembourg, Romania, Slovakia, Slovenia, Spain and Sweden adopted Resolution (99) 5 establishing the GRECO governed by the Statute appended to the Resolution. For its current membership, see www.coe.int/t/dghl/monitoring/greco/general/members_en.asp (last visited 29 April 2012).

1311 GRECO Statute, Art. 1. The functioning of GRECO is governed by its Statute and Rules of Procedure. GRECO Rules of Procedure, adopted by GRECO at its 1st Plenary Meeting, Strasbourg, 4–6 October 1999, amended at its 4th, 7th, 12th, 13th, 14th and 22nd Plenary Meetings (Strasbourg, 12–15 December 2000, 17–20 December 2001, 9–13 December 2002, 24–28 March 2003, 7–11 July 2003, 14–18 March 2005).

1312 GRECO Statute, Art. 4(3). Membership of GRECO is not limited to Council of Europe Member States; for example the United States is a Member State of GRECO. Any State which took part in the elaboration of the enlarged partial agreement may join. GRECO Statute, Art. 4(2). Each Member State appoints up to two representatives, who participate in GRECO plenary meetings with a right to vote. Each member also provides GRECO with a list of experts available to take part in GRECO's evaluations. Other Council of Europe bodies may also appoint representatives (such as the Parliamentary Assembly of the Council of Europe). GRECO has granted observer status to the OECD and the UNODC.

monitoring mechanism consists of an evaluation procedure and a compliance procedure. Under the evaluation procedure, all members are evaluated in an evaluation round that gives rise to recommendations aimed at furthering the necessary legislative, institutional and practical reforms.[1313] The compliance procedure is designed to assess the measures taken by members to implement the recommendations made. Assessment of whether a recommendation has been implemented satisfactorily is based on a situation report, accompanied by supporting documents submitted by the member under scrutiny 18 months after the adoption of the evaluation report. In cases where not all recommendations have been given effect, GRECO re-examines the outstanding recommendations. Compliance reports and the addenda thereto adopted by GRECO also contain an overall conclusion on the implementation of all the recommendations, the purpose of which is to decide whether to terminate the compliance procedure in respect of a particular member.

GRECO works in cycles or evaluation rounds, each covering specific themes.[1314] GRECO's first evaluation round (2000-2002) dealt with the independence, specialization and means of national bodies engaged in the prevention and fight against corruption. It also dealt with the extent and scope of the immunities of public officials from arrest and prosecution. The second evaluation round (2003–2006) focused on numerous issues, such as the identification, seizure and confiscation of the proceeds of corruption proceeds, the prevention and detection of corruption in public administration, the prevention of legal persons from being used as shields for corruption, account offences, corporate liability and sanctions for corruption. The third evaluation round (2007–2012) addresses the incriminations set out in the Criminal Law Convention on Corruption and the Transparency of Party Funding. The fourth evaluation round (launched in 2012) focuses on corruption prevention in respect of Members of Parliament, judges and prosecutors.[1315] The overall balance of the effectiveness of the GRECO evaluations is positive in terms of its scope in relation to both the provisions of the treaties monitored and the States under review. However, as with other monitoring mechanisms, GRECO has not resulted in progress in effective compliance at the national level in terms of anti-corruption prosecutions.

1313 The evaluation process follows a well-defined procedure, under which a team of experts is appointed by GRECO for the evaluation of a particular member. The analysis of the situation in each country is carried out on the basis of written replies to a questionnaire and the information gathered in meetings with public officials and representatives of civil society during an on site visit to the country. Following the on site visit, the team of experts drafts a report with conclusions. The conclusions of evaluation reports may lead to recommendations, which require action within 18 months, or to observations which members are supposed to take into account, but are not formally required to report on in the subsequent compliance procedure.

1314 GRECO Statute, Art. 10.

1315 For the evaluation and compliance reports of all the rounds and other documents on the mutual evaluation procedure, see www.coe.int/t/dghl/monitoring/greco/evaluations/index_en.asp (last visited 29 April 2012).

3. THE EUROPEAN UNION CONVENTIONS

The European Commission has not been in favour of setting up a separate evaluation and monitoring mechanism for the European Union conventions, in order to avoid duplication with GRECO.[1316] However, the Commission has also contributed to the development of anti-corruption action in the European Union by exercising a quasi-monitoring role over the implementation by Member States of certain anti-corruption instruments. Article 10 of the Convention on the Protection of the European Communities' Financial Interests and its Protocols requires Member States to transmit to the Commission the text of the provisions transposing into their domestic law the obligations imposed upon them by the Convention and its Protocols. The Commission has adopted and published two reports evaluating compliance by Member States with these instruments.[1317] Similarly, the Commission also issued a report in 2007 on the Council Framework Decision on Combating Corruption in the Private Sector. These efforts have contributed to raising awareness of which Members have not ratified the instruments or when their actions fall short from what is expected of them. More recently, in its Communication on the Stockholm Programme, the European Commission proposed to set up a mechanism for the regular evaluation of efforts to combat corruption across the European Union. There are therefore indications that a new mechanism will soon be set up to monitor the implementation of the European Union anti-corruption conventions by the 27 Member States.[1318]

4. THE INTER-AMERICAN CONVENTION AGAINST CORRUPTION

The Inter-American Convention against Corruption does not itself establish a mechanism to follow-up its implementation, and only in 2001 was a mechanism to monitor the implementation of the Convention established.[1319] The Follow-Up

---

1316 Commission of the European Communities, Communication from the Commission to the Council, the European Parliament and the European Economic and Social Committee on a Comprehensive European Union Policy against Corruption, COM(2003)317 Final, 28 May 2003, 9.

1317 See, Commission of the European Communities, Report from the Commission: Implementation by Member States of the Convention on the Protection of the European Communities' Financial Interests and its Protocols, Article 10 of the Convention {SEC(2004) 1299}, COM(2004) 709 Final, 25 October 2004; and Second Report from the Commission: Implementation of the Convention on the Protection of the European Communities' Financial Interests and its Protocols, Article 10 of the Convention {SEC(2008) 188}, COM(2008) 77 Final, 14 February 2008, and Annex.

1318 European Commission, *9 December – International Anti-Corruption Day: Say 'No' to corruption*, Press Release, 9 December 2009.

1319 Organization of American States, General Assembly Resolution AG/RES 1784 (XXXI-O/01) "Mechanism for Follow-Up on Implementation of the Inter-American Convention against

Mechanism for the Implementation of the Inter-American Convention against Corruption (MESICIC) constitutes the main anti-corruption activity in the OAS arena.[1320] This mechanism is composed of two bodies: (i) the Conference of States Parties, which is the political body of the mechanism, and handles the most important decisions and guidelines to set the mechanism in motion;[1321] and (ii) the Committee of Experts, which is the technical body that carries out the reviews of each State Party. The experts are members of institutions which exercise legal or political responsibility in the fight against corruption in their respective country. Each government can appoint a lead expert and all the alternate experts that it deems appropriate.[1322]

MESICIC reviews the legislation of States Parties in the context of action to combat corruption and promotes changes in national legislation to comply with the obligations deriving from the Inter-American Convention against Corruption. The monitoring is carried out in rounds, in which specific provisions are reviewed by the experts. For example, the following were reviewed in the first round: the provisions of the Convention pertaining to preventive measures (Article 3), assistance and cooperation (Article 14) and central authorities (Article 18). The Committee of Experts conducted reviews of pertinent legislation in States Parties related to the three above issues and adopted reports by country with the details of their studies, findings and recommendations.[1323] A similar procedure was followed in the second round with regard to preventive measures (Article 3, paragraphs 5 and 8) and the criminalization of certain

---

Corruption," adopted at the third plenary session, 5 June 2001 (endorsing the Buenos Aires Document). The Third Summit of the Americas supported the establishment as soon as possible of a mechanism for follow-up on the implementation of the Inter-American Convention against Corruption. In compliance with that mandate, on 4 May 2001 States Parties approved the Buenos Aires Document, which sets forth the purposes, principles and basic provisions on the organization and functioning of MESICIC.

1320 It was established by the Conference of States Parties to the Inter-American Convention against Corruption. However, not all the States Parties to the Convention are Parties to MESICIC. For more information on MESICIC, see General Assembly Resolution AG/RES 1784 (XXXI-O/01) 'Mechanism for Follow-Up on Implementation of the Inter-American Convention against Corruption', adopted at the third plenary session, 5 June 2001 (endorsing the Buenos Aires Document).

1321 The body is composed of the representatives of the States Parties to MESISIC, who must meet at least once a year. See, Rules of Procedure of the Conference of States Parties to the Mechanism for Follow-Up on Implementation of the Inter-American Convention against Corruption, SG/MESICIC/doc.58/04 rev.7, 2 April 2004.

1322 See, Rules of Procedure and Other Provisions of the Committee of Experts of the MESICIC, SG/MESICIC/doc.9/04 rev. 2, 30 September 2005. Secretarial services are provided by the General Secretariat of the OAS, through its Department of Legal Affairs and Services, and more specifically the Office of Inter-American Law and Programs.

1323 Reports adopted by the Committee of Experts on the Provisions Selected for Analysis in the Framework of the First Round, available at www.oas.org/juridico/english/mesicic_reports.htm (last visited 29 April 2012).

corrupt acts (Article 6).[1324] A third round of the review has dealt with the denial or prevention of favourable tax treatment for expenditures made in violation of anti-corruption laws (Article 3(7)), the prevention of bribery (Article 3(10), the criminalization of transnational bribery (Article 7), the criminalization of illicit enrichment (Article 9), notification of the criminalization of the above crimes (Article 10) and extradition (Article 13).[1325] The fourth round focuses on oversight bodies, with a view to implementing modern mechanisms for preventing, detecting, punishing, and eradicating corrupt acts (Article 9(iii)).

Although the monitoring mechanism of the Inter-American Convention against Corruption was slow to start, it is currently more active. However, a major negative element of this monitoring mechanism is that until now it has not monitored the actual enforcement of the law, and a report by Transparency International shows weak implementation in several Latin American countries.[1326] Conversely, one advantage of the monitoring mechanism of the Inter-American Convention against Corruption in comparison with other mechanisms is that the Technical Secretariat of the MESICIC has created a technical assistance programme to support States Parties in the creation of a national Plan of Action to implement the recommendations formulated by the Committee of Experts.[1327] This means that MESICIC is also involved in reforming the law, and not solely in identifying areas in which reforms are required.

5. THE AFRICAN UNION CONVENTION AND THE SADC PROTOCOL

A new body has been designated under the African Union Convention against Corruption to monitor the implementation of the Convention, namely the

---

1324 Reports adopted by the Committee of Experts on the Provisions Selected for Analysis in the Framework of the Second Round, available at www.oas.org/juridico/english/mesicic_reports.htm (last visited 29 April 2012).

1325 Reports adopted by the Committee of Experts on the Provisions Selected for Analysis in the Framework of the Second Round, available at www.oas.org/juridico/english/mesicic_reports.htm (last visited 29 April 2012). Following the completion of the two first rounds, the Committee of Experts issued a comprehensive report on the Inter-American region. See, *Hemispheric Report on the First Round of Review of the Committee of Experts of the Mechanism for Follow-Up on the Implementation of the Inter-American Convention against Corruption (MESICIC)*, SG/MESICIC/doc.170/06 rev. 1, 31 March 2006; and *Hemispheric Report on the Second Round of Review of the Committee of Experts of the Mechanism for Follow-Up on the Implementation of the Inter-American Convention against Corruption*, SG/MESICIC/doc.227/08 rev. 1, 11 December 2008.

1326 Transparency International, *Evaluación de la acción gubernamental contra la corrupción*, 2009.

1327 For the detailed plans of action for several countries, see the website of the OAS Department of Legal Cooperation, available at www.oas.org/juridico/english/mesicic_rounds.htm (last visited 29 April 2012).

Advisory Board on Corruption.[1328] However, this body has only been recently operational.[1329] Similarly, the SADC Protocol provides for an implementation mechanism that is to be overseen by a Committee consisting of States Parties, which is not yet in operation. For that reason, it is useful to make reference to the African Peer Review Mechanism (APRM), which is a mutually agreed instrument to which the Member States of the African Union (AU) may accede voluntarily as a self-monitoring mechanism.[1330] The mandate of the African Peer Review Mechanism is to ensure that the policies and practices of participating States are in conformity with the agreed political, economic and corporate governance values, codes and standards contained in the Declaration on Democracy, Political, Economic and Corporate Governance.[1331] The APRM process is based on a "self-assessment" questionnaire developed by the APR Secretariat. It is divided into four sections: democracy and political governance, economic governance and management, corporate governance, and socio-economic development. Its questions are designed to assess the compliance of States with a wide range of African and international human rights treaties and standards. The issue of corruption evidently falls within the area of democracy and political governance. However, reviews in the area of corporate governance also usually address corruption in the private sector. The APRM indirectly in practice deals with action to combat corruption in certain African countries. This functions both as a monitoring mechanism of the fight against corruption in African countries and raises awareness of the level of corruption and the steps that need to be taken to improve the situation. For example, South Africa was criticized for its system for the funding of political parties, which was not transparent.[1332] In addition, the report on South Africa provided a detailed account of the levels of corruption and the initiatives taken by the State to combat it. The review panel finally made recommendations to South Africa on how to decrease its level of corruption.[1333]

Nevertheless, the APRM is not a mechanism established to monitor the implementation of African conventions against corruption, and its role in the implementation of African anti-corruption treaty obligations is therefore extremely limited. In view of the enormous resources that are required to set up

---

1328 AU Convention against Corruption, Art. 22.

1329 The Members of the Advisory Board were designated in 2009 at the 12th Ordinary Summit of the AU Heads of State and Government.

1330 See, Memorandum of Understanding of the African Peer Review Mechanism ("The MOU"), NEPAD/HSGIC/03-2003/APRM/MOU, 9 March 2003; African Peer Review Mechanism Base Document AHG/235(XXXVIII), Annex II.

1331 Declaration on Democracy, Political, Economic and Corporate Governance, AHG/235 (XXXVIII) Annex, I.

1332 South Africa Country Review Report No 5 – September 2007, 19 October 2007, 86.

1333 South Africa Country Review Report No 5 – September 2007, 19 October 2007, 109–112 and 283–284.

and maintain such a monitoring mechanism, it would seem to be preferable for the African continent only to be reviewed by the mechanism developed to monitor the implementation of the UNCAC, with special provision also being made to monitor the obligations arising exclusively out of the African Union Convention and the SADC Protocol.

6. THE UNITED NATIONS CONVENTION

The mechanism to review the implementation of the UNCAC is potentially the most comprehensive of all monitoring systems of the anti-corruption conventions, as it has almost universal coverage and deals with a broad range of international anti-corruption obligations. After three years of intense negotiations by States Parties, the mechanism was adopted at the Third Session of the Conference of States Parties to UNCAC, held in Doha in November 2009.[1334] In accordance with the Terms of Reference of the mechanism,[1335] it consists of an intergovernmental process under the authority of the Conference of the States Parties based on review phases composed of two review cycles of five years each. The first cycle reviews Chapters III (Criminalization and Law Enforcement) and IV (International Cooperation) and the second cycle deals with chapter II (Preventive Measures) and V (Asset Recovery). A State is reviewed by two other States Parties, one of which is from the same geographical region as the State under review. The information on States under review is gathered through a self-assessment check list and the responses are analysed by the two reviewing States. On the basis of this analysis and a further exchange of information, the reviewing States Parties prepare a country review report in agreement with the State under review. In principle the report is confidential and is only made public if the State under review chooses to do so. Input by civil society or other relevant stakeholders to the procedure is not mandatory, and the State Party under review is only called upon to endeavour to prepare its responses to the self-assessment check list through broad consultations at the national level with non-governmental actors. No country visits are envisaged, except if the country under review wishes to accept such a visit or a joint meeting at the United Nations Office in Vienna.

1334 The Conference of States Parties was established to, inter alia, promote and review the implementation of the UNCAC and establish an appropriate mechanism. UNCAC, Art. 63(1) and 63(7).

1335 For a detailed description of the monitoring mechanism, see the Terms of Reference of the Mechanism for the Review of Implementation of the United Nations Convention against Corruption, Unofficial Resolution of the Third Session of the Conference of States Parties to UNCAC held in Doha on 9–13 November 2009, Annex 1, available at www.unodc.org/unodc/en/treaties/CAC/CAC-COSP-session3.html (last visited 29 April 2012).

As the mechanism has only been operational recently it is only therefore possible to speculate about its efficiency. The mechanism has clearly fallen short of the expectations of civil society organisations.[1336] It is less intrusive and potentially less effective than other existing mechanisms to monitor the implementation of anti-corruption conventions. The mechanism is overly respectful of the sovereignty of States. It is claimed to be non-adversarial and non-punitive,[1337] and is not intended to serve as an instrument interfering in the domestic affairs of States Parties and has to respect the principles of equality and the sovereignty of States Parties.[1338] It is clearly a compromise reached after years of deadlock between the States Parties, during which the majority of States had to give in to the conditions set by a small group of States, namely no mandatory civil society input into the process, no public reports and no on site visits.[1339] Nevertheless, a flawed mechanism is better than no mechanism at all and, although many of its provisions are not mandatory, States may in practice accept input from civil society, country visits and the publication of the reports. With the exception of the few States that opposed these provisions, the mechanism may still result in other States in a meaningful and constructive procedure. Only time will tell whether the monitoring of the UNCAC will contribute to the effective implementation of international anti-corruption obligations by the States Parties to the UNCAC.

III. SETTLEMENT OF DISPUTES BY INTERNATIONAL COURTS

The monitoring of the implementation of the international anti-corruption obligations is inherently a non-confrontational mechanism aimed at achieving their full implementation. However, what happens if a State does not comply with one or more of its obligations? The theoretical answer is straightforward: it is in violation of the treaty and incurs its international responsibility.[1340] In

---

1336 This was shown by the amount of criticisms received when it was adopted. See, for example, Transparency International Press Release, *UN Convention against Corruption review mechanism: A flawed step forward*, 13 November 2009, available at http://archive.transparency.org/news_room/latest_news/press_releases/2009/2009_11_13_review_mechanism_flawed (last visited 29 April 2012), and Global Witness Press Release, *UN anti-corruption convention rendered toothless*, 13 November 2009, available at www.globalwitness.org/library/un-anti-corruption-convention-rendered-toothless (last visited 29 April 2012).

1337 The terms of Reference of the Mechanism for the Review of Implementation of the United Nations Convention against Corruption, para. 3(f).

1338 Ibid., para. 5.

1339 The countries that stood out for this condition in order to accept a review mechanisms included Algeria, Angola, China, Egypt, Islamic Republic of Iran, Pakistan, Russian Federation, Venezuela, and Zimbabwe.

1340 The breach of an international obligation that is attributable to a State constitutes an internationally wrongful act by that State. And every internationally wrongful act of a State

Accordance with international law of State responsibility, the State must cease the internationally wrongful act (or in other words, it has to comply with its anti-corruption treaty law obligations), offer appropriate assurances and guarantees of non-repetition[1341] and make full reparation for the injury caused by the internationally wrongful act.[1342] However, as a result of the horizontal nature of international law, which lacks a supreme authority and the centralized use of force and law enforcement, when a State incurs its international responsibility for failure to comply with an international obligation, there is no international organ or court which can be seized. In other words, when a State violates an international obligation, there is no formal procedure to enforce compliance. How could the international anti-corruption obligations then be enforced?

There are several possible adjudicatory organs that could enforce international obligations relating to anti-corruption. The section below analyses the principal international courts that could potentially hear a case on corruption. The first section examines this possibility in relation to the International Court of Justice (ICJ), the European Court of Justice and the SADC Tribunal. Their jurisdiction *ratione materiae* is mainly established by the international anti-corruption conventions. While most international courts are closed for individuals, the second section below describes the ways in which individuals or groups of individuals can bring claims against States before international human rights courts. In the context of corruption, this is extremely important in order to empower the principal beneficiaries of international anti-corruption obligations to hold States accountable. The final section of this Chapter analyses whether the WTO dispute settlement mechanism, considered to be one of the most effective of such mechanisms due to its sanctions system, constitutes a valid alternative to enforcing international anti-corruption obligations.

1. THE INTERNATIONAL COURT OF JUSTICE AND OTHER INTERNATIONAL TRIBUNALS

With the exception of the OECD Convention, the African Union Convention, and the Inter-American Convention, all the other anti-corruption treaties explicitly envisage a dispute settlement mechanism for disputes relating to the interpretation and application of the conventions. In general, anti-corruption treaties establish relatively similar procedures. States are called upon to try to

entails its international responsibility. International Law Commission's Draft Articles on Responsibility of States for Internationally Wrongful Acts, Articles 2 and 1 respectively.

1341 Draft Articles on Responsibility of States for Internationally Wrongful Acts, Art. 30.

1342 Ibid., Art. 31.

resolve the dispute first through negotiation. This method is the best for settling a dispute in a direct manner without the involvement of a third party.[1343] In practice, negotiation is used more frequently than any other method of dispute settlement and is usually successful. A basic requirement of negotiation is that it has to be conducted in good faith,[1344] and the obligation to negotiate persists for a reasonable time depending on the circumstances of the case.

If negotiation fails, the second step in dispute settlement in accordance with the anti-corruption conventions is arbitration, a procedure consisting of the settlement of a dispute by a third party in an obligatory and definitive manner based on international law.[1345] The arbitration tribunal is an ad hoc tribunal which requires the explicit consent of the parties to the dispute. The main advantage of arbitration procedures is their flexibility, as the parties can freely define all the procedural matters, such as the competence of the tribunal or the applicable law. However, this very flexibility may also constitute a disadvantage, as the parties may never agree on the members of the tribunal or certain procedural issues. For that reason, some treaties establish a deadline for the organization of the arbitration procedure and, once the deadline has passed, the dispute has to be submitted for judicial settlement. This is where the anti-corruption treaties differ, with each providing for a different judicial tribunal.

The European Union anti-corruption conventions and protocols provide that disputes are to be submitted to the Council of the European Union and, if no solution has been reached in six months, a State or the European Commission may refer the dispute to the Court of Justice of the European Union.[1346] The SADC Protocol calls for disputes to be referred to the SADC Tribunal,[1347] which is the judicial organ of the SADC.[1348] The added advantage of the SADC Tribunal is that it has jurisdiction to receive claims from States, but also from

[1343] John Graham Merrills, *International Dispute Settlement*, 3rd ed. (Cambridge [etc.]: Cambridge Univ. Pr, 1998), Chapter I.

[1344] North Sea Continental Shelf Cases, ICJ Reports 1969, 3, 47, and Cameroon v. Nigeria, ICJ Reports 2002, para. 244.

[1345] Merrills, *International Dispute Settlement*, Chapter 5.

[1346] EU Convention against Corruption, Art. 12; EU Convention on the Protection of the European Communities' Financial Interests, Art. 8; First Protocol to the EU Convention on the Protection of the European Communities' Financial Interests, Art. 8; and Second Protocol to the EU Convention on the Protection of the European Communities' Financial Interests, Art. 13.

[1347] SADC Protocol against Corruption, Art. 22; Protocol on Tribunal and the Rules of Procedure Thereof (adopted on 7 August 2000), Art. 14.

[1348] Treaty of the Southern African Development Community (adopted in 1992 and amended in August 2001), Arts. 9 and 16. Despite the ratification requirements in the Protocol on Tribunal and the Rules of Procedure Thereof, the Protocol entered into force with the signature of the Agreement Amending the Treaty of SADC in August 2001. The Agreement Amending the Treaty made the Protocol on the Tribunal an integral part of the Treaty and thus automatically applicable to all Member States.

natural and legal persons.[1349] Individuals and corporations wishing to bring a case against a State first need to exhaust local remedies.[1350] Similarly, the ECOWAS Protocol calls for disputes to be brought before the ECOWAS Community Court of Justice,[1351] which also has jurisdiction in cases brought by both States and natural and legal persons. It therefore offers considerable potential to enforce the ECOWAS Protocol against corruption once it enters into force. The Council of Europe Criminal and Civil Law Conventions provide that a dispute may be brought to the jurisdiction of the International Court of Justice, but only with the agreement of the Parties in the specific case.[1352] The conventions also provide that the dispute should first be submitted to the European Committee on Crime Problems when it concerns the Criminal Law Convention, or to the European Committee on Legal Co-operation when it relates to the Civil Law Convention.

The UNCAC provides for the competence of the International Court of Justice (ICJ) to settle disputes concerning its interpretation or application.[1353] Any State Party can refer a dispute to the ICJ in accordance with the Statute of the Court.[1354] The UNCAC explicitly provides that States may declare that they do not consider themselves bound by the provision on arbitration and the jurisdiction of the ICJ to resolve disputes.[1355] As of April 2012, a total of 33 States Parties to UNCAC had made a reservation or declaration upon ratification or accession excluding the jurisdiction of the International Court of Justice to settle disputes on the interpretation or application of the UNCAC.[1356] This means that, of the 160 States Parties, disputes among 127 States could be referred to the International Court of Justice. This is a significant number.

The Court has jurisdiction in contentious cases between States on the basis of the consent of the Parties.[1357] A high number of States have accepted the jurisdiction of the ICJ to resolve disputes concerning the UNCAC. In the case of States that

1349 Protocol on Tribunal and the Rules of Procedure Thereof, Art. 15.
1350 Ibid., Art. 15(2).
1351 ECOWAS Protocol against Corruption, Art. 27.
1352 CoE Criminal Law Convention, Art. 40; CoE Civil Law Convention, Art. 21.
1353 UNCAC, Art. 66.
1354 UNCAC, Art. 66(2).
1355 UNCAC, Art. 66(3).
1356 Algeria, Azerbaijan, Bahamas, Bahrain, Bangladesh, Brunei Darussalam, China, Colombia, Cuba, El Salvador, Georgia, India, Indonesia, Islamic Republic of Iran, Israel, Kuwait, Malaysia, Malta, Republic of Moldova, Mozambique, Nepal, Pakistan, Panama, Qatar, South Africa, St. Lucia, Thailand, Tunisia, United Arab Emirates, United States of America, Uzbekistan, Viet Nam and Yemen. Kenya had originally made a reservation to the jurisdiction of the ICJ, but subsequently withdrew it. Kenya: Withdrawal of Reservation Lodged in Respect of Article 66(2), Reference: C.N.542.2009.TREATIES-18 (Depositary Notification), 9 September 2009.
1357 ICJ Statute, Arts. 34(1) and 36(1).

have explicitly refused the jurisdiction of the ICJ through a reservation to UNCAC, nothing prevents them from accepting its jurisdiction through an ad hoc agreement or *compromis* for a specific case. The rulings of the ICJ are final and cannot be appealed. Unfortunately, although all of the United Nations Members undertake to comply with the decisions of the ICJ, if they fail to do so there is no way of enforcing such a ruling. One option is for the party seeking enforcement of the judgment to bring the issue to the United Nations Security Council which may, if it deems it necessary, make recommendations or decide upon measures to be taken.[1358]

There are therefore several mechanisms through which the enforcement of international anti-corruption obligations can be sought, and the question is far from being confined to the theoretical. Although part of the international obligations of States arising out of the anti-corruption treaties concern the internal sphere of the State, in the sense that they are aimed at promoting and strengthening measures to prevent and combat corruption within the State itself, other obligations are aimed at facilitating the prevention and at combating corruption in other States. The former are owed to the citizens of the State, and the latter to another State. Failure to comply with these latter obligations could undoubtedly give rise to a dispute between two or more States Parties to anti-corruption conventions. If these obligations are not met, a foreign State could suffer damage. For example, in accordance with the UNCAC, States are under the international obligation to return confiscated assets to the requesting State Party in the case of embezzlement of public funds or of laundering of embezzled public funds, when confiscation was duly executed.[1359] If a State refused to return the assets to the requesting State, this would damage the requesting State and create a serious dispute between them. The requesting State could bring a case before the ICJ against the requested State to obtain the return of the assets. A similar situation could arise if, for instance, a State refused to extradite a person accused of bribery because that person was a national of that State, and the person concerned was not submitted for prosecution. This would violate the State's obligation to extradite or prosecute.[1360] In this case, the requesting State could bring a claim before the ICJ for the requested State to comply with its obligation and extradite or prosecute the accused.[1361]

1358 UN Charter, Art. 94(2).

1359 UNCAC, Art. 57(3)(a).

1360 UNCAC, Arts. 42(3) and 44(11); Inter-American Convention against Corruption, Arts. 5(3) and 13(6); CoE Criminal Law Convention, Arts. 17(3) and 27(5); AU Convention against Corruption, Arts. 13(1)(c) and 15(6) UNCAC, Art. 44(11); OECD Convention, Art. 10(3); SADC Protocol against Corruption, Art. 9(7).

1361 A similar case outside the context of corruption is before the ICJ in which Belgium instituted proceedings against Senegal for not complying with its obligation to extradite or prosecute the former President of Chad, Hissène Habré. See, International Court of Justice, Belgium v. Senegal, Questions relating to the Obligation to Prosecute or Extradite, 16 February 2009.

As indicated above, States can have recourse to international dispute settlement mechanisms to seek compliance by another State. But when an international anti-corruption obligation is not met and produces damage to a foreign citizen or corporation, what recourse do these foreign parties have to seek redress? Currently, with the exception of the SADC Tribunal, all of the other courts that have jurisdiction over disputes relating to anti-corruption obligations only accept claims made by States. Hence, a person or corporation in the SADC region could bring a claim against a State before the SADC Tribunal for the enforcement of an anti-corruption obligation based on the SADC Protocol. In the case of the other courts, the only option for persons to gain access to them is through diplomatic protection. Diplomatic protection consists of the invocation by a State, through diplomatic action or other means of peaceful settlement, of the responsibility of another State for an injury caused by an internationally wrongful act of that State to a natural or legal person that is a national of the former State with a view to the implementation of such responsibility.[1362] A State may therefore make a claim to protect the interests of its nationals. Such claims are usually settled by negotiation although, in the context of corruption, could be taken to the ICJ. Diplomatic protection for corruption could arise, for instance, if in the case of a public procurement procedure, a foreign corporation does not win the tender because of widespread corruption in the tendering procedure, even though its proposal was the most competitive in terms of price and quality. In this situation, the State could be in violation of its international obligation to establish appropriate and transparent systems of procurement.[1363] The State of the corporation could exercise its right to diplomatic protection and bring a claim before the ICJ, for example, against the State that had not met its international obligation.

Nevertheless, such international anti-corruption obligations only rarely concern and affect foreign persons. The majority of international anti-corruption obligations are owed by States to their own citizens and foreign States therefore suffer no damage and have no interest in enforcing such obligations before an international court such as the ICJ, either directly or through diplomatic protection. With the exception of the SADC Tribunal, the above international courts do not allow the citizens of a State to bring a case against their own State for failure to comply with their international anti-corruption obligations. This does not mean, however, that individuals are completely powerless in advancing the enforcement of international obligations. In addition to the jurisdictional

[1362] Draft Articles on Diplomatic Protection, adopted by the International Law Commission at its Fifty-eighth Session, in 2006, Official Records of the General Assembly, Sixty-first Session, Supplement No. 10 (A/61/10). Art. 1.

[1363] UNCAC, Art. 9(1); AU Convention against Corruption Art. 7(4) and 5(4). Under the Inter-American Convention against Corruption this is an obligation of best endeavour. See Inter-American Convention against Corruption, Art. 3(5).

mechanisms that may be available at the national level, individuals and groups of individuals can make use of international human rights courts to seek the enforcement of international anti-corruption obligations.

2. INTERNATIONAL HUMAN RIGHTS COURTS

Corruption is still seen by many as a systemic problem which affects society in general in economic, political and moral terms. However, in recent years, a shift in perspective has added a social approach to the consideration of corruption, and accordingly an undoubted connection to individuals and their human rights. Hence, voices have increasingly been heard concerning the links between corruption and human rights and the ways in which corruption violates human rights.[1364] Clearly, there is no human rights guarantee that prohibits corruption.[1365] There are, however, human rights provisions that allude to corruption. The African Charter is the only human rights treaty which explicitly addresses corruption as a human rights issue. The relevant paragraphs of Article 21 provide that:

> "1. All peoples shall freely dispose of their wealth and natural resources. This right shall be exercised in the exclusive interest of the people. In no case shall a people be deprived of it.
> 2. In case of spoliation, the dispossessed people shall have the right to the lawful recovery of its property as well as to an adequate compensation."[1366]

Similarly, the right of peoples to self-determination under Article 1 of the International Covenant on Civil and Political Rights (ICCPR) and the International Covenant on Economic Social and Cultural Rights (ICESCR) can also be interpreted as anti-corruptions provision, under the terms of which "in

---

1364 See for example, Nihal Jayawickrama, *Corruption--A Violation of Human Rights?* (Transparency International Working Paper, 1998); Marella Buckley, "Anti Corruption Initiatives and Human Rights: The Potentials," in *Human Rights and Good Governance*, ed. Hans Otto Sano and Gudmundur Alfredsson (The Hague, London, New York: Kluwer Law International, 2002), 173–201; Jarmila Lajcakova, "Violation of Human Rights through State Tolerance of Street-level Bribery: Case Study: Slovakia," *Buffalo Human Rights Law Review* 9 (2003): 111–160; Asbjørn Eide et al., eds., "Economic, Social and Cultural Rights: A Universal Challenge," in *Economic, Social and Cultural Rights*, 2nd ed. (Dordrecht: Martinus Nijhoff Publishers, 2001).

1365 For a contrary view, see Ndiva Kofele-Kale, "The Right to a Corruption-Free Society as an Individual and Collective Human Right: Elevating Official Corruption to a Crime under International Law," *The International Lawyer* 34, no. 1 (2000): 149–178; C. Raj Kumar, "The Human Right to Corruption-Free Service, Some Constitutional and International Perspectives," *Frontline*, 2002.

1366 African Charter on Human and Peoples' Rights (adopted on 27 June 1981, entered into force on 21 October 1986) 21 I.L.M. 58, Art. 21(1) and (2).

no case may a people be deprived of its own means of subsistence."[1367] Nevertheless, the effect of corruption on human rights is broader in scope, as it may potentially affect any of the recognized human rights.

Even though it has been repeatedly argued that corruption constitutes a violation of human rights, these claims are generally framed in broad terms without demonstrating in detail how exactly a corrupt act violates a specific human right. In practice in most cases, corruption leads to human rights violations, but does not in itself constitute a violation of a human right. In addition, many cases of corruption, particularly within the private sector, may have no impact on human rights. For instance, when an employee in a private company awards a contract to a less competitive, more expensive contractor as a result of bribery, there would appear to be no consequences on human rights.

A study on corruption and human rights has drawn a distinction between cases in which corruption is at the origin of subsequent violations of human rights from those in which corruption is itself part of the violation or a means of effecting a violation.[1368] In the former cases, corruption is a factor that fuels human rights violations, but is only distantly linked to the infringement of human rights. For example, the presidential elections in Kenya in 2007 demonstrated that corruption during an electoral process can raise concerns about the accuracy of the final result, social unrest and protests may occur and these may be repressed violently. In such a case, the right to political participation may be directly violated, and repression of the social protests may also cause serious violations of human rights. Nevertheless, electoral corruption is not necessarily the only or determining cause of such riots or their repression.[1369] Many other factors may have contributed and, in that sense, corruption has a more remote link to the violations in question.

On the other hand, it may be argued that corruption is a violation of human rights when it is itself part of the violation or a means of effecting a violation. Corruption is directly connected to a violation of human rights when the corrupt act is deliberately used as a means to violate the right.[1370] Corruption in such cases affects the enjoyment of the right. For example, a bribe offered to a judge *per se* affects the independence and impartiality of that judge, and is accordingly

---

1367 International Covenant on Civil and Political Rights (G.A. res. 2200A (XXI), 21 U.N. GAOR Supp. (No. 16) at 52, UN Doc. A/6316 (1966), entered into force Mar. 23, 1976) 999 U.N.T.S. 171, Art. 1; International Covenant on Economic, Social and Cultural Rights (GA res. 2200A (XXI), 21 U.N. GAOR Supp. (No. 16) at 49, UN Doc. A/6316 (1966), entered into force Jan. 3, 1976) 993 U.N.T.S. 3, Art. 1.

1368 International Council on Human Rights Policy, *Corruption and Human Rights: Making the Connection*, 2009, 23–29.

1369 Ibid., 28.

1370 Ibid., 27.

in violation of the right to a fair trial.[1371] The right to a fair trial, also called the right to procedural guarantees in trials or rights of due process, is composed of a broad range of rights which provide for the fair, effective and efficient administration of justice and implies that all individuals are entitled to equality before the courts and tribunals, and have the right to a fair and public hearing by a competent, independent and impartial tribunal established by law.[1372] In other cases, corruption is a direct violation of a human right when an act or omission of by state authority has prevented individuals from having access to their right. The violation is produced by the conditionality of access to the human right. For example, with regard to the right to health,[1373] it is usually considered that accessibility is an essential element of such right. Health facilities, as well as goods and services, must be accessible to everyone without discrimination. Accessibility not only entails physical accessibility, but also economic acceptability.[1374] However, a common corrupt practice in hospitals is the payment of bribes or so-called "informal payments," whereby patients are forced to offer bribes at hospitals to be treated, x-rayed, allocated a bed in a ward or operated upon.[1375] This example shows that when bribes are requested from patients, their access to health is conditional upon partaking in a corrupt practice, and thus the right to health is infringed by corruption. Similar reasoning can be followed with regard to accessibility to other economic and social rights, and particularly the right to education.[1376]

1371 Ibid.

1372 ICCPR, Art. 14.

1373 ICESCR, Art. 12. The right to health, also known by its more technical name, the right to the highest attainable standard of physical and mental health, is defined as the "right to the enjoyment of a variety of facilities, goods, services and conditions necessary for the realisation of the highest attainable standard of health." See, also, UN Committee on Economic Social and Cultural Rights, General Comment No. 14: The Right to the Highest Attainable Standard of Health (Article 12 of the International Covenant on Economic, Social and Cultural Rights), UN Doc. E/C.12/2000/4, 11 August 2000.

1374 UN Committee on Economic Social and Cultural Rights, General Comment No. 14, para. 12. The Committee on Economic, Social and Cultural Rights has emphasized that equality of access to health care and health services is of the utmost importance. See, General Comment No. 14, paras. 19 and 43.

1375 A survey carried out by Transparency International Morocco revealed that of those who had been in contact with members of the public health service, 40 per cent admitted to making an illicit payment for a service or supply that was supposed to be free of charge. See, Azedine Akesbi, Siham Benchekroun and Kamal El Mesbahi, Transparency International Morocco, "Informal Payment Take a Toll on Moroccan Patients," in *Transparency International, Global Corruption Report 2006*, 75. Similar cases have also been reported in Bangladesh and Uganda. See, Iftekhar Zaman, Alim Abdul, "Corruption in the Public Health Service in Bangladesh," in *Transparency International, Global Corruption Report 2006*, 343–345.

1376 Julio Bacio Terracino, *Hard Law Connections between Corruption and Human Rights*, Working Paper for ICHRP Project on Corruption and Human Rights (International Council on Human Rights Policy, 2007), 45–47.

In other situations, corruption may be considered to violate human rights indirectly. When a corrupt practice constitutes an essential contributing factor in a chain of events that eventually leads to a violation of a right, corruption can still be blamed for violating human rights. In this case, the right is violated by an act that derives from a corrupt act. But, the act of corruption constitutes a necessary condition for the violation. Corruption often leads to violations of children's rights in this way. For example, children have to be protected against all forms of sexual exploitation and sexual abuse,[1377] as well as from abduction, sale and trafficking.[1378] However, these rights are violated by the human trafficking of children (particularly for sexual exploitation and abuse, abduction, sale, prostitution and pornography), and corruption usually plays an essential role in such violations.[1379] Those responsible commonly bribe officials to obtain the documents required to cross borders, or so that the authorities turn a blind eye to the trafficking. Without corruption, the majority of human traffickers would be out of business and the human rights of the victims would not therefore be violated.

Evidently, the question of whether a corrupt practice is remotely, indirectly or directly connected to a human rights violation needs to be determined on a case by case basis.[1380] Cases in which corruption directly or indirectly constitutes a violation of human rights can be remedied before an international human rights mechanism. One option is to have recourse to various human rights monitoring mechanisms in the United Nations system, which are divided into so-called charter-based bodies and treaty-based bodies. The former, which are based on the United Nations Charter, are the Human Rights Council, its Special Procedures and the Universal Periodic Review. To differing forms and degrees, these bodies are entitled to receive certain forms of complaints from individuals concerning violations of human rights. However, the most substantial quasi-judicial work is carried out by the treaty-based bodies. Five of the human rights treaty bodies (the Committee on Civil and Political Rights, the Committee on the Elimination of Racial Discrimination, Committee against Torture, the Committee on the Elimination of Discrimination against Women and the

---

1377 Convention on the Rights of the Child (G.A. res. 44/25, Annex, 44 UN GAOR Supp. (No. 49) at 167, UN Doc. A/44/49 (1989), entered into force Sept. 2, 1990) 1577 U.N.T.S. 3, Art. 34.

1378 Convention on the Rights of the Child, Art. 35; Optional Protocol to the Convention on the Rights of the Child on the Sale of Children, Child Prostitution and Child Pornography, adopted and opened for signature, ratification and accession by General Assembly resolution, UN General Assembly Resolution 54/263 of 25 May 2000, entered into force on 18 January 2002.

1379 International Council on Human Rights Policy, *Corruption and Human Rights: Making the Connection*, 27.

1380 For numerous examples of how different corrupt practices violate specific human rights see, Bacio Terracino, *Hard Law Connections between Corruption and Human Rights*, 9–47.

Committee on the Rights of Persons with Disabilities) may consider individual complaints or communications from individuals.

In cases where a corrupt act directly or indirectly violates one or more of the rights set out in the ICCPR, International Convention on the Elimination of All Forms of Racial Discrimination, Convention against Torture, Convention on the Elimination of all Forms of Discrimination against Women and Convention on the Rights of Persons with Disabilities, a victim of such an act can bring a complaint against the State responsible before the corresponding treaty body, provided that the State has recognized the competence of the committee to receive such complaints. A cardinal principle governing the admissibility of a complaint is that the victim has exhausted all the remedies in his or her own State before bringing a claim. The decisions of the treaty bodies are final and if they hold that a human rights violation has occurred, they may ask the State in question to provide an effective remedy and may order the payment of compensation. Although the United Nations human rights monitoring system is commonly criticized for its findings and recommendations being too general or diplomatic, they still constitute a valid alternative for individuals to seek redress for corruption outside their States. Most importantly, such actions expose the issue of corruption and help in raising awareness of its detrimental effects at the personal level.

As an alternative to the United Nations human rights mechanisms, if a corrupt act directly or indirectly violates one or more rights contained in regional human rights treaties, the victims can instead bring a complaint to the corresponding body, following the exhaustion of domestic remedies. An individual or group of individuals, or an NGO in the Americas region, in a case of corruption that is in violation of the American Convention on Human Rights, can bring the case before the Inter-American Commission on Human Rights,[1381] which can produce recommendations and may in turn refer it to the Inter-American Court of Human Rights.[1382] A similar procedure can be followed in Africa under the African Charter on Human and Peoples' Rights, where an individual or NGO can bring a case before the African Commission on Human and Peoples' Rights, which will pronounce on the case and may refer it to the African Court of Human and Peoples' Rights.[1383] In Europe, a case may be

1381 Under the Convention, cases can be referred to the Court either by the Inter-American Commission on Human Rights or a State Party. Individuals first have to lodge a complaint with the Commission so that it can rule on the admissibility of the claim. American Convention on Human rights (adopted on 22 November 1969) 1144 U.N.T.S. 123, Arts. 44–51.

1382 Provided that the State complained against has accepted the jurisdiction of the Court. American Convention on Human Rights, Art. 62.

1383 African Charter on Human and Peoples' Rights, Art. 55; Protocol to the African Charter on Human and Peoples' Rights on the Establishment of an African Court on Human and

brought directly before the European Court of Human Rights under the European Convention on Human Rights.[1384]

Interestingly, a communication on corruption as a violation of human rights has already been lodged with the African Commission concerning Equatorial Guinea. Even more interestingly, it was a Spanish NGO, Asociación pro Derechos Humanos de España (APDHE), which brought the communication before the African Commission.[1385] The communication alleges violations of the right of the peoples of Equatorial Guinea to "freely dispose of their wealth and natural resources" under Article 21 of the African Charter on Human and Peoples' Rights.[1386] More specifically, the communication alleges that the Government of Equatorial Guinea has violated the Charter by permitting the family of the President, Teodoro Obiang Nguema Mbasogo, and his entourage to divert for their own private benefit the revenue from natural resources belonging to the people of Equatorial Guinea.[1387] APDHE further argues that the corruption system sustained by the Government is also in violation of other rights under the African Charter, namely the guarantee of the independence of the Judiciary (Article 26), the right to have a cause heard (Article 7.1), the right to development (Article 22), the right to health (Article 16), the right to education (Article 17.1) and the right to lawfully acquired private property (Article 14). As remedies, the communication calls upon the African Commission to issue recommendations to the Government of Equatorial Guinea requiring it to: (i) engage with civil society to ensure genuine oversight of revenues, investments and expenditures comprising or deriving from the peoples' resources; (ii) establish and enforce a compulsory system of financial disclosure of all government departments under the direct monitoring of the Commission; (iii) ensure the right of appeal and compensation regarding land condemnation decisions; (iv) and ensure the provision in the government's budget of adequate resources for health, education and housing services.[1388] The African Commission decided that it could be seized of the communication, but has not

---

Peoples' Rights, entered into force on 25 January 2004, Arts. 5 and 34(6). Only individuals and NGOs can bring a claim directly to the African Court, provided that the State concerned has accepted the competence of the Court to that effect.

1384 European Convention for the Protection of Human Rights and Fundamental Freedoms, 213 U.N.T.S. 222, entered into force 3 September 1953, as amended by Protocols Nos. 3, 5, 8, and 11, which entered into force on 21 September 1970, 20 December 1971, 1 January 1990, and 1 November 1998 respectively, Arts. 34–35.

1385 The NGO stated, that among its objectives, it advocates human rights in Equatorial Guinea through its Equatorial Guinea Working Group and that it counts among its members many nationals of Equatorial Guinea who are resident in Spain. See Communication 347/07 submitted by the Asociación Pro Derechos Humanos de España regarding the Republic of Equatorial Guinea, under Article 55 of the African Charter on Human and Peoples' Rights, 12 October 2007, 1.

1386 Ibid.

1387 Ibid.

1388 Ibid., 10.

yet ruled on its admissibility. This case is clearly groundbreaking, as it would open the door to countless similar cases in the African region, and probably in other regions as well.

The potential to link corruption to human rights has only recently started to be examined. Since corruption clearly has effects on the enjoyment of human rights, it is only natural that mechanisms for the protection and promotion of human rights are beginning to address the problem of corruption. A better understanding of the links between corruption and human rights clearly does not only serve the purpose of adding an extra adjudicatory proceeding to the anti-corruption tools. The relevance of linking corruption and human rights rests more on the realization that human rights can function as allies in preventing and combating corruption and can empower and influence public attitudes to make a stronger stand against corruption.

3. THE WTO DISPUTE SETTLEMENT BODY

In view of the existence of the WTO's famous "teeth" (its Dispute Settlement Body), there are constant calls to expand its agenda to include issues such as labour, investment, human rights and the environment. Although the basic documents of the WTO limit its jurisdiction to matters relating to international trade, many issues are in practice somehow related to international trade, and could therefore be interpreted as coming within the jurisdiction of the WTO. Corruption is one of those issues. As already indicated in Chapter V, corruption has been dealt with by the WTO indirectly in the context of Government procurement. However, it is necessary to examine whether there are other areas of international trade law that could be related to international anti-corruption obligations. In other words, in addition to government procurement, which of the trade obligations are most closely related to corruption?

Peter Eigen, one of the founders of the NGO Transparency International, claims that corruption has been linked to international trade since at least the Havana Charter of 1947, Article 10 of which refers to transparency in laws, regulations and decisions related to trade.[1389] Indeed, some provisions of WTO agreements could have the effect of indirectly constituting obstacles to corruption. This is the case of three treaties regulating procedures governing certain stages or types of trade: the Agreement on Import Licensing Procedures,[1390] the Agreement on

---

1389 Peter Eigen, *Las redes de la corrupción: La sociedad civil contra los abusos del poder* (Buenos Aires: Planeta, 2004), 217–222. However, the Havanna Charter was never adopted.

1390 Agreement on Import Licensing Procedures, Annex 1A to the Marrakesh Agreement Establishing the World Trade Organization, done at Marrakesh on 15 April 1994, took effect on 1 January 1996, 1868 U.N.T.S. 436.

Pre-Shipment Inspection[1391] and the Agreement on Government Procurement.[1392] The objectives of these agreements are to ensure that administrative decisions are more predictable and accountable by calling on Members to ensure that their responsible officials act on publicly available criteria when taking decisions and are able to provide written explanations of their final decisions.[1393] Already in 1995, it was claimed that the WTO should address the problem of corruption as a trade issue. It has been argued that corruption blocks trade by acting as a surcharge on goods and services, and by creating de facto monopolies.[1394]

While all of the above arguments concerning corruption and international trade are undoubtedly true, it may not in practice be possible to remedy a corrupt act which affects international trade through the WTO dispute settlement body. In accordance with the examples referred to above, the fact remains that, while a corrupt act may be assimilated to a de facto monopoly or a surcharge on goods and services, it is not technically a monopoly or a tariff as defined and interpreted by the WTO agreements. The Dispute Settlement Mechanism is triggered by a Member which considers that a benefit accruing to it under the WTO Agreements is being nullified or impaired as a result of an action or omission by another Member.[1395] Even if a corrupt act is considered to constitute an act or omission by a Member, it can only be remotely interpreted as nullifying or impairing one or more of the provisions of the WTO Agreements. Further research needs to be carried out, probably in the form of scenarios, to determine how remote the connection is between corruption and the international trade obligations and rights accruing from the WTO Agreements.

With regard to public procurement, as indicated in Chapter V, the WTO has an agreement on public procurement recently amended, namely the Agreement on Government Procurement. The Agreement is designed to make laws, regulations,

---

1391 Agreement on Pre-Shipment Inspection, Annex 1A to the Marrakesh Agreement Establishing the World Trade Organization, done at Marrakesh on 15 April 1994, took effect on 1 January 1996, 1868 U.N.T.S. 368.

1392 Agreement on Government Procurement, Annex 4(b) to the Marrakesh Agreement Establishing the World Trade Organization, done at Marrakesh on 15 April 1994, took effect on 1 January 1996, 1915 U.N.T.S. 103. See, Krista Nadakavukaren Schefer, "Corruption and the WTO Legal System" (Society of International Economic Law (SIEL) Inaugural Conference 2008 Paper, June 13, 2008), 6–16.

1393 Ibid.

1394 Philip M. Nichols, "Outlawing Transnational Bribery through the WTO," *Law and Policy in International Business* 28 (1997): 333–337; Philip M. Nichols, "Corruption in the World Trade Organization: Discerning the Limits of the World Trade Organization's Authority," *N.Y.U. Journal of International Law and Politics* 28 (1995): 711–784.

1395 General Agreement on Tariffs and Trade, Annex 1A to the Marrakesh Agreement Establishing the World Trade Organization, done at Marrakesh on 15 April 1994, took effect on 1 January 1996, 1867 U.N.T.S. 18, Art. 23.

procedures and practices regarding government procurement more transparent, mostly with the aim of ensuring that they do not protect domestic products or suppliers, or discriminate against foreign products or suppliers.[1396] Moreover, as stated earlier the WTO has recently amended the Agreement which now establishes that procurement must be conducted in a transparent and impartial manner that avoids conflict of interest and prevents corrupt practices.[1397] Yet, the main purpose of the Agreement is clearly to open up procurement as much as possible to international competition.

The Agreement on Government Procurement is however not an integral part of the Marrakesh Agreement establishing the WTO, which is binding on all WTO Members. The Agreement is part of the so-called "Plurilateral Trade Agreements", the ratification or accession of which is negotiated separately, and WTO Members can therefore choose not to become Parties to it. The Agreement is therefore only binding on WTO Members which have ratified it.[1398] The Agreement on Government Procurement has only been ratified by 41 WTO Members, the majority of which are developed nations.[1399]

As a result, it would be possible to bring a case on corruption in government procurement to the WTO dispute settlement system. It could be argued by a State Party to this Agreement that a corrupt procurement procedure violates several provisions of the Agreement. An example might be if a company A bribes a public official responsible for organizing a public tender, and who then awards the contract to that company without a tendering procedure, and company B is therefore excluded. Another example would be when during a tendering procedure, company A bribes the person responsible for awarding the contract, who then awards it to that company, even though another company B submitted the lowest and most advantageous tender. These overly simplistic examples illustrate the ways in which corruption may violate the provisions of the Agreement, thereby creating a tendering procedure that is corrupt, discriminatory, non-competitive and unfair. In such cases, the home State of company B, if it can provide evidence of corrupt acts which nullify or impair the benefit accruing to it under the Government Procurement Agreement, or which impede the attainment of any object of the Agreement, can refer the State that organized the tendering procedure to the WTO Dispute Settlement Body.[1400]

1396 Agreement on Government Procurement, Art. IV.

1397 Ibid., Art. IV(4).

1398 World Trade Organization, Marrakesh Agreement Establishing the World Trade Organization, 1867 U.N.T.S. 154, Art. 2(3).

1399 Although a number of Members are currently negotiating accession. For the list of States Parties, see www.wto.org/english/tratop_e/gproc_e/memobs_e.htm (last visited 29 April 2012).

1400 Agreement on Government Procurement, Art. XX.

CONCLUSION

As indicated by the late international lawyer and Professor at Columbia University Oscar Schachter, "[i]mplementation and accountability are now regarded as essential elements of normative declarations, whether soft or hard law. Reporting, monitoring, transparency are emphasised by governments and international organisations."[1401] This tendency, already identified by Professor Schachter in 1988, has only intensified in recent years and as shown in this Chapter is particularly relevant to anti-corruption normative declarations.

There are numerous international obligations based on the anti-corruption treaties, which may in turn be divided into two groups. On the one hand, some of the obligations are aimed at improving the general anti-corruption situation in the State. These obligations are principally owed to the population. On the other hand, other anti-corruption obligations are aimed at improving the anti-corruption situation in other States. These obligations are mostly owed to other States.

This conceptual framework is important in understanding the different methods of implementation and enforcement available for international anti-corruption obligations. The first group of obligations, which a State owes to its own population, are mostly enforced through the collaborative and peer review mechanisms of monitoring and follow-up. It should be emphasized that these are the most important mechanisms for the long-term enforcement of anti-corruption obligations. In addition, as indicated in this Chapter, the population of the State may have recourse to human rights accountability mechanisms to call on the State to meet its anti-corruption obligations. The second group of international anti-corruption obligations which are owed to foreign States can also be indirectly enforced through the monitoring mechanisms. However, if these should fail, States may have recourse to the traditional dispute settlement procedure of negotiation, arbitration and finally adjudication. As noted in this Chapter, States could bring a case on corruption to the International Court of Justice.

The potential of international law enforcement is immense since, for the first time in history, the fight against corruption does not rest solely within the internal sphere of States and their governments. Through the monitoring and enforcement of the international legal framework against corruption, non-governmental and foreign actors, including individuals and foreign States, may now play a meaningful role in forcing unwilling governments to curb corruption effectively.

1401 Oscar Schachter, "Recent Trends in International Law Making," *Australian Yearbook of International Law* 12 (1988): 14.

GENERAL CONCLUSION

It is now unquestionable that corruption has become an issue of international concern. With fourteen international anti-corruption conventions, together with anti-corruption soft law instruments, and particularly resolutions of international organizations, a complex set of substantive and procedural rules has emerged concerning the prevention and repression of corruption, which represents the international legal framework against corruption. However, although this international regulation constitutes the core of the international legal framework, other hard law and soft law instruments that are not specifically or directly designed to fight corruption also form part of the international legal framework against corruption. These consist of other general rules of international law or instruments that are relevant tools to supplement specific international anti-corruption obligations, and are also instrumental in their interpretation and implementation. For example, the international anti-corruption obligations concerning access to information, jurisdiction, immunities or extradition, are supplemented by, and have to be interpreted in the light of other applicable rules of international law. In other words, the international legal framework against corruption is composed of international anti-corruption rules and general customary and conventional rules of international law. An analysis of the interaction between these rules is at the core of the present study.

At the outset, the scope of application of the international legal framework has been clearly delimited. It applies to the corrupt acts of bribery, embezzlement, illicit enrichment, trading in influence and abuse of functions, as defined by the anti-corruption conventions. The most common elements of each of the corrupt acts have been described with the objective of clarifying the exact content of the international obligation of States when it comes to their criminalization. While each legal system has a different definition of corrupt acts, the internationalization of the problem of corruption is resulting in a process of the harmonization of domestic substantive law against corruption with international law providing the standard. However, the above list of corrupt acts is not exhaustive, and in practice only bribery and embezzlement are quasi-universal corrupt acts. The rest are widely accepted and their criminalization is called for by several international conventions, but they have not yet attained universal acceptance.

The main goal of the international legal framework against corruption is clearly to both compel and assist States to combat corruption more effectively. The approach taken is to strengthen national capacities for the prevention and repression of corruption. While more emphasis is placed on the latter, the prevention of corruption constitutes an important pillar, and the international legal framework against corruption therefore creates obligations for States concerning the prevention of corruption. However, the obligations relating to prevention are far from constituting a strong and complete package of measures for the realistic prevention of corruption. Unfortunately, most of the obligations only call upon States to endeavour to adopt measures, but do not impose on them a duty to achieve the necessary result of meaningfully preventing corruption. On the positive side, international anti-corruption preventive obligations do touch upon some of the usual systemic weaknesses that facilitate corrupt practices, such as access to information and transparency measures in the public sector and especially in the judiciary. If adequately implemented, they could significantly reinforce the necessary institutions for the prevention of corruption. Preventive measures have the potential of making corruption riskier and more difficult, and at the same time lay the basis for anti-corruption law enforcement.

ANTI-CORRUPTION LAW ENFORCEMENT AT THE NATIONAL LEVEL

One of the main problems of the fight against corruption is that in practice corruption and impunity have almost gone hand in hand. When corruption occurs, there are few investigations, even fewer trials and hardly any convictions. Hence, the main focus of the international legal framework against corruption is undoubtedly on law enforcement, which has consequently created a wide variety of international anti-corruption law enforcement obligations for States aimed at reducing impunity for corruption. In this connection, the international obligations concerning jurisdiction constitute a traditional set of measures with a minimum degree of novelty. Criminal jurisdiction for corruption remains largely territorial, although States may choose to apply extraterritorial grounds, such as active or passive nationality and the essential interests of the State. Nevertheless, such provisions should be interpreted in a way that reinforces the enforcement of anti-corruption law. Criminal territorial jurisdiction needs to be interpreted broadly so that an extensive physical connection to the corrupt act is not required. States are also encouraged to exercise their criminal jurisdiction, even when neither a part of the corrupt act nor its effects take place in their territory. Moreover, with regard to jurisdictional immunities, even though States are solely asked to apply an appropriate balance between immunities and adjudication, the interpretation of the law of immunities has shown that, in the majority of cases, jurisdictional immunities should not constitute a barrier to the prosecution of corruption or civil litigations.

Moreover, the international legal framework has to a certain extent enhanced the use of certain jurisdictional tools which reinforce the fight against corruption. The most important jurisdictional aspect of the international legal framework is undoubtedly the reinforcement of anti-corruption civil litigation, including at the international level. Moreover, the international legal framework has indirectly created a *permissive* form of quasi-universal jurisdiction. States may prosecute offenders on the basis of a number of stated jurisdictional grounds, ranging from territoriality to nationality, and protective principles. When combined with the obligation to extradite or prosecute, this has created a treaty based quasi-universal jurisdiction over corruption.

In anti-corruption law enforcement several of the international obligations constitute traditional elements of law enforcement mechanisms, with which most States are already familiar. This is the case, for example, with the criminalization of corrupt acts, money laundering and the application of criminal sanctions. However, the strength of the international legal framework with regard to law enforcement rests on the more innovative elements with which most States are not familiar, but which are particularly useful in combating corruption, such as the creation of special investigative techniques, enhancing the reporting of corrupt practices, stepping up confiscation regimes and the provision of liability for legal persons.

In addition to law enforcement, an essential part of the international legal framework against corruption consists of the obligations relating to international cooperation in criminal matters. These do not only cover traditional forms of cooperation, such as extradition, mutual legal assistance (MLA) and law enforcement cooperation, but also extend to other relatively new options in transnational criminal justice in relation to corruption, including the transfer of proceedings in criminal matters, assistance in establishing joint investigative bodies, and cooperation for the appropriate use of special investigative techniques. However, in line with other transnational crimes, the two most important aspects of international cooperation in criminal matters are extradition and MLA, to which the international legal framework therefore dedicates considerable attention.

International anti-corruption obligations regarding extradition supplement pre-existing extradition treaties. The obligations for States differ depending on whether or not they make extradition conditional on the existence of a treaty. When they do not, i.e. when they rely on their own laws, States have to ensure that corrupt acts are extraditable offences under their national law, preferably even in the absence of dual criminality. This group of States is therefore equipped with a solid legal framework for extradition. On the other hand, States that make extradition conditional on the existence of a treaty have to regard corrupt acts as being included in all extradition treaties existing between States Parties to anti-corruption conventions. Obviously, a State may still refuse extradition, except on the ground of the nationality of the offender where the obligation on States to extradite or prosecute corrupt individuals is relatively weak.

MLA international obligations are composed of traditional MLA provisions, which supplement pre-existing MLA treaties and are subsidiary to them. States that are Party to an MLA treaty have to apply the rules of such treaty, and only minor obligations arising from the international legal framework against corruption apply, such as the impossibility of declining MLA on the grounds of bank secrecy. States that have no MLA treaty need to apply all the international MLA obligations covering all relevant MLA issues, such as how to make requests, how to execute them, grounds for refusal, etc. Unfortunately, the international legal framework cannot resolve the problem that many developing States simply do not have the means to provide effective MLA. This is an issue that needs to be considered in future, particularly under the umbrella of international technical assistance obligations. Clearly, most obligations relating to extradition and MLA remain at the traditional level and, while they have advanced the potential for inter-State cooperation in the investigation and prosecution of corruption, they have not created extraordinary or revolutionary legal tools.

The international legal framework against corruption has been most innovative in its provisions concerning asset recovery. The return of assets in the past essentially depended on the good will of the State where the assets were found. The international legal framework has now established this as an international obligation, although only for assets stolen through the embezzlement of public funds. In the case of all other corrupt acts, the requesting State needs to demonstrate its ownership over the assets or its right to compensation. In addition, a framework has been created to enhance the practical aspect of recovery. It specifies how cooperation and assistance should be provided, how the proceeds of corruption are to be returned to a requesting State and how the interests of other victims or legitimate owners are to be considered. Notwithstanding its flaws, the international legal framework against corruption in practice constitutes a step forward towards a more solid web of legal tools to enhance international cooperation in criminal matters relating to corruption, especially with regard to the recovery of stolen assets.

ENFORCEMENT OF THE INTERNATIONAL LEGAL FRAMEWORK AT THE INTERNATIONAL LEVEL

Analysis of the bases and content of the international legal framework against corruption shows the emergence of numerous international anti-corruption obligations for States concerning the prevention and repression of corruption. As indicated throughout this study, these obligations may consist of two types: obligations to achieve a certain objective (obligations of result) and obligations of best endeavour (obligations of conduct). In addition, there are numerous optional recommendations. It is essential that obligations of best endeavour are not underestimated. States Parties are required to endeavour to adopt certain measures, and are therefore under a certain level of obligation. While there is no obligation to achieve a specific result, States are under the obligation to at least consider or to endeavour to achieve a specific result (an obligation of conduct). As demonstrated in this study, there are ways of knowing whether a State has pondered a particular course of action required by an obligation of conduct. Paying attention solely to the anti-corruption obligations of result would therefore ignore part of the potential of the international legal framework against corruption.

In order to obtain a complete picture of the potential of this international legal framework, it is essential to explore the different means for its enforcement. For this purpose, a new conceptual framework relating to obligations is used in order to understand the different methods of implementation and enforcement available. International anti-corruption obligations need to be divided into two groups. On the one hand, some of the obligations are aimed at improving the general anti-corruption situation in the State. These obligations are principally owed to the population. On the other hand, there are other anti-corruption obligations that are aimed at improving the anti-corruption situation in other States. These obligations are mostly owed to other States. The first group of obligations, which a State owes to its own population, are mostly enforced through the collaborative and peer review mechanisms of monitoring and follow-up. It should be emphasized that these are the most important mechanisms for the long-term enforcement of anti-corruption obligations. In addition, affected individuals in the State may also have recourse to the human rights accountability mechanism to require the State meets its anti-corruption obligations.

The second group of international anti-corruption obligations, which are owed to foreign States, can also be indirectly enforced through monitoring mechanisms. However, if these should fail, States may have recourse to the traditional dispute settlement procedures of negotiation, arbitration and ultimately adjudication. For example, States can now bring a case concerning corruption before the International Court of Justice. The potential of international law enforcement is immense since, for the first time in history, anti-corruption does not solely rest within the internal sphere of a State and its government. Through the monitoring and enforcement of the international legal framework against corruption, non-governmental and foreign actors, such as foreign States and international institutions can now play a meaningful role in forcing unwilling governments to curb corruption effectively.

OTHER USES OF THE INTERNATIONAL LEGAL FRAMEWORK AGAINST CORRUPTION

An analysis of the international legal framework against corruption shows that bringing corruption to the attention of international actors and developing an international legal framework may revolutionize the fight against corruption around the world. What therefore has international law added to the fight against corruption? The principal contribution of the regulation of corruption by international law does not solely reside in an improved network of inter-State cooperation for the repression of corruption, but in its effects in combating corruption at the purely domestic level. International law demands anti-corruption changes "from the inside out." The implementation of the international legal framework at the national level is already improving the legal and institutional framework to combat corruption within countries. And at times these changes have even happened at the core of criminal justice systems. For example, countries which have historically refused to criminalize legal persons, have now introduced such a concept into their legal systems, or at least some form of non-criminal responsibility. The effect of the international legal framework on anti-corruption national legal systems is clearly significant in this respect.

Yet, laws and institutions alone fall short of producing really effective action against corruption. The biggest challenge lies in the application of those laws and in the independent work of institutions which are usually deficient due to the lack of long-term and regular political will by the Government. Here, the international legal framework may also be of assistance. The UNCAC, for example, could provide political cover or leverage for national actors fighting corruption, such as prosecutors and civil society organizations. Anti-corruption conventions and their monitoring mechanisms can also be used to raise public awareness at the domestic level of the problem of corruption and what the government is required to do to address it. The monitoring mechanisms of anti-corruption conventions have proven especially efficient in encouraging dialogue between governmental and non-governmental actors. In addition, it may also prove effective to frame pending anti-corruption efforts in terms of international obligations with a view to influencing public opinion and furthering anti-corruption policy.

The real potential of the international legal framework in the overall fight against corruption is still uncertain. A first step towards the adoption and harmonization of the necessary laws at the domestic level is already taking place. The subsequent application of those laws constitutes the next challenge. Moreover, most interested parties, and particularly anti-corruption civil society organizations, are still adapting to the existence of the international legal framework and have yet to discover and exploit its full potential. The present study has shown some of its strengths and weaknesses and has aimed to untangle the network of international anti-corruption obligations with a view to improving understanding and implementation of the international legal framework, and ultimately holding States accountable for complying with their international anti-corruption commitments.

SELECTED BIBLIOGRAPHY

I. PRIMARY SOURCES

A. *International Treaties*

1. United Nations

United Nations Convention on Jurisdictional Immunities of States and Their Property (adopted by the UN General Assembly Resolution 59/38 on 16 December 2004, not yet entered into force) 44 I.L.M. 803

Convention against Corruption (adopted by the UN General Assembly by resolution 58/4 on 31 October 2003, entered into force 14 December 2005) 2349 U.N.T.S. 41

Convention against Transnational Organized Crime (adopted by the UN General Assembly by resolution 55/25 on 8 January 2001, entered into force 29 September 2003) 2225 U.N.T.S. 209

International Convention for the Suppression of the Financing of Terrorism (adopted by the UN General Assembly by resolution 54/109 on 9 December 1999, entered into force 10 April 2002) 39 I.L.M. 270

Convention on Access to Information, Public Participation and Access to Justice in Environmental Matters (adopted on 26 June 1998 by the United Nations Economic Commission for Europe, entered into force on 30 October 2001) 2161 U.N.T.S. 447

Convention on the Rights of the Child (adopted by the UN General Assembly by resolution 44/25 on 20 November 1989, entered into force 2 September 1990) 1577 U.N.T.S. 3

Convention against the Illicit Traffic of Narcotic Drugs and Psychotropic Substances (adopted by the UN Conference for the Adoption of a Convention against the Illicit Traffic of Narcotic Drugs and Psychotropic Substances (E/CONF.82/15) on 20 December 1988, entered into force 11 November 1990) 28 I.L.M. 493

International Covenant on Civil and Political Rights (adopted by the UN General Assembly by resolution 2200A (XXI) on 16 December 1966, entered into force 23 March 1976) 999 U.N.T.S. 171

International Covenant on Economic, Social and Cultural Rights (adopted by the UN General Assembly by resolution 2200A (XXI) on 16 December 1966, entered into force 3 January 1976) 993 U.N.T.S. 3

2. Council of Europe

Convention on Access to Official Documents (adopted by the Committee of Ministers on 27 November 2008 at the 1042*bis* meeting of the Ministers' Deputies, not yet entered into force) C.E.T.S. 205

Convention on Laundering, Search, Seizure and Confiscation of the Proceeds from Crime and on the Financing of Terrorism (adopted by the Committee of Ministers of the Council of Europe on 16 May 2005) C.E.T.S. 198

Additional Protocol to the Criminal Law Convention on Corruption (adopted by the Committee of Ministers of the Council of Europe on 15 May 2003, entered into force 1 February 2005) E.T.S. 191

Civil Law Convention on Corruption (adopted by the Committee of Ministers of the Council of Europe on 4 November 1999, entered into force 1 November 2003) 2246 U.N.T.S. 3

Criminal Law Convention on Corruption (adopted by the Committee of Ministers of the Council of Europe on 27 January 1999, entered into force 1 July 2002) 2216 U.N.T.S. 225

Convention on the Protection of the Environment through Criminal Law (adopted by the Committee of Ministers of the Council of Europe on 4 November 1998) C.E.T.S. 172

Convention on Laundering, Search, Seizure and Confiscation of the Proceeds from Crime (adopted by the Committee of Ministers of the Council of Europe on 8 November 1990, entered into force 1 September 1993) 1862 U.N.T.S. 69

Convention on the Transfer of Proceedings in Criminal Matters (adopted by the Committee of Ministers of the Council of Europe on 15 May 1972) 1137 U.N.T.S. 30

European Convention on Mutual Assistance in Criminal Matters (adopted by the Committee of Ministers of the Council of Europe on 20 April 1959) 472 U.N.T.S. 185 and its two Additional Protocols of 1978, 1495 U.N.T.S. 350 and 2001, 2297 U.N.T.S. 24

European Convention on Extradition (adopted by the Committee of Ministers of the Council of Europe on 13 December 1957) 359 U.N.T.S. 273 and its two Additional Protocols of 1975, 1161 U.N.T.S. 450 and 1978, 1496 U.N.T.S. 328

Convention for the Protection of Human Rights and Fundamental Freedoms (adopted by the Committee of Ministers of the Council of Europe on 4 November 1950, entered into force 3 September 1953, as amended by Protocols Nos 3, 5, 8, and 11 which entered into force on 21 September 1970, 20 December 1971, 1 January 1990, and 1 November 1998 respectively) 213 U.N.T.S. 222

3. European Union

Convention on Jurisdiction and Enforcement of Judgments in Civil and Commercial Matters (adopted on 30 October 2007) Official Journal L 339/3

Convention established by the Council in accordance with Article 34 of the Treaty on European Union, on Mutual Assistance in Criminal Matters between the Member States of the European Union (adopted on 19 May 2000) Official Journal C 197, 12 July 2000, 3–23; and its Protocol (adopted on 16 October 2001) Official Journal C 326 of 21 November 2001

Convention on Mutual Assistance and Co-operation between Customs Administrations of the Member States (adopted on 18 December 1997) Official Journal C024. 23 January 1998, 1–22

Second Protocol, drawn up on the basis of Article K.3 of the treaty on European Union, to the Convention on the protection of the European Communities' financial interests – Joint Declaration on Article 13 (2) – Commission Declaration on Article 7 (adopted by Council Act of 19 June 1997) Official Journal C 221, 19 July 1997, 11–22

Convention drawn up on the basis of Article K.3 (2) (c) of the Treaty on European Union on the fight against corruption involving officials of the European Communities or officials of Member States of the European Union (adopted by Council Act of 26 May 1997) Official Journal C 195, 25 June 1997, 1–11

Protocol drawn up on the basis of Article K.3 of the Treaty on European Union, on the interpretation, by way of preliminary rulings, by the Court of Justice of the European Communities of the Convention on the protection of the European Communities' financial interests – Declaration concerning the simultaneous adoption of the Convention on the protection of the European Communities' financial interests and the Protocol on the interpretation by way of preliminary rulings, by the Court of Justice of the European Communities, of that Convention – Declaration made pursuant to Article 2 (adopted by Council Act of 29 November 1996) Official Journal C 151, 20 May 1997, 1–14

Protocol drawn up of the basis of Article K.3 of the Treaty on European Union to the Convention on the protection of the European Communities' financial interests – Statements made by Member States on the adoption of the Act drawing up the Protocol (adopted by Council Act of 27 September 1996, entered into force 17 October 2002) Official Journal C 313, 23 October 1996, 1–10

Convention drawn up on the basis of Article K.3 of the Treaty on European Union, on the protection of the European Communities' financial interests (adopted by Council Act of 26 July 1995) Official Journal C 316, 27 November 1995, 48–57

Convention on jurisdiction and the enforcement of judgments in civil and commercial matters (adopted on 16 September 1988) Official Journal L319/9

Hague Convention on the Taking of Evidence Abroad in Civil or Commercial Matters (adopted on 18 March 1970) 847 U.N.T.S. 231

Convention on Jurisdiction and the Enforcement of Judgments in Civil and Commercial Matters (adopted on 27 September 1968) 1262 U.N.T.S. 153

Hague Convention on the Service Abroad of Judicial and Extra-Judicial Documents in Civil or Commercial Matters (adopted 15 November 1965) 658 U.N.T.S. 163

4. Organization of American States

Inter-American Convention against Corruption (adopted at the third plenary session of the Organization of American States, 29 March 1996, entered into force 3 June 1997) 35 I.L.M. 724

Inter-American Convention on Mutual Assistance in Criminal Matters (adopted on 23 May 1992) Treaty Series, OAS, No.75; and its Optional Protocol (adopted 11 June 1993)

Inter-American Convention on Extradition (Adopted on 25 February 1982) 1752 U.N.T.S. 190

Inter-American Convention on the Taking of Evidence Abroad (adopted on 30 January 1975) 1438 U.N.T.S. 287; and its Additional Protocol (adopted on 24 May 1984) 24 I.L.M. 472
American Convention on Human rights (adopted on 22 November 1969) 1144 U.N.T.S. 123

5. Organisation for Economic Cooperation and Development

Convention on Combating Bribery of Foreign Public Officials in International Business Transactions (adopted on 21 November 1997, entered into force 15 February 1999) 37 I.L.M. 1

6. African Union

African Union Convention on Preventing and Combating Corruption (adopted by the 2nd Ordinary Session of the Assembly of the Union on 11 July 2003, entered into force 5 August 2006) 43. I.L.M. 1
African Charter on Human and Peoples' Rights (adopted on 27 June 1981, entered into force on 21 October 1986) 21 I.L.M. 58

7. Southern African Development Community

Southern African Development Community Protocol against Corruption (adopted 14 August 2001, entered into force 6 July 2005)
Protocol on Tribunal and the Rules of Procedure Thereof (adopted on 7 August 2000)
Treaty of the Southern African Development Community (adopted in 1992 and amended in August 2001)

8. Economic Community of West African States

Economic Community of West African States Protocol on the Fight against Corruption (adopted 21 December 2001, not yet entered into force)

9. World Trade Organization

World Trade Organisation, Marrakesh Agreement Establishing the World Trade Organisation, done at Marrakesh on 15 April 1994, took effect on 1 January 1996, 1867 U.N.T.S. 154
Agreement on Government Procurement, adoption of the results of the negotiations under article XXIV:7 of the agreement on government procurement, following their verification and review, as required by the ministerial decision of 15 December 2011 (GPA/112), paragraph 5: Action taken by the parties to the WTO agreement on government procurement at a formal meeting of the committee, at the level of Geneva heads of Delegations, on 30 march 2012

Agreement on Import Licensing Procedures, Annex 1A to the Marrakesh Agreement Establishing the World Trade Organization, done at Marrakesh on 15 April 1994, took effect on 1 January 1996, 1868 U.N.T.S. 436

Agreement on Pre-Shipment Inspection, Annex 1A to the Marrakesh Agreement Establishing the World Trade Organization, done at Marrakesh on 15 April 1994, took effect on 1 January 1996, 1868 U.N.T.S. 368

General Agreement on Tariffs and Trade, Annex 1A to the Marrakesh Agreement Establishing the World Trade Organization, done at Marrakesh on 15 April 1994, took effect on 1 January 1996, 1867 U.N.T.S. 18

B. *Other International Instruments*

1. United Nations

A) General Assembly

i) Resolutions of the General Assembly

The right to development, A/RES/59/185, 8 March 2005

Preventing and combating corrupt practices and transfer of assets of illicit origin and returning such assets to the countries of origin, A/RES/59/242, 28 February 2005

Action against corruption: assistance to States in capacity-building with a view to facilitating the entry into force and subsequent implementation of the United Nations Convention against Corruption, A/RES/59/155, 3 February 2005

Assistance to least developed countries to ensure their participation in the sessions of the Commission on Crime Prevention and Criminal Justice and the sessions of conferences of States parties, A/RES/59/152, 1 February 2005

The right to development, A/RES/58/172, 11 March 2004

Implementation of the first United Nations Decade for the Eradication of Poverty (1997–2006), A/RES/58/222, 19 February 2004

Preventing and combating corrupt practices and transfer of assets of illicit origin and returning such assets to the countries of origin, A/RES/58/205, 11 February 2004

United Nations Convention against Corruption, A/RES/58/4, 21 November 2003

The right to development, A/RES/57/223, 27 February 2003

Preventing and combating corrupt practices and transfer of funds of illicit origin and returning such funds to the countries of origin, A/RES/57/244, 7 February 2003

High-level political conference for the purpose of signing the United Nations convention against corruption, A/RES/57/169, 16 January 2003

Terms of reference for the negotiation of an international legal instrument against corruption, A/RES/56/260, 9 April 2002

The right to development, A/RES/56/150, 8 February 2002

Preventing and combating corrupt practices and transfer of funds of illicit origin and returning such funds to the countries of origin, A/RES/56/186, 31 January 2002

Strengthening of the United Nations Crime Prevention and Criminal Justice Programme, in particular its technical cooperation capacity, A/RES/55/64, 26 January 2001

Preventing and combating corrupt practices and illegal transfer of funds and repatriation of such funds to the countries of origin, A/RES/55/188, 25 January 2001
An effective international legal instrument against corruption, A/RES/55/61, 22 January 2001
Indicative list of international legal instruments, documents and recommendations against corruption, A/RES/55/61, Annex, 22 January 2001
United Nations Convention against Transnational Organized Crime, A/RES/55/25, 8 January 2001
Action against corruption, A/RES/54/128, 28 January 2000
Prevention of corrupt practices and illegal transfer of funds, A/RES/54/205, 27 January 2000
Action against corruption and bribery in international commercial transactions, A/RES/53/176, 25 January 1999
Model Treaty on Mutual Assistance in Criminal Matters, A/RES/45/117, Annex, 14 December 1990, amended by A/RES/53/112, 9 December 1998
International cooperation against corruption and bribery in international commercial transactions, A/RES/52/87, 2 February 1998
United Nations Declaration against Corruption and Bribery in International Commercial Transactions, A/RES/51/191, 21 February 1997
Action against corruption, A/RES/51/59, 12 December 1996
International Code of Conduct for Public Officials, A/RES/51/59, Annex, 12 December 1996
Model Treaty on Extradition, A/RES/45/116, Annex, 14 December 1990, amended by A/RES/52/88, 12 December 1997
Code of Conduct for Law Enforcement Officials, A/RES/34/169, Annex, 17 December 1979
Measures against Corrupt Practices of Transnational and Other Corporations, their Intermediaries and Others Involved, A/RES/3514(XXX), 15 December 1975
Universal Declaration of Human Rights, General Assembly Resolution 217A (III), U.N. Doc A/810 at 71, 1948

ii) Other Documents of the General Assembly

Revised Draft Rules of Procedure for the Conference of the States Parties to the United Nations Convention against Corruption, A/AC.261/L.259, 26 January 2006
Corruption: Threats and Trends in the 21st Century, Working Paper prepared by the Secretariat, A/CONF.203/6, 16 March 2005
Report of the High-level Political Conference for the Purpose of Signing the United Nations Convention against Corruption, held in Merida, Mexico, from 9 to 11 December 2003, A/59/77, 29 April 2004
Report of the Ad Hoc Committee for the Negotiation of a Convention against Corruption on its seventh session, held in Vienna from 29 September to 1 October 2003, Ad Hoc Committee on the Negotiation of a Convention against Corruption, Seventh Session, Vienna, 29 September-1 October 2003, A/AC.261/25, 17 October 2003
Report of the Ad Hoc Committee for the Negotiation of a Convention against Corruption on the work of its first to seventh sessions: Addendum: Interpretative notes for the

official records (travaux préparatoires) of the negotiation of the United Nations Convention against Corruption, A/58/422/Add.1, 7 October 2003
Report of the Ad Hoc Committee for the Negotiation of a Convention against Corruption on the work of its first to seventh sessions, A/58/422, 7 October 2003
Report of the consistency group, Ad Hoc Committee on the Negotiation of a Convention against Corruption, Seventh Session, Vienna, 29 September-1 October 2003, A/AC.261/24, 2 September 2003
Report of the Ad Hoc Committee for the Negotiation of a Convention against Corruption on its sixth session, held in Vienna from 21 July to 8 August 2003, Ad Hoc Committee on the Negotiation of a Convention against Corruption, Seventh Session, Vienna, 29 September-1 October 2003, A/AC.261/22, 22 August 2003
Revised draft United Nations Convention against Corruption, Ad Hoc Committee on the Negotiation of a Convention against Corruption, Seventh Session, Vienna, 29 September-1 October 2003, A/AC.261/3/Rev.5, 15 August 2003
Revised draft United Nations Convention against Corruption, Ad Hoc Committee on the Negotiation of a Convention against Corruption, Sixth Session, Vienna, 21 July-8 August 2003, A/AC.261/3/Rev.4, 12 May 2003
Proposals and contributions received from Governments Morocco: amendments to articles 8 and 12, Ad Hoc Committee on the Negotiation of a Convention against Corruption, Sixth Session, Vienna, 21 July-8 August 2003, A/AC.261/21, 8 May 2003
Proposals and contributions received from Governments Pakistan and Philippines: amendment to article 3, Ad Hoc Committee on the Negotiation of a Convention against Corruption, Sixth Session, Vienna, 21 July-8 August 2003, A/AC.261/20, 7 May 2003
Report of the Ad Hoc Committee for the Negotiation of a Convention against Corruption on its fifth session, held in Vienna from 10 to 21 March 2003, Ad Hoc Committee on the Negotiation of a Convention against Corruption, Sixth Session, Vienna, 21 July-8 August 2003, A/AC.261/16, 14 April 2003
Proposals and contributions received from Governments Libyan Arab Jamahiriya: amendment to article 21, Ad Hoc Committee on the Negotiation of a Convention against Corruption, Sixth Session, Vienna, 21 July-8 August 2003, A/AC.261/18, 10 April 2003
Proposals and contributions received from Governments Pakistan: amendments to the proposal on article 61 contained in document A/AC.261/15 and Corr.1, Ad Hoc Committee on the Negotiation of a Convention against Corruption, Sixth Session, Vienna, 21 July-8 August 2003, A/AC.261/19, 10 April 2003
Proposals and contributions received from Governments Switzerland: amendment to article 61, Ad Hoc Committee on the Negotiation of a Convention against Corruption, Fifth Session, Vienna, 10–21 March 2003, A/AC.261/15/Corr.1, 26 February 2003
Revised draft United Nations Convention against Corruption, Ad Hoc Committee on the Negotiation of a Convention against Corruption, Fifth Session, Vienna, 10–21 March 2003, A/AC.261/3/Rev.3, 5 February 2003
Report of the Ad Hoc Committee for the Negotiation of a Convention against Corruption on its fourth session, held in Vienna from 13 to 24 January 2003, Ad Hoc

Committee on the Negotiation of a Convention against Corruption, Fifth Session, Vienna, 10–21 March 2003, A/AC.261/13, 3 February 2003

Global study on the transfer of funds of illicit origin, especially funds derived from acts of corruption, Ad Hoc Committee on the Negotiation of a Convention against Corruption, Fourth Session, Vienna, 13–24 January 2003, A/AC.261/12, 28 November 2002

Report of the Ad Hoc Committee for the Negotiation of a Convention against Corruption on its third session, held in Vienna from 30 September to 11 October 2002, Ad Hoc Committee on the Negotiation of a Convention against Corruption, Fourth Session, Vienna, 13–24 January 2003, A/AC.261/9, 26 November 2002

Revised draft United Nations Convention against Corruption, Ad Hoc Committee on the Negotiation of a Convention against Corruption, Fourth Session, Vienna, 13–24 January 2003, A/AC.261/3/Rev.2, 19 November 2002

Proposals and contributions received from Governments, Ad Hoc Committee on the Negotiation of a Convention against Corruption, Fourth Session, Vienna, 13–24 January 2003, A/AC.261/11, 4 November 2002

Revised draft United Nations Convention against Corruption, Ad Hoc Committee on the Negotiation of a Convention against Corruption, Third Session, Vienna, 30 September-11 October 2002, A/AC.261/3/Rev.1/Corr.1, 24 September 2002

Revised draft United Nations Convention against Corruption, Ad Hoc Committee on the Negotiation of a Convention against Corruption, Third Session, Vienna, 30 September-11 October 2002, A/AC.261/3/Rev.1/Add.1, 5 July 2002

Report of the Ad Hoc Committee for the Negotiation of a Convention against Corruption on its second session, held in Vienna from 17 to 28 June 2002, Ad Hoc Committee on the Negotiation of a Convention against Corruption, Third Session, Vienna, 30 September-11 October 2002, A/AC.261/7, 5 July 200

Revised draft United Nations Convention against Corruption, Ad Hoc Committee on the Negotiation of a Convention against Corruption, Second Session, Vienna, 17 June-28 June 2002, A/AC.261/3/Rev.1, March 2002

Report of the Ad Hoc Committee for the Negotiation of a Convention against Corruption on its first session, held in Vienna from 21 January to 1 February 2002, Ad Hoc Committee on the Negotiation of a Convention against Corruption, Second Session, Vienna, 17 June-28 June 2002, A/AC.261/4, 14 March 2002

Draft United Nations Convention against Corruption, Ad Hoc Committee on the Negotiation of a Convention against Corruption, First Session, Vienna, 21 January-1 February, 2002, A/AC.261/3 (Part I-IV), 27 December 2001

Report of the Informal Preparatory Meeting of the Ad Hoc Committee for the Negotiation of a Convention against Corruption, held in Buenos Aires from 4 to 7 December 2001, Ad Hoc Committee on the Negotiation of a Convention against Corruption, First Session, Vienna, 21 January-1 February, 2002, A/AC.261/2 and A/AC.261/2/Corr.1, 21 December 2001

Informal Preparatory Meeting of the Ad Hoc Committee for the Negotiation of a Convention against Corruption, Buenos Aires, 4–7 December 2001, Proposals and contributions received from Governments, A/AC.261/IPM/2 – A/AC.261/IMP/27

Report of the Meeting of the Intergovernmental Open-Ended Expert Group to Prepare Draft Terms of Reference for the Negotiation of an International Legal Instrument against Corruption, A/AC.260/2, 8 August 2001

Report of the Ad Hoc Committee on the Elaboration of a Convention against Transnational Organized Crime on the Work of its First to Eleventh Sessions, UN Doc. A/55/383, 2 November 2000

B) Economic and Social Council (ECOSOC)

i) Commission on Crime Prevention and Criminal Justice

United Nations Convention against Corruption: Report of the Secretary General, E/CN.15/2005/9, 23 March 2005

United Nations Convention against Corruption: Report of the Secretary General, E/CN.15/2004/6, 19 March 2004

Work of the Ad Hoc Committee for the Negotiation of a Convention against Corruption: Report of the Secretary General, E/CN.15/2003/6, 12 March 2003

Implementation of the United Nations Declaration against Corruption and Bribery in International Commercial Transactions: Report of the Secretary General, E/CN.15/2002/6, 15 February 2002

Existing international legal instruments, recommendations and other documents addressing corruption: Report of the Secretary-General: Corrigendum, E/CN.15/2001/3/Corr.1, 8 June 2001

Existing international legal instruments, recommendations and other documents addressing corruption: Report of the Secretary General, E/CN.15/2001/3, 2 April 2001

Report of the Expert Group Meeting on Corruption and its Financial Channels, held in Paris from 30 March to 1 April 1999, E/CN.15/1999/10, 8 April 1999

ii) Other Subsidiary Organs of ECOSOC

Corruption and its Impact on the Full Enjoyment of Human Rights, in Particular, Economic, Social and Cultural Rights, Progress Report Submitted by the Special Rapporteur, Christy Mbonu, E/CN.4/Sub.2/2005/18, 22 Junes 2005

Corruption and its Impact on the Full Enjoyment of Human Rights, in Particular, Economic, Social and Cultural Rights, Preliminary Report of the Special Rapporteur, Ms. Christy Mbonu, E/CN.4/Sub.2/2004/23, 7 July 2004

Corruption and its Impact on the Full Enjoyment of Human Rights, in Particular, Economic, Social and Cultural Rights, Working Paper Submitted by Ms. Christy Mbonu in Accordance with Sub-Commission Decision 2002/106, E/CN.4/Sub.2/2003/18, 14 May 2003

C) Security Council

Resolution 1377, S/RES/1377, 12 November 2001

Resolution 1373, S/RES/1373, 28 September 2001

Resolution 1267, S/RES/1267, 15 October 1999

2. Council of Europe

A) GRECO

Albania: Third Evaluation Round: Evaluation Report on Albania on Incriminations (ETS 173 and 191, GPC 2) (Theme I) and Evaluation Report on Albania on Transparency of Party Funding (Theme II), 15 May 2009; Second Evaluation Round: Addendum to the Compliance Report on Albania, 8 October 2009; Compliance Report on Albania, 19 October 2007; Evaluation Report on Albania, 18 March 2005; First Evaluation Round: Addendum to the Compliance Report on Albania, 21 March 2007; Compliance Report on Albania, December 2004; Evaluation Report on Albania, 13 December 2002

Armenia: Joint First and Second Evaluation Round: Compliance Report on Armenia, 13 June 2008; Evaluation Report on Armenia, 10 March 2006;

Austria: Joint First and Second Evaluation Round: Evaluation Report on Austria, 13 June 2008

Azerbaijan: Joint First and Second Evaluation Round: Compliance Report on Azerbaijan, 10 October 2008; Evaluation Report on Azerbaijan, 23 June 2006

Belgium: Third Evaluation Round: Evaluation Report on Belgium on Incriminations (ETS 173 and 191, GPC 2) (Theme I) and Evaluation Report on Belgium on Transparency of Party Funding (Theme II), 15 May 2009; Second Evaluation Round: Addendum to the Compliance Report on Belgium, 15 May 2009; Compliance Report on Belgium, 1 June 2007; Evaluation Report on Belgium, 2 December 2004; First Evaluation Round: Compliance Report on Belgium, 11 July 2003; Evaluation Report on Belgium, 15 December 2000

Bosnia and Herzegovina: Second Evaluation Round: Compliance Report on Bosnia and Herzegovina, 10 October 2008; Evaluation Report on Bosnia and Herzegovina, 8 December 2006; First Evaluation Round: Addendum to the Compliance Report on Bosnia and Herzegovina, 19 October 2007; Compliance Report on Bosnia and Herzegovina, 20 May 2005; Evaluation Report on Bosnia and Herzegovina, 11 July 2003

Bulgaria: Second Evaluation Round: Addendum to the Compliance Report on Bulgaria, 3 July 2009; Compliance Report on Bulgaria, 1 June 2007; Evaluation Report on Bulgaria, 1 July 2005; First Evaluation Round: Addendum to the Compliance Report on Bulgaria, 23 June 2006; Compliance Report on Bulgaria, 14 May 2004; Evaluation Report on Bulgaria, 17 May 2002

Croatia: Third Evaluation Round: Evaluation Report on Croatia on Incriminations (ETS 173 and 191, GPC 2) (Theme I) and Evaluation Report on Croatia on Transparency of Party Funding (Theme II), 4 December 2009; Second Evaluation Round: Addendum to the Compliance Report on Croatia, 8 October 2009; Compliance Report on Croatia, 7 December 2007; Evaluation Report on Croatia, 9 December 2005; First Evaluation Round: Addendum to the Compliance Report on Croatia, 8 December 2006; Compliance Report on Croatia, 2 December 2004; Evaluation Report on Croatia, 17 May 2002

Czech Republic: Second Evaluation Round: Compliance Report on the Czech Republic, 13 June 2008; Evaluation Report on the Czech Republic, 12 May 2006; First

Evaluation Round: Addendum to the Compliance Report on the Czech Republic, 23 March 2007; Compliance Report on the Czech Republic, 18 March 2005; Evaluation Report on the Czech Republic, 28 March 2003

Denmark: Third Evaluation Round: Evaluation Report on Denmark on Incriminations (ETS 173 and 191, GPC 2) (Theme I) and Evaluation Report on Denmark on Transparency of Party Funding (Theme II), 2 July 2009; Second Evaluation Round: Addendum to the Compliance Report on Denmark, 15 May 2009; Compliance Report on Denmark, 23 March 2007; Evaluation Report on Denmark, 18 March 2005; First Evaluation Round: Addendum to the Compliance Report on Denmark, 13 October 2006; Compliance Report on Denmark, 30 September 2004; Evaluation Report on Denmark, 12 July 2002

Estonia: Third Evaluation Round: Evaluation Report on Estonia on Incriminations (ETS 173 and 191, GPC 2) (Theme I) and Evaluation Report on Estonia on Transparency of Party Funding (Theme II), 4 April 2008; Second Evaluation Round: Addendum to the Compliance Report on Estonia, 5 December 2008; Compliance Report on Estonia, 13 October 2006; Evaluation Report on Estonia, 2 July 2004; First Evaluation Round: Addendum to the Compliance Report on Estonia, 14 October 2005; Compliance Report on Estonia, 11 July 2003; Evaluation Report on Estonia, 14 September 2001

Finland: Third Evaluation Round: Evaluation Report on Finland on Incriminations (ETS 173 and 191, GPC 2) (Theme I) and Evaluation Report on Finland on Transparency of Party Funding (Theme II), 7 December 2007; Second Evaluation Round: Addendum to the Compliance Report on Finland, 13 June 2008; Compliance Report on Finland, 23 June 2006; Evaluation Report on Finland, 2 July 2004; First Evaluation Round: Addendum to the Compliance Report on Finland, 20 May 2005; Compliance Report on Finland, 11 July 2003; Evaluation Report on Finland, 15 June 2001

France: Third Evaluation Round: Evaluation Report on France on Incriminations (ETS 173 and 191, GPC 2) (Theme I) and Evaluation Report on France on Transparency of Party Funding (Theme II), 19 February 2009; Second Evaluation Round: Addendum to the Compliance Report on France, 15 May 2009; Compliance Report on France, 23 March 2007; Evaluation Report on France, 2 December 2004; First Evaluation Round: Addendum to the Compliance Report on France, 23 June 2006; Compliance Report on France, 17 October 2003; Evaluation Report on France, 14 September 2001

Germany: Third Evaluation Round: Evaluation Report on Germany on Incriminations (ETS 173 and 191, GPC 2) (Theme I) and Evaluation Report on Germany on Transparency of Party Funding (Theme II), 4 December 2009; Second Evaluation Round: Addendum to the Compliance Report on Germany, 3 July 2009; Compliance Report on Germany, 1 June 2007; Evaluation Report on Germany, 1 July 2005; First Evaluation Round: Addendum to the Compliance Report on Germany, 23 June 2006; Compliance Report on Germany, 14 May 2004; Evaluation Report on Germany, 8 March 2002

Greece: Second Evaluation Round: Compliance Report on Greece, 15 February 2008; Evaluation Report on Greece, 9 December 2005; First Evaluation Round:

Addendum to the Compliance Report on Greece, 7 December 2007; Compliance Report on Greece, 2 December 2004; Evaluation Report on Greece, 17 May 2002

Hungary: Second Evaluation Round: Compliance Report on Hungary, 4 April 2008; Evaluation Report on Hungary, 10 March 2006; First Evaluation Round: Addendum to the Compliance Report on Hungary, 23 March 2007; Compliance Report on Hungary, 18 March 2005; Evaluation Report on Hungary, 28 March 2003

Iceland: Third Evaluation Round: Evaluation Report on Iceland on Incriminations (ETS 173 and 191, GPC 2) (Theme I) and Evaluation Report on Iceland on Transparency of Party Funding (Theme II), 4 April 2008; Second Evaluation Round: Addendum to the Compliance Report on Iceland, 19 February 2009; Compliance Report on Iceland, 13 October 2006; Evaluation Report on Iceland, 2 July 2004; First Evaluation Round: Addendum to the Compliance Report on Iceland, 9 December 2005; Compliance Report on Iceland, 17 October 2003; Evaluation Report on Iceland, 14 September 2001

Ireland: Third Evaluation Round: Evaluation Report on Ireland on Incriminations (ETS 173 and 191, GPC 2) (Theme I) and Evaluation Report on Ireland on Transparency of Party Funding (Theme II), 4 December 2009; Second Evaluation Round: Compliance Report on Ireland, 15 February 2008; Evaluation Report on Ireland, 9 December 2005; First Evaluation Round: Addendum to the Compliance Report on Ireland, 14 October 2005; Compliance Report on Ireland, 12 December 2003; Evaluation Report on Ireland, 20 December 2001

Italy: Joint First and Second Evaluation Round: Evaluation Report on Italy, 3 July 2009;

Latvia: Third Evaluation Round: Evaluation Report on Latvia on Incriminations (ETS 173 and 191, GPC 2) (Theme I) and Evaluation Report on Latvia on Transparency of Party Funding (Theme II), 10 October 2008; Second Evaluation Round: Addendum to the Compliance Report on Latvia, 19 February 2009; Compliance Report on Latvia, 13 October 2006; Evaluation Report on Latvia, 2 July 2004; First Evaluation Round: Addendum to the Compliance Report on Latvia, 13 October 2006; Compliance Report on Latvia, 30 September 2004; Evaluation Report on Latvia, 17 May 2002

Lithuania: Third Evaluation Round: Evaluation Report on Lithuania on Incriminations (ETS 173 and 191, GPC 2) (Theme I) and Evaluation Report on Lithuania on Transparency of Party Funding (Theme II), 2 July 2009; Second Evaluation Round: Addendum to the Compliance Report on Lithuania, 3 July 2009; Compliance Report on Lithuania, 1 June 2007; Evaluation Report on Lithuania, 20 May 2005; First Evaluation Round: Addendum to the Compliance Report on Lithuania, 23 March 2007; Compliance Report on Lithuania, 2 July 2004; Evaluation Report on Lithuania, 8 March 2002

Luxembourg: Third Evaluation Round: Evaluation Report on Luxembourg on Incriminations (ETS 173 and 191, GPC 2) (Theme I) and Evaluation Report on Luxembourg on Transparency of Party Funding (Theme II), 13 June 2008; Second Evaluation Round: Addendum to the Compliance Report on Luxembourg, 13 June 2008; Compliance Report on Luxembourg, 12 May 2006; Evaluation Report on Luxembourg, 14 May 2004; First Evaluation Round: Addendum to the Compliance

Report on Luxembourg, 1 July 2005; Compliance Report on Luxembourg, 11 July 2003; Evaluation Report on Luxembourg, 15 June 2001

Malta: Third Evaluation Round: Evaluation Report on Malta on Incriminations (ETS 173 and 191, GPC 2) (Theme I) and Evaluation Report on Malta on Transparency of Party Funding (Theme II), 8 October 2009; Second Evaluation Round: Addendum to the Compliance Report on Malta, 3 July 2009; Compliance Report on Malta, 1 June 2007; Evaluation Report on Malta, 1 July 2005; First Evaluation Round: Addendum to the Compliance Report on Malta, 19 October 2007; Compliance Report on Malta, 20 May 2005; Evaluation Report on Malta, 15 June 2001

Netherlands: Third Evaluation Round: Evaluation Report on the Netherlands on Incriminations (ETS 173 and 191, GPC 2) (Theme I) and Evaluation Report on the Netherlands on Transparency of Party Funding (Theme II), 13 June 2008; Second Evaluation Round: Addendum to the Compliance Report on the Netherlands, 8 October 2009; Compliance Report on the Netherlands, 19 October 2007; Evaluation Report on the Netherlands, 14 October 2005; First Evaluation Round: Addendum to the Compliance Report on the Netherlands, 23 March 2007; Compliance Report on the Netherlands, 18 March 2005; Evaluation Report on the Netherlands, 28 March 2003

Norway: Third Evaluation Round: Evaluation Report on Norway on Incriminations (ETS 173 and 191, GPC 2) (Theme I) and Evaluation Report on Norway on Transparency of Party Funding (Theme II), 19 February 2009; Second Evaluation Round: Compliance Report on Norway, 13 October 2006; Evaluation Report on Norway, 30 September 2004; First Evaluation Round: Addendum to the Compliance Report on Norway, 13 October 2006; Compliance Report on Norway, 30 September 2004; Evaluation Report on Norway, 12 July 2002

Poland: Third Evaluation Round: Evaluation Report on Poland on Incriminations (ETS 173 and 191, GPC 2) (Theme I) and Evaluation Report on Poland on Transparency of Party Funding (Theme II), 5 December 2008; Second Evaluation Round: Addendum to the Compliance Report on Poland, 10 October 2008; Compliance Report on Poland, 23 June 2006; Evaluation Report on Poland, 14 May 2004; First Evaluation Round: Addendum to the Compliance Report on Poland, 13 October 2006; Compliance Report on Poland, 2 July 2004; Evaluation Report on Poland, 8 March 2002

Romania: Second Evaluation Round: Addendum to the Compliance Report on Romania, 4 December 2009; Compliance Report on Romania, 7 December 2007; Evaluation Report on Romania, 14 October 2005; First Evaluation Round: Addendum to the Compliance Report on Romania, 13 October 2006; Compliance Report on Romania, 2 July 2004; Evaluation Report on Romania, 8 March 2002

Russian Federation: Joint First and Second Evaluation Round: Evaluation Report on the Russian Federation, 5 December 2008

Slovakia: Third Evaluation Round: Evaluation Report on Slovakia on Incriminations (ETS 173 and 191, GPC 2) (Theme I) and Evaluation Report on Slovakia on Transparency of Party Funding (Theme II), 15 February 2008; Second Evaluation Round: Addendum to the Compliance Report on Slovakia, 13 June 2008; Compliance Report on Slovakia, 12 May 2006; Evaluation Report on Slovakia, 25 March 2004; First Evaluation Round: Addendum to the Compliance Report on

Slovakia, 13 October 2005; Compliance Report on Slovakia, 28 March 2003; Evaluation Report on Slovakia, 15 December 2000

Slovenia: Third Evaluation Round: Evaluation Report on Slovenia on Incriminations (ETS 173 and 191, GPC 2) (Theme I) and Evaluation Report on Slovenia on Transparency of Party Funding (Theme II), 7 December 2007; Second Evaluation Round: Addendum to the Compliance Report on Slovenia, 13 June 2008; Compliance Report on Slovenia, 12 May 2006; Evaluation Report on Slovenia, 12 December 2003; First Evaluation Round: Addendum to the Compliance Report on Slovenia, 9 December 2005; Compliance Report on Slovenia, 28 March 2003; Evaluation Report on Slovenia, 15 December 2000

Spain: Third Evaluation Round: Evaluation Report on Spain on Incriminations (ETS 173 and 191, GPC 2) (Theme I) and Evaluation Report on Spain on Transparency of Party Funding (Theme II), 15 May 2009; Second Evaluation Round: Addendum to the Compliance Report on Spain, 8 October 2009; Compliance Report on Spain, 19 October 2007; Evaluation Report on Spain, 20 May 2005; First Evaluation Round: Addendum to the Compliance Report on Spain, 1 July 2005; Compliance Report on Spain, 17 October 2003; Evaluation Report on Spain, 15 June 2001

Sweden: Third Evaluation Round: Evaluation Report on Sweden on Incriminations (ETS 173 and 191, GPC 2) (Theme I) and Evaluation Report on Sweden on Transparency of Party Funding (Theme II), 19 February 2009; Second Evaluation Round: Addendum to the Compliance Report on Sweden, 3 July 2009; Compliance Report on Sweden, 1 June 2007; Evaluation Report on Sweden, 18 March 2005; First Evaluation Round: Addendum to the Compliance Report on Sweden, 12 May 2006; Compliance Report on Sweden, 25 March 2004; Evaluation Report on Sweden, 15 June 2001

Switzerland: Joint First and Second Evaluation Round: Evaluation Report on Switzerland, 4 April 2008

Turkey: Joint First and Third Evaluation Round: Evaluation Report on Turkey on Incriminations (ETS 173 and 191, GPC 2) (Theme I) and Evaluation Report on Turkey on Transparency of Party Funding (Theme II), 26 March 2010; Second Evaluation Round: Compliance Report on Turkey, 4 April 2008; Evaluation Report on Turkey, 10 March 2006

Ukraine: Joint First and Second Evaluation Round: Compliance Report on Ukraine, 15 May 2009; Evaluation Report on Ukraine, 23 March 2007

United Kingdom: Third Evaluation Round: Evaluation Report on the United Kingdom on Incriminations (ETS 173 and 191, GPC 2) (Theme I) and Evaluation Report on the United Kingdom on Transparency of Party Funding (Theme II), 15 February 2008; Second Evaluation Round: Addendum to the Compliance Report on the United Kingdom, 19 February 2009; Compliance Report on the United Kingdom, 13 October 2006; Evaluation Report on the United Kingdom, 30 September 2004; First Evaluation Round: Addendum to the Compliance Report on the United Kingdom, 1 July 2005; Compliance Report on the United Kingdom, 11 July 2003; Evaluation Report on the United Kingdom, 14 September 2001

United States: Second Evaluation Round: Compliance Report on the United States, 5 December 2008; Evaluation Report on the United States, 13 October 2006; First Evaluation Round: Addendum to the Compliance Report on the United States,

13 June 2008; Compliance Report on the United States, 12 May 2006; Evaluation Report on the United States, 25 March 2004

B) Other Organs of the Council of Europe

Recommendation Rec(2005)9 of the Committee of Ministers to member states on the protection of witnesses and collaborators of justice, 20 April 2005

Recommendation Rec(2003)4 of the Committee of Ministers to Member States on Common Rules against Corruption in the Funding of Political Parties and Electoral Campaigns, adopted by the Committee of Ministers on 8 April 2003 at the 835th Meeting of the Ministers' Deputies. See also, Recommendation 1516 (2001) on the Financing of Political Parties, adopted on 22 May 2001 by the Council of Europe's Parliamentary Assembly.

Recommendation No. R (2003) 4 of the Committee of Ministers to Member States on Common Rules against Corruption in the Funding of Political Parties and Electoral Campaigns and Annex, adopted by the Committee of Ministers at the 835th meeting of the Ministers' Deputies, 8 April 2003

Recommendation 2002(2) on access to official documents, adopted by the Committee of Ministers of the Council of Europe on 21 February 2002

Recommendation No. R (2000) 10 of the Committee of Ministers to Member states on codes of conduct for public officials and Model code of conduct for public officials (Appendix to the Recommendation), adopted by the Committee of Ministers at its 106th Session, 11 May 2000

Resolution 1214 (2000): Role of parliaments in fighting corruption, adopted by the Parliamentary Assembly at its 13th Sitting, 5 April 2000

Council of Europe Recommendation No. R (2000) 10 on Codes of Conduct for Public Officials, Annex

Resolution (99) 5 establishing the "Group of States against Corruption - GRECO" and Statute of GRECO (Appendix to the Resolution), adopted at the 668th meeting of the Ministers' Deputies, 1st May 1999

Resolution (98) 7 authorizing the partial and enlarged Agreement establishing the "Group of States against Corruption - GRECO", adopted by the Committee of Ministers at its 102nd Session, 5 May 1998

Resolution (97) 24 on the twenty Guiding Principles for the fight against corruption, Adopted by the Committee of Ministers at its 101st session, 6 November 1997

Programme of action against corruption, adopted by the Committee of Ministers at its 578th Session, 18–21 November 1996

Conference of European Ministers of Justice, and Council of Europe: Administrative, Civil, and Penal Aspects, Including the Role of the Judiciary, of the Fight Against Corruption: Proceedings, 19th Conference of European Ministers of Justice, Valletta, Malta, 14–15 June 1994

3. European Union

European Parliament, Resolution on Aid Effectiveness and Corruption in Developing Countries (2005/2141(INI)), Official Journal C 293 E, 2 December 2006

Directive 2005/60/EC adopted by the European Parliament and the Council of the European Union, 26 October 2005

Decision No 26/2004 of the Committee of the Regions of 10 February 2004 relating to the conditions and procedures for internal investigations in relation to the prevention of fraud, corruption and any illegal activity detrimental to the Communities' interests, took effect 1 March 2004, Official Journal L 102, 7 April 2004, 84–86

Council Framework Decision 2003/568/JHA of 22 July 2003 on combating corruption in the private sector, entered into force 31 July 2003, Official Journal L 192, 31 July 2003, 54–56

Communication from the Commission to the Council, the European Parliament and the European Economic and Social Committee: On a Comprehensive EU Policy against Corruption, 28 May 2003, COM(2003) 317 final

Council Decision of 28 February 2002 setting up Eurojust with a view to reinforcing the fight against serious crime, (2002/187/JHA), entered into force 6 March 2002, Official Journal L 063, 6 March 2002, 1–13

EU Council Regulation (EC) No 44/2001 of 22 December 2000 on Jurisdiction and the Recognition and Enforcement of Judgments in Civil and Commercial Matters, Official Journal of the European Communities L 12/1, 16 January 2001

Guide to the obligations of officials and other servants of the European Parliament (Code of conduct) Official Journal C 097, 5 April 2000, 1–12

Regulation (EC) No 1073/1999 of the European Parliament and of the Council of 25 May 1999 concerning investigations conducted by the European Anti-Fraud Office (OLAF), entered into force 1 June 1999, Official Journal L 136, 31 May 1999, 1–7

Council Regulation (Euratom) No 1074/1999 of 25 May 1999 concerning investigations conducted by the European Anti-Fraud Office (OCAF), entered into force 1 June 1999, Official Journal L 136, 31 May 1999, 8–14

Interinstitutional Agreement of 25 May 1999 between the European Parliament, the Council of the European Union and the Commission of the European Communities concerning internal investigations by the European Anti-fraud Office (OLAF), took effect 1 June 1999, Official Journal L 136, 31 May 1999, 15–19

1999/352/EC, ECSC, Euratom: Commission Decision of 28 April 1999 establishing the European Anti-fraud Office (OLAF) (notified under document number SEC(1999) 802), took effect 1 June 1999, Official Journal L 136, 31 May 1999, 20–22

1999/235/JHA: Joint Position of 29 March 1999 defined by the Council on the basis of Article K.3 of the Treaty on European Union, on the proposed United Nations convention against organised crime, Official Journal L 087, 31 March 1999, 1–2

98/742/JHA: Joint Action of 22 December 1998 adopted by the Council on the basis of Article K.3 of the Treaty on European Union, on corruption in the private sector, Official Journal L 358, 31 December 1998, 2–4

Explanatory Report on the Convention on the fight against corruption involving official of the European Communities or officials of Member States of the European Union (Text approved by the Council on 3 December 1998), Official Journal C 391, 15 December 1998, 1–12

Resolution on the communication from the Commission to the Council and the European Parliament on a Union policy against corruption (COM(97)0192 C4–0273/97), Official Journal C 328, 26 October 1998, 46

97/783/JHA: Second Joint Position of 13 November 1997 defined by the Council on the basis of Article K.3 of the Treaty on European Union on negotiations held in the Council of Europe and the OECD on the fight against corruption, Official Journal L 320, 21 November 1997, 1–2

97/661/JHA: Common Position of 6 October 1997 defined by the Council on the basis of Article K.3 of the Treaty on European Union on negotiations in the Council of Europe and the OECD relating to corruption, Official Journal L 279, 13 October 1997, 1–2

Council Resolution of 20 December 1996 on individuals who cooperate with the judicial process in the fight against international organized crime, Official Journal C 010, 11 January 1997, 1–2

Resolution of 15 December 1995 on Combating Corruption in Europe, Official Journal C 017, 22 January 1996

Council Regulation (EC, Euratom) No 2988/95 of 18 December 1995 on the protection of the European Communities financial interests, entered into force 26 December 1995, Official Journal L 312, 23 December 1995, 1–4

Resolution of the Council of 23 November 1995 on the protection of witnesses in the fight against international organized crime, Official Journal C 327, 7 December 1995, 5

Resolution of the Council of the European Union of 23 of November of 1995 on the Protection of Witnesses in the Fight against Organized Crime

4. Organization of American States

a) Resolutions of the General Assembly

Follow-up on the Inter-American Convention against Corruption and on the Inter-American Program for Cooperation in the Fight against Corruption, adopted at the fourth plenary session, held on June 4, 2009, AG/RES. 2516 (XXXIX-O/09)

Organisation of American States, Inter-American Judicial Committee, Principles on the Right of Access to Information, CJI/RES. 147 (LXXIII-O/08), 7 August 2008

Follow-up on the Inter-American Convention against Corruption and on the Inter-American Program for Cooperation in the Fight against Corruption, adopted at the fourth plenary session, held on June 3, 2008 AG/RES. 2410 (XXXVIII-O/08)

Follow-up on the Inter-American Convention against Corruption and the Inter-American Program for Cooperation in the Fight against Corruption, adopted at the fourth plenary session, held on June 5, 2007 AG/RES. 2275 (XXXVII-O/07)

Follow-up on the Inter-American Convention against Corruption and Its Program for Cooperation, adopted at the fourth plenary session, held on June 6, 2006 AG/RES. 2219 (XXXVI-O/06)

Cooperation among the Member States in the Fight against Corruption and Impunity, adopted at the fourth plenary session, held on June 6, 2006AG/RES. 2222 (XXXVI-O/06)

The Role of the Legislative Branch in Combating Corruption and Impunity in the Hemisphere, adopted at the fourth plenary session, held on June 7, 2005, AG/RES. 2064 (XXXV-O/05)

2006: Inter-American Year of the Fight against Corruption, adopted at the fourth plenary session, held on June 7, 2005, AG/RES. 2071 (XXXV-O/05)
Follow-up on the Inter-American Convention against Corruption and Its Program for Cooperation, adopted at the fourth plenary session, held on June 7, 2005, AG/RES. 2076 (XXXV-O/05)
Follow-up to the Inter-American Convention against Corruption and its Program for Cooperation, adopted at the fourth plenary session, 8 June 2004, AG/RES. 2034 (XXXIV-O/04)
Follow-up to the Inter-American Convention against Corruption and its Program for Cooperation, adopted at the fourth plenary session, 10 June 2003, AG/RES. 1943 (XXXIII-O/03)
Follow-up to the Inter-American Convention against Corruption and its Program for Cooperation, adopted at the fourth plenary session, 4 June 2002, AG/RES. 1870 (XXXII-O/02)
Inter-American Democratic Charter, Resolution AG/RES. 1 (XXVIII-E/01), adopted at the twenty-eighth special session of the General Assembly, 11 September 2001
Mechanism for Follow-up on Implementation of the Inter-American Convention against Corruption, adopted at the third plenary session, 5 June 2001, AG/RES. 1784 (XXXI-O/01)
Enhancement of Probity in the Hemisphere and Follow-up on the Inter-American Program for Cooperation in the Fight Against Corruption, adopted at the third plenary session, 5 June 2001, AG/RES. 1785 (XXXI-O/01)
Enhancement of Probity in the Hemisphere and Follow-up on the Inter-American Program for Cooperation in the Fight Against Corruption, adopted at the first plenary session, 5 June 2000, AG/RES. 1723 (XXX-O/00)
Enhancement of Probity in the Hemisphere and Follow-Up on the Inter-American Program for Cooperation in the Fight Against Corruption, adopted at the first plenary session, 7 June 1999, AG/RES. 1649 (XXIX-0/99)
Enhancement of Probity in the Hemisphere and Follow-Up on the Inter-American Program for Cooperation in the Fight Against Corruption, adopted at the third plenary session, 2 June 1998, AG/RES. 1552 (XXVIII-0/98)
Inter-American Program for Cooperation in the Fight Against Corruption, adopted at the seventh plenary session, 5 June 1997, AG/RES. 1477 (XXVII-0/97)
Probity and Public Ethics, adopted at the eighth plenary session, 7 June 1996, AG/RES. 1397 (XXVI-0/96)
Inter-American Convention Against Corruption, adopted at the eighth plenary session, 7 June 1996, AG/RES.1398 (XXVI-0/96)
Annual Report of the Inter-American Juridical Committee, adopted at the eighth plenary session, 7 June 1996, AG/RES.1395 (XXVI-0/96)
Probity and Public Ethics, adopted at the ninth plenary session, 9 June 1995, AG/RES.1346 (XXV-0/95)
Annual Report of the Inter-American Juridical Committee, adopted at the ninth plenary session, 9 June 1995, AG/RES.1328 (XXV-0/95)
Probity and Public Ethics, adopted at the tenth plenary session, 10 June 1994, AG/RES. 1294 (XXIV-0/94)
Corrupt International Trade Practices, adopted at the seventh plenary session, 22 May 1992, AG/ RES.1159 (XXII-0/92)

b) Other Documents of the Organization of American States

Rules of Procedure and Other Provisions of the Committee of Experts of the MESICIC, adopted by the Committee of Experts of the MESICIC at its first meeting, 30 September 2005, SG/MESICIC/doc.9/04 rev.2

Declaration of Nuevo Leon, Special Summit of the Americas, Monterrey, Mexico, 13 January 2004

Declaration of Quito on Social Development and Democracy, and the Impact of Corruption, adopted at the fourth plenary session, 8 June 2004, AG/DEC. 36 (XXXIV-O/04)

Rules of Procedure of the Conference of the States Parties to the Mechanism for Follow-Up on Implementation of the Inter-American Convention against Corruption, 2 April 2004, SG/MESICIC/doc.58/04 rev.7

Conclusions and Recommendations on Concrete Measures to Strengthen MESICIC, 2 April 2004, SG/MESICIC/doc.103/04 rev.6

Support for Ecuador in its Fight against Corruption, Declaration adopted at the fourth plenary session, 10 June 2003, AG/DEC. 35 (XXXIII-O/03)

Support for Peru in its Fight against Corruption and Impunity, Declaration adopted at the fourth plenary session, 10 June 2003, AG/DEC. 33 (XXXIII-O/03)

Report of Buenos Aires on the Mechanism for Follow-Up on Implementation of the Inter-American Convention against Corruption, Conference of the States Parties, Buenos Aires, Argentina, 4 May 2001

Declaration of Principles and Plan of Action, Third Summit of the Americas, Quebec, Canada, 20–22 April 2001

Recommendation of the Permanent Council to States Parties on the Mechanism for Follow-Up of Implementation of the Inter-American Convention against Corruption, 18 January 2001, CP/RES. 783 (1260/01)

Declaration of Santiago and Plan of Action, Second Summit of the Americas, Santiago, Chile, 18–19 April 1998

Declaration of Principles and Plan of Action, First Summit of the Americas, Miami, United States of America, 9–11 December 1994

5. Organisation for Economic Co-operation and Development (OECD)

a) Council

Recommendation of the Council on Principles for Transparency and Integrity in Lobbying, C(2010)16, adopted by the Council on 18 February 2010

Recommendation of the Council for Further Combating Bribery of Foreign Public Officials in International Business Transactions, adopted by the Council on 26 November 2009

Recommendation of the Council on Tax Measures for Further Combating Bribery of Foreign Public Officials in International Business Transactions, Annex I, C(2009)64, adopted by the Council on 25 May 2009

Recommendation of the Council on Enhancing Integrity in Public Procurement, C(2008)105, adopted by the Council in October 2008

Recommendation of the Council on OECD Guidelines for Managing Conflict of Interest in the Public Service, C(2003)107, adopted by the Council on 28 May 2003

Recommendation of the Council on Improving Ethical Conduct in the Public Service Including Principles for Managing Ethics in the Public Service, 1998-C(98)70/FINAL, adopted by the Council on 23 April 1998

Revised Recommendation of the Council on Combating Bribery in International Business Transactions, C(97)123/FINAL, adopted by the Council on 23 May 1997

Agreed Common Elements of Criminal Legislation and Related Action, Annex to the Revised Recommendation of the Council on Combating Bribery in International Business Transactions, C(97)123/FINAL, adopted by the Council on 23 May 1997

Recommendation of the Council on the Tax Deductibility of Bribes to Foreign Public Officials, C(96)27/FINAL, adopted by the Council on 11 April 1996

Recommendation of the Council on Bribery in International Business Transactions, C(94)75/FINAL, adopted by the Council on 27 May 1994

b) Directorate for Financial and Enterprise Affairs (DAF)

i) Working Group on Bribery in International Business Transactions

Argentina: Phase 2 Report on the Application of the Convention on Combating Bribery of Foreign Public Officials in International Business Transactions and the 1997 Recommendation on Combating Bribery in International Business Transactions, June 2008; Phase 1 Review of the Implementation of the Convention and 1997 Recommendation, April 2001

Australia: Phase 2: Follow-Up Report on the Implementation of the Phase 2 Recommendations on the Application of the Convention and the 1997 Recommendation on Combating Bribery in International Business Transactions, 29 August 2008; Phase 2: Report on the Application of the Convention on Combating Bribery of Foreign Public Officials in International Business Transactions and the 1997 Recommendation on Combating Bribery in International Business Transactions, Implementation of the OECD Anti-Bribery Convention, 4 January 2006; Phase 1: Review of the Implementation of the Convention and 1997 Recommendation, December 1999

Belgium: Phase 2: Follow-Up Report on the Implementation of the Phase 2 Recommendations on the Application of the Convention and the 1997 Recommendation on Combating Bribery in International Business Transactions, 10 January 2008; Phase 2: Report on the Application of the Convention on Combating Bribery of Foreign Public Officials in International Business Transactions and the 1997 Recommendation on Combating Bribery in International Business Transactions, Implementation of the OECD Anti-Bribery Convention, 21 July 2005; Phase 1 Review of the Implementation of the Convention and 1997 Recommendation, October 1999

Brazil: Phase 2: Report on the Application of the Convention on Combating Bribery of Foreign Public Officials in International Business Transactions and the 1997 Recommendation on Combating Bribery in International Business Transactions, Implementation of the OECD Anti-Bribery Convention, 7 December 2007; Phase 1

Review of the Implementation of the Convention and 1997 Recommendation, 31 August 2004

Bulgaria: Phase 2: Follow-Up Report on the Implementation of the Phase 2 Recommendations on the Application of the Convention and the 1997 Recommendation on Combating Bribery in International Business Transactions, 26 January 2006; Phase 2: Report on the Application of the Convention on Combating Bribery of Foreign Public Officials in International Business Transactions and the 1997 Recommendation on Combating Bribery in International Business Transactions, Implementation of the OECD Anti-Bribery Convention, 6 June 2003; Phase 1 Review of the Implementation of the Convention and 1997 Recommendation, July 1999

Canada: Phase 2: Follow-Up Report on the Implementation of the Phase 2 Recommendations on the Application of the Convention and the 1997 Recommendation on Combating Bribery in International Business Transactions, 21 June 2006; Phase 2: Report on the Application of the Convention on Combating Bribery of Foreign Public Officials in International Business Transactions and the 1997 Recommendation on Combating Bribery in International Business Transactions, Implementation of the OECD Anti-Bribery Convention, 25 March 2004; Phase 1 Review of the Implementation of the Convention and 1997 Recommendation, July 1999

Chile: Phase 2: Follow-Up Report on the Implementation of the Phase 2 Recommendations on the Application of the Convention and the 1997 Recommendation on Combating Bribery in International Business Transactions, October 2009; Phase 2: Report on the Application of the Convention on Combating Bribery of Foreign Public Officials in International Business Transactions and the 1997 Recommendation on Combating Bribery in International Business Transactions, Implementation of the OECD Anti-Bribery Convention, 11 October 2007; Phase 1*ter*: Review of Implementation of the Convention and 1997 Recommendation, December 1009; Phase 1*bis*: Review of Implementation of the Convention and 1997 Recommendation, October 2009; Phase 1 Review of the Implementation of the Convention and 1997 Recommendation, 24 August 2004

Czech Republic: Phase 2: Follow-Up Report on the Implementation of the Phase 2 Recommendations on the Application of the Convention and the 1997 Recommendation on Combating Bribery in International Business Transactions, 13 February 2009; Phase 2: Report on the Application of the Convention on Combating Bribery of Foreign Public Officials in International Business Transactions and the 1997 Recommendation on Combating Bribery in International Business Transactions, Implementation of the OECD Anti-Bribery Convention, 27 October 2006; Phase 1 Review of the Implementation of the Convention and 1997 Recommendation, March 2000

Denmark: Phase 2: Follow-Up Report on the Implementation of the Phase 2 Recommendations on the Application of the Convention and the 1997 Recommendation on Combating Bribery in International Business Transactions, 29 July 2008; Phase 2: Report on the Application of the Convention on Combating Bribery of Foreign Public Officials in International Business Transactions and the 1997 Recommendation on Combating Bribery in International Business

Transactions, Implementation of the OECD Anti-Bribery Convention, 15 June 2006; Phase 1 Review of the Implementation of the Convention and 1997 Recommendation, December 2000

Estonia: Phase 2: Report on the Application of the Convention on Combating Bribery of Foreign Public Officials in International Business Transactions and the 1997 Recommendation on Combating Bribery in International Business Transactions, Implementation of the OECD Anti-Bribery Convention, 20 June 2008; Phase 1 Review of the Implementation of the Convention and 1997 Recommendation, March 2006

Finland: Phase 2: Follow-Up Report on the Implementation of the Phase 2 Recommendations on the Application of the Convention and the 1997 Recommendation on Combating Bribery in International Business Transactions, 23 February 2006; Phase 2: Report on the Application of the Convention on Combating Bribery of Foreign Public Officials in International Business Transactions and the 1997 Recommendation on Combating Bribery in International Business Transactions, Implementation of the OECD Anti-Bribery Convention, May 2002; Phase 1 Review of the Implementation of the Convention and 1997 Recommendation, July 1999

France: Phase 2: Follow-Up Report on the Implementation of the Phase 2 Recommendations on the Application of the Convention and the 1997 Recommendation on Combating Bribery in International Business Transactions, 30 March 2006; Phase 2: Report on the Application of the Convention on Combating Bribery of Foreign Public Officials in International Business Transactions and the 1997 Recommendation on Combating Bribery in International Business Transactions, 22 January 2004; Phase 1 Review of the Implementation of the Convention and 1997 Recommendation, December 2000

Germany: Phase 2: Follow-Up Report on the Implementation of the Phase 2 Recommendations on the Application of the Convention and the 1997 Recommendation on Combating Bribery in International Business Transactions, 8 December 2005; Phase 2: Report on the Application of the Convention on Combating Bribery of Foreign Public Officials in International Business Transactions and the 1997 Recommendation on Combating Bribery in International Business Transactions, 4 June 2003; Phase 1 Review of the Implementation of the Convention and 1997 Recommendation, April 1999

Greece: Phase 2: Follow-Up Report on the Implementation of the Phase 2 Recommendations on the Application of the Convention and the 1997 Recommendation on Combating Bribery in International Business Transactions, 12 September 2007; Phase 2: Report on the Application of the Convention on Combating Bribery of Foreign Public Officials in International Business Transactions and the 1997 Recommendation on Combating Bribery in International Business Transactions, 26 April 2005; Phase 1 Review of the Implementation of the Convention and 1997 Recommendation, July 1999

Hungary: Phase 2: Follow-Up Report on the Implementation of the Phase 2 Recommendations on the Application of the Convention and the 1997 Recommendation on Combating Bribery in International Business Transactions, 7 September 2007; Phase 2: Report on the Application of the Convention on

Combating Bribery of Foreign Public Officials in International Business Transactions and the 1997 Recommendation on Combating Bribery in International Business Transactions, Implementation of the OECD Anti-Bribery Convention, 6 May 2005; Phase 1*bis*: Review of Implementation of the Convention and 1997 Recommendation, February 2004; Phase 1 Review of the Implementation of the Convention and 1997 Recommendation, March 2003

Iceland: Phase 2: Follow-Up Report on the Implementation of the Phase 2 Recommendations on the Application of the Convention and the 1997 Recommendation on Combating Bribery in International Business Transactions, 11 May 2006; Phase 2: Report on the Application of the Convention on Combating Bribery of Foreign Public Officials in International Business Transactions and the 1997 Recommendation on Combating Bribery in International Business Transactions, 24 February 2003; Phase 1 Review of the Implementation of the Convention and 1997 Recommendation, October 1999

Ireland: Phase 2 and 2*bis*: Follow-Up Report on the Implementation of the Phase 2 and 2*bis* Recommendations on the Application of the Convention and the 1997 Recommendation on Combating Bribery in International Business Transactions, 19 March 2010; Phase 2*bis*: Report on the Application of the Convention on Combating Bribery of Foreign Public Officials in International Business Transactions and the 1997 Recommendation on Combating Bribery in International Business Transactions, 11 December 2008; Phase 2: Report on the Application of the Convention on Combating Bribery of Foreign Public Officials in International Business Transactions and the 1997 Recommendation on Combating Bribery in International Business Transactions, Implementation of the OECD Anti-Bribery Convention, 14 March 2007; Phase 1 Review of the Implementation of the Convention and 1997 Recommendation, June 2002

Israel: Phase 2: Report on the Application of the Convention on Combating Bribery of Foreign Public Officials in International Business Transactions and the 1997 Recommendation on Combating Bribery in International Business Transactions, 11 December 2009; Phase 1 Review of the Implementation of the Convention and 1997 Recommendation, March 2009

Italy: Phase 2: Follow-Up Report on the Implementation of the Phase 2 Recommendations on the Application of the Convention and the 1997 Recommendation on Combating Bribery in International Business Transactions, 23 March 2007; Phase 2: Report on the Application of the Convention on Combating Bribery of Foreign Public Officials in International Business Transactions and the 1997 Recommendation on Combating Bribery in International Business Transactions, Implementation of the OECD Anti-Bribery Convention, 29 November 2004; Phase 1 Review of the Implementation of the Convention and 1997 Recommendation, April 2001

Japan: Phase 2: Follow-Up Report on the Implementation of the Phase 2 Recommendations on the Application of the Convention and the 1997 Recommendation on Combating Bribery in International Business Transactions, 10 October 2007; Phase 2*bis*: Report on the Application of the Convention on Combating Bribery of Foreign Public Officials in International Business Transactions and the 1997 Recommendation on Combating Bribery in

International Business Transactions, 15 June 2006; Phase 2: Report on the Application of the Convention on Combating Bribery of Foreign Public Officials in International Business Transactions and the 1997 Recommendation on Combating Bribery in International Business Transactions, Implementation of the OECD Anti-Bribery Convention, 7 March 2005; Phase 1 Review of the Implementation of the Convention and 1997 Recommendation, May 2002

Korea: Phase 2: Follow-Up Report on the Implementation of the Phase 2 Recommendations on the Application of the Convention and the 1997 Recommendation on Combating Bribery in International Business Transactions, 2 March 2007; Phase 2: Report on the Application of the Convention on Combating Bribery of Foreign Public Officials in International Business Transactions and the 1997 Recommendation on Combating Bribery in International Business Transactions, Implementation of the OECD Anti-Bribery Convention, 5 November 2004; Phase 1 Review of the Implementation of the Convention and 1997 Recommendation, July 1999

Luxembourg: Phase 2*bis*: Follow-Up Report on the Implementation of the Phase 2*bis* Recommendations on the Application of the Convention and the 1997 Recommendation on Combating Bribery in International Business Transactions, 1 October 2009; Phase 2*bis*: Report on the Application of the Convention on Combating Bribery of Foreign Public Officials in International Business Transactions and the 1997 Recommendation on Combating Bribery in International Business Transactions, 20 March 2008; Phase 2: Follow-Up Report on the Implementation of the Phase 2*bis* Recommendations on the Application of the Convention and the 1997 Recommendation on Combating Bribery in International Business Transactions, 2 August 2006; Phase 2: Report on the Application of the Convention on Combating Bribery of Foreign Public Officials in International Business Transactions and the 1997 Recommendation on Combating Bribery in International Business Transactions, Implementation of the OECD Anti-Bribery Convention, 28 May 2004; Phase 1 Review of the Implementation of the Convention and 1997 Recommendation, February 2001

Mexico: Phase 2: Follow-Up Report on the Implementation of the Phase 2 Recommendations on the Application of the Convention and the 1997 Recommendation on Combating Bribery in International Business Transactions, 4 April 2007; Phase 2: Report on the Application of the Convention on Combating Bribery of Foreign Public Officials in International Business Transactions and the 1997 Recommendation on Combating Bribery in International Business Transactions, Implementation of the OECD Anti-Bribery Convention, 2 September 2004; Phase 1 Review of the Implementation of the Convention and 1997 Recommendation, February 2000

Netherlands: Phase 2: Follow-Up Report on the Implementation of the Phase 2 Recommendations on the Application of the Convention and the 1997 Recommendation on Combating Bribery in International Business Transactions, 17 December 2008; Phase 2: Report on the Application of the Convention on Combating Bribery of Foreign Public Officials in International Business Transactions and the 1997 Recommendation on Combating Bribery in International Business Transactions, Implementation of the OECD Anti-Bribery

Convention, 15 June 2006; Phase 1 Review of the Implementation of the Convention and 1997 Recommendation, February 2001

Norway: Phase 2: Follow-Up Report on the Implementation of the Phase 2 Recommendations on the Application of the Convention and the 1997 Recommendation on Combating Bribery in International Business Transactions, 15 March 2007; Phase 2: Report on the Application of the Convention on Combating Bribery of Foreign Public Officials in International Business Transactions and the 1997 Recommendation on Combating Bribery in International Business Transactions, Implementation of the OECD Anti-Bribery Convention, 12 April 2004; Phase 1 Review of the Implementation of the Convention and 1997 Recommendation, April 1999

Poland: Phase 2: Follow-Up Report on the Implementation of the Phase 2 Recommendations on the Application of the Convention and the 1997 Recommendation on Combating Bribery in International Business Transactions, 1 October 2009; Phase 2: Report on the Application of the Convention on Combating Bribery of Foreign Public Officials in International Business Transactions and the 1997 Recommendation on Combating Bribery in International Business Transactions, Implementation of the OECD Anti-Bribery Convention, 18 January 2007; Phase 1 Review of the Implementation of the Convention and 1997 Recommendation, February 2001

Portugal: Phase 2: Follow-Up Report on the Implementation of the Phase 2 Recommendations on the Application of the Convention and the 1997 Recommendation on Combating Bribery in International Business Transactions, 6 October 2009; Phase 2: Follow-Up Report on the Implementation of the Phase 2 Recommendations on the Application of the Convention and the 1997 Recommendation on Combating Bribery in International Business Transactions, 1 October 2009; Phase 2: Report on the Application of the Convention on Combating Bribery of Foreign Public Officials in International Business Transactions and the 1997 Recommendation on Combating Bribery in International Business Transactions, Implementation of the OECD Anti-Bribery Convention, 14 March 2007; Phase 1 Review of the Implementation of the Convention and 1997 Recommendation, May 2002

Slovak Republic: Phase 2: Follow-Up Report on the Implementation of the Phase 2 Recommendations on the Application of the Convention and the 1997 Recommendation on Combating Bribery in International Business Transactions, 30 January 2008; Phase 2: Report on the Application of the Convention on Combating Bribery of Foreign Public Officials in International Business Transactions and the 1997 Recommendation on Combating Bribery in International Business Transactions, Implementation of the OECD Anti-Bribery Convention, 9 November 2005; Phase 1 Review of the Implementation of the Convention and 1997 Recommendation, February 2003

Slovenia: Phase 2: Follow-Up Report on the Implementation of the Phase 2 Recommendations on the Application of the Convention and the 1997 Recommendation on Combating Bribery in International Business Transactions, 6 October 2009; Phase 2: Report on the Application of the Convention on Combating Bribery of Foreign Public Officials in International Business

Transactions and the 1997 Recommendation on Combating Bribery in International Business Transactions, Implementation of the OECD Anti-Bribery Convention, 21 June 2007; Phase 1 Review of the Implementation of the Convention and 1997 Recommendation, March 2005

South Africa: Phase 1 Review of the Implementation of the Convention and 1997 Recommendation, June 2008

Spain: Phase 2: Follow-Up Report on the Implementation of the Phase 2 Recommendations on the Application of the Convention and the 1997 Recommendation on Combating Bribery in International Business Transactions, 6 October 2008; Phase 2: Report on the Application of the Convention on Combating Bribery of Foreign Public Officials in International Business Transactions and the 1997 Recommendation on Combating Bribery in International Business Transactions, Implementation of the OECD Anti-Bribery Convention, 24 March 2006; Phase 1 Review of the Implementation of the Convention and 1997 Recommendation, March 2000

Sweden: Phase 2: Follow-Up Report on the Implementation of the Phase 2 Recommendations on the Application of the Convention and the 1997 Recommendation on Combating Bribery in International Business Transactions, 9 October 2007; Phase 2: Report on the Application of the Convention on Combating Bribery of Foreign Public Officials in International Business Transactions and the 1997 Recommendation on Combating Bribery in International Business Transactions, Implementation of the OECD Anti-Bribery Convention, 21 September 2005; Phase 1 Review of the Implementation of the Convention and 1997 Recommendation, October 1999

Switzerland: Phase 2: Follow-Up Report on the Implementation of the Phase 2 Recommendations on the Application of the Convention and the 1997 Recommendation on Combating Bribery in International Business Transactions, 2 May 2007; Phase 2: Report on the Application of the Convention on Combating Bribery of Foreign Public Officials in International Business Transactions and the 1997 Recommendation on Combating Bribery in International Business Transactions, Implementation of the OECD Anti-Bribery Convention, 24 December 2004; Phase 1 Review of the Implementation of the Convention and 1997 Recommendation, February 2000

Turkey: Phase 2*bis*: Report on the Application of the Convention on Combating Bribery of Foreign Public Officials in International Business Transactions and the 1997 Recommendation on Combating Bribery in International Business Transactions, 18 June 2009; Phase 2: Report on the Application of the Convention on Combating Bribery of Foreign Public Officials in International Business Transactions and the 1997 Recommendation on Combating Bribery in International Business Transactions, Implementation of the OECD Anti-Bribery Convention, 7 December 2007; Phase 1 Review of the Implementation of the Convention and 1997 Recommendation, November 2004

United Kingdom: Phase 2*bis*: Report on the Application of the Convention on Combating Bribery of Foreign Public Officials in International Business Transactions and the 1997 Recommendation on Combating Bribery in International Business Transactions, 16 October 2008; Phase 2: Follow-Up Report on the Implementation of the Phase 2 Recommendations on the Application of the Convention and the 1997 Recommendation on Combating Bribery in International Business Transactions, 21 June 2007; Phase 2: Report on the Application of the Convention on Combating Bribery of Foreign Public Officials in International Business Transactions and the 1997 Recommendation on Combating Bribery in International Business Transactions, Implementation of the OECD Anti-Bribery Convention, 17 March 2005; Phase 1*bis* Review of the Implementation of the Convention and 1997 Recommendation, March 2003; Phase 1 Review of the Implementation of the Convention and 1997 Recommendation, December 1999

United States: Phase 2: Follow-Up Report on the Implementation of the Phase 2 Recommendations on the Application of the Convention and the 1997 Recommendation on Combating Bribery of Foreign Public Officials in International Business Transactions, 1 June 2005; Phase 2: Report on the Application of the Convention on Combating Bribery of Foreign Public Officials in International Business Transactions and the 1997 Recommendation on Combating Bribery in International Business Transactions, Implementation of the OECD Anti-Bribery Convention, October 2002; Phase 1 Review of the Implementation of the Convention and 1997 Recommendation, April 1999

ii) Regional Initiatives of the OECD DAF

Review of Legal and Institutional Framework for Fighting Corruption: Summary Assessment and Recommendations for Kazakhstan, 21 October 2005

Review of Legal and Institutional Framework for Fighting Corruption: Summary Assessment and Recommendations for Azerbaijan, 18 June 2004

Review of Legal and Institutional Framework for Fighting Corruption: Summary Assessment and Recommendations for Armenia, 18 June 2004

Review of Legal and Institutional Framework for Fighting Corruption: Summary Assessment and Recommendations for Ukraine, 21 January 2004

Review of Legal and Institutional Framework for Fighting Corruption: Summary Assessment and Recommendations for Georgia, 21 January 2004

Anti-Corruption Policies in Asia and the Pacific: The Legal and Institutional Frameworks for Fighting Corruption in Twenty-one Asian and Pacific Countries, Asian Development Bank; Organisation for Economic Co-operation and Development, 2004

Effective Prosecution of Corruption, Asian Development Bank; Organisation for Economic Co-operation and Development, Manila, November 2003

iii) Other Documents of the OECD DAF

OECD Principles of Corporate Governance, 2004

The OECD Guidelines for Multinational Enterprises, Text, Commentary and Clarifications, 31 October 2002, DAFFE/IME/WPG(2000)15/FINAL

Commentaries on the Convention on Combating Bribery of Foreign Public Officials in International Business Transactions, adopted by the Negotiating Conference on 21 November 1997, DAFFE/IME/BR(97)20

OECD, Why is Procurement Important? Factsheet December 2006

c) Trade Directorate, Working Party on Export Credits and Credit Guarantees

Export Credits and Bribery: Review of Responses to the 2004 Revised Survey on Measures Taken to Combat Bribery in Officially Supported Export Credits – Situation as of 30 September 2005, 29 September 2005, TD/ECG(2005)4/REV

Action Statement on Bribery and Officially Supported Export Credits, adopted by the Working Party on Export Credits and Credit Guarantees, Trade Directorate, 20 February 2003, TD/ECG(2999)15

6. World Trade Organization

Report (2003) of the Working Group on Transparency in Government Procurement to the General Council, WT/WGTGP/7, 15 July 2003

Working Group on Transparency in Government Procurement, Report of the Meeting of 18 June 2003, WT/WGTGP/M/18, 7 July 2003

Working Group on Transparency in Government Procurement, Work of the Working Group on the Matters Related to Items VI-XII of the List of the Issues Raised and Points Made, WT/WGTGP/W/33, 3 October 2002

Working Group on Transparency in Government Procurement, Work of the Working Group on the Matters Related to Items I-V of the List of the Issues Raised and Points Made, WT/WGTGP/W/32, 23 May 2002

Working Group on Transparency in Government Procurement, Report (1999) to the General Council, WT/WGTGP/3 12 October 1999

Working Group on Transparency in Government Procurement, Report of the Meeting of 24–25 February 1999, WT/WGTGP/M/7, 25 May 1999

Singapore Ministerial Declaration, adopted on 13 December 1996 (WT/MIN(96)/DEC, 18 December 1996)

7. Financial Action Task Force (FATF)

FATF 40 Recommendations, 16 February 2012

C. International Case Law

1. International Court of Justice

Application Instituting Proceedings, Belgium v. Senegal, Questions relating to the Obligation to Prosecute or Extradite, 16 February 2009

Arrest Warrant of 11 April 2000 (Democratic Republic of the Congo v. Belgium), Judgment, I.C.J. Reports 2002, 3

Treatment of Polish Nationals and Other Persons of Polish Origin or Speech in the Danzig Territory, Advisory Opinion, 1932, P.C.I.J. (Ser. A/B) No. 44

The Greco-Bulgarian "Communities", Advisory Opinion, 1930, P.C.I.J. (Ser. B), No. 17, 31 July, 32

Free Zones of Upper Savoy and the District of Gex, P.C.I.J. (Ser. A) No. 24 (Order of 6 December 1930), 12; and ibid., Judgment, 1932, P.C.I.J. (Ser. A/B) No. 46, 7 June, 167

2. International Arbitration

World Duty Free Company Ltd. v. Kenya, ICSID Case No. ARB/00/7, 4 October 2006,

ICC Case No. 8891, 1998, Journal du droit international, Vol. 127(4), 2000 p. 1076–1084, 1080

Westacre v. Jugoimport-SPDR Holding Co. Ltd. And Others, [1998] 2 Lloyd's Law Reports, 111, 131

Westacre v. Jugoimport, ICC Case No. 7047, Bulletin de l'Association suisse de l'arbitrage, 1995, 332

ICC Case No. 6248, 19 Yearbook of Commercial Arbitration, 1994, 124–140

ICC Case No. 5622 Hilmarton Ltd. v. Omnium de Traitement et de Valorisation S.A., 19 August 1988, 19 Yearbook of Commercial Arbitration, 1994, 105–123

ICC Case No. 2730, Journal du Droit International 1984, 914

ICC Case No. 1110, 1963, reproduced in Annex of J. Gillis Wetter, "Issues of Corruption before International Arbitral Tribunals: The Authentic Text and True Meaning of Judge Gunnar Lagergren's 1963 Award in ICC Case No. 1110," Arbitration International 10, no. 3 (1994): 282–294

3. European Court of Human Rights

Ramanauskas v. Lithuania, Eur. Ct. H.R., Judgment of 5 February 2008 (not yet published).

Murray v. U.K., 22 Eur. Ct. H.R. Rep. 29 (1996)

Doorson v. The Netherlands (1996) 22 Eur. Ct. H.R. 330

Lüdi v. Switzerland (1992) 15 Eur. Ct. H.R. 173.

Pham Hoang v France, Eur. Ct. H.R. (ser. A) 243 (1992)

Windisch v. Austria (1990) 13 Eur. Ct. H.R. 281

Kostovski v. The Netherlands (1989) 12 Eur. Ct. H.R. 434

Salabiaku v. France, Eur. Ct. H.R. (ser. A) 141-A (1988)

4. Inter-American Court of Human Rights

Claude Reyes et al. v. Chile, Inter-Am. Ct. H.R. Serie C No. 151, Judgment of 19 September 2006

5. African Commission on Human and Peoples' Rights

Communication 347/07 Submitted by the Asociación Pro Derechos Humanos de España Regarding the Republic of Equatorial Guinea, under Article 55 of the African Charter on Human and Peoples' Rights, 12 October 2007,

6. European Court of Justice

Case C-281/02, Andrew Owusu v. N.B. Jackson, trading as 'Villa Holidays Bal-Inn Villas' and Others, 1 March 2005, E.C.R. 2005 I-01383

Group Josi Reinsurance Company S.A. v. Universal General Insurance Company (UGIC), Case no. C-412/98, 13 July 2000

Case 21/76, Handelskwekerij Gj Bier NV v. SA Mines de Potasse d'Alsace [1976] ECR 1735

D. National Case Law

1. Hong Kong

Attorney General v. Hui King-hong [1995] 1 H.K.C.L.R.

Attorney General v. Lee Kwong-Kut [1993] A.C. 951.

Cheung Chee-kwong v. The Queen [1971] 1 W.L.R. 1454.

2. Lesotho

Ephraim Masupha Sole v. The Crown [Court of Appeal of Lesotho], 14 April 2003

Rex v. Ephraim Masupha Sole [High Court of Lesotho] 20 May 2002

3. Mexico

Case XXXIV/2002, Pleno de la Suprema Corte de Justicia [S.C.J.N.] [Supreme Court], Semanario Judicial de la Federación y su Gaceta, Novena Época, Tomo XVI, Agosto 2002, Tesis P. XXXVII/2002

4. Netherlands

Hoge Raad der Nederlanden [HR] [Supreme Court of the Netherlands], 20 June 2006, LJN AW3584, 01804/05

5. Switzerland

Tribunal fédéral [Federal Court] Fondation Brouilly v. Office federal de la justice, 12 January 2010, 1C_374/2009

Tribunal fédéral [Federal Court] affaire République du Kazakhstan, 25 June 2001, réf. 1A.94/2001
Tribunal fédéral [Federal Court] affaire République du Kazakhstan, 8 December 2000, réf. 1P.582/2000, 9
Tribunal fédéral [Federal Court] A. et B. c. Chambre d'accusation de Genève, 8 March 1999, réf. 1P.631/1998 and 1P.633/1998
Tribunal fédéral [Federal Court] Ferdinand and Imelda Marcos v. Office fédéral de la police, 2 November 1989, ATF 115 Ib 496

6. United Kingdom

Attorney General of Zambia for and on behalf of the Republic of Zambia v. Meer Care and Desai and Ors [2007] EWHC 952
Regina v. Bartle and the Commissioner of Police for the Metropolis and others Ex parte Pinochet, 28 ILM 581 (H.L. 1999),
R. v. Andrews-Weatherfoil Ltd. (1972) 56 Cr App R 31, CA

7. United States

United States Securities and Exchange Commission (SEC) v. Monsanto Company, No. 05-0014 (D.D.C. complaint filed 6 January 2005)
Sosa v. Alvarez-Machain, 124 S.Ct. 2739 (2004)
Presbyterian Church of Sudan v. Talisman Energy, 244 F.Supp. 2d 289, 296 (S.D.N.Y. 2003)
United States v. Sun-Diamond Growers of California, 526 U.S. 398 (1999)
United States v. Jennings, 160 F.3d 1006, 1013 (4th Cir. 1999)
United States v. McDade (ED Pa) 827 F Supp 1153 (E.D. Pa. 1993)
United States v. Liebo, 923 F.2d 1308, 1310–11 (8th Cir. 1991)
Lamb v. Phillip Morris, Inc., 915 F.2d 1024 (6th Cir. 1990), cert. denied, 111 S. Ct. 961 (1991))
W.S. Kirkpatrick and Co., Inc., v. Environmental Tectonics Corp. Int., 493 U.S. 400 (1990)
United States v. Secord (DC Dist Col) 726 F Supp 845 (D.D.C. 1989)
Republic of Philippines v. Marcos, United States Court of Appeals, 9th Cir., 818 F 2d 1473 (9th Cir 1988)
Republic of Philippines v. Marcos, 806 F.2d 344 (2d Cir. 1987)
Islamic Republic of Iran v. Pahlavi, 62 N.Y.2d 474, 477 (1984), cert. denied, 469 U.S. 1108 (1985)
Clayco Petroleum Corp. v. Occidental Petroleum Corp., 712 F.2d 404 (9th Cir. 1983), cert. denied, 104 S. Ct. 703 (1984)
Piper Aircraft Co. v. Reyno, 454 USS 235 (1981)
Sage International, Ltd v. Cadillac Gage Co., 534 F.Supp. 896 (E.D. Mich. 1981).
Court of Ulster County, New York v Allen, 442 U.S. 140 (1979)
United States v. Niederberger, 580 F.2d 63 (3d Cir.), cert. denied, 439 *U.S.* 980 (1978)
Jimenez v. Aristeguieta, 311 F.2d 547 (5th Cir. 1962), cert. denied sub nom. Jimenez v. Hixon, 373 U.S. 914 (1963)

E. *National Legislation*

1. Algeria

Law No. 06–01, 20 February 2006 on Prevention and Fight against Corruption

2. Argentina

Law No. 24.759 (17 January 1997)
Law 25.188 (1 November 1999)
Law 25.825 (11 December 2003)

3. Armenia

Law on Banking Secrecy of 2007

4. Belgium

Bribery Prevention Act of 10 February 1999

5. Brazil

Law 10.467 (June 11, 2002)

6. Canada

Corruption of Foreign Public Officials Act (CFPOA) 14 February 1999
Witness Protection Act

7. Chile

Executive Decree No. 496, 30 January 2002
Law No. 19,829 amending the Chilean Criminal Code

8. China

Chinese Supplementary Regulations on Suppression of Corruption and Bribery 1998, Promulgated by Standing Committee of the National People‘s Congress on 21 January 21 1988, by Order Number 63 of President Li Xiannian of the People‘s Republic of China.

9. Costa Rica

Law against Corruption and Illicit Enrichment in the Public Function, Law No. 8422, 26 May 2004

10. Indonesia

Law No. 30 of 2002

11. Japan

Unfair Competition Prevention Law, Act No. 47 of 1993

12. Kenya

Anti-Corruption and Economic Crimes Acts, Act No. 3 of 2003
Public Officer Ethics Act 2003

13. Korea

Act on Preventing Bribery of Foreign Public Officials in International Business Transaction (28 December 1998)
The Anti-corruption Act (25 January 2002)

14. Lesotho

Prevention of Corruption and Economic Offences Act 1999

15. Paraguay

Law 2.523 of 2004

16. Pakistan

National Accountability Bureau Ordinance No. XVIII of 1999, 16 November 1999, as amended
National Reconciliation Ordinance of 5 October 2007

17. Peru

Law 27.378, 20 December 2000
Law 27379, 20 December 2000

18. Poland

Act of 9 September 2000 (O.J. 2000 No 93, it. 1027)
Act of 28 October 2002 on Liability of Collective Entities for Acts Prohibited under Penalty (OJ 2002No 197, it. 1661)

19. South Africa

Promotion of National Unity and Reconciliation Act, No. 34 of 1995
Promotion of Access to Information Act 2000

20. Switzerland

Swiss Federal Banking Act of 8 November 1934
Federal Asset Sharing Act of 19 March 2004 (Loi fédéralesur le partage des valeurs patrimoniales confisquées, RS 312.4)

21. Turkey

Law 3628 of 4 May 1990

22. Uganda

Prevention of Corruption Act
Uganda Amnesty Act 2000

23. United States of America

U.S. Code of Federal Regulations, Title 5, Part 2635 (Standards of Ethical Conduct for Employees of the Executive Branch) Sections 201–205
Foreign Corrupt Practices Act (FCPA) 15 US Code Section 78dd-1–3 78m, 78ff, as amended by the International Anti-Bribery and Fair Competition Act of 1998, Pub. L 105–366, signed on 10 November 1998
The Civil Asset Forfeiture Reform Act (CAFRA) of 2000
Alien Tort Statute, 28 US Code Section 1350

24. Venezuela

Law against Corruption, Official Journal 5637, 7 April 2003,

II. SECONDARY SOURCES

Abed, George T., and Sanjeev Gupta. "The Economics of Corruption: An Overview." In *Governance, Corruption, and Economic Performance*, edited by George T. Abed and Sanjeev Gupta, 1–16. Washington, D.C.: International Monetary Fund, 2002.

ADB/OECD Anti-Corruption Initiative for Asia and the Pacific. *Anti-Corruption Policies in Asia and the Pacific: Progress in Legal and Institutional Reform in 25 Countries.* Manila: ADB/OECD, 2006.

— . *Controlling Corruption in Asia and the Pacific: Proceedings of the 4th Regional Anti-Corruption Conference held in Kuala Lumpur, Malaysia, in December 2003.* Manila: ADB/OECD, 2005.

—. *Effective Prosecution of Corruption*. Manila: ADB/OECD, 2003.
—. *Knowledge-Commitment-Action Against Corruption in Asia and the Pacific*. Manila: ADB/OECD, 2006.
—. *Mutual Legal Assistance, Extradition and Recovery of Proceeds of Corruption in Asia and the Pacific*. Manila: ADB/OECD, 2004.
—. *Asset Recovery and Mutual Legal Assistance in Asia and the Pacific*. Manila: ADB/OECD, 2008.
—. *Denying Safe Haven to the Corrupt and the Proceeds of Corruption: Enhancing Asia-Pacific Cooperation on Mutual Legal Assistance, Extradition, and Return of the Proceeds of Corruption: Capacity Building Program: Papers Presented at the 4th Master Training Seminar of the ADB-OECD Anti-Corruption Inititative for Asia and the Pacific, Kuala Lumpur, Malaysia, 28–30 March 2006*. Manila: ADB/OECD, 2006.
Ades, Alberto, and Rafael Di Tella. "The New Economics of Corruption: A Survey and Some New Results." *Political Studies* 45, no. 3 (1997): 496–515.
Aidt, Toke S. "Economic Analysis of Corruption: A Survey." *The Economic Journal* 113 (2003): 632–652.
Akakpo, Martial. *Review of the Political and Legal Challenges Involved in Implementing Anticorruption Conventions in Togo*. Transparency International, 2006.
Ala'i, Padideh. "The Legacy of Geographical Morality and Colonialism: A Historical Assessment of the Current Crusade against Corruption." *Vanderbilt Journal of Transnational Law* (2000): 877–932.
Alam, M. Shahid. "Anatomy of Corruption: An Approach to the Political Economy of Underdevelopment." *American Journal of Economics and Sociology* 48, no. 4 (1989): 441–456.
Alatas, Hussein. *Corruption and the Destiny of Asia*. Petaling Jaya: Prentice Hall, 1999.
—. *The Sociology of Corruption: The Nature, Function, Causes and Prevention of Corruption*. Singapore: D. Moore Press, 1968.
Altamirano, Giorleny. "The Impact of the Inter-American Convention against Corruption." *University of Miami Inter-American Law Review* 38, no. 3 (2007): 487–547.
Amadi, Johnson. "Corruption and Corruption Control: Focus on Nigeria." *Recht in Afrika*, no. 2 (2002): 111–140.
Amanbaev, Anarkul. "Corruption and Related Offences in International Economic Activities: Individual Reports: Corruption Preventing: Kyrgyz." *Revue Internationale de Droit Pénal* 74, no. 1 & 2 (2003): 493–497.
American Bar Association. *Report to the House of Delegates: Recommendation*. Undated.
Amin, Hasan. "Anti-Corruption Laws: The Gulf States and Iran." *Islamic and Comparative Law Quarterly* 9, no. 2–4 (1989): 93–100.
Amundsen, Inge. *Corruption: Definitions and Concepts*. Bergen: Chr. Michelsen Institute Development Studies and Human Rights, 2000.
—. *Political Corruption: An Introduction to the Issues*. Bergen: Chr. Michelsen Institute, 1999.
Andersen, Robert, and Pierre Nihoul. "La corruption: problématique générale et état de la question." *Annales de Droit de Louvain*, no. 2 (1998): 147–175.

Andreski, Stanislav. *The African Predicament: A Study in the Pathology of Modernisation*. London: Joseph, 1968.

Anechiarico, Frank. "End-Runs and Hairy Eyeballs: The Costs of Corruption Control in Market Democracies." *Connecticut Journal of International Law* 14, no. 2 (1999): 379–391.

Argandoña, Antonio. "Private-to-private Corruption." *Journal of Business Ethics* 47, no. 3 (2003): 253–267.

Arjon Schütte, Sofie. "The Fight Against Corruption in Indonesia." *Südostasien aktuell* 26, no. 4 (2007): 57–66.

Arrowsmith, Sue. "Towards a Multilateral Agreement on Transparency in Government Procurement." *International and Comparative Law Quarterly* (1998): 793–816.

Askin, Steve, and Carole Collins. "External Collusion with Kleptocracy: Can Zaïre Recapture Its Stolen Wealth?." *Review of African Political Economy*, no. 57 (July 1993): 72–85.

Ayee, Joseph R. A. "Corruption and the Future of the Public Service in Africa." *Verfassung und Recht in Übersee* 35, no. 1 (2002): 6–22.

Ayres, Margaret. "Development in U.S. and International Efforts to Prevent Corruption." *The International Lawyer* 41, no. 2 (2007): 597–611.

Bacio Terracino, Julio. *Hard Law Connections between Corruption and Human Rights*. Working Paper for ICHRP Project on Corruption and Human Rights. International Council on Human Rights Policy, 2007.

Baigún, David. "Corruption and Related Offences in International Economic Activities: National Reports: Argentina." *Revue Internationale de Droit Pénal* 74, no. 1 & 2 (2003): 93–115.

Balmelli, Tiziano. "La restitution internationale des avoirs acquis par la corruption: de l'obligation morale à lobligation juridique." In *Les traités internationaux contre la corruption: L'ONU, l'OCDE, le Conseil de l'Europe et la Suisse*, edited by Tiziano Balmelli and Bernard Jaggy, 63–90. Lausanne, Bern, Lugano: Editions interuniversitaires suisses – Edis, 2004.

Banfield, Edward. "Corruption as a Feature of Government Organization." *Journal of Law and Economics* 18 (1975): 587–605.

Banisar, David. "Whistleblowing: International Standards and Developments." Instituto de Investigaciones Sociales UNAM, March 2006.

Bantekas, Ilias. "Corruption as an International Crime and Crime against Humanity." *Journal of International Criminal Justice* 4 (2006): 466–484.

Bardhan, Pranab. "Corruption and Development: A Review of Issues." *Journal of Economic Literature* 35, no. 3 (September 1997): 1320–1346.

Basel Institute on Governance. *Summary of Recommendations: Experts Workshop on Asset Recovery* (Basel, Switzerland, 15–16 May 2007).

Basel Institute on Governance – International Centre for Asset Recovery. *Tracing Stolen Assets: A Practitioner's Handbook*. Basel: Basel Institute on Governance, 2009.

Bassiouni, M. Cherif, and Eduardo Vetere. "Organized Crime and Its Transnational Manifestations." In *International Criminal Law: Crimes*, 883–903. 2nd ed. The Hague: Transnational Publishers, Inc., 1999.

Bauer, Hans-Peter. "How to Deal with Politically Exposed Persons." In *Recovering Stolen Assets*, edited by Mark Pieth, 195–217. Bern: Peter Lang, 2008.

Bayley, David H. "The Effects of Corruption in a Developing Nation." *Western Political Quarterly* 19, no. 4 (1966): 719–732.

Becker, Gary S. "Crime and Punishment: An Economic Approach." *Journal of Political Economy* 76, no. 2 (1968): 169–217.

Béhar-Touchais, M. "Morale et contrats internationaux." In *La morale et le droit des affaires: Actes du colloque organisé à l'Université des sciences sociales de Toulouse le 12 mai 1995*, 185. Paris: Montchrestien, 1996.

Ben-Dor, Gabriel. "Corruption, Institutionalization, and Political Development: The Revisionist Theses Revisited." *Comparative Political Studies* 7, no. 1 (1974): 63–83.

Benson, George Charles Sumner. *Political Corruption in America.* Lexington, Mass: Lexington Books, 1978.

Benton, Leslie. "Anti-Corruption." *The International Lawyer* 42, no. 2 (2008): 709–727.

Berg, Larry L., Harlan Hahn, and John R. Schmidhauser. *Corruption in the American Political System.* Morristown, N.J.: General Learning Press, 1976.

Bhagwati, Jagdish N. "Directly Unproductive, Profit-Seeking (DUP) Activities." *The Journal of Political Economy* 90, no. 5 (October 1982): 988–1002.

Bhargava, Vinay, and Bolongaita, Emil. *Challenging Corruption in Asia: Case Studies and a Framework.* World Bank. Washington, D.C.: World Bank, 2004.

Blois, Alexis. "Infraction de corruption d'agent public étranger et procédure pénale nationale." *Revue de Droit des Affaires Internationales*, no. 2 (2006): 217–228.

Borghi, Alvaro. "Corruption et immunité des dirigeants politiques." In *Les traités internationaux contre la corruption: L'ONU, l'OCDE, le Conseil de l'Europe et la Suisse*, edited by Tiziano Balmelli and Bernard Jaggy, 91–109. Lausanne, Bern, Lugano: Editions interuniversitaires suisses – Edis, 2004.

Borlini, Leonardo. "La lotta alla corruzione internazionale dall'ambito OCSE alla dimensione ONU." *Diritto del commercio internazionale* 21, no. 1 (2007): 15–126.

Boylan, Scott. "Organized Crime and Corruption in Russia: Implications for U.S. and International Law." *Fordham International Law Journal* 19 (1995): 1999–2027.

Brooks, Robert Clarkson. *Corruption in American Politics and Life.* New York: Dodd, Mead, 1910.

Brown, H. Lowel. "Extraterritorial Jurisdiction Under the 1998 Amendments to the Foreign Corrupt Practices Act: Does the Government's Reach Now Exceed its Grasp?." *North Carolina Journal of International Law and Commercial Regulation* 26 (2000): 239–360.

Bruns, Rudolf, and Henry Motulsky. "Tendances et perspectives de l'arbitrage international (A propos de la réforme de la Convention de Genève de 1927)." *Revue Internationale de droit comparé* (1957): 717–727.

Burdescu, Ruxandra, Gary J. Reid, Stuart Gilman, and Stephanie Trapnell. *Stolen Asset Recovery: Income and Asset Declarations: Tools and Trade-Offs.* Washington, D.C.: World Bank, 2009.

Burger, Ethan S. "Corruption in the Russian Arbitrazh Courts: will there be significant progress in the near term?." *The International Lawyer* 38, no. 1 (2004): 15–34.

Bushell, Simon. "UK's Anti-Corruption Law – Filling in the Gaps." *International Business Lawyer* 28 (2000): 435–438.

Cabogo, Sarassoro Hyacinthe. "La corruption et l'enrichissement sans cause en Afrique aujourd'hui quel antidote?." *African Journal of International and Comparative Law* 2, no. 3 (1990): 384–422.

Caflisch, Lucius. "La Pratique Suisse en Matière de Droit International Public 1990." *Revue suisse de droit international et de droit européen* 1, no. 4 (1991): 533–537.

— . "La Pratique Suisse en Matière de Droit International Public 1998." *Revue suisse de droit international et de droit européen* 9, no. 4/5 (1999): 639–715.

Caiden, Gerald E. "A Cautionary Tale: Ten Major Flaws in Combating Corruption." *Southwestern Journal of Law and Trade in the Americas* 10, no. 2 (2004): 269–293.

— . "La democracia y la corrupción." *Revista del CLAD Reforma y Democracia* 8, no. May (1997): 7–36.

— . and Naomi J. Caiden. "Administrative Corruption." *Public Administration Review* 37, no. 3 (1977): 301–309.

Calderon Navarro, Nelly. "Fighting Corruption: The Peruvian Experience." *Journal of International Criminal Justice* 4 (2006): 488–509.

Campos, Nauro F. *In Pursuit of Policy Influence: Can Lobbying Be a Legitimate Alternative to Corruption in Developing Countries?.* U4 Brief, January 2009.

— . and Francesco Giovannoni. *Lobbying, Corruption and Other Banes.* William Davidson Institute Working Paper No. 930, 1 September 2008.

Candler, Linda J. "Tracing and Recovering Proceeds of Crime in Fraud Cases: A Comparison of U.S. and U.K. Legislation." *International Law* 31 (1997): 3.

Capus, Nadja. "Fighting International and National Corruption by Means of Criminal Law." *Rapports Suisses présentés au XVIème Congrès international de droit comparé, Brisbane, 14–20 juillet 2002* 44, no. 2 (2002): 633–669.

Cárdenas Rioseco, Raúl F. *El Delito De Enriquecimiento Ilícito Ante La Suprema Corte De Justicia De La Nación: Una Postura Inquietante.* México, D.F: Editorial Porrúa, 2003.

Carlberg, Christopher K. "A Truly Level Playing Field for International Business: Improving the OECD Convention on Combating Bribery Using Clear Standards." *Boston College International and Comparative Law Review* 26, no. 1 (2003): 95–111.

Carr, Indira. "Corruption in Africa: Is the African Union Convention on Combating Corruption the Answer?." *Journal of Business Law*, no. March (2007): 111–136.

— . "Fighting Corruption in International Trade: Towards Improving Strategy." In *Issues in International Commercial Law*, edited by Iwan Davies, 197–216. Aldershot, Hampshire, England: Ashgate, 2005.

— . "Fighting Corruption through Regional and International Conventions: A Satisfactory Solution?." *European Journal of Crime, Criminal Law and Criminal Justice* 15, no. 2 (2007): 121–153.

Carrera, Daniel P. *Peculado (de bienes publicos y de trabajos o servicios, art. 261 del Cod. penal).* Buenos Aires: Ediciones Depalma, 1968.

Carver, Jeremy. "Combating Corruption: The Emergence of New International Law." *International Law Forum du droit international* 5, no. 2 (2003): 119–123.

Cassani, Ursula. "La corruption de fonctionnaire: répression pénale d'un pacte." In *Pacte, convention, contrat: Mélanges en l'honneur du Professeur Bruno Schmidlin*, 207–226. Basel: Helbing & Lichtenhahn, 1998.

Cassuto, Thomas. "Effective Legal and Practical Measures for Combating Corruption: The French System." *Resource Material Series (UNAFEI)* 77 (March 2009): 23–37.

Castillo González, Francisco. *El Delito De Peculado.* 1st ed. San José, Costa Rica: Editorial Juritexto, 2000.

Centre d'étude pour l'application du droit communautaire en matière pénale et financière. *Corruption de fonctionnaires et fraude europénne: Actes du colloque de Bruxelles 21 et 22 novembre 1996.* Bruxelles: Bruylant, 1998.

Chaikin, David A, and J. C Sharman. *Corruption and Money Laundering: A Symbiotic Relationship.* New York: Palgrave-Macmillan, 2009.

Chari, Raj, Gary Murphy, and John Hogan. "Regulating Lobbyists: A Comparative Analysis of the United States, Canada, Germany and the European Union." *The Political Quarterly* 78 (September 2007): 422–438.

Charney, Jonathan. "International Agreements and the Development of International Law." *Washington Law Review* 61 (1986): 971.

Chêne, Marie. *African Experience of Asset Declarations.* U4 Anti-Corruption Resource Centre Expert Answer, April 21, 2008.

— . *Good Practice in Whistleblowing Protection Legislation (WPL).* U4 Anti-Corruption Resource Centre Expert Answer, July 2009.

— . *Mutual Legal Assistance Treaties and Money Laundering.* U4 Expert Answer, July 29, 2008.

Clapham, Andrew. "Corporate Complicity in Violations of International Law: Beyond Unocal." In *From Government to Governance: The Growing Impact of Non-State Actors on the International and European Legal System*, edited by Wybo P. Heere, 227–238. Proceedings of the Sixth Hague Joint Conference Held in The Hague, the Netherlands, 3–5 July 2003. The Hague: T.M.C. Asser Press, 2004.

— . *Human Rights in the Private Sphere.* Oxford: Clarendon Press, 1993.

— . "Terrorism, National Measures and International Supervision." In *Enforcing International Law Norms Against Terrorism*, edited by Andrea Bianchi, 282–305. Oxford: Hart Pub, 2004.

Colares, Juscelino F. "The Evolving Domestic and International Law against Foreign Corruption: Some New and Old Dilemmas Facing the International Lawyer." *Washington University Global Studies Law Review* 5, no. 1 (2006). To Read at Home.

Collins, Lawrence, and Claude Reymond. "Recovery of Stolen Property from Deposed Rulers." In *Etudes de droit international en l'honneur de Pierre Lalive*, edited by Christian Dominicé and Robert Patry, 221–230. Bâle: Helbing & Lichtenhahn, 1993.

Commonwealth Secretariat. *Asset Recovery: Draft Report*, June 2005.

Commonwealth Secretariat, and Chatham House. *Anti-Corruption Conference: The UN Convention against Corruption Implementation & Enforcement: Meeting the Challenges.* Report of the Meeting Held in London, 24–25 April 2006. London, 2006.

Conteh, Sonkita. *Country Review of Legal and Political Challenges to the Domestication of the Anti-corruption Conventions in Sierra Leone.* Transparency International, 2006.

Corr, Christopher, and Judd Lawler. "Damned if You Do, Damned if You Don't: The OECD Convention and the Globalization of Anti-bribery Measures." *Vanderbilt Journal of Transnational Law* 32, no. 5 (1999): 1249–1344.

Corruption Eradication Commission, The Republic of Indonesia. *Gap Analysis Study Report: Identification of Gap between Laws/Regulations of the Republic of Indonesia and the United Nations Convention against Corruption.* Jakarta: Komisi Penberantasan Korupsi, 2006.

Crawford, James. "Prospects for the Codification and Development of International Law by the United Nations: The Work of the International Law Commission." *Finnish Yearbook of International Law*, no. IX (1998): 9–15.

Czaplinski, Wladyslaw. "Sources of International Law in the Nicaragua Case." *International and Comparative Law Quarterly* 38, no. 1 (1989): 151–166.

Daniel, Tim, and James Maton. "Civil Proceedings to Recover Corruptly Acquired Assets of Public Officials." In *Recovering Stolen Assets*, edited by Mark Pieth, 243–266. Bern: Peter Lang, 2008.

—. "Recovering the Proceeds of Corruption: General Sani Abacha – A Nation's Thief." In *Recovering Stolen Assets*, edited by Mark Pieth, 63–78. Bern: Peter Lang, 2008.

Davis, Kevin E. *Civil Remedies for Corruption in Government Contracting: Zero Tolerance Versus Proportional Liability.* International Law and Justice Working Papers 2009/4, 2009.

De Maria, William. "Whistleblower protection: Is Africa ready?" *Public Administration and Development* 25, no. 3 (2005): 217–226.

De Michele, Roberto. "The Follow-Up Mechanism of the Inter-American Convention Against Corruption: Absoluteness Preliminary Assessment: Is the Glass Half Empty?" *Southwestern Journal of Law and Trade in the Americas* 10, no. 2 (2004): 295–318.

Delaney, Patrick X. "Transnational Corruption: Regulation across Borders." *Virginia Journal of International Law* 47, no. 2 (2007): 413–461.

Della Porta, Donatella, and Alberto Vannucci. *Un Paese Anormale: Come La Classe Politica Ha Perso L'occasione Di Mani Pulite.* 1st ed. Saggi tascabili Laterza. Roma: GLF editori Laterza, 1999.

Deming, Stuart H. *The Foreign Corrupt Practices Act and the New International Norms.* International Practitioner's Deskbook Series. Chicago: Section of International Law and Practice, American Bar Association, 2005.

Deming, Stuart H. "The Potent and Broad-Ranging Implications of the Accounting and Record-Keeping Provisions of the Foreign Corrupt Practices Act." *Journal of Criminal Law and Criminology* 96 (2005): 465.

Derains, Yves. "La lutte contre la corruption – Le point de vue de l'arbitre international." In *Contribution au Congrès AIJA, Montreux*, 1996.

Deysine, Anne. "Political Corruption: A Review of the Literature." *European Journal of Political Research* 8, no. 4 (December 336): 447–462.

D'Hollander, Juliette. "Ethics in Business: The New OECD Convention on Bribery." *Revue Juridique Themis* 33, no. 1 (1999): 147–166.

Díaz, Rodolfo. "La lucha contra la corrupción." *Aportes para el Estado y la Administración Gubernamental* 16, no. Primavera (2000): 105–115.

Doig, Alan, David Watt, and Robert Williams. *Measuring 'Success' in Five African Anti-Corruption Commissions: The Cases of Ghana, Malawi, Tanzania, Uganda and Zambia.* U4 Anti-Corruption Resource Centre Research Report. Bergen: Chr. Michelsen Institute, May 2005.

Dolinger, Jacob. "World Public Policy: Real International Public Policy in the Conflict of Laws." *Texas International Law Journal* 17, no. 2 (1982): 167–193.

Dominicé, Christian. "Quelques Observations sur l'immunité de Juridiction Pénale de l'ancien Chef d'Etat." *Revue Générale de Droit International Public* 103, no. 2 (1999): 297-308.

Dommel, Daniel. *Les défis de la corruption.* Transparency International Working Paper, 1999.

Dorobant, Alina. "Corruption and Related Offences in International Economic Activities: Individual Reports: Report on Fighting Corruption in Romania." *Revue Internationale de Droit Pénal* 74, no. 1 & 2 (2003): 535–542.

Douence, Jean-Claude. "La loi du 29 janvier 1993 relative à la prévention de la corruption et à la transparence de la vie économique et des procédures publiques: Les contrats de délégation de service public." *Revue Française de Droit Administratif* 9, no. 5 (1993): 936–951.

Dowd, Maureen A., and Theodore B. Eichelberger. "Recent Decisions: International Law: Act of State Doctrine: An Emerging Corruption Exception in Antitrust Cases?" *Notre Dame Law Review* 59 (1983): 455–470.

Draetta, Ugo. "La lutte contre la corruption des fonctionnaires publics étrangers: premières observations sur les examens de la phase 2 au titre de la Convention OCDE." *Revue de droit des affaires internationales*, no. 1 (2005): 99–102.

— . "The European Union and the Fight against Corruption in International Trade." *Revue de Droit des Affaires Internationales*, no. 6 (1995): 699–713.

Dulin, Antoine. *Biens mal acquis ... profitent trop souvent: La fortune des dictateurs et les complaisances occidentales.* Paris: Comité Catholique contre la Faim et pour le Développement, 2007.

Dwivedi, O.P. "Bureaucratic Corruption in Developing Countries." *Asian Survey* 7, no. 4 (1967): 245–253.

Eboe-Osuji, Chile. "Kleptocracy: A Desired Subject of International Criminal Law that is in Dire Need of Prosecution by Universal Jurisdiction." In *African Perspectives on International Criminal Justice*, edited by Edward K Kwakwa and Evelyn A Ankumah, 121–132. Accra: Africa Legal Aid, 2005.

Ehsan, Mohammad. "When Implementation Fails: The Case of Anti-Corruption Commission (ACC) and Corruption Control in Bangladesh." *Asian Affairs* 28, no. 3 (2006): 40–63.

Eigen, Peter. "Controlling Corruption: A Key to Development-Oriented Trade." *Trade, Equity, and Development*, no. 4 (November 2002).

— . *Las redes de la corrupción: La sociedad civil contra los abusos del poder.* Buenos Aires: Planeta, 2004.

— . "Préface: Changer les règles du jeu." In *Les traités internationaux contre la corruption: L'ONU, l'OCDE, le Conseil de l'Europe et la Suisse*, edited by Tiziano Balmelli and Bernard Jaggy, 1–6. Lausanne, Bern, Lugano: Editions interuniversitaires suisses – Edis, 2004.

Ekeanyanwu, Lilian. *Review of Legal and Political Challenges to the Domestication of the Anti-Corruption Conventions in Nigeria*. Transparency International, 2006.

Elliott, Kimberly Ann, ed. *Corruption and the Global Economy*. Washington D.C.: Institute for International Economics, 1997.

Evrard, Sébastien. "La loi du 10 février 1999 relative à la répression de la corruption." *Journal des Tribunaux* 118, no. 5926 (1999): 337–340.

Fabrizy, Ernst Eugen. "Corruption and Related Offences in International Economic Activities: National Reports: Austria." *Revue Internationale de Droit Pénal* 74, no. 1 & 2 (2003): 117–131.

Fariza, Binti Hamzah. "Corruption and Related Offences in International Economic Activities: Individual Reports: Malaysia." *Revue Internationale de Droit Pénal* 74, no. 1 & 2 (2003): 505–508.

Fendo, Julie. "Attacking the Tools of Corruption: The Foreign Money Laundering Deterrence and Anti-Corruption Act of 1999." *Fordham International Law Journal* 23 (1999): 1540–1576.

Fenwick, Stewart. "Measuring up?: Indonesia's Anti-Corruption Commission and the New Corruption Agenda." In *Indonesia, Law and Society*, edited by Timothy Lindsey, 406–429. Federation Press, 2008.

Fenyk, Jaroslav. "Corruption and Related Offences in International Economic Activities: National Reports: Czech Republic." *Revue Internationale de Droit Pénal* 74, no. 1 & 2 (2003): 417–455.

Ferola, Laura. "The Action of the European Union against Corruption." *Legal Issues of European Integration* 26, no. 1 & 2 (1999): 123–156.

Flore, D. *L'incrimination de la corruption: Les nouveaux instruments internationaux: La nouvelle loi belge du 10 février 1999*. Brussels: La Charte, 1999.

Ford, Henry Jones. "Municipal Corruption." *Political Science Quarterly* 19, no. 4 (December 1904): 673–686.

Forget, Louis. "The Criminal Law Convention on Corruption of the Council of Europe." In *Liber Amicorum Ibrahim F.I. Shihata: International Finance and Development Law*, edited by Sabine Schlemmer-Schulte and Ko-Yung Tung, 235–263. The Hague, London, Boston, New York: Kluer Law International, 2001.

Forti, Gabrio, ed. *Il Prezzo Della Tangente: La Corruzione Come Sistema a Dieci Anni Da Mani Pulite*. Milano: Vita e Pensiero, 2003.

Friedmann, Wolfgang Gaston. "Human Welfare and International Law: A Reordering of Priorities." In *Transnational Law in a Changing Society: Essays in Honor of Philip C. Jessup*, edited by Louis Henkin, Wolfgang Gaston Friedmann, and Oliver Lissitzyn, 113–134. New York: Columbia University Press, 1972.

Friedrich, Carl J. *The Pathology of Politics; Violence, Betrayal, Corruption, Secrecy, and Propaganda*. 1st ed. New York: Harper & Row, 1972.

— . "Corruption Concepts in Historical Perspective." In *Political Corruption: Concepts and Contexts*, edited by Arnold J. Heidenheimer and Michael Johnston, 15–23. 3rd ed. New Brunswick, N.J: Transaction Publishers, 2002.

Frisancho Aparicio, Manuel, and Raúl Peña Cabrera. *Tratado De Derecho Penal: Delitos Contra La Administración Pública*. Lima: Editora Fecat, 1999.

Gaetner, Gilles. *L'argent facile: Dictionnaire de la corruption en France*. Au vif. Paris: Stock, 1992.

Gash, Norman. *Politics in the Age of Peel: A Study in the Technique of Parliamentary Representation, 1830–1850.* 2nd ed. Hassocks, Sussex, Eng: Harvester Press, 1977.

Génaux, Maryvonne. "La corruption avant la lettre: le vocabulaire de la déviance publique dans l'ancien droit pénal." *Revue historique de droit français et étranger* 81, no. 1 (2003): 15–32.

George Crutchfield, Barbara, and Kathleen A. Lacey. "Investigation of Halliburton Co./TSKJ's Nigerian Business Practices: Model for Analysis of the Current Anti-Corruption Environment on Foreign Corrupt Practices Act Enforcement (The Changing Face of White-Collar Crime)." *Journal of Criminal Law and Criminology* 96, no. 2 (2006): 503–525.

— . Barbara, and Kathleen A. Birmele Jutta Lacey. "On the Threshold of the Adoption of Global Antibribery Legislation: A Critical Analysis of Current Domestic and International Efforts Toward the Reduction of Business Corruption." *Vanderbilt Journal of Transnational Law* 32 (1999): 1–48.

— . "The 1998 OECD Convention: An Impetus for Worldwide Changes in Attitudes Toward Corruption in Business Transactions." *American Business Law Journal* 37, no. 3 (2000): 485–525.

Global Witness. *Country for Sale: How Cambodia's Elite Has Captured the Country's Extractive Industries*, February 2009.

— . *Undue Diligence: How Banks Do Business with Corrupt Regimes*, March 2009.

Glynn, Patrick, Stephen J. Kobrin, and Moisés Naím. "The Globalization of Corruption." In *Corruption and the Global Economy*, edited by Kimberly Ann Elliott, 7–29. Washington D.C.: Institute for International Economics, 1997.

Goldman, Berthold. "L'action complémentaire des juges et des arbitres en vue d'assurer l'efficacité de l'arbitrage commercial international." In *Arbitrage international: 60 ans après, regard sur l'avenir*, 271. ICC publishing, 1984.

— . "Le droit applicable selon la Convention de la BIRD, du 18 mars 1965, pour le règlement des différends relatifs aux investissements entre Etats et ressortissants d'autres Etats." In *Investissements étrangers et arbitrage entre états et personnes privées: La Convention B.I.R.D. du 18 mars 1965*, 196. CREDIMI. Paris: Pedone, 1969.

— . "Les conflits de lois dans l'arbitrage international de droit privé." *Recueil des cours* 109, no. 2 (1963): 347–485.

Goldman, Marshall. "The Pitfalls of Russian Privatization." *Challenge* 40, no. May-June (1997): 35–49.

Gossin, Pascal. "International Mutual Legal Assistance in Switzerland." *Resource Material Series (UNAFEI)* 77 (March 2009): 19–22.

Graf Lambsdorff, Arvind K. "Corruption in Comparative Perception." In *Economics of Corruption*, edited by Arvind K. Jain, 81–109. Boston: Kluwer Academic Publishers, 1998.

Greenberg, Theodore S., Larissa Gray, Delphine Schantz, Michael Latham, and Caroline Gardner. *Stolen Asset Recovery: Politically Exposed Persons: A Policy Paper on Strengthening Preventive Measures*. Washington D.C.: World Bank, 2009.

Greenberg, Theodore S., Linda Samuel, Wingate Grant, and Larissa Gray. *Stolen Asset Recovery: A Good Practice Guide for Non-Conviction Based Asset Forfeiture*. World Bank Publications, 2009.

GTZ. "A Comparison of Compliance Reviews Based on the UN Convention against Corruption: Indonesia, Colombia, Cameroon and Germany." 2007.

—. *Asset Recovery – A Breakthrough by the UN Convention against Corruption (UNCAC)*. 2007

—. "How are the Paris Declaration and the Millennium Development Goals Linked to Corruption Prevention and Control?" 2007.

—. *Supporting the Implementation of the United Nations Convention against Corruption: What Technical Assistance Can Do: South Africa, Ghana, Indonesia and Latin American Countries*, 2007.

—. "The UN Convention against Corruption and Development Cooperation – Corruption Prevention by More Efficient Law Enforcement?" 2007.

Guerrero-Cabrera, Julio Cesar. "Corruption and Related Offences in International Economic Activities: Individual Reports: Corruption Control in Criminal Justice of the Country of Venezuela." *Revue Internationale de Droit Pénal* 74, no. 1 & 2 (2003): 557–561.

Gully-Hart, P. "The Function of State and Diplomatic Privileges and Immunities in International Cooperation in Criminal Matters: The Position of Switzerland." *Fordham International Law Journal* 23 (2000): 1334–1343

Gupta, Sanjeev, Hamid Davoodi, and Rosa Alonso-Terme. *Does Corruption Affect Inequality and Poverty?* IMF Working Paper WP/98/76, 1998.

—. Hamid Davoodi, and Erwin R. Tiongson. "Corruption and the Provision of Health Care and Education Services." In *Governance, Corruption and Economic Performance*, edited by George T. Abed and Sanjeev Gupta, 245–279. Washington, D.C: International Monetary Fund, 2002.

—. Luiz de Mello, and Raju Sharan. *Corruption and Military Spending*. IMF Working Paper WP/00/23, 2000.

Hadjadj, Djilali. *Etude sur la promotion en Algérie des Conventions internationales contre la corruption*. Transparency International, 2007.

Hamann, Kathleen M., Philip Urofsky, Nicole M. Healy, Alexandra Wrage, and Margaret Ayres. "Developments in U.S. and International Efforts to Prevent Corruption." *The International Lawyer* 40, no. 2 (2006): 417–431.

Harari, Maurice, and Corinne Corminboeuf. "Corruption à l'étranger: quel sort réserver aux fonds saisis en Suisse." *Revue pénale suisse* 116, no. 1 (1998): 1–25.

Harms, Brian C. "Holding Public Officials Accountable in the International Realm: A New Multi-Layered Strategy to Combat Corruption." *Cornell International Law Journal* 33 (2000): 159–209.

Hatchard, John. "Recent Developments in Combating the Bribery of Foreign Public Officials: A Cause for Optimism?" *University of Detroit Mercy Law Review* 85, no. 1 (2007).

—. "Strengthening Presidential Accountability: Attorney General of Zambia V Meer Care & Desai & Others." *Journal of Commonwealth Law and Legal Education* 5, no. 1 (2007): 69.

Haule, Romuald. "Preventing and Combating Corruption: An Analysis of Tanzanian Laws and International Conventions." *Journal of African and International Law* 1, no. 1 (2008).

Heidenheimer, Arnold J. "The Context of Analysis." In *Political Corruption: Readings in Comparative Analysis on Definition*, edited by Arnold J. Heidenheimer, 3–28. New Brunswick: Transaction Books, 1970.

— . and Michael Johnston, eds. *Political Corruption: Concepts and Contexts.* 3rd ed. New Brunswick, N.J: Transaction Publishers, 2002.

Heilbrunn, John. *Anti-Corruption Commissions: Panacea or Real Medicine to Fight Corruption?* World Bank Institute, 2004.

Heimann, Fritz, and Gillian Dell. *Transparency International Progress Report 2009: Enforcement of the OECD Convention on Combating Bribery of Foreign Public Officials in International Business Transactions.* Berlin: Transparency International, June 23, 2009.

Heine, Gunter, Barbara Huber, and Tomas O. Rose. *Private Commercial Bribery: A Comparison of National and Supranational Legal Structures.* Freiburg: Edition iuscrim, 2003.

Hellman, Joel S., Geraint Jones, and Daniel Kaufmann. *Seize the State, Seize the Day: State Capture, Corruption and Influence in Transition.* World Bank Policy Research Working Paper No. 2444, September 2000.

Henning, Peter. "Corruption and Related Offences in International Economic Activities: National Reports: United States." *Revue Internationale de Droit Pénal* 74, no. 1 & 2 (2003): 169–193.

Henzelin, Marc. "L'immunité pénale dans le domaine économique, bancaire et financier: Un état de la pratique suisse et internationale." In *Le droit international des immunités: contestation ou consolidation?*, edited by Verhoeven Joe, 219–251. Bruxelles: Larcier, 2004.

— . "L'immunité pénale des chefs d'Etat en matière financière. Vers une exception pour les actes de pillage de ressources et de corruption?." *Revue suisse de droit international et de droit européen* 12, no. 2 (2002): 179–212.

Herzfeld, Thomas, and Christoph Weiss. "Corruption and Legal (In)effectiveness: An Empirical Investigation." *European Journal of Political Economy* 19 (2003): 621–632.

Hess, David, and Thomas W. Dunfee. "Fighting Corruption: A Principled Approach: The C2 Principles (Combating Corruption.)." *Cornell International Law Journal* 33, no. 3 (2000): 595–628.

Hill, Thomas W. "Foreign Representatives: Saudi Law and the Foreign Corrupt Practices Act (FCPA)." *Arab Law Quarterly* 4 (1989): 291–325.

Hislope, Robert. *When Being Bad is Good: Corrupt Exchange in Divided Societies.* Conference on Post Communist States and Societies: Transnational and National Politics. Maxwell School of Syracuse University, October 30, 2005.

Honoré, Tony. "The Dependence of Morality On Law." *Oxford Journal of Legal Studies* 13, no. 1 (1993): 1–17.

Horpisbulsuk, Sakulyouth. "Corruption and Related Offences in International Economic Activities: Individual Reports: Anti-Corruption in Thailand." *Revue Internationale de Droit Pénal* 74, no. 1 & 2 (2003): 543–555.

Hosseini, Sadeghi. "Corruption and Related Offences in International Economic Activities: National Reports: Iran." *Revue Internationale de Droit Pénal* 74, no. 1 & 2 (2003): 325–336.

— . "Internationalisation du droit pénal en Iran: le cas de la corruption." *Archives de politique criminelle* 2003/1, no. 25: 213–236.

Houston, Douglas A. "Can Corruption Ever Improve an Economy?." *Cato Journal* 27, no. 3 (2007): 325–342.

Huber, Barbara. "Supranational Measures." In *Private Commercial Bribery: A Comparison of National and Supranational Legal Structures*, edited by Günter Heine, Barbara Huber, and Thomas O Rose, 559–600. Freiburg im Breisgau: Iuscrim, 2003.

Human Rights Watch. *Some Transparency, No Accountability: The Use of Oil Revenue in Angola and Its Impact on Human Rights*, 2004.

Huntington, Samuel P. "Modernization and Corruption." In *Political Order in Changing Societies*, 59–71. New Haven: Yale University Press, 1968.

Hussmann, Karen. *Anti-Corruption Policy Making in Practice: What Can Be Learned for the Implementation of Article 5 of UNCAC?* U4 Report 1:2007. Bergen: Anti-Corruption Resource Centre, 2007.

Hussmann, Karen, Hannes Hechler, and Miguel Peñailillo. *Institutional Arrangements for Corruption Prevention: Considerations for the Implementation of the United Nations Convention against Corruption Article 6*. U4 Anti-Corruption Resource Centre Report, 2009.

Iglesias Rio, Miguel Angel. "Herramientas preventives en la lucha contra la corrupción en el ambito de la Union Europea." *Anuario de derecho consitucional latinoamericano* 10 (2004): 905–936.

International Commission of Jurists Expert Panel on Corporate Complicity in International Crimes. *Corporate Complicity and Legal Accountability: Volume 3 Civil Remedies*. Geneva, 2008.

International Council on Human Rights Policy. *Corruption and Human Rights: Making the Connection*, 2009.

Iqbal, Zafar, and Mervyn K. Lewis. "Governance and Corruption: Can Islamic Societies and the West Learn from Each Other?." *American Journal of Islamic Social Sciences* 19, no. 2 (2002): 1–33.

Jabbarov, Fakhriyar. "Corruption and Related Offences in International Economic Activities: Individual Reports: Information on Measures Undertaken for Combating Corruption in Azerbaijan." *Revue Internationale de Droit Pénal* 74, no. 1 & 2 (2003): 459–467.

Jacobs, Benjamin B. Wagner & Leslie Gielow, and Wagner. "Retooling Law Enforcement to Investigate and Prosecute Entrenched Corruption: Key Criminal Procedure Reforms for Indonesia and Other Nations." *University of Pennsylvania Journal of International Law* 30, no. 1 (2008): 183.

Jaenicke, Günther. "International Public Order." In *Encyclopedia of Public International Law*, edited by Rudolf Bernhardt, II:1348–1351. Consolidated library ed. Amsterdam: North-Holland, 1992.

Jaggy, Bernard. "La Convention de l'ONU contre la corruption: Autopsie d'une négociation." In *Les traités internationaux contre la corruption: L'ONU, l'OCDE, le Conseil de l'Europe et la Suisse*, edited by Tiziano Balmelli and Bernard Jaggy, 47–62. Lausanne, Bern, Lugano: Editions interuniversitaires suisses - Edis, 2004.

Jain, Arvind K. "Corruption: Quantitative Estimates." In *Economics of Corruption*, edited by Arvind K. Jain, 61–79. Boston: Kluwer Academic Publishers, 1998.
— . "Corruption: A Review." *Journal of Economic Surveys* 15, no. 1 (February 1, 2001): 71–121.
— . "Models of Corruption." In *Economics of Corruption*, edited by Arvind K. Jain, 13–34. Boston: Kluwer Academic Publishers, 1998.
Jakulin, Vid, and Matjaz Jager. "Corruption and Related Offences in International Economic Activities: National Reports: Slovenia." *Revue Internationale de Droit Pénal* 74, no. 1 & 2 (2003): 383–406.
Jarvin, Sigvard, and Yves Derains, eds. *Collection of ICC Arbitral Awards 1974–1985*. 1st ed. Kluwer Law International, 1994.
Jayawickrama, Nihal, Jeremy Pope, and Oliver Stolpe. "Legal Provisions to Facilitate the Gathering of Evidence in Corruption Cases: Easing the Burden of Proof." *Forum on Crime and Society (UNODC)* 2, no. 1 (2002): 23–32.
Jenks, C. Wilfred. "The Will of the World Community as the Basis of Obligation in International Law." In *Hommage d'une génération de juristes au Président Basdevant*, 280–299. Paris: Pedone, 1960.
Jimenez, Luis F. "The Inter-American Conveention against Corruption." *American Society of International Law: Proceedings of the 92nd Annual Meeting* 92 (1998): 157–162.
Johnson, O. Thomas, and Donald J. Ridings. "The OECD Convention and the Emergence of an International Anti-Bribery Regime." *Private Investments Abroad-Problems and Solutions in International Business in 1998* 41 (1998): 325–399.
Johnston, Michael. "A Brief History of Anticorruption Agencies." In *The Self-Restraining State: Power and Accountability in New Democracies*, edited by Andreas Schedler, Larry Diamond, and Marc F. Plattner, 217–226. Boulder, Colorado: Lynne Rienner Publishers, Inc., 1999.
— . "Fighting Systemic Corruption: Social Foundations for Institutional Reform." *European Journal of Development Research* 10, no. 1 (June 1998): 85.
— . "Right and Wrong in British Politics: 'Fits of Morality' in Comparative Perspective." *Polity* 24, no. 1 (Autumn 1991): 1–25.
— . *Syndromes of Corruption: Wealth, Power, and Democracy*. Cambridge: Cambridge University Press, 2005.
— . "The Political Consequences of Corruption: A Reassessment." *Comparative Politics* 18, no. 4 (1986): 459–477.
— . "The Search for Definitions: The Vitality of Politics and the Issue of Corruption." *International Social Science Journal* 149 (1996): 321–335.
Jones, Jessica. "India Versus the United Nations: the Central Vigilance Commission Act Does Not Satisfy the U. N. Convention Against Corruption." *Emory International Law Review* 22, no. 2 (2008): 799–856.
Jorge, Guillermo. *The Effects of International Anti-money Laundering Initiatives in Repatriating Proceeds from Corruption*, 2003.
— . *The Romanian Legal Framework on Illicit Enrichment*. American Bar Association Central European and Eurasian Law Initiative (ABA/CEELI), July 2007.
Kahn, Philippe. "A propos de l'ordre public transnational: Quelques observations." In *Mélanges Fritz Sturm offerts par ses collègues et ses amis à l'occasion de son*

soixante-dixième anniversaire, edited by Jean-François Gerkens, II:1539–1550. Lausanne: Faculté de droit de Lausanne, 1999.
— . "Les principes généraux du droit devant les arbitres du commerce international." *Journal du droit international* 116, no. 2 (1989): 305–327.
Kaufmann, Daniel. "10 Myths about Governance and Corruption." *Finance & Development* 42, no. 3 (2005).
— . "Corruption: The Facts." *Foreign Policy*, no. Summer (1997): 114–131.
— . "Research on Corruption: Critical Empirical Issues." In *Economics of Corruption*, edited by Arvind K. Jain, 129–176. Boston: Kluwer Academic Publishers, 1998.
— . "Rethinking Governance: Empirical Lessons Challenge Orthodoxy." In *Global Competitiveness Report 2002–2003*. Geneva: World Economic Forum, 2003.
— . and Paul Siegelbaum. "Privatization and Corruption in Transition Economies." *Journal of International Affairs* 50, no. 2 (1997): 419–458.
— . and Pedro C. Vicente. "Legal Corruption," November 24, 2005. http://papers.ssrn.com/sol3/papers.cfm?abstract_id=829844.
— . and Shang-Jin Wei. *Does 'Grease Money' Speed Up the Wheels of Commerce?* National Bureau of Economic Research Working Paper no. 7093, 1999.
Kennedy, David. *The Dark Sides of Virtue: Reassessing International Humanitarianism*. Princeton, N.J: Princeton University Press, 2004.
— . "The International Anti-Corruption Campaign." *Connecticut Journal of International Law* 14 (1999): 455–465.
Kessedjian, Catherine. "La norme juridique est-elle apte à lutter contre la corruption?." In *Souveraineté étatique et marchés internationaux à la fin du 20ème siècle: à propos de 30 ans de recherche du CREDIMI: Mélanges en l'honneur de Philippe Kahn*, Volume 20:601–611. Travaux du Centre de recherche sur le droit des marchés et des investissements internationaux. Dijon: Litec, 2000.
— . "Transnational Public Policy." In *International Arbitration 2006: back to Basics?*, edited by A. J. van den Berg, 857–870. ICCA Congress Series. Alphen aan den Rijn, The Netherlands: Kluwer Law International, 2007.
Kichana, Philip. *Country Review of Legal and Practical Challenges to the Domestication of the Anti-Corruption Conventions: Kenya*. Transparency International, 2006.
Kim, Jong Bum. "Korean Implementation of the OECD Bribery Convention: Implications for Global Efforts to Fight Corruption." *Pacific Basin Law Journal* 17, no. 2 & 3 (1999): 245–275.
Klein, Charles B. "What Exactly is an Unlawful Gratuity after United States v. Sun-Diamond Growers?." *George Washington Law Review* 68 (1999): 116–133.
Klitgaard, Robert. "Bribes, Tribes and Markets that Fail: Rethinking the Economics of Underdevelopment." *Development Southern Africa* 11, no. 4 (1994): 481–493.
— . *Controlling Corruption*. Berkeley: University of California Press, 1988.
— . "International Cooperation against Corruption." *Finance & Development* (March 1998): 3–6.
— . "Introduction: Subverting Corruption." *Global Crime* 7, no. 3 & 4 (2006): 299–307.
Knoepfler, François. "Corruption et arbitrage international." In *Les contrats de distribution, Contributions offertes au Professeur Dessemontet*, edited by I. Cherpillod, 357–380. Lausanne: Publication CEDIDAC 38, 1998.

Kofele-Kale, Ndiva. *International Law of Responsibility for Economic Crimes: Holding Heads of State and Other High Ranking State Officials Individually Liable for Acts of Fraudulent Enrichment.* The Hague: Kluwer Law International, 1995.

— . "Patrimonicide: The International Economic Crime of Indigenous Spoliation." *Vanderbilt Journal of Transnational Law* 28 (1995): 45–118.

— . "Presumed Guilty: Balancing Competing Rights and Interests in Combating Economic Crimes." *The International Lawyer* 40, no. 4 (2006): 909–944.

— . "The Right to a Corruption-Free Society as an Individual and Collective Human Right: Elevating Official Corruption to a Crime under International Law." *The International Lawyer* 34, no. 1 (2000): 149–178.

Konstantopoulou, Zoe. "Corruption and Related Offences in International Economic Activities: National Reports: Greece." *Revue Internationale de Droit Pénal* 74, no. 1 & 2 (2003): 255–289.

Kubiciel, Michael. "Core Criminal Law Provisions in the United Nations Convention Against Corruption." *International Criminal Law Review* 9 (February 2009): 139–155.

Kumar, C. Raj. "The human right to corruption-free service, some constitutional and international perspectives." *Frontline*, 2002.

Kunaka, Constance, Noria Mashumba, and Philliat Matsheza. *The Southern African Development Community Protocol against Corruption: A Regional Framework to Combat Corruption.* Harare: Human Rights Trust of Southern Africa, 2002.

Kunicka-Michalska, Barbara. "Corruption and Related Offences in International Economic Activities: National Reports: Poland." *Revue Internationale de Droit Pénal* 74, no. 1 & 2 (2003): 351–382.

Laje Anaya, Justo. *Delitos Contra La Administración Pública.* Colección de derecho penal y derecho procesal penal. Córdoba: M. Lerner Editora Córdoba, 2001.

Lalive, Pierre. "Transnational (or Truly International) Public Policy and International Arbitration." In *Comparative Arbitration Practive and Public Policy in Arbitration*, edited by Pieter Sanders, 257–318. International Council for Commercial Arbitration, Congress Series No. 3, VIIIth International Arbitration Congress, New York, 6–9 May 1986. Deventer, The Netherlands: Kluwer Law and Taxation Publishers, 1987.

Latimer, Paul, and A.J. Brown. "Whistleblower Laws: International Best Practice." *University of New South Wales Law Journal* 31, no. 3 (2008): 766–794.

Lawrence, Richard. "US Anti-Corruption Drive Pays." *Journal of Commerce*, June 20, 1996.

Lawson, Letitia. "The Politics of Anti-Corruption Reform in Africa." *The Journal of Modern African Studies* 47, no. 01 (2009): 73–100.

Leff, Nathaniel H. "Economic Development through Bureaucratic Corruption." *American Behavioral Scientist* 8, no. 3 (1964): 8–14.

Leiken, Robert S. "Controlling the Global Corruption Epidemic." *Foreign Policy*, no. 105 (December 1996): 55.

LeVine, Victor. "Transnational Aspects of Political Corruption." In *Political Corruption: A Handbook*, edited by Arnold J Heidenheimer, Michael Johnston, and Victor LeVine, 685–700. New Brunswick, N.J: Transaction Books, 1989.

Leys, Colin. "What is the Problem about Corruption?" *Journal of Modern African Studies* 3, no. 2 (1965): 215–230.

Ligeti, Katalin. "Corruption and Related Offences in International Economic Activities: National Reports: Hungary." *Revue Internationale de Droit Pénal* 74, no. 1 & 2 (2003): 291–323.

Lo Kwok-chung, Jeremy. "Combating Corruption in Hong Kong." *Resource Material Series (UNAFEI)* 77 (March 2009): 3–10.

Lomjaria, Levan. "Corruption and Related Offences in International Economic Activities: Individual Reports: Report on the Present Situation, Problems and Solutions in the Legal System Related to Corruption Control and Corruption Cases in Georgia." *Revue Internationale de Droit Pénal* 74, no. 1 & 2 (2003): 485–491.

Looney, Robert. "Profiles of Corruption in the Middle East." *Journal of South Asian and Middle Eastern Studies* 28, no. 4 (2005): 1–20.

Loquiun, Eric. "Les manifestations de l'illicite." In *L'illicité dans le commerce international*, edited by Philippe Kahn and Catherine Kessedjian, 604. Travaux du Centre de recherche sur le droit des marchés et des investissements internationaux. Paris: Litec, 1996.

Low, Lucinda A. "Milestones in Mutual Evaluation: the Phase 2 Review of the United States under the OECD Antibribery Convention." *International Law Forum du droit international* 5, no. 2 (2003).

— . "Transnational Corruption: New Rules for Old Temptations, New Players to Combat a Prennial Evil." *American Society of International Law: Proceedings of the 92nd Annual Meeting* 92 (1998): 151–156.

— . Andrea K. Bjorklund, and Kathryn Cameron Atkinson. "The Inter-American Convention against Corruption: A Comparison with the United States Foreign Corrupt Practices Act." *Virginia Journal of International Law* 38 (1997): 243–292.

Lugon-Moulin, Anne. "Lutte contre la corruption et coopération au développment – Synthèse, enjeux et perspectives." In *Les traités internationaux contre la corruption: L'ONU, l'OCDE, le Conseil de l'Europe et la Suisse*, edited by Tiziano Balmelli and Bernard Jaggy, 139–165. Lausanne, Bern, Lugano: Editions interuniversitaires suisses – Edis, 2004.

Manzetti, Luigi, and Charles Blake. "Market Reforms and Corruption in Latin America." *Review of International Political Economy* 3, no. Winter (1997): 662–697.

Marican, Y. Mansoor. "Combating Corruption: The Malaysian Experience." *Asian Survey* 19, no. 6 (1979): 597–610.

Martin, A. Timothy. *Canadian Law on Corruption of Foreign Public Officials.*

— . "International Arbitration and Corruption: An Evolving Standard." *Transnational Dispute Management* I, no. 2-May (2004).

Masabo, Michel. *Country Review of Legal and Practical Challenges to the Domestication of the Anti-Corruption Conventions in Burundi.* Transparency International, 2007.

— . *Les défis politiques et légaux relatifs a la mise en application des conventions de lutte contre la corruption au Burundi.* Transparency International, 2005.

Matsheza, Philliat, Heather Mupita, and Kenyatta Nyirenda, eds. *SADC Anti-Corruption Laws: A Case for Harmonisation.* Harare: Human Rights Trust of Southern Africa, 2004.

Mauro, Paolo. "Corruption and Growth." *Quarterly Journal of Economics* 110, no. 3 (1995): 681–712.

— . "Corruption and the Composition of Government Expenditure." *Journal of Public Economics* 69, no. 2 (1998): 263–279.

Meagher, Patrick. *Anti-Corruption Agencies: A Review of Experience.* Center for Institutional Reform and the Informal Sector, March 2004.

Messick, Richard. *Income and Assets Declarations: Issues to Consider in Developing a Disclosure Regime.* U4 Issue 2009:6. Bergen: Anti-Corruption Resource Centre, 2009.

— . and Rachel Kleinfeld. "Writing an Effective Anticorruption Law." World Bank, October 2001.

Michael, Bryane. "Depoliticising Anti-Corruption in Bolivia: Local International Intervention and the State." *International Journal of Public Administration* 29, no. 13 (2006): 1311–1336.

— . "Drafting Implementing Regulations for International Anti-Corruption Conventions." *QEH Working Paper Series* Working Paper 150.

— . "Suing against Corruption: The Role of Civil Law." Policy Innovations, 23 July 2007. www.policyinnovations.org/ideas/innovations/data/000015.

— . *What Does the UN Convention on Corruption Teach Us About International Regulatory Harmonisation?* SSRN Working Paper, 2007.

— . and Habit Hajredini. "The Effective Implementation of International Anti-Corruption Conventions." *eucrim*, no. 3–4 (2007): 128–133.

Mikkelsen-Löth, Jorge Federico. *Enriquecimiento Ilícito: El Desafío Para La Ciencia Jurídico-penal En La Sociedad Actual De Enfrentar a La Corrupción En La Administración Pública.* Buenos Aires: La Ley, 2001.

Milovanovic, Milic. *Endogenous Corruption in Privatized Companies.* 2001.

Mir Puig, Carlos. *Los Delitos Contra La Administración Pública En El Nuevo Código Penal.* Biblioteca de derecho penal. Barcelona: J.M. Bosch, 2000.

Miranda, Anibal. *Legislación Anticorrupción: Convenios, Leyes, Decretos-leyes Y Otros Instrumentos Contra La Corrupción, El Enriquecimiento Ilegítimo, Crimen Organizado Y Delitos Conexos: Anotados Y Comentados.* 2003rd ed. Asunción, Paraguay: Miranda & Asociados, 2003.

Misbah-ul-Hassan, Qazi, and Pakistan. *The National Accountability Ordinance, 1999: As Amended up to Date with Relevant Notifications, Case-law and Commentary.* Lahore: PLD Publishers, 2006.

Miyasaki-Miyamae, Mirta Rika. "Corruption and Related Offences in International Economic Activities: Individual Reports: Corruption in Paraguay." *Revue Internationale de Droit Pénal* 74, no. 1 & 2 (2003): 527–533.

Molina Arrubla, Carlos Mario, and Colombia. *Comentarios Al Nuevo Código Penal: Delitos Contra La Administración Pública.* Bogotá: Editorial Leyer, 2001.

Moodie, Graeme C. "On Political Scandals and Corruption." *Government and Opposition* 15, no. 2 (April 1980): 208–222.

Moody-Stuart, George. *Grand Corruption: How Business Bribes Damage Developing Countries.* 3rd ed. Oxford: WorldView Publishing, 1997.

Moore Dickerson, Claire. "Culture and Transborder Effects: Northern Individualism Meets Third Generation Human Rights." *Rutgers Law Review* 54 (2001): 865–880.

Morrissey, David. "The Fight against Corruption by International Organizations." *The George Washington International Law Review* 39, no. 1 (2007): 165–198.

Mosler, Hermann. "General Principles of Law." In *Encyclopaedia of Public International Law*, edited by Rudolf Bernhardt, II:511–527. Consolidated library ed. Amsterdam: North-Holland, 1992.

— . *The International Society as a Legal Community*. Alphen aan den Rijn, The Netherlands: Sijthoff & Noordhoff, 1980.

Muxart, Anne. *La restitution internationale des biens publics détournés par d'anciens chefs d'État*. Paris I, 2003.

Mwenda, Kenneth Kaoma. *Legal Aspects of Combating Corruption: The Case of Zambia*. Youngstown, N.Y: Cambria Press, 2007.

Myrdal, Gunnar. "Corruption: Its Causes and Effects." In *Asian Drama: An Inquiry into the Poverty of Nations*, 2:937–958. New York: Twentieth Century Fund, 1968.

— . "Corruption: Its Causes and Effects." In *The Economics of Corruption*, edited by Ajit Mishra, 37–62. New Delhi: Oxford University Press, 2005.

— . *The Challenge of World Poverty: A World Anti-Poverty Program in Outline*. The Christian A. Herter lecture series. New York: Pantheon Books, 1970.

Naeen, Mohamed. "Corruption and Related Offences in International Economic Activities: Individual Reports: Maldives: Corruption Control in Criminal Justice." *Revue Internationale de Droit Pénal* 74, no. 1 & 2 (2003): 509–514.

Naím, Moisés. "Bad Medicine." *Foreign Policy*, 2005.

— . "The Corruption Eruption." *Brown Journal of World Affairs* 2, no. 2 (1995): 245–261.

— . "Tunnel Vision on Corruption." *Washington Post*, February 20, 2005.

Nasreen, Begum. "Corruption and Related Offences in International Economic Activities: Individual Reports: The Present Situation, Problems and Solutions in the Legal System Related to Corruption Control: Bangladesh." *Revue Internationale de Droit Pénal* 74, no. 1 & 2 (2003): 469–478.

Nicholls, Colin, Tim Daniel, and John Hatchard. *Corruption and Misuse of Public Office*. Oxford: Oxford University Press, 2006.

Nichols, Philip M. "Corruption in the World Trade Organization: Discerning the Limits of the World Trade Organization's Authority." *N.Y.U. Journal of International Law and Politics* 28 (1995): 711–784.

— . "Outlawing Transnational Bribery through the WTO." *Law and Policy in International Business* 28 (1997): 305–381.

Nilsson, Hans G. "Special Investigation Techniques and Developments in Mutual Legal Assistance: the Crossroads between Police Cooperation and Judicial Cooperation." *Resource Material Series* (2005).

Noonan, John T. *Bribes*. Berkeley: University of California Press, 1984.

Nordio, Carlo. *Giustizia*. 1st ed. Milano: Cantiere Italia, 1997.

Nye, Joseph S. "Corruption and Political Development: A Cost-Benefit Analysis." *American Political Science Review* 61, no. 2 (1967): 417–427.

Ocheje, Paul D. "Refocusing International Law on the Quest for Accountability in Africa: The Case against the Impunity." *Leiden Journal of International Law* 15, no. 04 (2002): 749–779.

OECD. *Armenia: Fighting Corruption in Transition Economies*. Paris: OECD Publications, 2005.

—. *Azerbaijan: Fighting Corruption in Transition Economies*. Paris: OECD Publications, 2005.
—. *Corruption: A Glossary of International Criminal Standards*. Paris: OECD Publishing, 2007.
—. *Enhancing Integrity in Public Procurement: a Checklist*, 2008.
—. "Fighting Corruption in Transition Economies Kazakhstan," 2007.
—. *Georgia: Fighting Corruption in Transition Economies*. Paris: OECD Publications, 2005.
—. *Integrity in Public Procurement: Good Practice from A to Z*. Paris: OECD Publishing, 2007.
—. *Kazakhstan: Fighting Corruption in Transition Economies*. Paris: OECD Publications, 2007.
—. *Lobbyists, Governments and Public Trust: Building a Legislative Framework for Enhancing Transparency and Accountability in Lobbying*, August 2008.
—. *OECD Principles for Integrity in Public Procurement*. Paris: OECD Publishing, 2009.
—. *Specialised Anti-Corruption Institutions: Review of Models*. Paris: OECD, 2007.
—. *Tajikistan: Fighting Corruption in Transition Economies*. Paris: OECD Publications, 2005.
—. *The Kyrgyz Republic: Fighting Corruption in Transition Economies*. Paris: OECD Publications, 2005.
—. *Typologies on the Role of Intermediaries in International Business Transactions*, October 2009.
—. *Ukraine: Fighting Corruption in Transition Economies*. Paris: OECD Publications, 2005.
Ofosu-Amaah, W. Paatii, Raj Soopramanien, and Kishor Uprety. *Combating Corruption: A Comparative Review of Selected Legal Aspects of State Practice and Major International Initiatives*. Washington, D.C.: World Bank, 1999.
Okuyucu-Ergün, Güne. "Anti-Corruption Legislation in Turkish Law." *German Law Journal* 8, no. 9 (2007): 903–914.
Olagoke, Olankunle O. "The Extra-territorial Scope of the Anti-corruption Legislation in Nigeria." *The International Lawyer* 38, no. 1 (2004): 71–88.
O'Leary, Cornelius. *The Elimination of Corrupt Practices in British Elections, 1868–1911*. Oxford: Clarendon Press, 1962.
Olinga, Alain Didier. *Les défis pratiques et légaux relatifs à la mise en application des conventions de lutte contre la corruption au Cameroun*. Transparency International, 2005.
Onoria, Henry. *Country Review of Legal and Practical Challenges to the Domestication of the Anti-Corruption Conventions in Uganda*. Transparency International. Kampala, March 2006.
Open Democracy Advice Centre. *Country Review of Legal and Practical Challenges to the domestication of the Anti-Corruption Conventions in South Africa*. Transparency International, 2006.
Open Society Justice Initiative. *Legal Remedies for the Resource Curse: A Digest of Experience in Using Law to Combat Natural Resource Corruption Legal Policy Series*. New York: Open Society Institute, 2005.

Oppetit, Bruno. "Droit du commerce international et valeurs non marchandes." In *Etudes de droit international en l'honneur de Pierre Lalive*, edited by Christian Dominicé, Robert Patry, and Claude Reymond, 309–319. Bâle: Helbing & Lichtenhahn, 1993.

— . "Le paradoxe de la corruption à l'épreuve du droit du commerce international." *Journal du droit international* (1987): 5–16.

Orakhelashvili, Alexander. "International Public Order and the International Court's Advisory Opinion on Legal Consequences of the Construction of a Wall in the Occupied Palestinian Territory." *Archiv des Völkerrechts* 43, no. 2 (2005): 240–256.

OSCE. "Bribery and Corruption in the OSCE Region: Hearing before the Commission of Security and Cooperation in Europe," 1999.

Osterfeld, David. *Prosperity Versus Planning: How Government Stifles Economic Growth*. New York: Oxford University Press, 1992.

O'Sullivan, Julie R. *Federal White Collar Crime: Cases and Materials*. 2nd ed. St. Paul: Thomson West, 2003.

Passas, Nikos. "Formalizing the Informal? Problems in the National and International Regulation of Hawala." In *Regulatory Frameworks for Hawala and Other Remittance Systems*, 7–16. Washington, D.C: International Monetary Fund, 2005.

— . "UNCAC, Technical Assistance and Development Efforts." In *Recovering Stolen Assets*, edited by Mark Pieth, 281–295. Bern: Peter Lang, 2008.

— . and Dimitri Vlassis, eds. *The United Nations Convention against Corruption as a Way of Life*. Milan: ISPAC, 2006.

Peña Cabrera Freyre, Alonso. *Comentarios a la Legislación Anti-Corrupción*. La Molina: Ediciones Legales, 2002.

Peñailillo, Miguel. *How Prepared Are We to Assess Real Implementation of Anti-Corruption Conventions? Lessons from the Americas*. U4 Issue 3:2009. Bergen: Anti-Corruption Resource Centre, 2009.

Penal Law Colloquim. "XVIIth International Congress of Penal Law Preparatory Colloquium Section IIICorruption and Related Offences in International Economic Activities, November 11–12, 2002, Tokyo (Japan) Resolution." *International Review of Penal Law* 74.

Peters, John G., and Susan Welch. "Political Corruption in America: A Search for Definitions and a Theory." *American Political Science Review* 72 (1978): 974–984.

Philp, Mark. "Defining Political Corruption." In *Political Corruption*, edited by Heywood Paul, 20–46. Oxford: Blackwell, 1997.

Pieth, Mark. "International Efforts to Combat Corruption in Business Transactions." *Middle East Executive Reports* 22, no. 11 (1999): 8–14.

— . "Preventing Corruption: A Case Study." In *Les chemins de l'harmonisation pénale = Harmonising Criminal Law*, edited by Mireille Delmas-Marty, Mark Pieth, Ulrich Sieber, and Juliette Lelieur, 15:225–252. UMR de droit comparé de Paris. Paris: Société de législation comparée, 2008.

— . Lucinda A. Low, and Peter J. Cullen, eds. *The OECD Convention on Bribery: A Commentary*. Cambridge University Press, 2007.

Pihlajamäki, Antti. "Corruption and Related Offences in International Economic Activities: National Reports: Finland." *Revue Internationale de Droit Pénal* 74, no. 1 & 2 (2003): 195–214.

Polaine, Martin. "General Sani Abacha – a Nation's Thief." Making international anti-corruption standards operational: Asset Recovery and mutual legal assistance, Regional Seminar for Asia-Pacific, September 2007.

—. "The 2003 United Nations Convention against Corruption: Criminalisation." London, 2006.

Pope, Jeremy. *TI Source Book: Confronting Corruption: The Elements of a National Integrity System*. Berlin: Transparency International, 2000.

Posadas, Alejandro. "Combating Corruption Under International Law." *Duke Journal of Comparative & International Law* 10, no. 2 (2000): 345–414.

Pouyaud, Dominique. "La loi du 29 janvier 1993 relative à la prévention de la corruption et à la transparence de la vie économique et des procédures publiques: Concurrence, transparence et libre administration: A propos de la décision de Conseil constitutionnel no. 92-316 DC de 20 janvier 1993." *Revue Française de Droit Administratif* 9, no. 5 (1993): 902–920.

Pritchard, John. "Introduction to the New South Wales Independent Commission against Corruption." *Resource Material Series (UNAFEI)* 69 (July 2006): 202–226.

Qadir, Mansoor. "Corruption and Related Offences in International Economic Activities: Individual Reports: Report on Present Situation, Problems and Solutions in the Legal System Related to Corruption Control and Corruption Cases in Pakistan." *Revue Internationale de Droit Pénal* 74, no. 1 & 2 (2003): 515–525.

Quah, Jon. *Defying Institutional Failure: Learning from the Experiences of Anti-Corruption Agencies in Four Asian Countries*. Centre for Research and Studies on Sociology (CIES), Conference: Empowering Anti-Corruption Agencies: Defying Institutional Failure and Strengthening Preventive and Repressive Capacities, May 14, 2008. SpringerLink.

Quinones, Enery. "L'evolution du droit international en matière de corruption: la Convention de l'OCDE." *Annuaire français de droit international* 49 (2003): 563–574.

Racine, Jean-Baptiste. *L'arbitrage commercial international et l'ordre public*. Paris: L.G.D.J., 1999.

Reed, Quentin. *Sitting on the Fence: Conflicts of Interest and How to Regulate Them*. U4 Issue 2008:6. Bergen: Anti-Corruption Resource Centre, 2008.

Reisman, Michael W. *Folded Lies, Bribery, Crusades, and Reforms*. New York: Free Press, 1979.

—. "Harnessing International Law to Restrain and Recapture Indigenous Spoliations." *American Journal of International Law* 83 (1989): 56–59.

Rider, Barry, ed. *Corruption: The Enemy Within*. The Hague, London, Boston: Kluwer Law International, 1997.

Riffault-Silk, Jacqueline. "La lutte contre la corruption nationale et internationale par les moyens du droit pénal." *Revue internationale de droit comparé* 54, no. 2 (2002): 639–661.

Rolin, Henri. "Vers un ordre public réellement international." In *Hommage d'une génération de juristes au Président Basdevant*, 441–462. Paris: Pedone, 1960.

Rose-Ackerman, Susan. *Corruption and Government: Causes, Consequences, and Reform*. Cambridge: Cambridge University Press, 1999.

—. *Grand Corruption and the Ethics of Global Business*. Working Paper No. 221, 1999.

— . "Political Corruption and Democracy." *Connecticut Journal of International Law* 14, no. 2 (1999): 363–378.
— . "The Economics of Corruption." *Journal of Public Economics* 4 (1975): 187–203.
— . "The Political Economy of Corruption." In *Corruption and the Global Economy*, edited by Kimberly Ann Elliott, 31–60. Washington, DC: Institute for International Economics, 1997.
Sacerdoti, Giorgio. "La convention de l'OCDE de 1997 sur la lutte contre la corruption des agents publics étrangers dans les transactions commerciales internationales." *Revue de Droit des Affaires Internationales*, no. 1 (1999): 3–17.
Sancinetti, Marcelo A. *El Delito De Enriquecimiento Ilícito De Funcionario Público--Art. 268 (2), C.P.: Un Tipo Penal Violatorio Del Estado De Derecho*. Buenos Aires: AD-HOC, 1994.
Saphos, Charles. "Something is Rotten in the State of Affairs between Nations: The Difficulties of Establishing the Rules of International Criminal Law because of Public Corruption." *Fordham International Law Journal* 19 (1995): 1947–1954.
Sayed, Abdulhay. *Corruption in International Trade and Commercial Arbitration*. The Hague, London, Boston: Kluwer Law International, 2004.
Scheppele, Kim Lane. "The Inevitable Corruption of Transition." *Connecticut Journal of International Law* 14, no. 2 (1999): 509–532.
Schleifer, Andrei, and Robert W. Vishny. "Corruption." *Quarterly Journal of Economics* 108, no. 3 (1993): 599–617.
Schroth, Peter W. "The African Union Convention on Preventing and Combating Corruption." *Journal of African Law* 49, no. 1 (2005): 24–38.
Schultz, Jessica. *The UNCAC and Judicial Corruption: Requirements and Avenues for Reform*. U4 Brief No. 18. Bergen: Anti-Corruption Resource Centre, 2009.
Scott, James C. "The Analysis of Corruption in Developing Nations." *Comparative Studies in Society and History* 11, no. 3 (1969): 315–341.
Seidl-Hohenveldern, Ignaz. "Ordre Public (Public Order)." *Encyclopaedia of Public International Law* III (1992): 788–790.
Seminario internacional sobre la corrupción y la convención interamericana. *Talleres de divulgación e implementación de la convención interamericana contra la corrupción*. Bogotá: Pontificia Universidad Javeriana, Facultad de Ciencias Jurídicas, 1999.
Shah, Anwar, ed. *Performance Accountability and Combating Corruption*. Public Sector Governance and Accountability Series. Washington, D.C.: World Bank, 2007.
Shams, Heba. *Legal Globalization: Money Laundering Law and Other Cases*. International financial law series. London: British Institute of International and Comparative Law, 2004.
Shleifer, Andrei, and Robert W Vishny. "Politicians and Firms." *The Quarterly Journal of Economics* 109, no. 4 (November 1994): 995–1025.
Simis, Konstantin M. *USSR: The Corrupt Society: The Secret World of Soviet Capitalism*. New York: Simon and Schuster, 1982.
Simon, Joel. "Clayco Petroleum Corp. v. Occidental Petroleum Corp.: Should there be a Bribery Exception to the Act of State Doctrine?" *Cornell International Law Journal* 17 (1984): 407–427.

Sinjela, Mpazi. "The African Union Takes a Legal Stand on Corruption." *African Yearbook of International Law* 11 (2003): 143–159.

Slaughter, Anne-Marie. *A New World Order.* Princeton, N.J: Princeton University Press, 2004.

Smith, Jack, Mark Pieth, and Guillermo Jorge. *The Recovery of Stolen Assets: A Fundamental Principle of the Un Convention Against Corruption.* U4 Brief. Anti-Corruption Resource Centre, February 2007.

Snider, Thomas R, and Won Kidane. "Combating Corruption through International Law in Africa: A Comparative Analysis." *Cornell International Law Journal* 40 (2007): 691.

Sonesavanh, Seng Aphey. "Corruption and Related Offences in International Economic Activities: Individual Reports: Corruption Control: Laos." *Revue Internationale de Droit Pénal* 74, no. 1 & 2 (2003): 499–503.

de Sousa, Luís. "Anti-Corruption Agencies: Between Empowerment and Irrelevance." European University Institute Working Papers, RSCAS 2009/08, 2009.

de Speville, Bertrand. *Reversing the Onus of Proof: Is it Compatible with Respect for Human Rights Norms.* Paper presented at the 8th International Anti-Corruption Conference, 1997.

Stancich, Rikki. "Deals in the Dark." *Ethical Corporation: Anti-Corruption Special Report*, April 2008.

Starr, Sonja B. *Extraordinary Crimes at Ordinary Times: International Justice Beyond Crisis Situations.* Harvard Public Law Working Paper No. 133, 2007.

Steffens, Lincoln. *The Shame of the Cities.* First American century series ed. American century series. New York: Hill and Wang, 1957.

Stephan, Paul B. "Rationality and Corruption in the Post-Socialist World." *Connecticut Journal of International Law* 14, no. 2 (1999): 533–549.

Stern, Brigitte. "Immunities for Heads of State: Where Do We Stand?" In *Justice for Crimes against Humanity*, 73–106. London: Hart Publishing, 2003.

Stessens, Guy. "Corruption and Related Offences in International Economic Activities: National Reports: Belgium." *Revue Internationale de Droit Pénal* 74, no. 1 & 2 (2003): 133–147.

— . *Money Laundering: A New International Law Enforcement Model.* Cambridge: Cambridge University Press, 2000.

— . "The International Fight against corruption." *Revue Internationale de Droit Pénal* 72, no. 3–4 (2001): 891–937.

Sundack, Tracie A. "Republic of Philippines v. Marcos: The Ninth Circuit Allows a Former Ruler to Invoke the Act of State Doctrine against a Resisting Sovereign." *American University Law Review* 38 (1988): 225.

Sundet, Geir. *Following the Money: Do Public Expenditure Tracking Surveys matter?* U4 Issue 2008:8. Bergen: Anti-Corruption Resource Centre, 2008.

Sur, Serge. "La coutume internationale: Sa vie, son ouvre." *Droits, Revue française de théorie juridique* 3 (1986).

Svensson, Jakob. "Eight Questions about Corruption." *Journal of Economic Perspectives* 19, no. 3 (2005): 19–42.

Tanzi, Vito. "Corruption around the World: Causes, Consequences, Scope, and Cures." In *Governance, Corruption, and Economic Performance*, edited by George T. Abed and Sanjeev Gupta, 19–58. Washington, D.C.: International Monetary Fund, 2002.

— . and Hamid Davoodi. "Corruption, Growth, and Public Finances." In *Governance, Corruption, and Economic Performance*, edited by George T. Abed and Sanjeev Gupta, 197–222. Washington D.C.: International Monetary Fund, 2002.

— . *Corruption, Public Investment, and Growth*. IMF Working Paper WP/97/139, 1997.

Thiankolu, Muthomi. *The Anti-Corruption and Economic Crimes Act, 2003; Has Kenya Discharged her Obligations to Her Peoples and the World*? December 2006.

Thomas, Chantal. "Does the 'Good Governance Policy' of the International Financial Institutions Privilege Markets at the Expense of Democracy?" *Connecticut Journal of International Law* 14, no. 2 (1999): 551–562.

Thompson, Dennis. *Ethics in Congress: From Individual to Institutional Corruption*. Washington, D.C.: Brookings Institution, 1995.

— . "Mediated Corruption: The Case of the Keating Five." *American Political Science Review* 87 (1993): 369–381.

Thuo Gathii, James. "Corruption and Donor Reforms: Expanding the Promises and Possibilities of the Rule of Law as an Anti-Corruption Strategy in Kenya." *Connecticut Journal of International Law* 14, no. 2 (1999): 407–453.

Tilman, Robert O. "Emergence of Black-Market Bureaucracy: Administration, Development and Corruption in the New States." *Public Administration Review* 28, no. 5 (1968): 432–444.

Transparencia Paraguay. "Politics and Nepotism Plague Paraguay's Courts." In *Global Corruption Report 2007*. Cambridge: Cambridge University Press, 2007.

Transparency International. *Accountability and Transparency in Political Finance: Why, How, and What For?* TI Working Paper No. 01/2008.

— . *Global Corruption Report 2007: Corruption in Judicial Systems*. Cambridge: Cambridge University Press, 2007.

— . *Global Corruption Report 2009: Corruption and the Private Sector*. Cambridge: Cambridge University Press, 2009.

— . *Political Finance Regulations: Bridging the Enforcement Gap*. TI Policy Position No. 02/2009.

— . *Standards on Political Funding and Favours*. TI Policy Position No. 01/2005.

— . *Using the Right to Information as an Anti-Corruption Tool*, 2006.

Transparency International, and The Carter Center. *The Crinis Project: Money in Politics, Everyone's Concern*, 2007.

Transparency International USA. *Compliance of the United States of America with the Inter-American Convention against Corruption*, 2007.

Tricot, Juliette. "Les figures de l'internationalisation en droit pénal des affaires: La criminalisation imposée au droit interne par le droit international: La corruption internationale." *Revue de science criminelle et de droit pénal comparé*, no. 4 (2005): 753–765.

Udombana, Nsongurua J. "Fighting Corruption Seriously? Africas Anti-corruption Convention." *Singapore Journal of International & Comparative Law* 7, no. 2 (2003): 447–488.

UNCTAD. *Illicit Payments*. UNCTAD Series on issues in international investment agreements. New York, Geneva: United Nations, 2001.

— . *Transparency*. UNCTAD Series on issues in international investment agreements. New York, Geneva: United Nations, 2003.

UNDP. *Anti-corruption: Practice Note*, 2004.

— . *Institutional Arrangements to Combat Corruption: A Comparative Study*. Thailand, 2005.

UNODC. *Good Practices for the Protection of Witnesses in Criminal Proceedings Involving Organized Crime*. Vienna, New York: United Nations, 2008.

— . and Nikos Passas *Legislative Guide for the Implementation of the United Nations Convention against Corruption*. Vienna, New York: United Nations, 2006.

— . *The Global Programme against Corruption: UN Anti-Corruption Toolkit*. 3rd ed. Vienna: UNODC, 2004.

— . and UNICRI. *Technical Guide to the United Nations Convention against Corruption*. Vienna, New York: United Nations, 2009.

Van Klaveren, Jacob. "Corruption as a Historical Phenomenon." In *Political Corruption: Concepts and Contexts*, edited by Arnold J. Heidenheimer and Michael Johnston, 83–94. 3rd ed. New Brunswick, N.J: Transaction Publishers, 2002.

Van Vuuren, Hennie. "Corruption, Perception and Foreign Direct Investment: Counting the Cost of Graft." *African Security Review* 11, no. 3 (2002).

Van Zyl, Albert, Vivek Ramkumar, and Paolo de Renzio. *Responding to challenges of Supreme Audit Instituions: Can legislatures and civil society help?* U4 Issue 2009:1. Bergen: Anti-Corruption Resource Centre, 2009.

Veglio, Pietro, and Peter Siegenthaler. "Monitoring the Restitution of Looted State Assets: The Role of Multilateral Development Banks (MDBs)." In *Recovering Stolen Assets*, edited by Mark Pieth, 315–329. Bern: Peter Lang, 2008.

Veloso Abueva, Jose. "The Contribution of Nepotism, Spoils and Graft to Political Development." *East-West Center Review* 3 (1966): 45–54.

Vermeulen, Gert, ed. *EU Standards in Witness Protection and Collaboration with Justice*. Maklu, 2005.

Villada, Jorge Luis. *Delitos Contra La Función Pública: Concordado Con Códigos Latinoamericanos*. Buenos Aires: Abeledo-Perrot, 1999.

Vincke, François. "L'anti-corruption après la Convention de Mérida." *Revue de Droit Pénal et de Criminologie* 85, no. 4 (2005): 351–386.

— . "The Business Community's Attitude towards Corruption: Special Focus on Private-to-Private Corruption." In *Liber Amicorum: Commission Droit et Vie des Affaires*, 177–194. Bruxelles: Bruylant, 1998.

Von Sydow, Annette. "Corruption and Related Offences in International Economic Activities: National Reports: Sweden." *Revue Internationale de Droit Pénal* 74, no. 1 & 2 (2003): 407–416.

Wang, Gyeltshen. "Corruption and Related Offences in International Economic Activities: Individual Reports: Corruption Control in Criminal Justice: Bhutan." *Revue Internationale de Droit Pénal* 74, no. 1 & 2 (2003): 479–483.

Ware, Glenn T. "Filling the Regulatory Gap: The Emerging Transnational Regulator." *Global Governance* 12 (2006): 135–139.

Warner, T. Negbalee. *Legal and Practical Challenges in Liberia to the Domestication of International Anti-Corruption Conventions: Liberia*. Transparency International, 2006.

Waterbury, John. "Corruption, Political Stability and Development: Comparative Evidence from Egypt and Morocco." *Government and Opposition* 11, no. 4 (October 275): 426–445.

—. "Endemic and Planned Corruption in a Monarchical Regime." *World Politics* 25, no. 4 (July 1973): 533–555.

Webb, Philippa. "The United Nations Convention Against Corruption: Global Achievement or Missed Opportunity." *Journal of International Economic Law* 8, no. 1 (2005): 191–229.

Wei, Shang-Jin. "How Taxing is Corruption on International Investors?" *Review of Economics and Statistics* 82, no. 1 (2000): 1–11.

Weigend, Thomas. "Corruption and Related Offences in International Economic Activities: National Reports: Germany." *Revue Internationale de Droit Pénal* 74, no. 1 & 2 (2003): 71–92.

Werlin, Herbert H. "The Roots of Corruption-The Ghanaian Enquiry." *Journal of Modern African Studies* 10, no. 2 (1972): 247–266.

Wetter, J. Gillis. "Issues of Corruption before International Arbitral Tribunals: The Authentic Text and True Meaning of Judge Gunnar Lagergren's 1963 Award in ICC Case No. 1110." *Arbitration International* 10, no. 3 (1994): 282–294.

Whitton, Howard. *Making Whistleblower Protection Work: Elements of an Effective Approach.* U4 Anti-Corruption Resource Centre Brief, December 2008.

Wilder, Martijn, and Michael Ahrens. "Australia's Implementation of the OECD Convention on Combating Bribery of Foreign Public Officials in International Business Transactions." *Melbourne Journal of International Law* 2, no. 2 (2001): 568–586.

Williams, Aled. *International Experience of Asset Declarations.* U4 Anti-Corruption Resource Centre Expert Answer, October 12, 2006.

Williams, James W., and Margaret E. Beare. "The Business of Bribery: Globalization, Economic Liberalization, and the 'Problem' of Corruption." *Crime, Law and Social Change* 32 (1999): 115–146.

Williams, Robert. "New Concepts for Old?" *Third World Quarterly* 30, no. 3 (1999): 503–513.

Williams, Robert, and Alan Doig, eds. *Controlling Corruption.* The Politics of Corruption 4. Cheltenham, UK: Edward Elgar Publishing Ltd., 2000.

Williams, Robert, Jonathan Moran, and Rachel Flanary, eds. *Corruption in the Developed World.* The Politics of Corruption 3. Cheltenham, UK: Edward Elgar Publishing Ltd., 2000.

Williams, Robert, and Robin Theobald, eds. *Corruption in the Developing World.* The Politics of Corruption 2. Cheltenham, UK: Edward Elgar Publishing Ltd., 2000.

Wilsher, Dan. "Inexplicable Wealth and Illicit Enrichment of Public Officials: A Model Draft That Respects Human Rights in Corruption Cases." *Crime, Law and Social Change* 45 (2006): 27–53.

Wolf, Sebastian. "Modernization of the German Anti-Corruption Criminal Law by International Legal Provisions." *German Law Journal* 7, no. 9 (2006): 785–792.

World Bank. *Strengthening Bank Group Engagement on Governance and Anticorruption*, 2006.

Wraith, Ronald E. *Corruption in Developing Countries.* London: Allen & Unwin, 1963.

Yamaguchi, Atsushi. "Corruption and Related Offences in International Economic Activities: National Reports: Japan." *Revue Internationale de Droit Pénal* 74, no. 1 & 2 (2003): 337–350.

Yukins, Christopher. "Integrating Integrity and Procurement: The United Nations Convention against Corruption and the UNCITRAL Model Procurement Law." *Public Contract Law Journal* 36, no. 3 (2007): 307–329.

Zachaël, Kl. *Lois contre corruption: Inventaire des dispositions réglementaires et juridiques relatives à la lutte contre la corruption au Burkina Faso.* Ouagadougou: Collection REN-LAC, 2002.

Zagaris, Bruce. *International White Collar Crime: Cases and Materials.* Cambridge: Cambridge University Press, 2010.

— . and Shaila Lakhani Ohri. "The Emergence of an International Enforcement Regime on Transnational Corruption in the Americas." *Law and Policy in International Business* 30 (1999): 53–93.

Zegarra Aranda, Zulema. "Convención Interamericana contra la Corrupción." In *25 aniversario de la Sociedad Boliviana de Ciencias Penales*, 82–113. La Paz: Sociedad Boliviana de Ciencias Penales, 2002.

Zerbes, Ingeborg. "Article 1: The Offence of Bribery of Foreign Public Officials." In *The OECD Convention on Bribery: A Commentary*, edited by Mark Pieth, Lucinda Low, and Peter J. Cullen, 45–172. Cambridge University Press, 2007.

Zhang, Zhihui, and Caiwei. "Corruption and Related Offences in International Economic Activities: National Reports: China." *Revue Internationale de Droit Pénal* 74, no. 1 & 2 (2003): 149–167.

www.ingramcontent.com/pod-product-compliance
Ingram Content Group UK Ltd.
Pitfield, Milton Keynes, MK11 3LW, UK
UKHW051044120926
8556IPUK00041B/1261

9 781780 680927